50 in50

50 Trades in 50 Weeks

One year of good ideas, dumb mistakes, and timeless trading lessons

Brent Donnelly

Foreword and editing by Justin Ross

First edition 2023
Editing: Justin Ross
Cover design, proofing and layout: Stephen K. Donnelly
Images: Brent and Stephen K. Donnelly
Author photo: Suvadip Bose

ISBN 979-8-9869805-1-5 (softcover)

ISBN 979-8-9869805-2-2 (e-book)

ISBN 979-8-9869805-3-9 (hardcover)

For more information go to www.spectramarkets.com

Justin's Substack is excellent. Check it out at https://squareman.substack.com

This book is dedicated to the Gitt.

Good friend, good mentor, good human.

All-in on the best ideas and honest about the bad ones.

Contents

Foreword

Once upon a time, I wanted to be a day trader. And so, likely, did you, and so did numerous other people you know.

Because who doesn't want to be a trader? It's exciting, it's fascinating… it's the game played by people who win at life. It's the game played by some of the people we most wish we were like. They're rich and they had fun getting there, and they continue to have fun doing it while still getting richer.

I'm the guy you hear about in stories who tried trading and failed at it. I quit my job with 40 grand to try my hand at the endlessly interesting game of stocks. I worked at my living room desk, traded my own money, and lost all of it.

I read books by Richard Wyckoff. I read books like John J. Murphy's *Technical Analysis of the Financial Markets.* I read books about strategy and candlesticks and historically-successful trading styles. And then I joined chat groups and paid thousands of dollars for how-to-trade courses. And those courses, I thought, taught me so much about how the stock market works. And how market participants behave. And about how to finally make money.

One of those "if I just find the right strategies, I'll be all set" things.

Alas, no such luck. Trading is not a journey of finding the right strategies.

Trading is not a journey of learning what and when to trade. Trading is a journey of *transforming oneself into the kind of person who would be a successful trader.* It's about learning how to think and behave and act.

After a while, I encountered Brent Donnelly's *Alpha Trader,* which, as I'm sure goes without saying at this point, was an instant trading classic. Not only because of its rich content with regards to analysis, but because it is a book about how to think and behave and act. I like to think that successful traders have to be obsessed with the market in order to win in the market; *Alpha Trader* was a book about how to be obsessed correctly. With trading, or with winning at anything.

And it wasn't long before Brent and I had interacted online a bit, simply because I was a fan and I saw that he was consistently putting out good nuggets of wisdom and commentary online.

And it wasn't long after that until Brent had hired me to be his business manager and I got to experience his trading and his macro analysis up close and in real time.

Which means that I've had the good fortune of being right here with Brent as the 50in50 project was active. And every step of the way, I have edited his work, provided whatever commentary and additions I could, and reminded him incessantly that I love how he's doing a real-time trading education project. Or at least, I hope I have reminded him of that enough.

Because that's what was missing from my trading education – and that's what, as far as I can tell after spending hundreds of weeks around thousands of traders, is most often missing from everyone's trading education. A real-time, hands-on glimpse into how a professional generates his trading ideas and runs his business. A real-time story of a professional's actual experience with the actual market. A glimpse into *what* he's watching and *why*. Into *when* feels like the right time to sit still, and *where* might be the best place to engage with the market. Into how, on a week-to-week basis, to actually think and act like someone who makes money.

50in50 offers the educational backdrop that is generally missing from people's rookie years (and some people's professional years). Because, no matter how many Wyckoff or Murphy or Graham books you read about stocks and other assets, trading is about much more than analysis. It's about running a creative business around a commerce of ideas.

Brent never tells me which charts to look at. He never tells me how to systematize my trading. And he won't do those things for you, either.

What he has taught me how to do is pay good attention and engage with the market the way an expert would. He has taught me how to think and behave like an expert. And for the first time, I can.

Justin Ross
Editor

Introduction

Hi, I'm Brent Donnelly. Welcome to Fifty Trades in Fifty Weeks.

In early 2022, I was looking for a new way to teach trading. My book *Alpha Trader* had been out for six months, and I wanted to do something different. In business school, I learned via the case study method, and I have always found that learning through specific, real-life examples is powerful. Over the years, many readers have asked me for a specific walkthrough of a trade from start to finish and so I realized that the case study method would be the perfect format for a trader education series.

So, Fifty Trades in Fifty weeks (aka 50in50) was born. 50in50 uses the case study method to go through one real-time trade in detail, about once per week. The idea came to life as a Substack and this two-book series is a permanent record of the weekly process that spanned from February 2022 to May 2023.

Each week, I shared a new trade idea and walked readers through it from start to finish. Fiftyish real-time trades in just over fifty weeks. Lessons covered a wide range of topics like tactics, strategy, mindset, risk management, and of course the psychology of successful trading. The idea was to let readers watch real trade ideas come to life in real time.

Remember those Prima guides for New Super Mario Bros. and Kirby's Epic Yarn, or those YouTube video game walkthroughs where they explain, step-by-step, how to clear each level of the game? That's the spirit here. Also, like I said, kinda inspired by Harvard Business School's case study method.

Each trade goes from start to finish, touching on aspects like:

Where did the idea come from? Why does it make sense?

- Narrative
- Fundamental analysis
- Technicals
- Pattern recognition
- Backtesting
- Positioning and sentiment

Risk management

- How to choose stop loss and take profit levels.
- Defining reassessment triggers—If *x* happens during the life of this trade, I will do *y*.
- How to determine position size—What is the appropriate amount of risk for this trade?

Psychology. How might this trade be ruined by mental errors and bias?

The alternative hypothesis

- What are the risks to the trade and reasons it might not work?
- Pre-mortem as we imagine the trade going horribly wrong and dissect the worst case before it happens.

Data collection. Monitoring and tracking trades.

Learning. What have we learned?

50in50 is a 1-year "Introduction to Trading" class full of new ideas, tactics, and strategies for trading.

The book follows the trades over time and concludes with some takeaways and lessons learned along the way. The target audience is traders with 0 to 5 years of experience, but I got a ton of feedback from experienced professionals who found the series valuable, too.

Good to know info before you dive in

The book and the lessons in 50in50 are all self-contained and self-explanatory, but here are a few notes that will give you useful context before you start.

I favored simplicity over complexity throughout the process. Each lesson could not delve into every intricacy of a trade, so I kept things simple. If the weekly lesson was about technical analysis, I didn't spend a lot of time on position sizing that week. The idea was to cover all the important topics over the course of fifty weeks—not cover every topic, every week for fifty weeks. This desire for simplicity means that I did not consider the portfolio of trades in 50in50 at any given time. I did not scale into or out of trades, or actively hedge options positions. Each trade and each week was written to stand alone.

I am a global macro trader. I wrote about many markets where I am not an expert. Most of my experience is in trading global macro narratives and currency markets. I have dabbled a bit in commodities and crypto, and I traded the NASDAQ bubble from 1998 to 2002 using a specific strategy that had a lot of edge from 1998 to 2001 and no edge in 2002. As such, I would say I'm expert in global macro but not in single name equities, commodities, or crypto.

To avoid a lot of repetition and overlap with my day job, **I mostly avoided global macro trading in 50in50** and used primarily examples from the world of single names. As such, my expectation was that the trades would deliver break even performance overall as I have no edge in trading individual stocks. The point was not to achieve profitability, it was to use a specific case study to explain a particular facet of trading each week. There is a discussion of the results at the end of Part 2.

My capital allocation per trade in 50in50 is very, very conservative. I imagined a portfolio value of $100,000 and allocated 2% ($2,000) per trade. The average trade lasted 33 days. This is an incredibly low risk level for a portfolio and is unlikely to produce useful alpha, even if you have good ideas. In real life, a common benchmark for day trader capital allocation is to risk 2% of your free capital each day. Free capital is the total amount of money you can afford to lose.

If you're at a bank or hedge fund, free capital is your stop loss. If you are retail, it's the size of your account. This concept is covered in depth in my book *Alpha Trader*. The point here is just for you to know that allocating 2% of your free capital, once per week is extremely conservative to the point of being nonsensical. And note that I didn't get into portfolio risk analytics in 50in50 because that subject is beyond the scope of the project. The idea is to explain individual trades, not portfolio management.

Don't copy other traders. Not even me. The best way to become a successful trader is to develop your own style and approach—an approach that makes sense given your personality, strengths, and weaknesses. I'm a good short-term trader because I have unlimited risk appetite, a lot of aggression, and fast video game fingers. On the flipside, this means I am impatient, and I overtrade. I am not well-suited to swing trading or long-term investing. I get bored easily and crave stimulation. Take whatever resonates with you from the 50in50 lessons, and add to a continuously-adapting approach.

The most likely path to success in trading is to choose one market and master everything you possibly can about that market, using a combination of data / quantitative analysis and subjective analysis of narratives, positioning, anecdotes, pattern recognition, and experience. Don't pick a methodology—different methodologies work in different regimes. Pick a market and master it. That approach is inherently adaptable over time, while mastery of a technique or strategy is much less flexible and much more regime dependent.

OK, that's all you need to know. But before we get started, let me answer a few common questions about this project.

Frequently Asked Questions

The Substack is free. Why are you charging for a book?

People asked for the book! I tried to make it as low cost as possible.

I already read *Alpha Trader* and *The Art of Currency Trading*. Is this different?

About 15-20% of 50in50 overlaps with one of those two books and the remaining 80% is original content. The concepts overlap significantly with *Alpha Trader*, but the examples and situations are all fresh. If you're nervous about this, check out the Substack first and if it seems fine, grab the book!

The trades are all closed now, and in the past. Is the info still useful?

Yes! Case studies are still useful, even after years have passed. This is why Harvard and many other business schools use the case study method. Real-life setups can be analyzed after the fact to see what went right and what went wrong. Many Harvard Business School case studies in use today are more than 20 years old. But they are still useful!

If you are such a good trader, why are you writing books and Substacks and a paid newsletter?

This is a common question and a smart question to ask. Before you read or learn about trading from anyone, you should know their background. Especially if you plan to give them cash money. Here is my trading background:

I have been trading non-stop since 1995, mostly currencies, but also futures and single name equities. I have been an FX market maker, a Managing Director and chief dealer at various commercial and investment banks, a portfolio manager at a hedge fund, and I traded my own money for five years. I have been writing about macro and markets just about every day since 2004.

I put my entire net worth of $25,000 into a day trading account in 1998 and turned it into $350,000 by 2000. Then, I spent the next two years spending and losing virtually all of it (you learn a lot when you blow up…). My best year I made just over $50 million trading FX in 2008. I worked at a hedge fund for three years but didn't love it because I couldn't write. My best day at Lehman Brothers I made more than $5,000,000. I have lost more than a million dollars in one day on many occasions and lost that much in one hour a few times.

I have had a successful 25-year trading career and continue to trade my own money while advising and providing liquidity for hedge funds and asset managers in FX.

BUT… I also love writing. I co-created and wrote a cartoon that was on TV in Canada for a while. I've written two books on trading, and I write fiction. As I hit the halfway mark of my 100-year lifespan, I find I get as much joy out of writing as I do out of trading. I want to do both, and I want to do both in a non-bureaucratic environment where I'm free to think and write what I want. My writing also taps me into the zeitgeist as readers respond to my ideas. That puts my ear to the ground on sentiment and positioning.

That's why I am building Spectra Markets, and that's why I write a newsletter and Substacks and probably other stuff in the future. Because it makes me happy and creates a virtuous writing and trading circle. But if my writing was free, I doubt I'd commit the effort to make a timely, high-quality product. Good writing takes time, and my time is not free. The fact that I'm good at trading is the reason I can charge people for my writing … So the original question is posed backwards. You should be asking people with no experience why they are charging for content.

The TLDR is: The way for me to live my most fun life is to combine my two passions: writing and trading. My time is worth money and if my thoughts have value to people and they want to pay money to read them... Perfect.

Hope that helps.

Each week couldn't be 5,000+ words long or it would get boring and I would die of carpal tunnel syndrome. Therefore, each week I picked one or two areas of focus and drilled into those while covering the other aspects of the trade in less detail.

OK, that's the preamble. Let's roll.

DISCLAIMER

Nothing in 50in50 is investment advice. Do your own research and consult your personal financial advisor. I'm putting out thoughts for people who want to learn. Trade your own view!

Thank you to TradingView for allowing me to use their beautiful charts in this book. TradingView is an absolutely excellent charting system and it's very reasonably priced.

Week 1: Short XAUEUR

Trade Number 1: Short XAUEUR

XAU is the symbol for gold, EUR is the euro. Normally, when you buy or sell XAU, you are implicitly doing so against the USD, but you can trade gold against any currency you want, depending on your view. Currently, I like the EUR better than the USD so I'm using that as my denominator. This will make all the explanations a little more complicated than a simple XAUUSD trade, but I want to be true to my real views. I prefer not to dumb things down too much.

Before I get into the reasons I like gold lower against the euro, I need to introduce my basic framework. Much of this is explained more deeply in my book *Alpha Trader* but you don't need to read that book to understand this book. I will walk through each step over the coming weeks. And if you did read *Alpha Trader*, you're like the kid that read the textbook during the summer, before school started. Winning.

Here is my framework from start to finish. You can grab Excel and PDF versions of this file at www.spectramarkets.com/tradetracker

Trader Framework and Checklist
Trade Description

The idea	Date			
	Security			
	Long, short, other			
	Idea source	Elevator pitch		
		Events or news		
		Deviation from fair value		
		Pattern recognition / indicators		
Filters	Tailwind or headwind and why?	Narrative cycle		
		Positioning and sentiment		
		Events and catalysts		
		Correlated markets		
		Technicals		
	Alternative hypothesis	What might go wrong? Pre-mortem		
Tactics	Trade structure	Best asset, market, structure?		
		Microstructure considerations		
		Entry		**Stick to the original plan**
		Stop loss		
		Take profit		
	Other reassessment triggers			
Risk management	Conviction level	TYPE I, II, or III		
	Free Capital			
	% of free capital			
	$ at risk			
	Solve for position size			
	Any issues with liquidity or capacity?			
Execution	Execution notes (limit, market, etc.)			
	Automate or outsource stop loss			
	Enter trade in journal			
Psychology	What emotions are involved here? Do I feel anything unusual? List emotions or possible pitfalls.			
Performance Analysis	Post-mortem			
	Lessons			
	What is working and what is not?			

I encourage you to fill one of these out each time you do a meaningful trade. If you are doing 100s of trades per day, that's not practical but if you're doing five or fewer trades per day, you can easily do it.

I like to print this thing out and use a pen. There is something about filling out an actual piece of physical paper that feels more serious and concrete than just clicking and scrolling around in another Excel sheet.

When you write something down, it solidifies. It transforms from abstract into concrete. All the sludge falls away and only the important information is left. When you write something down, you have made a choice to select that particular information as more relevant than the rest. This highlights it for your brain. You signal to your brain "THIS IS IMPORTANT".

Your brain records it as such.

The pathways and connections developed in your brain are different when you write it down because the encoding process is different. The encoding is deeper, more robust, and information is recalled more easily. If you want a message to stick, write it down.

Where the idea came from

The short gold idea comes as the narrative around global central bank easing has changed dramatically and the European Central Bank (ECB) is taking the lead in pushing global rates higher. This is a surprise! Just a month or so ago, nobody expected anything from the ECB. German 2-year rates were bobbing around down in a -75 to -55 range. Then, last Thursday, they did this:

Germany 2-year yield (hourly back to March 2021)

Why does this matter for gold?

Gold is one of the most difficult markets to understand and predict because it's not a safe haven and it's not a risky asset. Instead, it's a quasi store of value and liquidity barometer that sometimes trades like a risky asset. Another strange feature of gold, compared to most assets, is that it's negative carry. You pay to own it. Most assets (like many stocks and bonds) generate cash flows and thus have an automatic built-in head start over gold or any negative carry asset.

If you invest $100 in gold and $100 in bonds at the current US 10-year yield (1.95%) and both assets go nowhere for 10 years, here's what your $100 looks like:

Year	$100 in gold	$100 in bonds
0	100.00	100.00
1	99.50	101.95
2	99.00	103.94
3	98.51	105.96
4	98.01	108.03
5	97.52	110.14
6	97.04	112.29
7	96.55	114.47
8	96.07	116.71
9	95.59	118.98
10	95.11	121.30

The power of positive and negative compounding means that any investment that produces cash flows will always start with a huge advantage over one that does not. That said, when gold rallied from $400 to $1800 from 2002 to 2011, nobody was worried about the negative carry!

An interesting thing happens, though, when interest rates fall toward, or below zero. *Gold becomes much more attractive.* If bonds are yielding below zero, gold's negative carry suddenly doesn't matter. And bonds with a negative yield are extremely unattractive given their negative carry AND their extreme valuation. Holders of negative-yielding bonds are very unlikely to make money (negative yield = very expensive bond because lower yields = higher price in bond land).[1] Sure gold has negative carry, but if your timing is good, you can make money on price appreciation.

As the quantity of negative-yielding bonds in the world increased from 2013 to 2021, gold became a better and better substitute as you can see here:

[1] If you don't have a good handle on how bonds work… here you go: https://europe.pimco.com/en-eu/resources/education/everything-you-need-to-know-about-bonds

Gold vs. % of global bonds with negative yields (2013 to August 2021)

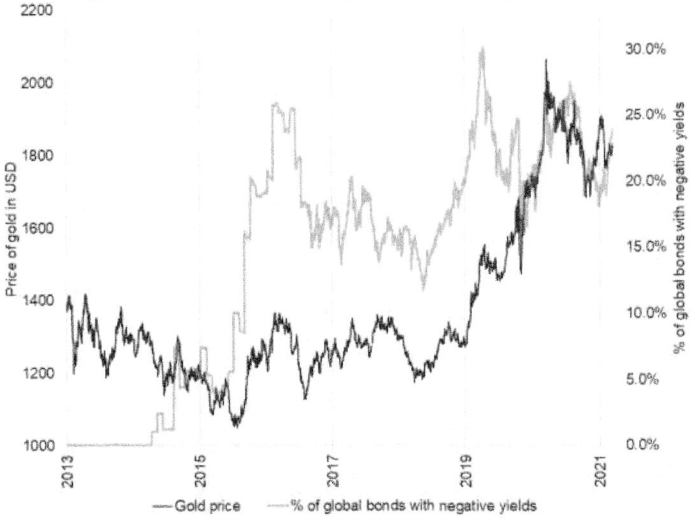

Denmark, Sweden, Switzerland, and other European countries started to experiment with negative rates in 2013 and they remained right through mid-2021. You can see in mid-2015, the percentage of negative-yielding bonds skyrocketed as the ECB announced QE and then Japan cut its benchmark interest rate below zero in early 2016.

You can also see that the more negative-yielding bonds were out there, the higher gold rallied. The ratio in these sorts of relationships is not 1:1. There is noise and leads and lags, but ultralow rates were almost certainly an important driver of higher gold in that period.

Let me show you what the chart looks like now.

Gold vs. % of global bonds with negative yields (2013 to now)

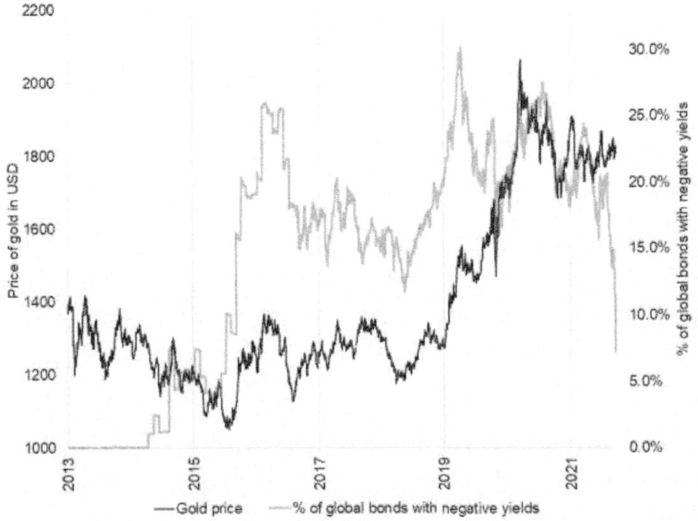

Wow! The "buy gold because central banks are crazy" narrative is stale. We are back to 2015 levels in negative-yielding bonds as rates rip higher. There are plenty of positive-yielding substitutes for gold again.

Another way of looking at this is to examine US real rates (market pricing of US yields, minus inflation) against gold. If real rates are falling and negative, that generally means that central banks are enacting extremely loose policy. Here is US 10-year real interest rates against gold.

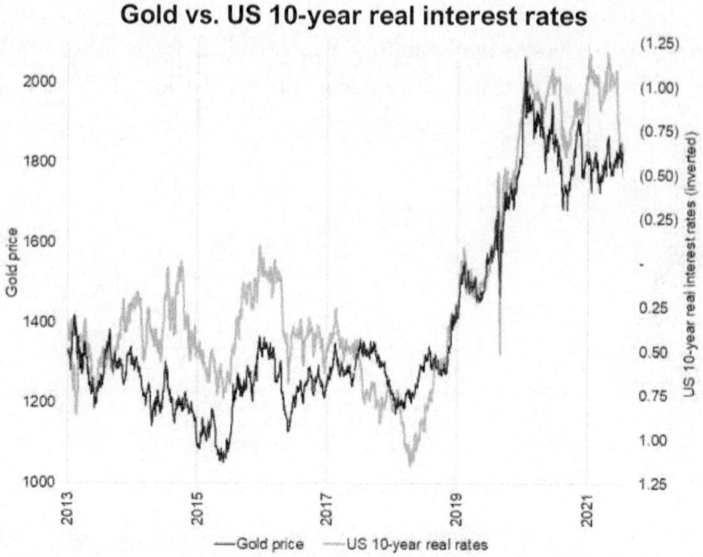

The signal from this chart is less dramatic, but also confirms that the direction of US real rates is probably bearish gold, not bullish. Some will argue that US real rates are still negative and thus gold is still OK but I generally believe that as traders, you should always focus on changes, not levels. The direction and momentum of US rates and US real rates is higher and that is generally bad for gold.

Global central banks just embarked on the greatest monetary and fiscal policy experiment in history and now that experiment is over. Normalization has begun. The biggest beneficiaries of loose policy are falling one by one. First it was ARKK, then crypto, then the NASDAQ. Next should be gold.

Let's take a quick pause here to talk about correlation trading. So far I have used various other markets like negative bond yields and US real interest rates to make a guesstimate of which direction gold might go next. This is similar to the way you can piece together what might happen next in the real world by pulling together a series of clues.

If you see clouds in the sky, hear thunder in the distance, and see an umbrella seller dude setting up outside the entrance to the subway, you can make a high probability guesstimate that it's going to rain soon. But… It might not! It's not that obvious in markets of course. The clues are much more confusing and ambiguous. As my first boss used to say:

"**If trading was easy, it wouldn't pay so well**, would it Burl?"[2]

So my initial thesis here is: The market has been buying gold for the past three years as a reaction to negative yields around the world and falling real rates in the USA. Now, real rates have turned higher, most debt is positive yield again and yet the price of gold has barely adjusted. Markets operate with leads and lags and this type of trade is sometimes called "lead/lag" or "cross-market" trading. You get clues from other markets and you determine that one of these things is not like the other. One of these things does not belong.

Now let's fill in page 1 of the "Trader Framework and Checklist."

			Trade 1 Short XAU/EUR
	Date		8-Feb-22
	Security		**XAU/EUR**
	Long, short, other		**Short**
The idea	Idea source	Elevator pitch	ECB raising rates this year is important new information. Monetary debasement arguments are beyond stale.
		Events or news	ECB meeting 03FEB22 is the catalyst but there is still time to get in
		Deviation from fair value	Negative yielding bonds and real rates suggest XAU overvalued
		Pattern recognition / indicators	When inflation falls from high levels, what does gold do? When CFTC sells aggressively, what does gold do?
Filters	Tailwind or headwind and why?	Narrative cycle	New narrative: Hawkish ECB. Old narrative: Fiat debasement
		Positioning and sentiment	CFTC has been selling gold aggressively.
		Events and catalysts	Next ECB meeting is March 10. There should be a runup trade into that.
		Correlated markets	Real rates skyrocketing. Negative yielding debt pile shrinking
		Technicals	Triangles inside triangles make it clear where the trade is wrong (above 1700)
	Alternative hypothesis	What might go wrong? Pre-mortem	Best argument against this trade is that gold has held in very well.

That is the story of why I like this trade. Now let's quickly look at some filters.

[2] He claimed I looked like Burl Ives because of my ginger goatee.

Positioning

Here is how I look at positioning.

The six positioning vs. market price regimes

Positioning	Bull Market	Bear Market
Long and increasing	Very Bullish	
Long and stable	Bullish	
Long but falling	BEARISH	
Short and stable		Bearish
Short and getting more short		Very bearish
Short but buying back		BULLISH

Currently, the market is long gold, and reducing, which is bearish. Here is a chart of the price of gold against CFTC speculative gold positions.

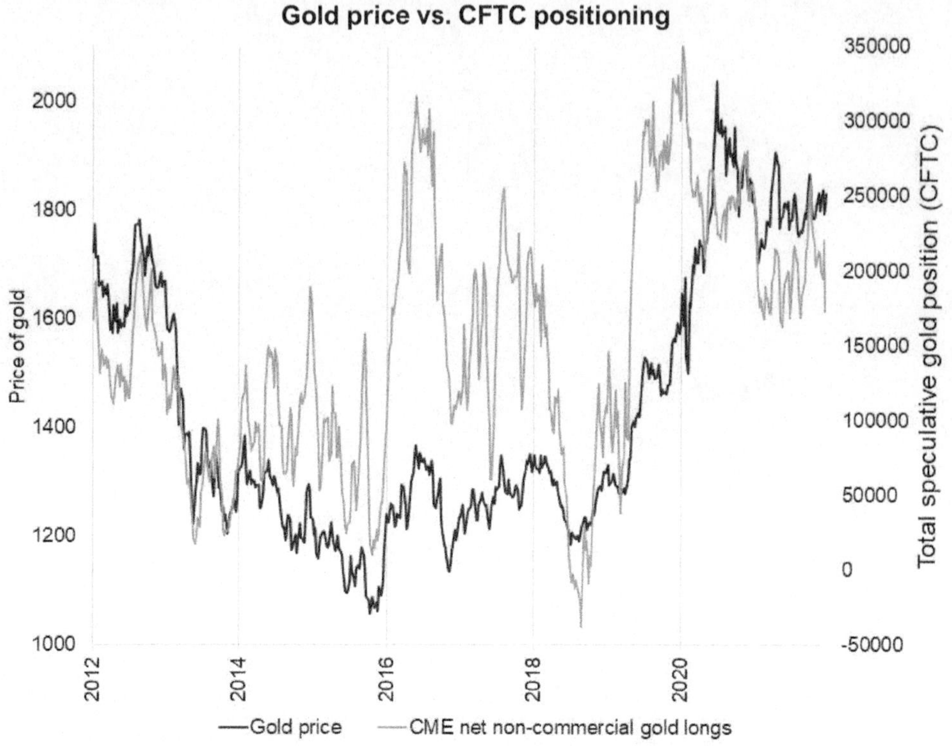

Events and catalysts

Last week's ECB was the appetizer and the March 10th ECB meeting could be the main course. When the market anticipates an upcoming event, it will tend to position in the direction of least regret. In this case, I would bet the market wants to position for a hawkish ECB meeting on March 10th as that is the direction that has been telegraphed by the central bank and it's the direction that "makes sense" macro-wise with inflation very high in the eurozone and the ECB abandoning its old dovish guidance. Given the massive move in European rates last week, the market will not want to be caught out in the same direction again.

Technical analysis

Gold has been tracing out a massive triangle formation. Triangles are symptomatic of a loss of interest as volatility falls and ranges contract more and more. Most traders view a break of a triangle as a "go with" and a potential signal that volatility is back and a large directional move is in play. Here is the chart of XAUEUR:

XAUEUR daily back to 2017

What is the alternative hypothesis?

Gold bulls say that gold has weathered rate hikes very well. This is true, but markets do not always move instantaneously toward equilibrium. There can be slow-moving, non-price-sensitive flows that keep price from adjusting to new information. If markets were always right, it would be impossible to make money. Markets are usually wise, but not always.

Now let's complete page 2 of the trader framework.

Trader framework and checklist, page 2				
Tactics	Trade structure	Best asset, market, structure?	Spot. It's hard to trade options (though certainly not impossible) and the stop loss is fairly obvious.	
		Microstructure considerations	Is this an XAU trade or a USD trade or a EUR trade? This is useful to understand.	
		Entry		**Stick to the original plan**
		Stop loss		
		Take profit		
		Target		
	Other reassessment triggers		Next ECB meeting is March 10. There should be a runup trade into that. Cut before ECB meeting.	
Risk management	Conviction level	TYPE I, II, or III		
	Free Capital			
	% of free capital			
	$ at risk			
	Solve for position size			
	Any issues with liquidity or capacity?			
Execution	Execution notes (limit, market, etc.)			
	Automate or outsource stop loss			
	Enter trade in journal			
Psychology	What emotions are involved here? Do I feel anything unusual? List emotions or possible pitfalls.		Be patient. This could chop around for a while.	
Performance Analysis	Post-mortem			
	Lessons			
	What is working and what is not?			

The trade is most simply executed through spot; no need to get fancy with options or anything. We could do XAUUSD but have decided to be long EUR against gold instead of USD because the ECB is acting very aggressively and is near the start of the hiking cycle, while the Fed pivoted last November and expectations for US rate hikes are high. XAUUSD and XAUEUR are mostly the same trade most of the time, but occasionally you are happy you chose the right denominator. Here is XAUUSD and XAUEUR:

XAUEUR (black) vs. XAUUSD (gray) since 2009

It takes a big move in EURUSD to make a difference here because XAU is much more volatile than EUR or USD and as such the metal drives the movements more than the currency rate. You can see in 2015, when EURUSD was cratering from 1.40 to 1.10, there was a big divergence between XAUUSD and XAUEUR but generally, it doesn't usually matter which one you pick. In this case, it might matter and it's worth thinking about because I am bullish EUR and bearish USD right now for various reasons covered in am/FX (my daily macro note).

The stop loss is 1702 (well through the top of the triangle and above all but the all-time high). I was tempted to put my stop loss ABOVE the all-time high, but I think if the triangle breaks, the idea is wrong, so there is no point tacking on another 50 EUR of P&L risk. My target is the Q1 2021 low at 1410 so I put my TP at 1421 (just ahead of that major support). My other reassessment trigger (other than stop loss and take profit) is that I want to exit the trade before the ECB meeting on March 10.

I have three levels of conviction in trading, TYPE I, II and III. I will explain those in a future 50in50, but this trade I'm going with TYPE II which is where about 60%-70% of my trades end up. I'm risking 2.5% of capital and for this 50in50 project, I'm going to assume $100,000 of free capital. Free capital is the amount of money you can afford to lose. So if you're at a hedge fund, your free capital is your stop loss. If you're retail, it's your account size. 2.5% of capital is reasonable but fairly conservative for an account this size.

Knowing where my stop is and how much money I want to risk ($2,500, or 2.5% of $100,000), I calculate my position size.

My P&L on XAUEUR will be in euros because all currency trades have P&L in the denominator currency. ($2500 / 1.1420 EURUSD exchange rate) means I am risking 2189 EUR.

> *% risk*
> = entry point minus stop loss / (entry point)
> = (1600 – 1705) / 1600
> = 6.6%

Note: I added 3 EUR onto my stop loss for estimated slippage.

> *Position size*
> = EUR at risk / risk%
> = 2189 / 6.6%
> = 33000 EUR

So we're gonna sell 33000 EUR worth of gold. If it goes to our stop, we lose $2,500. If it goes to our take profit we make 11.2% or 3692 EUR = $4,230. Risk/reward of about 1.7:1. If this sounds complicated, don't worry, it just takes a bit of practice.

You determine how many USD you want to risk on the trade, say $X. Then, you figure out what position size will lose you $X based on the stop loss level you determined beforehand using technical analysis or whatever methodology. That's it. In this chapter's appendix, I have presented two more position sizing walkthroughs, in case you would like a bit more.

Once you have the position size, log in to your system, set the notional to 33000 EUR and sell the gold. Boom. If you can't trade XAUEUR on whatever platform you use, simply sell gold and buy EURUSD (in the same USD notional) and voila! You have XAUEUR.

I would also write down a few feelings at this point like "I'm extra nervous on this one because it's the first trade of the 50in50 series and I will look stupid if I'm wrong" or something like that.

Conclusion

50in50 goes short XAUEUR at 1600. Stop loss 1702. Take profit 1421.

I will monitor the performance and offer detailed updates as we progress.

APPENDIX: Extra position sizing exercises

One of the most common questions I get from new traders is: How do you size your positions? For me, the answer is pretty simple. Here are the five steps:

You have a trade idea. Let's say you think bonds are going to sell off in the days leading up to non-farm payrolls (aka The US Jobs Report) because the market is massively long, everyone has been super bullish for months and the whisper number for the jobs number is creeping higher and higher in recent days. This is a classic run-up trade. You have decided the best way to trade this is to buy TBT, the ultrashort bond ETF. While TBT is not a good way to short the bond market for more than a day or two, your time horizon is just two days so you have decided this will be the easiest, most liquid, and levered way to execute the trade.

Determine your conviction level. You think this is a classic run-up trade and you love a good run-up trade. You decide this is a Type II trade, which this month means $250,000 of risk would normally be allocated to this idea.

Decide how much to risk. You are up $1.0 million this year and have a particularly strong feeling about this trade. The chart set up is great, too, so you can take a big position. Since you plan to cover the trade BEFORE the non-farm payrolls release, you don't have to worry about gap risk through the number. You decide to risk the standard $250,000, plus 10% of your YTD P&L ($1 million X 10% = $100,000) so you are risking $350,000 on the trade.

Determine the stop loss. Use technical analysis and other inputs (average daily range, expected volatility, an understanding of round number bias, etc.) to determine the stop loss on the trade. You have a rule that you always place your stop loss at least one average day's range away from your entry point. This is a good rule of thumb for new traders. If I know absolutely nothing about a security, the first thing I do when looking to put in a stop loss is calculate the security's average daily range. Any stop loss closer than 1-day's range away is at high risk of getting dinged by short-term noise.

Determine the position size. To make the math easy, let's say TBT is trading at $100.00 and you have determined, after looking at the charts and studying the volatility of TBT, that the appropriate stop loss is $102.02. Liquidity is excellent and slippage is not an issue. You estimate 3 cents of slippage on your stop. So you are risking $2.05 / share and you decided in step 3 to risk $350,000. Here is how you calculate the correct sizing:

Position size
= $ at risk / (entry point - stop loss level)
= $350,000 / (102.05 - 100.00)
= 170,731

Therefore, the trader in this example should buy 170,731 shares of TBT. The formula for determining position size is always the same:

Position size
= $ at risk / (entry point - stop loss level)

Let's do one more just to make sure it's clear.

I am a retail trader and I want to sell AUDUSD because: reasons. The currency pair is trading at 0.7500 right now and after studying the pair's volatility and doing 20 minutes of technical analysis, I have determined that 0.7572 is the correct stop loss. My trading account balance is currently $165,000 and I always risk 2% of capital on every trade. I never run more than one trade at a time so this is a safe way to run my account. I will add 3 pips to my stop loss level to allow for slippage on execution.

2% of 165,000 is $3,300.

Position size
= $ at risk / (entry point - stop loss level)
= $3,300 / (0.7500 - 0.7575)
= $3,300 / -0.0075
= - 440,000

So our short position in AUDUSD should be 440,000 AUD. If we get stopped out, we will lose $3,300, which is 2% of capital.

Bad traders work in the opposite direction. They say: I'm short 2 million AUDUSD at 0.7500 but I can't afford to lose more than $10,000 so my stop loss will be 0.7550. This makes no sense because 0.7550 is a totally arbitrary level that does not take market factors like volatility or technical analysis into consideration. Always start with $ at risk, then determine your stop loss by analyzing the market. The position size is the output, not the input.

To summarize the five steps explained above:

1. You have a trade idea.
2. Determine your conviction level (TYPE I, II or III).
3. Decide how much to risk. This amount to risk can be in USD or in basis points, depending on where you work. This amount is determined by your conviction level, YTD P&L, and your risk management system.
4. Determine your stop loss using technical analysis and other inputs.
5. Do the math to back out the correct position size.
6. Using this methodology, your position size can vary substantially. A low conviction position with a wide stop loss for a good hedge fund trade might be 20 million AUDUSD while a high conviction trade with a tighter stop loss for the same trader could be 200 million AUDUSD.

Good traders vary bet size. Good traders vary bet size.
Good traders vary bet size. Good traders vary bet size.

Week 2: Short Oil

Volume spike failure, steep curve, resistance in 10-year yields and more

Trader Error

Oops.

Last week, 50in50 went short XAUEUR (short gold vs. euro) and I didn't put "Russia invades Ukraine" on my list of risks. That is a fail on my part. It was a known risk, but unfortunately, it had been kicking around for a few weeks and I failed to take it into account. That's not good.

A few people asked if I would exit the trade or hedge it, etc. but this being a weekly blog, I will not be dynamically hedging or rebalancing. While I want to approach realism here, I only have so much time and the incremental value add of monitoring and updating in real-time is not worth the massive increase in effort.

The purpose of this exercise is not to create a real-time portfolio of winners.

The purpose of this exercise is to explain the process of trading. Whether I am writing a Substack or managing a $400 million hedge fund portfolio, I always try to focus on process, not outcomes. That is the winning approach in trading, poker, golf, and any probabilistic pursuit. A golfer can practice, prepare, center her mind, go through all her mental exercises, step up to the tee… And still shank the ball into the pond. That's just how life goes. Focus on process and not on outcomes.

By the way, process over outcome is a great way to live a less stressful life and it's also the thesis of the book "Thinking in Bets" by Annie Duke. I highly recommend that book to anyone serious about trading or poker.

Before we get to the trade idea, a fairly detailed explainer is in order as I outline how I use correlation to trade. I introduced a few correlation concepts last week when I explained how negative-yielding debt and US real rates are correlated to the price of gold. Today, I am going deeper into cross-market correlation, continuing with some themes from Trade 1.

I watch all markets and attempt to make sense of what micro moves in markets might mean for forward-looking global macro.

Correlation is useful, even when it's not causal

Whenever I point out a less obvious correlation between two markets, the most common skeptical reaction is "correlation does not imply causation". Tyler Vigen's famous website has some excellent examples of strong correlations between series that are clearly not causal. These are called spurious correlations. Here's one:

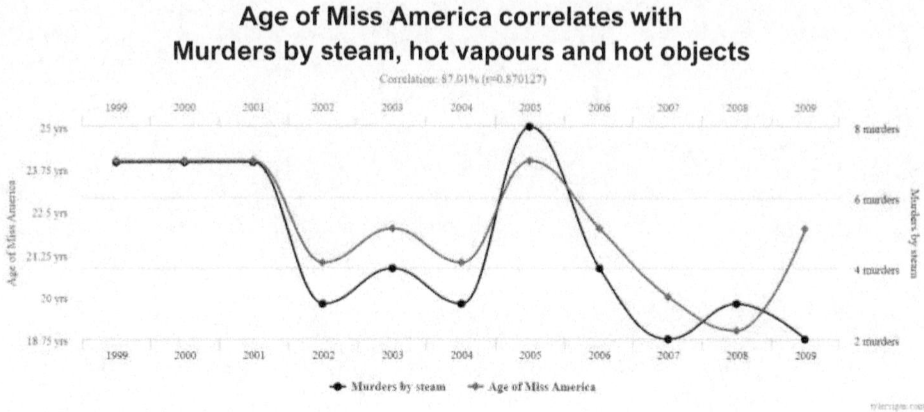

The word spurious means "not being what it purports to be; false or fake." But is this correlation spurious?

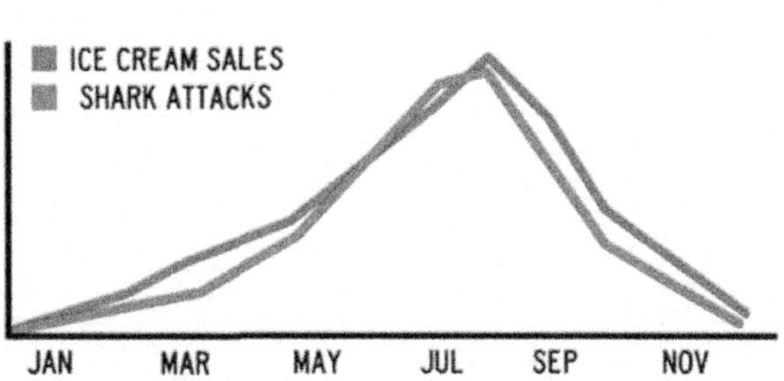

Well, there is certainly no causation between ice cream sales and shark attacks. People do not get attacked by sharks because sharks smell ice cream in swimmers' bellies, right? But the relationship is not a nonsensical coincidence, either.

There is a third variable (seasonality) that drives both series. During the summer, people go swimming more, get attacked by sharks more, and buy more ice cream. Outdoor temperatures drive both series and generate the high correlation.

Another correlation like this would be "Starbucks Pumpkin Spice Latte advertising budget vs. Buzz Lightyear costume sales." Both spike around Halloween. Seasonality can also drive markets. For example, natural gas prices rise in winter as demand peaks.

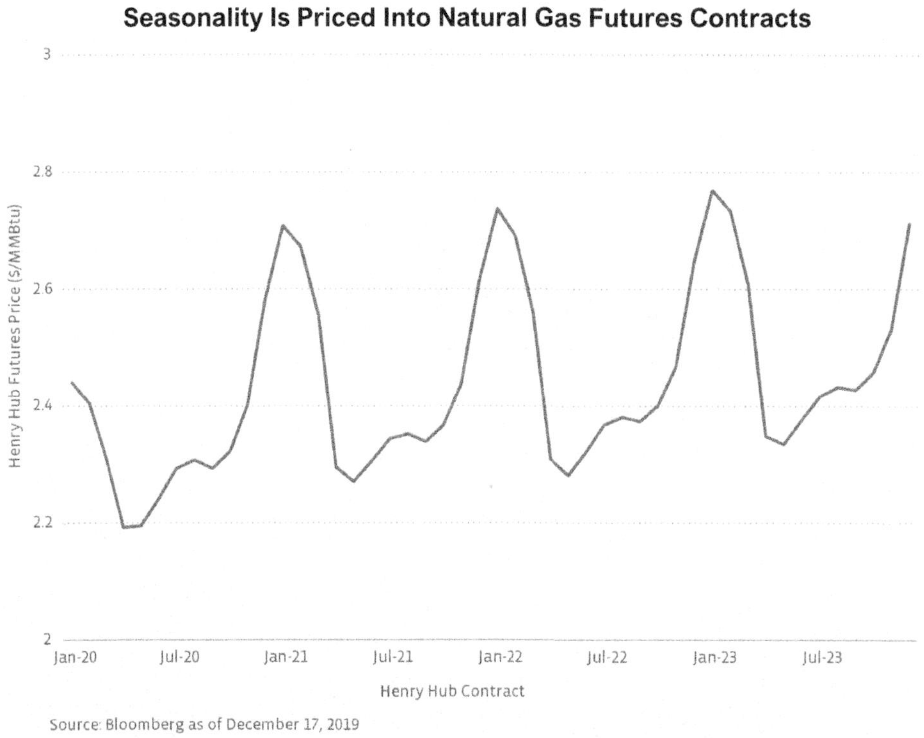

https://insights.alerian.com/seasons-greetings-energy-seasonality-and-midstream

Stock markets also exhibit persistent seasonality and (much to the dismay of the haters and the EMH acolytes), that seasonality works in and out of sample, across almost every geography, for the past 300 years.[3] The next chart shows the average seasonality of US stocks since 1990 along with the actual path that stocks took in 2021. Amazing!

This is not hindsight… I was writing about this in am/FX in September 2021 as a reason to be bearish and in mid-October as a reason to be bullish. Like every input, seasonality is not the be-all, end-all… It's one of many clues. It works on average, but not every year of course.

---

[3] http://www-stat.wharton.upenn.edu/~steele/ Courses/434/434Context/Calendar%20Effects/SellInMayGoAway.pdf

There are many third variables that can drive financial markets. For example, Canadian interest rates, Canadian equity markets, and the Canadian dollar will all move in predictable ways in reaction to Canadian GDP growth and inflation. If growth in Canada is strong and there is high inflation, you would expect Canadian yields, equities, and CAD to do well. This is a simplistic view of the world and not always true, but it's a good starting point.

Most markets move up and down in response to the same underlying drivers, such as:

- Economic growth and inflation
- Monetary Policy
- Geopolitics
- Global risk appetite

So there is a reason that markets are correlated. People yelling "CORRELATION IS NOT CAUSATION!" in all caps are technically right but practically not very helpful. There often is no causation, but there is a ton of information contained in the correlation between assets.

Here are six other ways the abstract concept of cross-market correlation plays out in the real world.

Arbitrage and substitution. This is an easy one in its simplest form. If bitcoin is selling at 57,500 on one platform and there is a bid at 57,600 on another platform, that's pure arbitrage.[4] There is also a more nuanced version of this that looks a lot like arbitrage but is not. This is usually called basis or RV trading.

Closest to arbitrage is the basis between two fungible or nearly-fungible products like futures and spot. You can sell gold futures and buy physical gold and at some point down the road, the prices are very likely to converge. This is not arbitrage though! There is a significant basis and mark to market risk. Still, this basis-related near-arbitrage is the reason nearly-fungible products like futures and spot, or ADRs and their underlying stock price, exhibit very high correlation.

Moving along the spectrum from arbitrage to basis to RV... If you build a curve of all the crude oil futures prices and there is a kink in the curve that puts the DEC 2023 high relative to the other contracts, you can sell DEC and buy a contract on or below the curve and have an excellent (but not risk-free) chance of making money.

Substitution is further out on the same spectrum. This is the dynamic where a rise in the price of one asset will lead consumers to buy a cheaper substitute. If corn doubles in price, those who can switch to soy will do so, pushing the price of soy futures higher. If Doordash rips higher and now looks overvalued, investors looking for food delivery apps to invest in might buy GrubHub instead.

Third variable. As briefly mentioned above, when two asset prices move up and down together, they could be responding to a third variable that drives them both. This is the most common driver of the correlations I talk about and it is the reason trading lead/lag is logical. Most of the assets moving around on your screen are responding to the same set of macro stimuli.

As outlined above, if there is rising optimism about Canadian growth, CAD will trade stronger, and Canadian interest rates will rise. The third variable (Canadian growth expectations) is the key driver of both USDCAD and Canadian rates. This will show up as high correlation between the two markets and the snazzy overlays that frequently decorate am/FX.

Opportunities arise as some markets move more slowly than others and the signal from one market provides clues as to the direction of the other. This could be because of non-price-sensitive flows against the grain in one market but not the other.

---

[4] Here is an excellent trading story involving arbitrage: https://www.linkedin.com/pulse/crazy-trading-story-from-year-2000-brent-donnelly/. Probably my favorite trading story of all time.

For example, if the outlook for China growth is improving and copper is ripping higher but a huge M&A is going through selling AUD, you might see a divergence develop. The moment the M&A transaction is complete, AUDUSD will snap higher to where it "should have been" given the rally in copper and the rosy outlook for China.

Cash flows. When one asset moves, it can generate cash flows in another asset. For example: When a Canadian crude oil producer sells their crude, they receive USD. They need CAD to pay their employees and shareholders so after they sell their crude, they need to sell USDCAD to convert the proceeds. If the price of crude doubles, the crude producer will have twice as many USD to sell and this will weigh on USDCAD.

This is one mechanism that drives the USDCAD vs. crude oil correlation. If you have ever worked at a bank with a strong Canadian presence, you know those flows are an important piece of the USDCAD puzzle.

While cash flows are a significant driver of the correlation between commodity currencies and commodities, cash flows can also be important in other pairs. If US yields move higher, Japanese investors will find those higher yields appealing and will buy US bonds. Those purchases will drive the USD higher and generate a correlation between US yields and USDJPY.

Higher yields tend to, but do not always, lead to higher USDJPY.

USDJPY (black) vs. US 10-year yield (gray), July to November 2021

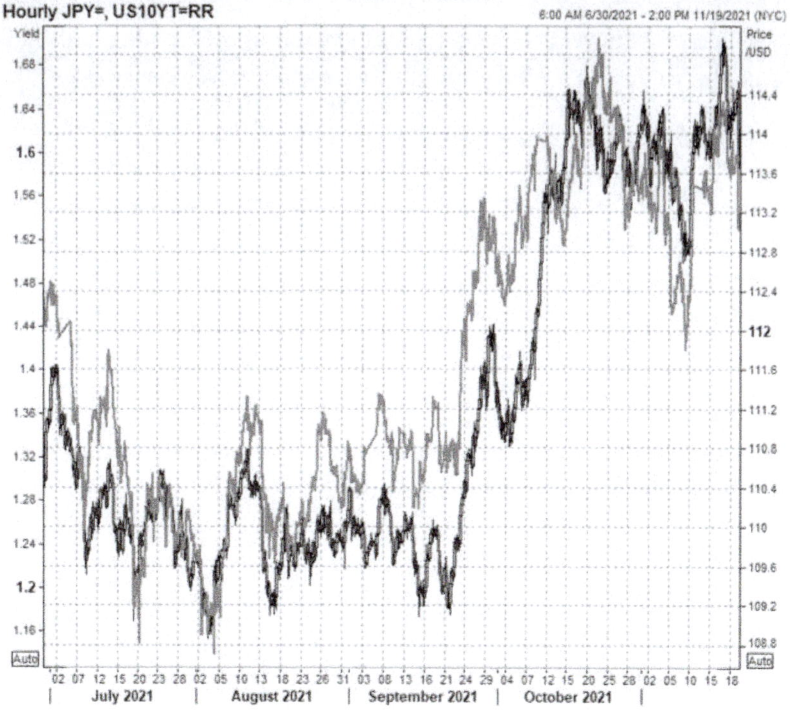

Cross ownership / liquidation / forced selling. Speculators tend to take positions relating to broad macroeconomic themes. For example, at the moment the theme is inflation so the macro positions are: short bonds, long USDJPY, long oil, and so on. When there is significant movement in one of those assets (even if views on the global growth outlook have not changed), it will trigger activity in the other markets as owners of the basket react to the changes in their P&L.

For example, if the market is positioned short bonds and long oil for the inflation trade (like they are right now), and bonds start to rally, you might see oil start to sell off as speculators feel the pain in their P&L. The more bonds rally, the more oil specs need to sell to manage their drawdown.

Correlation traders and algos (self-fulfilling prophecy). Since people know that certain products are correlated, they won't wait for the cash flows or cross-ownership flows to kick in. If oil rips $2 higher, algos and humans all over the world will sell USDCAD.

Volatility and systemic risk. As systemic risk rises and risky assets fall, correlations rise. Every asset has an idiosyncratic risk component and a systemic or macro risk component. Idiosyncratic risk (say, supply and demand for copper) loses importance when systemic risk is high. Intense risk aversion pushes all correlation towards one as the only thing that matters is the rise or fall of the systemic risk.

Like many high school relationships, correlations are fun, but unstable, and unreliable. They can bring you great joy and inspiration one day and then leave you sad and confused the next. That is why I never present correlation factors as the be-all-end-all. They are the clues that might get you to a good idea, but they are never the answer.

Trading is probabilistic, not deterministic.

No matter how confident you are in your trade idea, always know there's a pretty good chance you might still be wrong. This gives you incredible freedom because once you acknowledge and accept you are going to be wrong rather frequently, you get used to it. It becomes part of the process and you don't really take an emotional hit when you stop out. There are no sure bets in trading and if you are 100% confident on a trade, or it seems like free money, you are probably about to get punched in the face by Mike Tyson.

That's the intro. Now let's get to the idea. I will keep it pretty tight from here because I promised you each 50in50 would be under 3000 words.

Trade 2: Sell Oil

Here's my completed framework template for this sell oil trade:

50 in50

Trade 2
Short oil

	Date		15-Feb-22
	Security		**April CL micro future (WMIJ2)**
	Long, short, other		**Short**
The idea		Elevator pitch	Crude making a choppy topping pattern just like last time Russia was threatening Ukraine.
	Idea source	Events or news	Russia / Ukraine has triggered high volume speculative frenzy. You are paid to take the other side.
		Deviation from fair value	US 10-year yields heading into strong resistance and very high correlation to oil right now. It's a distraction.
		Pattern recognition / indicators	Front month crude extension is the same pattern as 2014.
Filters	Tailwind or headwind and why?	Narrative cycle	No strong view on whether or not this is peak commodity narrative but feels like a short-term top.
		Positioning and sentiment	BAML survey shows market bearish tech and bonds and bullish commodities, eurostoxx, and banks.
		Events and catalysts	Russia / Ukraine simmering, obviously. Iran deal could help this trade.
		Correlated markets	10-year yields at mega resistance.
		Technicals	Volume spike and bearish divergence.
	Alternative hypothesis	What might go wrong? Pre-mortem	Russia invades Ukraine or just another huge leg higher.

50 Trader framework and checklist, page 2 50

Tactics	Trade structure	Best asset, market, structure?	Futures or ETF
		Microstructure considerations	CL is liquid, not much gap risk during the week but careful on the weekend. An invasion on a Saturday could create huge gap risk.
		Entry	**91.05**
		Stop loss	**95.45**
		Take profit	**79.05**
	Other reassessment triggers		None. Stick to the plan.
Risk management	Conviction level	TYPE I, II, or III	**TYPE I**
	Free Capital		**$ 100,000**
	% of free capital		**1.50%**
	$ at risk		1,644
	Solve for position size		4 contracts of WMIJ2
	Any issues with liquidity or capacity?		No. Tiny position.
Execution	Execution notes (limit, market, etc.)		91.05 limit
	Automate or outsource stop loss		Yes
	Enter trade in journal		Yes
Psychology	What emotions are involved here? Do I feel anything unusual? List emotions or possible pitfalls.		Doubling down on Russia story which could lead to regret. BUT! Sometimes the hard trade is the right trade.

Stick to the original plan

I am using micro oil futures in the spreadsheet because the position size is too small for regular futures. CME micro futures are 1/10th the size of normal ones. Note, I am not an expert in retail execution (!!) so **make sure you know what you are doing before you trade**. None of this is investment advice. This is an educational product. Seriously.

Figure out how much you want to risk in $ and then back out your position size as explained in Week 1. There is a futures P&L calculator at www.danielstrading.com/trading-resources/futures-calculator. There is a chance I could make a mistake when discussing particular products like micro crude futures, which I am familiar with conceptually, but have never traded because I worked at a bank or hedge fund for most of my life.

Here's a quick run through of the logic of the trade. Note, **this is not a big picture global macro trade**. It's a quick attempt to pick a top in a market that looks like it's blown off to the topside. Risking 4 dollars to make 12.

Blow-off top on high volume

As you can see from the chart, the hourly volume in crude futures this week hit a three-month spike high. Spikes in volume can often be indicative of panic and forced buying or selling and they make great turning points. When there is a massive surge of volume and the price rejects that location, you can then pinpoint that location as a critical pivot. In this case, it's the high. Then, you set your stop loss above that. Note the sweet, sweet megavolume low in early December.

Crude oil fails on huge volume spike

Front end contracts megabid but contracts further out not so much

There are dozens of crude oil futures contracts that expire as early as this month and as late as 2033. You can plot a curve of the prices and sometimes it slopes up and sometimes it slopes down.

Here's the curve right now:

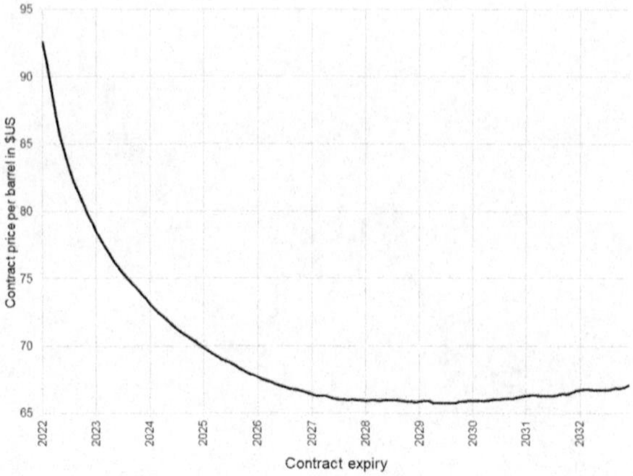

A deep dive into the importance of the shape of the crude curve is beyond the scope of this piece, but believe me when I say a steep downward slope like that is rare. The next chart gives you a sense of some history.

This chart shows the first contract (CL1) minus the contract that expires five years later (currently 93 minus 68 = 25, roughly). When crude markets are tight and there are shortages, you tend to see the first contract trade at a huge premium. Generally, that is unsustainable and it's a sign of unsustainable upward price pressure.

Front NYMEX crude (CL) minus CL contract expiring in five years

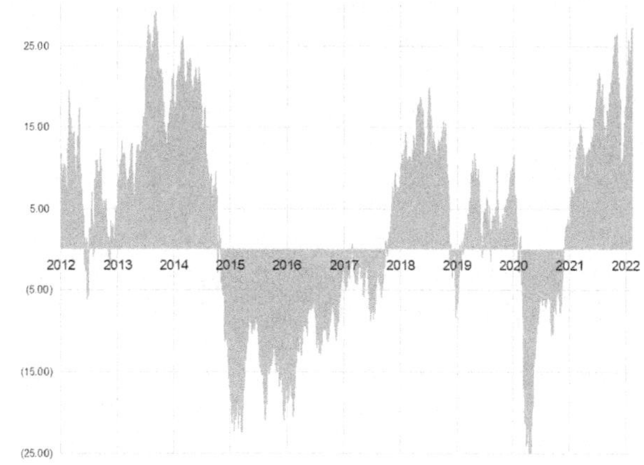

Pull up a chart of crude oil and you will see that prior times when the front end was super bid (late 2013, 2014, and 2018) were horrendous times to own crude. Extreme moves in the crude curve tend to (but do not always) signal potential mean reversion.

US 10-year yields and crude oil have been moving in lockstep for months as you can see in this chart (black bars are US yields, the line is crude oil).

And we are entering a big zone of interest here in US 10-year yields. 2.04% was the post-GFC low and the 2017 low (see chart) and the last spike before the Fed started easing then COVID hit was 2.15%. As such, I think 10-year yields will start to struggle up here. The implication, given the correlation between rates and oil, is that if yields slow their ascent, the entire reflation trade will too, and that should take a bit of pressure off oil.

US 10-year yields in a big resistance zone

And, finally, the Economist is asking "How High Will Interest Rates Go?"[5] which can often, but not always, be a contrarian indicator.

I would never trade off any single one of the reasons I have listed here today, but in combination, this looks like a nice setup. If you are wondering why the Economist cover is contrarian, check out the web page in the footnote.[6]

Risks

This is another Russia invasion risk trade, in theory. I don't really believe that a Russian invasion means much for crude beyond a kneejerk reaction, but the market seems to think so. The good thing about this setup is that Russia invasion odds have shot higher and you are now selling AFTER the high volume spike and failure in crude. If oil can get back up and make new highs, it deserves to stop me out!

There is a positive kicker risk on this trade: If there is a deal on Iran nuclear, that could bring more supply to market and hit oil.

I put this as a TYPE I trade because it is correlated risk to Trade 1 and because my conviction is a bit lower given the risk of a random headline that could take me out at the knees without warning. Then again, I like placing trades like this where you have a very clearly-defined exit level and a good entry point.

It's way too complicated for me to consider the 50in50 trades as a portfolio, so generally, I will **NOT** be factoring in the correlation between live 50in50 trades.

I don't know retail trading platforms

The point of this book is not to teach you the micro specifics of how to press buttons on your specific platform. I want to explain to you the general idea and you figure out how to do it on Interactive Brokers or TD Ameritrade or whatever platform. I'm no expert on that. I worked as a market maker at a bank and traded OTC for most of my life and even when I traded futures in the past, it was at a hedge fund.

Be very careful with your weekend risk. A stop loss doesn't help you much if you're short at $91, Russia invades on Saturday and you get filled at $101. Either square up on the weekends, or size it so you are not ruined by a $15 or $20 weekend worst-case scenario gap. Unlikely but pointless risk.

If you want to do this trade, micro CL futures should work, but you could also structure it your own way through Brent crude, XLE, or whatever else is correlated to crude oil. I

---

[5] https://www.economist.com/weeklyedition/2022-02-05

[6] https://medium.com/@mbrentdonnelly/a-somewhat-empirical-look-at-the-magazine-cover-indicator-2d0ca835f7d1

used April micro futures (WMIJ2 on Bloomberg) because March futures are about roll off. That's why my entry point is $91.00.

Trade idea summary:

- TYPE I conviction sell oil futures
- Short-term blowoff top on high volume gives a nice entry
- The curve is steep like it was at prior highs
- Correlated asset (yields) entering massive resistance

Final thoughts

Some will not like this trade because I am doubling down on Russia risk. I think it's worth it.

I have to say of the hundreds of geopolitical flare-ups I have seen (including the March 2014 annexation of Crimea)... Very few have had a lasting impact on markets.

I acknowledge that this is like saying "very few earthquakes destroy cities." When it happens, it's a massive deal but you can't spend the rest of 2022 under the desk hiding from Putin. He might stack the border with materiel for the next 12 months in a Sword of Damocles kind of strategy. If Russia invades, my trades will get stopped out. That's life.

Week 3: Short DOCS

Great companies can be terrible investments

Update: Open trades

The XAUEUR trade continues to suck wind as Russia risk hangs over markets like the Sword of Damocles.

Side note: The story of the Sword of Damocles[7] *is more interesting than I expected it to be. Many lessons.*

As explained last week, I strongly prefer to stick to the plan on trades like this; so that's what I'll do.

The short oil trade is flat; nothing significant to report there, really. The entry point in April crude was $92.20 and the current level is $92.34. For record-keeping and tracking, I will always use the market price when I hit send on the trade idea. This might differ slightly from the write-up because it takes me a while to write these things.

Update complete. This week, my focus is on technical analysis.

[7] https://en.wikipedia.org/wiki/Damocles

Intro to technical analysis

A good intro to technical analysis (aka, techs) could fill 30 pages but today I'm going to boil it down to 1,500 words or so. If you want to learn more about technical analysis, my three favorite books on the topic are:

Technical Analysis of the Futures Markets by John Murphy

Mind Over Markets by Dalton, Jones, and Dalton

Japanese Candlestick Charting Techniques by Steven Nison

Also, both my books have extensive sections on technical analysis. Pages 107 to 178 of *The Art of Currency Trading* and Chapter 10 of *Alpha Trader* are all about techs.

What is technical analysis?

Technical analysis is the study of chart patterns in an attempt to forecast future price movements. The theory is that in a natural system composed of many human beings, price patterns will repeat and echo as humans tend to behave in similar and predictable ways over time. This psychological regularity should generate patterns that can be seen in real-time and used as predictors of future market moves.

There are literally hundreds of technical patterns ranging from generic (support and resistance levels) to very esoteric patterns like the "Abandoned Baby" or the "Three Buddha Bottom". Anything involving charts and pattern recognition usually falls under the heading of technical analysis.

Does technical analysis work?

There is a ton of research on technical analysis out there, but unfortunately no conclusive evidence. There is some modest evidence of persistent trend and tradable patterns in certain markets over time, but it is unclear how much of this works in real-time (it could just be hindsight and data snooping). Trend following models in FX have performed poorly since the 1990s and the evidence generally suggests that some patterns worked for some periods but profitable technical patterns are arbitraged away over time.

Some people think technical analysis is useless—a complete joke. Other traders think technical analysis is the only tool you need to trade successfully. My philosophy on technical analysis is somewhere in the middle.

I think technical analysis is a valuable tool but does not work well as a standalone trade selection or forecasting methodology. The more years I trade, the more strongly I believe that technical analysis should be used as a tactical and risk management tool and not as a trade selection tool. This comes from years of trading experience, from watching many people trade, and from reading volumes of research on the topic.

While there are examples out there of successful purely technical traders, in more than 20 years of trading on both the buy side and the sell side, I have never worked with a purely technical trader who made real money. Every successful trader I have worked with over the years either trades macro or uses a multifactor approach. And I have seen many traders who use only technical analysis fail miserably.

A majority of the most successful traders of all time: Soros, Tudor-Jones, Bacon, Druckenmiller, etc… Are macro or hybrid guys, not pure technicians. They supplement their analysis with charts but their ideas come from all over the place. Again, I'm not saying it's impossible to trade purely techs, but success rates are microscopic.

Do you really think it passes the common-sense sniff test that you can just look at a chart, see a simple pattern, trade it, and consistently make money? Given the thousands of traders and billions of lines of code, you are competing with… Probably not. There were systematic funds that profited from simple technical analysis in the 1980s and 1990s but those days are long gone. Systematic funds now compete on a much more complex playing field and the profitability of simple trend following and other technical systems has converged towards zero.

There is a simple reason that using technical analysis is inherently risky for humans: Humans are designed to see patterns. It's how our biology works. It allows us to simplify and process a complex world. This human tendency to perceive meaningful patterns within random data is called "apophenia."

For example, this faucet which looks nothing at all like a face:

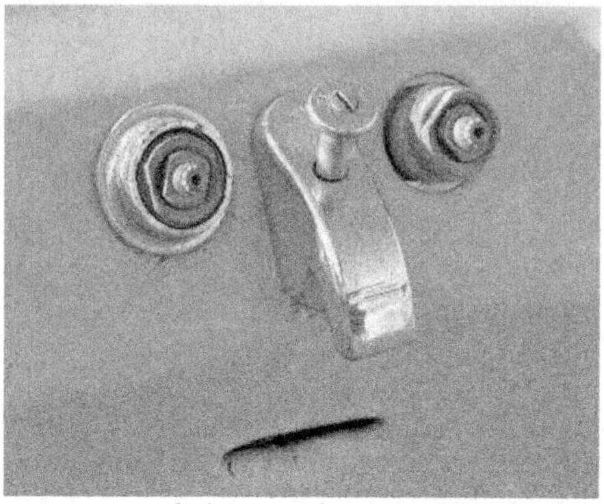

Just a simple faucet, right? Face? What face??

The human brain is designed to see patterns! Even where they do not exist.

If you are bullish some security, I can guarantee that if you look at a chart long enough you will find a pattern that confirms your bullish view. In other words, another problem with technical analysis is that it is subject to confirmation bias. You see what you want to see. A friend of mine once said "Charts are like clouds. If you stare long enough, you will eventually see something interesting!"

Furthermore, most of the empirical evidence from research shows that if you trade popular technical patterns like Head and Shoulders systematically, *you do not make money*. So I strongly believe that technical analysis is best used for risk management and tactical considerations and not as a primary trade selection tool.

While my belief is that the value of technical analysis as a forecasting tool is limited, **I use technical analysis every day**. I come up with my trade ideas elsewhere and then go to the technicals to determine optimal tactics such as entry level, stop loss, take profit, and position size.

Without technical analysis skills, you are too often entering trades at midrange with no clear concept of where to get out. Techs give you clear-cut risk management levels and allow you to maximize your leverage and determine the point at which you will admit you are wrong. Note that my approach also meshes with research that shows that portfolio managers who use technical analysis outperform those who do not.

I strongly advise you to learn about technical analysis—but consider it a risk management and tactical tool, not a trade selection or forecasting tool. Never do a trade just because a chart looks good or because something is on a big support or Fibonacci level.

From personal experience, observation of 100s of other traders over 25 years, and reading the research… I believe:

1. Technical analysis is an important part of almost every excellent trader's toolkit.
2. Technical analysis is overrated and overused, especially by new traders.

Think of technical indicators the way you think of the rearview mirror and dashboard indicators in your car. They tell you where you have been, how fast you are going, when you might run out of gas, and so on. But they don't tell you where you are going. For that, you need to piece all the indicators together, then look out the front window.

Technical indicators that I like

When it comes to technical indicators, here's what I like and why.

I like: Simple and objective

The more complicated something is, the less I like it because subjective and complicated approaches tend to be time-consuming and poisoned by confirmation bias.

If an Elliott Wave practitioner is subconsciously bullish NASDAQ because of her secret crush on Cathie Wood, she will always be able to find a bullish wave count.

Permabears with expert knowledge of Elliott Wave can always find a bearish count.

In contrast, if your system is (for example) "don't be long anything that is trading below the 50-day moving average"… It doesn't matter what your bias is because your system is simple and objective.

Also, the self-fulfilling prophecy aspect of technical analysis works best with simple approaches. Part of the reason a level might hold is that everyone believes it will hold—and so everyone puts their bids there. If you are using PhD quantum physics and homological mirror symmetry to find your tech levels, and nobody else in the known universe is, the levels you find just might not mean much in the market.

Open-ended approaches that are not objective can yield way too much noise. For example, traders like to use Fibonacci levels as support and resistance. I don't mind a bit of numerology and there is an appealing concept behind Fibonacci (or fibo) levels: When something drops a lot, you wait for a big bounce to sell it. That, in itself has some value. Instead of chasing something lower, practitioners of Fibonacci retracements will wait for a bounce of 61.8% or 76.4% of the down move and sell there. This can be good!

On the other hand, here is a EURUSD daily chart marked with all the daily fibos. Separating noise from signal can be difficult. If you're bullish on the way down, you can always find another fibo to justify it.

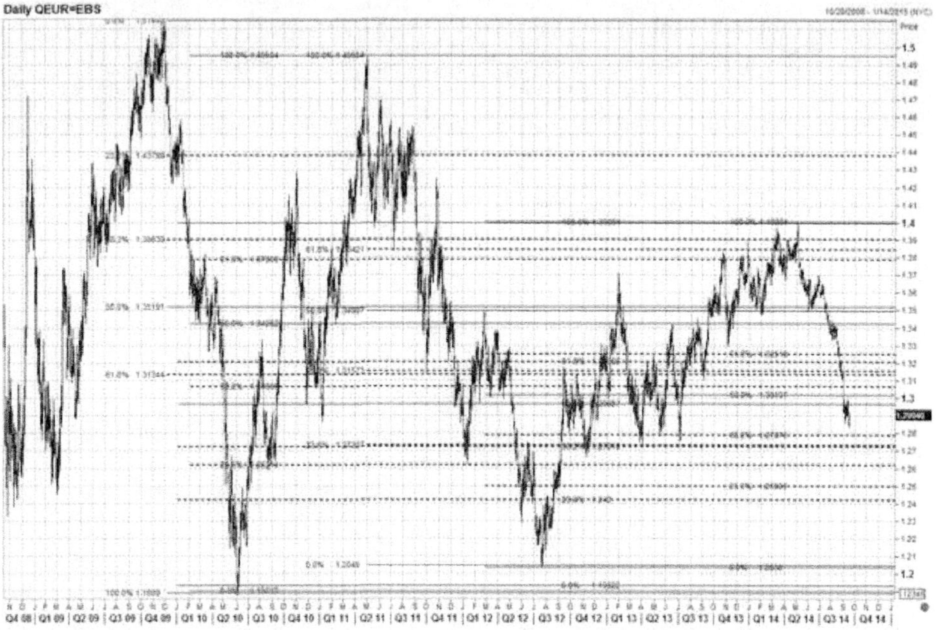

I like: Approaches that reveal underlying reality in the market

Some technical setups directly reveal a reality in the market. Horizontal lines could reflect large orders out there. Slingshot reversals can reflect a final capitulation of speculators through a key level. Gaps can reflect where the liquidity is (or isn't). Let's take a look at a few ways techs can reveal underlying market reality.

1. Horizontal lines

Most of the technical approaches that I use reflect something about the underlying structure of the market in a particular area. For example, the beauty of simple horizontal lines is that they very often reflect the presence of large orders. Let's say a Japanese auto exporter needs to sell 5 billion USDJPY, and they have left an order with a bank to sell at 116.33. They are patient and don't mind waiting. You might get a chart that looks like this:

USDJPY double touch of horizontal resistance at 116.33

There's very often a reason horizontal lines work: They are reflecting the reality of large bids and offers in the market. Remember that because support and resistance are simple and not subject to much interpretation, most people in the market will be monitoring roughly the same support and resistance levels.

Therefore, you need to think about the metagame and leave your stops far enough below support (or above resistance) that you are not dinged by a weak stop loss run that takes out an obvious level. **It is often best to place your stop loss about a half-day's range below a major level to avoid any noisy whipsaws around that point.**

2. Volume spikes

Another approach that I like is to look for volume spikes at price extremes.

High volumes reinforce the importance of a support or resistance level or can signal that it has been decisively broken. **High volumes provide signal confirmation for technical patterns.**

The next chart shows a massive volume spike at a turning point. Note the huge volume as EURNOK made a low in late August 2021. That marked the ding dong low in the pair. If you squint, you can also see the second-largest volume bar coincides with an important low in mid-June.

Volume spikes at a price extreme are super useful indicators that huge volume has gone through and the move was rejected or accepted by the market.

EURNOK hourly, April 2020 to September 2020

Top pane is EURNOK price, bottom pane is volume

3. **Moving averages**

One of the easiest ways to make sure you are not fighting the market is to implement a simple moving average (MA) rule. For example: *I will only be long if the market is above the 50-day moving average. I will only be short if the market is below the 200-hour moving average.* And so on.

I have a 200-hour moving average on all my charts because that matches my time horizon, but it's kind of arbitrary. You can backtest and find the best fit for trend and that's a good starting point just don't forget that out of sample, the best fit will probably not be the exact MA you found in your backtest. The idea with MA's is not to seek the false precision of an exact lookback period, it's to find a moving average that roughly matches the ebbs and flows of your market so you don't get a million noisy signals every day, but you also don't get one or two signals a year.

One hedge fund that I know uses a very simple rule which I like. They are bigger picture than me, so they use a 100-day MA filter, and then they simply apply that to all their macro views. They have a bunch of analysts and portfolio managers who come up with all the discretionary views but they only execute those views which are on the correct side of the 100-day MA.

This avoids the problem of: "I loved it at 10, now it's at 7… So I must really love it now!" A rigorous approach to technical analysis leads to good risk management and tells you "You're wrong, it's time to get out." Very often, fundamental analysis will never tell you to get out and might tell you to keep doubling down as prices get more and more attractive. You see this in crypto a lot.

Alright, that's the background material for this week's trade idea.

To be clear: **I never do a trade purely on technicals.** Technicals are a good risk management tool but not a great forecasting tool. My ideas come from my read on changing narratives, from cross-market correlation, pattern recognition, backtesting, positioning, and other fundamental or microstructure analysis. Then, I use technical analysis to hone my tactics, maximize leverage, put up risk management guard rails, and determine the stop loss and take profit. Sometimes, I'll find a trade I love and then the techs don't line up, so I'll wait. *Strategy vs. tactics.*

Trade 3: Short DOCS

I will run through the narrative explanation for this trade very quickly as the focus this week is on technicals. Please don't email me what a great company DOCS is, or how telehealth is the future. I'm sure it is!

My view here is short-term (2-4 week time horizon) and anyway… **Great companies can make terrible investments.** When I was screaming about Zoom and Shopify being terrible investments last year, Twitter would fire back with cringe replies like:

Cringe

In the midst of heavily hyped narratives, people forget that stock investments are a combination of:

a) how good is the company, and
b) what are you paying for it?

A BMW M5 is a great car, but not good value at $1,800,000.

Christine, if you're reading this… Birthday gift idea.

ZM and SHOP can be great companies and wildly overvalued at the same time. If you want to read more about this, I had a conversation with Howard Marks on this topic in March 2021. You can read it on Epsilon Theory.[8]

---

[8] https://www.epsilontheory.com/a-conversation-with-howard-marks/

Regardless, this is a short-term trade. The market is punishing high-priced stocks and I expect that to continue. Babies out with bathwater.

My thesis is:

- All COVID darlings getting taken to the woodshed one by one
- Teladoc, DOCS main competitor, crashing to new lows
- Market is dumping expensive stocks. DOCS trades at 35x sales, making it the 15th most-expensive US-listed large cap. I like price-to-sales as a simple valuation metric because earnings are much easier to manipulate/obfuscate than sales. It's not perfect; it's a simple heuristic. If you're curious, the average stock in the US trades around 1.5X sales.
- Big spike on earnings offers a better entry point for shorts compared to most COVID favorites which are mostly down 50% to 80% at this point. Telehealth is one of the sexy narratives around COVID and while I'm certain it's a massive trend in health care, the stocks of highly-valued megatrend disruptors are under severe pressure and are likely to remain under severe pressure. ARKK's price performance has shown (just like 1999 showed)... Great companies can be terrible investments, especially in the short and medium run.
- Massive **volume spike** high rejected on good news (earnings). I will discuss this below.
- Strong **horizontal line resistance** at $58/$60 over the past two weeks
- Target the bottom of the huge gap ($50) and the 200-hour MA at $49.10.

Let me be crystal clear here: I am not a stock analyst. I look at narratives, short-term indicators, microstructure, and other factors to make trading decisions. I don't know who the CEO of DOCS is and for the purposes of this trade, I don't care. Big picture fundamentals are irrelevant on a 2-4 week time horizon.

Trading and investing are completely different sports.

Also please note: This is an educational blog (book). Don't copy my trades. Learn from my process and develop your own trading style that has edge. Thanks.

Explaining the tech setup

Take a look at the hourly chart below. You can see that there was a massive volume spike in November and that marked the absolute high. Now, we have another massive volume spike high at $65 on the earnings announcement (plus DOCS buying Amion). Everyone that wanted to buy on the earnings release has done so and is almost surely trapped out of the money having bought $60/$62ish.

DOCS common equity hourly chart with 200-hour MA in gray

If we zoom in a bit, and look at 5-minute chart, we see two important bits of info. There is a second volume surge when DOCS broke back down below $60 (this is the weakest of the headline buyers stopping out, where price breaks below the black line 10/11FEB) and we now have nice horizontal resistance at $60. This persistent distribution near $60 is probably a major institutional investor trying to reduce or exit a large stake.

DOCS common equity 5-minute chart with horizontal resistance

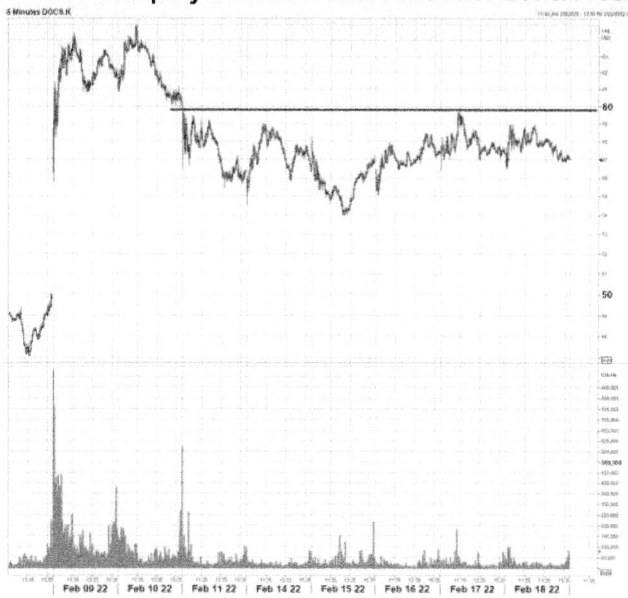

This gives us a nice setup where we can go short here and put a stop loss at $60.51 (above the horizontal line with a bit of room for noise). The take profit is $50.21 as we want to be in front of both the bottom of the huge news gap, and the 200-hour MA at $49.20. Based on Friday's close ($57) that would be risking $3.50 to make $6.80 for a gain of about 2x the loss.

I will use the NYSE open on 22FEB22 for the entry point (for tracking purposes) since I'm sending this on a holiday Monday in the USA. My trade is to sell $56 or better because selling worse than $56 just messes up the risk/reward too much. If DOCS opens below $56, this becomes a limit order to sell at $56.

Conclusion

50in50 goes short DOCS at the open 22FEB @ $56 or better. Stop loss $60.51. Take profit at $50.21.

Risking $2,000 this week, or 2% of capital. Therefore, short 443 shares ($2,000 divided by $4.51 per share of risk = 443 shares.) As is the case with most stock trades, there is gap risk here if DOCS releases news overnight.

Week 4: A Respite from Winter

Long BTC for a 2-week to 4-week tactical rebound

Update: Open trades

The XAUEUR and oil trades got stopped out on the Russian invasion. This is a bummer, but that's trading. I was wrong about the Russian risk and thought it was a risk worth selling. There is no shame in being wrong. In fact, if you are ashamed to be wrong, it will be hard to succeed as a trader. The best traders in the world are wrong, all the time.

Sadly, short XAUEUR and short oil both look like amazing trades now so perhaps the lesson is "wait for the climactic news before you try to take the other side of a geopolitical event." I got in front of a known risk and got run over. Then again, if they never invaded, I would have regretted waiting and Hindsight Harry is the best trader in the world.

DOCS is flying around but going nowhere for now.

Update complete! This week, my focus is on the narrative cycle.

Bullish world

I have been leaning mostly bearish risky assets since last November when Powell dropped "transitory", the crypto/GameFi/Web3 sentiment bubble was raging out of control and the bulls controlled the narrative cycle.

Now, all the GameFi tokens have crashed, Web3 haters have a voice, crypto is off 50% to 60% from the highs, the Fed is priced for 7 or 8 hikes, Russia has invaded Ukraine, ARKK is back to where it was two years ago, it's cool to make fun of Cathie Wood on Twitter, and so on.

The narrative and zeitgeist now are a mirror image of where we stood in November. This is all *textbook* narrative cycle.

What is the narrative cycle?

The narrative is the story the market tells itself to explain movements in price. Like any good story, there is usually the main plot and then a few subplots. The main arc is the most important to understand because markets tend to focus on one thing at a time. But you also need to be ready for the next story as it elbows today's narrative out of the way.

Understanding narrative is what most people used to call fundamental analysis but there is an important nuance. Narrative analysis is about studying not just what *you* think is the story, but (more importantly) what story market players are telling and what story the market itself is trying to tell. When it is done well, narrative analysis is a coherent and fluid combination of ever-changing macroeconomic fundamentals and behavioral factors. It is often about nailing down the one, most important story the market wants to trade and then tracking the evolution of that story.

For example, 2010 to 2012 was a remarkable period in FX markets as the market watched the near implosion of the eurozone at the same time as the US Federal Reserve enacted a series of quantitative easing (QE) programs. The eurozone crisis was bearish EUR and US QE was bearish USD. During this period, EURUSD was known as "two garbage trucks colliding" because both currencies had huge issues.

The interesting thing about trading that period, though, was that one story or the other clearly dominated most of the time. The market was either freaking out about the eurozone or going bananas over US QE but it was usually clear which theme was in the driver's seat. This is typical. It is very difficult for markets to hold two competing themes in its collective hivemind at once, and so the focus oscillates back and forth instead of going in two directions at once.

Understanding the narrative cycle is important because when you are good at it, it is a critical tool that helps you identify turning points and trends. You see the psychology and storytelling at work in the market and you can predict where price is going to go. Surprisingly, the **narrative often turns before price** because price has momentum of its own and a propensity to overshoot.

Here is the general narrative cycle:

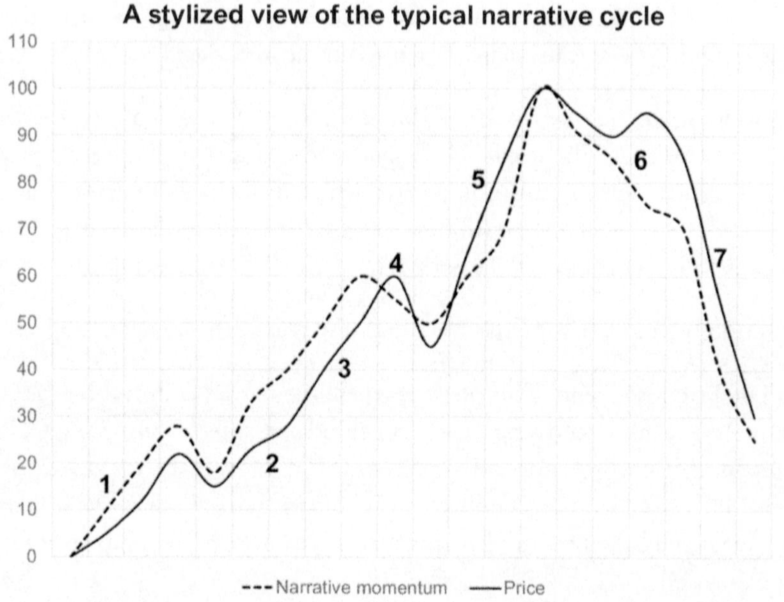

The numbers on that chart refer to the following section in which I will briefly describe each phase of the narrative cycle. You might recognize this as similar to other cycle analysis like the panic/euphoria model or the famous "SELL? SELL? SELL? BUY! BUY!" comic by Kal. It also rhymes a fair bit with Elliott Wave analysis.

Think about the narrative arc of Cathie Woods' ARKK ETF as you read this. It fits perfectly.

Stage 1: Under the radar. At this point, there is a new narrative forming, but very few traders have heard about it. Some smart, independent thinkers and research-oriented people are talking about it and a few contrarians are putting on the position.

Stage 2: Momentum Builds. At this point, the narrative goes a bit viral (at least among professionals or experts) and the price jumps to reflect the new zeitgeist. Remember that at every stage of the narrative cycle, there is a dynamic interplay between price and narrative. The story drives the price and the price drives the story and often it is hard to tell which one is causing the movement. For example, say a stock has a good story but it's still in Stage 1 of the narrative cycle. Nobody is paying attention. A fund manager reads some three-week-old research and decides he loves the story. He starts buying stock and liquidity is poor. The price rallies 4%. Some stale shorts stop out and the fund manager keeps buying and soon the stock is up 11% over the course of two days.

Because the stock rallied, it appears on a few radars (many firms and individuals run scans for stocks with unusual volatility) and this generates some new interest. Traders and investors look it up and some of them like what they see (great story!) and that triggers more buying. In this little description, the price is now feeding the narrative, not the other way around. The narrative already existed three weeks ago.

As momentum builds and the stock hits (for example) a 60-day high, trend followers and CTAs will start to buy. This feedback loop where changes in price influence investor expectations, which influence the narrative, which influences the price, is a form of reflexivity. Reflexivity is a concept from sociology that was transferred over to finance by George Soros. It is a fancier way of saying "circularity" or "feedback loops".

As momentum buying feeds the narrative and feeds on itself, we enter Stage 3.

Stage 3: The Primary Trend. This phase is where the narrative drumbeat takes hold and there are more and more converts lined up behind the apostles from Stage 1. Pullbacks are bought and the news reinforces the price which reinforces the trend which reinforces the buying. This stage is often the most profitable in a strong narrative because Stage 3 can last a surprisingly long time. Just because a narrative is well-known, that does not mean it's exhausted.

Stage 3 involves a lot of hype, usually from financial media and tourists who have joined the party fairly early. Again, just because there is hype, don't think the story is over. The hype phase can accompany dramatic price moves as demand outstrips supply for an extended period and the market ignores bad news and doubles down on good news.

Stage 4: First cracks. At this stage, some cracks appear. Bad news hits that threatens the narrative. The story is crowded, and early entrants think maybe the story is over so they take some profits. There is a meaningful pullback in price. This pullback shakes off the weaker and more recent buyers but those that believe in the narrative appear on the bid and the price stabilizes. Slowly, the importance of the bad news dissipates and price climbs back towards the highs.

Stage 5: The final hype wave. As price breaks through and makes new highs, the narrative often goes into overdrive. Longs are emboldened by the price action and a strong feeling of FOMO comes over anyone who is not participating. Depending on the story, you will often see the narrative cross over from financial media to the mainstream media at this point if the narrative is interesting and important enough.

Non-experts will join the party (retail and macro tourists) and this will push price aggressively higher. Stage 5 is usually the most surprising and volatile part of the narrative cycle as sellers step away and buyers get desperate. Magazine covers and fawning media profiles tend to appear at this stage.

Stage 6: The Peak and the Turn. The top in the narrative and price can be a long-drawn-out process or an impulsive overshoot and collapse. Often, it's like the climax in a movie with a huge flashy rip higher followed by a rapid reversal that catches everyone on the wrong side.

Excellent traders will realize there has been a meaningful turn in the narrative here, even when price continues to make new highs. Bad traders hate to give up on winning trades and great stories and will fall victim to powerful confirmation bias. As long as price continues to rise, most traders will ignore information that goes against the narrative.

It's important to realize that markets are not always correct. The wisdom of the crowd is powerful but not infallible.

Stage 7: The End. As a narrative expires, people lose interest and only those with bad discipline hang on. Shorts hammer the price down and longs slowly but surely get out. Market themes are like fashion trends. The market's interest is fickle and limited. People get bored of a theme, and they move on. Sometimes this will be justified by fundamentals and sometimes it will simply be that a sexier, more interesting theme came along.

That is the narrative cycle.

Remember, I am not an investor and this is not about investing. It is about understanding the current stage of the narrative cycle so that as new information arrives, you can capitalize. If you know where you are in the story and understand current positioning, you will have an edge as the cycle moves from stage to stage. These narrative cycles can last hours, days, or weeks.

Understand the stories the market is telling itself and learn to identify when the market is falling in or out of love with a narrative.

Here's the narrative arc for ARKK. It has gone through the seven stages of my narrative cycle. Cathie Wood has gone from fawning media profiles and God-like status to a handy punching bag for all the retail-driven Fed-gasoline-fueled excess of 2021.

The arc of ARKK: Textbook!

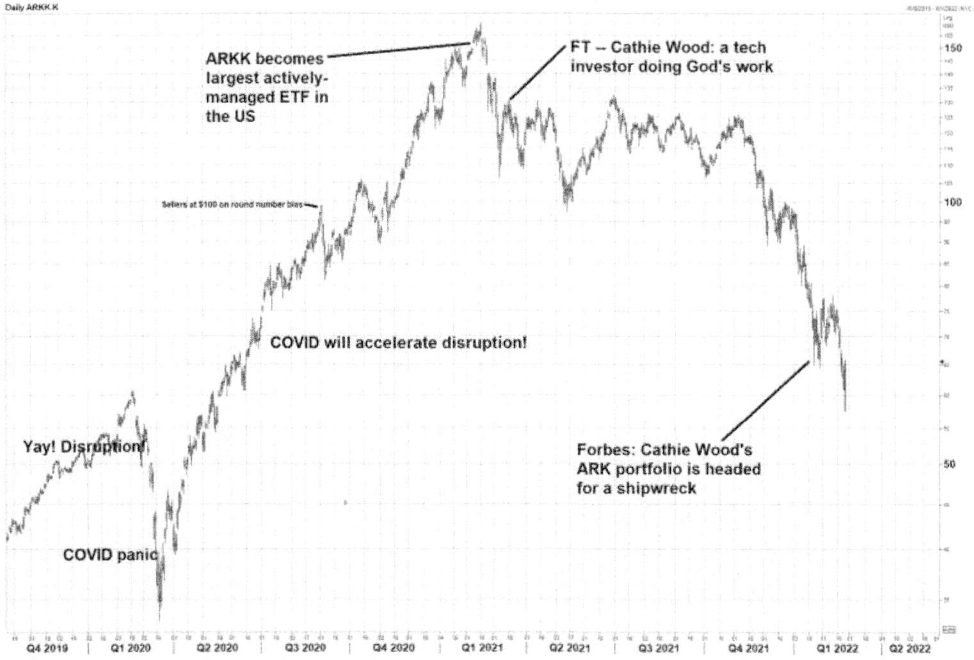

Crypto

I have been bearish crypto since November 2021 based on the narrative cycle and its relationship to the economic and halving cycles of bitcoin. The narrative cycle stayed bullish due to FOMO and price momentum in Q4 2021 even as it was becoming obvious that headwinds for crypto were increasing. Massively.

Now, I feel that we hit peak fear yesterday as the market sold risky assets indiscriminately on the Russian invasion, even though empirically most military actions have been buying opportunities in risky assets, not selling opportunities. The initial invasions of Vietnam, Iraq, and Crimea were all times to buy, not sell. The simple reason for this is that the human toll of war is terrifying but the economic impact on US and global growth tends to be minimal. As such, markets tend to overreact to scary military stuff.

The VIX made a nice double top, gold made a massive fake breakout and reversal, and SPX and NASDAQ made bull hammer bottoms. See these three charts.

VIX gapped higher and formed a double top on Russia

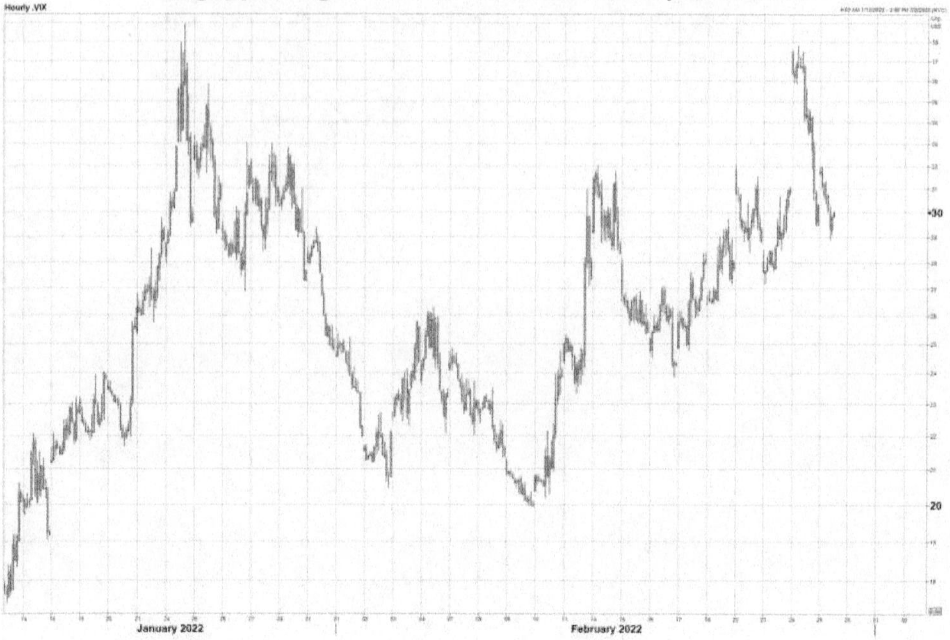

Gold daily chart: False break and massive reversal

S&P Futures slingshot reversal and bull hammer through key 4225 level

Even more interesting is that as SPX and NASDAQ broke aggressively through the lows, bitcoin (also a levered risky asset) didn't even come close to making a new low. That is a bullish divergence. When something makes higher lows while all its peers (or its indicators like RSI) are making deep new lows… That's bullish.

Trade 4: Long bitcoin at 39200

I sent something out on this yesterday at 3:08PM (sent to am/FX and MacroTactical Crypto subscribers)[9] and went long BTC at 38220, but for this blog, I will always mark to market at the level the asset trades when I hit send on the email. Again, the point of this particular writing is not to post strings of winning trades; it's an educational series. So here I'm long at worse levels than IRL. It doesn't matter.

My stop loss is 31400, which would be a new low -$1600. I always like to give it a bit of room through the support in case there is a choppy move. There is giant support at 28500/30000 so you could put your stop below 28500, in theory, but I think that if 31400 breaks, my thesis is wrong and I should get out. I will also get out if SPX goes below 4100.

---

[9] At the time I was writing this, I was also writing a crypto newsletter called MacroTactical Crypto. That newsletter was discontinued in September 2022, but the references will remain because it helps highlight what I was seeing and writing about at the time of these 50in50 posts.

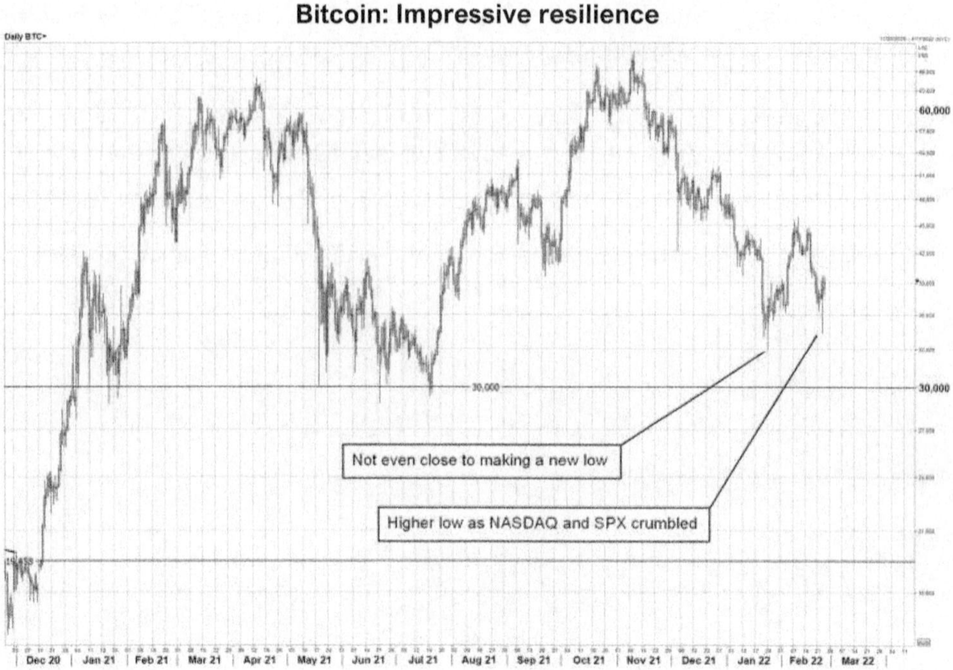

In the interest of brevity, let me outline my view here in bullet point form as most of the idea has already been laid out above. I am bullish bitcoin because:

- The narrative cycle in risky assets and crypto has rolled over massively and crypto market cap is down almost 50% from the highs. Web3 skeptics abound these days, the GameFi hype machine has quieted down, and all the while, bitcoin never made a new low, even when NASDAQ soiled the bedsheets (bullish divergence).
- Climactic low in risky assets on Russian invasion of Ukraine. History shows military invasions often lead to high-velocity selloff and then bottoms for risky assets.
- The market has made its peace with 6 or 7 Fed hikes.
- Hammer bottoms in SPX and NASDAQ.
- Double top in VIX.
- Gold mega reversal and oil unchanged from pre-invasion levels.
- US economic data stabilizing after omicron scare in January.
- NOTE: QT is on the horizon, and that is a bearish risk for crypto and risky assets, but I think we could get a tradable rally here for the next 4 weeks or so.

This is a 2-week to 1-month time horizon trade. Target is anywhere close to 50,000. This is a TYPE II trade, so let's allocate $2,000 out of $100,000 free capital. Note that I'm using $100,000 as the free capital number for every trade as I am not revalling the entire portfolio in real-time… It's too much work for not enough educational upside… and that's not the point of 50in50. Risking $2,000 and the stop loss is $7,800 away so that means 0.25 BTC is the position size.

Note: in the interest of saving space in this book, I won't paste in all of my trade frameworks/checklists. But I still do strongly recommend you use them or something like them.

As always, I will monitor the performance and offer detailed updates as we progress.

Week 5: Add Moar Bitcoin

Understand variance and volatility

Mr. Nakomoto has set the price

Update: Open trades

The first three trades are stopped out and BTC is around 4k in the money. Not a great start to this process but that's trading. The odds of the first three trades getting stopped out are about 12.5% so it's disappointing but nothing to make me question whether or not this is a bad idea. Even if it is… I'm doing this for 50 weeks no matter what! Again, I like to provide updates for transparency but the idea here is to teach the process and not worry about the outcome.

Update complete! This week, my focus is on P&L variance and market volatility.

Fooled by randomness

Traders who do not understand randomness and variance overestimate the importance of skill in the short run and will react more emotionally to the ups and downs of their P&L. Some days, you're going to get lucky. Some days you will be unlucky. And in the long run, we are all dead. But somewhere in the middle of those two time horizons is the place where trading results are signal, not noise.

The starting point to understanding signal vs. noise in markets and in your P&L is a basic understanding of statistics. If you don't have much of a math background and don't know much about statistics, take an intro to stats course or read Darrel Huff's *How to Lie with Statistics* or Charles Wheelan's *Naked Statistics*. You need to know the primary statistical analysis topics like standard deviation, mean vs. median, variance, volatility, and expected value.

Why variance matters

Your P&L is going to go up and down and you won't always know why. Unlike poker or other forms of skill-based gambling, the odds in trading are not static or defined. You are constantly estimating odds of success in a game you don't ever fully understand or know you can win. Here are some examples of negative variance outside trading:

Example 1: You are playing poker. You have two aces and your opponent has a junk hand like 9-5. The player with 9-5 is drunk and goes all in and you obviously call. The flop is 9-9-5 and you lose to the full house.

Example 2: A tennis player hits a perfect shot down the line and the umpire calls it out, even though it was clearly on the line.

Example 3: A baseball player hits a line drive that looks like a clear home run but the opposing center fielder climbs the wall and grabs it for a very loud out.

A professional poker, tennis, or baseball player in these situations will tend to understand that they did everything they were supposed to do and ran into a very unfortunate bit of bad short-term luck. They understand that if you re-run the same event 1,000,000 times, the result would be a success more than 99% of the time. They can shrug it off and understand that their process was good and while the outcome clearly stunk, they have nothing to feel bad about.

On the other hand, a weak player or someone who does not understand process vs. outcome or what they control vs. what they do not control will be enraged. "I can't believe that guy flopped a full house! I am the unluckiest person in the world!" etc. That is what Annie Duke calls "resulting". When you focus on results, you fail to understand what you control and what you do not control—this is a major fault. In life, trading, sports, and everywhere, you need to understand what you control and what you do not.

What is most important is to make the distinction between those things that we do and do not control. This is captured nicely in the Serenity Prayer, a mantra popularized by Alcoholics Anonymous but relevant to everyone:

God, grant me the serenity to accept the things I cannot change, the courage to change the things I can, and the wisdom to know the difference.

The last line is key. Think about what parts of the system you control. You control the inputs, not the outputs. In trading, this means focus on good thinking and rational decision-making and don't get upset when you hit a bad run.

People waste way too much time worrying about random stuff they can't control. This is often true in trading but it is true out there in the world, too. A big part of my personal philosophy is to not waste time on things I cannot control. For example, when I was younger, I would spend months obsessing about what my bonus was going to be in January. As discussions started in September and expectations management took hold into October and November, I listened to all the speculation about the bonus pool and tried to keep my ear to the ground to get a sense of what my bonus might be.

As years passed, I realized something. If I come into work and try my best and perform well and do a good job… The bonuses take care of themselves. There is no correlation between how much you worry about what your bonus is going to be and how much you get paid. There is, though, a strong correlation between your bonus and: how hard you work, how well you prepare, how disciplined you are, and what kind of attitude you have.

Come in and trade each day with a positive attitude. Do the work. Focus. Behave rationally. Go home. Do it again tomorrow.

That is the 22-word recipe for trading success.

Is it variance… Or do I just suck at this?

P&L variance

The best way to shield yourself from variance (and negative thinking about variance) is: collect data. The more data you have about your trading, the less frightening it will be when you hit a losing streak. People have a hard time believing that streaks are the result of randomness, even though random data contains many streaks![10]

In statistics and probability, variance is the concept that in a series of numbers with a given average, individual data points will be spread out away from the average. So even if your average daily P&L over the last 10 years is +$23,000, you might still lose $25,000 five days in a row sometimes. This may not mean you did anything wrong. It's just variance.

Variance is a prominent feature in poker. A well-rested professional poker player will inevitably beat a drunk amateur over a long period, say 12 hours. But over any 10-minute or even 30-minute period, the drunk amateur might prevail. The key to understanding

[10] Read about the Clustering Illusion at https://en.wikipedia.org/wiki/Clustering_illusion

variance is that it is most visible in short samples. The larger the sample, the closer the aggregate data will approach the true average.

Luck is a short-term thing. In the long run, skill prevails.

Then again, as Keynes famously said... "In the long run, we are all dead." A very solid trading strategy with a significant edge generates substantial variance, even year to year. This is why it is incredibly difficult to evaluate traders, portfolio managers, and hedge funds. Was it luck or was it skill? Michael Mauboussin's book, *The Luck Equation: Untangling Skill and Luck in Business* is the go-to book on this topic.

To give you a sense of how variance impacts a year of performance in trading, let's run a few simulations. For simplicity, we'll use a static risk management approach where the trader does not change their risk appetite during the year, regardless of performance. That said, I strongly advocate increasing your risk as your P&L rises.

I include these simulations because I think very few people, even expert traders, truly appreciate just how dramatic the impact of variance can be on performance. It is probably a defense mechanism. If we truly appreciated how important variance was, we would feel like we barely control our own fate. And humans love to believe they are in control.

The first simulation approximates the performance of a retail trader. She makes money 50% of days and loses money 50% of days. Her average winning day (net P&L) is +$2,000 and her average losing day is -$1,200. Based on these figures, she will expect to make $100,800 in an average year. Here is her cumulative YTD P&L simulated 100 times.

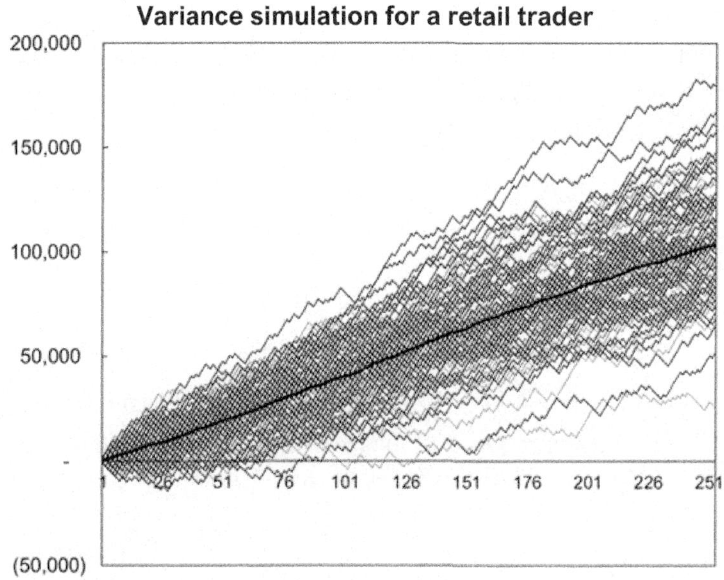

The same trader using the same strategy in a world with the same probabilities might make $50,000 one year and $150,000 the next, with variance—and literally nothing else—to blame.

The second simulation represents a bank trader. He makes money 55% of days and loses money 45% of days. His average winning day (net P&L) is +$150,000 and his average losing day is minus $120,000. Based on these figures, his expected value is +$7.2 million. But here is how he fares in 100 simulations:

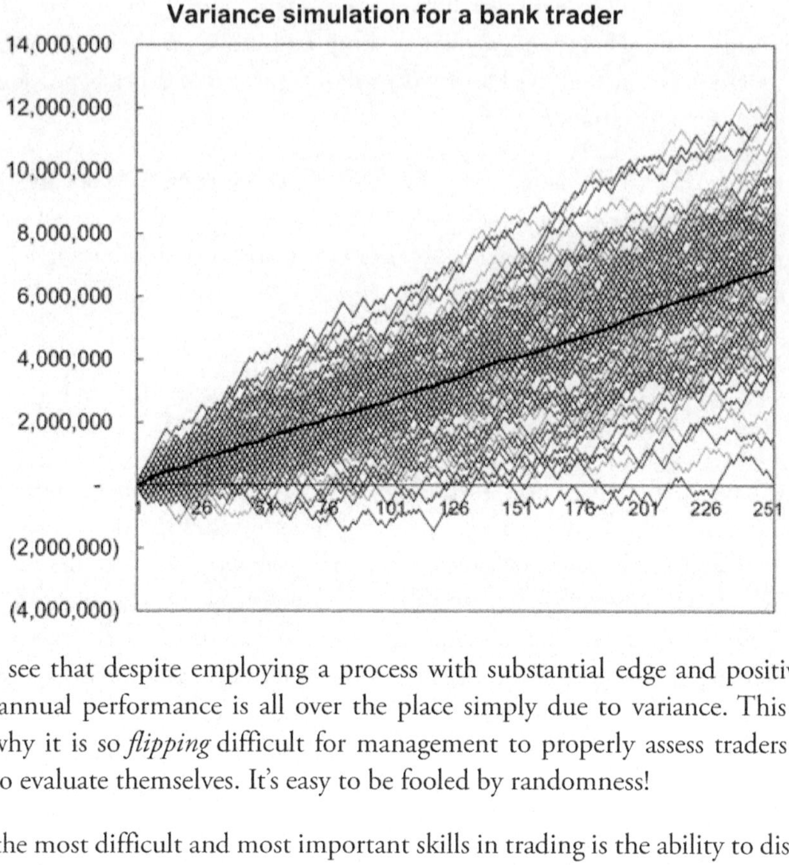

You can see that despite employing a process with substantial edge and positive EV, a trader's annual performance is all over the place simply due to variance. This is a big reason why it is so *flipping* difficult for management to properly assess traders and for traders to evaluate themselves. It's easy to be fooled by randomness!

One of the most difficult and most important skills in trading is the ability to distinguish between variance and bad decision making. If you are losing money right now, is it because your process has broken down, your discipline sucks and the market has completely changed? Or is it because of the inevitable variance within the P&L distribution?

When you are on a bad streak, you need to ask yourself this. The longer you have been trading, the easier this is to answer (usually). For me, I can usually look back on a losing streak and determine with a fair amount of confidence whether it was variance. When you are starting out, it's almost impossible to tell.

Here are some examples of how I look at a losing streak and determine whether it's a product of variance or bad process.

Variance

1. I was wrong a lot. Being wrong is part of trading. It's OK to be wrong!
2. I got unlucky. I was long and some bad news came out yesterday. Today, I got stopped out at the highs.

When I am wrong and I lose money, I barely care. That's trading. As long as I have been sticking to my risk management system, I shrug and move on. Being wrong is where variance comes from in trading. Don't worry about it. On the other hand, some things can't be attributed to variance.

The first three trades I did all got stopped out on some sort of variance attributable to Russia headlines and news. At some point, you can't keep exposing yourself to the same randomness and so I am now making an effort to focus on trades that are less likely to get smoked on Russia headlines.

Not variance

Here are negative outcomes that are NOT explained by variance.

1. I have been right, but I am losing money. This is a strong indicator there is something wrong with my process. For much of 2020, I was in sync with the market and my percentage of accurate calls was very high. But my performance was disappointing because of multiple breakdowns in discipline and process. I was wrong-sizing my trades and bleeding on random, low conviction ideas. **If you are reading the market well and losing money, that's a red flag**: something is wrong with your process and it's not just variance.
2. I traded with no plan. I walked in each day and started hitting buttons without a good sense of what I was trying to do. I cut out of good ideas early because I was bored.
3. I keep fading the same news event or trading close to known, potentially random risk events.
4. I am overtrading. I should be tight/aggressive but instead, I'm making a series of small bets on random, dumb ideas and leaking money every day.
5. I left a stale order in the system overnight and it triggered a loss. Poor attention to detail is not bad luck.
6. My discipline is poor. I broke my risk management rules. My positions were way too big. I kept moving my stop lower instead of cutting. I doubled a losing position.
7. The market regime has changed and I have not adapted.

8. My boss is giving me a hard time and making me nervous.
9. I am tired. I am arguing with my spouse or children. I think I might get a divorce. I am drinking too much. I feel depressed. I don't want to do this anymore.

If losses stem from any of 1 to 9 above; that's not variance. That is bad trading, bad process, or bad mindset. Cut all your risk and figure out how to get things back on track. When you trust yourself to do the right thing, you are trading well. It should not matter all that much whether you make or lose money on any given day.

When you are trading with a good mindset, you see each trade and each day as a series of independent events with a probabilistic nature and you understand that some trades and some days you will lose money. Each day, you come in and do your best without getting too high or too low. You invest most of your energy in the process and very little in the outcome. Each trade, you go through a thoughtful process and execute in a rational and systematic way.

Get comfortable with variance.

If you understand your edge and can confidently explain it, you will be much more comfortable with variance. Furthermore, if you continually spend time thinking about the current regime and how to adapt to present market conditions, you will reduce your variance and maintain steadier performance over time. No matter how good you are, though, you still need to understand that variance is a thing.

Signal or noise?

Market volatility

Markets are noisy, complex systems. Sometimes they trend; sometimes they chop around; sometimes they go nowhere. People say price is always right, or markets are always right, or "the bond market knows something"… But that's not always true. Often, markets are just quasi-random distributions that are pushed around by random flows, emotional human outbursts, and forced or non-price-sensitive buying and selling.

One key to understanding your market is to understand how it moves. Before you trade any market, you need a good understanding of volatility. I am not a huge fan of paper trading in general but one benefit of paper trading is that it allows you to watch a market and get in sync with its ebbs and flows so that you understand how it moves. You should watch a market for at least a month or two before you trade it. This will give you a sense not only of general volatility but also of what constitutes a fast market or a quiet market.

Another important way to familiarize yourself with a market is to analyze the market statistically before trading it. Note that volatility and liquidity are not static; they change over time and therefore historical measures of volatility are by definition backward-looking.

Volatility is a statistical measure of how an asset price moves. It uses historical data to analyze the standard deviation of past moves. Assets with higher volatility tend to be riskier by nature. Volatility is usually expressed as an annual percentage. It can also be expressed as a standard deviation or histogram of returns. The higher the number, the more volatile the asset.

The reason that volatility matters is that it relates directly to position sizing. You cannot trade as large a position in an asset that is more volatile, because your risk of ruin is larger. Many experienced traders that I have worked with over the years never fully understood this concept.

For example, many bank traders I worked with simply ran 10 lots all the time. In other words, they would tend to be comfortable long or short 10 million NZDUSD or 10 million EURUSD or 10 million USDMXN, completely disregarding the fact that each of these currency pairs has different volatility and therefore the amount of P&L dollars at risk on each position of 10 million is different. You need to normalize your position size based on volatility. Take smaller positions when volatility is high and larger positions when volatility is low.

Trade 5: Double the BTC position

Let's go to Trade 5.

I'm doubling the bitcoin long position.

The random volatility triggered by the ongoing conflict in Ukraine has been making a mess of my positions and while bitcoin has historically been a risky asset, it may attract some safe-haven flows as the EU and the US weaponize their financial systems against Russia.

Recent news about the weaponization of the global payments system (along with guilty until proven innocent financial seizures in Canada) has buttressed the idea of a parallel financial system that can at least partially avert arbitrary government freezes and seizures. This should provide a strong short-term tailwind for BTC as money exits EUR and USD and looks for a safe home in a world where there are very few safe homes. I wrote about this in am/FX.

I don't mind doubling down on a trade like this. I will record and track the trades as two separate line items. Risking 2% of free capital again and the stop is much closer so the position size is 0.5BTC this time (vs. 0.25 last time). The trades are obviously correlated since they are the same product, but the different entry and exit parameters mean they can be treated as two different ideas for the sake of risk management. Obviously, you cannot just keep piling on the same idea but doubling my position from 2% to 4% of capital with two different stop losses isn't overly insane.

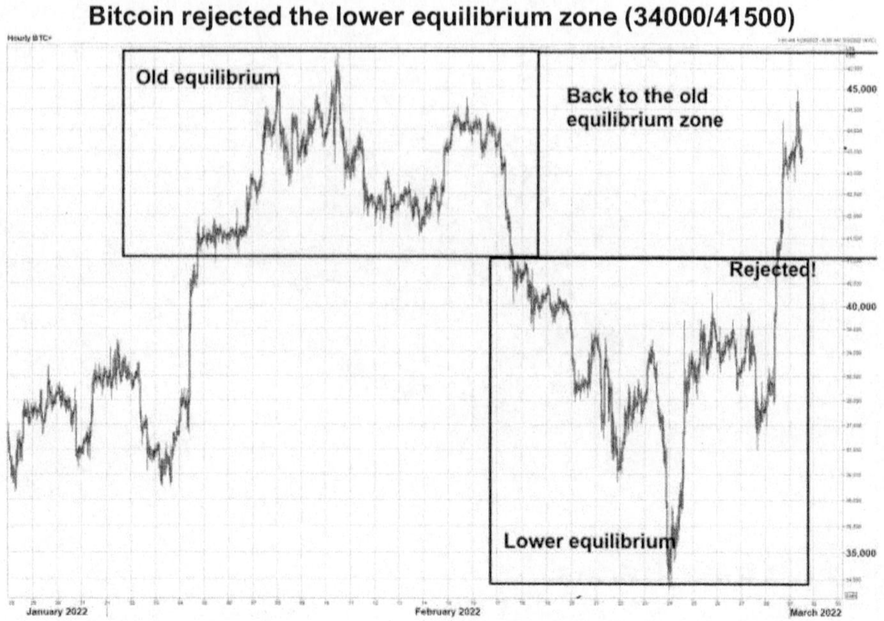

As you can see in the lower box on that chart, the 34000/41500 equilibrium zone has been rejected in favor of the previous, higher equilibrium. As such, we should stay above the 41500 level again as was the case in the second half of January. I will put my stop on this piece at 38900 and the take profit is 51900.

50in50 goes long more BTC. Long at 43500 with a stop at 38900.

Doubling the position with a tight stop as the narrative momentum and price momentum work in favor of the idea—and I try to avoid Russia headline risk after that triggered too much random variance in the first three trades.

Week 6: Options or Cash?

Poutine on a long Canada trade via EWC

Update: Open Trades

It has been one hell of a start for this book. While it's tempting to attribute the bad start to bad luck, that's not the correct explanation. The main reason the trades have not worked out is that I tend to fade geopolitical events and that has not been a good strategy in 2022.

I have been too blasé about the financial market implications of the Russian invasion of Ukraine. I don't particularly hate myself for this; fading geopolitical moves has been the right strategy most of the time throughout my career and so it was a logical process that I followed despite the suboptimal outcomes.

The gold and oil trades were directly blown up by Russia and the DOCS trade was stopped out in a wave of countertrend optimism before the sanctions hit. The double down in bitcoin is now stopped out too, so I am oh-for-four so far. Even if I'm oh-for-49… I'm going to do all 50 trades. Come hell or high water.

Worst case scenario here is: you learn some stuff and I learn my only edge is in FX.

With the DOCS trade, my target level hit soon after the stop loss triggered, and so in hindsight, it was a perfect trade for options, but not for cash. That brings us to this week's topic: Trade structuring… When should I use options? I have given myself a most difficult task this week, not because the question is complicated (it is) but because I could literally write an entire book on this topic and today I'm going to try to do it for you in under 3000 words. Let's go!

When should I use options?

While investing generally involves mostly a one-dimensional decision of "what to buy?"… Trading sits at the other end of the decision complexity spectrum. The trader's decision process has many dimensions:

- Long or short? At what price?
- Where to stop loss and take profit?
- How long do I hold?
- How to structure it: Cash, futures, or options?

Trade structuring has many dimensions, and I have covered some of them already in prior posts. For example: position sizing, stop losses, entry tactics, and so on. Today, inspired by a missed opportunity in DOCS (the trade from Week 3), I am going to look at a larger and more complicated question: When to use vanilla options instead of cash or spot.

First, take a look at this summary of my DOCS trade:

DOCS: Good idea, bad structure

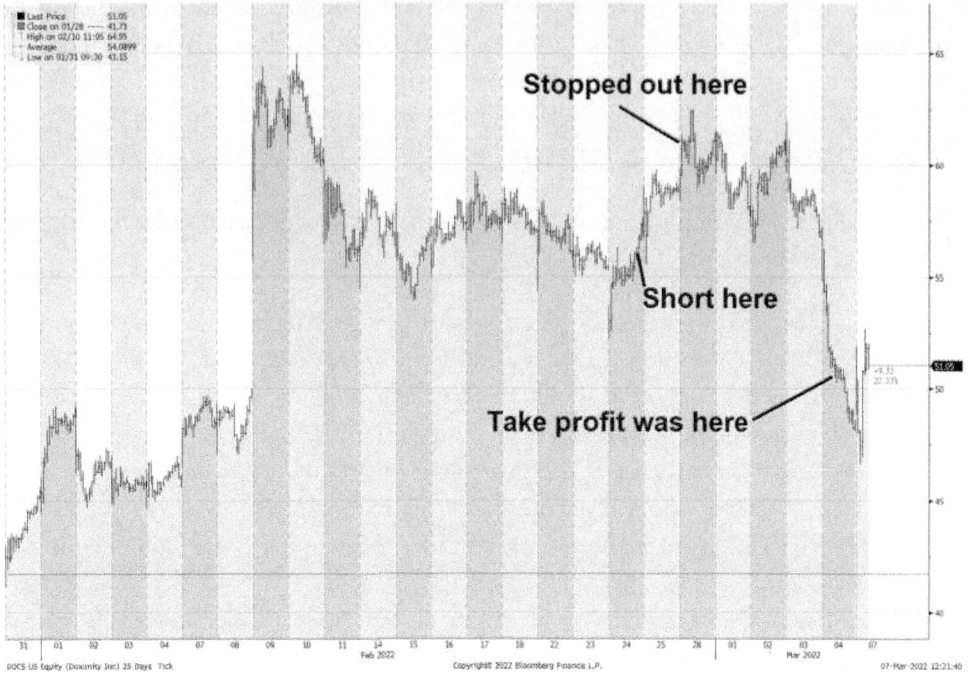

I went short at $56 and stopped out above $60. A few days later it dropped more than ten bucks in a straight line and hit my take profit. On March 4th, reader @svilkoni tweeted he had expressed the bearish DOCS idea via puts and done extremely well on it. Two things about that:

1. That's how this is supposed to work! Readers don't copy my ideas, they incorporate them into their process and do what they think is best.
2. This is a good example of a trade where options worked better than cash. Since I trade a lot of options, this is a good time to cover that!

My DOCS time horizon was 2-4 weeks, so let's see what would have happened if I had bought the 1-month put option instead of doing the cash trade. (Note: "cash" or "spot" means trading the actual thing… Not a derivative of the thing. DOCS common stock is a cash (or margin) trade and DOCS options are a derivatives trade.)

I assume a working knowledge of options in this piece. If you don't know what a put and a call are, read an introduction to options trading before you tackle this one. Vanilla just means simple puts and calls. More complex structures are useful but beyond the scope of today's note. At some point, I will probably do a 50in50 on some other options strategies but for today we're talking the simple stuff: Buying puts and buying calls. By the way, simple is not an insult in trading.

Simple ideas almost always work better than complicated ones.

Everything I discuss here applies to trading, not investing. I pretty much never buy options beyond a three-month time horizon, so that gives you a sense of what I'm talking about here. My normal trading time horizon is 1-10 days.

Why options can be better

Options help you accomplish specific goals in a trade. Here are situations where options can work better than cash:

1. To avoid getting stopped out. Once you buy an option, you are in the position until the option expires. In a cash trade, you might get stopped out right before the trade idea goes your way. That's what happened to me in DOCS. In choppy, headline-driven markets, options can keep you in the trade.
2. To achieve more leverage. If you buy an option and there is a gigantic move in the market… Your option will generally make more money than a cash position would have. I will go through this in detail in the P&L comparison section coming up next.
3. Take very large positions more easily. If you want to be short 500 million AUDUSD, it's tough to run a cash position with a stop loss. But you can (fairly) easily strap on a billion AUD of puts that give you a delta of 500 million. Options are good for putting on huge trades.

4. Avoids gap risk and offers defined risk. If you went short ZM into earnings in 2021, you are probably reading this on your phone while on break from your job at Krusty Burger because you blew up your trading account. If you bought ZM puts, they went to zero and your risk was finite. When you buy an option, you decide how much money to spend and then you either lose that much, or less. When you go long or short in cash markets, you expose yourself to gap risk on news, weekends, or when markets are closed.
5. To achieve custom payout profiles. Let's say you think a stock is going to go up but it's not going to the moon. You could trade a spread that gives you very high leverage for your specific view while substantially reducing your premium outlay.

Why options can be worse

1. **Timing is critical**, especially on short-dated options. If your option expires, you are out!
2. **If the market goes nowhere, you lose money**. This is called time decay, or theta. Each day you wait, you bleed.
3. **You can be right and lose money**. If the asset moves in your direction, but not enough to cover the option premium, you lose money. The price you pay and the strike you choose are key. Note you can be right and lose money in cash too, like I was on my DOCS trade. There is no free lunch.
4. **Bid/offer is wider in options.** This can actually be a benefit though! As a person who overtrades, I like that options are harder to get in and out because once I'm in an options trade, I tend to stick with it longer. Because the cost to get out is higher, the bar to chop a trade for no reason is higher.
5. **Events and obvious catalysts tend to be overpriced.** Events and catalysts are the two setups where you most want to use options and they are the most expensive. Buying USDJPY options through nonfarm payrolls was a sucker's game through the 2010s, even though USDJPY moved a lot on payrolls. The dream scenario for option buyers is when you have a view on an event or catalyst but that view is not priced into the options market.

   For example, say there is a big speech from the deputy governor of the RBNZ tonight. People know about it, but nobody cares. You believe the central bank could be about to pivot and there is a decent chance the assistant governor may say something important. In this case, **you have a divergent view on volatility**.

   The market thinks the speech is a nothingburger and you think it's important. Those are the best setups for buying options. Sure, buying calls through Zoom earnings might work, but it's not a positive expected value play. The options market knows the earnings are coming out and it's going to price that in by charging you through the nose for the privilege of participating.

Less obvious events and catalysts can be bargains in the short-term options market. In the case of the DOCS trade, earnings had passed and options prices were relatively reasonable.

Those are the main points on options vs. cash. The key to understanding whether cash or options provide a better expression of a trade you like is to build a spreadsheet. It's not super hard, and it forces you to truly understand what the heck you're getting into.

It all comes down to three things:

- Where do you think the market is going?
- What path do you think it will take to get there?
- How much do options cost?

A quick example, using DOCS

In Trade 3, I went short at $56 with a stop at $60.50 and got stopped out of DOCS. Instead, I could have bought the March 18 $50 puts for $1.70. Here is a chart of the stock (black) and the option (gray) with some key moments tagged.

DOCS stock and the March 18 $50 put in DOCS

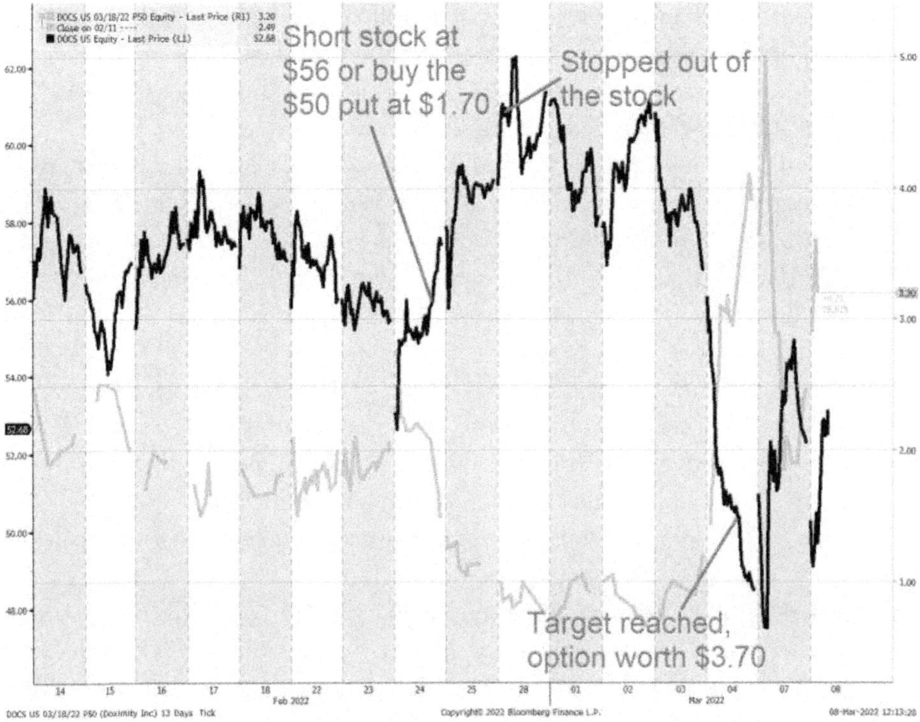

So clearly, in this case, the put was better. It saved me from getting stopped out and turned my $2,000 into $4,400 in the options market. My $2,000 turned into zero on the cash trade. If you want to understand what an option's going to look like vs. cash… The first thing to do is make a spreadsheet that shows your P&L at each level the option could expire. For example, here's one for this DOCS trade:

P&L at expiry of short DOCS at $56 vs. buying the 18MAR21 $50 put

Entry price:	56.00	
Option strike:	50.00	
Option contracts	12	
Cost per contract	1.70	
Cash position	(443)	shares
Stop loss	60.50	
Ladder increment	1.5000	
	Buy put	**Short stock**
68.00	(2,040)	(1,994)
66.50	(2,040)	(1,994)
65.00	(2,040)	(1,994)
63.50	(2,040)	(1,994)
62.00	(2,040)	(1,994)
60.50	(2,040)	(1,994)
59.00	(2,040)	(1,329)
57.50	(2,040)	(665)
56.00	(2,040)	-
54.50	(2,040)	665
53.00	(2,040)	1,329
51.50	(2,040)	1,994
50.00	(2,040)	2,658
48.50	(240)	3,323
47.00	1,560	3,987
45.50	3,360	4,652
44.00	5,160	5,316
42.50	6,960	5,981
41.00	8,760	6,645
39.50	10,560	7,310
38.00	12,360	7,974
36.50	14,160	8,639

The stock position and options position size are both plugged so each has $2,000 of risk. And here is the chart of that spreadsheet:

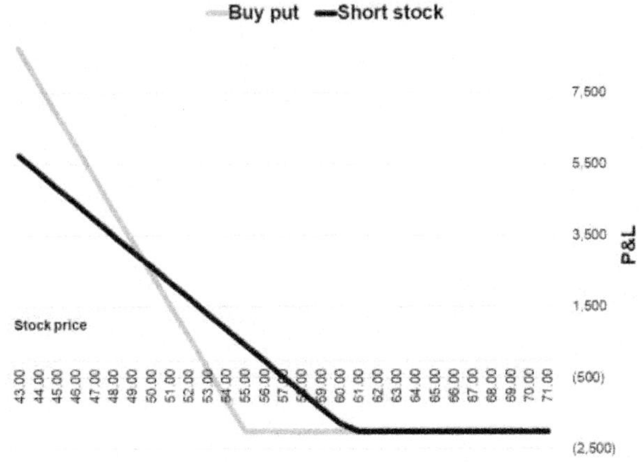

This tells you a few things:

1. As you move from left to right on the chart, that is the stock price going up, and you are losing money on the bearish position. If the stock goes straight up, you lose $2000 on either structure. As you go left, the P&L goes up because we're cheering for a lower stock price.
2. If the stock ends around $44 at expiry, both trades have the same P&L. That's the place where the dark gray and light gray lines cross. Once the stock falls below there, the put (the steeper, dark gray line) makes more money (that's when leverage kicks in). Since our take profit was $50, buying the $50 strike is pretty aggressive—you need a quick move to the target for this option to work. In this case, it worked out but the option trade was extremely risky, just in different ways. In hindsight, the option worked, but ex-ante it probably would not have looked all that amazing because my target was not ambitious.
3. If the stock is above $50 on expiry day, you lose the whole 2k on the option and you're *flat or positive* on the cash trade (if you didn't get stopped out). There is a huge tradeoff here!

The chart captures only the final destination (expiry), not the path. It shows what happens if you put the trade on and then you cover on the day the option expires. This ignores the path that the security follows in real life which in this case was that the stock price shot higher, stopping out the cash trade, then cratered, hitting the TP.

You can see that while in this case, the option worked out better because the cash got stopped out, the tradeoffs you had to make to get the optionality were significant. Anywhere above $44 at expiry, the cash position was better.

BUT… You also see how the path matters. The quick move lower meant the $50 put option still had tons of value so instead of losing $2,000 on the trade, the option would have allowed us to take profit and make good money (sell the option at $3.70 when the stock hit our $50.21 target).

In that case, when the target hits, you sell the option for a profit and move on. In a whippy, up / down / up scenario, the option is much better and that certainly was the case here. The cash trade lost $2,000 and the option trade made $2,400. On $100,000 of capital, that's a massive swing.

The way you structure trades can make or break your P&L.

When I say "structure trades" I mean everything from *cash or option* right down to your choice of entry and exit points. If my stop loss on the DOCS trade had been above the old high, I would have survived and hit my target. BUT, my position would have been half the size and my risk/reward would have been sus.

There is always tension between maximizing position size and maximizing leverage while optimizing trade structure. In this case, I did a bad job. An option, or a wider stop loss, would have allowed me to be a winner here, instead of a loser.

Trade 6: Bullish EWC

EWC is the US-traded ETF that tracks Canadian equities. Here is a brief thesis on the trade and then I'll talk about whether or not an option makes sense to express the bullish view.

1. Canadian equities are showing tremendous relative strength. As global equities slump, the Toronto Stock Exchange is near the all-time highs as it's a geopolitically stable supplier of commodities in a world caught short commodities. If global equities stabilize, Canada should outperform as oil prices remain elevated and commodities like wheat remain in short supply. By the way, one of the most famous songs by one of the most famous Canadian bands is called "Wheat Kings." It's a beautiful song.
2. The world needs somewhere to put their money. EWC is dominated by bank stocks and oil companies… In a world of rising commodities and rising rates, it makes sense that Canadian stocks are performing well. Money is flying out of Europe and emerging markets at a crazy pace and it needs to find a new home.

To give you a sense of how money is flying out of Europe and into "other"…

Check out this chart from am/FX today.

Distance from Kyiv in miles vs. currency performance since 25FEB

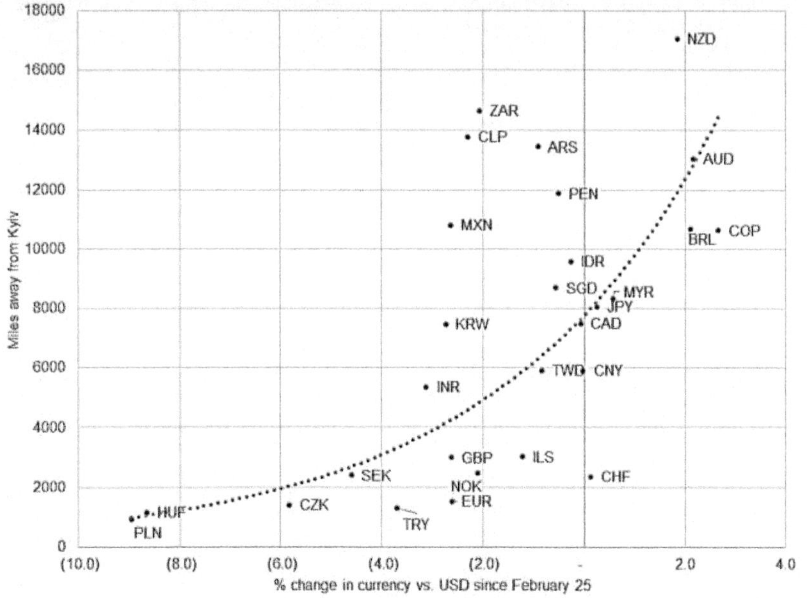

3. In a world of geopolitical uncertainty, Canada is a natural safe haven. Bonds are scary in inflationary times and US tech is even scarier. If things in the world improve, stocks should rally broadly and EWC should do well so this makes EWC a bit of an all-weather trade right now as it has commodity exposure and bank and risky asset exposure, all in about the right balance.
4. US bans Russian oil imports. It's a token gesture but helps the US oil-exporting neighbors a bit.

It makes sense that money will continue to flow into Canada and this should support Canadian equity prices. I am not 100% sure if this is a bullish oil trade… I think there are scenarios where oil could sell off, global equities rally, and EWC still goes higher.

Should we buy the stock, or buy an option?

First, we need to choose our target and stop loss and punch all the info into the spreadsheet. The stop loss is fairly easy as the daily chart has been consolidating for ages and looks like this:

EWC daily since Q4 2019

So a stop loss below all those lows would be $35.19. The take profit is $44.80, which is simply the top of the current range ($40.00) plus the width of the current consolidation ($4.80). That is a semi-standard way of projecting breakouts from a consolidation.

To compare this to an option, we need to decide on the holding period. The nearby options expire March 18th and April 18th. This trade needs a bit of time to work; $44.80 is not a chip shot and March 18th is way too tight. So let's look at April expiry options. Then, we pick a strike. Since the breakout level is clearly $40 on this chart, that's a nice level to pick. One might reasonably expect price to accelerate once it breaks $40.

The April $40 EWC calls are thinly traded but trade around $0.60 with EWC at current levels ($38.00). We set the number of shares to equal a $2,000 loss at the stop loss level and we set the number of contracts to cost $2,000 so that both trades are equivalent risk.

P&L at expiry comparison to spot trade

Entry price:	38.00	
Option strike:	40.00	18-Apr
Option contracts	33	
Cost per contract	0.60	
Cash position	687	shares
Stop loss	35.19	
Ladder increment	0.3000	
	Buy call	**Long stock**
42.50	6,270	3,091
42.20	5,280	2,885
41.90	4,290	2,679
41.60	3,300	2,473
41.30	2,310	2,267
41.00	1,320	2,061
40.70	330	1,855
40.40	(660)	1,649
40.10	(1,650)	1,443
39.80	(1,980)	1,237
39.50	(1,980)	1,030
39.20	(1,980)	824
38.90	(1,980)	618
38.60	(1,980)	412
38.30	(1,980)	206
38.00	(1,980)	-
37.70	(1,980)	(206)
37.40	(1,980)	(412)
37.10	(1,980)	(618)
36.80	(1,980)	(824)
36.50	(1,980)	(1,030)
36.20	(1,980)	(1,237)
35.90	(1,980)	(1,443)
35.60	(1,980)	(1,649)
35.30	(1,980)	(1,855)
35.00	(1,980)	(1,930)
34.70	(1,980)	(1,930)
34.40	(1,980)	(1,930)
34.10	(1,980)	(1,930)

So here we see the crossover point for the option to outperform the stock is around $41.40. EWC is moving around in a $2/$3 range so a 8.9% rally from $38 to $41.40 feels like a lot to ask. In fact, since we know April 18th is 38 days away, we can check the data and see how many times the stock has rallied more than 8.9% in 38 days. I looked back to 2018, and the answer is less than 10% of the time. And that is in a period where EWC rallied a fair bit! Based on that data and a simple eye-balling of the chart, $41.40 feels like a long way away. Here is the rolling 1-month low/high range for the ETF:

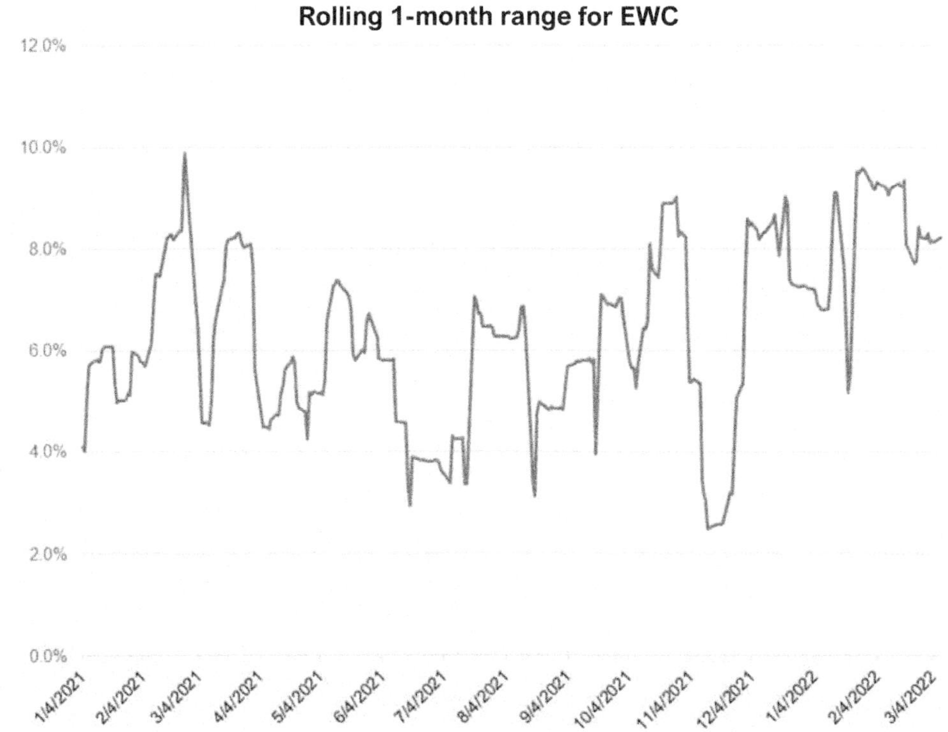

I don't have any special reason to think EWC volatility is about to skyrocket. It's a basket of a bunch of stocks and even through the Russia news, the drop in global stocks, and the rise in oil prices has created opposite pressure on EWC and kept it somewhat pinned.

Options don't appear to offer much leverage here. If we were doing a more expert-level piece, we could compare implied to realized volatility and see the options look expensive using that methodology too. Implied vol is above 25% and historical is 18%.

You don't need an advanced degree in applied math to make reasonable estimates of future volatility. I'm putting my finger in the air and into a few spreadsheets and determining that an option is unlikely to work better than cash.

The other question I need to answer (as we saw in the case of the DOCS trade) is: What is the chance I get stopped out, and then it hits my target? Again, in one month and one week, it seems highly unlikely to me that we trade down to $35.19 and then back up and through the top of the old range.

My target on the trade is not feasible by April 18th, so I looked at the June expiry options too, but again, you need a huge move before it's worthwhile. The breakeven between spot and option on the June $41 calls is around $43.10 so yes, if EWC goes to $44.80 by June, you are better off in the option, but I strongly doubt I will want to hold this trade that long and holding an option like that severely reduces my flexibility. Especially as these are thinly-traded options with poor liquidity.

In this case, you are not purchasing an expected volatility catalyst, you are simply giving yourself staying power in a choppy market and leverage if EWC breaks out. The stop loss on a cash position is clear, the options are expensive given the ETF hasn't been moving, and if it continues to consolidate for another month or two… You lose everything in the option and lose nothing on the cash trade.

Don't buy the option

In this case, the answer was pretty obvious to me. The cash long is better than the option because:

- I strongly doubt EWC hits both my stop **and** my take profit in the next 38 days. It's just not that volatile. The stop loss is pretty easy to determine given it has been a clear range trade.
- There is a meaningful chance EWC stays in this range. If I own the option, it will be worthless on April 18th. If I buy the stock and it goes nowhere, I have lost nothing.
- The leverage is not impressive. For something that frequently trades monthly ranges less than 5% wide, an 8.9% directional move in 38 days is asking a lot.

Conclusion

The option is too expensive and doesn't provide a real benefit vs. cash.

Today I have presented a simple way to evaluate whether you should buy an option, or trade a cash position instead. Please understand this is a starting point for further exploration and I have approached the question in a fairly simple way. Still, simple is good! Sure you can compare historical to implied in a more rigorous way than I have done here… But your answers should converge if you have a decent sense of what you are doing.

To decide between cash or options: look at the destination the stock needs to reach for your option to pay off… And then make your best guess as to the path the stock will take on its way to that destination. If there's zero chance you're gonna get stopped out, and the stop is close enough to give you decent leverage... The option is not a good bet.

If you're worried about getting stopped out, or you have a target that is aggressive in terms of both distance from market and the speed you expect it to hit... An option will be superior.

The simple way to start looking at options is to create a payoff spreadsheet like the ones I made above and then make a realistic estimate of where you think the stock might go. Don't salivate at the huge pile of coins that might come out of the slot machine if the very unlikely tail outcome takes place. Think about the most likely scenarios and the distribution of probabilities around the other scenarios and then make your decision. And live with it.

Don't do a bunch of woulda coulda shoulda afterward.

Write down your plan, execute it, and let the chips fall.

50in50 goes long EWC at $38.00 with a stop at $35.19 and take profit at $44.80

That's it. As always, I will monitor the performance and offer detailed updates as we progress. See you next week!

Week 7: The Plural of Anecdote Is Often Data

This was a popular meme in 2007… but the euro did not stay on top for long

Update: Open trades

1. EWC long at 37.85 is doing OK despite further global weakness in equities.
2. I'm cutting the bitcoin long. You got every piece of positive news you could have hoped for from that trade and yet it has not performed. Sanctions, gold exploded higher, stocks stabilized for a while, and BTC is… Unch. It has had plenty of time to rally (and it did, in fact, rally to $44k) but it looks abysmal now and with the Fed this week, I hate it now. Cutting at flat. I am not sticking with the plan here because the upcoming event risk is significant (The Fed) and the thesis has played out and is now stale. So I don't mind cutting it and moving on.

Once I am out of a position, I don't have a lot of psychological attachment to it. If BTC goes to $50k now, I'll feel a brief pang of FOMO but it will be short-lived. As a short-term trader, there are hundreds if not thousands of opportunities every year.

Today, we cover one of my favorite areas of behavioral finance.

Anecdotal evidence

Anecdotal evidence is any information you gather by personal observation. It normally involves behavioral observations and sentiment red flags. Some signposts marking human behavioral extremes can be predictive.

There is a wide range of anecdotal evidence you can incorporate into your analysis of the financial markets and use to confirm existing views or establish new conclusions. Analyzing anecdotal evidence is fun, but can also be unscientific and often unreliable.

There is a saying you hear now and then: "the plural of anecdote is not data."

Weirdly, that saying, while commonly tossed around, is a misquote and is **the exact opposite of the original quote**[11] by UCal professor Raymond Wolfinger. The fact is, singular anecdotes, when approached judiciously and aggregated with other confirming evidence, can lead us to meaningful conclusions and predictions. Often anecdotes are the n=1 that lead us to find a larger sample of evidence to support a thesis that we never would have thought of had it not been for the original anecdote.

Perhaps the most accurate saying would be: **The plural of anecdote is often data.** Anecdotes do not exist in a vacuum. Data does not emerge out of nowhere.

The risk with anecdotal evidence is that it is fraught with the potential for sample size issues, confirmation bias, and cherry-picking. If you are bearish, you are going to notice bearish anecdotes more readily than bullish ones, for example. The advantage of anecdotal evidence is that it can be observed in real-time and can be easy to understand. It is logical and intuitive.

The Magazine Cover Indicator

The most famous anecdotal indicator is The Magazine Cover Indicator. The indicator says that when a financial story or market theme is displayed on the cover of a mainstream magazine, that theme or the related trend is near exhaustion. In other words, magazine covers are reverse indicators.

Two famous examples of this phenomenon are when BusinessWeek's cover hollered: "The Death of Equities", right as the stock market made a major bottom in August 1979 and when The Economist proclaimed the world to be: "Drowning in Oil" just as oil bottomed in 1999.

---

[11] http://blog.danwin.com/don-t-forget-the-plural-of-anecdote-is-data/

S&P 500, 1958 to 2000

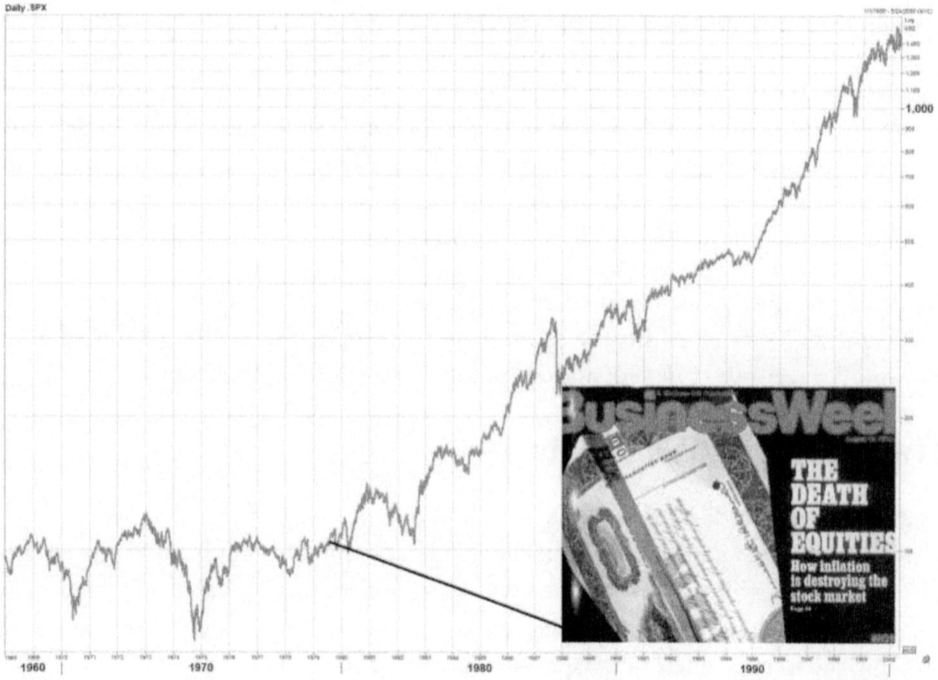

Crude oil, 1997 to 2008

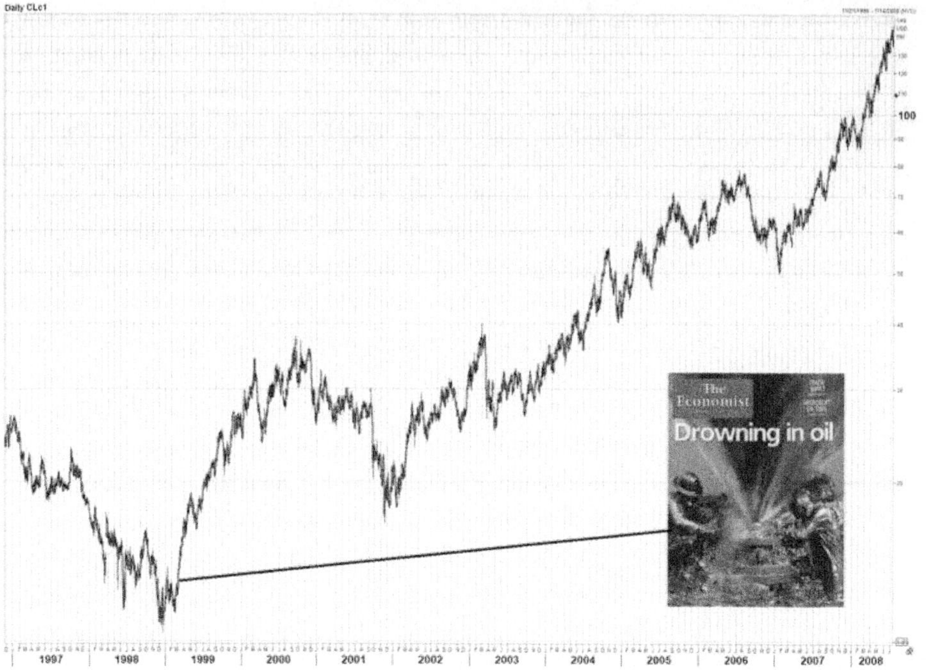

Two other well-known examples of the Magazine Cover Indicator are the appearance of Jeff Bezos as Time's Man of the Year in 2000 just before the tech bubble burst and Russian

President Vladimir Putin as Man of the Year in 2007 right before the collapse of oil brought down the Russian economy.

The premise behind the indicator is that when a journalist or editor finally devotes a cover to a market trend, company, country, or person, the story or theme has been in the market for some time and is likely past its peak. Positioning and sentiment should already fully reflect the story on the cover of the publication. In other words, by the time a magazine features a trend, it is not news. The story is priced in.

To avoid the cherry-picking problem, I did an empirical study of all covers of The Economist to see whether they are contrarian in aggregate. **The evidence shows that they are.** You can read the complete study in a post of mine on Medium.[12]

The Skyscraper Indicator

The Skyscraper Indicator suggests that when a country builds the world's tallest skyscraper, it is a sign of overconfidence and a potentially imminent financial crisis. Countries build world-record-setting skyscrapers only during bull markets when credit is plentiful, and thus historically there have been many instances where the country building the world's tallest skyscraper subsequently fell upon hard times.

Some salient examples are 1929: The Empire State Building (followed by Great Depression), 1972: the World Trade Center and Sears Tower (1970s stagflation), 1997: the Petronas Tower (Asian Financial Crisis) and 2005: the Burj Dubai (Real Estate collapse and financial crisis). The indicator doesn't produce many signals, of course, but it has an impressive track record.

Instead of focusing on a single anecdotal indicator, you can also observe extremes in sentiment when many anecdotes come together at once. A good example of this was in 2007 when fears of a dollar collapse raged because of the twin US deficits (trade deficit and budget deficit) and massive dollar selling by central banks like China and Saudi Arabia. The following three anecdotes appeared around the same time:

1. November 6, 2007: Supermodel Gisele Bunchen asks for her contracts to be modified and paid in euros instead of dollars.
2. November 17, 2007: Jay-Z is featured making it rain euro notes in his new rap video instead of the traditional Benjamins (US dollars).

[12] https://medium.com/@mbrentdonnelly/a-somewhat-empirical-look-at-the-magazine-cover-indicator-2d0ca835f7d1

3. November 2007: This meme goes viral:

The EUR hit an all-time high shortly after these three anecdotes circulated. The weak dollar was part of the mainstream narrative and these anecdotes were evidence that the theme was popular, well known, priced in, and at risk of turning stale. The dollar peaked four months later and the EUR never traded higher again.

Overall, anecdotal evidence is interesting and fun and can be a useful input into your big-picture macro analysis. Just be aware that anecdotal evidence is unscientific and fraught with pitfalls. The power of contrarian anecdotes tends to be evident in hindsight but my experience is that people are constantly pointing out anecdotal evidence to support their contrary view during strong trends and some of it works, and some of it doesn't.

Don't get too excited about anecdotes. Treat them as one extremely fascinating, but not very predictive input into your process. Those with experience will recognize when history repeats or rhymes and anecdotes from the present market will match past anecdotes and help the experienced trader to see patterns that may have some forecasting value. If you find yourself thinking "I've seen this movie before" … You probably have.

Think rationally about whether the anecdote you have observed could be representative of the underlying data/reality.

The IPO Indicator

A massive Initial Public Offering (IPO) can be another indicator to watch for as the sign of a top in a specific industry or for the stock market as a whole. By definition, the only time the market will absorb a very large IPO is when sentiment is bullish and the market is trading extremely well. Companies will rarely go public in a weak market because they want to sell shares in their company for the highest price possible.

IPOs tend to be plentiful in the late stages of a bull market as owners of companies see their market value rise and decide to cash out. IPOs are often seen as smart money selling out to dumb money. After all, if you strongly believed that your stock was cheap and your company was set to grow dramatically, why would you sell?

A great example of the IPO indicator is when Glencore sold its initial public offering in 2011. Glencore is one of the largest commodity producers in the world and in 2011 the world was in the midst of the second wave of an extreme bull run in commodities known as the Commodity Supercycle. Chinese and speculative demand had pushed commodity prices to new peaks and investor appetite for anything commodity-related was insatiable.

The insiders at Glencore were smart and realized that if they ever wanted to sell their company (which was massive at the time, valued at about $60B) this was a great time to do so. It is not hindsight to talk about how they sold the top—many observers and analysts (including me) pointed out at the time that the IPO could be a textbook sign of a top for commodities.

Take a look at the next chart which shows the Glencore IPO marked on a chart of the CRB. The CRB is the benchmark commodities index. Note how the Glencore IPO marked the exact top tick for commodity markets.

Daily CRB Index, 2009 to 2017

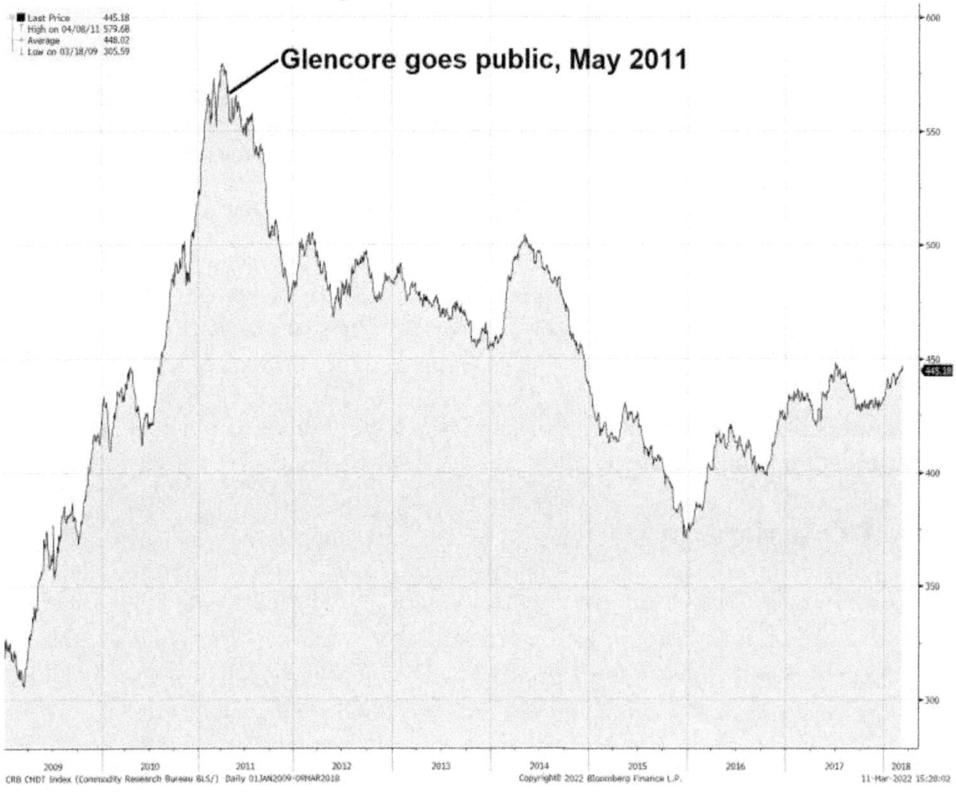

Monster IPOs do not happen often but the signals are so powerful that it is worth keeping this indicator in the back of your mind in case you see something similar in the future. The Coinbase IPO in April 2021 is another example. The day of the COIN IPO marked the first of two major peaks for crypto. The second peak was marked by another famous anecdotal setup: The Stadium Curse.

Bitcoin, 2020 to now

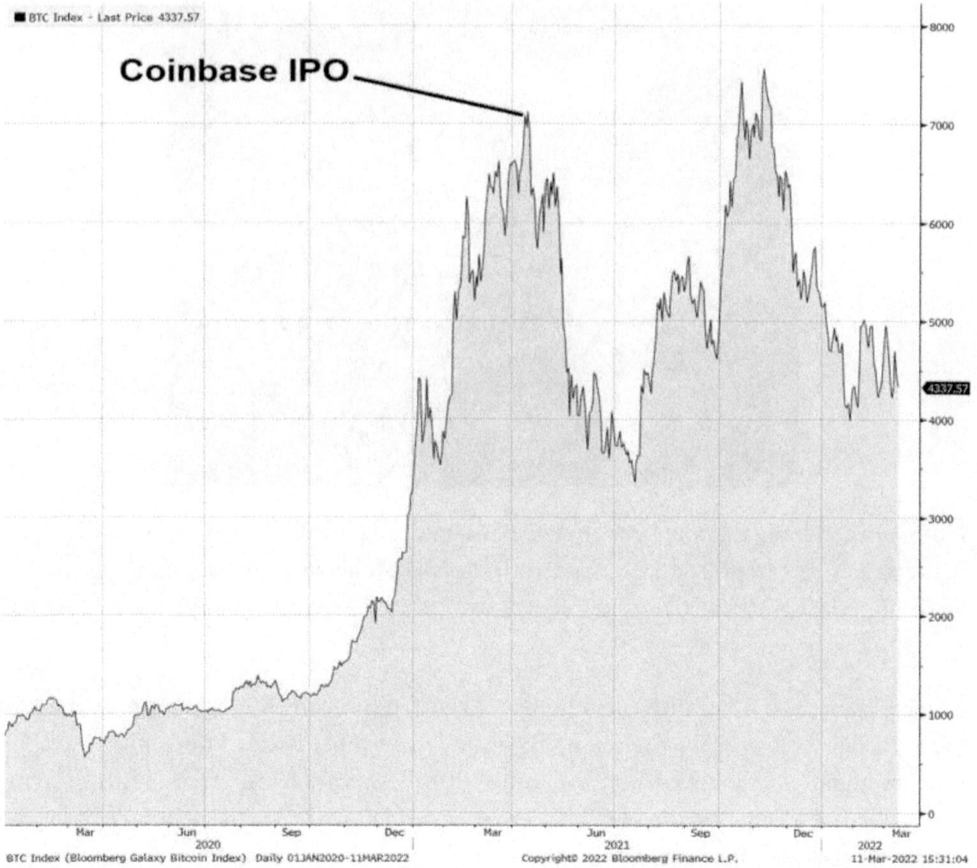

The Stadium Curse

A feature of epic bull markets and booming industries that are overearning and pumping out extraordinary excess cashflow is: at, or near, peak levels of optimism, you start to see the names of companies from that industry on stadiums. The 2000 dotcom mania provides many examples including Enron Field, CMGI Field, the MCI Center, the Corel Center, and PSINet Stadium. Those are all companies that boomed in the internet bubble and went bankrupt (or almost bankrupt) afterward. Needless to say, those stadiums all have different names now. Then, you had Citi Field and Barclays Center, both named in 2007 at the peak of the bank stock and housing bubbles.

Oops

Not every company that puts its name on a stadium goes bust, of course, but it's a signpost marking possible hubris and excessive cash on hand. They even have a name for it: The Stadium Curse. Much like the Skyscraper Index, stadium naming is a potential overconfidence indicator.

There was never a more obvious one than when Crypto.com became the new name of the LA Lakers' arena at the ding dong highs mid-November 2021. This is not hindsight: I wrote about it as part of my November 2021 cyclical bearish crypto thesis in my MacroTactical Crypto newsletter. That event coincided with a massive bubble in crypto sentiment and a straight-up mania of utopian Web3 visions.

Oops, I did it again

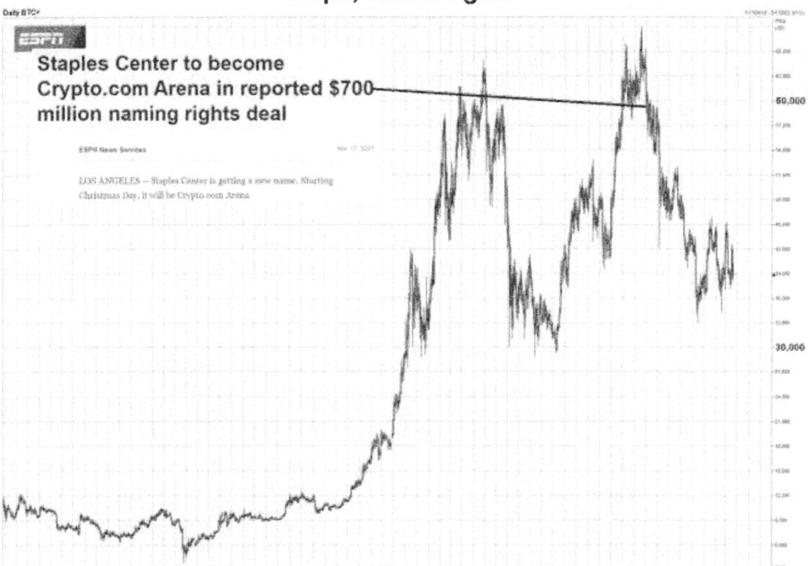

I hope this quick intro has given you a solid introductory understanding of anecdotal evidence and opened your mind to a particular type of behavioral indicator.

Now, let's get to today's trade idea...

Trade 7: Short XPO

On Friday, March 11, **French logistics company Geodis signed a contract to put its name on the largest soccer stadium in North America.**[13] This is pretty random and certainly a meaningful sign that logistics companies have never been more confident and flush with cash!

Oops, I did it again (again)

While I would not use this as a reason to go short logistics companies all on its own, there have been quite a few other reasons to think we may have hit an extreme in the commodity shortage, supply chain bottlenecks / logistics story.

- We are about to rotate back to a services-led economy. For the past two years, we have been locked in our homes, buying junk we don't need from Amazon. Now, as we line up to buy concert tickets to go see Kendrick Lamar or Phoebe Bridgers or whoever, plan client dinners in Miami, and just generally crawl out of our caves and into the light... Shipping and logistics are not going to be as important. You could probably put logistics in the "obvious COVID beneficiary" category and the stocks of most obvious COVID beneficiaries have now collapsed as that narrative has expired. ARRK, Robinhood, PTON, etc. etc. etc.
- "Chinese metals tycoon faces steep losses on nickel price surge" (FT).[14] Blowups and margin calls tend to be late-stage dynamics in a bull market. By the time people

---

[13] https://www.tennessean.com/story/sports/nashvillesc/2022/03/10/ nashville-sc-stadium-name-geodis-park-largest-soccer-stadium/9376673002/

[14] https://www.ft.com/content/0269cdda-ef67-43c8-b820-a919c919b5fa

are blowing up and being forced to cover shorts, it's usually near the end of the move. The inverse of this is the famous Sumitomo Copper Affair, where forced selling to unwind a rogue trade put in a major bottom in copper in 1996.

- CPI goods inflation relative to services has started to come off. This is another sign that we're past peak goods and moving back to services.
- Oil made a classic Sunday night gap high at $130 has not been there since. Sunday gaps tend to often make multi-month extremes as liquidity is horrendous on the open and markets tend to find max overshoot on the Asia open.
- Gold and other commodities making blow-off tops all over the place.

The global macro story is slowly but surely going to turn away from goods and back to services. This will take pressure off supply chains and reduce the premium paid for logistics companies.

I'll be perfectly honest, I'm not qualified to do a deep dive on XPO fundamentals. That isn't really the point of this trade. I chose XPO mostly because I like the entry point vs. other logistics companies like GXO (an XPO spinoff). XPO recently announced another spinoff and that triggered a big jump in the stock. To me, it's a great spike to sell as the good news is out of the way and you are selling into a 15% jump. This is in contrast to the other logistics companies, where you are selling the exact lows.

The chart is an absolute mess but there is a horizontal pivot at $73.75 and some nice downtrend channels in the same area. The spinoff news triggered an extremely aggressive blastoff through all the resistance and that blastoff failed to launch like Matthew McConaughey's character in the 2006 film with Sarah Jessica Parker.

XPO cannot take out $73.75 despite a valiant effort

One, two, three, four attempts to take out the $74 area

These anecdotal sort of trades tend to take a few months to play out so let's compare two ways to structure this thing:

Short the stock at $70 with a stop at $81.25, target $53.50. I put the stop loss above the last four daily highs (76, 78, 81, 81) and about four times an average day's range away. That gives it some breathing room since the goal is to get all the way down to $53.50. Risking 11.25 to make 16.50. Note these take a while to write. The stock is around $68.70 now. I will always mark to market the trade at the price when I hit "publish."

Or…Buy the May $60 puts for $2.60.

If we risk $2,080, we get this spreadsheet (normally risking $2,000 on these trades in 50in50 but 8 option contracts costs $2,080, close enough):

Entry price:	70.00	
Option strike:	60.00	
Option contracts	8	
Cost per contract	2.60	
Cash position	(185)	shares
Stop loss	81.25	
Ladder increment	2.0000	
	Buy put	**Short stock**
86.00	(2,025)	(2,081)
84.00	(2,025)	(2,081)
82.00	(2,025)	(2,081)
80.00	(2,025)	(1,850)
78.00	(2,025)	(1,480)
76.00	(2,025)	(1,110)
74.00	(2,025)	(740)
72.00	(2,025)	(370)
70.00	(2,025)	-
68.00	(2,025)	370
66.00	(2,025)	740
64.00	(2,025)	1,110
62.00	(2,025)	1,480
60.00	(2,025)	1,850
58.00	(2,025)	2,220
56.00	(2,025)	2,590
54.00	(1,125)	2,960
52.00	675	3,330
50.00	2,475	3,700
48.00	4,275	4,070
46.00	6,075	4,440
44.00	7,875	4,810

And the chart of the P&L looks like this:

This chart probably has too many gridlines.

If you are not familiar with how to compare cash and options positions, please see the last 50in50 (which is now the previous chapter).

The leverage looks pretty good on the puts here so I will go for the option. The odds of getting stopped out at $81.25 before it subsequently collapses to $50 are not zero, either. The stock sometimes moves 10% in a day.

Over the last 60 days, historical volatility has been around 60% while the implied vol on the puts is 50% so it passes the sniff test there, too. I wouldn't say the option is obvious here, but a quick move lower gives us extra leverage and protection from a whipsaw so the option looks marginally more attractive. Also, this isn't the kind of trade where it sits there and does nothing (like EWC might be, see 50in50 Trade 6). XPO is flying all over the place.

Conclusion

50in50 goes short XPO, buying 8 contracts of the May 2022 $60 put at $2.60

The target is $53.50 and there is no stop loss because we own the option. The summary of the reasoning is:

- The largest soccer stadium in North America sells naming rights to a logistics company. The stadium curse is a good indicator! It implies we may have hit the peak of the bull market in logistics.
- We have just had a 2-year orgy of goods buying. People are out of breath and can't buy any more goods for a while. That suggests pressure on logistics should abate.
- Commodity markets are breaking and margin calls are coming in. This usually happens near the end of a trend, not the beginning.
- Oil made a textbook top on last Sunday's open.
- Commodity blowoff tops.

As always, I will monitor the performance and offer detailed updates as we progress.

Week 8: Top-Down vs. Bottom-Up

I am more of a top down guy.

Update: Open and recently closed trades

1. EWC long at 37.85 is doing OK currently trading at 40.09.
2. The bitcoin long was a good idea but I got bored and cut it at flat. Classic bad decision / bad outcome. It is almost always better to stick to the plan because markets don't always move at the speed you wish they would! I acknowledge and inspect that little lump of frustration I feel in my throat—and I move on.
3. The May XPO puts are worth about 70 cents (paid $2.60). Plenty of time left on the clock. Despite the rally in XPO, I still think this is a good trade.

Update complete!

Today, I am going to talk about the idea generation process and how I try to deal with conflicts between top-down and bottom-up reasoning.

Top-down vs. bottom-up

I am a currency trader and the natural way to approach FX is from the top down. You look at the global macro picture, drill down into country specifics, look at asset classes within each country, develop a thesis, then implement it through various currency pairs or derivatives thereof. If you think global growth looks good, you buy commodity currencies, for example. If you think US rates and oil are going higher, you buy USDJPY. And so on.

In contrast, equity traders tend to be more bottom-up. They will analyze companies and make determinations on individual stocks based on their assessment of the company, its future earnings prospects, quality of management, and so on. For what it's worth, here's my opinion of three styles of bottom-up equity analysis:

Source: @Bardamu_31 on Twitter

Neither top-down nor bottom-up is necessarily the right or wrong approach. I believe the combination of both is almost always best.

That can mean different things, depending on what you trade, but in isolation, bottom-up analysis often leaves much to be desired because global macro beta very often dominates the performance of individual securities and currencies. For example, you can be the best RBA analyst in the world, but if China goes into recession, copper drops 40%, and the Fed hikes 100 bps in May… Your hawkish RBA call isn't going to help you much.

You can do all the work on supply and demand in the copper market, but if 16 countries all do fiscal stimulus at the same time, your bearish "copper overcapacity thesis" isn't going to work.

This goes to my overall philosophy which is that you need to specialize in one market but understand how other markets and variables influence your domain of expertise. If your job is to pick stocks, fine, bottom-up works. If your job is to truly understand why your market is moving, you have to study each fractal from the bottom to the top.

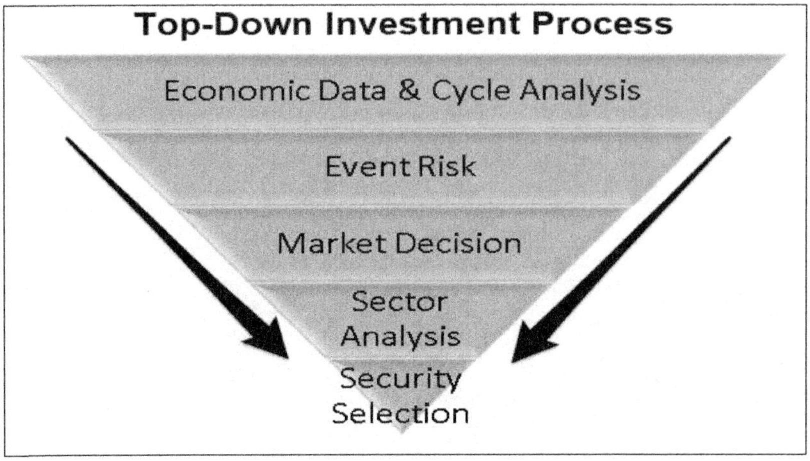

Top-down vs. bottom-up is usually a framework people apply to the stock market and it looks like this diagram at right from David Nelson at *Seeking Alpha.*

Bottom-up analysis makes more sense in equities than in other markets because those analysts are often working for firms or investors who want to buy and hold. They want the best investments and the best companies, not a long or short decision. If you're choosing stocks for a long-only portfolio, a focus on microeconomics makes sense.

But there is a similar pyramid for every asset class. For example, this is a rough sketch of the same thing for a global macro trader looking at Australia. Say someone is bullish on Australia… They might look bottom-up or top-down like this:

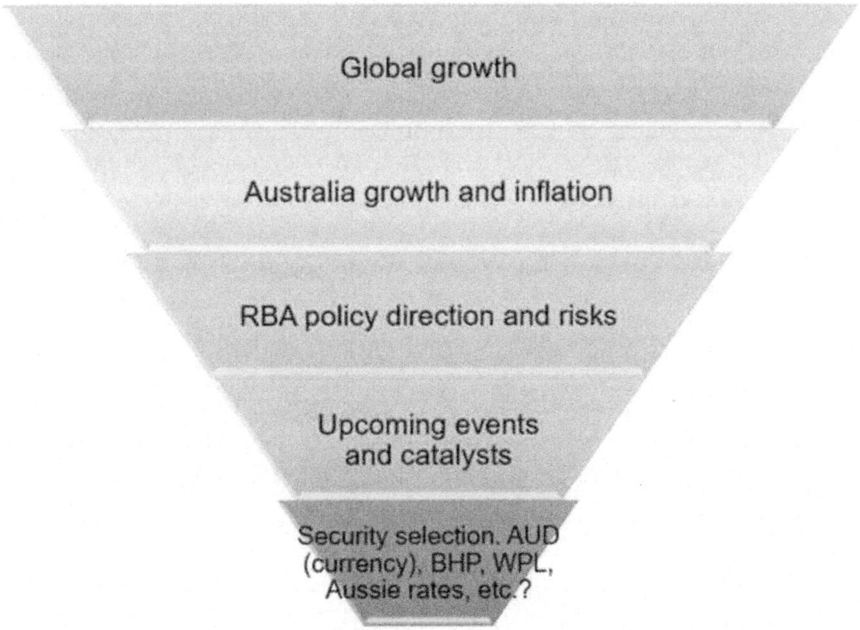

Top-down obviously makes more sense on this pyramid, and in reality, most traders will do analysis that goes up down and sideways all around the pyramid as they circle toward a better and better thesis.

Why would anyone go bottom-up on that second pyramid? Perhaps because they can only trade a specific asset class. Maybe they really like the AUDUSD chart setup and that was the inspiration for a deeper dive. Maybe long AUD is a good portfolio hedge for their Chilean assets. The point here is to look at all the fractals. Nano, micro, and macro. Go into depth on all the drivers that will (or might) move your market.

If you stay too micro, you will miss the forest for the trees. If you are too macro, your security selection, structuring, and tactics will suck wind.

Dealing with beta

A good example of the importance of macro vs. micro can be seen in the two most recent 50in50 trades: long EWC and short XPO. In the period since I put out those two trade ideas, the S&P 500 has rallied from ~4200 to 4500.

Guess which trade is working and which one is not!? Of course, the long is working and the short is getting bamboozled. The net result of the two trades is a small profit, but close to flat. The beta (S&P 500 moves) is more important than the alpha for now.

Once you have done your top-down and bottom-up analysis, there are a few ways to implement and execute:

Find trades that work all the way down the pyramid. This is the dream scenario and where most of my good trades come from. I go down the pyramid and across the different types of analysis (technicals, positioning, narrative cycle, correlation, etc.) and find the wind blowing in the same direction on most indicators. Those are the best trades. When you have a ton of crosswinds, go find a better trade idea.

Put on **relative value (RV) trades** that benefit from variations in the pyramid. For example, say you are bullish the Australian dollar and bearish the US dollar (i.e., bullish AUDUSD), but you're worried there is a bullish speculative mania in copper and a ton of new supply is about to come on. You know AUDUSD is correlated to copper. In that case, you might go long AUD and short copper. These two trades have the same directional macro drivers (primarily global growth) but have idiosyncratic drivers further down the pyramid.

Personally, I do not love RV trading. It's hard to risk manage, and often very hard to use leverage. It's a completely different style of trading from directional macro and requires a different set of skills. The best way to do it is to have a bunch of ideas and employ them all as a big, uncorrelated blob. Individual RV trades just make me annoyed and I tend to strip the leg that doesn't jibe with the rest of my macro view. If I think global growth is going to be strong, why not just be long AUDUSD and forget about the copper short. Hedging is for gardeners, as they say.

Macro overlay. This is a type of RV trading, but it's way simpler and easier to risk manage and execute. Say you have two longs and one short position in the stock market, giving you net long exposure... And that was fine, because you were bullish...

But now you are bearish for whatever reason. Your bearish view is tactical and nimble, though, so you don't want to mess around with your existing long and short stock positions which are all carefully thought out and have stop losses and take profits of their own that make sense. You might sell some S&P futures here as a macro overlay.

Wait. So how is "macro overlay" different from "hedging"?

I mean... It isn't all that different really. The subtle difference is that hedging implies a direct offset of an existing risk, whereas macro overlay involves layering on a new risk that offers some form of diversification or protection but will still be risk-managed as a separate trade. Macro overlay is often much less precise than hedging. You are temporarily offsetting some of your risk, often by putting on a different position that you also like (maybe for different reasons) but in a way that you feel reduces some unwanted directional risk in your overall portfolio. This may sound a bit complicated but in reality, it can be done in a simplistic way. My overlays are never super complicated.

Macro overlay is not just for stonks. If you're long AUDUSD and worried about the USD for the next few days, you might turn your AUDUSD into EURAUD for a bit. Or go short GBPUSD against it. Or sell copper. etc.

This is getting into portfolio management, kinda, but what I am discussing here is much more simplistic. You are simply adding a new trade that goes in the opposite direction of your other trades and giving that new trade its own set of parameters. I will very often do this in FX.

Since March 16th, for example, I have been long AUDUSD as discussed in my daily note, am/FX. Friday, March 25th, I started to get nervous about the USD side. At the same time, I was getting more bearish GBP as interest rate differentials moved hard against GBP and in favor of the USD. So I sold GBPUSD.

Selling GBPUSD when you are long AUDUSD is effectively short GBPAUD... But I ran them as two completely different positions with separate time horizons, take profits and stop losses. Then, on March 28th, I took off the AUDUSD long for a profit and stuck with the GBPUSD short, which is now 100 pips+ in the money. When done well, **macro overlay is like an elaborate dance** as you add and subtract risk according to the evolution of your views.

The more you can assign risk management parameters to every trade you do, the easier it is to manage your risk and avoid the complexity and uncertainty associated with more complicated forms of portfolio management. When individual trades remain independent, you can treat them all as separate ideas, even if they provide some diversification or hedging benefit to one another. That way, you get the benefits of a portfolio (once in a while when you want it), but you don't need 14 engineers from RIT doing stress tests and VAR simulations on your 327 line items.

One of the best traders I ever worked with is the master of this overlay style. He would have a strong view on KRW and MYR or whatever and strap on 200 million USD of long Asia positions… Then some news would come out that was bad for Asia and he'd sell 300 million AUDUSD against his KRW and MYR. Four hours later, he'd strip the AUD at the perfect time, and then his KRW and MYR would start to perform soon after. Sometimes he'd be making money on both sides because his timing and intuition on what legs to run, strip, or hedge was so crazy bananas good.

When I first saw the guy trade, I assumed he would blow up. He had so much risk going back and forth sometimes, it was incomprehensible. But, turns out *it was only incomprehensible to me,* not him! He's still going strong 15 years later.

Finally, one last way to deal with the bottom-up vs. top-down issue is to simply **be a long-only investor** and pick stocks. This isn't trading and is not what this series is about, but it's a perfectly reasonable approach and explains why many investors are mostly bottom-up. They assume US innovation and growth and stocks for the long run and then pick the companies and stocks they like best.

In prior 50in50s, I have talked about finding a thesis supported by many styles of analysis: fundamentals, narrative, microstructure, technicals, sentiment, correlation, positioning, and so on. Here I want you to understand the idea that trades should work through most or all of those lenses and also work on most slices of the top-down/bottom-up pyramid.

My process is all about looking for trades that tick as many boxes as humanly possible. The times when many planets are in line. But I also utilize strategy #3 (macro overlay) now and then when I feel like my book is not balanced the way I want it to be vis-a-vis the USD, risky assets, rates, commodities, or whatever.

Don't copy down those pyramid diagrams. Yours might look different, depending on what you trade. The two diagrams I included are just simplified schematics to give you an idea of what I'm talking about. If you are going deep, you might find pyramids within the pyramid. For example, you can break the "Global Growth" slice into its major components and think about US, German, Japanese and Chinese growth (for example) and how each country's economic momentum might influence the price of your security.

I'm not saying you need to do a complete unpack of the entire global economy every time you do a trade! That's crazy talk. But the more you can break your trade down and think about the variables that will or might impact it... The better. Simple thoughts like these can work:

- Shanghai locked down last night. That's probably a negative for Chinese growth. That doesn't help my AUD trade.
- German investor and executive sentiment have been abysmal and there is a strong Europe / China link. Not amazing for AUD.
- US financial conditions are tightening faster now than they were a few weeks ago. That might underpin the dollar.

And so on. The core idea here is to analyze your market on as many dimensions as possible. Come at it from above, below, and sideways. Be creative and figure out all the variables that you think matter for the price of the asset you are trading.

The more you know at each level of zoom, the more clear your thesis will become, and the better you will understand the risks, catalysts, and drivers of the trade after you put it on.

OK! That's today's lesson. Now let me overlay a top-down view over these two other existing trades.

Trade 8: Sell NASDAQ Futures (NQM2)

I said at the start of 50in50 that I am not running this as a big portfolio. It's too complicated to do so. Still, it's impossible for me not to notice the beta of the portfolio and want to manage it.

I am slowly becoming more bearish risky assets again after a period of trading nimble/agnostic with a bullish bias. Here is the basic evolution of my views on risky assets.

- November 2021 to early February: Bearish. Most of am/FX and MacroTactical Crypto was about Fed tightening and the importance of QT as it entered the narrative for the first time early in 2022. This year set up a lot like 2018 and I was surprised how complacent many were given the obvious 100mph approach of the QT train.
- In February I shifted to neutral and on February 24 I turned bullish. My main view at that time was that geopolitical events are scary for markets but generally do not have a huge impact on US growth or corporate earnings and thus the market tends to overreact to them. This is generally, but not always true and this blasé view cost me before the invasion as I went short both gold and oil. So I'm not claiming to

be some genius here, I am just biased against trading geopolitics from the short side. It cost me initially and then it helped me lean the right way over the last few weeks.

- Now, the bad shorts put on for the Russian invasion are out. The shorts that were trading on WW3 fears are out. The bad portfolio hedges and underweights have given up on the now 1-month-old Russia story and that is what has pushed stocks from 4100 to 4500. Thing is, Russia is a red herring. The real story this year, in my opinion, is the Fed—and we are headed for a tightening in financial conditions similar to what we saw in 2018.

  The market can only focus on one theme at a time. The hawkish Fed theme (bearish) cascaded into the Russia invasion theme (bearish) and there was a big puke. Now, we've seen a short squeeze as commodity prices rise, risk aversion subsides, and people realize the human devastation in Ukraine is unlikely to massively impact (for example) JPM or TSLA earnings.

  With the shorts rinsed, we can go back to focusing on the Fed. When we do so, the view will not be pretty. We are priced for chunky 50bp hikes and demand destruction and inverted yield curves and plenty of stuff that is not great for stocks.

I've got EWC long and XPO short and the obvious thing I could do here is just cut the EWC. But I always much, much prefer to stick to the original plan on trades whenever I can, so another option here is to simply do a macro overlay. The question is, can I do some kind of overlay that is simple and easy to risk manage?

Yes! I can because I have been noticing over the past week that the 4585 level in SPX and the 200-day in NASDAQ (15,111) are both nearby. There also happen to be two major tops in NASDAQ at 15100 (mid-February) and 15260 (early February). So in this case, short ES or NQ (S&P futures or NASDAQ futures) are both reasonable cash trades that are easy to risk manage.

In this case, I like the NASDAQ chart better and I also believe that higher rates are ultimately more negative for tech than they are for the broad market. Tech stocks are long-duration assets while banks and oil (for example) are sectors that might be fine in a rising commodities, rising interest rate world.

Here's a daily chart of NQ. You can see the 200-day defined the trend pretty well on the way up and we are about to kiss it.

And here's the same chart, but hourly, back to when the Fed dumped "transitory."

On the hourly chart, it's pretty clear that the old broken support and early February tops around 15230/15260 are the pivots to watch. The average day's range in NASDAQ futures has been around 200 handles so if we add two of those to 15260 we get a stop loss of 15660. That's plenty of room on a trade like this and puts us well above the 100-day, the 200-day, and the February tops. The target is back into that choppy bottoming zone around 13k and I'll add two day's ranges above the bottom to come up with a target of 13344. Risking 690 to make 1626.

Finally, if you needed one more reason to be bearish the NASDAQ: Those horrendous QQQ freeze-frame ads during the NCAA Basketball are enough to make me hit a bid. The Official ETF of the NCAA®?

Bleh.

Anyway........................ That's it for this week.

50in50 goes short NQM2 (June NASDAQ futures) at 14970 with a stop at 15660 and take profit at 13344.

Week 9: Buy High, Sell Higher

Elon Musk puts it bluntly.

Update: Open and recently closed trades

1. Short NQM2 is just about flat (small underwater). *Note: I forgot to do the position sizing exercise in 50in50 last week; I'm sorry. Micro NQ futures or short QQQ were fine for the trade but for retail traders, NQ futures are too large. I should have clarified that.*
2. EWC long at 37.85 is doing OK currently trading at 40.40.
3. The May $60 XPO puts are worth about $1.40 (paid $2.60). Plenty of time left on the clock. XPO has come way off the highs and trades pretty soft. No change to the plan.

Update complete!

Today, I am going to talk about adaptation and why it's good to avoid devoting yourself too religiously to one style of trading.

Adaptation

Good traders keep learning. They adapt. They want to improve every day and have a growth mindset. They don't sit there and complain about how the market sucks; they identify new market regimes and try to understand whether their current process will work as the regime shifts. This ability to adapt has been especially important in the last 10 years as market microstructure has changed dramatically with the rise of the algos.

As trading was increasingly automated during the 2000s, there were two groups of traders: one group complained every day about the algos and how they were messing up the market and changing the game in unfair ways. The other group of traders analyzed the new market structure and adapted, changing their trading style to fit the new regime. Guess which group of traders lost their jobs?

When volatility, liquidity, microstructure, and correlations change, good traders see it happening and adapt their process. Those who do not adapt are eliminated by natural selection.

For the first 10 years or so of my trading career, I tended to favor mean reversion over breakout trading. This is often a feature of traders who fancy themselves as smarter than average, because the feeling of fading the crowd and "swimming against the tide" is something that can make you feel super smart. When it works.

On the other hand, reflexive contrarians get buried during major trends as positioning, sentiment, and price can move in the same direction for prolonged periods when the story is real and the narrative is strong. In big macro trends, you don't want to be the smartest person in the world, you want to see the trend and ride it with everyone else.

That's the underlying message of the various IQ memes like this one:

Trend following!

When it comes to independent thinking, Peter Thiel nails it with this quote (from his book *Zero to One*):

The most contrarian thing of all is not to oppose the crowd but to think for yourself.

Many traders are good in a specific type of market. Some are good breakout traders, or range traders or flow traders. Maybe they do well when stocks are falling but not when stocks rally. Some traders were great before the algos but have no idea how to trade algo-driven markets. The challenge is that markets are always changing. If you're really good at one type of market, it is almost guaranteed that you will be a dinosaur at some point.

Don't say "I'm a great breakout trader but I can't do mean reversion." Or "I'm a mean reversion guy." Be aware that markets change and be the type of trader that adapts in real-time. Trade according to the empirical facts and the external setups and regimes, not a pre-programmed internal bias.

No trading method works always and forever. No matter how well your methodology works right now, there is a chance it won't work tomorrow. Be vigilant to see changes in the market and monitor the success of different trading strategies. For example, if you notice that breakout trading has not been working for you over the past two years, spend some time thinking about why. Has your methodology changed? Did you stop following your own rules? Or… are there new algorithms doing the same thing you used to do, but faster? Are the basic breakout trading strategies such common knowledge that they no longer provide any edge?

William Faulkner's advice to fiction writers was: "Kill your darlings." What he meant was that no matter how much you love some paragraph or character or scene you've written, if it doesn't work in the bigger picture: *cut it.* The same applies to trading strategies. Don't be the trader that is a one-trick pony and can't drop a strategy even though she knows (and the P&L shows) that it doesn't work. Do not fall in love with strategies that made you money in the past. Kill your darlings.

Example: Traders that made money buying calls on WFH stocks before earnings releases in 2020 will have a hard time abandoning that strategy in 2021 or 2022. But it is highly likely that they should do so.

I tell you this from experience because, for the majority of my career, my bread and butter was trading lead/lag and correlation between currencies and variables like oil, gold, interest rates, and equities. This served me well from 2003 to 2013 or so, but since then it has been much more difficult to extract profit from this approach. Too many people know about the methodology, too many blogs post about it, and too many algos trade it.

In 2006, very few FX traders had live feeds for gold, oil, and single-name equities. Now every single trader does. In 2006 there might have been a few expensive, PhD-built algorithms trading correlation; now you can build a correlation trading algo in Excel in two hours and plug it directly into the market through an online broker.

Efficient markets eventually prevail. *Always.*

It took me a few years to transition, but now I use correlation more selectively and question the logic more aggressively before I employ it as a tactical or strategic decision-making tool. My first assumption now is to assume lead/lag will *not* work, and see if I can find reasons why it *might work* in this particular instance. In the past, my base assumption was the opposite. I'd assume it would work and then try to think of reasons it might not.

So I still use lead/lag… But my approach and assumptions have changed as the market changed.

If there is a major change to the structure of markets, STOP AND THINK.

How is this going to impact me? Here are a few examples of major structural changes that have changed markets in my lifetime.

1996: Currency trading moves from voice brokers to electronic brokers.

2001: US stock markets stop trading in fractions and trade decimals instead.

2002 - 2005: Algorithmic trading becomes an important part of markets.

2010 - 2015: Flash crashes become an important risk in many markets.

October 2019: Free stock trading for retail traders triggers several euphoric "runnings of the bulls" in US stocks.

I believe that adaptation is one of the keys to survival and professional longevity in almost every industry. A good athlete adapts as her sport changes, just like a good trader adapts as markets change. Be thoughtful about the current environment, how it is changing and how it might change in the future. Think about how you can adapt your trading to stay ahead.

As the Red Queen in *Through the Looking-Glass* (Lewis Carroll) says:

> *Now, here, you see, it takes all the running you can do, to keep in the same place.*
> *If you want to get somewhere else, you must run at least twice as fast as that!*

You need to work twice as hard as everyone else if you want to get ahead. Understand the market regime and fit your trading strategy to that regime. Don't embrace a trading style and hope the market complies with it. "Trading style" should describe your time horizon, risk management approach, asset class focus, and preferred analysis methodology; it should *not* describe the specific strategies you prefer. Specific strategies work in specific market regimes and you need to adapt your overall style to the regime.

Don't fall in love with the first thing that works for you and stick with it long after it stops working.

Trade 9: Long TWTR

Today Elon Musk announced that he has bought 9.2% of Twitter. Here is the reaction in the stock:

TWTR stock hourly since November 2021

If I saw this story and stock chart 15 years ago, I can absolutely guarantee you that I would be dying to **short** the gap higher because "it's moved too much!" or "too far too fast!" or whatever.

Unless you have a specific measure for "too far too fast" that you like to use systematically (RSI below 10, for example)… The concept of "too far, too fast" is vague and useless in trading.

In this case, this is what I see:

- Richest person in the world and wildly successful entrepreneur buying into a company that…
- Has an excellent brand name but…
- Has generally disappointed investors.

It's a classic activist shareholder situation (kinda) and definitely not something you want to sell into on Day One. In fact, I think you plug your nose and buy it, despite the huge gap.

Reminder: This is an educational book. None of this is investment advice. The idea here is to share how I think… Not to tell you how to think.

The Elon Musk brand name is good enough to put a multi-day or multi-week bid under TWTR. Not to mention, Musk is an active and well-known user of the product and so his interest probably extends further than a simple pump of the stock. It looks to me like a classic: **buy high, sell higher** setup where the hard trade is the right trade.

I acknowledge that past pumps by Elon (Doge, etc.) have sometimes led to huge investor losses as the frenzy met gravitational reality much faster than longs could take profit. In this case, I think there should be another huge leg higher in the stock as the market slowly processes the new information.

The stock made a nice island today with 46.85 the low and 48.80 holding firm since about 10:30am. Here is the chart for today:

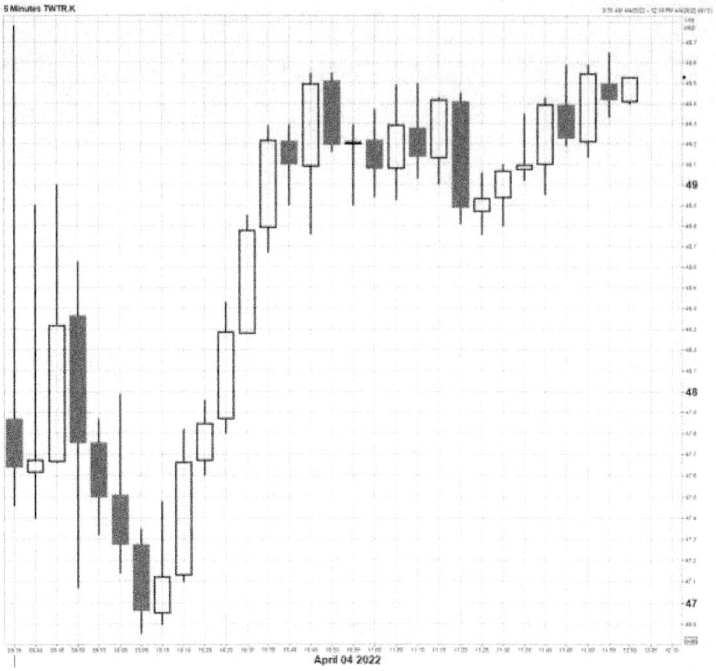

The risk management here is pretty simple. Buy the stock with a stop below $46, targeting $58/$68. I got the target by looking at the old equilibrium zone for the stock before it dumped.

You can see that here:

Options don't look particularly attractive compared to cash so I'm going to keep it simple. Long at 50.00 with a stop at 45.84 and take profit at 57.77. Risking 4.16 to make 8.52. As always, I will mark to market the trades at the point I hit send. So the entry point is at market; it won't be exactly $50.00. It's trading $50 as I type but could be better or worse depending on how long it takes me to finish writing and recording the audio!

Be Nimble

The ability to both **go with … or fade** large market moves is a learned skill. As you grow as a trader, you should be equally comfortable jumping on a big move or going against it. Sure, most will have a built-in bias, but the key is to know your bias and overcome it in situations where you believe the market will reward you for doing so.

I think this is a situation where I should overcome my mean reversion bias and buy TWTR high in the hope of selling it higher.

That's it for this week! **50in50 goes long TWTR at 50.00 with a stop at 45.84 and take profit at 57.77.**

Week 10: The Metagame

Play the actual game, not the imaginary game you wish was real

Cringe

Update: Open and recently closed trades

1. Short NQM2 is in the money and halfway to the take profit as risky assets slump and Fed fears mount. Move the stop loss to 15301 now (above the 100-day, 200-day, and late March tops)
2. EWC long at 37.85 is doing OK currently trading at 39.65, which isn't bad considering broad equity market weakness. **Take profit on EWC** here as oil is slumping, global financials are not trading well, and the Bank of Canada meeting this week could hurt CAD. The thesis was that Canadian stocks are heavily weighted to financials and oil and thus should do well. As bank stocks fail to benefit from rising rates and oil slumps to $94 after touching $130 on the Russia panic… The thesis feels stale. Take the money and run.
3. Twitter long is stopped out. Another doge-like failed Elon pump, in the end.
4. The May $60 XPO puts are worth about $4.10 (cost was $2.60). Plenty of time left on the clock. XPO has come way off the highs and trades pretty soft. No change to the plan.

Update complete!

This week, I am going to talk about understanding the metagame, especially as it relates to messages from policymakers.

The metagame

Good traders understand the game and they don't play some other fictional game that only exists in their heads. This is similar to sports where weak competitors will complain about a new rule while others will find ways to adapt to it and capitalize on it. Or in school where high-performing students predict what will be on the test and low-performance students complain that the teacher is bad.

In markets: you can complain about central bank intervention and the death of free markets and crazy dovish policies and so on… Or you can attempt to understand them and trade profitably. It doesn't matter what the Fed "should do"; it matters what the Fed **will do**. It doesn't matter what is right or wrong. It only matters what is.

One classic example of this is in 2010 when the market was still gripped by post-GFC permabearishness. To give you a sense of how bearish the world was, there were **two** celebrity forecaster economists with the nickname "Dr. Doom" on TV. All the time. LOL.

Every headline was like:

STOCKS AND BONDS

U.S. Stocks Drop on New Jitters About Global Growth

June 29, 2010

New York Times

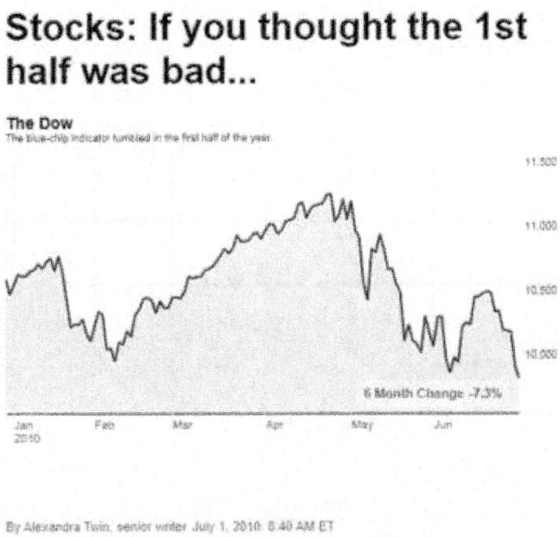

CNN

Market Comment

July 26, 2010

Betting on a Bubble, Bracing for a Fall

John Hussman

Everyone was focused on the old game (economic performance, future growth, earnings estimates…). Meanwhile, up there on CNBC, hedge fund manager David Tepper and famed strategist David Zervos were bullish. All they cared about was liquidity. Obviously, Tepper and Zervos had the right framework while the majority of traders and investors did not.

There's a video on YouTube of Tepper with the best read on the market at the time.[15] His framework was: Economy up: Good for stocks. Economy down: More QE, good for stocks. He was right! Almost everyone else was wrong. What did Tepper understand that nobody else did? The Fed put was the only game in town. He had no idea where the economy was going but he understood that forecasting the economy was not important.

While many in the market stuck with bearish outlooks on stocks for years after that, Tepper correctly identified that liquidity was the only thing that mattered and he performed incredibly well.

In the 2012-2015 period, there was constant shouting at the TV from rates traders who were paid rates and criticizing the Fed because "they should be hiking!" Same story in 2021. Too many traders were positioned for a move they thought the Fed *should* make, instead of trying to predict the move the Fed *would* make. The important thing is to understand that it's fine to debate what the Fed should be doing, but to make money, you must predict what the Fed **will do**. Not what it **should do**.

Intervention

There is a long and rich history of central banks putting a floor under domestic equity markets. Japan conducted "price-keeping operations" (PKOs) from August 1992 to November 1993.

---

[15] https://www.youtube.com/watch?v=eMx8QimKaMY

Japan Nikkei, 1990 to 1995

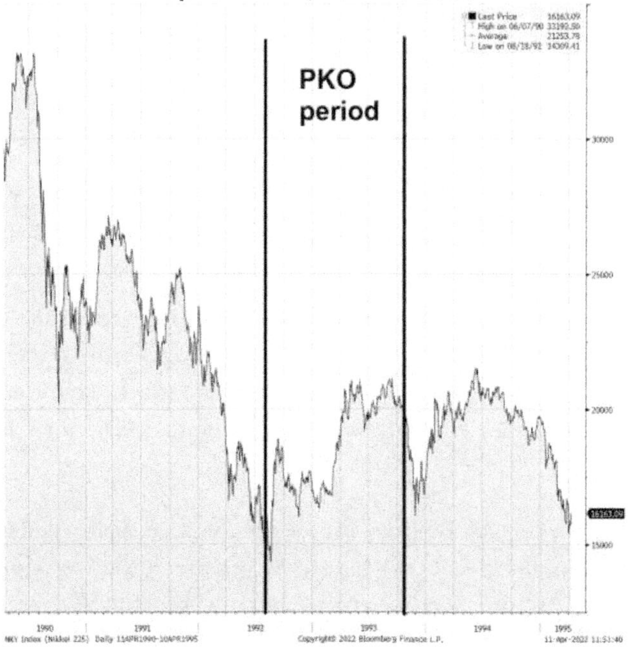

The most famous example is when Hong Kong enacted price-keeping operations, buying HK equities directly in 1998. This operation was no secret. Joseph Yam explained it in a WSJ editorial on August 20, 1998. The editorial is interesting and informative. Here's how the Hang Seng responded:

Hang Seng Index, 1995 to 2000

While conspiracy theorists love to ruminate over the existence of a US Plunge Protection Team,[16] no proof has yet emerged that this group actually intervened in US stock markets at some point. Personally, I would not be surprised, but whatever.

Fed Chairman Ben Bernanke pretty much announced the Fed added a third mandate: "make stocks go up" with this WaPo editorial in November 2010.[17] That editorial ratified Tepper's view that the Fed was all that mattered. By the way, the June 29, 2010 headline from the NYT (featured above) was the exact low in the SPX (1030) and stocks doubled by the end of 2014.

Over and over, the lesson has been: governments have more money than you do. Be careful trading from the short side when the government says "no más." In some cases like Japan 1993, the government eventually let stocks fall again as the risks to financial stability eased, but in most cases, an important low is put in when the government intervenes. Either way, there is always a trade.

So where are we now? **The US government could not care less about stocks**. They want inflation down and they don't care what the cost. There is no Fed put… If anything, there is a Fed call as the higher stocks go, the more Fed hikes the market will price, and the more the Fed will hike in response. There have only been two US presidents that wanted higher interest rates: Jimmy Carter and Joe Biden.

Trade 10: Long ASHR

On the other side of the world, we got this headline from China today:

China Securities Regulator Says Supports Social Security Fund, Pension Funds, Trust, Insurance, and Wealth Management Institutions to Allocate More Funds to Equity Assets and Increase Capital Market Investment - Reuters

This is after the mid-March announcements from China that they vowed to support the economy and financial market stability. Those two announcements in tandem are about as close as you can get to China announcing PKOs without announcing PKOs.

While many people trade FXI as a US-listed China proxy, ASHR has a much higher correlation to the CSI 300 (75% vs. 46%). Both FXI and ASHR had absolutely gargantuan volume spikes in mid-March and that sets up a good tradable low for ASHR. The old highs are all around $31 as well so this sets up a great pivot.

---

16 https://en.wikipedia.org/wiki/ Working_Group_on_Financial_Markets

17 https://www.federalreserve.gov/ newsevents/files/bernanke_post_op_ed_20101104.pdf

31 is a major pivot

There is no such thing as free money. It's possible that the Chinese intervention is not as aggressive as it needs to be and it's also possible that they just put a floor under Chinese stocks, but supply remains heavy and the bounces are minimal. You need to risk manage every trade.

In this case, you can get really nice risk/reward by putting the stop loss at $29.89 (below the pivot with a bit of room for an overshoot—I always like having my stops on the right side of the large round numbers, too). A rally back to $35 seems like the chip shot target and $40 is the more hopeful objective. In mid-February, there was a series of tops around 36.50 and so I think a TP at 36.44 makes sense.

As you know if you read my daily (am/FX) or my crypto notes, I have been bearish risky assets and bullish USD since April 4. I think the path of least resistance into the May 4th FOMC is: lower risky assets and a higher dollar. As such, you could pair this long China idea against short SPX and be market neutral. For the sake of simplicity, I'm just going to run this as one trade but I acknowledge that ASHR has some beta to US equity direction. I could double my NQ short or whatever, but the point of 50in50 is not to create an optimal portfolio, it's to isolate where ideas come from and how to structure them.

The right framework and the right game

The real lesson today is that **the most important tool for any trader is the right framework.**

If someone has been bearish equities since 2010 based on valuation or comparisons of US household net worth to stock market capitalization… They have the wrong framework.

If someone was playing for Fed hikes in 2013 and 2014 because they thought the Fed was crazy to keep rates at zero… They had the wrong framework.

If people are shorting USDJPY right now because equities are going down. They have the wrong framework. *USDJPY is a rates trade, not an equities trade.*

In late 2021 and through 2022, people screaming "too much is priced in for the Fed!" have had the wrong framework. *When the Fed is following market pricing instead of leading it, pricing can go almost anywhere. The market gave the Fed 25 in March and they took it. Now the market is giving them 50 in May and they'll take it. Playing the "too much is priced" game is not very fun when the Fed and the US government both want higher rates.*

What is the right game?

Another way to think about this is to ponder: What is the right game to be playing here? A famous hedge fund manager stuck a Post-It note to his monitor in 2009 after the Fed and Treasury changed all the mark-to-market and stock shorting rules. It said "Long or flat." He knew the game had changed and now it was time to profit from the coming bull market as governments had declared an end to the financial calamity of 2008. Sometimes just avoiding the hard trade is half the battle.

Separate your philosophy on free markets from this reality: The US is a mixed economy that has both capitalist and socialist characteristics. The government plays an important role in every global economy. Canada, Europe, and other "free market" economies too. There is no pure free market. To wish otherwise can be expensive.

Recognize the moments when the government is intervening in markets, and have a healthy respect for it, even if you find it morally repugnant.

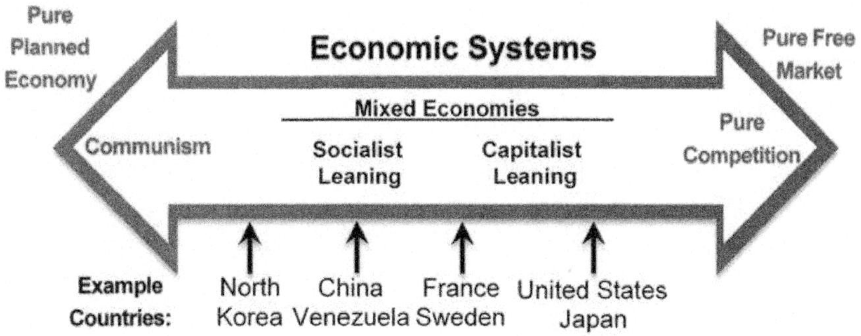

Source: adamsmith.org

Right now, in the USA, the government wants lower inflation at almost any cost. They don't care what AAPL stock or GME or TSLA do. They care what CPI does.

At the other end of the planned vs. free market spectrum, China has just signaled they want higher stock prices. While they may or may not get their wish in the long run, I think it sets up an excellent risk/reward trade over the next few months.

The alternate hypothesis

I could write 2000 words about the alternate (bearish China) hypothesis here. China's economy is dumping, the stock market there is nearly uninvestable, Russia is making them look bad, real estate is collapsing, and so on. All true! This trade is a pure play on government intervention being more important than all those economic fundamentals in China (for the short-term).

If ASHR makes a new low and I get stopped out, my idea is wrong, and life goes on.

50in50 goes long ASHR at 32.18 with a stop loss at 29.84 and take profit at 36.44

Risking 2.34 to make 4.26. Given the high frequency of these trades and the fact I'm going outside of my main asset class (FX)… My conviction level has been about the same on all the trades. Risking 2% of capital every time. Same thing this time.

As always, I will monitor the performance and offer detailed updates as we progress. I will also do a detailed recap of the P&L after every 10 trades. That is, next week!

Week 11: Sentiment and Positioning

Can't ignore it, but don't overhype it

Grizzly Bull

Update after ten trades

1. Taking profit on the XPO puts and the NASDAQ short. Full explanation below.
2. Only open trade remains the ASHR long.
3. Full results so far in the grid
4. After 10 trades, the results are not great, but not horrendous. Started 0-4 and 3-for-4 more recently. There is a lack of big winners so far and therefore the P&L is negative. My edge is in FX and it remains to be seen if it translates to single names, equity indexes, and commodities. If it doesn't, that's OK, the point is to teach tactics and methodologies and give you tools. Then, you apply those tools to markets where you have an edge. I still think it's useful to collect and display the data, though, for intellectual honesty and also so you can see how to collect and organize trade-by-trade data.

50in50 results to date

	Entry date	L/S	Asset	Entry	USD at risk	Stop loss	Take profit	Actual exit	P&L
1	2/9/22	Short	XAUEUR	1,602	2,000	1,702	1,421	1,704	(2,000)
2	2/16/22	Short	CLK2	91	1,000	95.45	79.05	95.55	(2,000)
3	2/21/22	Short	DOCS	56.00	2,000	60.51	50.21	60.58	(2,000)
4	2/25/22	Long	BTC	39,200	2,000	31,400	49,800	39,200	
5	3/1/22	Long	BTC	43,400	2,000	38,900	49,800	38,870	(2,000)
6	3/8/22	Long	EWC	37.85	2,000	35.19	44.80	39.65	1,353
7	3/14/22	Long	XPO May $60 puts	2.60	2,000	-	53.50	6.10	2,692
8	3/28/22	Short	NQ	14,970	2,000	15,660	13,344	13,930	3,014
9	4/4/22	Long	TWTR	50.85	2,000	45.84	57.77	45.80	(2,000)
10	4/11/22	Long	ASHR	32.18	2,000	29.84	36.44		
								TOTAL	(2,940)
								Win%	38%
								AVGwin	2,353
								AVGloss	(2,000)

All P&L is calculated assuming full USD at risk deployed on each trade. For simplicity, I am not taking into account issues around contract sizes and the granularity of specific security pricing. For example, you can't deploy exactly $2,000 in micro NASDAQ futures, but I'm using 2000 at risk here anyway. It won't change the end result much so don't worry about it.

Sentiment and positioning

First of all, I want to preface this whole thing by saying: People tend to overweight positioning. **It is very often totally irrelevant.** But then, once in a while, positioning and sentiment are the only things that matter. As such, the bar for me to care about or factor in positioning is very high, but at the mega-extremes, I give it high or even dominant importance in my framework.

While I believe sentiment and positioning are important variables to consider in every trade, and can sometimes be the main driver of a trade idea, I also believe they are overrated as indicators by many traders. Here are the key points on sentiment and positioning:

1. Sentiment and positioning matter sometimes, but not most of the time.
2. 80-90% of the time, sentiment just follows price so if you trade against sentiment and positioning you are often just fighting the trend.
3. At inflection points, a tuned-in feel for positioning and sentiment can be a huge source of edge.

Positioning is packed with potential energy, like fuel for a future fire. Positioning unwinds are like fires. They need heat (a spark or catalyst), fuel (large positions), and oxygen (more bad news, or mark-to-market losses that trigger feedback loops that lead to more position unwinds).

You need large positions, a catalyst, and mark-to-market losses all at once and then you get a chain reaction that continues until it finally burns itself out (or is put out by a central bank). When I was in grade school, they taught us this process with the fire triangle.

Large positions are like piles of dry tinder that can potentially burst into flame at any moment, but probably won't. Remember, just because you have a large stack of dry wood next to an open can of gasoline… That does not mean there will be a fire.

Here is my basic positioning and sentiment framework:

The six sentiment vs. market price regimes

Sentiment	Bull Market	Bear Market
Bullish and increasing	Very Bullish	
Bullish and stable	Bullish	
Bullish but falling	BEARISH	
Bearish and stable		Bearish
Bearish and getting more bearish		Very bearish
Bearish but getting less bearish		BULLISH

In other words, going against sentiment works at the turning points but not during the trend. If you can identify a palpable turn in sentiment via observation of behavior or via data analysis, you can position ahead of the crowd.

Sources of sentiment and positioning data

The most commonly-used positioning data comes from the CFTC. This data shows the positioning of non-commercial speculators, and while it is closely followed and can be interesting information, it has no predictive power on its own. If you see "Copper longs on CFTC hit all-time high" your instinct is probably to go short copper but the inconvenient truth is that a setup like that is actually modestly bullish on all time horizons.

The CFTC data is slow-moving and trend-following and directional, not contrarian. Do not use CFTC data by itself as a contrarian indicator.

A source of sentiment data that *is* contrarian is the Daily Sentiment Index, produced by Jake Bernstein since the 1980s. That data is the output from a survey of retail traders that simply asks: "Are you bullish or bearish on X?" It shows what percentage of survey respondents are bulls. When bulls get below 10 or above 90, that is a good indicator of a near-term extreme. DSI data is available only via subscription.

Options markets often contain important positioning information. For example, when stocks rise and VIX rises at the same time, you know that something unusual is going on because the correlation is almost always inverted between those two. Stocks up / VIX up is a sign that the market is so bullish it is adding to upside with calls, instead of hedging the downside with puts. You can also look at the put/call ratio for a read on equity sentiment. In currency markets, people look at the risk reversal to see if traders have a strong preference for puts or calls, and how that preference is changing.

Positioning surveys can be a useful source of information. They are timely and fast moving. People change their minds quickly, as opposed to trend-following systems which move much more slowly as they wait for price confirmation. Again, with surveys, most of the time they are directional, and the only time they are contrarian is when they hit an extreme. In the positioning surveys I have done when working at banks, I found that when sentiment made a record high or low for the past year, that could often be a good sign of a turn.

In the stock market, there are many sentiment surveys and indicators available. I like the AAII survey (bulls vs. bears). CNN's Fear and Greed indicator is also a nice simple snapshot of equity sentiment. As you become expert in your market, you will learn the best sentiment and positioning indicators to follow.

Finally, magazine covers can be the ultimate contrarian indicator. When a financial theme hits the cover of a mainstream magazine, always take note. By the time journalists believe a theme is worthy of a cover story, that theme is (by definition) well-known. That means the theme is probably also crowded.

How to use sentiment and positioning data

"You can't escape the madness of crowds by dogmatically rejecting them... The most contrarian thing of all is not to oppose the crowd but to think for yourself."

- Peter Thiel, *Zero to One*

Sentiment and positioning data can be the difference maker at turning points. The number one takeaway on sentiment and positioning, whether you are using surveys, options markets, or other sources of information, is that only the super-mega-extremes are times when you should consider fading. Otherwise, positioning and sentiment are mostly just trend indicators and they move up and down with the price.

Positioning and sentiment are part of the picture, NOT THE WHOLE PICTURE.

"Sentiment" is not always synonymous with "positioning"

While they tend to mostly move in lockstep, it is important to understand the difference between sentiment and positioning. Many traders and analysts use the two terms interchangeably but they are not always the same thing.

Sentiment is how people view the market. If you take a poll of traders, you will get a sentiment reading. An example of this sort of reading is the Daily Sentiment Index (DSI).

Positioning is a metric that measures *actual positions*. An example of this type of data is the Commitment of Traders report, which comes out every Friday and summarizes futures positions held by commercial and non-commercial traders.

You can have a market that is extremely bearish, but not heavily positioned and this is different from a market that is extremely bearish and extremely short. The difference is that the skew of future moves is completely different in the two situations. The reason is simple: A market that is bearish but not yet positioned is primed to go down as people take new positions to reflect their bearish view. On the other hand, a market that is bearish but heavily positioned short is more at risk of a short squeeze or reversal because there could be nobody left to sell.

Why would a market see extreme sentiment but not extreme positioning? There are many possible reasons. For example:

1. **The theme is new**. It takes a while for positions in one direction to become extreme. Sentiment moves faster than positioning. Many traders will build into a position as their conviction rises and as new information substantiates their view. As a general rule, sentiment leads positioning because it is faster and easier for a trader to get bearish than it is for her to put on a sizeable bearish trade.

2. **Major event risk upcoming**. This is one of the most common and highly profitable setups. Let's say the market is extremely bearish EURUSD but there is an ECB meeting. Nobody wants to go into the ECB meeting short EURUSD because there is gap risk or event risk if they are hawkish.

   The moment the ECB statement comes out, the EUR might drop aggressively as traders put on the trade they wanted to have all along. Traders were just waiting for the event to get out of the way and did not really care about the outcome of the event. This can lead to surprising moves where you get, for example, a somewhat hawkish ECB meeting (which should be bullish EURUSD) and EURUSD drops aggressively because traders care less about the ECB and more about the fact that the event risk is out of the way and now it's safer to get short EURUSD.

If you can identify moments where the market has a very strong view but does not have the position yet because they are waiting for an upcoming event to pass, you can often profit by simply putting on the position faster than others once the event is out of the way.

3. **Time of year**. A trader's risk appetite varies depending on her profitability and the time of year. For example, as we get close to the end of the year, traders like to reduce risk and book profits to start the new year with a clean slate. Therefore, you might see a situation at the end of the year where the market is extremely bullish USDJPY but flat because of an unwillingness to commit. In this case, the turn of the year could trigger substantial USDJPY buying even though nothing macro has changed between December 31 and January 1.

4. **Positioning clear outs**. From time to time, crowded positions will get rinsed by sharp counter moves. The market might hit a point where traders cannot take any more pain and the majority cut their losses. While they still hold the macro view, they cannot afford to hold the position any longer and so they cut it. This is called a stop loss run.

A good example of this is the price action in interest rate and FX markets in Fall 2014. Throughout 2014, the market was heavily positioned for higher US interest rates and a stronger dollar. In mid-October, however, the market started to lose faith in the interest rate trade as global and US inflation fell.

This reached a tipping point on October 15th as a weak US Retail Sales release was the final straw and the market stopped out of most of its dollar and interest rate positions all at once. In the weeks following this positioning wipeout, the market came to the conclusion that while US rates were not set to rise, the dollar should continue to benefit as the ECB and BOJ embarked on quantitative easing (QE) programs.

This led to a situation a few weeks later where the market was very bullish USD (sentiment) but flat (positioning) as they simply could not bring themselves to get long USD again as they were scarred by the pain of October 15th. Once new catalysts pointed to further USD gains, the market went from extremely bullish and lightly positioned back to extremely bullish and extremely long USD and the dollar shot higher.

While sentiment and positioning move together, it is important to remember that they are not always the same thing. Most of the time sentiment and positioning will match fairly closely but it is the times when they do not match that can be most important.

Understand positioning

In FX, there are many proprietary positioning indicators published by the major banks and there is the Commitment of Traders (COT) report from the Chicago Mercantile Exchange (CME).

There are many potential sampling issues with the COT data but it is still generally regarded as the best aggregate measure of FX positioning available. Have a look at how positioning and price move together:

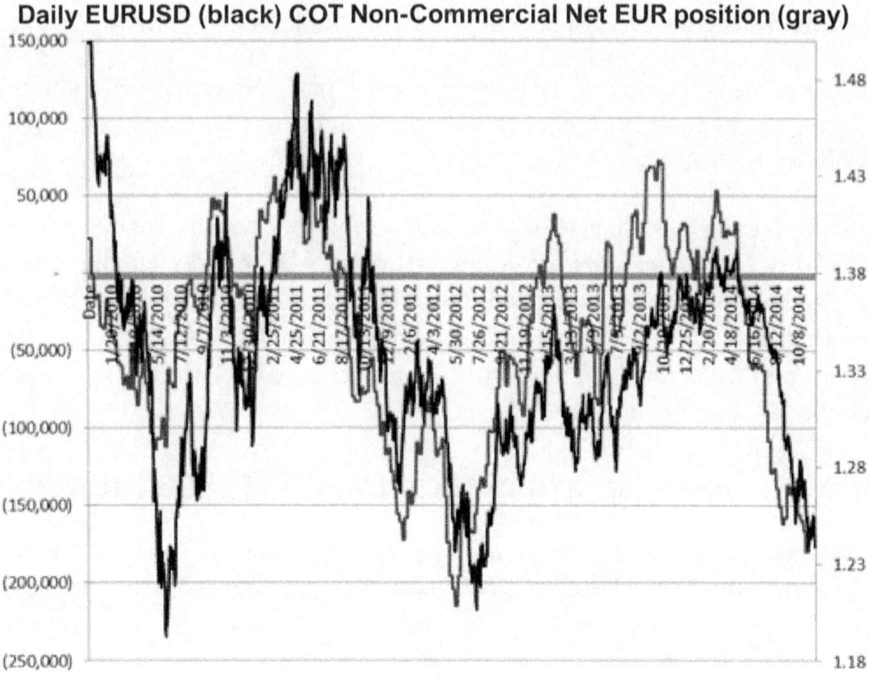

2009 - 2014

A few observations here that apply broadly to positioning:

1. Positions and price normally trend in the same direction.
2. Positioning often leads price at turning points. If you look at the lows in mid-2012, for example, you can see that positioning (the gray line) led the move off the lows in spot (the black line).
3. Positioning can trend for a long time. The market took more than a year to get from the highs in positioning (and price) to the lows between May 2011 and June 2012.
4. Absolute levels of positioning mean less than the rate of change of positioning. In May 2010, you can see that short EUR positioning reached what was then an extreme level of more than 100,000 contracts. This then led to a very aggressive reversal from 1.18 to 1.48 in EURUSD. The next time positioning reached short

100,000 contracts (early 2012), many traders took that as an indication that positioning again could go no further. Positions then went from short 100,000 to more than 200,000 contracts and EURUSD kept going down from 1.28 to 1.22 before it bottomed.

When you hear someone say that positioning is extreme, don't get too excited. Usually, all that means is that the market is in a strong trend. Ask more questions: Can positioning get more extreme? How long has it been extreme? Is the price continuing to go in favor of those who are positioned with the trend (i.e., do price and positioning confirm each other?) Are the variables and narrative that led to the big position still in play? Or are the fundamentals changing? What upcoming catalysts could lead to a turn in positioning?

Finally, as a market maker, I have often noticed that you can get a good read on positioning by the number of inquiries you get when the market moves. You can get the same vibe on Twitter.

If people are generally asking "what the??" about a move, or saying the move is "stupid" or "dumb" or "ridiculous" you can assume they are NOT on the winning side of the move. Similarly, if you are at a hedge fund and you get 11 different "BUY USDCAD!" recommendations in your inbox; you should probably hit a bid. The deeper your involvement in the market and the greater your experience level, the better your sense of positioning and sentiment.

Trade 11: Cover shorts and go long S&P 500 futures

Late last week, the American Association of Individual Investors (AAII) published its weekly sentiment survey. Here are two charts. The first one shows BULLS dropped to a 30-year low. The second one shows BULLS minus BEARS also at an extreme.

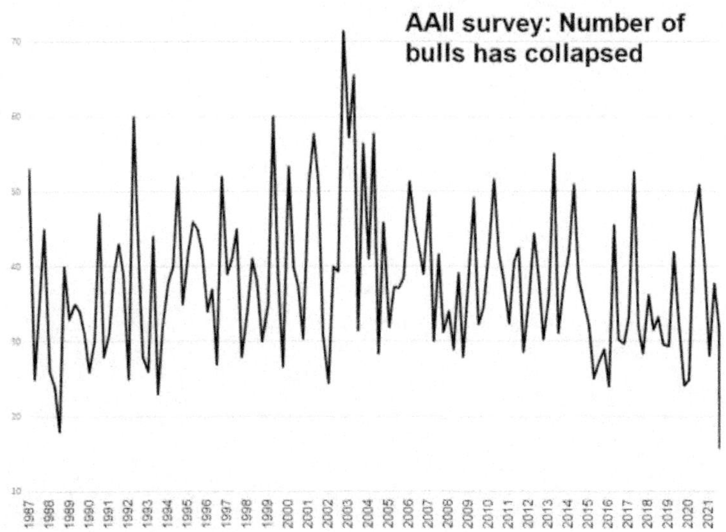

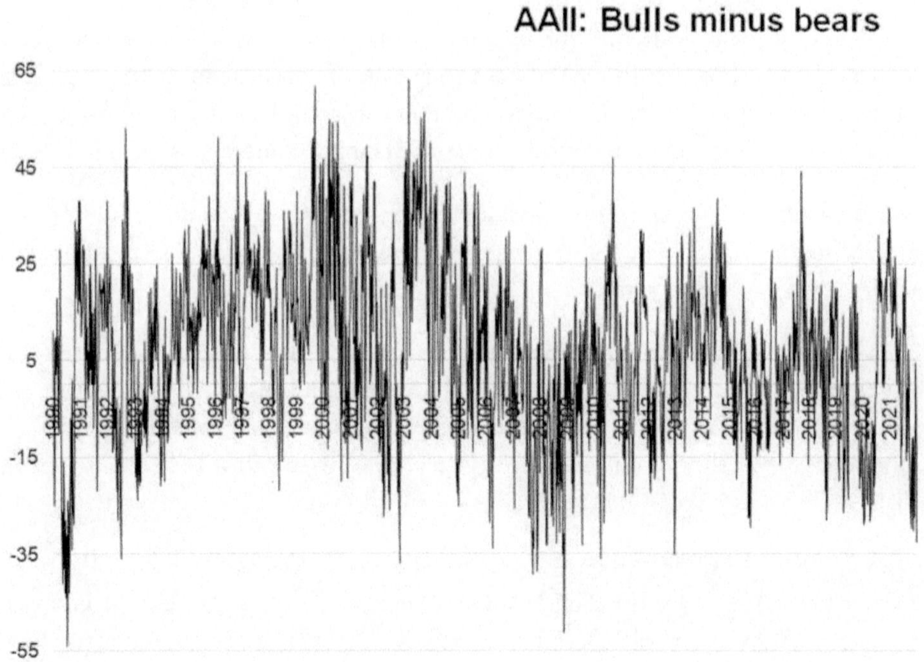

How do we know if this matters? The simplest way is to backtest the setup and see what the forward performance looked like other times readings were this extreme. So I did that. Here is the performance of (long US equities when BULLS minus BEARS is below -25). The current reading is -33.

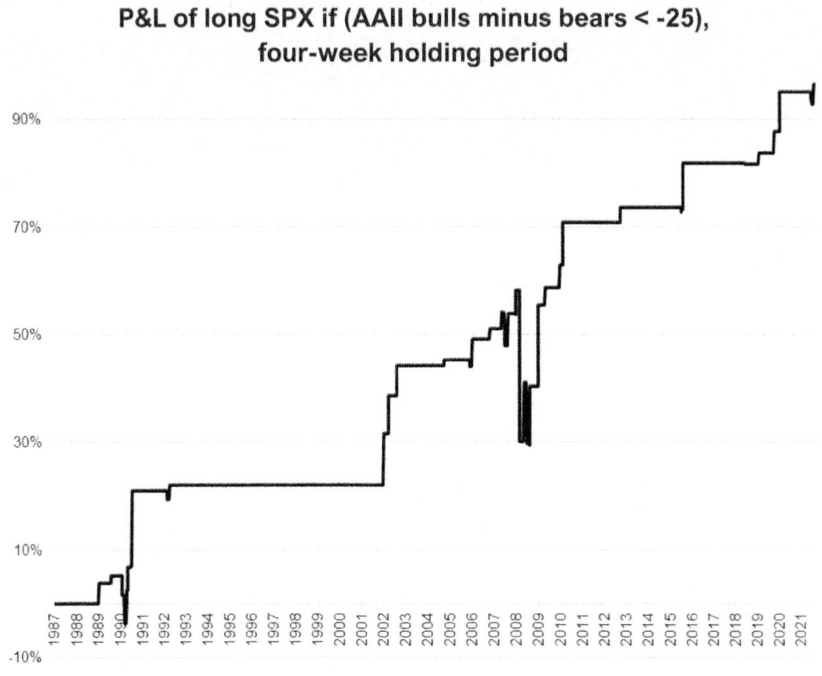

The win rate is 66% vs. 62% in all other 4-week periods, the sample size is 38 non-overlapping 4-week periods, and the median return is +2.9% vs. +1.2% in all other 4-week periods. The effect is strong and hard to ignore. If you take out 2008, the effect is gigantic. Today (April 18) is also tax day, and that can often be a low point for stocks in periods of heavy retail involvement because retail selling to fund tax payments dries up.

While the FOMC is coming in a few weeks and the overall macro setup still looks extremely suspect to me, I'm going to close my eyes, plug my nose, and flip from short NASDAQ to long S&P futures.

Seasonals work very well here too as stocks tend to rally after tax day (today) and into May. Every April and every May since 2017 have been bullish S&P. Furthermore, there is nothing major going on this week, event-wise, and bear markets tend to need fuel to keep going. "Never short a dull market" as they say. The stop loss is 4279 and the take profit is 4579.

We also cover the XPO puts (the stock was getting pretty close to the take profit anyway) and cover the NASDAQ short. The NASDAQ short and XPO puts were the best trades so far (NASDAQ short at 14970, out at 13908; XPO puts in at $2.60, out at $6.10).

I'm using TYPE II sizing here for the S&P long, risking 2% of capital ($2,000). I have not been varying my sizing much as my conviction is about equal most weeks. That is probably a function of doing a weekly piece instead of just trading whenever I have conviction. In real life, I vary my position size more.

50in50 goes long ESM2 at 4385 with a stop loss at 4279 and take profit at 4579.

Risking 106 to make 194.

Week 12: Euphoria, Panic, and Despair

Almost time to go dumpster diving for Disruptive Innovators™

Update on previous trades

ASHR and SPX trade are both stopped out as China, Europe, NFLX, and the breakdown in copper trigger concerns about global growth.

Pattern recognition

Pattern recognition can be useful in trading, as "I've seen this movie before!" can often be the feeling right before "I know what's going to happen next!". That said, it's also important to remember that human beings are biased to see patterns, even where none exist.

Today, I look at one of the most well-known patterns in markets, the euphoria/panic cycle that defines speculative bubbles.

Speculative bubbles follow two primary patterns.

1. Inflate / collapse / prosper, or

2. Inflate / collapse / die.

Let's start with two examples where the bubble laid the seeds for a subsequent, epic bull market. Here is the NASDAQ bubble, which laid the groundwork for the massive tech bull market of the 2010s.

And here is the bitcoin bubble in 2017, which was the seed for massive crypto prosperity in the 2020s:

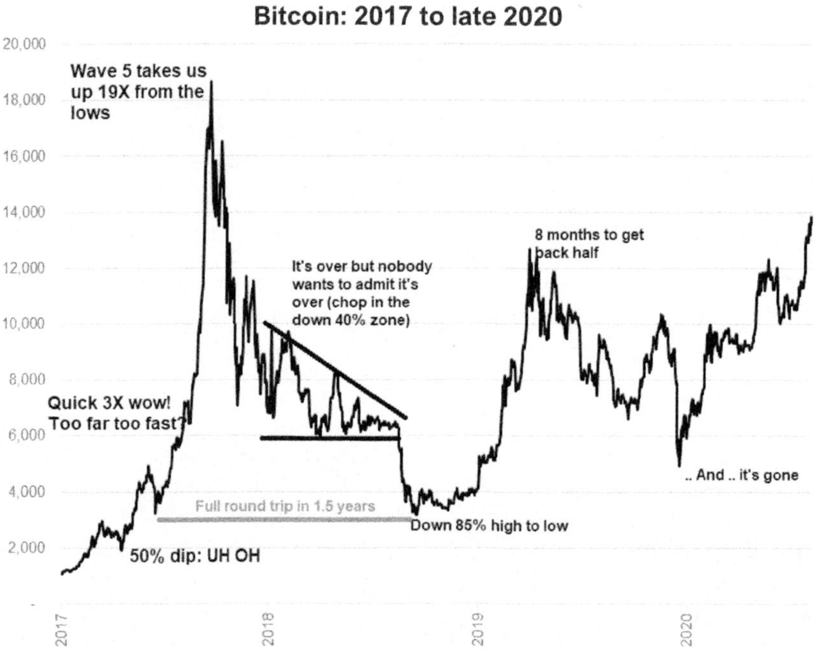

The bitcoin and NASDAQ bubbles are virtually identical if you account for the fact that bitcoin is much higher vol than NASDAQ.

Not all movies have happy endings, though! Other bubbles, like gold in 1980, and the Nikkei in 1990, were dead money for decades. You may have noticed that the pattern on those two charts is similar to the textbook speculative bubble asset pattern:

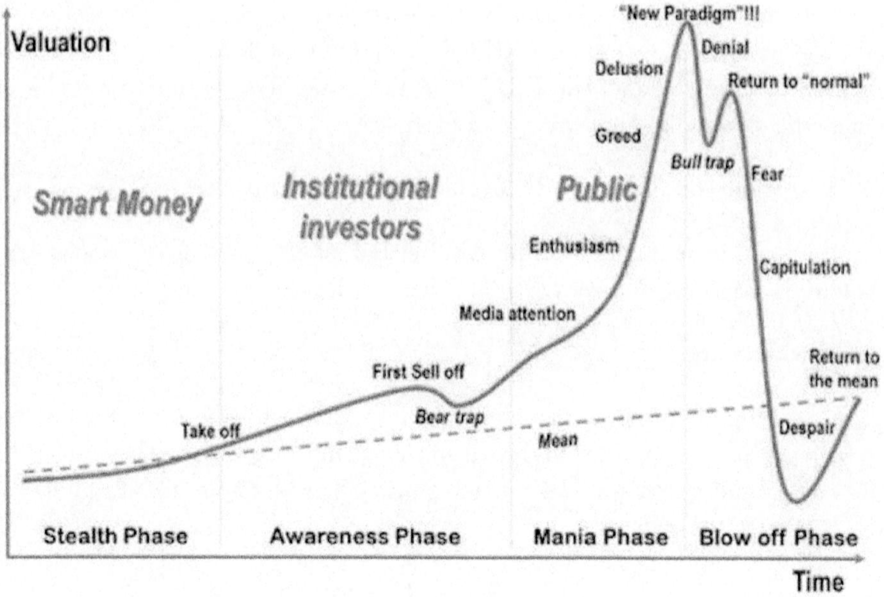

It is truly uncanny how every bubble looks pretty much the same. And here's a chart of the ARKK bubble so far:

The two most likely paths for a bubble asset after it bursts are:

1. Complete the round trip, stabilize, and rally. This is what happened with the NASDAQ in 1999, US housing in 2006, and 2017 bitcoin bubbles (for example).
2. Fizzle and grind towards zero or go nowhere for literally decades. This is what happened with the 1980 gold bubble, the 1990 Nikkei bubble, CMGI in 1999. And the tulips.

The heavily-marketed *Disruptive Innovators*™ narrative, the deification of Cathie Wood, and the run-up and collapse in the ARKK ETF all rhyme perfectly with 1999. The whole thing looked, smelled, and felt EXACTLY the same. This is not hindsight; many commentators (including me) wrote about it in 2021.

Using 1999 as the comparison, ARKK is likely to follow one of two analogs.

1. Janus (complete the round trip, stabilize, and rally).
2. CMGI (fizzle towards zero or go nowhere for literally decades)

Let's start with Janus.

Janus was the high-flying fund manager most associated with the 1999 dotcom bubble. They were heavily concentrated in the stocks that went to the moon. They rode the wave all the way up and all the way back down. So did their investors. This headline is peak Janus.

February 9, 2000

Janus' Extraordinary 1999 Powered by Small Group of Favored Stocks

The average Janus fund gained 81.6%, thanks to an appetite for large-cap growth and tech stocks.

IAN MCDONALD • FEB 9, 2000 11:39 AM EST

And a few years later…

January 12, 2003

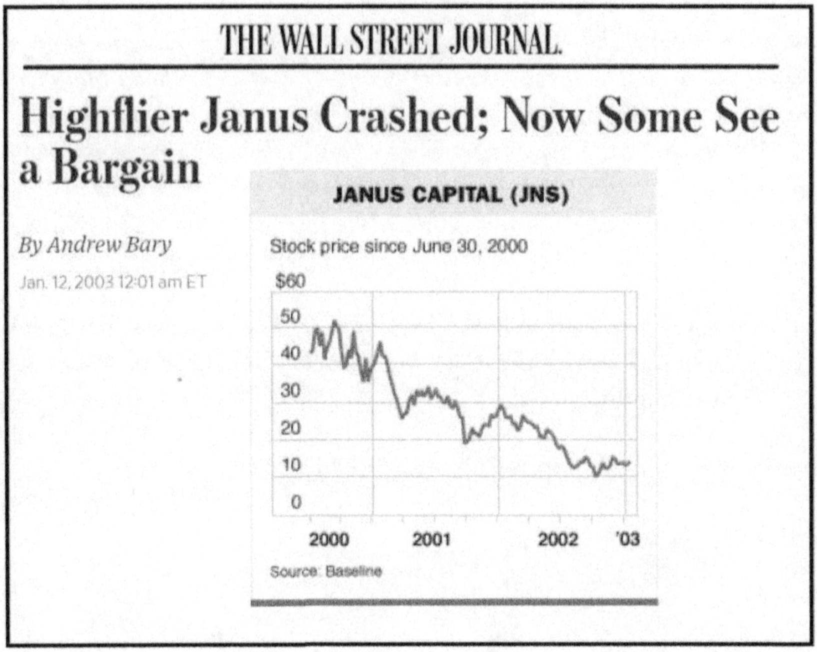
THE WALL STREET JOURNAL.

Highflier Janus Crashed; Now Some See a Bargain

By Andrew Bary

Jan. 12, 2003 12:01 am ET

As I said, ARK's[18] concentration and the manic herding of bullish retail in 2021 was nothing new. It was recognized well before ARKK peaked, for example in a January 2021 Bloomberg article.[19] The article was prescient; ARKK peaked about a month later.

January 7, 2021

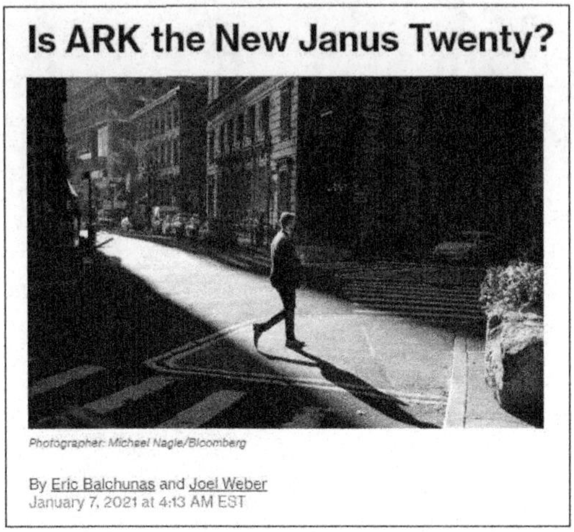
Is ARK the New Janus Twenty?

Photographer: Michael Nagle/Bloomberg

By Eric Balchunas and Joel Weber
January 7, 2021 at 4:13 AM EST

[18] Note: ARK Invest (with one K) is Cathie Wood's investment management firm; ARKK (with two Ks) is their flagship "disruptive innovators" ETF.

[19] https://www.bloomberg.com/news/articles/2021-01-07/is-ark-the-new-janus-twenty

Here is an excerpt:

> *"Cathie Wood of ARK is not the first highly concentrated active manager to shoot the lights out for half a decade while sparking a stampede of flows into their funds. There have been many throughout history but perhaps the one that most echoes ARK today is the famous Janus Twenty Fund, which dominated the latter half of the '90s and early 2000s with very similar returns and flows to what ARK is experiencing, albeit one met with a 50% downturn when the Internet bubble burst."*

The next chart shows the path followed by Janus 20. The fund was mostly invested in megatech, so it rebounded with the indexes. Those that bought in the 30s, after the full round trip 30-90-30, did very well.

Janus 20 Fund, 1989 to 2015

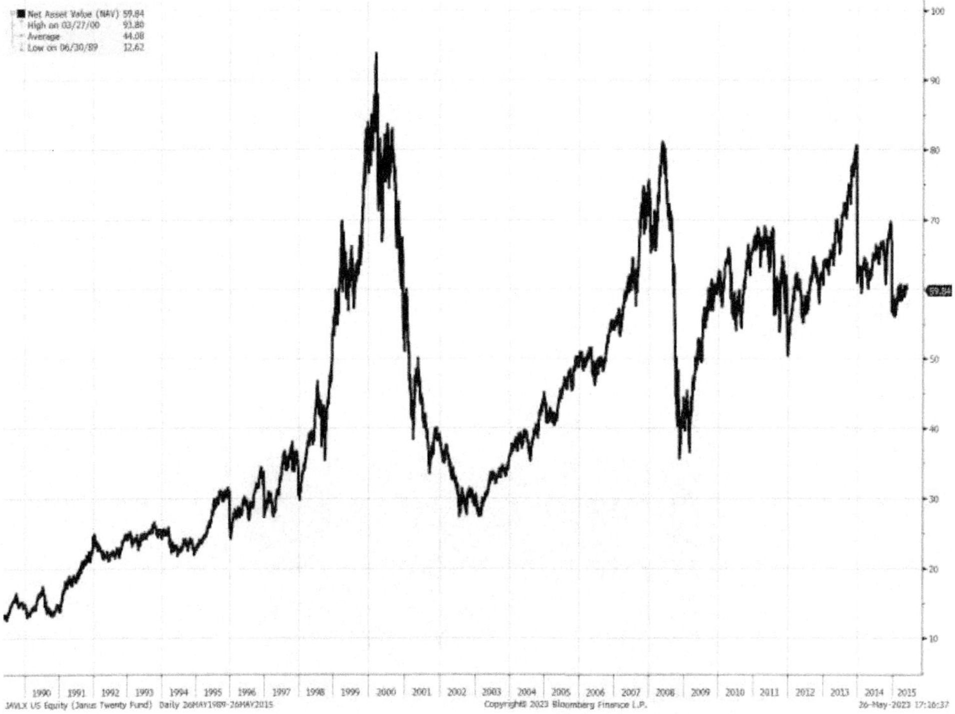

A less flattering comparison for ARKK would be CMGI.

CMGI was also one of the most famous internet names of the late 1990s. You could describe it as a hybrid of ARKK and SoftBank. It was a holding company and active investor running a concentrated portfolio of internet favorites. This is from a 1999 press release:

About CMGI

With nearly 50 companies, CMGI, Inc. (Nasdaq:CMGI) represents the largest, most diverse network of Internet companies in the world. This network includes both CMGI operating companies and a growing number of synergistic investments. CMGI leverages the technologies, content, and market reach of its extended family of companies to foster rapid growth and industry leadership across its network, and the larger Internet Economy.

CMGI's majority-owned subsidiaries include Engage Technologies (Nasdaq:ENGA), Activerse, Adsmart, AltaVista, Cha! Technologies, iCAST, Magnitude Network, NaviSite, NaviNet, Planet Direct and ZineZone. The company's @Ventures affiliates have ownership interests in Lycos, Inc. (Nasdaq:LCOS), Critical Path (Nasdaq:CPTH), Silknet (Nasdaq:SILK), Chemdex (Nasdaq:CMDX), Ancestry.com, Asimba, AuctionWatch, Aureate Media, blaxxun, BizBuyer.com, buyingedge.com, CarParts.com, CraftShop.com, eCircles.com, EXP.com, FindLaw, Furniture.com, HotLinks, Intelligent/Digital, KOZ.com, Mondera.com, MotherNature.com, NextMonet.com, NextPlanetOver.com, OneCore.com, ONElist, PlanetOutdoors.com, Productopia, Promedix.com, Raging Bull, Softway Systems, Speech Machines, ThingWorld.com, Vicinity, Virtual Ink, Visto and WebCT.

Here's how CMGI stock has fared (there were a few restructurings and renamings along the way):

CMGI stock, 1985 to now

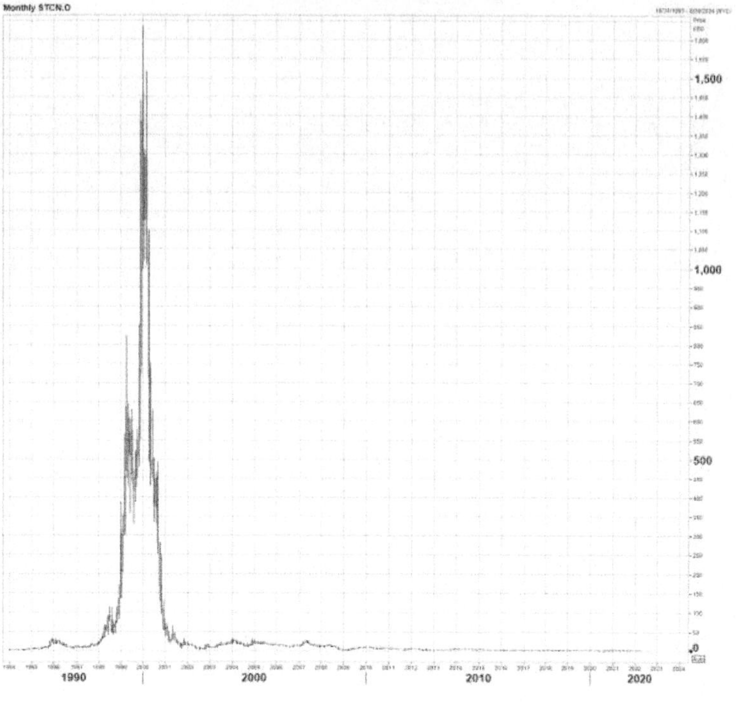

CMGI was invested in a pile of high-burn-rate up-and-comers and the bets didn't pay off as most of the names in the portfolio went bust. CMGI's holdings were competed out of business or the companies burned through all their cash and what looked like infinite funding in 1999 dried up by 2001. If I go through that list of CMGI companies, I can't think of one that is still alive.

Does ARKK remind you more of CMGI (a list of random high-burn-rate companies) or Janus 20 (a list of megacaps)? **It's more like CMGI than Janus 20**, but you could argue it's somewhere in between. Here are the top 10 holdings in ARKK:

Tesla, Zoom, Teladoc, Roku, Coinbase, Square, Exact Sciences, Unity Technologies, Spotify, Twilio, CRISPR and UiPath.

After Tesla, the average market cap is $24B. Not tiny but not mega.

If you think ARKK rebounds, the buy zone is the full round trip: The $40/$50 zone that defined the stock's equilibrium through the pre-COVID 2019 period. If you think ARKK is CMGI, don't touch it. If you think it's somewhere in between, there's a middle way.

Trade 12: Buy ARKK at 49, 45, and 43 with a stop loss at 29

I like the middle way. Attempt to participate in the upside, but control the downside.

Go long at 49 / 45 / 43 (scaling in as the ARKK ETF goes back to where it started pre-COVID—that is: round trip complete!) with a stop loss at 29 (below the 2020 COVID lows). This gives you the upside if the round trip completes and Cathie Wood rises from the ashes like Janus. But it allows you to manage the risk if TSLA is massively overvalued and the rest of the basket turns out to be full of cow dung, not chocolates.

Buy and hold is way too risky with a potential value trap like this but the opportunity to buy the epic dip that rhymes perfectly with 1999 is too attractive to ignore. You want to own the upside, but use a stop loss to control the downside.

Fun Math Fact

Another reason to take a shot at a long in ARKK (at the right level) is that burst bubbles tend to see incredibly large countertrend bounces, even if they eventually go to zero. Here's the pattern of a stock that goes down 50% then up 50% over and over:

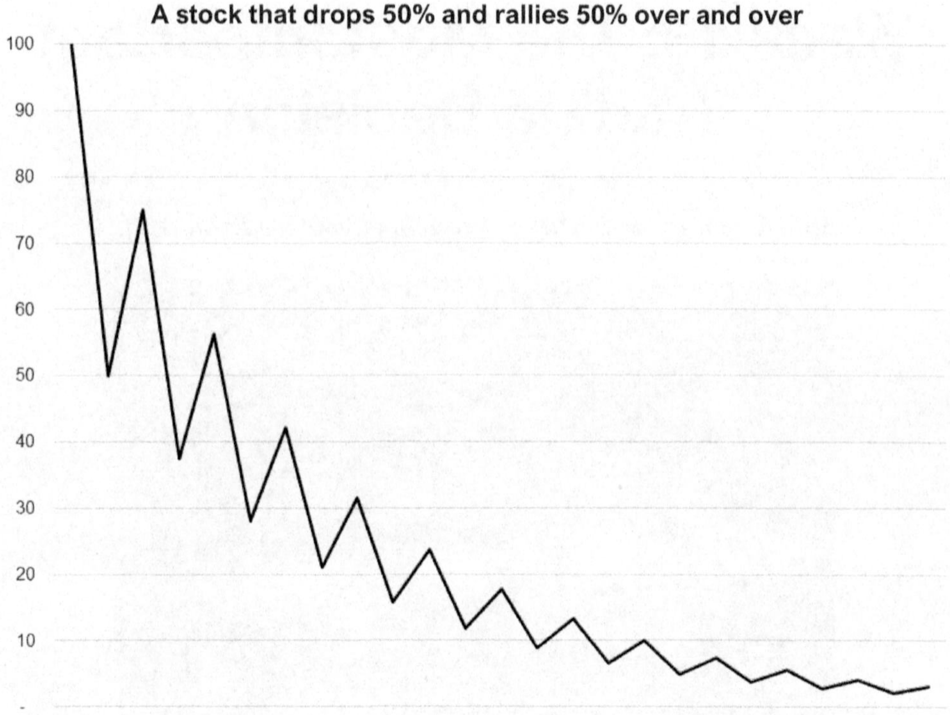

Conclusion

Pattern recognition can be a useful tool when analyzing markets. The euphoria, panic, and despair cycle traced out by speculative bubbles is common and well-known.

Establishing where you are in a clear pattern or cycle can give you a useful starting point for analyzing the market and forecasting future moves. In this case, we are near the full round trip point for ARKK.

And that means it's almost time to start dumpster diving.

Week 13: The Most Important Trading Decision

Where you trade matters as much as how well you trade

Update on previous trades

Not much to update. We got 1/3 filled on the ARKK idea from last week and that's it! Today, I am cheating because the trade recommendation explains how to think about trading one trading job for another. This is super important stuff, in my opinion, much more important than understanding support and resistance!

The most important trading decision

The biggest trading decisions of my life were when I had to decide whether or not to leave a trading job where I was no longer fully happy. You spend so much of your time working; ideally you want to choose a job that is intellectually satisfying and where your day-to-day experience of coming into work is mostly positive. A perfect job is an unrealistic goal, of course, and we don't always have a choice of jobs. But when there is a choice, here's how I think about it.

Trading is hard. Your odds of success are heavily influenced by the seat you choose. I have worked as a retail trader, and for a variety of institutions over the years. My decision to switch jobs was usually driven by a failure on one of the metrics I describe below. Here are common features of the best places to work as a trader.

- Healthy trading environment (this is the big one; I go into detail below)
- The company or division you work for targets revenue growth more than cost cuts. It's much more enjoyable to work for a company that is trying to grow, not one that is trying to cut. And you'll get paid better.
- Your manager believes in you and gives you enough runway to screw up now and then. You will screw up at some point and what goes down between you and the firm at that point is critical.
- No micromanaging. A great trading manager who trusts his peeps checks the P&L once a week, not four times a day.
- Passionate peers and a mentor who all love trading as much as you do.
- Filled with people who are hungry, smart, and humble.

Nothing matters more than a healthy trading environment, so let me go into detail on that. Most of the section below is from my book, *Alpha Trader*.

Healthy Trading Environment

You cannot succeed in an unhealthy trading environment. You must have a risk-taking environment that is not hostile to risk and is not thinly capitalized. In the wrong environment, even the most rational, disciplined, skilled and self-aware trader will fail. There are many features of a trading environment that can be desirable but there are two that are absolutely necessary for survival and success:

1. Appropriate capital
2. Healthy and supportive risk-taking environment

Let's look at each one separately.

Appropriate Capital

In terms of external factors, sufficient capital is an absolute prerequisite for successful trading. Let's look at what this means for the three main types of trader.

Retail Traders

No retail trader can succeed with a $1,000 trading account because the income generated from the most successful strategy will be too small to move the needle. Even a 300% return will not be enough to make a difference and so the trader is very likely to employ too much leverage and blow up the account via gambling.

A tiny trading account is OK for learning the markets and much better than paper trading. It might give you a sense of the emotional and psychological hurdles that come with live trading, but it will never give you a chance to learn what kind of trader you are.

In general, position sizing can account for most issues around insufficient capital. If your capital is small, you need to take smaller positions. But there are thresholds below which you cannot hope to succeed. For a young retail trader with no family to support and low expenses, this amount could be as low as $25,000. For a dentist with three kids in private school looking to quit his job and trade full time, this number would be significantly higher.

Bank Traders

If you work in a bank, you don't have a fixed amount of capital. Instead, you have risk limits. As such, your risk limits need to be properly aligned with your performance expectations or budget. If you have a $30,000 daily stop loss and a budget of $10,000,000, you will fail. It's impossible to make ten million dollars in a year with such a tight daily stop.

The easiest way to determine whether your risk limits are appropriate in a bank is to run simulations. You can set up simple simulations in a spreadsheet to look at a 252-day period and spit out ranges of outcomes based on various inputs. Retail traders can do this as well to determine risk of ruin. The greater idea you have of your prior performance statistics, the more accurate the simulation will be.

Portfolio managers

Capital or assets under management is a critical variable for every hedge fund and real money portfolio manager (PM). Good PMs can scale their strategy substantially and tend to think of performance in terms of basis points, not dollars. Good PMs comfortably scale their risk up or down as necessary based on the capital they are managing. On the other hand, PMs that think about P&L in terms of dollars tend to have trouble sizing up (or sizing down) because they are anchored on various P&L thresholds. If you think of a good day as $1 million of P&L, you won't adjust very smoothly as your capital increases from $100 million to $1 billion. On the other hand, if you think of a good day as 100 basis points, you will.

Note that it is possible to have too much capital. In fact, a common issue with hedge fund portfolio managers is that they have too much capital, not too little. Many traders at hedge funds are pressured to take on more and more capital, regardless of the capacity of their trading strategy. And it takes a trader with courageous integrity to say "no" to more capital. It is a bit like refusing a promotion—quite often it could be the right decision, but it can feel strange and potentially risky to do so.

Every trader and every trading strategy has an optimal level of capital. The more capital you take on, the worse your returns will be after a certain point, because your best strategies will reach capacity and additional capital will need to be allocated to inferior strategies. If you are a PM at a hedge fund, you should target your optimal level of capital, not just look to increase your capital year after year.

Capacity depends to a great extent on the products you trade. A boutique institutional trader specializing in microcap stocks will have much lower capacity than a hedge fund PM trading G10 currencies. Capacity is mostly determined by liquidity.

Research shows there is a sweet spot for hedge fund size in the $250 million to $1 billion assets-under-management range. Below $250m, costs are hard to cover and above $1 billion, returns and Sharpe ratios fall. This is logically true for individual managers as well. This does not mean all increases in capital are bad. You need to think about what your optimal capitalization level looks like and aim for that, not higher. As your capital rises to higher than optimal levels, the opportunity set is diluted and transaction costs increase disproportionately. The high-alpha opportunities are slowly drowned out by inferior trades.

A Healthy Risk-Taking Environment

A healthy environment breeds successful risk takers. Even the best trader is unlikely to succeed in a toxic environment. A healthy risk-taking environment means different things for different types of traders.

Retail Traders

For people trading their own money, a healthy environment means enough runway to learn, make mistakes, bounce back and eventually prosper. Capital is crucial, as mentioned in the last section, but so is support from family, financial flexibility, and the ability to focus and get in the zone all day.

If you want to be a trader, but your wife wants you to get a "real" job and you have twins screaming from the other room and no money to pay rent next month… You should come back when you have a more conducive environment. Trading is hard enough; anything that makes it harder usually makes it impossible.

You own your life, so if you want to be a trader, do it. But pick the right time and circumstances to do it so that you give yourself a proper shot at success. There is nothing worse than wondering what could have been. Quite often, you can work full time and find ways to trade on the side (and more importantly, study trading) so that as you gain experience and confidence in trading you are still earning a steady income. Then, once you have a decent amount of money in the bank, you have a bit of runway to trade full time and see if you have what it takes.

Bank Traders

You would think that most or all bank traders would operate in a healthy risk-taking environment, but this is absolutely not the case. Banks have different levels of risk appetite and managers within those banks can have dramatically different incentives.

Let's say you trade 10-year bonds at a large commercial bank. Imagine two environments:

- The manager that hired you and mentored you got a job offer at an investment bank and just left under somewhat acrimonious circumstances. Instead of replacing the head of trading, the bank has given the current head of sales responsibility for your group. He never liked your old boss, he has never traded before, and he plans to retire in a few years. He just wants to survive the last few years of his career and pay for his kid's last few years of college. He is extremely risk averse. He views the business model as an agency where clients do trades, the bank goes to market and offloads the risk, and the bank earns a small, nearly risk-free commission.

Or...

- Your manager is fired up and entrepreneurial and previously ran global macro at a big hedge fund. He wants that kind of ambitious risk culture at your bank because he believes a strong, healthy risk culture best serves the clients of the bank. By employing meaningful risk appetite, the bank can provide best-in-class pricing to clients, world class trade ideas and expert market intelligence. Customers get superior service from the bank and the bank makes more money than the competition in the process. Win/win.

It is obvious which trader is going to have a greater chance of success and most enjoy coming to work each day. If you work at a bank, you should regularly evaluate your environment and study where your incentives are aligned with the bank's and where they are not. To succeed, you need clear risk limits and rules of engagement so that no one is ever second-guessing your actions, and you don't have to second guess them yourself.

Portfolio Managers

Portfolio managers are most likely to work in a healthy risk-taking environment. Since hedge funds and asset managers are often exclusively in the business of taking risk, they best understand the nature of risk and they are usually good at creating a clear set of rules and then letting traders trade.

Still, it's important to understand where your incentives align with those of the firm and where they do not, so that you don't misfire. The most important example of this is that many hedge fund risk managers focus as much or more on volatility of returns than on absolute returns. This is because the risk manager at a pod-based hedge fund sees each trader as part of a portfolio.

If the returns of each PM look approximately like those of a call option (small downside with unlimited upside), then the aggregate performance of all those traders at the end of the year is likely to look pretty good. If, on the other hand, most traders are targeting 6% volatility while two or three are realizing 25% volatility, the business model does not work as well.

While you are paid a percentage of your absolute returns, quite often your manager is almost as concerned about your volatility as she is about the headline returns number. This makes perfect sense, especially as risk managers are constantly trying to separate luck from skill. A trader that makes money consistently with low volatility is much more likely to be displaying skill than a PM that puts up three years like: +70%, -24%, + 35%. Furthermore, the risk of ruin of a Steady Eddie is significantly lower than the PM I just mentioned, and nobody wants to be the one managing a trader when he blows up.

This is not an argument for you to target a specific level of volatility and forget about returns. All I am saying is that you should be acutely aware of your manager's (and your investors') incentives, not just your own.

A related phenomenon you will see at many hedge funds is that while your contract may have a stop loss, your real stop loss might be much tighter. Contractual risk limits are often wider than reality, depending on the personality of the business and risk managers involved. If you are new at a hedge fund, make sure you fully understand all the written and unwritten rules the fund follows. Your official stop loss might be -15%, but if every other trader that ever went down 9% at the fund got a shoulder tap, you should probably calibrate to a 9% stop loss (or tighter)!

Think about your manager's (and investors') incentives. Does your strategy and behavior align?

This advice applies to traders at every type of institution. When you understand the incentives of management, you can make sure you are playing by the correct rules and that you will not put yourself or your manager in an unwanted or awkward position. It's not just playing the game well, but also playing the correct game.

Other features of a healthy risk-taking environment:

Rule-based limits and risk-taking framework. The clearer the rules of engagement, the easier it is to develop a clear process and proper risk management. You don't want an environment where a loss is fine one day, but the same loss two weeks later results in a bunch of emails flying around asking what happened. Ask for clear, numerical limits and goals.

Peers. There are other good risk takers to talk with and bounce ideas off. Hopefully there is at least one trader that is more experienced and/or more skilled than you. Otherwise, you are always the mentor and never the mentee. For retail traders, I believe there is a huge benefit to working in a trading office, not at home. You learn from others, have people to share ideas with and share the pain with when things go wrong. A robust network of peers gives you a chance to talk about specific trades, general risk management and other trading-related topics.

Make a concerted effort to build a strong network of trading peers. This can be online or IRL. Learning takes longer if you have to figure everything out yourself.

Management risk appetite. Management knows if you take real risk, you will lose money sometimes. It is common to hear bank traders joke about the "Take risk, but don't lose money" business model. This is a model that works for management as it means they can sleep well at night knowing that traders are monetizing client flow but not taking meaningful risk. It is less attractive for individual traders because their leeway to express views is severely limited. The only time traders can take "risk" in this model is when they are already profitable (usually from a client trade). This model lets traders risk money earned but not take real financial risk that may result in losses.

A mentor to teach you, support your risk taking and help you maintain confidence during the inevitable down times.

A clear connection between performance and pay. Risk appetite fizzles when traders don't get paid for alpha. Taking real risk requires significant mental effort and endurance and traders will not give their all to a business they do not believe will compensate them for doing so.

Remember: the biggest trade you will ever do is when you sign an employment contract or quit your job.

Week 14: BTC Slingshot

Wait for the falling knife to hit the ground before you grab it

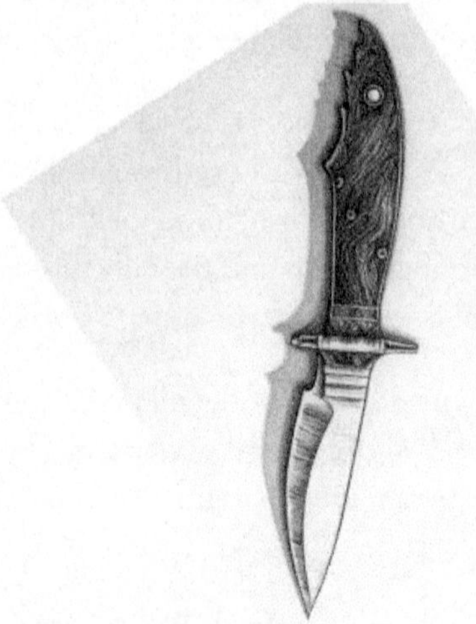

A picture of a slingshot would make more sense here but knives look cooler.

Update on previous trades

The three slices of the ARKK long position are on and the stop is $29. The stock is trading around $40 right now so the trade is underwater. This is the nature of catching falling knives… You usually feel some pain.

Slingshot Reversal

All the technical setups and formations that I use and believe in reflect, in some way, the underlying structure of the market. They reveal something about the behind-the-scenes activity happening on trading floors.

Conversely, this also explains the common feature of styles and approaches to technical analysis that **do not** appeal to me. Those approaches do not match something that happens in the market IRL. A highly-complex and mathematical approach that operates at 15,000 feet and does not directly mirror underlying trading activity will never appeal to me. Elliott Wave does not appeal to me. Gann fans do not appeal to me.

Perhaps subconsciously I have concluded that this feature of some approaches and not others is the difference between technical analysis as a "study of underlying market structure" vs. technical analysis as pig entrail reading/astrology.

An excellent example of a setup that makes sense in the context of real-life actions and reactions from traders is the Slingshot Reversal.

What is a Slingshot Reversal?

In this section, I will introduce the Slingshot Reversal, discuss how the pattern is traded, and provide an ancient example from the AUD/USD (Australian dollar) market.

A slingshot reversal occurs when a major support is broken but the price does not follow through and the market then reverses, going back up through the old support level. Here I am referring to a broken support but everything described in this piece also applies to the opposite formation, where resistance breaks and the rally fails and reverses back below the resistance. A Slingshot Reversal is a specific type of false break reversal.

The pattern works because the downside break of the major technical level clears existing long positions and creates new weak shorts. Breakout traders, bearish speculators, and momentum models pile in on the break, but use tight risk management. They are weak hands.

The chart below shows a textbook slingshot reversal. This chart is ancient because I took it from the original article I wrote about Slingshot Reversals in 2007. Amazingly, the pattern is still useful 15 years later. I could have used charts from 2022 but I like the throwback vibe of the old school chart. My bio from 2007:

Brent Donnelly trades the Australian, Canadian, and New Zealand dollars for Lehman Brothers New York. He has been trading foreign exchange for seven years. He also traded equities for five years and created a television cartoon, which aired nationally in Canada. ***He may be reached at brent.donnelly@lehman.com.***

Don't email me there; it will bounce back.

Anyway, have a look at the chart. From July 27 to August 8, 2006, the Australian dollar traced out a boring range between 0.7585 and 0.7685 (points 1 and 2). Many traders were excited about the possibility of a breakdown below 0.7585 and the level was attracting a ton of hype. Every spot trader on the street was bearish and ready to sell the break.

Finally, on August 8, Oz broke lower (point 3). This created a wave of new selling as longs cut their positions, new shorts entered, and black box models sold the technical break.

The Stages of a Slingshot

Then, whoosh! Slingshot Reversal! As the sellers ran out of bullets below 0.7585, buyers gained the upper hand, and soon, the AUD/USD started ripping higher (4). The rapid reversal took the Australian unit back toward the top of the range before a brief failure (5), then a topside break (6). Finally, the Slingshot lost momentum and the Aussie dropped all the way back to the old support (7) before bouncing. Both false breaks were excellent indicators.

The beauty of the slingshot reversal is that instead of catching a falling knife, it's more like waiting for the falling knife to hit the ground, then picking it up. Not my best analogy ever. Also not my worst.

How I trade the Slingshot

Here's how I trade the Slingshot Reversal:

- Identify a significant level that many traders are watching (in this example, the support at 0.7585)
- Wait for the market to trade clearly through the level. In this case, I used 10 points below the key level, then put a stop entry order 10 pips above. So when 0.7575 trades, input an order to stop enter; buy AUD/USD @ 0.7595 (point 4)
- If done, stop-loss out of the position five pips under the previous low (in this case, 0.7563 is the low, so stop at 0.7558) (point 3)

- You calculate the take-profit by taking the potential loss and multiplying it by 3 to create a 3-to-1 risk/reward. Here, the take-profit is (0.7595 - 0.7563) x 3 + 0.7595 = 0.7691. Alternatively, you can use other forms of technical analysis to come up with a logical target. I usually prefer market-based take profits, not ratio-based ones, but either approach is reasonable.

The Slingshot Reversal is a highly reliable pattern with a strong logic because of its effect on market positioning. Look for major levels that could yield Slingshot Reversals. **The more that people are talking about a particular level, the better your odds of finding a Slingshot.**

In real life, here's what's happening as a Slingshot plays out:

A narrative builds about the importance of the level and traders attach importance to it. The more hype and chatter about the level, the better the setup.

- Bulls get long as the support level approaches.
- Existing and new longs enter stop-loss orders below the level.
- Shorts reduce risk (take profit) as the level nears.
- When the level breaks, longs bail and shorts add so the positioning rapidly flips. The market goes from long to short in a hurry and most of those shorts are in the weak hands of breakout traders looking for an easy win.

When a Slingshot Reversal happens, you can hear the screams of the newly-added shorts from a mile away.

This image is not pixelated. YOU are pixelated.

Trade 14: BTC Slingshot

Rarely has there been a level in markets that has attracted as much focus as the 30,000 level in bitcoin. Let me show you the chart at two levels of zoom.

Bitcoin 2017 To Now (Log)

Bitcoin Q3 2020 to Now (With 9 Touches of 30k Marked)

You can see the nine probes of 30k, all rejected with great vigor. The absolute low on all those little breakdowns is 28,800.

I think it's somewhat remarkable that 30k held again yesterday on the LUNA / NASDAQ meltdowns and one could make the argument to simply go long here with a stop below 28000. But I'm waiting for **one last purge**.

Here, I will define the Slingshot Reversal as follows:

- BTC trades below 28,500, and then...
- BTC trades above 30,300

Once this happens, the trade is to go long at market (stop into the topside trade through 30,300). The simple way to execute this is to wait for 28,499 to trade, then place a stop entry trade at 30,300. The stop loss on the long would be below whatever the low was when 28,500 broke. The position will be sized to risk 2% of capital based on the entry and the stop loss. Take profit will be (($ at risk) X 3).

If <25k trades, the whole idea is canceled as that's not a false break anymore, that's a straight-up hull breach.

Techs are not enough

I would never do a trade just because of a technical setup. In this case, the trade is consistent with my long-term view that bitcoin is the one cryptocurrency worth owning. BTC has no competition on the store of value use case IMO and it has the security credibility and true decentralization lacking in most other coins and tokens. Bitcoin is like a first edition. There can only ever be one first edition.

I have been mostly bearish BTC because of the macro cycle (as I've been writing about in MTC), but things are getting scary enough out there that I'm willing to dabble from the long side in some risky assets.

If your fundamental view is that crypto is worthless, this is not a trade you should be doing. None of this is investment advice, ever. Since the trade fits my bigger picture view of buy the megadips in crypto, I'm interested in the Slingshot setup here.

Conclusion

The less scary, and often higher expected value way to trade a falling market is to wait for a super well-known level to false break, then get involved. This puts you in a strong position when everyone else is weak and offers up trades that have easy risk management parameters and good risk/reward.

Slingshot Reversals don't happen all the time. You need to find situations where the market is hyper-focused on a particular level and then get ready to pounce. A false break of the 30,000 level (which I define as a touch sub-28,500) could be the final cathartic washout we need to get bullish BTC.

Week 15:
RV Trading Is Hard

A lesson about alpha, beta, and dodging global macro

"Dude, are you swimming naked?"... "You'll see when the tide goes out!"

Update on previous trades

1. The slingshot reversal in BTC triggered the long at 30300. It was messy in both directions. The stop loss is 24850, which is below the 2022 low (25390) and below the round number: 25000.
2. The three slices of the ARKK long are on and the stop is $29. The stock is trading around $42 right now so the trade is underwater. This is the nature of catching falling knives... You usually feel some pain.

RV Trading is hard

Markets go up and down for many reasons, but very often traders and investors focus too much on their favorite investments, sectors, or asset classes, and fail to recognize the importance of global liquidity and beta. Liquidity is such an important concept, it has spawned many clichés:

- A rising tide lifts all boats
- Only when the tide goes out do you find out who is swimming naked
- Everyone is a genius in a bull market
- Don't fight the Fed

Stan Druckenmiller, one of the most famous traders of the current era, once said: "Earnings don't move the overall market; it's the Federal Reserve Board... focus on the central banks, and focus on the movement of liquidity... most people in the market are looking for earnings and conventional measures. It's liquidity that moves markets."

This Druckenmiller statement is an exaggeration, but it's not far off. If you don't get liquidity right, your world-class earnings estimates won't matter.

Whatever product you trade, you need to figure out what is driving that market and to what extent. For example, my main market is currency trading... Any time I trade a currency, I will always know how it will be impacted by changes in:

- Fed or global monetary policy
- Market interest rates
- Commodity prices
- Stock prices and global risk sentiment
- Geopolitics

That is global macro in five bullets and those factors drive every asset class to some extent.

If you are trading single stocks, you need to know how much of your stock's movement comes from global macro and market beta and how much comes from idiosyncratic factors.

Before we go any further, let me define alpha and beta, because they are two terms you will see all the time in finance and you need to know what they mean. We are not concerned here with the specific mathematical definitions of alpha and beta, we just want to know what the heck the words usually mean in common discussion. If you want more precision, just Google "finance alpha definition" or "finance beta definition" and I'll see you in 45 minutes when you get back.

Here is how I use "alpha" and "beta".

Alpha is excess or abnormal returns. If the market is up 20% and you are up 30%, that is (theoretically) alpha of 10%. In reality, it might not be alpha but we'll get back to that in a sec.

Beta is the amount a security generally moves when the broader market moves. A stock with a beta of 1.0 will be about as volatile as the overall market while a stock with a beta of 0.5 will be less volatile and one with a beta of 1.5 will be more volatile. Portfolios also have a measure of beta.

Beta can also refer to index-hugging returns. If you closely match market returns, a critic might argue that your fund is all beta. If you massively outperform the market, you might have generated alpha.

When is alpha not alpha? Alpha is not always actually alpha because there are other ways to generate excess return besides skillful trading or security selection. The simplest way to outperform an index is to follow it, but use leverage. If you give me $100 and I use 2X margin to buy $200 worth of S&P futures and the S&P goes up 10%, I made $20 and your return on your $100 is 20%. That's not alpha. That's leverage. Very often, people confuse alpha with leverage or (more dangerously) with hidden leverage. There is more to this discussion but I don't want to go too far off track here.

The main point is: You can do all the analysis you want on a single stock, and if the stonk market tanks, your stock is probably going to tank too. You can do all the supply/demand analysis you want on the copper market, but if China shuts down, copper is probably going lower.

I discuss this today because I find many newer traders become enamored with their micro analysis in crypto, commodities, or equities, and completely ignore or forget about the macro influences that might help or hurt them. You can be a master of L1 and L2 narratives in crypto, but if you don't know that 70% of the movement in every coin is driven by the broad ups and downs of crypto… NGMI.

I went through some of this in Trade 8: Top-down vs. Bottom-up so if you don't know the difference between top-down analysis and bottom-up analysis, please revisit that chapter.

How to deal with beta and global liquidity

Not everyone needs to be a global macro trader! If you want to learn global macro, that's great (best way to learn global macro: sign up for my global macro daily, am/FX). If you are focused on your particular market, where you have an edge, that is excellent… But you still need to have global conditions in the back of your mind when you put on trades.

The big takeaway from this piece should be: You can't just pick a thing and be bullish or bearish based on that thing's fundamentals or technicals or correlation, etc.. You need to know what big picture factors matter and what might drive the price of your thing up and down whether or not your analysis is correct.

Obviously, if you're a global macro trader, your whole existence is predicated on forecasting and reacting to cycles and regime shifts in various asset classes. But not everyone is supposed to trade global macro. Many traders find much more success by focusing on a particular security or asset class and developing expertise and an edge there. But those traders can often get blindsided by global macro and so the point of this piece is to help you **not** be that trader that gets blindsided.

Here are some ways to deal with global macro when you're not a global macro trader:

One: Trade super short term

For short-term traders that don't trade macroeconomic events, global macro matters the least. You need to know when the big economic events are coming so you don't get your face ripped off through FOMC, or a Powell speech, or the USDA reports or other high-vol events... But you don't really need to know much more than that.

Square up through the big events and trade short-term like a banshee. Be agnostic and flexible about long vs. short and trade products where you have no bias. If you are a huge Elon fan, don't trade TSLA stock short-term or you'll find yourself biased to the long side. Excellent short-term traders are equally happy long or short whatever they trade. If you can never be long EURUSD... Don't trade EURUSD. In short-term trading, max flexibility and zero bias are key.

Two: Be long only

This is the simplest way to avoid ever having to care about macro but it's also the least likely to make you a successful trader. This is more like investing than trading, but it can still work.

If you are a crypto or equity permabull, just pick the best longs and always trade from the long side. You can be long, or you can be flat. This is a low-stress way to trade in the direction of your fundamental core view and add alpha onto beta. If you are a crypto megabull and you dabble from the short side, you will notice that you always cut your shorts way too fast and white-knuckle every tiny rally because your brain is dripping with cognitive dissonance.

The problem is, during the down cycles, long only traders will face 20% to 80% drawdowns, depending on the asset class, no matter how solid the security selection. The beta will destroy the alpha. And if you're not paying attention to the macro, you won't really know what hit you. All your analysis of L1 vs. L2 or relative demand for your commodity or whatever isn't going to help you if liquidity dries up or the Fed hoses down the markets with 10T of QE.

When it's a liquidity story, it's all the same trade and it doesn't matter much which longs you've chosen. For example:

BTC, ETH, BNB, XRP, ADA, SOL, DOT, DOGE (Sept. 2021 to Now)

Long only is mostly beta. Some alpha, if you're good. But mostly beta.

Three: Trade RV

The simplest way to avoid the ups and downs of global markets and the falling and rising tides of global macro liquidity is to trade relative value (RV). RV trading is an entire industry and you could fill books with explanations of how to do it but in its simplest form, it works like this: You buy one thing and sell another thing. It's a bet that the long will outperform the short.

If you do this with two stocks in the same industry (let's say short FB, long GOOG), you eliminate a ton of macro risk such as:

- Where is the broad market going to go? (doesn't matter)
- How will the bond market impact megacap technology stocks? (doesn't matter)
- What does Fed policy look like going forward? (doesn't matter)
- How will a Republican win in the midterms impact tech regulation? (doesn't matter)

I'm saying "doesn't matter" though it's not 100% accurate since of course tech regulation can impact FB more than GOOG or Fed policy could impact GOOG more than FB, etc. But generally, you cancel out most macro and top-down risk when you pair two assets that operate in the same silo of the same asset class.

RV trading is much more complex than directional trading because there are a bunch of new factors to consider, especially when it comes to sizing and risk management. RV trading can be accomplished by going long one thing and short another or by doing baskets of longs and shorts. You can also (for example), go short a basket of stocks and go long index futures to hedge it.

For the purposes of this note, I am calling RV anything where you put on offsetting trades to minimize market or macro risk in an attempt to isolate the idiosyncratic risks of particular assets or securities.

Short ETH, long BTC would be RV. Or short copper and long AUD (they are correlated due to the global growth beta shared by both). Long USDJPY and long US 10-year bonds is a common RV trade, too (because USDJPY and US yields are correlated).

An industrial strength version of RV is when a fund will look at a universe of say, 100 assets and compare how they all trade relative to one another. Imagine a huge matrix of 100 assets X 100 assets and the correlation and beta of all those assets compared to each other in real-time. The machine will attempt to buy things that are cheap and sell things that are rich and continuously rebalance as assets move closer to, or further away from fair value. Some of these funds make money but it's a tough biz and it's very sensitive to regime shifts because correlation, volatility, and beta are not stable.

Personally, I hate RV. But many people love it and it's a perfectly valid approach.

I almost always have a global macro view and prefer to trade in the direction of that view. When I put RV trades on, I tend to get annoyed with the risk management, the difficulty in applying leverage, and the cognitive dissonance of leaning in two directions at once.

Whenever I do an RV trade like short copper and long AUD… I always end up stripping one leg and turning it into a directional trade. If I'm bullish world, I'll end up keeping the long AUD and somehow that pesky short copper always disappears from my blotter.

But that's just me! It's worth knowing how RV works. Some people love it.

Thinking about RV trades

OK so yes, RV can be complicated. But! You can also do RV in a simple way without a team of quants estimating correlation and volatility… and survive to tell about it (if you're careful).

I'm going to provide a simple example here, but I really want to emphasize: RV trading is hard. I am going to explain a risk-averse way to do a single pair RV trade where you cannot blow up, no matter how much my idea stinks.

I'm going to pick two companies as my example today, but I have not done the deep dive on company fundamentals that you would do if you were really into this sort of thing. I'm going to make a simple observation and then see how you might trade it.

Trade 15: Short CVNA, long RBLX

We are at the stage of the tech cycle where companies either make it, or they don't. A wave of bankruptcies will hit over the next 12 months as Powell's firehose of unlimited, free funding has dried up and companies that cannot generate cash or quickly rightsize will burn through their remaining moneys at alarming speed.

It's the point in the cycle where you start to guess who is going bankrupt and who is not. I'm not a CFA, and I'm not a securities analyst. I'm going to make a bunch of statements here that are theoretical so that I might describe to you how to think about an RV trade. This is not investment advice. OK, ready? Here we go.

I think Carvana is going bankrupt. They had massive negative cash flow in what should have been a dream year (2021), they overbuilt, and the recent layoffs via Zoom show poor governance and a company that is flailing.

Watch the video of that mass layoff video call and tell me you don't want to be short this company! Please open your books and turn to Chapter 11.

But… I don't want to be straight short CVNA because it has already come off so much and the NASDAQ is already 20% off the high. A short squeeze in the NASDAQ or a change in the global macro picture (peace in Ukraine, less hawkish Fed, etc.) could take me out of my short.

On the other hand, I think Roblox is a strong brand that will survive this tech wipeout and live to fight another day. They have cash, etc. CVNA and RBLX are not in the same industry (one is auto sales, one is video games/metaverse) but they are both beaten down COVID favorites and they move somewhat in sync because of that. RBLX has a 54% correlation to CVNA but only 28% to AAPL, for example.

Some facts:

Carvana just issued a huge slug of debt

◆ WSJ NEWS EXCLUSIVE | FINANCE

Carvana, Once a Market Darling, Forced to Turn to Apollo for Cash

April 27, 2022

Online used-car retailer was spurned by lenders to fund deal

Carvana debt is not trading well compared to Roblox debt

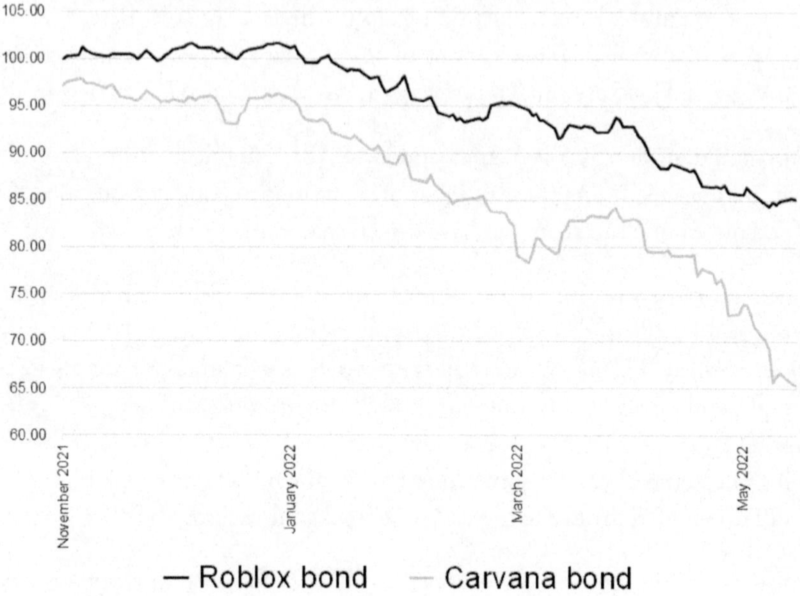

Roblox has more cash than CVNA

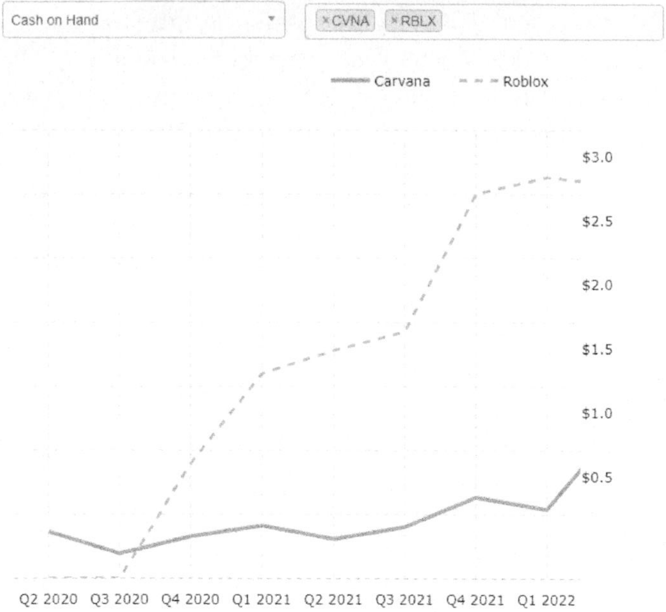

Do I get a free CFA for that analysis? Making Dr. Parik Patel proud.

Anyhoo. Let's say I want to risk $3,000 on this idea, which is a bit more than usual because I think it's going to work and that TikTok layoff video really sends a strong doom signal to my Spidey Senses. How do I structure it?

This is the hard part with RV trades!

Again, I want to emphasize, I'm just doing tip of the iceberg stuff here. RV trading is a huge, complex field that employs zillions of smart quanty types. I'm just giving you the basics. Anyway... There are three main ways to structure and risk manage an RV trade.

ONE: You could go short CVNA stock and long RBLX and leave a stop loss on each leg, risking $1,500 per leg = $3,000. But what do you do if one leg gets stopped out? If you get stopped out of one leg, then you have directional market risk, which you didn't want.

Also, when shorting massively beaten-down stocks, the upside gap risk is larger than usual. You could walk in tomorrow and Apple buys CVNA for a 100% premium and you're dead. Gap risk is always something to worry about in single stocks because they close at night and on weekends, but with beaten-down stocks, the gap risk is much larger because they tend to have insane countertrend rallies, even as they asymptotically approach zero. Remember that something that is down 90% from the highs can double and it's still down 80% from the highs! **Dead stocks know how to fly.**

TWO: You can size each leg using estimated volatility and stop out when the combined P&L hits -$3,000. This is how professional RV trading is normally done. You use historical or implied volatility to size each leg appropriately. That is, if one stock is more volatile than the other, you take a smaller position in that instrument. Less volatile = bigger position. This is called volatility adjustment or vol-adjusting. The big issue with vol-adjusting and then letting the two-legged position run is that you don't have fixed P&L downside. You might lose more than $3,000.

Also, it's a pain in the butt to monitor because you generally cannot automate this sort of risk management. You have to be watching. I always prefer automated risk management because it makes fewer mistakes and leads to more rigorous discipline.

THREE: Another way to do this RV trade is to buy options. The options on these stocks are not cheap, but I'm going to do it anyway. If you have the knowledge, you could probably sell put spreads on RBLX and sell call spreads on CVNA and that is probably a better trade but this chapter is getting way too long and that's way too complicated for our purposes here. So keeping it simple, I am going to buy some long-dated options:

Buy January 20, 2023 CVNA $20 PUT for $4.70 (implied vol of around 140 lol)

Buy January 20, 2023 RBLX $40 CALL for $7

I spend $1,500 on each side. The target on CVNA stock is basically zero. RBLX is 2x current levels (~$60).

I can sleep at night because I don't have to white-knuckle two separate stop losses or a combined P&L stop on the trade. I paid crazy high vols for those options, but I honestly believe that both options could pay off. Sometimes, buying expensive options is OK, but it's a hard way to make a consistent living.

Conclusion

If you are not a global macro trader, you need to either factor in global macro, hedge it away, or explain why you are happy to ignore it. Selecting individual securities, cryptocurrencies, or commodities is great… But always consider the macro and cyclical landscape and how that might blindside you, provide a headwind, or (ideally) work as a tailwind.

Week 16: Don't Blow Up

If you don't properly manage risk of ruin, nothing else matters

A delightful image from the Long-Term Capital Management investor brochure

Update on previous trades

1. The slingshot reversal in BTC triggered the long at 30300. It was messy in both directions. The stop loss is 24850, which is below the 2022 low (25390) and below the round number: 25000.
2. The three slices of the ARKK long position are on and the stop is $29. The stock is trading around $44 right now so the trade is tiny underwater.
3. January 2023 CVNA puts bought for $4.70 are unch. The $40 RBLX calls (bought for $7) are around $6.20. So there is a tiny loss on the RV trade but not much happening yet.

Don't blow up

This is Week 16 of 50 Trades in 50 Weeks and I hope you are enjoying it so far. I feel like the format is working well and it's taking me in some interesting and random educational directions.

In hindsight, I wish I started with today's note as Week 1 because it's the most important aspect of trading, by far. "Don't Blow Up!" is fairly straightforward advice but there are literally hundreds of examples of traders that did not follow this most simple and ultimately important consideration.

No matter how awesome your strategy, and no matter how gigantic your edge… If you blow up, none of it matters. You will be bankrupt or unemployed. Avoid risk of ruin above all else. Every other consideration comes after…

Rule #1 of Trading: Avoid Risk of Ruin

There are many ways to blow up, but most trader and hedge fund wipeouts have common features. The majority of this note is about how traders blow up, and how to avoid the primary land mines. Note that blowups often have more than one driver, and the factors I list overlap somewhat. Funds and traders that blow up will often tick more than one of the boxes I am about to list.

Here are the main reasons traders and hedge funds blow up:

Leverage

The number one reason people blow up is leverage. Their positions are too large relative to the amount of capital they employ. When your positions are too large, you cannot weather adverse shocks or unexpected jumps in volatility because your margin for error is tiny.

This one is pretty easy to understand so I won't spend too much time on it. The most famous example of a fund blowup due to leverage is Long Term Capital Management (LTCM) in the late 1990s. That fund employed a variety of carry strategies that were analogous to picking up pennies in front of a steam roller. You can still find their delightful promotional brochure online.[20]

The simplest way to operate with the appropriate level of leverage is to size each trade as a percentage of free capital and use stop losses. I put a stop loss on every single trade that I do and I strongly recommend that everyone do so. This is not always possible for large,

---

[20] https://www.spectramarkets.com/wp-content/uploads/2022/05/ltcm.pdf

complicated portfolios, RV traders, and traders of illiquid assets, but since the audience here is traders with 0-5 years of experience, that most likely does not apply.

Regardless, even very large PMs at very large hedge funds often can and do use stop losses. Trading crypto at 100:1 leverage means your stop loss is going to be super close and your probability of running into noise issues (random market jiggles take you out) is high. If you're not sure what you're doing, just risk 2% of your free capital on every trade. Free capital is your account size or the amount you are allowed to lose before you get shut down. That's a simple and effective starting point for risk management.

You should never be in a trade that is going to cost you more than 10% of your capital in the worst-case scenario. Ever. If you are debating between a range of position sizes, err on the low side until you have high confidence that your leverage is appropriate. Good traders use rigorous, systematic risk management and don't get in over their heads on trades out of excitement, bad discipline, or inexperience.

"When in trouble, double" is a trading aphorism mostly used as a joke because every good trader knows that adding to losing positions (unless it's as part of a pre-planned scaling in strategy) can be deadly. Emotional doubling down on bad positions is often a source of excess leverage that happens in a fit of rage as a position goes hard the wrong way. Doubling down is a behavior associated with problem gamblers.

Four famous leverage-related blowups: LTCM, Amaranth, Bear Stearns Asset Management, and Archegos

Gambling

People don't just trade to make money. There are all sorts of other less obvious reasons traders trade. Trading can be incredibly fun. That's good. But that is also a problem! Enjoyment should always be a side benefit of trading and not the primary objective. The first objective must always be profit.

How powerful is trading as a stimulant? *Very*. This is from a 2001 study:[21]

The psychological processes underlying the anticipation and experience of monetary prospects and outcomes would appear to play an important role in gambling and in other behaviors that entail decision making under uncertainty. In this regard, it is striking that the activations seen in the NAc, SLEA, VT, and GOb in response to monetary prospects and outcomes overlap those observed in response to cocaine infusions in subjects addicted to cocaine.

---

[21] https://www.cell.com/neuron/pdf/S0896-6273%2801%2900303-8.pdf

In case you are wondering: NAc (nucleus accumbens), SLEA, VT, and GOb are four reward-related brain regions. And the following is from Andrew Lo's testimony to Congress on Hedge Funds, Systemic Risk, and the Crisis of 2007-2008:

... the same neural circuitry that responds to cocaine, food, and sex—the mesolimbic dopamine reward system that releases dopamine in the nucleus accumbens—has been shown to be activated by monetary gain as well.

Both the anticipation and receipt of monetary gains trigger the reward circuitry of the brain. Human nature is to seek activation of this circuitry both consciously and unconsciously. You must come to grips with the fact that trading often involves sitting there doing nothing, just waiting for a great opportunity. Unfortunately, the numbers moving up and down on that screen are like squirrels, and you are a dog.

Various commentators, including Jean-Paul Sartre, have commented that war is "...hours of boredom interspersed with moments of terror". Trading can often be the same. There is a strange temporal rhythm to trading where time speeds up and slows down depending on what is going on.

Sensation-seeking and gambling often go hand in hand. To get a sense of whether you are trading to feed your desire for excitement (i.e., as a form of gambling) take a look at the following excerpt from the DSM-V. The DSM-V or DSM5 is the Diagnostic and Statistical Manual of Mental Disorders. It contains descriptions, symptoms, and other criteria for identifying mental disorders and it is the authoritative guide to mental illness used by psychologists throughout most of the world.

Here, I have taken the section on identifying gambling disorder[22] (previously known as pathological gambling) and replaced the word "gambling" with "trading." Do any of these line items sound familiar to you?

1. Need to trade with increasing amount of money to achieve the desired excitement
3. Restless or irritable when trying to cut down or stop trading
4. Repeated unsuccessful efforts to control, cut back on or stop trading
5. Frequent thoughts about trading (such as reliving past trading experiences, planning the next trade, thinking of ways to get money to trade)
6. After losing money trading, often returning to get even (referred to as "chasing" one's losses)
7. Lying to conceal trading activity
8. Jeopardizing or losing a significant relationship, job, or educational/career opportunity because of trading

[22] https://www.psychiatry.org/patients-families/gambling-disorder/what-is-gambling-disorder

Jesse Livermore is celebrated as a trading hero but it is worth remembering that he took his own life after going bankrupt for a third time, after his second divorce. He is a trading hero and a cautionary tale wrapped into one. He blew up three times because he was gambling and there were times when he could not stop himself.

The process and mechanics of trading and gambling overlap. Both involve risk management, probability, randomness, risk of ruin, emotion, bias, and irrational human beings. Bad trading can often be very much like casino gambling. It is impulsive, emotional, and has a negative expected value. Gamblers in the market tend to blow up.

If you want to gamble, go to a casino.

Two famous gambling-related blowups: Jesse Livermore (a few times) and Barings Bank (Nick Leeson)

Selling options and tail risk

Selling options is a hidden form of excessive leverage. When you sell an option, you usually receive a premium that is smaller than the downside if things go terribly wrong. Often, this downside can be multiples larger than the premium you collect. Selling options is great when it works, and in fact, selling S&P puts is one of the highest-Sharpe trading strategies in the history of finance. But there is a reason for that. It's incredibly expensive when stocks dump.

Some of the most famous blowups in finance were the result of traders and funds selling options. Victor Niederhoffer is a famous example, but there are many others. Here's Malcolm Gladwell on Niederhoffer's 1997 blowup.

> *Victor Niederhoffer sold a very large number of options on the S&P index, taking millions of dollars from other traders in exchange for promising to buy a basket of stocks from them at current prices if the market ever fell. It was an unhedged bet, a "naked put," meaning he bet in favor of the large probability of making a small amount of money, and against the small probability of losing a large amount of money and he lost. On October 27, 1997, the market plummeted eight percent. He ran through a hundred and thirty million dollars — his cash reserves, his savings, his other stocks — and when his broker came and asked for still more he didn't have it. In a day, one of the most successful hedge funds in America was wiped out. Niederhoffer had to shut down his firm. He had to mortgage his house. He had to borrow money from his children. He had to call Sotheby's and sell his prized silver collection.*

Niederhoffer's next blow-up was in 2007 and The New Yorker wrote a massive feature on him called "The Blow-Up Artist".[23] Anyway, not to pick on him specifically, but anyone generating steady returns by selling options needs to know EXACTLY what they are doing because stock market returns (and financial market returns in general) are not normally distributed. Tail events happen much more often than a normal distribution would suggest. That is one of the key takeaways from Nassim Taleb's book *Fooled by Randomness.*

Selling options doesn't always mean *selling options.* It can also mean taking a position that has the same risk/reward as selling options. This is normally called being short tail risk. An excellent example of selling tail risk is when traders bet on a pegged currency.

Because price action around the peg is non-linear, you don't know what your exit will be if the peg breaks. We saw this type of ruin recently in the LUNA market and in 2015 as many hedge funds and retail traders were destroyed when the Swiss National Bank unexpectedly pulled its 1.2000 floor in EURCHF.

Sure, there was profit to be made trading long EURCHF for several years, but the problem was that while the rewards were clear, the risks were not measurable. Many people expected that if 1.20 broke, they would be able to sell their EURCHF at 1.15 or maybe 1.12 as a worst case. Instead, the first trades were around 1.0100 and the pair quickly traded down to 0.8500 within minutes! It's shocking to look at the insane **1-second** chart of that event.[24]

The first priority for every trader is to avoid risk of ruin. Live to trade another day. It is possible that a tail risk could appear out of nowhere, but that was not the case with the CHF move. It was a well-known risk and yet still it ruined many traders' careers and cost shareholders and investors hundreds of millions of dollars. Don't place trades in products where you can't know your exit with high certainty in advance. No matter how juicy the yield or payoff… It's never worth it.

Three famous option-selling and tail risk blowups: Fortress Macro, Victor Niederhoffer X 2, and LUNA.

Liquidity vacuum

Liquidity, leverage, and tail risk are often tightly linked and you cannot always single out liquidity as a problem all on its own. When markets go bananas and tail moves happen, liquidity dries up. You may have thought you were using prudent leverage and you might have thought you understood the tail risk… Then, whoops.

---

[23] https://www.newyorker.com/magazine/2007/10/15/the-blow-up-artist

[24] https://www.spectramarkets.com/wp-content/uploads/2022/05/eurchf.png

Let's say you want to short stock XYZ because you think the company is the next Blockbuster Video. Crappy in-store experience, dwindling customer base, technological disruption from more nimble competitors. Sensible thesis. OK, how big should the position be? You look at some historical data. A lot of historical data. And you see this:

Stock XYZ: 10-day change in price, 2002 - 2019

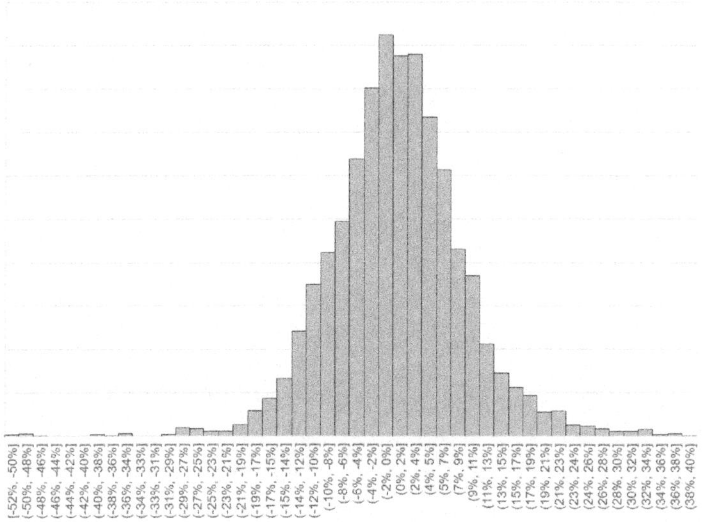

OK cool, so out of 5000 ten-day periods, you have a very tiny chance of a move over 30% or -50% with almost all the data showing ten-day moves of -30% to +30%. You size your position accordingly. Here is the distribution of 10-day returns for the following two years. Note the extreme moves (tiny, thin bars).

Stock XYZ: 10-day change in price, 2020 - 2022

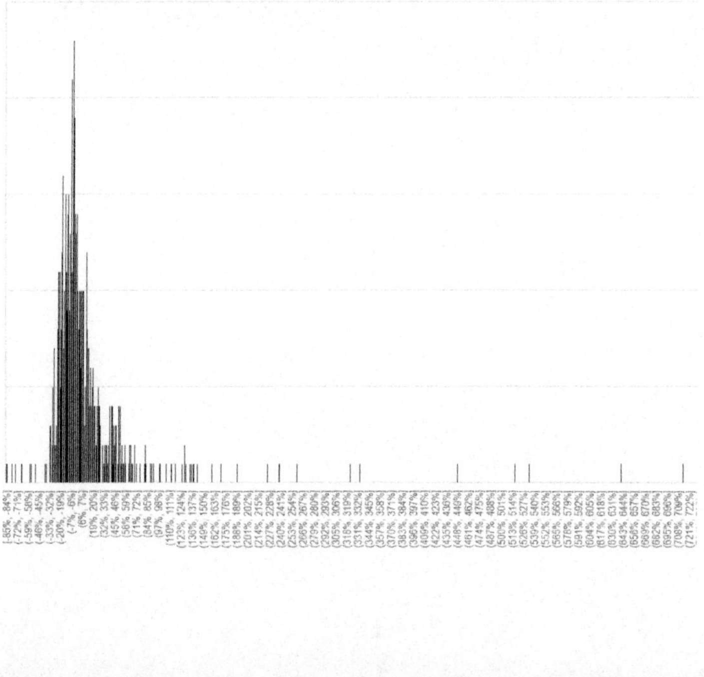

Those are moves of 100%, 200%, 300%, 400%, 500%, 600%, all the way up to 1642%. I truncated the x-axis just so you can see the results a bit better.

This is GameStop common stock I'm talking about here, but you probably knew that already. When the apes went nuts on WSB in 2021, the old rules disappeared. Melvin Capital, and other shorts, may have had a plan to stop out at $20 or something, but liquidity completely disappeared. Using 20 years of historical data, the funds would have sized for a worst-case scenario of something like a 50% rally in 10 days. Instead, the stock rallied ten times that. There was no liquidity and the shorts were decimated.

On a much smaller scale, here's a quick true story from my book, *Alpha Trader*.

Jerry, the greatest trader who never was

Jerry was one of the best pure traders I have ever seen. But he drove so fast that we all knew that eventually, he would slam into the wall…

Jerry was a 21-year-old college dropout who worked in the same day trading office as I did in the late 1990s. He had no financial markets background. He was a pure gambler who found his way onto the trading floor because of a few lucky coincidences. He loved to go out clubbing until 3 a.m. and then come in and trade the pre-open at 8 a.m. He was hilarious and immature and knew very little about markets.

Despite all this, he had incredible instincts. He had a professional gambler's eye for risk/reward and opportunity. He was like a modern-day Jesse Livermore who could read the tape and sentiment and price action and make money in ways that were incredibly skillful and fun to watch. Jerry could feel what was going to happen before it happened. He was so obviously good at trading that the 40-year-old trader that was randomly seated next to him decided to close his own account and back Jerry instead.

But Jerry couldn't stay away from the thinly-traded names. He would yell out "Look at -*insert ticker symbol of a thinly-traded stock nobody has ever heard of here-*. It's exploding!" We would bring up the chart and see some random microcap trading at $5.25, up 361% on the day. Instead of trading one cent wide in 500 or more shares like most stocks, these stocks jumped around in $1 increments, trading 30 cents wide in 100 shares. Jerry would sell 3,000 shares, taking it down from $5.25 to $4.25 and this would often trigger a waterfall move that let him quickly take profit at, say, $3.10.

There was yelling involved and it was incredibly fun to watch. He would then go back to trading normal stocks and making money and someone would say to him: "Jerry, you can't trade those microcaps. One day, one of them will just keep going up and you will get carted out of here."

He would listen closely and nod his head and say: "Yeah dude. You're right. I'll stop doing that. For sure."

Then three days later Jerry's yelling across the floor: "Oh boy! I'm short a lot of this one! This is not good!"

A stock went from $2 to $4, and he got short 7,000 shares. A few minutes later it was $6, and he sells a bit more. Then it's $7. Then $8. His $50,000 account was suddenly worth minus $6,000. The manager of the trading floor issued a margin call and forced Jerry to buy back all the shares at an average of $8.20. The stock closed the day at $3.45.

Jerry was such an obviously talented kid that even after that incident, a different trader seeded him another $50,000. Four months later, guess what… The same thing happened. Jerry had amazing natural skill as a trader but it didn't matter. He blew up. Twice.

Jerry and Melvin Capital are edge cases, but both true stories of how risk of ruin is the first and most important risk to manage. Never enter a trade unless you know you can get out. One of my previous bosses once said:

Trading is like driving a race car. You want to drive as fast as possible, but you can never lose control or crash into the wall.

Don't be like Jerry. Don't crash into the wall.

Ruin from lack of liquidity can happen because positions are too large as liquidity disappears and it can also happen due to gaps. Not every gap can be predicted, but some can. For example:

- Most assets have weekend gap risk. If there's big Saudi news over the weekend, for example, oil might close at $70 on Friday and open at $85 on Monday. It always makes sense for traders to reduce risk into the weekend.
- Stocks have gap risk around the times they are closed. If seventeen investment banks announce before-the-open upgrades of a stock you're short—you face gap risk. Holding any position when the market is closed is always going to present gap risk. Can you measure it? Are you comfortable with it?
- Assets have gap risk through events. If you're short ZM stock through earnings, there's gap risk. If you're long bonds through the nonfarm payrolls release, there's gap risk.

Not all gaps can be forecasted, but most can. Avoid gap risk or reduce positions ahead of time to avoid the risk of ruin.

Famous liquidity-related blowups: Melvin Capital and Proshares XIV.

Fraud and bad ethics

This is a simple one. Don't do fraud. Don't use privileged, non-public information. It will eventually bite you in the ass. Even if it doesn't, your mind will be racing and your hands will be trembling every time the doorbell rings. Is that SEC Enforcement? Maybe the DOJ? Not worth it.

Famous fraud-related blowups: Bernard L. Madoff Investment Securities, LLC and Galleon.

So ummm... What's the trade?

The main point of today's note is you need to constantly scan for risk of ruin and avoid it and eliminate it from your trading. Don't take risk of ruin. It is never worth it.

The flipside (and the idea for today's trade) is that if you can find cheap convexity, gap risk, crash risk, or liquidity risk out there, can you take the other side? Those can be very nice trades! In other words, where might others blow up, and can you be long that risk instead of short?

You can't just buy every tail risk. Tail risk options are generally overpriced because people overpay for lotto tickets and market makers don't like to sell tails.

But the genius of traders like Roaring Kitty[25] who got into GME early was that they saw a trade with a ton of upside and fixed downside. That's cheap convexity. I see similar (though less extreme) potential in ETH/BTC.

In MacroTactical Crypto (MTC), I often discuss why I have a strong preference for BTC over ETH. In my most recent MTC, I explained why I think there is growing crash risk in ETH. The very brief bear case for ETH/BTC is this:

- Most of DeFi relies on ETH as collateral and most of that collateral is set to automatically liquidate to meet margin calls. Automatic liquidation is the root cause of many market crashes. A spontaneous liquidation waterfall is not out of the question. ETH crash risk is not zero.
- BTC has no competitors. ETH has infinite competitors.
- The Merge is a potential bullish catalyst but it's been punted and delayed so many times, it's a downside catalyst too. It shows how semi-centralized cryptocurrency protocol decisions can be a negative and can create credibility issues.

By selling ETH/BTC, you buy the crash potential of ETH, but avoid outright short crypto exposure. I like it. The chart looks horrendous too.

---

[25] https://fortune.com/40-under-40/2021/roaring-kitty-keith-gill/

I'm not saying ETH is going to crash. **It's a risk, not the base case.** But even if it doesn't crash, short ETH/BTC could easily work anyway.

Conclusion

If you are long ETH, do you understand your risk of ruin? If it gapped to $500, will you be OK? What about if it crashed to $200? I think ETH crash risk is a known tail risk at this point. Best to be prepared for it. If ETH crashes, BTC will outperform and ETH/BTC could go back to 0.033, where it was in mid-2021.

Short at 0.061, stop loss 0.077 (out the top of the triangle).

Take profit 0.033.

ETH at 800 and BTC at 24000 would get you there.

Week 17: Good News/Bad Price

Counterintuitive price action can send an important message

The price is wrong.

Update On Previous Trades

There are four active trades right now and they are all hovering just above or below break even. Long BTC, long ARKK, --CVNA/++RBLX (RV trade), and short ETHBTC. Nothing significant to report, really. I will update in more detail when larger moves happen and larger P&L is generated!

Good news/bad price

Price action is mostly meaningless. Markets go up, down, and sideways for all sorts of reasons. The numbers on the screen jiggle and flicker in constant motion, but there is barely any signal in all that noise. Erratic and semi-random flows create bid/offer bounce and the illusion of meaningful market movement as randomness dominates.

Traders often come away from reading a book like *Reminiscences of a Stock Operator* with a feeling like they, too, might learn to get a visceral sense of where a market is headed just by watching it go up and down for a while. But that is rarely the case. Reading the tape is barely a thing.

Still, while I believe price action is **mostly** meaningless, it's not **completely** meaningless. The way price reacts to news can sometimes contain information. Every time news comes out or a market correlated to yours goes up or down, you have an expectation of what will happen in your market. Good traders have a good sense of the range of possible catalysts and news items that might come out, and they have a range of expectations for how those catalysts will impact price.

For example, traders in these markets should know the answers to these questions right now:

- If Boris Johnson loses the vote of confidence... Is that good or bad for GBPUSD?
- If the SEC announces that ETH fails the Howey Test[26] and is ruled to be a security, how will various altcoins trade? How far will ETH drop? What will BTC do?
- If the ECB meeting this week signals a 25 basis point hike in July, not 50... What will German bunds do?

When price does something other than what you thought it would... That's a potential signal.

Trade the news

The price of the security or market you trade is an equilibrium determined by the sum total of all the available information in the world. When new information arrives, the market will move to reflect that new information, but the market won't find a new equilibrium instantaneously. Different market participants will have different opinions of what the new info means, and they will have different positions, incentives, and risk tolerance.

Trading the news can be a major edge if you know your market extremely well and have an expert understanding of how new information matters (or doesn't matter). Important information will create opportunities to jump on a move quickly, before it's fully played out. Many of the successful traders in Jack Schwager's latest book *Unknown Market Wizards* trade the news prolifically.

I will write a piece on how to trade the news at some point in this series, but today I want to discuss a specific setup that sometimes unfolds after news comes out. It is a setup that can be extremely useful and will help you play both better offense and better defense.

---

26 https://fisherhudson.com/decentralized-cryptocurrencies-typically-fail-the-howey-test/

Good news/bad price

In brief, good news/bad price is a scenario where a market doesn't react logically to a clear piece of news. For example, great news comes out in your favorite stock, and the stock closes lower on the day. Or bad news comes out on the economy, and yields go **up**. I called this note "Good news/bad price", but bad news/good price is obviously the same setup in reverse. If bad news comes out, and the price goes up, that's the same concept as good news/bad price, just flipped.

To be clear, the counterintuitive reaction in the market does not have to be instantaneous. For example, an unexpected bullish headline hits and your favorite stock rallies 4%. But then momentum quickly starts to fade. Now the stock is only up 3%. Now just 1.5%. Now flat on the day. And… It's gone. That's good news/bad price.

What are we to make of seemingly nonsensical days when there is good news and the price goes down?

Before we answer that, you first need to be close to 100% sure that you are interpreting the news correctly. Only unexpected news moves markets. If AMZN is expected to report record earnings, and they report record earnings… That's not news and it's not bullish. It's neutral. The record earnings should already be factored into the price.

If everyone expects the central bank to hike rates by 0.25% and they hike rates by 0.25%, the market shouldn't move much when the hike is announced. On the other hand, if nobody expects the central bank to hike rates and they hike rates, you can expect a massive market reaction.

This concept is known as news being "priced in."

To trade good news/bad price, you first need to rule out a) you misinterpreted the news and b) the news was already priced in.

Key Concept: Understand what's priced in

Before you can trade or interpret the market's reaction to a surprise headline, economic data, central bank meetings, or any other news event, you need to understand what is priced in. This is an absolutely critical concept for anyone who trades any financial market. **If you trade or ever plan to trade any security in any market, you need to fully and completely get the concept of "Priced In"**. If you read this section and still don't really get it, ask someone to explain it more fully. Every trader must be completely comfortable with the concept of what is priced in to a market.

Financial market prices are generally set by the sum total of all the buying and selling done by every human and computer market participant in a giant, unending series of auctions. Different buyers and sellers will decide to buy or sell depending on the price, and as prices move different actors with different time frames will enter or exit the market.

Decisions to buy and sell are generally driven by the market's assessment of fair value for the security and this assessment should (in theory) be composed of all the available information that relates to that security. As new information comes in, prices move in real-time and should quickly incorporate and reflect that new info. Let's look at an example.

Currencies are highly sensitive to interest rate movements. Therefore, it makes sense that currencies should move when central banks adjust their primary interest rate. Here is an example of how a currency can move when a central bank unexpectedly changes interest rates.

Hourly USDCAD on a 2015 surprise interest rate cut from the Bank of Canada

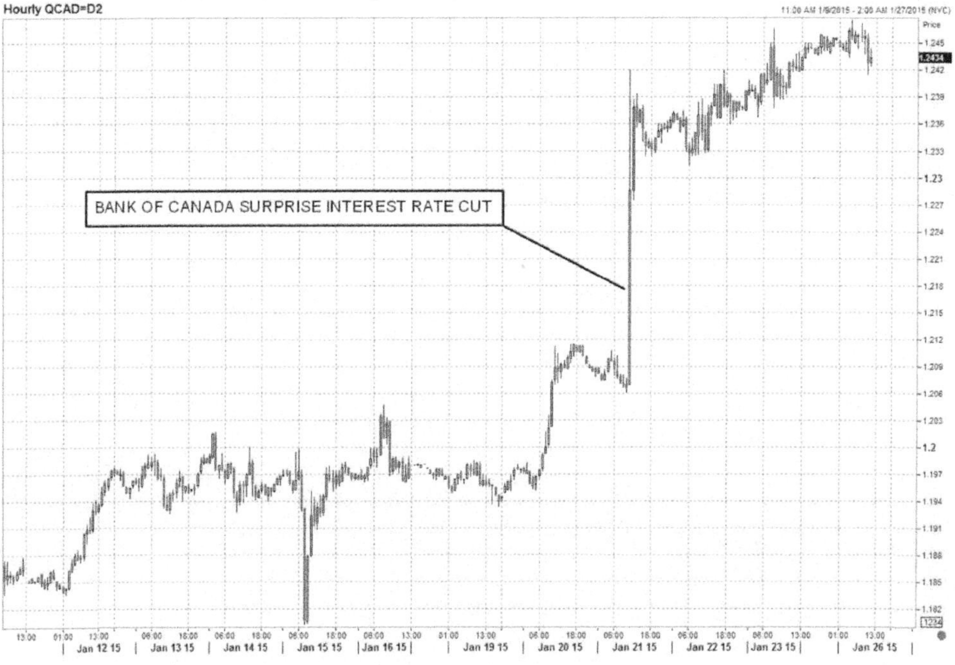

Note USDCAD higher = weaker CAD, stronger USD

When something unexpected like this happens, it is **not priced in**. This move higher in the USD vs. CAD is what you would anticipate because an unexpected rate cut by the Bank of Canada makes holding Canadian dollars less attractive given the lower yield. The market sells CAD and buys USD, driving USDCAD higher because the cut was a surprise, and *not priced in*.

In contrast, let's say six months ago, rumors start that Apple's self-driving car is coming soon, probably in the next six months. Apple stock rallied 5% on those rumors. Three months ago, images of the car were leaked online, confirming the rumors. Apple stock rallied another 15%. Two weeks ago, five Apple insiders confirmed to the WSJ that Apple's self-driving car announcement was imminent. Apple stock rallied another 12%!

Today, Apple announces yes, they will be releasing a self-driving car tomorrow. Do you buy Apple stock? … Probably not! The news of the self-driving car is known and is already reflected in the higher price of Apple stock. In other words: **It's priced in.** If anything, Apple stock is more likely to sell off today in a pattern known as "Buy the rumor, sell the fact." I will discuss "buy the rumor/sell the fact" in a future 50in50; so don't worry about that for now.

With earnings reports and economic releases, you can nail down almost exactly what is priced in because there are surveys that establish the expectation. With other news events and headlines, it helps to be expert in your product and talk to as many people as possible. If you talk to dozens of traders who trade your asset class, you're going to have a pretty good intuitive idea of what's priced in for almost any scenario. Reading and following experts on Twitter also helps you identify what's priced in.

OK, so you understand the concept of what is priced in.

You are trading your favorite fake meat stock, BYND. The stock is trading at $25. Good news comes out — Outback Steakhouse will soon put the "Beyond Filet Mignon" on the menu at every one of its 700 US locations. Crikey! You are certain this news is unexpected. It is not priced in. BYND gaps up 9% in an instant, but then it immediately turns aggressively lower. By the end of the day, the stock is DOWN 1.5%

What the actual???

That price action is extremely important. When a market cannot rally on good news or it cannot sell off on bad news, it is revealing information. What could that information be?

1. Positioning is heavily one-sided. If everyone is already max long BYND and they come out with a huge positive announcement… There is nobody left to buy. In that scenario, the price might rally a bit on the kneejerk, but then sellers will come in one by one to use the headline liquidity as an exit.
2. A large seller is lurking and wants to take advantage of any surges in liquidity. Let's say I'm a Boston asset manager and I'm long 4,000,000 shares of BYND. I decided today that I want to get out of all my BYND because I believe lab-grown meat is going to take over from plant-based meat. I'm talking tactics with the execution desk when DING DING DING a bullish headline comes out. Sure, it's good news, but it doesn't alter my longer-term thesis. The stock rips to $27 on high volume. I tell the execution trader to run a 60-minute TWAP with a $25 limit for 4 million shares. The headline buyers run into my supply and the stock slowly rolls

over. Soon, it's back below $25, and I managed to slide out almost 2 million shares. Nice. By the end of the day, the longs are stopping out at $24.

3. There is event risk coming up. If US economic data comes out super strong, people will generally buy the USD and sell bonds. But let's say ISM comes in three standard deviations stronger than expected, but there is a US Presidential election tomorrow. Is the market going to pile into the USD, given there is a more important event in less than 24 hours? Probably not. You will very often see weird price action into events as the market is more concerned about reducing whatever risk it has on, than trading in the direction of the logical macro narrative.

There are other reasons a market might not rally on good news, but the main point is to identify those moments and understand what they mean. **Good news/bad price is bearish**. The market should have rallied, and it didn't. That is going to make bulls nervous and give shorts confidence. Let's look at a recent example.

Last week's jobs report

Nonfarm payrolls (the US jobs market report) came out Friday, June 3 and the market reaction on the release was just about unanimous. It went something like this: Strong headline jobs, and lower wages = goldilocks. A goldilocks number is one that signals the economy is not too hot and not too cold and strong jobs growth with lower earnings growth is just that. I am in a ton of Bloomberg chats with various hedge funds and banks and every single one read the report as Goldilocks and good for stocks.

Here is what happened:

5-minute chart of S&P futures after nonfarm payrolls

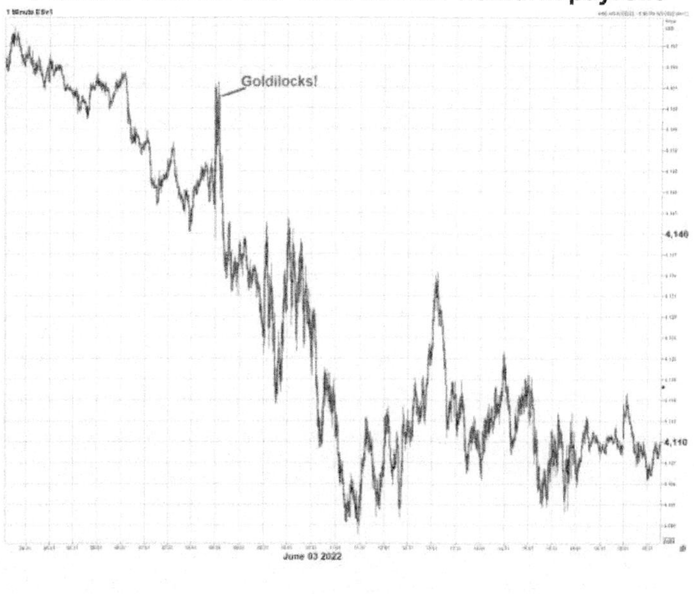

Stocks went up for about four minutes, then down for the remainder of the day.

Let's look at an even more dramatic version from last week, this time bad news/good price. Before I show the chart, let me give a bit of background. The market is excited about the prospect that the Swiss National Bank (SNB) might hike rates soon. All the market was waiting for was one more CPI number to confirm the thesis.

If you think the SNB is ready to hike rates, the trade is to sell EURCHF (that is sell euros, buy Swiss francs). Swiss CPI was coming out, and if it was strong, it was the best excuse in the world to sell EURCHF. CPI came out, and it was a monster. One of the biggest topside misses ever in the history of the series. Here is what EURCHF did:

EURCHF 1-minute chart around CPI

Whoops. EURCHF dropped a full day's range in one minute, then spent the rest of the day going up, up, and away.

How to trade bad news/good price

How do you know when to pull the trigger on a bad news/good price setup? The simple starting point is you always identify the level of your market just before a major headline or news item. This level is called the NewsPivot. In that EURCHF example, the market was trading 1.0270 before the CPI data came out so that's your NewsPivot.

If news like this comes out that is massively bearish EURCHF, the pair should never go back above the NewsPivot. If it breaches the NewsPivot, that's bad news/good price. If you are short, get out. If you were bullish for some other reason, get long!

Here is what EURCHF did after:

EURCHF 1-minute chart around and after CPI

And for the record, this is not hindsight. I wrote about this bad news/good price setup in am/FX when EURCHF was still 1.0670, after the CPI release. Some of the clients I cover exited their shorts at that point because the setup was clearly bullish EURCHF.

I do not trade the good news/bad price setup systematically. I watch how markets trade around each NewsPivot and monitor closely for weird reactions. When I see one, I use it as a trigger to either initiate a trade I was interested in anyway, or to get out of existing risk.

Unambiguous news should trigger unambiguous directional moves in the market. If it doesn't, something or someone else is in control.

Effective on many fractals

Price reaction to news isn't just an intraday trading thing. Quite often, you will see a major turn in a market after it fails to respond logically to news. A counterintuitive and important concept that every trader needs to remember is this:

Major lows come on bad news. Major highs come on good news. It's very rare that a market is at the lows, good news comes out, and it rallies and starts a new up trend. Very often, it's the opposite. Bad news triggers a push to new lows and that push cannot sustain, signaling that sellers have run out of ammo. That's the rebar on which bottoms are built.

An example of this that I will never forget is the day that Osama bin Laden was killed. At the time, the killing of bin Laden was viewed as super bullish news as it eliminated the head of one of the great threats to US national security. Stocks initially blasted higher on the news, but then the market slowly drifted lower for the rest of the day. Here is the chart:

The day Osama bin Laden was killed marked a medium-term high in US stocks

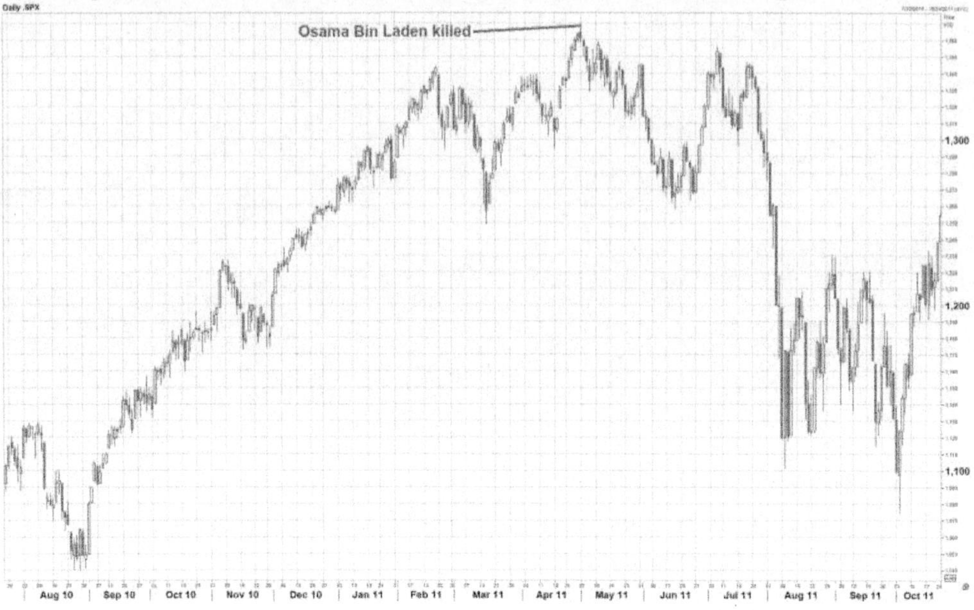

I remember at the end of that day, many traders turned super bearish stocks because it was stunning to see the SPX close in the red on such apparently important news. It worked! Good news/bad price.

The recent price action in gold after the Russian SWIFT announcement is another example. The weaponization of the USD was seen as great news for gold yet gold went up for a few days and is now much lower.

A possible good news/bad price setup in LLY

Eli Lilly (NYSE: LLY) closed at 301.60 yesterday and rallied to 315.13 today on promising news about a weight-loss drug. Let's say I was bearish LLY for whatever reason and I see the chart looks like this:

LLY stock for the past 10 days

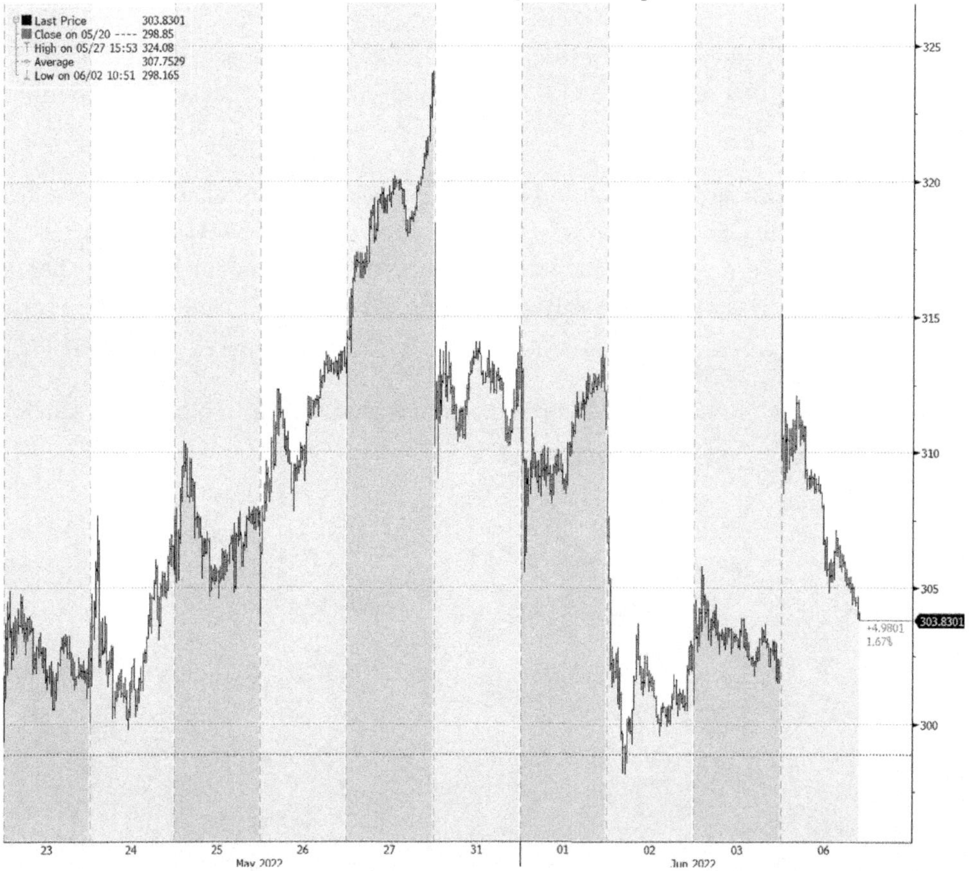

The reason I said "Let's say I was bearish LLY for whatever reason…" is that I don't do trades purely on a tech setup like this. I use these types of tech setups (volume spike at price extreme, slingshot reversal, etc.) to determine tactics, not strategy.

So the good news came out at a price of 301.60. Below there, the price action is not good. Given we have a low of 298.20 on June 2, I will leave a stop entry to go short LLY at 297.99. If done, stop loss at 306.25. That stop loss is above the old 298.20/305.85 equilibrium zone that dominated in the two days before the positive news came out. Zooming out a bit, the chart has mostly been in a 280/315 range since mid-March so I put the take profit at 283.10. Risking 8 to make 15.

If the stop entry order is not executed by the close this Friday, June 10, I will cancel it and forget about the idea. Good news/bad price setups don't last very long because the more time that passes after a new headline, the less relevant it is to the price action or psychology of the market. That is, super quick rejections of news are more valid than rejections that take a long time.

Conclusion

When unambiguous good news about a company comes out, the stock should go up and stay up. If it doesn't, there is often some signal and forecasting value in the price action. Any time price doesn't do what you think it should be doing:

- First, question your underlying assumptions. Do you fully grok what is driving the stock and what news is important? Is the market doing something truly weird, or is it just that you don't understand what's going on?
- Second, pay attention! Good news/bad price is often an early warning signal telling you to be careful. It can be a sign of large positions in the market, large flows in the market, and counterintuitive supply/demand imbalances that run counter to the primary news flow.

Use good news/bad price to get into trades you like, and out of trades you don't. Once a market crosses back through a NewsPivot after a major event, headline, or announcement, get ready for a quick, painful, and aggressive move the other way.

Week 18: Fun with Quadrants

Simple frameworks help us understand complex systems (part 1)

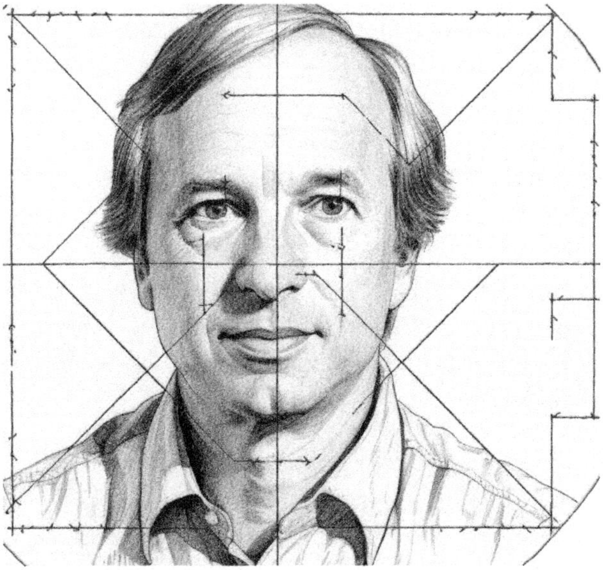

Update on previous trades

The bitcoin long was stopped as risky assets continue to crumble under the weight of high inflation (and the presumed Fed reaction function). ARKK is nosediving.

The LLY short is 8 bucks in the money and --CVNA/++RBLX (the RV trade), and short ETHBTC are doing well. Those last two trades show the beauty of market-neutral positions vs. trades where the returns are derived mostly from the overall direction of the market.

Only shorts and RV trades are making money right now and there is no particular reason to think the risky asset pain ends anytime soon. As a reminder, every 10 weeks, I post the full results spreadsheet with all the gory details.

Fun with quadrants

When studying extremely complex systems, we look for heuristics or shortcuts that can help us strip out complexity and see only the most important underlying dynamics. A popular way to do this in finance is through the use of quadrants. Very often, we can slurp out the two most important variables in a system, put them on an x/y axis, and use the four quadrants produced by the matrix to better understand where we are and where we're going.

If this sounds overly simplistic, it's not. If it is good enough for Ray Dalio and some of the best macro analysts in the world… It's good enough for me!

Bridgewater

The OG quadrant guy was Ray Dalio, who developed a simple matrix to better understand the economic machine. Most of what Ray Dalio writes and says resonates with me on some level. When I started in the 1990s, getting your hands on good quality macro research was difficult and mostly we just got Bridgewater's "Daily Observations," The Gartman Letter, and Bob Savage's daily note. Two out of three of those were excellent!

The four-box framework that Dalio developed in the early days of Bridgewater is outlined in an excellent essay on their website.[27]

It looks like this…

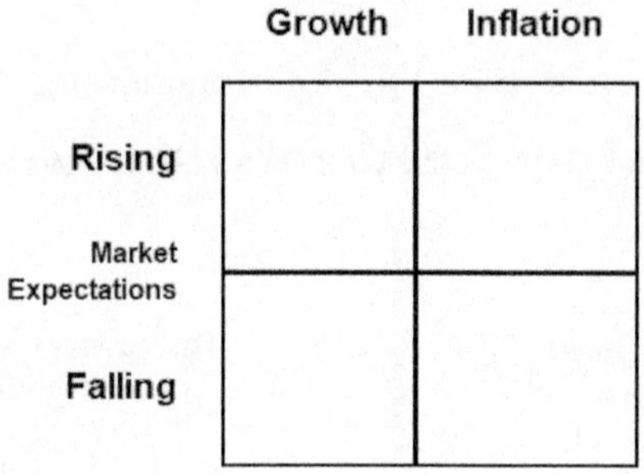

If you can identify where your economy (or the world economy) sits in these four boxes… You're 60% or 70% of the way to getting the macro story right. It's not as simple as solving this framework because once you do, you still have to figure out what it means for various asset classes. But most macro traders, analysts, and strategists start with a framework like this, whether they do so explicitly or implicitly.

By weird coincidence, I was halfway through writing this note when I received an email from Bridgewater updating their quadrants. This is flukey since I only get about one email per month from them.

[27] https://www.bridgewater.com/research-and-insights/the-all-weather-story

Here is their update:[28]

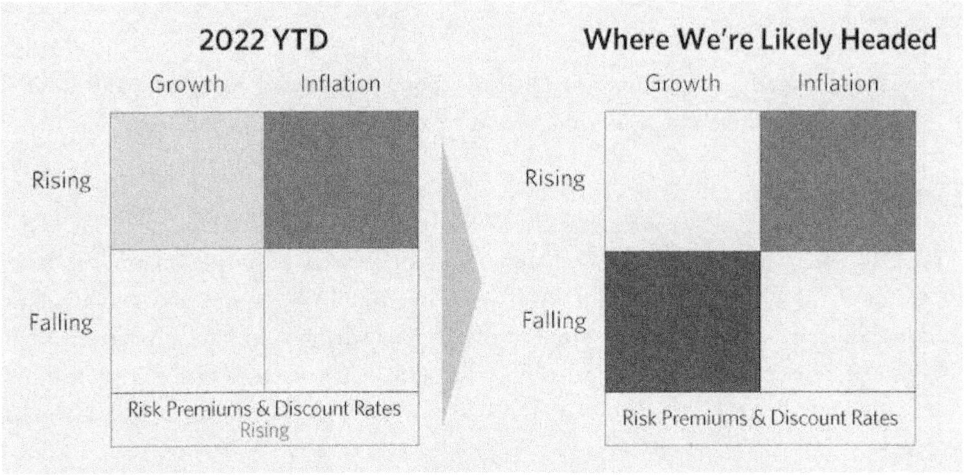

Once the most basic questions are answered (i.e., is the market's expectation of growth rising or falling? Is the market's expectation of inflation rising or falling?), strategists will outline which assets do well in each quadrant. Most analysts use quadrants where only one of four boxes is ever lit up at one time. That's easier to understand.

For example, here is the Gavekal Four Quadrants framework:

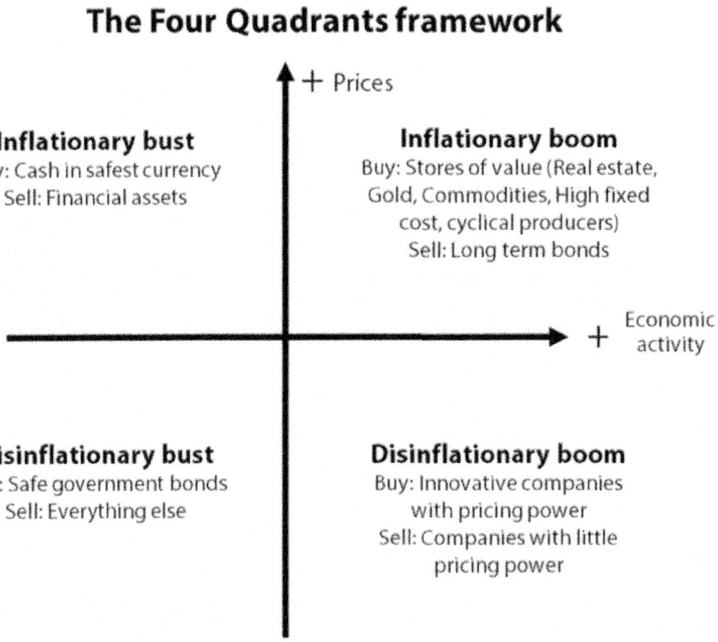

[28] https://www.bridgewater.com/research-and-insights/current-challenges-investors-face

You can use empirical data and common sense logic to build a four quadrants framework of your own. Alfonso Peccatiello (@MacroAlf on Twitter) uses a slightly different approach with axes labeled "Global Credit Impulse" and "Relative Monetary Stance."

This is a nuanced difference. He substitutes "monetary policy stance" for "inflation", and "global credit impulse" for growth. This says that in his framework, the way central banks react to inflation is more important than inflation itself. And that the global credit impulse is more important than real-time growth because credit impulse leads growth. Makes sense!

Here are Alf's quadrants as of May 2022 (from his Macro Compass):

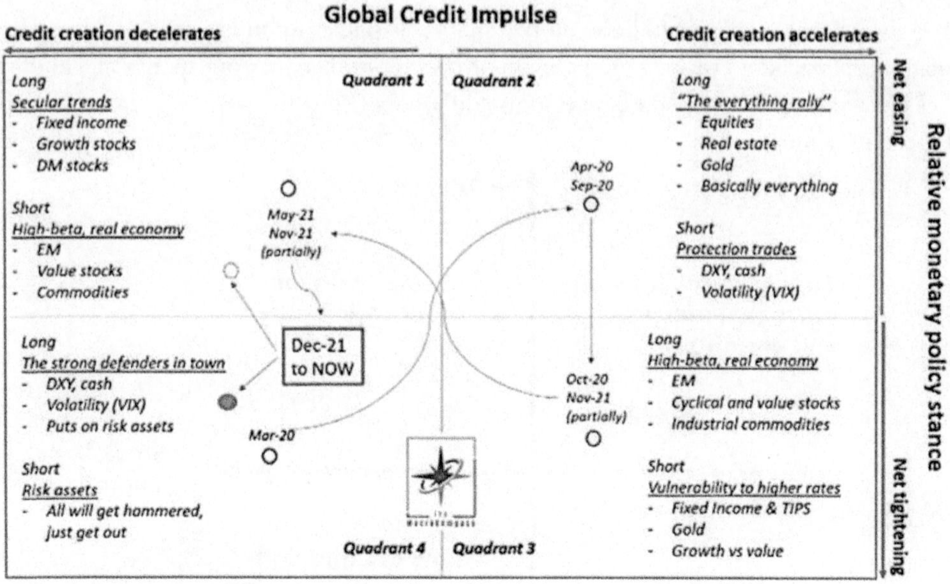

However you structure the quadrants, the basic principle is the same: Growth and inflation drive macro and there are four main scenarios in every economy:

1. Inflationary bust
2. Inflationary boom
3. Disinflationary bust
4. Disinflationary boom

We move around from quadrant to quadrant and you can mostly define recent years as follows:

- **1990 to 2000** - Inflationary boom
- **2000 to 2002** - Disinflationary bust
- **2003 to 2007** - Disinflationary boom

- **2008** - Disinflationary bust
- **2009 to 2020** - Disinflationary boom
- **2021** Inflationary boom
- **2022** Inflationary bust transitioning to disinflationary bust (?)

This is a nice simple macro framework. My point in this piece isn't to teach this specific framework, but to present a super simple way of looking at the economy or markets through an easy-to-understand filter. Obviously, a lot of detail gets lost in this filtering process, but a lot of noise gets eliminated too.

Oil vs. stocks

You can use the relationship between two market variables to build useful quadrant-style matrices as well. And very often, there can be cool tie-ins between one matrix and another. Let's look at the relationship between oil and stocks. I put the year of a strong example for each regime in gray.

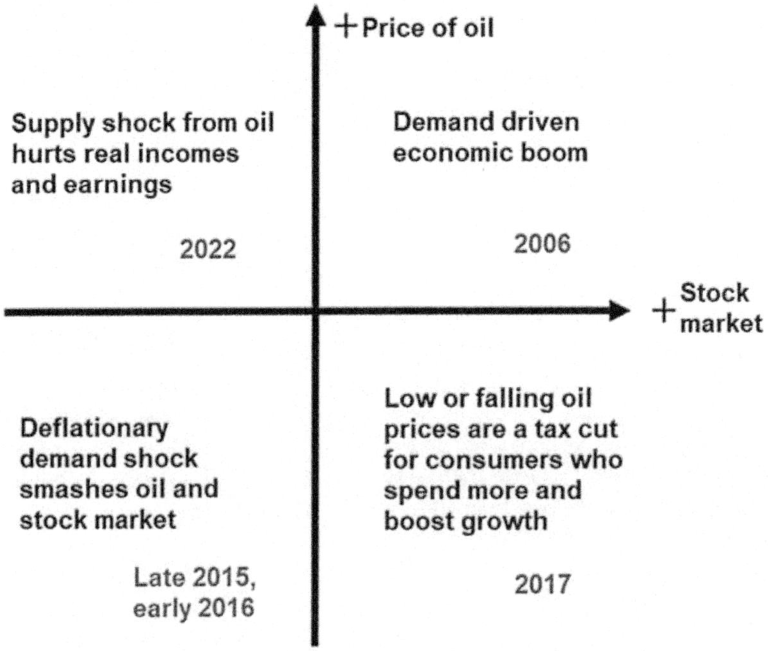

There is much more complexity than a 2X2 matrix will allow, though. These matrices focus on changes because changes are always more important than levels. But levels can still matter! Falling oil is usually a signal of falling demand (bad for stocks) but low, stable oil prices can be a fat tax cut for consumers (good for stocks).

Also, velocity matters. If oil is going up four cents per day, and stocks are rallying 0.1% per day, that's the top right quadrant, but not meaningful. If stocks and oil both rallied

10% this month, that's turbo top right quadrant action. You can't just split stuff into a 2X2 and ignore the underlying complexity presented by rate of change and levels.

Another example of this is that rates rising 1% off zero probably matter a lot more than rates going from 7% to 8%. So even velocity in isolation isn't enough. Starting points, levels and velocity (rate of change) all matter, even while direction is the most important factor of all.

Remember like in high school calculus, you have: Level, change, rate of change, rate of rate of change, and so on. The biggest driver for markets is usually **changes**, but levels and rates of change and even rates of rates of change can also matter.

You might have noticed that my oil vs. stocks matrix mirrors the other matrices very well because oil is a good proxy for inflation and the stock market is an OK proxy for growth (not always true!!!!!). Inflationary booms are usually also periods where the stock market goes up and oil goes up.

But quadrant maps don't always have to be about growth and inflation or related market moves. They can be useful for identifying all sorts of regimes.

Regime switcher

So far, the takeaway should be that you can create useful shorthand models for the economy and for markets in a simple way: Create a 2X2 matrix and solve for what you think each quadrant means. This is a useful way of breaking down the economy and market relationships.

These matrices help you identify the current regime and they should also help you identify regime switches in advance or at least in real time. **Adaptive regime-switching is a trading superpower. To survive as a trader in the long run, you must be able to adapt as economic and market regimes change.** If your strategy was to buy short-dated calls before disruptortech earnings announcements and you didn't recognize that there was a regime shift around 2021, you probably made a lot of money for a while … then lost a lot of money, really fast.

One of the greatest advantages humans have over computers is our ability to make creative, non-linear, non-obvious judgments about regime shifts, especially shifts into regimes that never existed in the past. For example, any human being could probably reason that COVID lockdowns would lead to more time playing video games. It is extremely unlikely that any algorithm or machine learning or AI model would have been able to make such a prediction because there would be no data to analyze as video games did not exist the last time a major pandemic swept the world.

Trading regimes

While economic regimes can be most simply boiled down to growth and inflation, trading regimes can be boiled down most simply to volatility and trend. Here's a matrix for those two variables with examples for SPX in gray. For example, 2021 was a high-volatility trend higher in stocks as everything ripped and call buyers kept volatility supported.

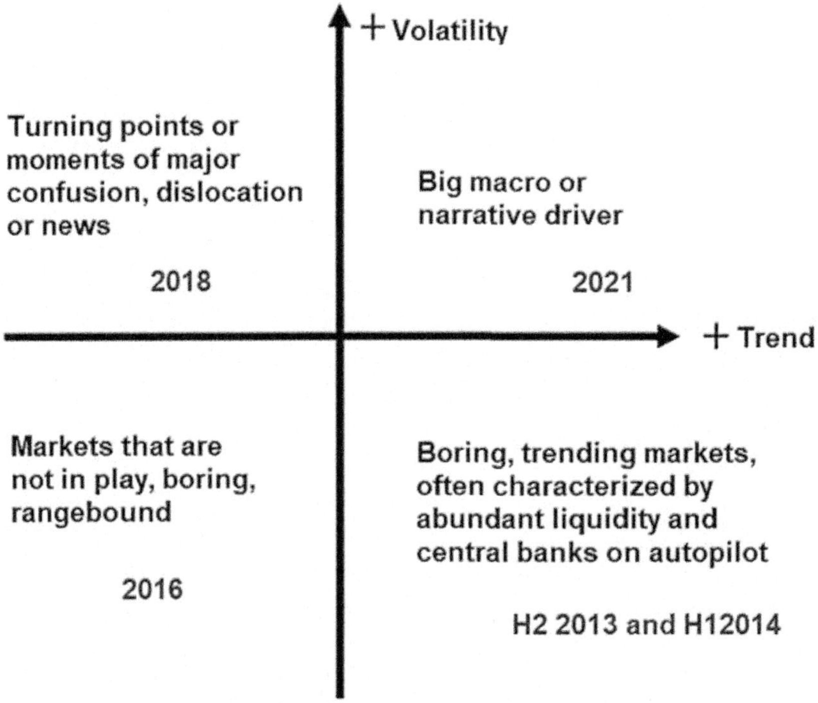

If we were making a 3D cube instead of a 2X2 matrix, we would add correlation, but as a general rule, correlation and volatility move together so the volatility axis partly accounts for correlation.

As a rule, super high correlation (aka, corr) between assets is a feature of high-volatility, fear-driven markets. When things are calm, correlations are lower and individual assets can express idiosyncratic directional moves. This is a general truth but not an ironclad law of global markets. The reason corr tends to go up during periods of fear is that every asset is made up of a systemic risk/liquidity component and an idiosyncratic component. As systemic risk rises, the idiosyncratic factor is crowded out and the systemic/fear component dominates. In a risk aversion regime, fear (and relief from fear) crowds out the idiosyncratic drivers of each asset class and pushes cross-asset corr towards 1.

For example, in crypto, nobody cares about bitcoin adoption, or Solana transaction speeds, or the promise of GameFi right now. All that matters now is macro and the Fed. Here is a quick analogy from a recent MacroTactical Crypto piece I wrote:

Imagine a music festival with four separate stages. The song being played on each stage will lead to idiosyncratic styles and speeds of dancing. People watching Kendrick Lamar will dance and walk around in styles and patterns that are totally independent of the movements of people watching the trance DJ, the pop singer, or the deep house DJ on the side stages (that is: the movement of people watching each stage is idiosyncratic and uncorrelated).

If there's light rain, you will see some people from each stage area head for cover (some correlation, but still low correlation of people movement as some portion of spectators at each stage heads for the tent).

But **if there's a massive lightning storm** (i.e., risk event), all the people at all four stages will run for cover, regardless of the style of music being performed on each stage (high correlation of people movement, most of the crowd rushing for cover).

During periods of calm and optimism, asset classes dance independently. During periods of fear, all asset classes move as one. That is: fear drives cross-market correlation higher. There are various names for this such as "risk on/risk off (aka RORO)", "The Blob" and so on.

In trading, it's absolutely critical to know what volatility regime you're in, and whether your market is rangebound or trending. I go into this stuff in great detail in *Alpha Trader*. Let me talk a bit more here about range vs. trend markets.

Rangebound vs. trending

Rangebound markets favor mean reversion strategies (buy low/sell high) while trending markets favor breakout or "go with" strategies (buy high/sell higher). You should always have a good sense of whether each market you trade is trending or rangebound. Identifying if you are in a range or trend regime is fairly easy, but forecasting when the regime will change is hard.

Volatility and trend are the two features you should always be able to describe with confidence for each market you trade. You should always know where volatility is relative to recent history, and whether your market is in a trend or a range. If you update your view of these two variables daily, you will adapt in real time better than most of your competitors.

One more matrix

Here is a matrix I use to trade the USD:

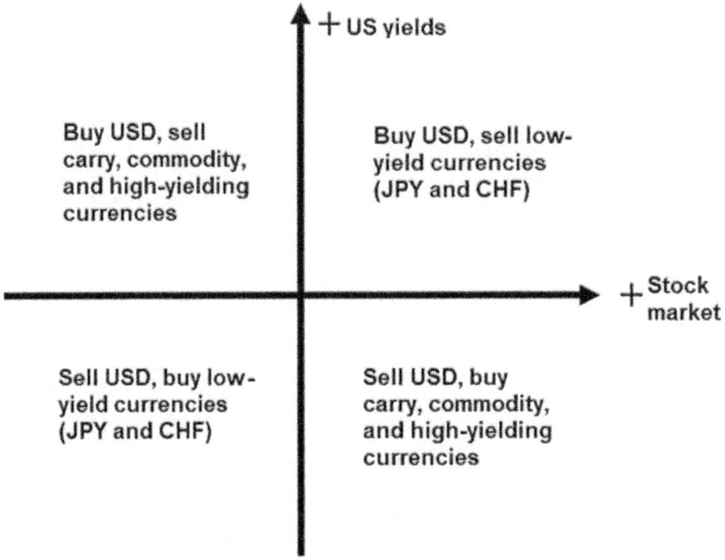

Yields up, stocks up = America, fk yea! Buy USDJPY. Yields up, stocks down = Inflation problem or liquidity issues, sell risky currencies like AUD, NZD, EMFX etc. And so on. Once you put together a matrix like this, you can back test it.

Let's look at average returns for USDJPY using this breakdown, but with a bit more detail so you can see what I mean. The JPY is a low-yield currency, so we would think top right corner action (stocks up, yields up) would be best for USDJPY. I'm going to look at data since 2010 because any analysis including data pre-2010 will tend to be distorted by the monster moves in 2008 and 2009.

		YIELDS	
		DOWN	UP
STOCKS	UP	**-0.4%**	**0.6%**
	DOWN	**-0.7%**	**0.4%**

Minimum yield move = 10bps to qualify for this analysis

This simple table tells you right away that USDJPY is a yields trade, and not an equity trade. People commonly believe that the JPY is a safe haven, but it's not. It's only a safe haven when bonds are a safe haven (and bonds are often not a safe haven in times of high inflation, like right now). If you care about JPY and its relationship to rates and equities, I have an am/FX note on the Spectra Markets website you can read for more.[29]

---

[29] https://www.spectramarkets.com/wp-content/uploads/2022/04/AMFX-Always-and-everywhere-14MAR22.pdf

The trade: buy bonds

The purpose of this lesson was to get you thinking about two-variable interactions and how you can reduce complex systems into a simple matrix for better understanding. These matrices can lead to trade ideas as you understand the current state of the world and forecast its future state.

The US economy has accelerated into the inflationary bust quadrant now as Bridgewater says in their email. That's rates up, stocks down. It's a good time to own cash and a terrible time to own almost all assets.

But my feeling is that we are soon going to transition **out of the inflationary bust** and **into a disinflationary bust** as the Fed accelerates its response to the CPI threat. The accelerating velocity of the Fed response is hitting stocks and will further decimate growth expectations. I envision an episode similar to May where US 10-year yields pull back 30-50bps. This is a *catch the falling knife* scenario in bonds, but my core view for the past 2 weeks (as described in am/FX) has been: one last soul-crushing capitulation push up through the 3.24% double top in US 10-year yields. We just got that.

Since bond futures are at the lows, there is no obvious technical point to leave a stop loss. I'm going to take 3X daily average range of 0.5 points in 2022 and put my stop loss 1.5 points below my entry.

The Fed meeting is tomorrow so there is serious event risk. I think the best result for this trade (counterintuitively, perhaps) would be 100bp (1%) hike from the Fed. To anchor inflation expectations and bond prices, the Fed must abandon their addiction to gradualism and go Volcker.

The trade parameters are: **Long TYU2 at 114 18/32**. Bond futures trade in 32nds so 114 18/32 is 114.56. My stop loss is 3 days' ranges away and below the round number of 113 so it will be at 112 27/32 or 112.84375. The take profit is a move back to where we were three days ago: 118.00. I am risking 1.7 points to make 3.4. Let's go.

Conclusion

A simple four-quadrant matrix can help you distill themes and reduce complexity. First, make sure you fully understand the popular macro quadrants framework developed by Bridgewater. Then, be creative and come up with your own 2X2 matrices.

Let me know if you think of any cool ones.

Week 19: Weigh the Pros and Cons

Simple frameworks help us understand complex systems (part 2)

This con is a pro

Update on previous trades

I am going to do the full .xlsx update next week as we hit Week 20, so I will keep it short here today. ARKK is on the comeback, CVNA/RBLX is doing OK, short ETHBTC is ITM, and the LLY short is stopped out.

And… Last week's long TY trade was about as perfect as they get. It already hit the take profit. Here's the chart:

US 10-year bond futures (hourly back to 07JUN)

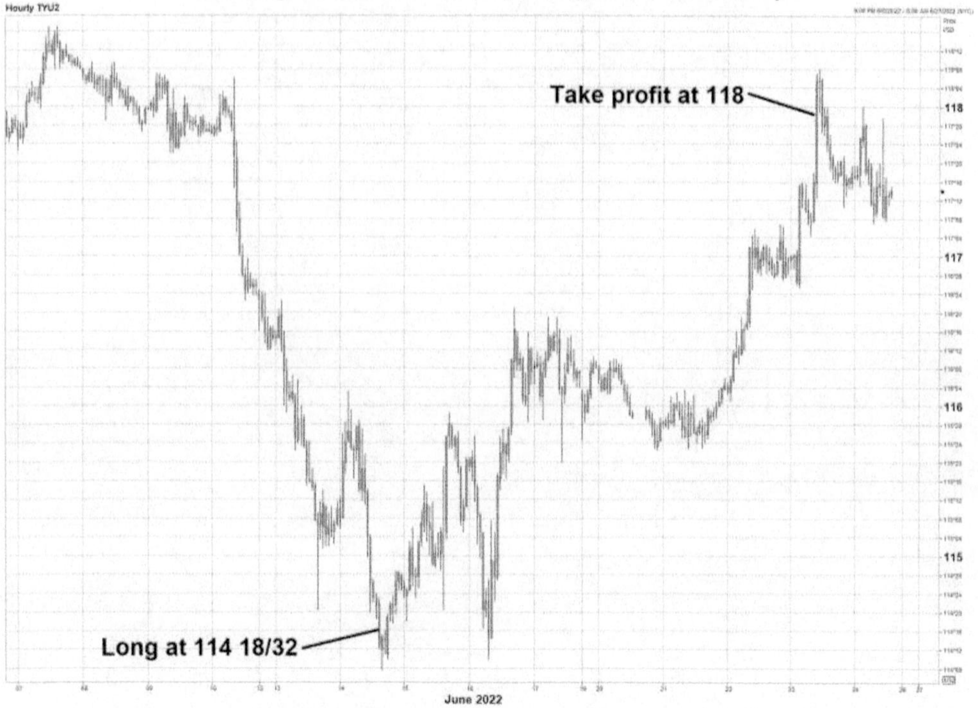

One interesting aspect of this whole Fifty Trades in Fifty Weeks exercise will be to see how the different trades play out by asset class. My expertise is global macro and FX but I am avoiding FX trades in here because I don't want my primary audience to confuse my core macro views (published in am/FX) with these more esoteric and scattershot 50in50 views where the primary purpose is instructional. A logical guess would be that whatever macro trades I do in here will outperform the micro trades (e.g., single name equities). But we shall see.

For transparency and accountability, I publish my P&L for all am/FX trades once per quarter. The most recent quarterly results are below. My P&L on the am/FX trades is mostly good-to-excellent with occasional periods of drawdown where I go ice cold for a month or two. It would make sense that since I'm a tourist in some of these 50in50 trades, I have less (or no) edge but I will be curious to see the final results. Full spreadsheet of 50in50 results to date next week. Here are the Q2 am/FX results:

AM/FX Trade Ideas since 08MAR22

Risking $100,000 on each trade   Free capital: 4,000,000 2.5% of free capital on each trade

		Asset	Entry	Stop loss	Position size	Take profit	Actual exit	P&L	Exit date	Holding period (days)	Notes
16-Mar	L	USDJPY	118.65	116.51	5,555,556	123.3300	123.33	223,149	28-Mar	12	
16-Mar	L	USDJPY	118.65	116.51	5,555,556	123.3300	123.33	223,149	28-Mar	12	
16-Mar	L	AUDUSD	0.7258	0.7127	7,516,610		0.7511	190,170	28-Mar	12	
16-Mar	L	EURUSD	1.1000	1.0802	4,959,596		1.0966	(16,863)	28-Mar	12	
16-Mar	S	USDCHF	0.9422	0.9592	5,424,656		0.9357	69,136	28-Mar	12	
16-Mar	S	USDCNH	6.3623	6.4768	6,042,539		6.3855	(21,954)	28-Mar	12	
25-Mar	S	GBPUSD	1.3215	1.3353	7,322,048	1.2811	1.3010	150,102	18-Apr	24	
30-Mar	L	EURGBP	0.8460	0.8369	8,453,085	0.8599	0.8366	(103,297)	5-Apr	6	
4-Apr	S	EURUSD	1.1000	1.1201	5,066,033	1.0755	1.0825	88,656	13-Apr	9	
11-Apr	L	USDCAD	1.2606	1.2539	18,714,925	1.2777	1.2537	(99,516)	14-Apr	3	
12-Apr	S	AUDNZD	1.0875	1.0976	15,232,292	1.0667	1.0945	(69,307)	14-Apr	2	
19-Apr	L	AUDUSD	0.7362	0.7289	13,562,797	0.7480	0.7377	20,344	21-Apr	2	
3-May	S	USDSEK	9.8350	9.9610	7,857,143	9.5510	9.9650	(102,502)	5-May	2	
4-May	L	AUDUSD	0.7135	0.7049	11,487,753	0.7245	0.7245	126,365	5-May	1	
9-May	S	CADJPY	101.21	102.61	7,229,286	97.11	100.88	23,250	17-May	8	moved stop way lower
18-May	Buy	GBPJPY	put spread	157/154				(100,000)			
24-May	S	NZDCHF	0.6240	0.6365	7,360,000	0.6085	0.6260	(16,000)	1-Jun	8	
31-May	S	EURUSD	1.0702	1.0801	10,194,451	1.0411	1.0411	296,659	13-Jun	13	
10-Jun	S	EURJPY	141.25	144.44	4,427,900	137.77	140.9500	9,197			
11-Jun	S	USDJPY	134.05	135.55	8,936,667	130.55	135.5700	(100,212)	15-Jun	4	

Total P&L	790,526	8.3 *average hodling period*
Winners	11	
Losers	9	
Win%	55%	
avgWIN	129,107	
avgLOSE	(69,961)	

Gray trade is still alive. Covers March 8 to June 12, 2022

Takeaways:

- An excellent quarter. The big trades were long USDJPY from 118 to 123 and short EURUSD most of the way from 1.10 to 1.04. Pretty good P&L for low-leverage approach risking only 2.5% of capital on each trade.
- In GBP, I had a nice short but was way too early on the EURGBP long and that was costly. GBPJPY also didn't work because the JPY leg kept going as rates kept going.
- You can't get JPY or JPY crosses right unless you get bonds right.
- The good trades mostly took around 10-14 days to pan out. The only exception was the bang bang AUDUSD long May 4 FOMC.

Weigh the Pros and Cons

Last week's lesson was about how to reduce extremely complex systems like the global economy into a simpler form using quadrants. The central idea was to look for heuristics or shortcuts that can help us strip out complexity and see only the most important underlying dynamics. This week, I want to look at another framework for thinking that helps me filter noise and unpack the important factors in a trade. Like the quadrants idea, it's another super simple metacognition framework that helps me think about my thinking.

Hi Mom

When I was a kid and I had a difficult decision to make, my mom would always tell me to make a list of pros and cons. That is a simple way to get the crazy buzzing flurry of contradictory information out of your head and distill it down into something workable. I am a big believer in physically writing stuff down when it's important. The process of writing stuff down (with a pen or pencil) has a different impact than typing something on a computer or thinking about it in your head.

Thoughts are abstract and fuzzy. Writing is solid and concrete. If you think, "I'm going to cut my AAPL short at $285", that is completely different from writing **CUT AAPL 285** on an index card and having those words stare up at you in thick black Sharpie ink as the stock rallies from $280.50 to $284.75.

The same goes for any plans or ideas you have. There is so much noise in your head, so many competing voices vying for airtime. Don't assume you can formulate a plan in there and then execute it successfully without writing anything down. Again, this doesn't have to mean anything more than scratching a few notes down on a piece of paper or recording some thoughts on an index card.

Research shows that when you write down a goal, you are more likely to achieve it.

When you write something down, it solidifies. It transforms from abstract into concrete. All the sludge falls away and only the important information is left. When you write something down, you have made a choice to select that particular information, goal, or action as more important than all the others. This highlights it for your brain. When you write something down, you signal to your brain "THIS IS IMPORTANT". Your brain records it as such.

The pathways and connections developed in your brain are different when you write something down because the encoding process is different. The encoding is stronger, and more robust, and information is recalled more easily.

For years after leaving home and venturing out into the big, bad world, I forgot about the pros and cons thing. Then, one day in 2011, I was thinking about changing jobs. I have changed jobs many times in my life and it's usually a fairly easy choice. Factors at the existing job are generating a push (I don't like the environment, business model, management, etc.) and factors at the new job are creating a pull (money, risk appetite, business model, management, etc.) But in this particular case, I couldn't decide. My mind froze up.

Then, I remembered my mom's pros and cons thing and decided "what the heck I might as well try that". It worked! Once I laid it all out, it was clear to me that the new job on offer was a suboptimal choice and I should reject it. This was a good call! I ended up getting a way better offer in a way better trading environment about three months later and soon I was an MD at Nomura.

The CIA knows

Not long after the pros and cons thing helped me with my employment decision, I was re-reading one of my favorite non-fiction books, *Psychology of Intelligence Analysis*, by CIA intelligence expert Richards J. Heuer. The book is pure gold; it is the best elucidation of good thinking I have read. The author worked for the CIA for 45 years in various roles including operations, counterintelligence, and intelligence analysis. The book explains how human bias impedes clear thinking. Much of it applies directly to trading.

Of particular relevance is Part Two: Tools for Thinking, especially Chapter 8: Analysis of Competing Hypotheses. If you want access to the full buffet of information, I suggest you read the whole book: it's less than 200 pages and it is not boring! If you want the quick meal, at least read Chapter 8.

For now, here's an appetizer… Heuer's summary of Chapter 8.

Step-by-Step Outline of Analysis of Competing Hypotheses

1. Identify the possible hypotheses to be considered. Use a group of analysts with different perspectives to brainstorm the possibilities.
2. Make a list of significant evidence and arguments for and against each hypothesis.
3. Prepare a matrix with hypotheses across the top and evidence down the side. Analyze the "diagnosticity" of the evidence and arguments— that is, identify which items are most helpful in judging the relative likelihood of the hypotheses.
4. Refine the matrix. Reconsider the hypotheses and delete evidence and arguments that have no diagnostic value.
5. Draw tentative conclusions about the relative likelihood of each hypothesis. Proceed by trying to disprove the hypotheses rather than prove them.
6. Analyze how sensitive your conclusion is to a few critical items of evidence. Consider the consequences for your analysis if that evidence were wrong, misleading, or subject to a different interpretation.
7. Report conclusions. Discuss the relative likelihood of all the hypotheses, not just the most likely one.
8. Identify milestones for future observation that may indicate events are taking a different course than expected.

I think you can use all eight of these points to help analyze trade ideas. But the simple takeaway for traders is: No matter how in love you are with your trade idea, spend time looking for disconfirming evidence. Your brain is biased to look for confirming evidence (i.e., confirmation bias). Look at alternative hypotheses with an open mind and try to figure out how and why you could be wrong. Lay out the arguments against your view and see how you feel about them. Do they make sense? Are they easily refuted?

Naturally, this process of examining alternative hypotheses reminded me of the pros and cons list. It's basically the same thing, just a super fancy version. And usually in trading you really only have two hypotheses: Bullish or bearish.

That's not precisely true and there are nuances around each way of thinking about the market but the point here is that if you are going to put on a trade, first do a pros and cons for it. Then go through the eight steps above as a means of clarifying your thought process. This will force you to think of what might go wrong. It will identify risks that you might have not fully taken the time to factor in.

Long GBTC

In MacroTactical Crypto 23: 3.4% of the Bitcoins Are 34% off, I wrote my hypothesis explaining why I want to scale into long GBTC in five clips of 20% each day next week. Here is the intro to MTC23:

"As discussed in MTC22, liquidation is a risk for the next 10 days. Funds with gates and various rules are getting month-end, quarter-end and half-year-end redemption requests right now. I presume these requests will be large. One particularly interesting liquidation play into month end is GBTC. That is the Grayscale Bitcoin Trust. It holds spot bitcoin and currently owns 654,885 BTC or 3.4% of all the bitcoin in circulation.

Pedantic sidenote: The plural of bitcoin can be bitcoin or bitcoins. It should be one or the other. I vote bitcoin.

The problem with GBTC is that it cannot be converted or redeemed into BTC and therefore it can trade at any premium or discount to net asset value. There is no mechanism to convert GBTC into BTC or to make GBTC trade near net asset value (NAV). So, the value of GBTC is correlated to, but also completely unanchored from, its NAV.

In theory, one share of GBTC is worth NAV, eventually. But since there is no way of converting GBTC into BTC, the price of GBTC reflects some combination of two things: The price of bitcoin, and the overall demand for an exchange-traded bitcoin proxy.

When crypto is hot, GBTC trades at a premium because people will pay anything to get exposure. When crypto is wintery, like now, GBTC trades at a discount because demand disappears. Here is the GBTC discount / premium to NAV over time:

GBTC premium or discount to NAV

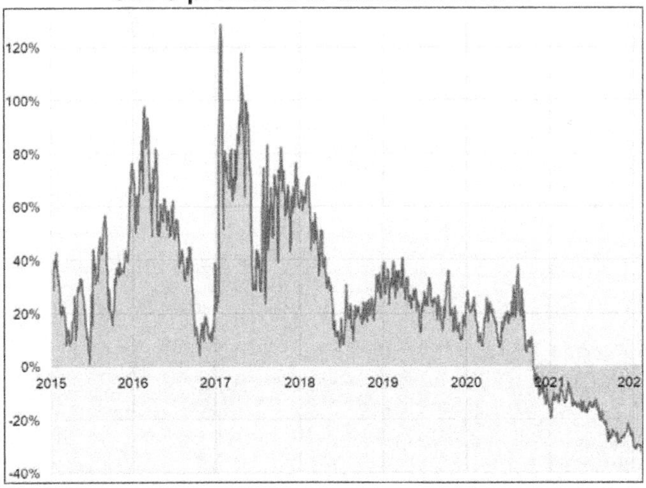

Expect large crypto fund liquidations into month-, quarter-, and half-year-end. These could hit crypto and hit GBTC particularly hard because insolvent hedge fund Three Arrows Capital is the biggest holder of GBTC. As of the most recent data, they hold 39 million shares and it trades 6 million shares/day.

To summarize the thesis:

- I am bullish bitcoin and this is an interesting way to get exposure in a tax-friendly way (not investment or tax advice!).
- This could work as a tactical trade (turn of the month and into a potential SEC announcement on July 6) or as a long-term investment. I see it working on both time horizons.

Here is my pros and cons sheet for the long GBTC trade:

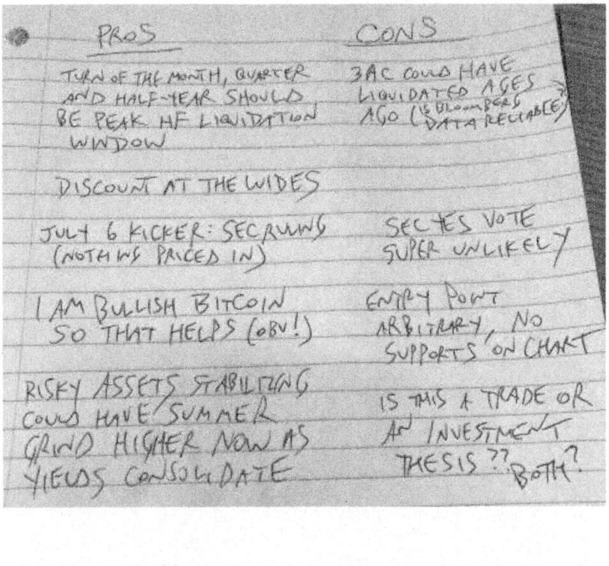

Once I have done this, I can actively debate the pros and cons. For example:

1. The "SEC YES vote super unlikely" kind of doesn't matter because nothing is priced in. I don't think GBTC will sell off much if the SEC rejects Grayscale's application to become a spot BTC ETF.
2. The two different time horizons is an important concern and consideration. By laying this out, I force myself to make a decision: Is this a trade or an investment? This avoids the possibility of entering it as a trade, then if it goes horribly wrong, deciding... er, actually... it's an investment.
3. The lack of chart support and technical support is not a problem. I had the same issue with the TY trade last week. You can simply use X number of average day's ranges to determine the stop loss, like I did last week.
4. My current "mildly bullish risky assets for a summer consolidation" view is low conviction, so it doesn't factor in as a strong "pro."

When all is said and done, I like the trade on both time horizons. The cons are not overly concerning. For 50in50, I will follow the short-term trade and I can also choose to do the trade in my 401k as an investment for optimal tax treatment because buying a trust at a discount like this is generally an unlimited time horizon, no stop loss kinda trade.

The parameters for the trade are: Buy 5 clips of GBTC, one at the close of each day next week (20% of $2,000 P&L risk per day so total $ at risk for the trade will be 2000). Therefore the average close for those 5 days will be my entry point.

The stop loss gets a bit complicated because you need to risk manage each clip as you get in, but for the sake of simplicity here let's just use the average rate of the five tickets and subtract 2.5 average day's ranges to get the stop loss. An average day's range in GBTC since January 2021 is 5.9% so the stop loss will be at entry minus 14.6% or average price X 0.854.

Take profit on July 31 or +30%, whichever comes first.

Conclusion

Simple frameworks are excellent tools. Nothing I'm describing in here is rocket science! It's more like 6th-grade 1/2 credit Life Skills Class type stuff. But it's important to have processes and frameworks that help you get to the root of the problem so that you don't get bogged down by information overload.

Use pros and cons to identify your thesis and compare it to the alternative hypothesis. This simple process can help you make better decisions.

Trading combines many fields, such as economics, behavioral science, probability, gambling, psychology, statistics, and decision theory. Incorporate literature and theories from all those fields (and others) to improve your trading.

For example, if you want to learn more about decision making, check out: *Thinking in Bets* (Annie Duke) and *Predictably Irrational* (Dan Ariely).

Week 20: Don't Get Squozen

How to structure equity shorts for max profit and min risk of ruin.

Update on previous trades

There is a lesson on variance in the recent LLY trade so I just want to point this out. The short LLY trade from week 17 was within 1 cent of the take profit! 283.11 was the low and my take profit was 283.10! Unreal. In real life, it is very unlikely that I would let a trade touch within one cent of a TP and then sit there and watch it take out my stop loss, but in this exercise, I'm not doing any real-time adjustments for logistical reasons. Check out the chart:

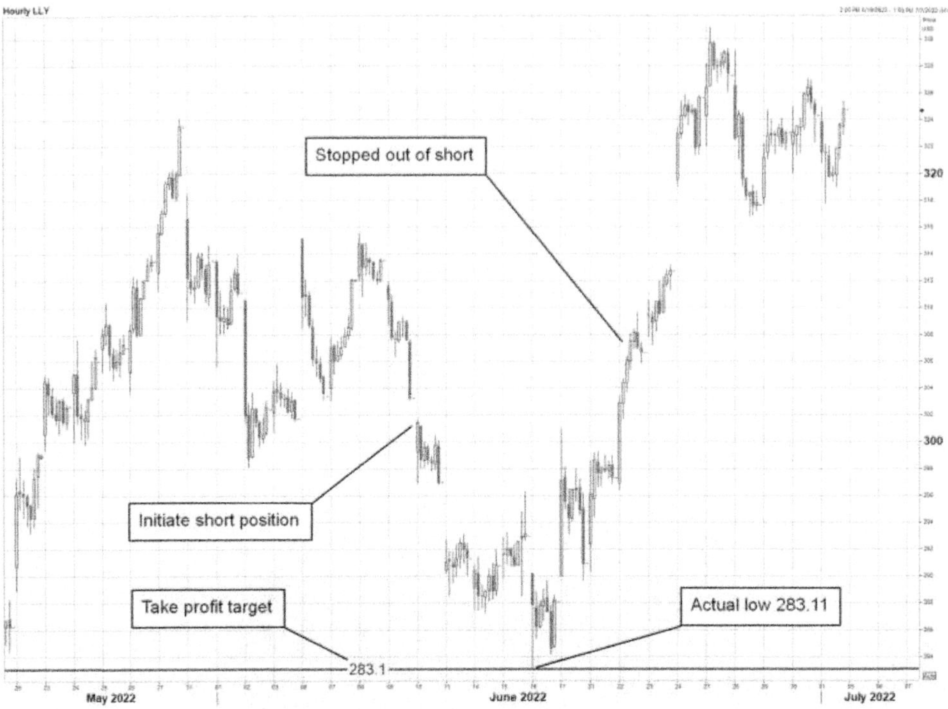

And here are the results of the trades so far (table below). I also included the stats for what would have happened if the LLY trade hit the TP instead of the SL so that you can see that even in a sample of 19 trades, the results can be sensitive to a single outcome.

	Entry date	L/S	Asset	Entry	USD at risk	Stop loss	Take profit	Exit or current level	P&L	Exit date	Holding period (days)	Notes
1	2/9/22	Short	XAUEUR	1,602	2,000	1,702	1,421	1,704	(2,000)	28-Feb	19	
2	2/16/22	Short	CLK2	90.50	1,000	95.45	79.05	95.55	(2,000)	1-Mar	13	
3	2/21/22	Short	DOCS	56.00	2,000	60.51	50.21	60.58	(2,000)	28-Feb	7	Wrong stop loss.
4	2/25/22	Long	BTC	39,200	2,000	31,400	49,800	39,200	-	14-Mar	17	
5	3/1/22	Long	BTC	43,400	2,000	38,900	49,800	38,870	(2,000)	14-Mar	13	
6	3/8/22	Long	EWC	37.85	2,000	35.19	44.80	39.65	1,353	11-Apr	34	
7	3/14/22	Long	XPO May $60 puts	2.60	2,000	-	53.50	6.10	2,692	18-Apr	35	
8	3/28/22	Short	NQ	14,970	2,000	15,660	13,344	13,908	3,078	18-Apr	21	
9	4/4/22	Long	TWTR	50.85	2,000	45.84	57.77	45.80	(2,000)	13-Apr	9	
10	4/11/22	Long	ASHR	32.18	2,000	29.84	36.44	29.80	(2,000)	25-Apr	14	Wrong stop loss.
11	4/18/22	Long	ESM2	4,381	2,000	4,279	4,579	4,276	(2,000)	5-May	17	
12	4/25/22	Long	ARKK	45.67	2,000	29.00		41.22	(534)	*1-Jul*	67	
14	5/15/22	Long	BTC	28,500	2,000	24,900	39,300	24,900	(2,000)	13-Jun	29	
15	5/18/22	Long	JAN23 CVNA 20 put	4.70	1,500	-	-	6.50	574	*1-Jul*	44	
15	5/18/22	Long	JAN23 RBLX 40 call	7.00	1,500	-	-	7.50	107	*1-Jul*	44	
16	5/27/22	Short	ETHBTC	0.061	2,000	0.077	0.033	0.055	750	*1-Jul*	35	
17	6/6/22	Short	LLY	297.99	2,000	306.25	283.10	306.25	(2,000)	22-Jun	16	Low was 1 cent from the take profit!!!!!!!
18	6/14/22	Long	TY	114.56	2,000	112.84	118.00	118.00	4,000	30-Jun	16	
19	6/24/22	Long	GBTC	12.77	2,000	10.90	16.60	12.25	(555)	*1-Jul*	7	

Total P&L	**(6,533)**
Winners	**7**
Losers	**11**
Win%	**39%**
avgWIN	**2,781**
avgLOSE	**(2,000)**
avg holding period	**24**

Total P&L	(928)
Winners	8
Losers	10
Win%	44%
avgWIN	2,946
avgLOSE	(1,709)
If LLY trade TP'd	

Trades in gray are still open.

I show this differential because it's important not to judge your own trading performance over a small sample. If you have been trading for five years with a 50% daily hit rate and you lose money six days in a row, that's probably variance. A bad week or even a bad month can be variance, not lack of skill. For a full discussion of the difference between variance and bad trading, see Chapter 11 of my book *Alpha Trader*.

The 50in50 results so far are not amazing, nor are they catastrophic. I am venturing into all kinds of trades where I have no particular edge just to show methods and tactics and ideas of how to look at the market. The idea is to apply solid strategies, tactics, and risk management in a market where you have an edge, as I do in short-term macro and FX. I will do another detailed update like this in Week 30.

Now let's talk about shorts.

Don't get squozen

The decimation of short-sellers in 2021 is one of many factors that set the table for the 2022 bear market. The capitulation of short sellers is an important signpost at the peak.

Whenever a fund blows up, or shuts down, it's worth considering whether it marks an extreme for that fund's style. The Russell Clark example is epic timing as was the closure of Julian Robertson's Tiger Global[30] at the **exact peak** of the 2000 tech bubble.

Short is not just the opposite of long

Shorting stocks presents unique risk management and trade structuring challenges and in today's 50in50 I will present a few simple structures and strategies you can use to short a stock while avoiding risk of ruin.

Shorting is hard

Three factors increase the degree of difficulty for shorts.

1. **You can only make 1X your money when you short, but you can lose much more.** When you are long you can make any multiple: 3X, 5X, 10X, etc. The mathematics work against you when you short a stock. You can never lose more than 100% on a long, but on a short, you can! If you short a stock at $5 and cut your losses at $100, you were risking 95 to make 5. That sounds extreme, but that's roughly what Melvin Capital did in GME.
2. **You pay a borrow fee plus any dividends the stock pays out while you are short.** You get paid to own stock and you must pay to short it. When you pay to hold a trade, that's called negative carry. Cost of carry is meaningless on short-term trades but adds up fast over time.
3. **Stocks generally go up.** Since 1946, stocks go up on 53.4% of all days, 60% of all months, and 71.6% of all years.

Not only are you peeing into the wind when you short a stock, you are paying a fee to do so! As such, the bar to short any stock must be high.

Defense first

Let's assume you have a company you want to short. Before you can pick a trade structure, you need to answer a bunch of questions about the microstructure of the stock you want to short. This allows you to play defense and protect against disaster.

- Is the stock liquid or illiquid? Check daily volume, bid/offer, volatility, and volatility of volatility.
- Does the stock have a history of gaps? Download OHLC data for the stock into Excel and create a formula for "today's open minus yesterday's close." What are the

---

[30] https://www.nytimes.com/2000/03/31/business/the-end-of-the-game-tiger-management-old-economy-advocate-is-closing.html

five largest gaps? This will give you a sense of your gap risk, though remember it's backward-looking and you should apply logic and common sense to consider whether a large gap is more likely in future.

- Is the stock a takeover candidate? If yes, don't short it. It's not worth the risk, no matter how bad you think the company is. Peloton would be a good example here. Sure, it's been an incredible short, but since it crossed $50 or so, the risk of a buyout was too high. Yes, you missed a big short by avoiding it, but that's life. If you want to be a good risk manager, sometimes you need to pass up positive EV opportunities in order to avoid tail risk.
- Are there any binary outcomes (like a drug approval for a biotech) that could rip your face off? If yes, do not short.
- What is the current short interest? If you go to a page like https://www.marketwatch.com/tools/screener/short-interest you can see the most shorted stocks. There is a conundrum here because the most-shorted stocks are most-shorted for a reason. They are crappy companies! But the most-shorted stocks are the most dangerous shorts because short interest is gasoline for a big explosion. My view is generally that it's not worth it to short the heavily-shorted stocks. Again, the trades are positive EV with a big tail risk. Not worth it!
- Is the stock trading below 10 bucks? Low-priced stocks have more topside convexity because retail likes them better.
- Are there options on the stock? If there are options to trade, you have more ways to play the downside.

These are practical questions that will determine your ability to rigorously manage your risk with a high level of certainty around your max downside. No matter how juicy a short looks, my philosophy is that if you're not sure if you can effectively manage your P&L risk, just pass. There are thousands of trading opportunities. Let someone else sell the tails. That's not the way to play the long game.

Structuring the trade

The best way to trade a bearish stock view depends on various factors, specifically your ability to identify the timing of a possible move, and your estimate of the size of the move.

Note: While what I am writing here today is about stocks, many of the trade structuring concepts apply to all asset classes. In particular, the question: "how far and how fast?" is the key input to the decision on whether to trade delta one (cash), or via an options structure (derivatives). For more on the question of whether to use cash or options, please read Week 6.

The two big questions are:

1. How much do you expect the stock to fall?
2. Do you have a specific time frame or catalyst in mind?

In other words: **How far and how fast?**

Very roughly speaking, there is an appropriate strategy for each speed and size of the expected drop. To take the most extreme example: if you expect a stock to drop to zero tomorrow, options will give you much more leverage and you don't have to worry much about timing or time decay (theta). And you want the farthest possible strike because that will give you the most leverage.

In contrast, if you expect a stock to do nothing for a while and eventually drop 20 percent or so at some unknown time... Options are not going to look as good and low-delta strikes are certainly no bueno.

This article is not a deep-in-the-weeds options lesson, it assumes you know the basics. But let me just give a quick definition of delta here because it's a critical term that you need to fully understand. There are two main ways I think about delta:

Delta is the market-implied odds that the option will finish in the money. So a 25 delta put has a 25% chance of finishing in the money. A 50 delta option is at the money and has a 50/50 shot of finishing in the money. There are nuances around skew and so on but for our purposes, this is a good, simple way to think about delta.

Delta tells you how much your P&L will change as the stock moves. For example, if you have 1 contract (representing 100 shares) of a 20 delta put option... Your delta is short 20 shares. Your P&L here will go up and down like you're short 20 shares of the stock. If the stock goes up $1 intraday, you will lose roughly $20. This is not exactly true because your delta changes as the stock moves. And volatility can change. But it's a good way to estimate how much exposure an option will give you when you buy it. For example, if you buy a 30-delta put option on 1000 shares of AMZN, your P&L risk today is similar to your P&L risk if you were short 300 shares.

The main factors that determine an option's delta are: 1) the distance from market level to the strike, 2) how much time is left on the option, and 3) the stock's volatility.

Four paths

Let's go through the four main ways a stock can go down and discuss the best structure for each. There is no correct answer, but this will give you a good starting point for how to think about trade structuring around single-name equity shorts.

There are four paths to consider:

1. Big drop, soon
2. Small or medium drop, soon
3. Big drop, eventually
4. Small or medium drop, eventually

Let's imagine we want to short Tesla. We think it's an overvalued stock that has not repriced like the other 2021 retail bubble favorites like PLTR, SQ, ZM, GME, AMC, SHOP, ARKK, PTON, bitcoin, etc.

TSLA trades at 12X sales compared to AMZN at 4X sales, UBER at 2X sales, and most automakers under 1X sales. ***I'm really just using TSLA as an example here and this lesson is about structuring a short when you're already bearish.*** **That said, I do believe that reversion to a lower valuation is a reasonable thesis** as TSLA lays off employees and their CEO forecasts recession[31], sending a signal that massive YoY sales growth is set to slow even as June was a great month for production numbers. Rapidly growing companies aren't usually laying off workforce or forecasting recession. And companies trading at 12X sales need to grow fast or disappoint.

For the sake of this lesson, it doesn't matter if you are bullish or bearish TSLA. The point is to think about the pros and cons of the different ways to play a bear view on a stock. TSLA is just a useful example.

Say I want to risk $20,000 on my bearish TSLA view (this is not the normal $ at risk for 50in50, but it's easier to use a larger number to explain these options examples). To give you an idea of how different strategies will pay off, I made two P&L graphs so you can see how different speed and size of moves in the stock will determine the right strategy.

In each chart, I compare shorting the stock (with a stop loss at $820) to an at-the-money put, a lower delta put, and a put spread. A put spread is a strategy where you buy a put, and sell a put with a lower strike to cheapen things up. In a put spread, your P&L is capped once you hit the bottom strike.

---

[31] https://www.theguardian.com/technology/2022/jun/21/elon-musk-says-a-us-recession-is-inevitable

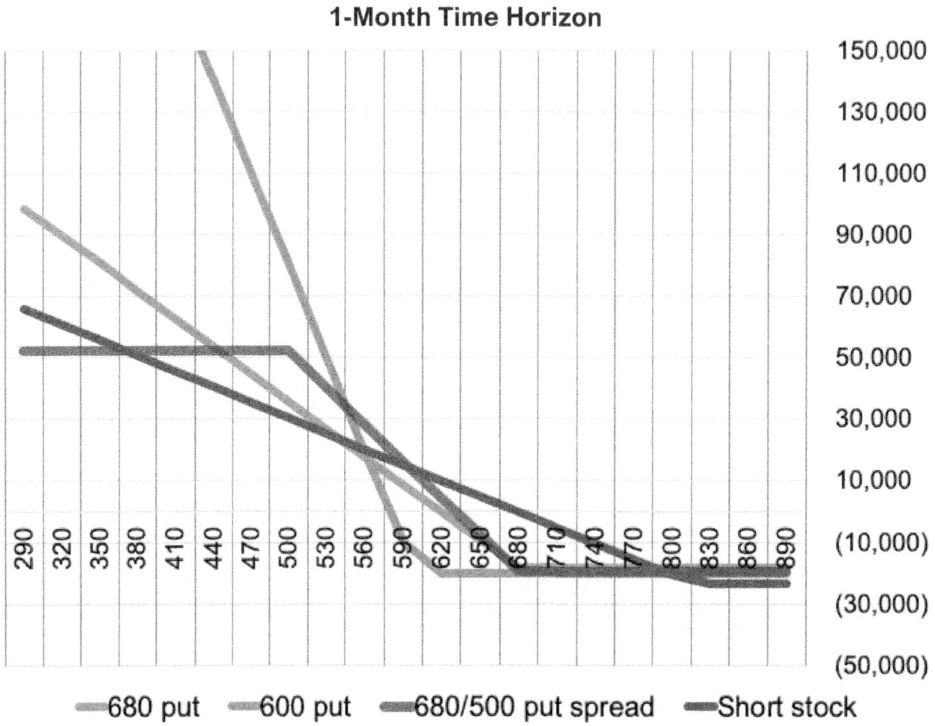
1-Month Time Horizon
150,000
130,000
110,000
90,000
70,000
50,000
30,000
10,000
(10,000)
(30,000)
(50,000)
290
320
350
380
410
440
470
500
530
560
590
620
650
680
710
740
770
800
830
860
890
680 put
600 put
680/500 put spread
Short stock

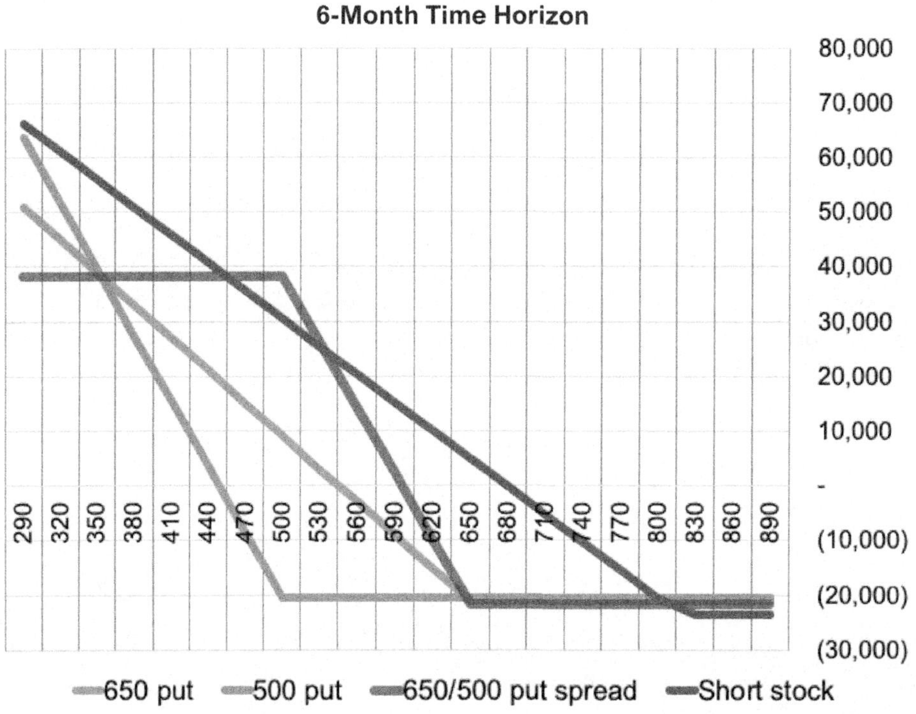
6-Month Time Horizon
80,000
70,000
60,000
50,000
40,000
30,000
20,000
10,000
-
(10,000)
(20,000)
(30,000)
290
320
350
380
410
440
470
500
530
560
590
620
650
680
710
740
770
800
830
860
890
650 put
500 put
650/500 put spread
Short stock

Takeaways:

1. You get much more leverage on the one-month option trade vs. the six-month trade. Check out the y-axis on each chart. You will always get paid much, much more if you can nail the timing, but if it was easy, it would not have such a huge payoff!
2. There is a point at which the put on its own massively outperforms the put spread. This is when the sloping lines break above the one that flatlines as it heads to the left.
3. If you nail the move on the 1-month option, it pays way better than the short stock position, but on the 6-month trade, it takes a huge move before the option is worthwhile. This makes sense.
4. Note how the "short stock" line is above the other lines in most cases in the 6-month time horizon. The longer the option, the more the payoff just looks like a cash position, where you are paying a premium so you don't have to worry about getting stopped out. This staying power has value. If TSLA goes from here, to \$850, to \$400 in the next six months, the option is gold and the cash short is a loser because it got stopped out at \$820. This is an important takeaway: **Short-dated options for leverage, long-dated options for staying power.** It's a spectrum, of course, and you could look at the 3-month option here as a compromise, for example.

There are, of course, many other options strategies. I'm covering the big ones here and to be honest, I question whether many other strategies are necessary. If you know how to short a stock, buy ATM puts, buy low-delta puts, and buy put spreads, you are pretty well set. **Selling naked calls, for example, is a recipe for disaster** and not a good bearish strategy for any trader who cares about risk of ruin.

Every time you are deciding how to structure a trade, you should build a payoff diagram like this. Then, think about the possible paths you think your stock could follow and which path is most likely. Then, match the payoffs on the chart to the path or paths you see as most likely, and choose your structure.

Note: Catalysts are generally priced in by the options market. You are going to pay a ton more for a short-dated option through earnings than you would pay for a short-dated option when nothing is going on. The dream scenario is when you find a catalyst that the market **isn't** pricing in correctly. This could be a major chart breakout, a poorly-understood catalyst (for example, a scheduled product announcement from a competitor that could hurt your stock, a court ruling that isn't well-known, etc.). Not every catalyst is well-understood and priced in by the market.

There are plenty of ways to be correct on your bearish stock view and still lose money. For example:

1. Your cash position gets stopped out before the stock goes down.
2. You buy a put and the stock falls after the option expires.
3. You buy a put and the stock ends up at your strike price (but not below) at expiry. This is called pinning the strike. It's one of the most frustrating outcomes because if you bought a 25-delta put and then pinned it, you correctly forecast a large move lower and yet you lost your entire option premium.
4. You short the stock, but it takes forever to fall and you pay more to borrow the stock and cover dividends than you make on the short position.

Choosing a strategy

The thesis for this lesson is pretty basic: We want to short TSLA on still-high valuation, catch up to peers, and a bearish chart formation. When we play the valuation game, we are looking for a large drop on an unknown time horizon, so there is no logic to buying a short-dated option.

Then again, looking at the chart of TSLA, it's been in a steady trend lower since mid-April and it looks to be consolidating in a nice bear pennant:

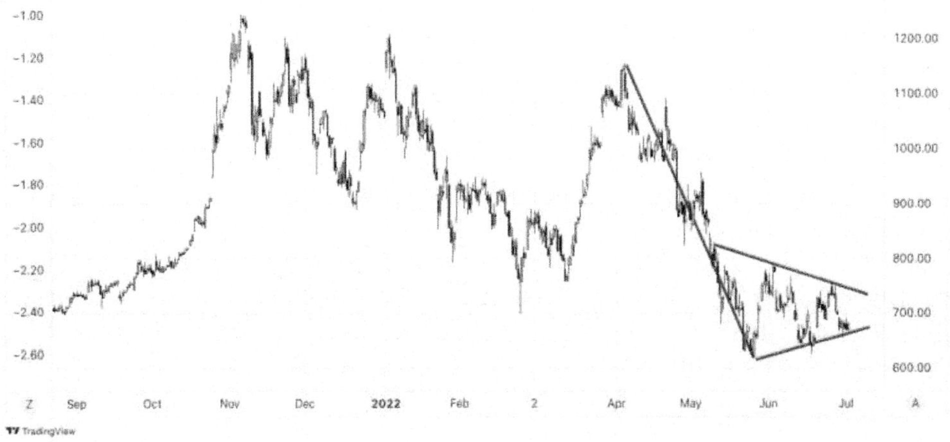

In theory, we might say that the narrowing triangle helps us with timing as breakout odds rise as the triangle narrows. This is reasonable, but I'd still be worried about two or three more weeks of rangebound consolidation like we saw in February 2022 and again in June. Therefore, the best structure here is to simply short the stock.

If we're going to short a stock, we first need to go through the checklist of no go's from the "defense first" section earlier in this note. Here is how it looks for TSLA: The stock is extremely liquid and high-priced, topside gaps do not suggest risk of ruin (the three biggest topside gaps in TSLA over the past 12 months are 10%, 9% and 6%). Risk of ruin is close to nil. It's not a takeover candidate, there are no binary outcomes of note, and short interest is tiny, just 3% of the float. So we're good. What about the risk of getting stopped out before the thing collapses?

The biggest disadvantage of shorting a stock instead of buying puts is that you might get stopped out before the stock drops. My view is that if we go back above $800, the idea is probably wrong anyway because that will take the price back up and out of the triangle. Therefore, in this case, the staying power offered by a put option is probably not worth much. That is, this is the kind of setup where TSLA should just keep going lower as it breaks down out of the triangle. Otherwise, the idea is probably wrong. I would rather take the risk of getting stopped out at $820 than take the risk that TSLA range trades for another month before it dumps and I have spent a load of cash on a worthless option. There are always tradeoffs when choosing a structure.

Choose your weapon

Once you decide you are bearish a particular stock, you need to choose a structure. It's all about the tradeoffs between timing, leverage, and the probability of getting stopped out on cash shorts. To summarize this note, here are the pros and cons of the four main ways to structure a single name equity short:

	Pros			Cons		
	1	2	3	1	2	3
Short the stock	No upfront cost	Timing not as critical	Profit increases as stock falls all the way to zero	Can get stopped out before the stock falls	Gap risk–you might lose more money than you expected (risk of ruin?)	Negative carry
Near or at-the-money put	Don't have to worry about getting stopped out	Don't need a huge move lower to get to your strike	Liquid with volume and reasonable bid/ask, usually	The longer dated the option, the greater the chance the stock goes down but you still lose money	A straight cash position is often better for most outcomes	Not much leverage
Low delta put		Big leverage gives it home run potential	High % returns when you are correct	Easy to be correct (stock falls) but lose money (it didn't fall enough)	Longer dates can still be expensive	Timing has to be good
Put spread		Cheaper than vanilla and nice compromise between low delta and ATM strategies	Less premium and more precision if you have a high-confidence downside target	P&L is capped by the short strike	Wide bid/offer if you change your mind it's expensive to square up	Can be tricky to manage short strike at expiry

Conclusion

We aren't clear on the timing of the TSLA short, so we don't want to touch options. **We go short the stock on the Monday open ($680 approx) with a stop loss at $820 and a take profit at $437** (TSLA gapped higher through that level as it commenced its voyage moonward in late 2020 so it's a nice round trip target). Risking $140 to make $243 on a position of 14 shares (~$2,000 at risk).

Short TSLA is a bit of a hedge for the ARKK long from Week 12. I don't have a strong view on broad market direction right now so partially-hedged feels reasonable. It's incredible how badly ARKK has performed when we consider that Cathie Wood's biggest holding and loudest rah-rah in 2021 was TSLA. Craziness. Maybe it's time for "TSLA down / ARKK up" mean reversion as most of Wood's holdings are thoroughly bombed out at this point. Something to consider.

Week 21: Overshoots and Pullbacks

Use mean reversion to improve entries and exits

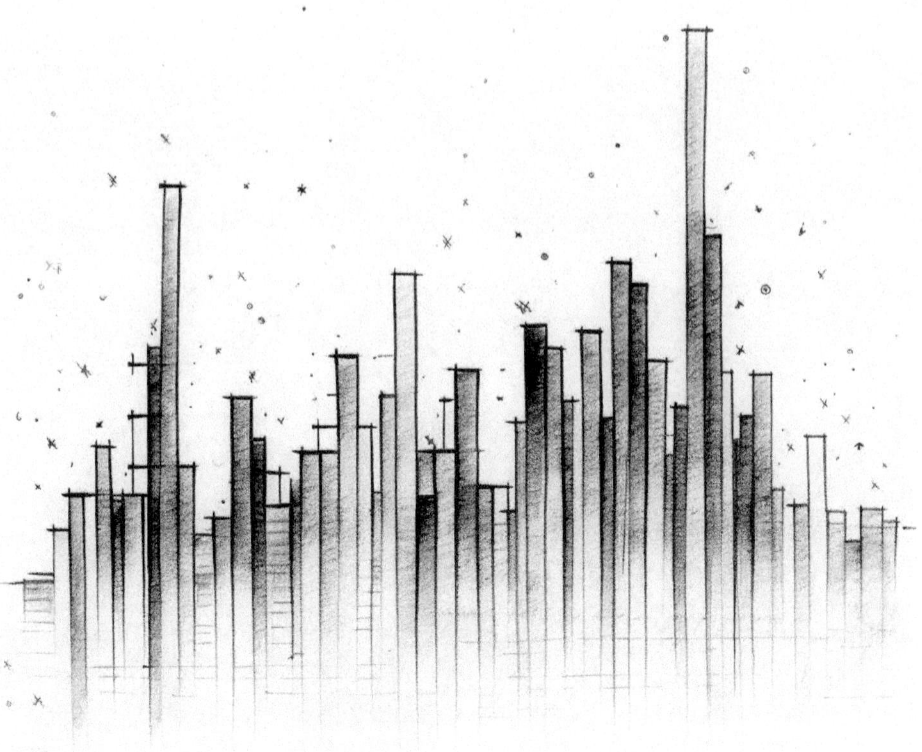

Update on Previous Trades

RBLX massively outperforming CVNA (good!—see chart). GBTC ripping ($16.60 TP target looks possible soonish).

50in50 is on a good run.

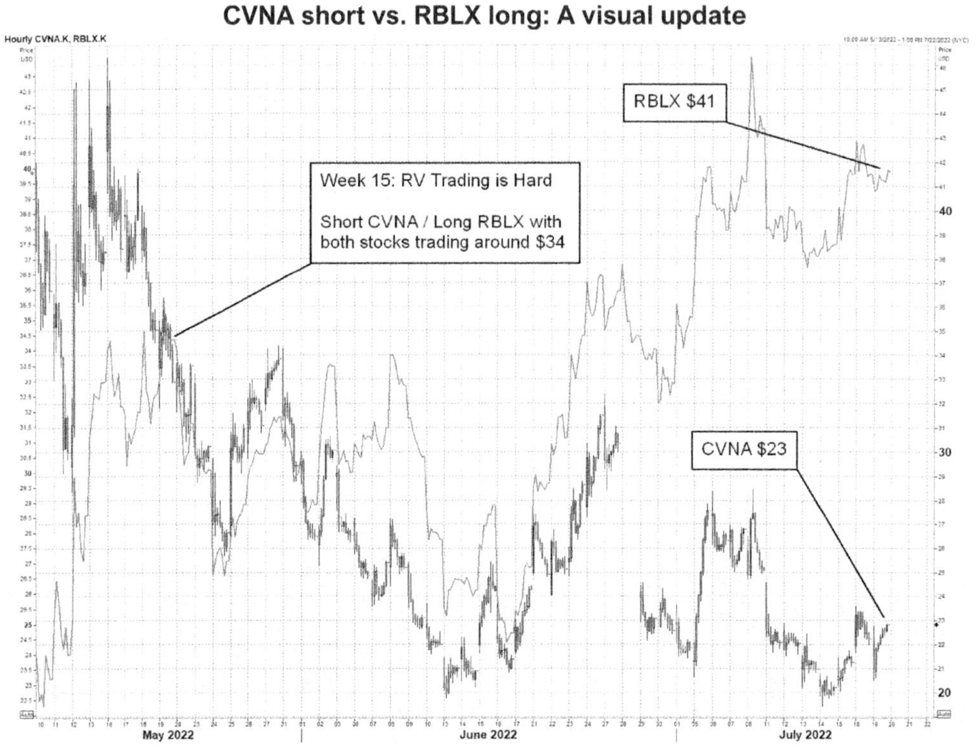

ARKK vs. TSLA not doing much. Let's talk mean reversion.

Overshoots and pullbacks

Excellent traders toggle successfully between trend following and mean reversion strategies. It is not always a good time to play breakouts and it's not always a good time to follow the trend. The ability to detect and switch between regimes is one of the hallmarks of a great trader.

Today, I'll focus on mean reversion. While some markets mean revert more than others, all markets display some combination of trend and mean reversion over time. Prices do not move in a straight line—even in a raging up trend, price will frequently revert back towards a rising trend or moving average.

For your info, there are generally two ways people think about mean reversion. One: price goes up or down, and then pulls back. Two: when two assets with similar underlying drivers diverge and then mean revert back towards each other. The first one is what we are talking about today (price mean reversion), the second one (reversion to "fair value") is more in the realm of correlation, intermarket, and lead/lag trading. That's a topic I write about quite often, but not today.

Snooping and Mining for Mean Reversion

There's a ton of research out there on mean reversion and there are systems that trade it, but one major challenge in testing and trading mean reversion systems is that they are highly regime sensitive. That is, you can easily find and backtest highly profitable mean reversion strategies but that does not mean they will work in the future, out of sample. Trading systematic mean reversion can be like picking up pennies in front of a steam roller (synthetic short carry or synthetic short options, essentially) or it can be fooled by randomness.

To give you a sense of what I mean, take a look at the P&L of the simplest possible mean reversion strategy which is long or short 1 unit as follows: (if market is down today, go long tomorrow / if market is up today, go short tomorrow). This simple UP / DOWN strategy could be traded in real life with minimal slippage in many markets. Here's the cumulative P&L of the strategy in AUDUSD:

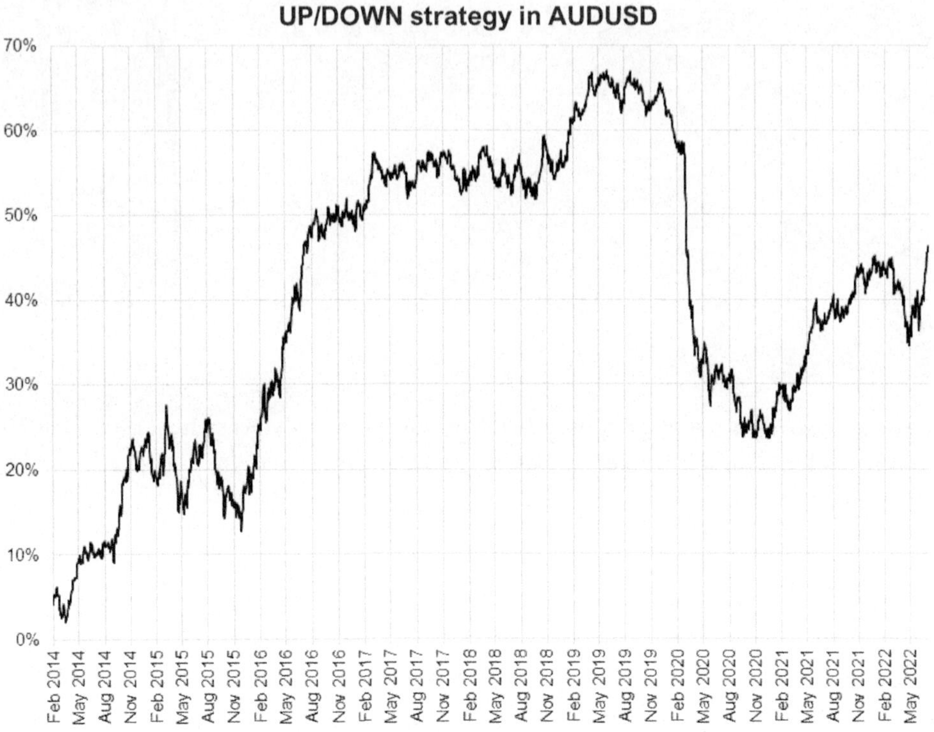

From 2016 to 2019, it looked pretty good but then when COVID happened, **not so much**. The COVID regime shift erased three years of returns in three months.

In contrast, **a good human trader would not be in mean reversion mode in March 2020**, even if they were mostly trading mean reversion in AUD in prior years. The game had changed and that was obvious. This P&L path for AUD mean reversion is a good example of how low and falling volatility regimes favor mean reversion. AUDUSD volatility fell steadily from 2016 to 2019 then exploded through COVID.

Here's the P&L of the same strat in GME common stock:

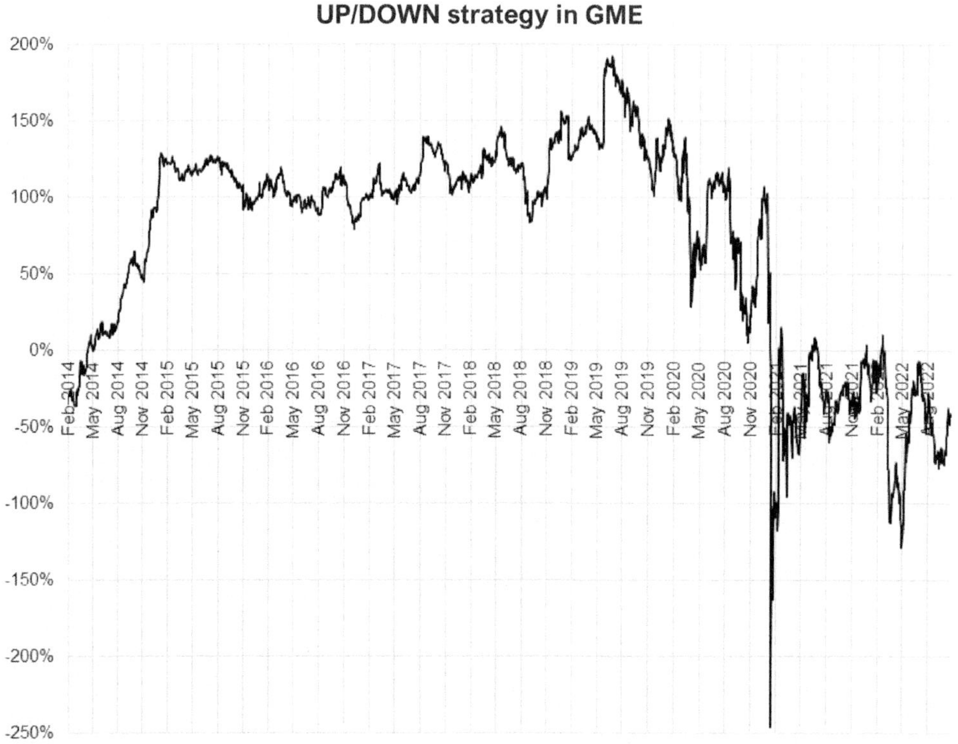

Mean reversion is not a good strategy during tail events! My point here is to show that you want to focus on mean reversion strategies more when volatility is low and there isn't some crazy thing happening in the world.

If Russia invades Ukraine, don't sell oil just because it's overbought. If a biotech's drug passes Phase 3 and it's a big surprise, don't short the stock just because it's overbought. **In tail and high volatility moments, overbought and oversold mean nothing.** While you can combine trend with mean reversion (as I'll show later)… Remember that a market trending upward, and a market dislocating higher on a major news event are two completely different kettles of fish.

Three ways to trade mean reversion

Now, let's look at three ways to profit from mean reversion. Most implementations of mean reversion involve some form of technical analysis and as I have explained in my other books[32] and in this one, I use techs for tactics and risk management, not for strategy. **I never get a trade idea from a chart.**

My ideas will come from macro, positioning, behavioral factors, events, and other inputs, and then I will use techs (like mean reversion signals) to fine-tune my tactics and maximize my leverage. Entering a trade at some random time just because you decided you're bullish mid-range is often not optimal. Deciding you're bullish, doing nothing for a while, then buying the highs after a 2% rally because of FOMO and you "knew this was going to happen!" is *definitely* not optimal.

Instead, when you have a market view, you should mentally fly up out of the trees, and into the clear sky above... To take a long, calm look at the forest below. What are the best tactics you can use to implement your 5-star strategy? That's where technical analysis can help you.

Remember that when you put on a trade, there is often a tension between "tightest possible stop loss for maximum leverage" and "risk of getting stopped out due to noise." Getting to the right answer takes some work.

Here are three mean reversion strategies you can use to better fine-tune your entry and exit tactics.

1: Pullback to a moving average

You are bullish XYZ but it just made a double top and seems to be losing momentum. You generally like going with the trend, not against it, but you hate the current entry point. A simple approach is to find one or two moving averages, drop them on a chart, and wait for XYZ to pull back to that moving average (MA).

Avoid false precision with moving averages. Whatever moving average fit in the past will probably not fit perfectly in the future, so don't waste time optimizing whether the 241-day MA or the 266-day MA is better. Find a moving average that defines the trend pretty well, and use it.

Another approach is to use two moving averages and scale into 1/2 your position at each. This helps with the false precision problem, and also avoids the all-or-nothing problem where the moving average is at (say) 146.10 and you bid there for your whole position and the low is 146.16.

Here is an example. It's June 2, 2022, and you are bullish oil because of the war in Ukraine and Russia's squeeze on the European energy markets. But the chart looks like this:

---

[32] https://amzn.to/3rngGo3

NYMEX crude, Q4 2020 to early June 2022

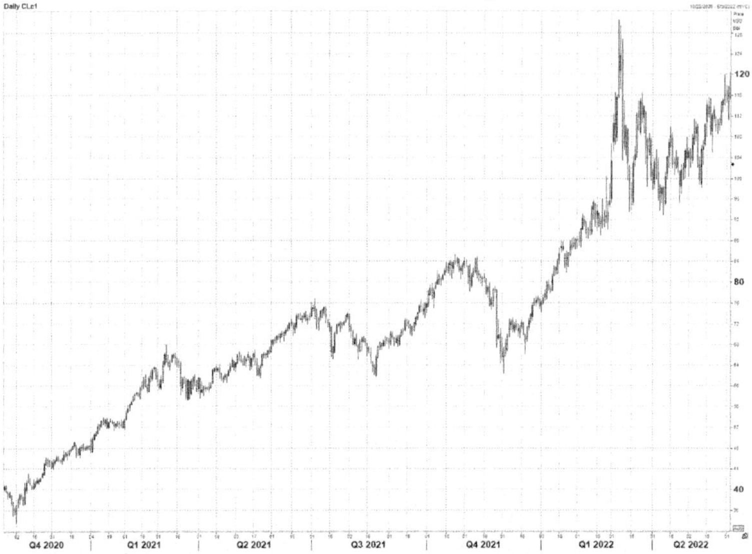

Oil is getting back toward the highs but not breaking through them and this just seems like a really bad entry point. As long as there is no peace treaty in Ukraine, you want to buy a dip.

Looking at the chart, you can see there is a slow trend in 2021, which was pretty smooth, followed by a steeper trend and a rip in 2022. You draw two moving averages on the chart, one that captures the lows of the first trend and one that catches the bottoms on the second, faster trend. Now the chart looks like this:

NYMEX crude, Q4 2020 to early June 2022 (with MAs)

Moving averages are 175-day and 265-day, to approximately catch the drops that defined trend higher.

You could also use trendlines in the exact way I am using MA's here, they tend to accomplish the same thing. I'm fitting my MA to the trend, so that's obviously conceptually similar to a trendline. Now, I have my "buy the dip" zone. I'll buy half at the first moving average line and half at the second one. Fast forward, and this is how the chart looks now.

NYMEX crude, Q4 2020 to now

Normally in educational things like this, someone would find an example where the price pulled back perfectly to the trendline and you would say "wow, what a great indicator" but in real life that might happen, or this might happen: Limit order at $94.40. Intraday low $95.50. Current price $103.50. Dang it! Sometimes you are going to miss your levels by a few ticks. That's life. This type of double moving average approach gives you a window or range to buy. In this case it's $87.80/$94.40.

Some people use more than two moving averages to further deal with the false precision problem. There is even the Guppy Multiple Moving Average system which I find is a bit nuts but produces super cool looking Mobius strip kinda charts like this:

GMMA of NYMEX crude

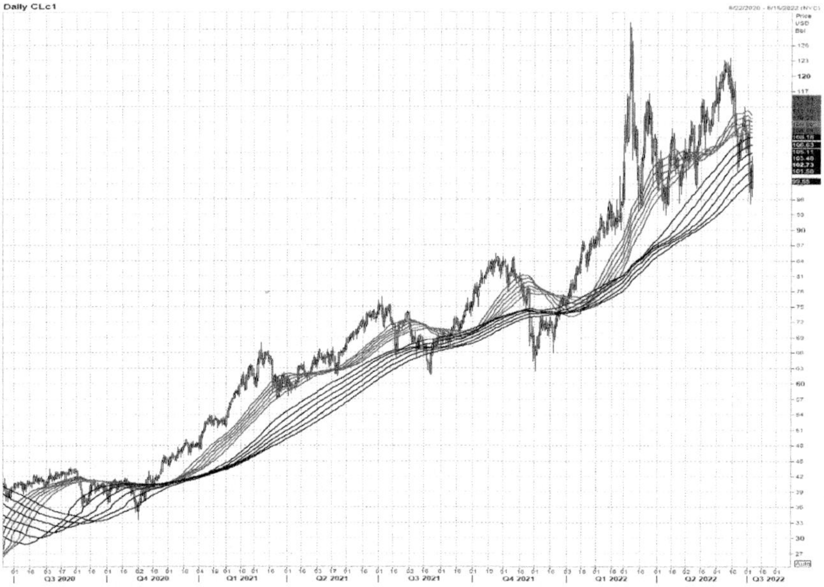

When we wait for a pullback to a moving average, we optimize our entry point based on the slope of the prior trend and avoid paying the highs or some random mid-range location. We benefit from mean reversion but stay with the direction of the trend.

2: The Deviation

If you want to play mean reversion directly and go against the trend, there are many overbought and oversold signals you can use. My favorite is called “The Deviation.” The technique is pretty simple, as usual. I take the price of the asset I’m trading and check how far it is from the 100-hour moving average. Then, I look as far back as possible and see if The Deviation tends to oscillate in a steady range or if it looks unreliable or random. For many markets, you will see that The Deviation tends to peak and trough around the same levels over and over as long as overall market volatility is fairly stable.

Here is an example using S&P minis. The top panel shows S&P 500 futures with 100-hour MA. The middle panel is the deviation from the 100-hour and the bottom panel shows buy / sell signal triggers if S&P is more than 3.5% above or below 100-hour MA.

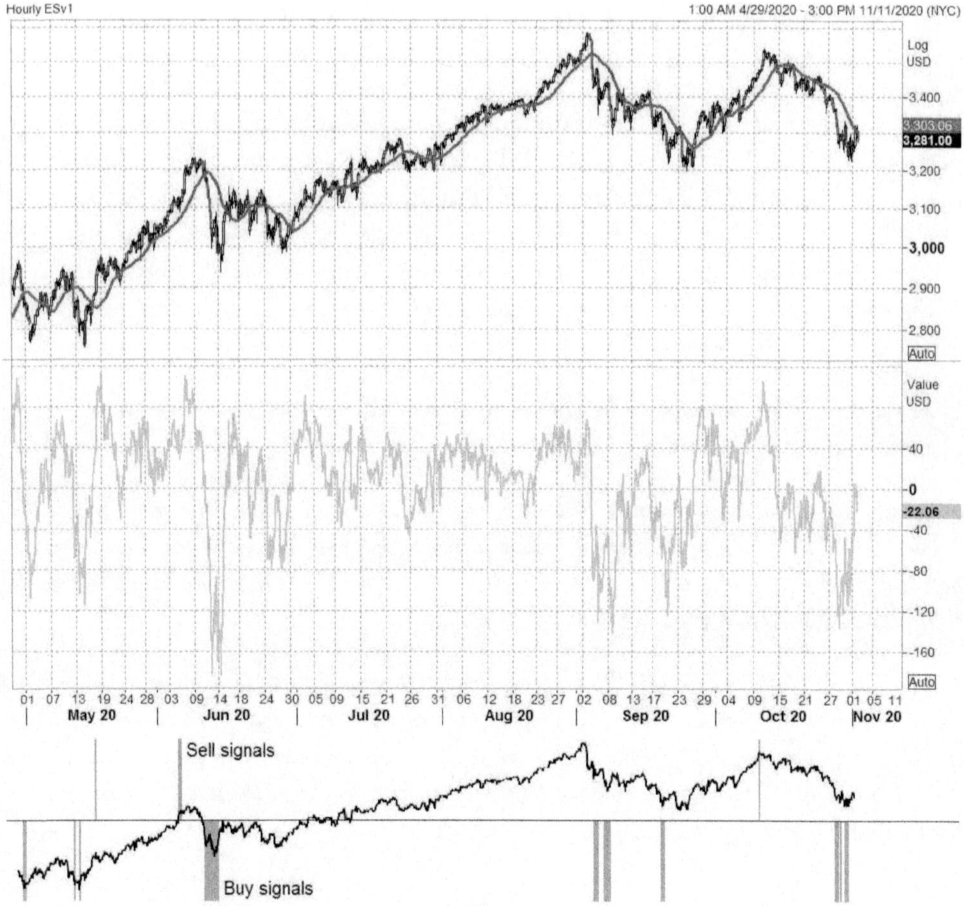

This is easy to set up on your trading system or in a spreadsheet. Use historical data to determine what the extremes are in The Deviation and then use those extremes going forward as reversal signals. In this case, I filtered for the 5% of most extreme values in the deviation and this represents a move in the S&P 500 of about 3.5%.

When using The Deviation, it is important to understand the skew of your market. Skew is the direction of the market that tends to happen faster and be more volatile. For example, stocks tend to sell off much more quickly than they rally, so you might want to use a more conservative entry point for your deviation signal on the downside or scale in gradually knowing that sell-offs can overshoot and are harder and more violent to fade. I use the Deviation regularly in my FX trading.

3: Relative strength index (RSI)

Every trader should have one or two indicators that tell them when their market is extremely oversold or overbought on the time horizon they trade. RSI is a standard indicator most people use, and the textbook strategy is that if it goes above 70, wait for it to fall back below 70 and then sell. I use it differently.

I take as much data as possible (using hourly data because that suits my trading time horizon) and find the extremes in the RSI going back as far as possible. I then calculate the top and bottom 5% most extreme and use these levels as "***get out no matter what***" levels. That is, if I'm long, and the RSI gets into the top 5% of the series, I cut. I find that at the mega RSI extremes, the risk of a reversal is too high so the risk-reward on staying in the trend is poor. If I am trying to trade against the trend, I will also use these mega extremes as an entry point.

Here's a super short excerpt from one of my dailies (December 2, 2020) where I use an extreme in the RSI to get short NZDUSD:

The textbook approach to trading RSI is to wait for it to rise above 70 and then fall back below 70 and then go short. I prefer to isolate the most extreme levels and use those as reversal points right away. While RSI is a trend indicator, generally, it can be an amazing reversal indicator at the MEGA extremes.

I sorted all the daily NZDUSD RSI data from 2010 to now and the most extreme readings occur when the RSI breaks above 75. That happened this week. With the dramatic repricing in NZ rates and the non-stop flood of good vaccine news, much goodness is in the price of NZDUSD now. The table below shows how the pair performed in the twelve instances where the RSI went above 75 (since 2010).

Date	x+1	x+3	x+5	x+10	x+20	x+30	x+60
average	0.0%	-0.4%	-0.8%	-0.7%	-0.7%	-2.0%	-2.7%
median	-0.1%	0.0%	-0.4%	-0.3%	0.1%	-1.1%	-1.2%
% of time it goes up	50%	50%	42%	42%	50%	33%	25%

x+1 means performance one day after the first RSI reading above 75, x+3 means three days later, x+5 means 5-day performance, etc.

You can see in this short example that if you isolate the times when the RSI is historically extreme, you can find points where you have high confidence to go the other way. When the NZD RSI is above 75, future performance is raging bearish as NZD averages a drop of 2.7% over the next 60 trading days and goes up only 25% of the time.

In this case, I was already bearish risky assets (NZD is a risky asset) so this just added to my thesis and gave me a way to play it. I went short NZDUSD at 0.7040 with a stop at 0.7111 and a take profit at 0.6911. A high RSI on its own would not be enough to get me involved, but it's a nice seed that might grow into a full trade idea.

Think about what you are doing

An important note about using overbought and oversold signals: ***think think think***. If the Fed just announced a massive QE program and stocks rip higher to extreme overbought… That is probably not a signal that it is time to go short. Things that are overbought can become more overbought and then more overbought again. Overbought on its own is not a reason to sell an asset. It's a warning sign that the future distribution of returns might be skewed lower and that's all.

An elevated RSI reading or a sexy stochastic are not reason enough to do a trade. Incorporate overbought and oversold indicators into your process and use them to fine-tune entries and exits, but don't be the trader who fades a move solely because "Too far, too fast, dude!" That is not a valid trading strategy. Remember we are using these technicals as guidance and tactical inputs and not as a systematic quantitative trading framework.

Long XME

Tony Greer writes a great daily macro letter with a focus on commodities at https://tgmacro.com. He has been long commods for a while and highlighted in his piece today that a ton of commodities have pulled back to support as defined by previous 2021 tops.

The Four Tops

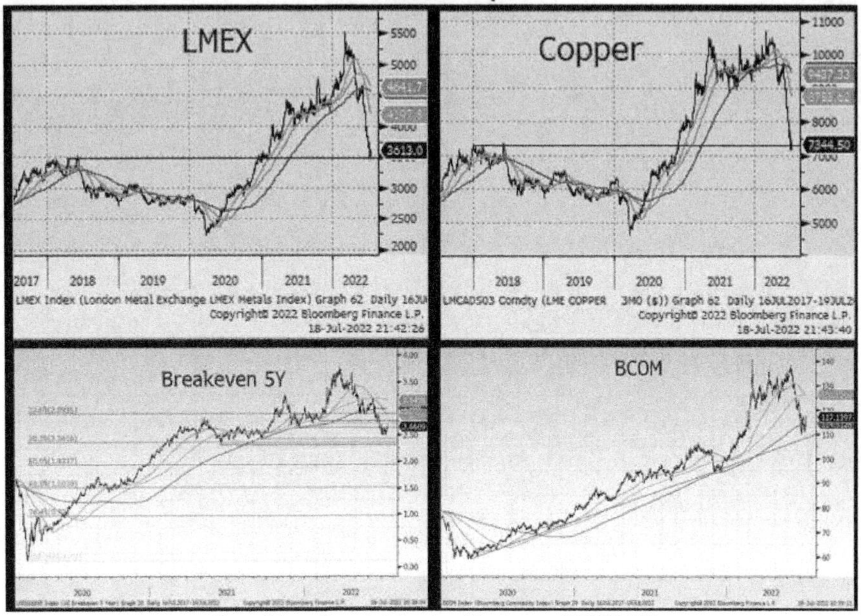

From Tony Greer's Morning Navigator (19JUL22)

Let's say I'm bullish commodities but flat right now. There's a lot of recession talk out there and maybe, just maybe the real story is more nuanced as the jobs market remains strong, inflation is still pretty sticky, and soft sentiment data could be overstating hard economic weakness due to the way consumers feel *real* vs. nominal pain. China and Europe are sucking wind, but maybe that's priced in by now?

So my thesis is bullish commodities as I think the worst of the bad economic vibes are priced in, and the mean reversion setup on XME (the metals ETF) looks especially attractive. The 504-day moving average (two years of daily data, because there are 252 trading days in a year) looks like this:

XME vs. 504-day Moving Average

This is a nice chart. Overshoot up to 66 then major mean reversion back to a moving average that has done an excellent job of defining the trends. I especially like how the break of the MA in Q4 2020 was an excellent straight-line breakout indicator. You also have a quadruple bottom $39/$40; that was the base for most of 2021.

Meanwhile, if we zoom in and look at The Deviation (from 100-hour MA), there is a consistent pattern where XME momentum fades when it gets more than $7 above or below the 100-hour. Here's the chart:

XME vs. 100-hour MA (top) and Deviation from 100-hour (bottom)

We held the oversold Deviation and have now rallied back above the 100-hour. The dream scenario is that we would have seen this when XME was at $40, trading $7 below the 100-hour, but I still like it here given the litany of supports and other greenlights.

There's so much to like here. In fact, if we zoom out to the daily chart again, you can see that a) we are bouncing off the old 2017 highs ($39.50—strong resistance becomes important support—see horizontal line)… And b) the deviation from the **100-day** has bottomed roughly the same place it bottomed during COVID.

This is not the PERFECT entry point; we have bounced a fair bit off the 504-day MA and we are way off the $7 deviation, but we also don't want to let perfect be the enemy of good. There are so many converging technical signals here, I'm not going to wait for another dip down to $40/$43.

Let's just plug our nose here and **buy at $44.50 with a stop loss at $34.95.** That stop loss is more than $7 below the current 100-hour MA, and it's well, well below the big support in the $39/$40 area. Note that of course, The Deviation and moving averages change over time, so the current Deviation is not the same as what it will be in a week. **Take profit at $63.70.**

Conclusion

Mean reversion is an important tactical tool that every trader needs to know how to use. I have suggested three specific methodologies in today's 50 in 50. Use these, and other mean reversion tactics, to focus your entries and exits, maximize leverage, and squeeze the most possible juice from your best trade ideas.

Week 22:
Time, the Forgotten Dimension

Being right or wrong, right away, lowers opportunity cost and preserves mental capital

Update on previous trades

Last week's XME idea is small ITM. The TSLA short is stopped out. CVNA vs. RBLX is still good. ARKK is boring.

I am cutting the short ETH vs. BTC trade because it makes no sense anymore. The crypto crash is over and ETH Merge excitement is building into 19SEP22 (this is fully explained in my MacroTactical Crypto piece at https://mtcbd.substack.com/p/bullishish. GBTC still doing well.

That's it. Let's talk about time.

Time, the Forgotten Dimension

In my travels on Twitter and the internet, I read many write-ups about trading every day. Naturally, after 25 years of doing this, and writing two books about it, I run into fewer "wow that's a great piece!" pieces. I do still find cool new stuff though. Always learning.

Today's 50in50 is mostly a guest post from a FinTwit Lord who goes by the handle "Horselover Fat". That is a reference to a Philip K. Dick novel, which made me like him right away. He's @Michigandolf on Twitter and his tag line is "Joking about life, serious about trading" which captures the vibe of his videos and Twitter. He trades a lot of ES and a bit of NQ and other stuff, and he likes talking and writing about trading much as I do.

Horse runs traderade.com. This is not a paid placement or endorsement, I have no financial or other relationship with Horse or Traderade. I just think the site is good and I like interacting with Horse. He's a smart guy, he's fun to talk to, and he knows what he's talking about.

Instead of me trying to explain Traderade, here is their landing page:

Horse wrote a piece a while ago that resonated with me because it addresses **a third dimension of risk management that I have always found prickly: Time**. How long do you leave a trade on if it's not getting stopped out but it's also not moving much into the green? This is an issue in FX when you trade pairs like AUDNZD and NOKSEK, as they can often sit there and do nothing for ages while you wait. Generally, my view is that you just wait for the plan to work, or not, but Fat provides some compelling logic in his piece for why that is not always optimal.

Many of these things come down to personal style and preference, but it's great to ingest as many viewpoints and approaches as possible and then digest what helps improve your process and discard what does not. Without further ado, I bring you (with permission) "Riffing on Risk" from the tradefat.com blog. I hope you like the piece! FYI, t*here are a few bad words in here. All typos are intentional.*

Riffing on Risk

by Horselover Fat

Since I started sharing with people how I trade, I've learned something that kind of surprised me:

Risk management is a difficult topic to discuss.

Probably because it means so many different things to different people. I often find myself feeling bad because I struggle to answer the most basic of questions people ask me, like "How many points should I risk on each trade?" or "How many contracts should I trade?"

I find myself thinking "Dude...I don't know!" I'm not you, I have no idea how you trade, what your goals are, what your experience is, etc. etc. etc. This is the conundrum with risk management: It's arguably the most important part of trading yet so universally difficult to teach because no two people trade exactly alike and there's no standard definition of what risk management means.

To help establish a baseline for this blog post, I'll define risk management in the most basic sense as **the process by which a trader attempts to avoid losing more than they make.**

If we can all agree on that basic definition, I'd like to share with you how I think about risk as a **trader**. As in, how I view risk management as a whole, not in regards to specific trades. As some of you know, I primarily trade futures intraday, but I also swing stocks and buy/sell options premium occasionally. So this blog post is about how I approach risk management in the long-term, which might help explain *why* I trade the way I do.

Ok, introduction over...let's get into it.

Let's start with 2 very basic factors in determining positional risk:

1. Likelihood that I am correct in my thesis
2. My position size

Logically, there should be a positive linear relationship between these two factors. The more likely I am to be correct when entering a trade, the larger my position size should be.

Some of you have watched the "How I Day Trade" videos I released and it should be no surprise that I approach trading like gambling. If you haven't seen the videos, I use the analogy of poker. In poker, you start with a stack of chips (i.e. your trading capital), and good poker players wait for hands where they know they have a statistical edge based on the strength of the cards. When they receive a "strong" hand they bet accordingly (i.e. heavily).

During tournament poker, a key part of any winning strategy is the ability to fold hands that are unlikely to win. To me, it's the same in trading. You have to be willing to cut losers and/or wait patiently for a setup that has demonstrated a high likelihood of success in the past. This core concept is what I'm referring to in Factor #1 (the likelihood that I'm correct in my thesis). If I'm entering a trade in the middle of nowhere, with no key Support/Resistance, no clear order flow information, etc., well that trade is essentially a coin toss...the market is just as likely to move against me as it is to move in my favor. To stay with the poker analogy, that's a hand I would fold.

But let's say the market is at a key area of confluence, and there's a VERY good chance it'll change direction, and I'm seeing order flow to support that thesis...well now I have a slight edge, so technically my position size should increase from whatever my minimum size currently is. We can represent this thinking with a basic graph:

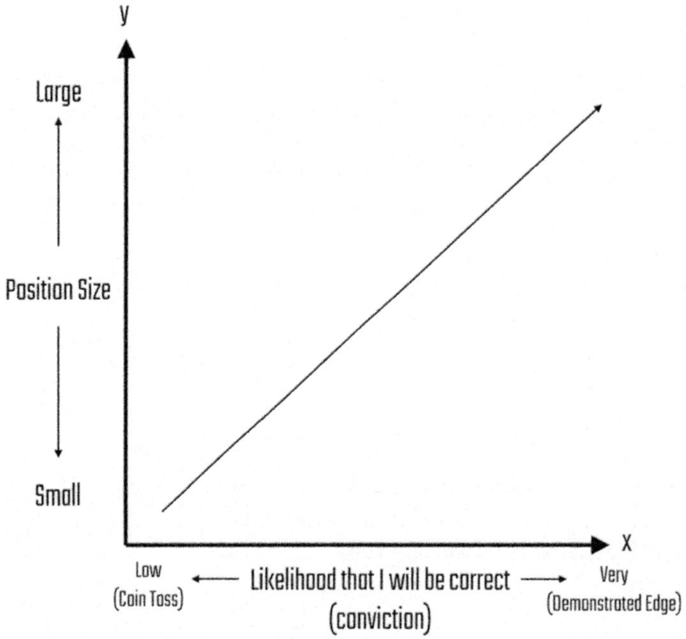

Wouldn't it be nice if risk management was just this simple? It's not. Now we have to introduce a third factor on our Z axis: **Time.**

Specifically, the time it will take me to know if I am right or wrong in my thesis.

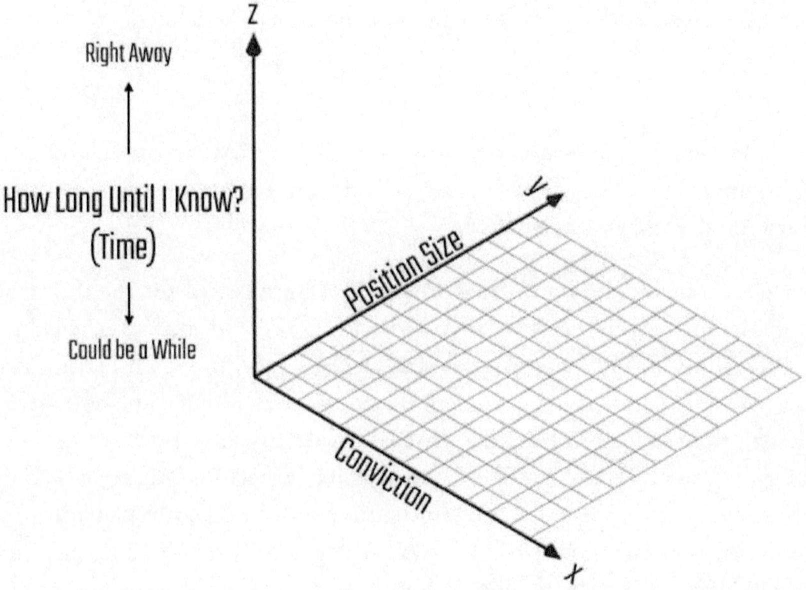

You might be thinking, "Horse what the hell does time have to do with risk management?"

That's a valid question. It has to do with opportunity cost.

Again, referencing our poker analogy, I have a limited stack of chips. I cannot place unlimited large bets with high conviction. I have to "manage" my chip stack, my capital. Therefore, I can't have too much tied up for an indeterminate amount of time hoping my thesis is correct. For me, it's sort of a "shit or get off the pot" scenario. The longer I have to wait to know if I'm correct absolutely impacts my likelihood of being correct AND my position size.

In my opinion, this is why macro investing is so difficult. You could enter a position with a very sound thesis, but over time things change and you end up being dead-ass wrong… through no fault of your own. The more time that elapses, the more opportunity for things to change that impact your initial thesis. Sometimes those unknown factors are positives, but more often than not they seem to be negatives because your initial thesis generally accounted for the positives, right?

Earlier I used the word "process" to describe risk management. I absolutely view it as an ongoing process. Things change in markets—therefore I need to be prepared to change as well in order to properly manage risk in the long term.

So back to opportunity cost. I'm a trader in this for the long haul, I need to adjust position sizes and stop-losses based on new information and time. Here's a couple of examples:

DWAC

One of my best equity trades this year was the DWAC SPAC (Note: Unintentional yet hilarious rhyme). Here's how it went down and how I thought about it in my weird "mental risk model" that we're discussing:

I developed a thesis for the trade after the markets were closed for the day. I heard the news about Trump possibly getting involved with a SPAC deal. I checked the price of DWAC after-hours and it was sitting almost at NAV (~$10), which had me scratching my head…why hadn't this thing run? Well the answer was simple: The news JUST broke and it wasn't priced in yet. So I decided that I'd take a very large position size pre-market the next day because I figured my likelihood of being correct (e.g. that it would pump on the news) was very high. I also factored in the time for our thesis to play out (our z axis) and determined that I'd know RIGHT away if I was right or not. The likelihood of it falling below NAV was extremely low, so it was "all systems go" for me and time to make an aggressive trade. The rest, as they say, is history.

GOLD

Another example that better showcases adjusting my risk management approach using the 3 factors we've discussed is a recent gold swing trade I took. In the final days of September, I started a large swing trade in gold micro futures (more on why I like the micros for gold some other time). The inflation narrative was picking back up, and even though gold is a bona fide piece of shit for an inflation hedge, my thesis was that the general public is too dumb to know that, plus gold had recently been beaten to a pulp and I figured it was oversold and there was an opportunity to BTFD.

I also figured portfolios would be getting rebalanced Sept 30-Oct 1 and IF gold was to run it would likely happen FAST due to EOM rebalancing. Additionally, the technicals looked good to me as well…so all of the factors I was looking for were there: A reasonable bull thesis based on the incompetence of Average Joe investors, likely bounce area from a technical perspective, and I'd know quickly if I was right or wrong due to EOM (plus some key FedTalks and inflation data drops were on the horizon).

Some of you may remember from my obnoxious Twitter bragging, but I practically bottom ticked it and gold took off on a nice ~7.5% bull run. But I'd be lying if I said I held that position full size for the entire run. I didn't.

I trimmed it and I'll tell you why: My mental model for long-term risk management changed. In early November gold started to slip again, so I naturally questioned 2 of my key factors: Likelihood of being correct and time.

At this point, I had been in the position for over a month and truthfully I thought it would run harder than it did given the intensity of the inflation narrative. The index futures were looking more and more attractive in early November, as I was anticipating seasonal bullishness and continuation of recent momentum. So things began to shift on my mental risk model. Did I really want that many of my "chips" tied up in that one "hand" anymore, or would it be better deployed somewhere else? I determined it was time to trim the position considerably…of course gold ended up ripping right after that because, well, fuck gold lol. But hopefully you get the point of this example: If I deem the likelihood of continuing to be correct has decreased AND the time it will take me to know is longer than anticipated, then I will actively manage my exposure (risk) and make changes.

The Evolution of my Swing Trade in Gold

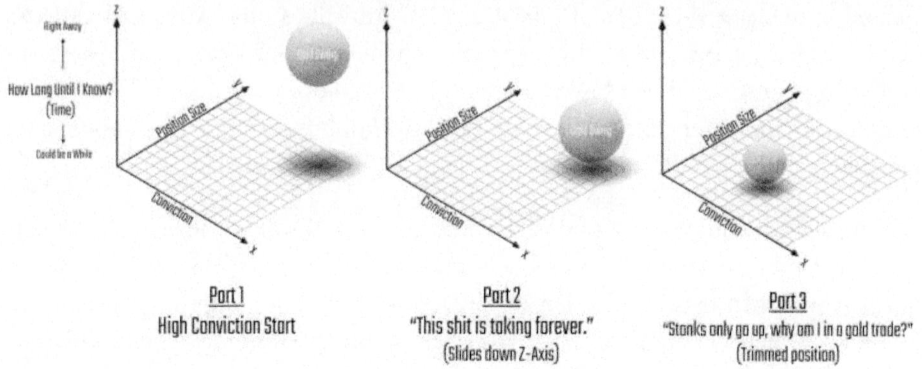

These are ever-changing factors. As soon as you enter a trade they begin to change. This is the main reason I prefer to trade futures intraday: I am better at it than equities/options (therefore I typically have a higher likelihood of being correct) and I know IMMEDIATELY if I am right or wrong. Since futures are a leveraged product, I am able to quickly size accordingly…and size large if the thesis is strong.

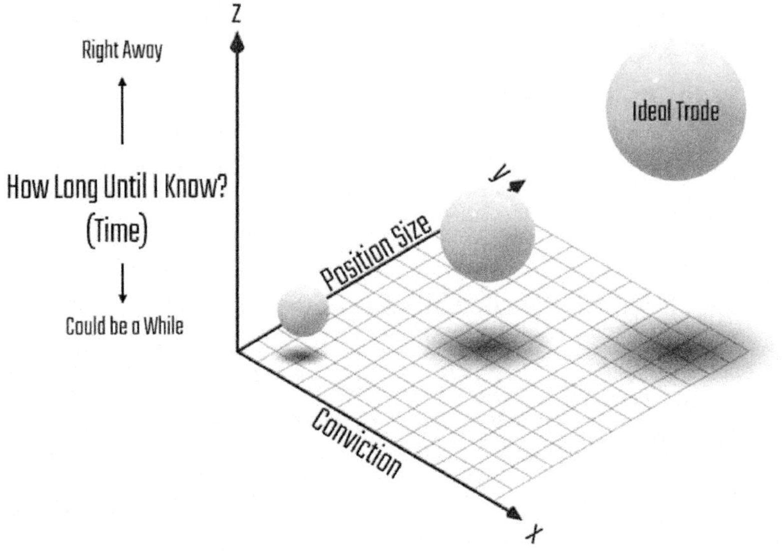

One of the reasons I decided to write this post is to help you better understand why I am not phased in the least when one of my "Quickies" (usually equity swing trades) doesn't pan out. The position size is typically negligible compared to day trading futures because my conviction is usually much lower and the time it takes me to know if I'm right or wrong is usually much longer. It may seem weird to you, but it's all part of a holistic way of managing risk throughout my trading journey.

I love seeing a great equity swing trade pan out over time. Absolutely love it. But I'm also very realistic about my strengths, so my risk management approach needs to align with that awareness. When I see large orders on the Limit Order Book tipping their hand at a key level of confluence, I am usually VERY certain what is about to happen in the next 5 to 10 minutes. I can't say the same for swing trading stocks, therefore I can't size the same.

Now, I don't want you to read this and leave thinking there's anything wrong with the classic "risk 1-2% of your capital per trade" approach to risk management…there isn't. Everyone is different. I'm just simply providing a different way of approaching risk management in its entirety. Even if you're very disciplined about only risking 1-2% per trade, things change once you take the position! All I'm suggesting is to view true risk management as a fluid process, not a stagnant one.

I'm a firm believer that to be a sustainable trader, risk needs to be viewed on a "macro" scale. For example, I mentioned in the "How I Day Trade" videos that my sizing for short trades is ALWAYS smaller than my sizing for long trades. Why? Because markets are inherently bullish due to the incredible amount of passive investing flows. Seems like a small detail, right? Maybe. But not if you plan to sustainably trade for years to come.

That's what I want to do, and that's what I want for you…no matter how you do it.

So I hope this post is at least thought-provoking if nothing else. I know we didn't get into the details of stop-losses and stuff, but I think that warrants its own post. For now, I just wanted to expand on how I think about risk management from a philosophical perspective.

Thanks for reading and thanks for being here.

Horse.

I was thinking about this piece because there is a trade like that this week. A trade where every single catalyst is rammed into a small window and you can put the trade on and you'll either be right or wrong just about right away.

Week 22: Short META

Facebook isn't doing well lately. Sheryl Sandberg is out, SNAP and TWTR have signaled ad revenues are at risk, **revenue growth could be negative for the first time when they announce earnings on 27JUL**, new measures to grow the user base look desperate, and it has lost to TikTok. The stock obviously reflects many of these harsh realities as it has collapsed from 386 to 165 in a year.

If 2001 (dotcom) and 2021 (ARKK and friends) taught us anything, it's that once-favored tech companies can drop 85% in pretty much a straight line if they want to. Selling something that's down 57% is a hard trade, but it's often also the right trade.

Short META right now either works or it doesn't work, just about right away because we have FOMC and then META earnings on Wednesday, July 27 (I am writing this on July 25). My view is that the market is too early on looking for a Fed pivot and that despite the swoon post SNAP earnings, there is still plenty of room for META to take another dump towards the 125/137 base formed in 2018 and 2019.

Here is my reasoning on the Fed, excerpted from this morning's am/FX.

•

Excerpt from am/FX: Trends Resume Tomorrow? (25JUL22)

I feel like the market is still locked into the old Fed framework which was: Fed turns dovish at the first whiff of trouble. I don't think that is the right framework anymore and the Fed is likely to remain much stickier and more hawkish than people currently think. This week's Fed meeting will reveal whether I'm right or wrong.

I don't see any scope for the Fed to back off at this week's meeting as the remaining scraps of their credibility are in jeopardy after a horrendous twelve months of bad forecasts (understandable, forgivable), slow pivot (still buying MBS in 2022, etc., nonsensical), and a spate of trading scandals and resignations (deplorable). For them to declare any sort of mission accomplished here with headline CPI at 9%, PPI at 18%, and Biden wishing gas prices lower on Twitter every day seems premature. Jackson Hole at the earliest.

The current market setup is:

- Everything got oversold
- Market got short and got squeezed
- Growth is slowing faster than economists thought
- QT is just starting and will double in September

The same way they bought MBS in February 2022 even though housing was blasting through the moon and towards Mars, they will be doubling QT in September even as the US economy may well be entering a third straight quarter of negative growth at that point. The implication for markets is that this year's primary trends—lower stocks and a higher USD—should resume Tuesday or Wednesday.

End of excerpt.

•

You have two big catalysts on Wednesday, and a horrible fundamental story and downtrend in META. Even if you think it's come a long way down, it's also 10 bucks off the June lows, so a move to 150/155 isn't hard to imagine. A cash trade is difficult to manage because of the gap risk, so the idea is to plug your nose and buy $1,000 worth of the July 29 expiry $160 puts for $6.30 and $1000 worth of the $155 puts for $4.60. A 15% drop in META to $142 on worse-than-expected earnings is not a crazy target … but we don't need a target because the whole trade is going to last a few days.

Instant gratification—or annihilation.

If the trade works, cover everything at 3:59 PM on July 28. The good news is, as Horse explained in the main part of this chapter, we know if we're wrong almost right away and the opportunity cost of this trade (and its drain on our mental capital) will be minimal. Right or wrong, we move on.

Conclusion

This is a bit of a lotto ticket trade, and Horse's approach is juicier when you can do the trade in cash with a reasonable expectation of enough liquidity to safely exit at your stop loss level. Trades with immediate right/wrong timing that involve chart breaks, or less obvious fundamental catalysts, are often better than this META idea because implied volatility will not be so high.

In this case, there has been a lot of bad news about META and there is bearish anticipation going into earnings. Therefore if I'm wrong, I could get my face ripped off with a short position as the stock gaps through $200 and delivers the pain. I don't like getting my face ripped off, so the only alternative here, despite eye-watering vol, is to buy the option and hope it realizes.

Week 23: Bear Markets Are Hard To Trade, Even When You're Bearish

Sell early and carry a wide stop

This little bear turns feisty when squeezed.

Update on previous trades

Here are some updates on past 50in50 trades:

1. Last week's META trade was a loser, even though META went straight down from inception. In real life, the trade was fine because the stock bounced off $155 twice and there was some ability to trade around the gamma. But the specific strategy laid out here lost money as there was no flexibility.
2. The XME trade is nice so far. Up around 7%.
3. The GBTC trade was good. Took profit at $14.80 (Friday close, as per the plan).
4. ARKK is boring.
5. RBLX is still substantially outperforming CVNA.

That's it! Full spreadsheet with all the results in Week 30. Now, let's talk about selling into bear market rallies.

Bear markets are hard to trade, even when you're bearish

Bear markets are hard to trade for a bunch of reasons:

Volatility is higher in bear markets. The volatility of volatility (vol of vol) is also higher. Therefore, the market switches between regimes faster. For example, stocks were cratering and VIX was 35 in May and again in June… Now we're grinding higher and the VIX is 22. Those are two completely different trading regimes in the space of two months. To give you a sense of the difference, here is the average daily range of S&P futures vs. the level of VIX the day before.

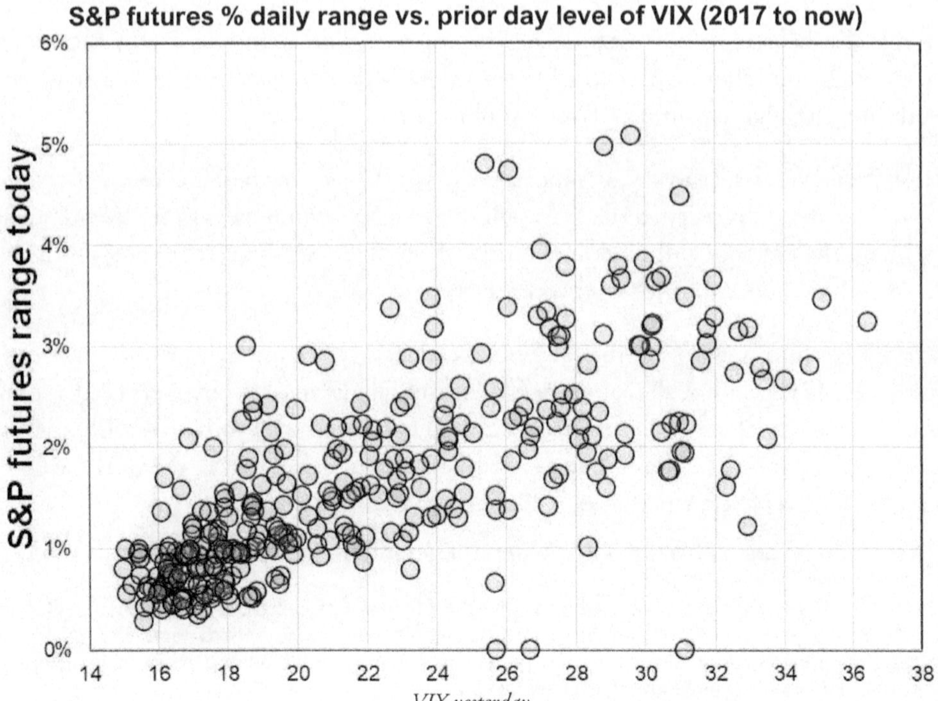

You can estimate from that chart that at the lows in stocks (the highs in VIX) in June, daily S&P ranges were in the 3%-5% area while now they are closer to 1%-2%. That's a totally different regime that requires different position sizes and a different trading approach. In a bull market, volatility doesn't change that quickly. In bear markets, you need to be good at real-time vol-adjustment.

Quite often, the exact moment you want to add to your shorts is the moment you should be taking profit. The most fun trade in the world is when you catch the right side of a bear market selloff and ride it down while adding. Unfortunately, this doesn't happen very often because stocks are in a bull market most of the time, and even when they're not, this trade requires perfect timing.

Bear market rallies are fast and soul-destroying and go farther than most people think is possible. When stocks are oversold, and everyone is bearish, the rips higher can be insane. There were solid 25% rallies in 2001 and 2008, even as it seemed pretty obvious that the world was ending. There does not have to be any fundamental catalyst for a bear market rally. It just happens when it's ready to happen.

I provide this intro as a warning because this piece is about selling the current rally in stocks.

Selling a bear market rally

Selling the hole in a bear market is fun when it works, but it barely ever works. Pyramiding into short equity trades is soooooooooooooooooooo much fun when it works. But it's high payoff, low EV most of the time.

Most of the successful short equity index trades that I have executed involved self-restraint to wait for the right entry, courage to pull the trigger, a willingness to trade with a wide stop, and the patience and discipline of Ernest Shackleton[33] to avoid adding on the way down and hold on until the target was reached.

Before I get into how to sell the rally in a bear market, let me first provide my bearish rationale. My view is not all that unique or creative; many market observers hold a similar bearish view. The thing is, that's fine. It's easy to talk about why you are bearish, the hard part is making money. For example, one of the biggest permabears in the world, who has been bearish every year since at least 2010 as per these sorts of comments…

These quotes are all from the same person. A famous person.

2010: "Investors dangerously underestimate the risk of an abrupt and severe equity market plunge."
2011: "The expected return/risk profile of the stock market has shifted to hard-negative."
2012: "The present menu of investment opportunities continues to be among the worst in history."
2013: "Stock returns prospectively are very low."
2014: "What concerns us beyond valuations is the overvalued, overbought, overbullish conditions."
2015: "Exit now."
2016: "Current extremes imply 40-55 percent market losses.... These are not worst-case scenarios, but run-of-the-mill expectations."
2017: "The most broadly overvalued moment in market history."
2018: "The music is fading out, and a trap-door has opened up in the floor, but they're still dancing."
2019: "A projected 50-65 percent market loss is actually somewhat optimistic."

… And he is down 3.4% on the year for 2022!

Whenever you see some kudos like "the man who called the 2008 crash" or some such nonsense… Try to find out whether that person made money. There is a very good chance they did not. You will see many prognosticators make aggressive directional forecasts but most of those forecasts involve an unlimited time horizon and no stop loss. That's a much easier game to play vs. trying to make money in real life.

---

33 https://en.wikipedia.org/wiki/Ernest_Shackleton

Anyway, I'm generally bearish stocks because:

1. The Fed will keep policy tight right into 2023 as they follow lagging indicators like CPI and US Unemployment.
2. Quantitative Tightening (QT) has just begun and will double in September. Fed balance sheet growth or shrinkage has been a pretty good univariate model for forecasting stock prices since 2008.
3. The Fed is tightening into a significant global growth slowdown with Europe and China weakening at the same time as the US stalls.
4. Valuations are high and bear markets normally end with cheap, not high valuations.
5. VIX has never gone to panic levels yet in this bear market; it keeps topping around 35. Bear markets usually climax with a blow-up in the VIX.
6. The period from August to October in mid-term years is seasonally weak. Here is a chart from Capital Group:

There are some other reasons to be bearish, but that is the basic gist.

Courage, patience, and discipline

Selling bear market rallies takes courage, patience, and discipline. First, let's talk about the courage part. It takes no brains or courage to sell into a collapsing market because that's what every trader's instinct is likely to be. On the other hand, when S&Ps bounce hard off 3650 and start climbing the wall of worry every day, it's strangely difficult to sell the rally at 4125.

This is a strange quirk of human nature. We love a bargain on Amazon Prime Day and we desperately want to sell our used car for top dollar… But we feel more comfortable buying SPX (and USDJPY) at the highs and selling it on the lows. Avoiding this sort of reflex to buy high and sell low is the number one way to avoid sucking wind as a trader and investor.

The two main reasons investors perform poorly are 1) transaction costs and 2) selling low and buying high. Check out this mind-blowing chart from JPAM:

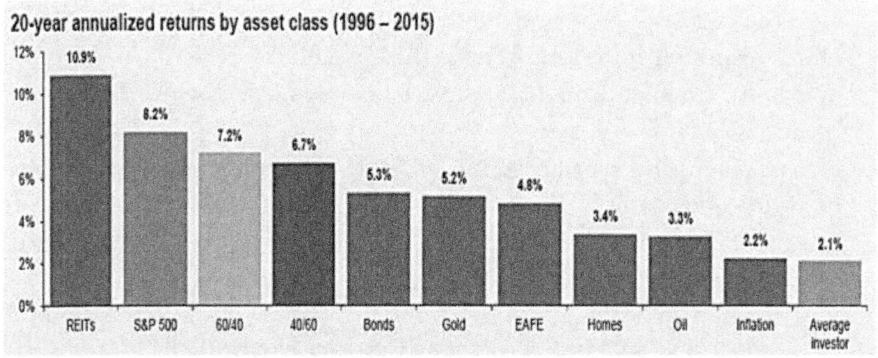

Anyway, it takes courage to sell the rally. That courage is abetted by analysis that convinces you that you are not just peeing in the wind, but instead taking a calculated shot in an attempt to determine when the direction of the wind is about to change. The simplest way to do this is to use some basic technical analysis.

Assuming you are not already short at bad levels, you want to wait as long as possible to sell the rally. There is tension, though, because if you wait too long, you miss it. One way I deal with this is to sell a bit early and use a wide stop.

The SPX chart right now looks like this:

That's a lot of lines lol! The purpose of the lines is to show points where I think there is likely to be meaningful resistance. As you can see by the three highs in late May, there looks to be a band of resistance right here 4160/4200. Then, the big papa resistance is 4300 where you had a triple top in April/May. Above that, you have the 4355 level (top of gap down in late May and old support) and then the huge trendline that comes down right at 4350.

So my strategy in a setup like this is to sell early and use a wide stop. There is a cost to selling early, but there's also a cost to missing it and then hitting a bid at 3900 cuz of FOMO! The main cost to selling early is that you can't lever up very much. If you're selling here with a 4366 stop loss, your position is not going to be very big.

But everything is always about tradeoffs. Here, it's better to sell ahead of the first batch of resistance, with a stop above the last batch of resistance, and give yourself the best odds of 1) catching it before it turns and 2) surviving the overshoot if there is one.

The more aggressive strategy would be to sell here (4125) and stop above the first layer of resistance (4225, for example). This gives you much more leverage but less staying power. It's always about tradeoffs. Leverage vs. staying power. Always a tradeoff.

Specific tactics for this trade

My view here is that stocks roll over and trade back to the lows by September or October. It's a three-month view, and I don't think we collapse in a disorderly fashion. I think we go back to 3600/3700 and at that point, I will want to cover.

In S&Ps that means I go short at 4125 with a stop at 4366. If we are using SPY (the S&P 500 ETF), we could go short at 412.50 with a stop at 436.60 and then look at selling some puts to make the risk/reward a bit better.

Selling S&P puts against short positions is often a good idea if you are not looking for a stock market collapse. S&P puts tend to be expensive, and selling SPX puts has produced abnormal returns over almost all extended time periods primarily because a) natural demand for SPX puts as insurance almost always exceeds natural supply and b) it's very hard to manage naked equity puts when you're wrong. Stocks go up slow and down fast.

As discussed in previous 50in50 episodes, if I'm comparing cash to options positions (or cash to a mix of cash and options,) I always plot the possible P&Ls in Excel. It's the easiest way to easily and quickly understand the payout profile of each strategy.

In this case, I think we go to 3700, so I'll take a look at selling the October 3600, 3700, or 3800 puts ($360, $370, and $380 in SPY) to see how the P&L changes.

Here is the result:

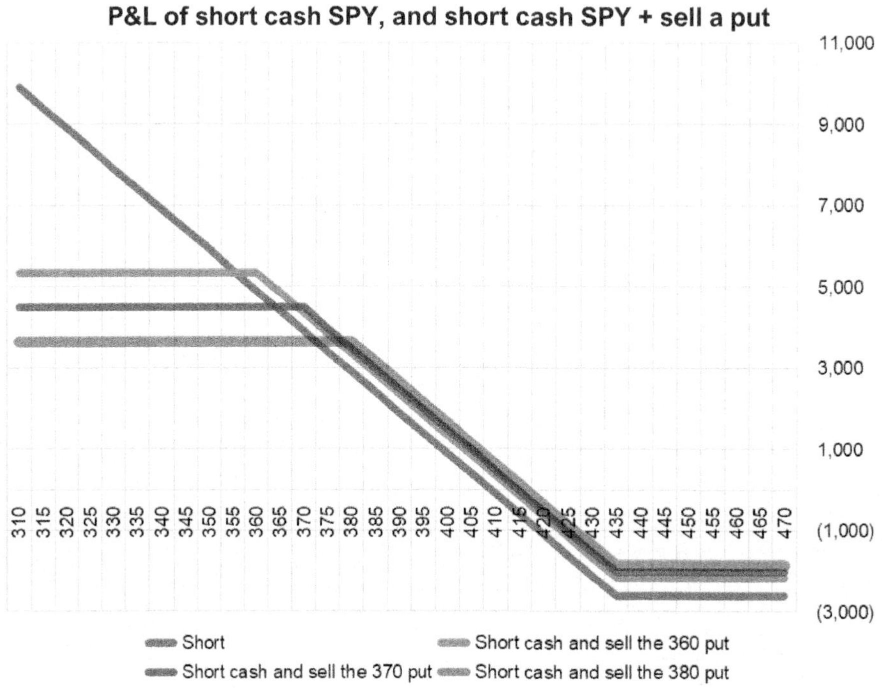

Premium on the puts is: $4.50, $5.85, and $7.44 (360, 370 and 380 strikes)

Since my plan is to cover around 3700 anyway, and I don't think we are going there in a straight line overnight… Selling the 370 put makes sense. The 380 put isn't terrible to sell, but that cuts off a bit too much of my P&L. The 360 put is similar to the 370, but since I plan to get out down there somewhere anyway, it honestly doesn't make much difference.

A few things to consider:

- If we get stopped out, we need to buy back the option. Presumably, it will be much cheaper, but depending on how quickly the stop-out happens, we are not going to collect the full premium sold in that case.
- If stocks collapse right now and go straight to 3700, I'm going to wish I didn't sell the put. That's life. **Once you have your view, you structure your trade around that view. Not around the path of least regret.**
- When SPX goes to 3900 next week, you'll be tempted to sell into that downward momentum. This is usually a recipe for a worse average and big frustration when it rallies back to 4100 and you cut the regrettable decision to add.
- That chart looks like it could be the new, modern logo for an NHL hockey team.

Conclusion

Selling rallies in a bear market is better than selling the hole. The best way to execute swing trades in stocks in a bear market is to wait for a rally into converging resistance, sell early as resistance nears, and put your stop loss on the far side of the next layer of tops.

This approach maximizes expected value but it does not maximize returns because the wide stop requires you to use less leverage. But: less leverage means a greater chance of survival and with the high volatility and high vol-of-vol in bear markets, the early and wide strategy is best.

Note that this is a 3-month view and there are more nimble and high-leverage ways to sell the rally in stonks. This is a swing trade methodology looking for a retest of the lows sometime before Halloween.

We go short SPY at 412.50 with a stop loss at 436.60 and sell an October 370 put to generate a bit better risk/reward. Target 370.

Week 24:
Do Good Traders Vary Bet Size?

The relationship between forecast confidence and forecast accuracy is uncertain.

Update on previous trades

Here are some updates on past 50in50 trades:

1. The short SPY trade got spanked by CPI but it's a 3-month view so let's see.
2. Roblox got smoked on earnings then ripped; Carvana is ripping too.
3. The XME long is more than 15% in the money.
4. **Take profit on the ARKK long.** It makes me physically ill to be long that thing as the company's public messaging and high fees make it highly questionable IMO. I regretted using it as an example trade from the second I hit send lol. :|

That's it! Full spreadsheet with all the results in Week 30.

Now, let's talk about bet sizing.

Today's 50in50 is a joint effort co-written by Justin Ross, my colleague here at Spectra Markets. Please check out his Substack: Square Man, Round World[34] *where he picks apart life's questions and struggles.*

Do good traders vary bet size?

In *Alpha Trader* and *The Art of Currency Trading*, there is detailed discussion of how to vary bet size according to market volatility, and according to conviction level. Varying bet size according to volatility is not controversial. If the S&P is moving 5%/day, you need to trade smaller than when it's trading 1%/day. And it also stands to reason that if you are extremely confident on a trade, you should invest more in that idea than a trade where your confidence is just 6 out of 10.

But maybe that's wrong!

The reason that could be wrong is that the idea is only sensible if there is a known, positive relationship between confidence and accuracy. If your highest conviction trades have the same hit ratio as your "I'm not totally sure on this one!" trades… There is no reason to vary your bet size.

The Bet Sizing Problem

Bet sizing is one of the most important topics in trading. Not only because it ties in with risk management, and not only because it allows you to leverage your best ideas… but also because there is not one clear correct answer or best methodology. While most everyone will agree that you need to vary your bet size based on *volatility*, the issue of whether to vary bet size according to *confidence level* is up for debate.

If you've read any trading books, or you spend time around experienced traders, you've probably heard somebody say: "good traders vary bet size." And by "varying bet size," they mean "bet bigger on better ideas, and smaller on lower-quality ideas." This is considered timeless wisdom in many trading circles – like "never revenge trade" and "always use a stop loss."

There are plenty of reasons why this makes perfect sense, especially for veteran traders who are good with probabilities and know their edge. However, there are also plenty of reasons that this advice just doesn't click with other traders. Perhaps 80% of traders believe you should vary bet size with conviction, but there are plenty of experienced vets who think otherwise.

[34] https://squareman.substack.com/

Let's take a look at some arguments for and against varying bet size according to confidence level.

Are Confidence And Accuracy Correlated?

Unfortunately, there is no monolithic answer to this question. Some think the answer is obvious. "Of course, higher confidence leads to higher accuracy!" But if you study the literature on this, it's not obvious. At all. Various accuracy/confidence scatter plots offer wildly different conclusions.

For example, one study asked participants to monitor their heart rate in reaction to various stimuli and then report on changes in their cardio state over time. They were also asked how confident they were in their assessment. Here is the scatter plot of confidence vs. accuracy:

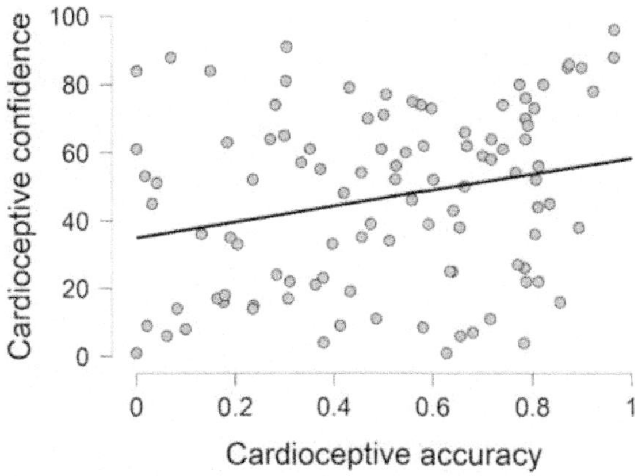

Noisy!

Here's a second chart, this time from a study of confidence vs. accuracy in the realm of avalanche prediction:

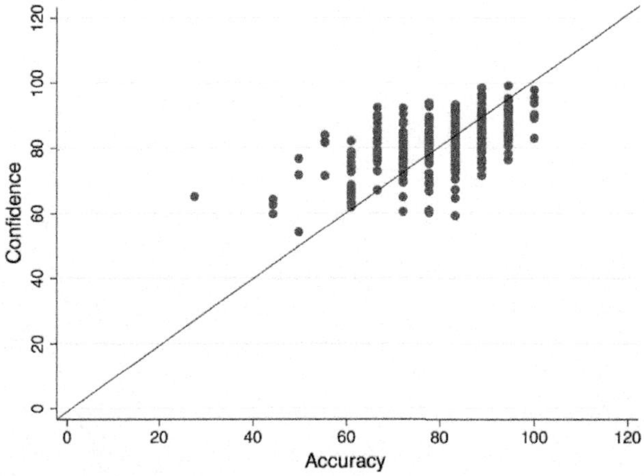

Again, there's a weak positive relationship there, but if it wasn't for that 45-degree line they drew, it would be hard to see. Confidence and accuracy are also much studied in the arena of eyewitness testimony because such testimony is often unreliable and highly problematic. Therefore, any way of increasing the reliability of eyewitness testimony through ex-ante confidence estimates would be useful for investigators and prosecutors and might help avoid wrongful convictions.

Here is the confidence vs. accuracy relationship from a Duke University article[35] about eyewitness testimony:

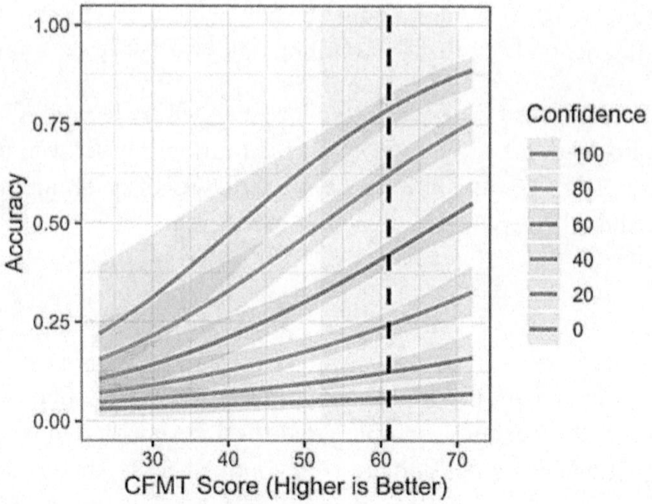

This time, there appears to be a strong positive relationship, but you can see that depending on the field you study, a correlation between confidence and accuracy is not guaranteed. It depends on the subject matter, task difficulty, expertise of the individual estimating, and the calibration level of the estimator. If the person estimating is wildly overconfident, that's going to impact the relationship between confidence and accuracy.

Confidence and Overconfidence

There is an enormous body of literature on biases and failures in human decision-making. There is a handful of essential books in the genres of decision theory and behavioral finance, including *Thinking, Fast and Slow* by Daniel Kahneman and Amos Tversky, and *Psychology of Intelligence Analysis* by Richards J. Heuer.

As these books (and countless other books and studies) detail, people are overconfident in almost all measurable aspects of human behavior. People think they're better at

---

35 https://judicature.duke.edu/articles/distinguishing-between-reliable-and-unreliable-eyewitnesses/

forecasting than they actually are. Clinicians think they're better at diagnosing than they actually are. Academic economists are still in demand.

So, the average trader might look at an opportunity and think he has a 70% chance of being right. But most traders actually realize closer to a 50-55% win rate, so it sounds like this trader might be a bit too optimistic. But he might not be. The only way to truly know the answer is to gather data.

I often advocate for collecting as much data as you can at as granular a level as possible, but I am sad to say that I have not collected data on my conviction level on trades or trading days over the years. While I know my daily win rate is close to 50% most years back to 2006, I have no idea if that win rate correlates with ex-ante confidence.

So the first lesson is: **Record your conviction level on each trade** in your journal to create a database of information that will show you the relationship between your confidence and your accuracy. Then, you will have a systematic way of determining the answer to the question: "Should I vary bet size based on conviction?" If you don't have data, you are guessing.

Kelly is Key

A critical concept in any optimal bet size discussion is the Kelly criterion[36], a formula in probability theory that maximizes gambling returns over time. It defines your edge, your payoff, and your available capital, and prescribes optimal bet size in any situation. It finds the mathematically ideal bet size that offers the best tradeoff between maximum return and least risk of ruin.

If you are not familiar with the Kelly criterion concept, it's worth taking some time to read about it. *Fortune's Formula* by William Poundstone[37] is a fun read that explains the history and use of Kelly and the book has strong application to both trading and gambling.

Here is a graphic from the Wikipedia page for Kelly criterion:

---

[36] https://en.wikipedia.org/wiki/Kelly_criterion

[37] https://amzn.to/3pb1PvX

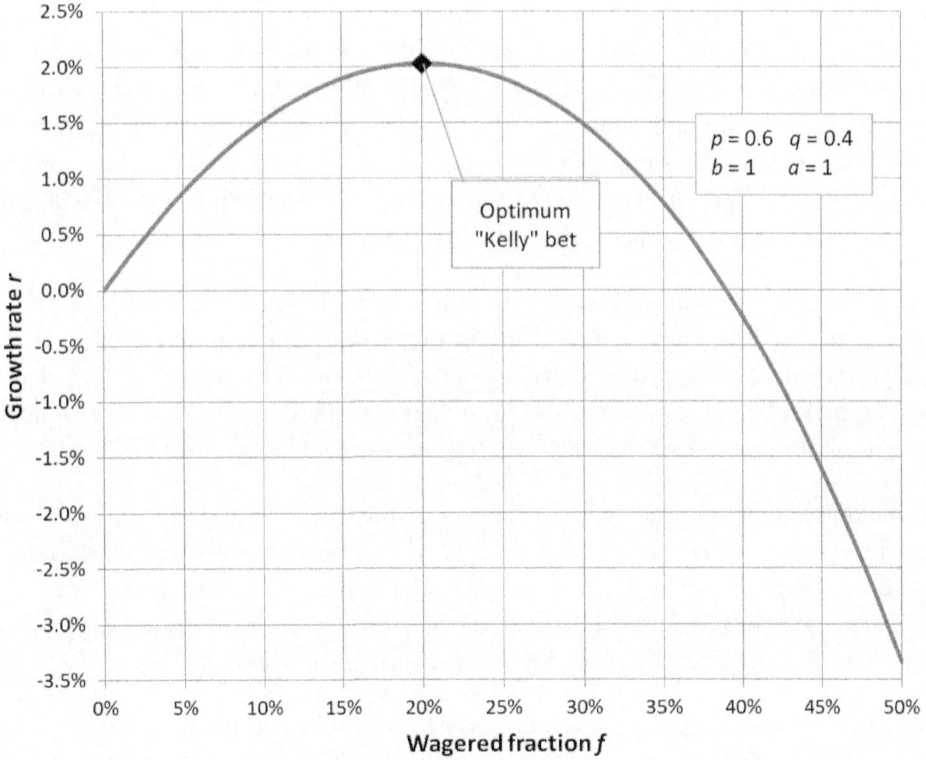

Here's a less mathy way of looking at it:

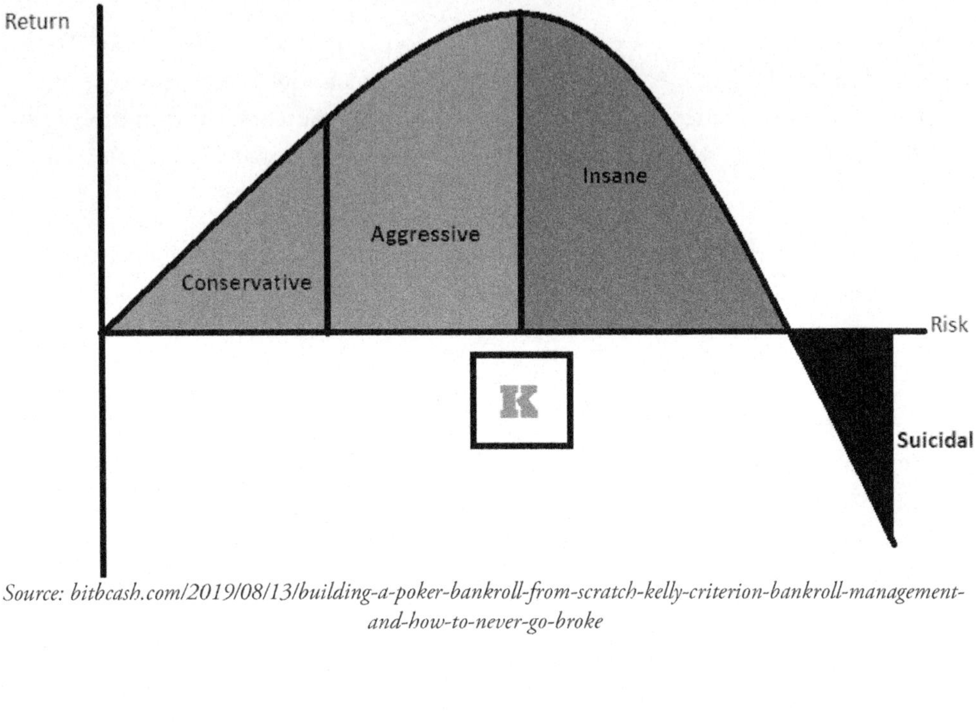

Source: bitbcash.com/2019/08/13/building-a-poker-bankroll-from-scratch-kelly-criterion-bankroll-management-and-how-to-never-go-broke

But there's an important caveat: the Kelly criterion maximizes returns *when the probability of the outcome is known*. In other words, it works for coin tosses – where, until the end of time, you will have exactly a 50% probability of winning. It works for card games, where despite the immense difficulty of *calculating* the odds, there *are defined odds*. Poker players can use the Kelly criterion. Even in sports gambling, Kelly is useful because there is a huge database of historical information that can be used to objectively and accurately estimate future odds before the event.

Can traders use the Kelly criterion? The answer, again, is not at all obvious. The market isn't a static or stable thing – **it doesn't offer us repeating opportunities,** strictly speaking. Every single tick, every second, every regime, is different from every other one that has ever happened before. Context is always different. Just because you had a 55% hit rate last month does not mean you will have the same hit rate this month.

So the question is: can traders realistically assess the ex-ante win probability of a trade? Maybe not new traders. But what about experienced traders with years of experience? Good traders get better at thinking probabilistically over time. And the skill associated with any endeavor goes up and to the right over time, as a rule. Also, those who know more are (at least slightly) better at knowing what they don't know[38].

But when it comes to the specifics of assessing probabilities in trading – we don't really know. Some traders we talk to are confident their high conviction trades out-earn their low conviction trades. But they don't have any hard data to back it up. So they might just be overconfident. Or they might be dead wrong.

This question must be answered, with data, on a trader-by-trader basis. Because everybody trades differently. Everybody looks at different criteria and senses the market in their own idiosyncratic ways. The only way to assess the outcomes of your probabilistic predictions over time is to journal about them every time you trade, *before you trade*.

Then, once you have a good idea of your win rate based on probability, you plug it into Kelly, adjust to a determined percentage of Kelly, and place your bet. This is the most sophisticated and difficult, but highest leverage way to size your trades.

A Second, Simpler Option

Until you have data that tells you whether your win rate and confidence level on trades are correlated, another approach is to use your historical win/loss statistics to figure out the ideal $ at risk for each trade and stick to that. You assume your conviction is not

[38] https://home.csulb.edu/~cwallis/382/certainty/overconfidence /The%20Role%20of%20Individual%20Differences%20in%20the.pdf

correlated with success rate and you bet the same amount every time. This makes life easier; one less variable to juggle and one less question to ask yourself every time.

For example, if you have a 57% win rate and your winning trades make 1.5X the average loss on your losing trades over the past three years, just use those stats in conjunction with a modified Kelly calculation to determine your sizing. There is something to be said for this level of simplicity. It doesn't allow you to increase leverage on higher confidence ideas ... but it preserves mental capital by reducing complexity.

Conviction level is one less dial to fine-tune, one less thought to fret over before you put on a trade. Mental capital is just as important as financial capital and simplicity can save you from overthinking and exhaustion.

If you think you know your trading stats pretty well (either trade-by-trade or daily stats), you can plug them into this formula.

% of Capital to Risk
= Win% - ((1-Win%)/(AverageWin/AverageLoss))

So let's say it's the first trading day of the year and you have $4,000,000 of free capital (free capital means how much you can lose... At a bank or hedge fund, that's your stop loss; as a retail trader, that's your account size).

You make money on 50% of your trades and your average winning trade is $370,000 and average losing trade is $300,000. You know this from collecting three years of historical P&L data. The figures here are realistic and approximately reflect real life daily trading performance data for someone generating around $10 million dollars per year of P&L at a commercial bank. Plugging these numbers into the Kelly formula we get:

% of Capital to Risk
= 0.50 - ((1 - 0.50)/(370,000/300,000))
= 9.4%

So 9.4% times $4,000,000 would suggest this trader should risk $378,400 on their first trade of the year. **The Kelly number tends to be very high** relative to what you might expect because it represents the most aggressive allocation possible to maximize upside. Understand that the Kelly Criterion was developed for gambling scenarios where you know the exact odds beforehand and every bet is made in a series. Kelly assumes you are making one bet at a time whereas in trading you might have multiple bets on at once. There are critical reasons why **the Kelly Criterion is better suited to gambling games than to trading.**

In trading, you use a past probability to estimate a future probability. To compensate for the fact that you don't know your real odds going forward (you can only estimate the future using historical odds) you should consider half-Kelly or quarter-Kelly sizing. This depends on how confident you are in your performance data and how consistent your performance has been over the years.

A Third, Simplest Option

The simplest approach is to assume a) conviction doesn't correlate with accuracy, and b) historical trading stats may not predict the future distribution of outcomes. Then, just bet a fixed percentage of your capital on each trade.

2% or 3% of free capital is conservative and will keep you out of trouble.

Simple Kelly, or Kelly adjusted for conviction level, is more aggressive and offers greater and more asymmetric upside than conservative, fixed bet sizing… But it's riskier and more complicated. There are always tradeoffs.

Systematic, Automatic

In Chapter 11 of *Alpha Trader*, a tiered sizing system is presented where confidence is the input and bet size is the output. In this system, a run-of-the-mill mean reversion trade merits a smaller bet than a once-a-year "perfect" macro setup with a tight stop loss. The latter trade gets the bigger bet size.

The math says that if you're aggressive on your "best bets," and your confidence is correlated to your accuracy, your winners will vastly outweigh your losers over time. Your P&L will grow dramatically as you capitalize more and more on your best ideas. *This* is why lots of veteran traders are telling you to vary bet size: because you want to leverage your best ideas.

In *The Art of Currency Trading*, there were five levels of confidence. In *Alpha Trader*, there were three. Now, we are debating whether there should be *any* variation in bet sizing by confidence. This is a hard question and that's why it's worth debating.

Whether you use five, three or just one level of conviction for trade sizing, you should always consider the possibility that one day there could still be the occasional outlier that deserves a bigger bet. If you're good, you will know it when you see it. And you'll record the results so that over time you learn what you know, what you think you know, and what you don't know. As the apocryphal Mark Twain quote says:

"It ain't what you don't know that gets you into trouble. It's what you know for sure that just ain't so."

So What's The Right Answer?

There is no right answer to the varied bet size question. It depends on the trader. It depends on your experience, confidence, calibration, and risk tolerance. You have to decide what kind of bet sizing protocol is right for you. As is often the case with questions of trading styles and methodologies, the answer varies by individual. You have to decide for yourself.

If you're the kind of person who is good at making snap judgments, and you're great with probabilities, and you already have an extended history of trade journaling that shows a strong confidence/accuracy connection… vary your bet sizes. If you're up 12 million dollars on the year and you seem to keep finding outstanding opportunities, then bigger bets might be for you. If you are confident, and your confidence is well-calibrated to reality, and you can afford to take some extra risk, you will benefit from varied bet sizing when you play your cards (candles) right.

But if you're not the kind of person who wants extra risk, higher variance, increased stress, or extra mental output, **that's okay too.** When extra complexity does not yield a clear and measurable benefit, take the simple route. Maybe you are self-aware enough to see you don't have a well-defined sense of which opportunities are better or worse. You simply have a binary way of looking at trades. They're either good enough to put on, or they're not. That's fine.

Conclusion

All good traders vary bet size according to **volatility**. But whether or not to vary bet size based on **conviction** is a subjective call that can be turned into an objective decision with enough data. Your goal should be to establish whether or not there is a correlation between your confidence and your accuracy in trading. Then, choose between one of three sizing methods:

Easy. Use a fixed percentage of free capital as your constant bet size on all trades. This is the simplest, lowest risk way to trade and that is not a bad thing. As you gain experience and collect data, you can experiment with other approaches.

Medium. Use historical win rates and trading stats and a modified Kelly criterion percentage to pick a bet size and stick to that every time. This is simple, it reduces the number of decisions you have to make every day, and it allows you to make quicker trading decisions by reducing complexity and making the sizing decision binary. Either you do the trade in size X, or you don't. If you ever do stray from fixed sizing (perhaps because of a watermelon-sized opportunity you sniff out), record the outcome in an effort to create your own confidence/accuracy scatter plot.

Hard. Vary bet size according to conviction. Use rigorously collected data on win/loss percentage, size of average win and loss, and modified Kelly to determine the appropriate risk on each trade. Design and implement an objective bet sizing procedure that uses historical trading stats and does not rely on guesswork about the relationship between confidence and accuracy in your trading. Scale your bets using the linear or geometric relationship between conviction and accuracy. Keep collecting data and update your system as you gain more insight.

One more thing

Instead of a trade this week, we're going to try something different and collect a bunch of data for the next few weeks. The goal is to collect accuracy vs. conviction data from as many people as possible over multiple weeks to determine whether the wisdom of the market crowd has a positive confidence/accuracy relationship.

Bonus Chart

Here is the accuracy/confidence scatter plot for 50in50 so far

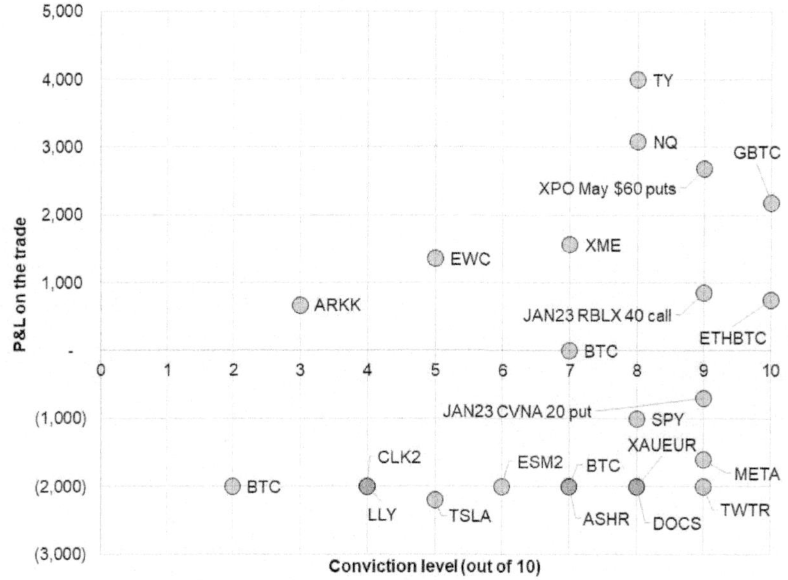

A few takeaways from that chart:

- There is a correlation, but it's early to tell with just 23 data points.
- Trades with a conviction level of 6 or lower have a 33% hit rate.
- Trades with a conviction level of 7 or higher have a 58% hit rate.
- Trades with a conviction level of 10 are 100% (sample size = 2).

- *Why would I do a trade with a conviction level below 5*? **In real life, I wouldn't.** But for this Substack (now book), sometimes it's hard to get a solid trade and attach it to a clear concept every week. In those cases, (like the LLY, CLK2, BTC slingshot reversal, and recent TSLA trades) I find a reasonable example that kinda made sense… But that was not an actionable "many planets in line" setup that would be worthy of a real capital allocation in real life.

Week 25: Horizontal Lines

Simplicity is the ultimate sophistication

This image makes my brain happy, but it hurts my eyes.

Update

Not too much news on the open trades, other than SPY ripping to 430 now and putting the 436.60 stop loss in some jeopardy. The sentiment survey was interesting last week. Here are the results:

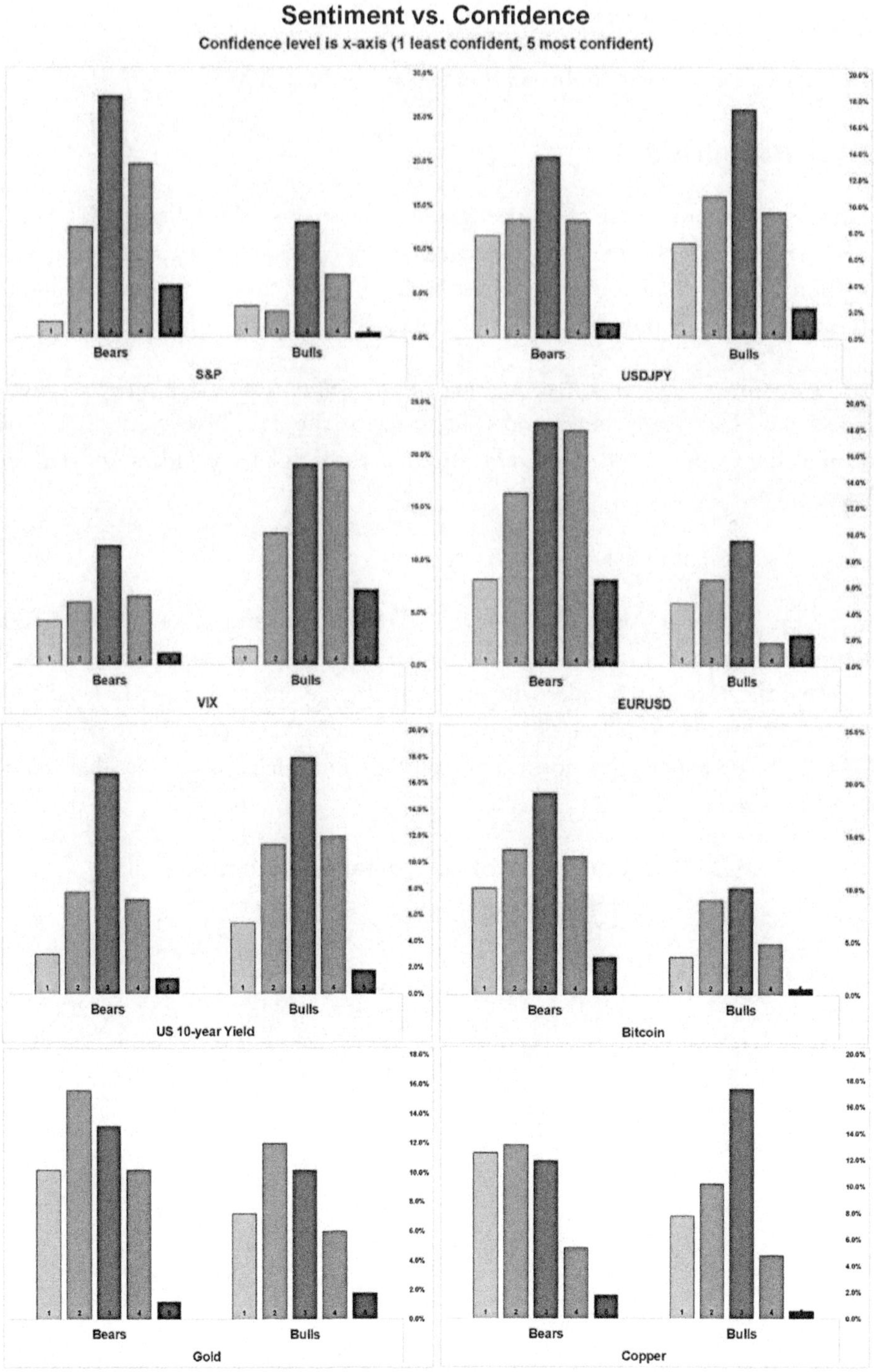

Two takeaways: People were mega bearish stocks, gold, and EURUSD last week. People don't feel confident predicting copper. The sample size was 217 respondents. Thanks to all those who filled it out.

Now, let's talk about simplicity.

"Simplicity is the ultimate sophistication." - Leonardo da Vinci

Horizontal lines

The idea for this book was to teach new traders how to trade. I feel like the last few notes have been pretty complicated, with advanced concepts like bet sizing, options, the fourth dimension of time, and so on. Let's get back to basics this week and talk about the simplest, but arguably most effective tool in technical analysis: Horizontal lines.

I have always preferred horizontal lines and simple support and resistance to trendlines, channels, arcs, Gann fans, and so on. The reason is simple. There's very often a reason horizontal lines work... They are reflecting the reality of large bids and offers in the market.

I like approaches that reveal an underlying reality in the market.

Most of the technical approaches that I use reflect something about the underlying structure of the market in a particular area. For example, the beauty of simple horizontal lines is that they very often reflect the presence of large orders. Let's say a Japanese auto exporter needs to sell 5 billion USDJPY, and they leave an order with a bank to sell at 116.33. They are patient and don't mind waiting. You might get a chart that looks like this:

USDJPY double touch of horizontal resistance at 116.33

Remember that because support and resistance are simple and not subject to much interpretation, most people in the market will be monitoring roughly the same support and resistance levels. This is the self-fulfilling prophecy aspect of technical analysis.

Because horizontal lines are obvious and easy to understand, you need to think about the metagame and leave your stops far enough below support (or above resistance) that you are not dinged by a weak stop loss run that takes out an obvious level. **It is often best to place your stop loss about a half-day's range above or below a major horizontal level to avoid any noisy whipsaws around that point.**

An example in EURUSD

Last week, an interesting thing happened as I was writing am/FX. I was sick of trading EURUSD from the short side for most of this year and wanted to open my mind to the alternate hypothesis.

This is what I do when I feel I have been stuck in one mode for too long and worry that confirmation bias might be creeping in. I consciously try to write a piece going the other way, or at least honestly explore the other direction. Here is the piece I wrote last Thursday.

•

am/FX, August 11, 2022

As someone who has the word "nimble" in his daily closing salute, I have not been particularly nimble of late as I have been either flat or bullish USD and either flat or bearish stocks for ages. This worked well in Q1 and Q2 but is leading to a lot of red P&L this quarter and so I'm going to try to keep an open mind.

The EURUSD chart still looks rather bearish, with the only real bullish angle being that the huge gamma pocket and round number at 1.00 held right at the peak of EUR bearishness. Here is the daily:

EURUSD daily since April 2021 with 60-day and 120-day moving average

A close above 1.04 would take out the 60-day moving average and would exceed the pivot marked by the last horizontal line. The horizontal lines show that each broken support has held as strong resistance with just one tiny exception in early April. Good trends find resistance at prior support, and this has been a good trend.

Selling at the horizontal line and the 60-day has been a good expression of the trend most of the way down. 1.0613 is the big daddy but that moving average was only tested once (in February 2022), and the 60-day has been way more actionable.

Rate differentials show nothing bullish for EURUSD (still near the lows), and relative equity performance has been in line with the currency. On the bullish side, BTPs are back to 200bps over Germany after twice testing 250bps… So you could argue the much-hated TPI (the ECB antifragmentation tool) has worked, to some extent. Then again, BTPs are mostly just a risky asset and they have performed worse than SPX on the massive recovery in risky asset sentiment since mid-June. SPX is making new 3-month highs while BTP spreads are nowhere near the tights printed in May.

It's not like lower crude prices have helped the idiosyncratic EU energy story. Here's Dutch Natural Gas:

Dutch Natural Gas

And the UK still has plenty to worry about:

https://www.bloomberg.com/news/articles/2022-08-11/liz-truss-s-plan-for-boe-seen-as-threat-to-pound-and-uk-bonds

To me, everything still points to EUR softness. Yesterday, I wanted to avoid the USD side, so I went short EURAUD because anything long AUD, or long carry makes sense as I expect we enter a two-week period of low vol, out of office emails, early departures, and family tripping.

I promised myself I would go into today's am/FX with an open mind and now my view is back to bearish EURUSD. **That's fine!** I believe my analysis and process were unbiased. I actually started writing this piece with the intent of outlining a bullish case for EURUSD in the spirit of examining the alternative hypothesis. And I found very little that was bullish.

The chart looks particularly nice, location-wise as you only have to risk 120 pips from here. **Short EURUSD here at 1.0346 with a stop loss at 1.0463 and take profit at 1.0166.** Risk 120 to make 180. The 1.0466 stop is above the 60-day moving average, the horizontal line, and the 05JUL22 high.

End of excerpt.

•

I think there are two takeaways here:

1. If you go in with an open mind, trust your conclusion, even if it's not what you were expecting! You need to be able to trust yourself to have an open mind and when you are questioning that ability, go hard towards the alternate hypothesis and see what happens. If you end up back at the original hypothesis, you followed the process and can feel more confident in your original view.
2. Horizontal lines are useful!

Here's what happened after I published that on August 11.

EURUSD hourly showing last two instances where support became resistance

EURUSD held the old support perfectly, failed at the horizontal line, and dumped 200 points in a straight line in three days. The take profit (1.0166) hit today.

The beauty of horizontal lines is:

1. **Horizontal lines are objective and simple, not arbitrary.** If the old low was 1.0550, the line goes straight across to 1.0550. You are not fudging around with angles and determining whether a trendline touched based on the width of the crayon you're using. When a method is objective and simple, there is less chance that confirmation bias will pollute your analysis. When someone uses Elliott Wave, for example, there are so many subjective interpretations and wave counts possible that if they started out bullish, they will probably find a bullish wave count!

2. **Horizontal lines reflect market reality.** When a market keeps bouncing off the same level, it's often because there is a huge order there. Central bank orders, barrier defense, corporate orders, M&A transactions, institutional demand, and other types of non-urgent limit orders from large patient participants create horizontal support and resistance. When the horizontal level breaks, the order is probably gone and the underlying supply/demand dynamic has changed. This isn't hocus pocus tech stuff, it's the reality of transaction level activity being directly reflected back at you in a chart.
3. **Horizontal lines are easy to use.** No protractor required! If the line breaks, you know it broke, and you can act accordingly.

Peter Brandt is one of the best-known technicians out there. Here is a quote from Jack Schwager's interview with Brandt in *Unknown Market Wizards*:

> *I used to trade any pattern I could see. I would trade 30 to 35 patterns a month. Now, I am much more selective. I used to trade patterns like symmetrical triangles and trendlines, which I no longer do. I only trade patterns where the breakout is through a horizontal boundary.*
>
> Why is that?
>
> *With horizontal boundaries, you can find out much more quickly whether you are right or wrong.*
>
> Was there a catalyst for that change?
>
> *No, it was just a gradual process of realizing that I was getting my best results trading rectangles, ascending triangles, and descending triangles. Give me a 10-week rectangle with a well-defined boundary that ends with a wide daily bar breakout out of that pattern, and now we're cooking.*

Let me reiterate an important concept that is critical to understanding something simple like how to use horizontal lines.

I never do a trade purely on technicals. Technicals are a good risk management tool but not a great forecasting tool. My ideas come from my read on changing narratives, from cross-market correlation, pattern recognition, backtesting, positioning, and other fundamental or microstructure analysis. Then, I use technical analysis to hone my tactics, maximize leverage, put up risk management guard rails, and determine the stop loss and take profit. Sometimes, I'll find a trade I love, but the techs don't line up, so I'll wait. *This is about strategy vs. tactics. Macro, cross-market, and behavioral stuff is for strategy, technical analysis is for tactics.*

The most useful way to use horizontal lines is to find setups that maximize leverage. Let's look at a simple trade using horizontal lines.

Short MSTR with a tight stop

In my crypto piece last week (MTC 29[39]), I showed how the price of MicroStrategy stock varies according to two main drivers. 1) the price of bitcoin and 2) the momentum in meme stocks. Here's a comparison of MSTR "fair value" (or, estimated intrinsic value) vs. its stock price.

If you know when past meme stock rallies happened, you can see that the premium on MSTR goes up and down with meme stock fever.

MSTR stock (lighter line) vs. "fair value" (darker line), with premium over fair value in the panel below

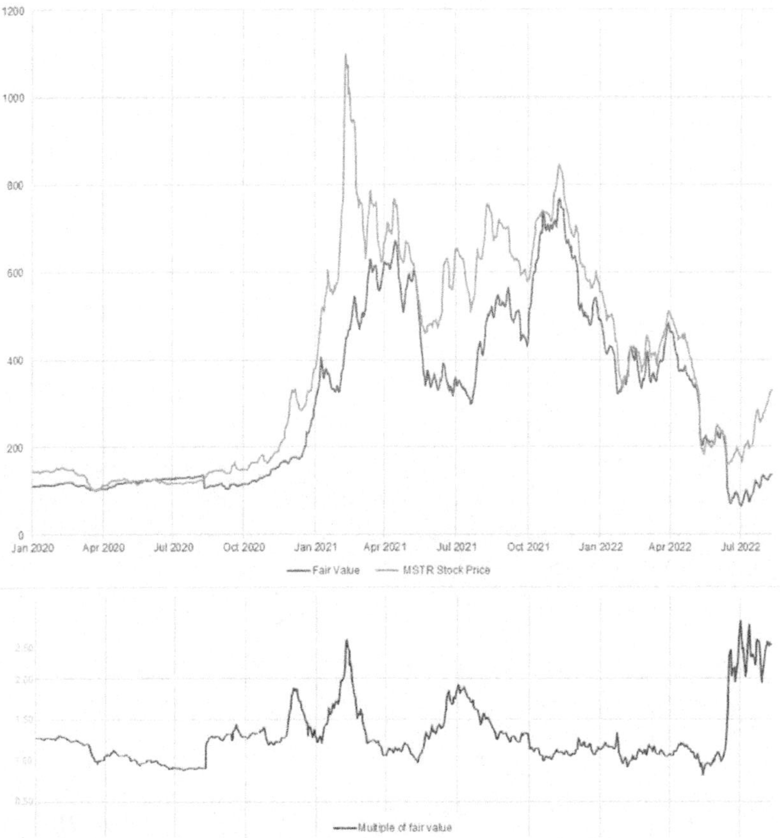

Let's say I'm getting bearish bitcoin here because I think risky assets are stretched, the dollar is strong, real interest rates are high and rising, and short MSTR looks nice because

[39] https://mtcbd.substack.com/p/the-bull-trade-continues-but-mstr

you are selling at an inflated premium level. 2.5X fair value is where MSTR trades now and that's where it peaked in the past.

When selling a raging mutant beast like this, there are two main approaches. Small position with wide stop (like in Week 23) or take a big position with a tight stop. In the second instance, you wait for what looks like a perfect entry, then take your shot with a fairly tight stop loss. If you time it perfectly, the asymmetrical payout is yours. If you time it wrong, you get stopped out and life goes on. Your mental theta is minimal because you are either going to time it right, or lose right away.

That "I'll know right away if I'm wrong" aspect has value, as discussed in Week 22. It's especially useful on an expensive short like MSTR where you could be paying 10%-15% / year for the borrow.

You've been waiting patiently as MSTR rallied… Now ETH has failed at 2000 (round number, and market is raging bullish), BTC has looked soggy the whole time (options open interest in the toilet), and we are back to a major level in MSTR. You draw a couple of horizontal lines and get this:

MSTR with two horizontal lines off March low support, May low bounce, and May triple top resistance

One line is off the March support, and one is off the last bottom in early May (and it also covers the triple top before the LUNA-driven collapse). Pre-LUNA, MSTR had a hard time getting below 363. Once it broke down, it never got back above 369. As such, you could do worse than selling here ($345) with a stop above both lines at $381. That's a tight stop loss on a stock that's trading an average daily range of $27 in 2022, but it's not ridiculous. "Tight but not ridiculous" is a good way of thinking about the right stop loss for a max leverage trade.

The current MSTR rally started at $240, so we will look for a full round trip and put the take profit at $251 (just ahead of $240 support). Risking $36 plus slippage to make about $98. There is always going to be gap risk with MSTR because it trades like a meme stock and tracks bitcoin (which moves over the weekend, when MSTR is closed). Also the short interest is large (37% of float). **Size accordingly!**

I will rate this trade 7 out of 10 conviction on the sheet, though someone pointed out to me that my conviction could be high on a trade like this as it pertains to expected value, but still less than 50% on the probability of being correct since the trade pays 3:1.

That is an inherent issue with any conviction vs. accuracy assessment of bets that are not 50/50. Are you describing your conviction as it pertains to the expected value of the trade or the probability of winning? Here, I'm saying as a trade (taking into account the probability of a win, and size of potential win) I rate this a 7 out of 10.

Conclusion

Horizontal lines are simple.

When it comes to technical analysis... Simple is good.

Part 1 Wrap-up

Justin here.

We hope you're enjoying the 50in50 story so far. After all, that's our favorite way to look at this project – not as a series of isolated lessons, but as one long lesson with lots of related parts.

So far we've talked about some of the most important things any trader should learn about. We've talked about risk, tactics, and what it takes for an everyday trade idea to become an excellent one.

We've talked about how to let your charts help you instead of hurting you. By looking for important price/behavior interactions like horizontal lines, news pivots, and slingshot reversals.

We've talked about how to develop a professional framework. How to build simple and regime-independent thought processes by using things like quadrants and narrative analysis.

We've talked about dislocations between price and public perception (good news, bad price) and how to trade those dislocations.

And we've talked about how time is an element of risk management that is easy to overlook.

Remember that each of these lessons, and each trading concept in general, is not the holy grail. None of these lessons on their own will fix your trading or make you suddenly see the market clearly. This project is about looking at the different things a professional has to think about and using that diverse wisdom to build a framework. A real, robust thinking framework that will earn you money across many strategies and many regimes.

In other words, the whole is much greater than the sum of the parts. And you can discard the parts you don't like, because nobody trades the same as anybody else.

In part 2, we're going to dig into psychology, by looking at topics like getting flat, maintaining an edge, and always being nimble. We're also going to go much deeper into analyzing the behavior of the market and its participants. We'll look at how sometimes the market misses obvious trades. We'll talk about how the market still rewards behavior that worked 100 years ago: behavior like buying the rumor and selling the fact, or trading mean reversion at the extremes.

But we'll also keep discussing simple and practical trading tools like overshoots, gaps, and coming up with sane stop losses. And we'll go over some basic back-testing, which can be one of the most useful things you'll ever do in trading.

We'll learn some new lessons from some trades that didn't go so well. And we'll also trade Tesla a few times, short Ford on narrative dislocation, trade options on MicroStrategy, and make a ton of profit going long bonds at the bottom.

And at the end of the second part there is a longer section that wraps up the entire project, with broad takeaways, bigger lessons, and a discussion of strengths and weaknesses.

Drink water, have fun, call your mom. See you in part 2.

Week 26: Pattern Recognition

Humans are pattern recognition machines. That's good and bad.

Quick Update

This is Week 26. Fifty weeks divided by 2 is 25 … and 26 is greater than 25 … so that puts us >50% of the way through this experiment! Nifty. I have been having fun and I hope you are learning specific skills and techniques that you can put directly into practice in your trading. If you have read every single episode so far, I admire your hard work and you deserve a sticker.

The short SPY trade is back from the dead as we peaked right into mega resistance at 4300/4330 in SPX. Last week's MSTR short is almost at the take profit already, while XME trades well in a down market. Overall, the 50in50 trades had a good week.

Here are the results from last week's sentiment vs. confidence survey. Similar to Week One, people are looking for lower stocks and generally tighter financial conditions. The consensus was generally correct last week.

Sentiment vs. confidence (1 is least confident, 5 is most confident)

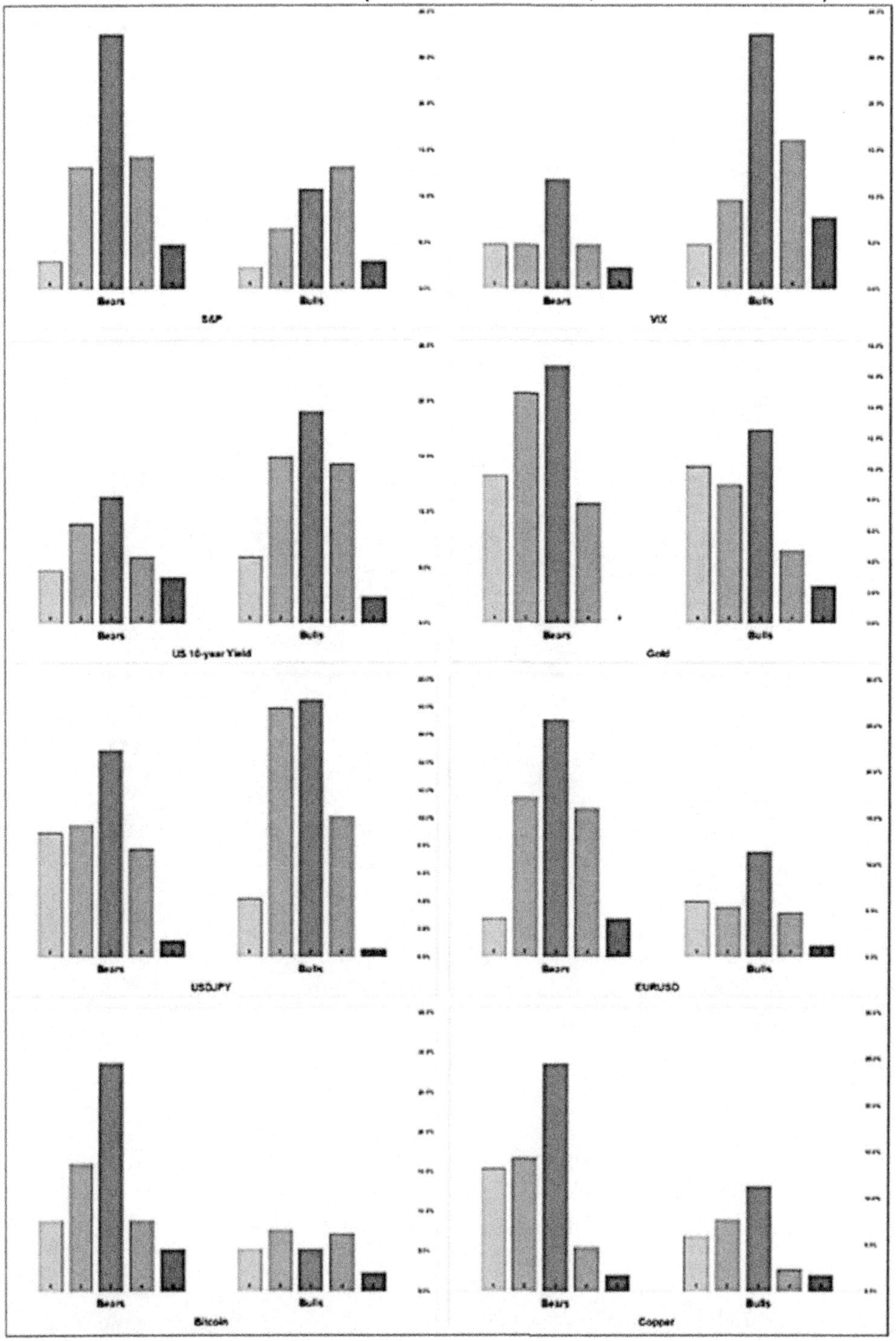

Now, let's talk about pattern recognition and backtesting.

Pattern Recognition

"Chaos is not dangerous until it begins to look orderly."
- Max Gunther, *The Zurich Axioms*

Great traders are masters of pattern recognition. They will see a setup and recognize it either consciously or unconsciously. I remember many times after great runs of trading that I felt like I knew what was going to happen before it happened. This ability comes from the incredible powers of human pattern recognition. The problem is:

Humans are built to see patterns, even when none exist.

Apophenia and patternicity are terms psychologists use to describe the human predisposition to see patterns or connections, even where none exist. Apophenia leads to many flaws in human thinking and explains why people see Jesus on toast, UFOs in the sky, bigfoot in the woods and so on. This human bias toward pattern recognition also leads gamblers who are on a winning streak to believe they will keep winning. Even smart, logical people often feel like they are "heating up" after a lucky series of hands at a poker table.

This is also known as clustering illusion. People have a hard time believing that streaks are the result of randomness, even though random data contains many streaks!

We are wired to find meaning and significance in random and meaningless data. Apophenia goes a long way toward explaining why humans believe conspiracy theories, suffer from paranoia, and embrace pseudoscience. When you see patterns everywhere, you see meaning and connections too. Understand that you are not immune! You are predisposed to see patterns, even where none exist.

The human ability to see patterns is a critical part of our evolution and allows us to understand the world without having to analyze every single new piece of information. If we have never seen a large black cat with large teeth on the savannah, a useful evolutionary trait was to assume that its behavior and risk profile is similar to other large animals with huge teeth we have encountered in the past.

We can correctly infer that the presence of dark clouds in the sky above us represents an increased probability of rain in the next few hours. We know a hissing sound nearby means snake bite risk is higher than normal and we dramatically increase our alert level.

Evolution favored false positives over false negatives because the cost of a false positive in the wild was much lower than a false negative. For example, there is a loud grumbly noise in the bush that Caveman Kror cannot clearly identify:

False positive (Type 1 error): That sounded like a lion, I think?! I'm out of here!

Cost: Kror may have used some unnecessary energy avoiding what could have been just a random sound.

False negative (Type 2 error): Hmm, I wonder what that grumbly noise was. It didn't sound exactly like a lion. I guess I'm good. (42 seconds later) Oh, dang, it was a lion.

Cost: Kror is dead.

Seeing patterns where there are none may be superior evolutionary behavior, but it's not helpful in trading. Given the very strong human instinct to see patterns, how useful do you think simple eyeballing of charts, basic trendlines, and breakout patterns is likely to be? What are the odds that chart break is just a standard false positive—like the loud noise in the bush? Now add on human confirmation bias... Are you just seeing what you want to see? Probably.

This does not mean that there are no patterns in the world. If you run into heavy traffic four days in a row at a particular interchange, it makes sense to consider whether there is causation. Investigating further, or temporarily changing your route is likely to be optimal. But you need to be aware that the way humans see patterns is biased to Type 1 errors. You need to be discriminating and use a tight filter when looking for patterns. You need to consider that what you are looking at could be random.

Let's say you see a headline on Bloomberg: "Death Cross in silver futures triggers bearish signal". You pull up the story and see a fugly chart where the 50-day moving average has just crossed below the 200-day. Is your first instinct to sell silver? Or to investigate more deeply? Patterns like this should not be taken at face value. Most of them are meaningless and have no empirical basis. Take half an hour to pull some data into Excel and backtest the pattern. Does it have any predictive value?

When I say "patterns" that does not just mean technical analysis. It is any cause-and-effect relationship that appears to exist in markets. Again, humans tend to ascribe causality to many things that are the result of pure chance.

On the other hand, patterns like the following examples could be meaningful, persistent, and predictive:

- Gold tends to go lower from 9 a.m. to 10 a.m. (maybe gold producers sell at this time?)
- Whenever US rates go lower, USDJPY goes lower (Japanese investors prefer higher rates?)
- AAPL tends to lead the QQQs (large caps lead indexes?)
- Highs and lows are more likely on round numbers than non-round numbers (humans exhibit round number bias)

- Bankrupt stocks usually rally on the open after being halted (nobody left to short and shorts wanna cover)
- Two days before the last day of the month, the USD tends to rally (this is the day many corporations buy USD to hedge foreign revenues)

And so on. Sophisticated pattern recognition can be a significant source of edge when it is free from bias.

Finding and analyzing patterns

I spend a good part of my time analyzing data in an attempt to determine whether patterns have predictive value or not. Most often, the answer is "not". Taking the time to analyze patterns and to determine whether or not they are useful for forecasting is a good way to overcome apophenia and discover useful tools for beating the market.

This is my simple four-step method for accepting or rejecting patterns:

1. Identify a pattern or relationship.
2. Generate a hypothesis.
   The best patterns have some sort of underlying logic. If gold goes down every day from 9 a.m. to 10 a.m., maybe that is the window when gold producers sell. If you can logically explain why a pattern works, it is much more likely to be non-random and persistent.
3. Analyze the data.
4. Accept or dismiss the pattern.

Anyone who took a science class as a kid should recognize this as a short-form version of the scientific method. Most patterns you analyze will be worthless. You will dismiss them and move on. On the other hand, the few patterns you find that are non-random can be incredibly valuable to your future trading.

Every time you notice a pattern, reduce it to something you can test and then get to work. You don't need sophisticated quantitative skills to do basic backtesting of simple theories. Once you backtest a pattern, you have a much deeper understanding of whether or not it is random, and you know whether to factor it into your trading decisions.

For example, I like to use moves in one market to predict moves in another market. Here is an example of how I will look at a pattern and try to determine whether or not it has meaning. This excerpt from am/FX also gives you an idea of how I pull together multiple reasons for a particular trade idea.

•

From am/FX on July 1, 2020

We had a rare setup at the close yesterday as US rates have dropped 8 bps in the last five days while USDJPY was up 1.3%. There have been 2610 trading days in the last 10 years and just 49 of them have satisfied the condition: (USDJPY up >1% and US 10-year yields down more than 7bps). Here is how USDJPY performed after:

USDJPY performance after two conditions met (sample = 49)

	t+1	t+3	t+5	t+10	t+20
Average return	-0.1%	-0.3%	-0.6%	-0.9%	-0.5%
% of time USDJPY goes down	56%	55%	63%	63%	65%

Two conditions: USDJPY up >1% in past 5 days and US 10-year yield down >7 bps in past 5 days

And note that USDJPY rallied from 88 to 107 in the last 10 years, so if you took any random sample it would show USDJPY going up, not down. That makes this result even more interesting. The medians are similar to the averages, so there is not a small group of instances skewing the average.

Overall, I think USDJPY is a sell based on yields, the move in gold, and USDJPY's consistent inability to take out 108.00. Also, there was a three-day run of buying madness in NY time from 7 a.m. to 11 a.m. and there is no evidence of that today. It was probably a major rebalance into month end. So that is over, which also helps.

Note in the chart below how USDJPY bashed against 108.00 four times (four arrows) before a huge false break and then it retested the 108.00 level again afterwards (fifth arrow).

I am therefore adding a short USDJPY recommendation. You could either sell here or leave an offer at 107.75 with a stop at 108.26. With ISM and payrolls tomorrow, there is a decent chance you get done. And with Yield Curve Control on the horizon and the explosion of coronavirus cases in the US South, I doubt strong US data will impact yields much.

Note by leaving an order to sell above market at 107.75 through nonfarm payrolls, I attempt to take advantage of the noisy volatility created by an event I think is meaningless to get set at a good level on a trade I like for a bunch of reasons. Here is the chart:

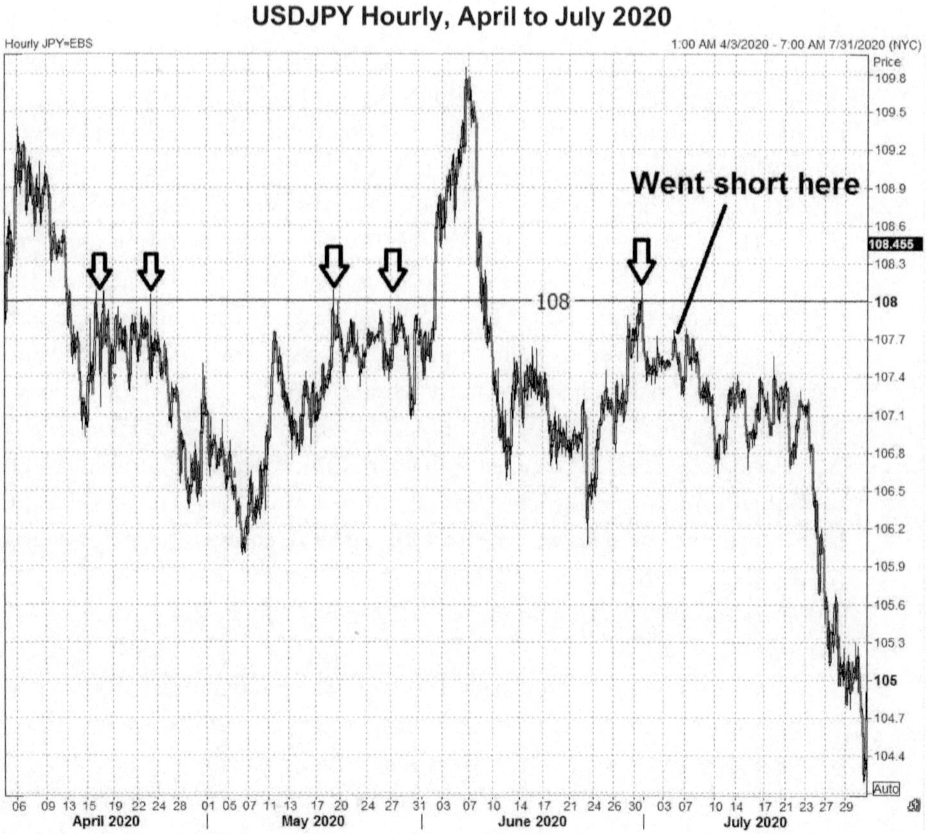

End of excerpt.

•

I got set on the trade the day after payrolls (at 107.75) and USDJPY went pretty much straight down.

Backtesting tips

Backtesting is an entire field of quantitative research and there is considerable complexity involved. I am not a computational finance or applied math expert, so I like to keep things as simple as possible. I come up with a theory, and then I test it. I don't tweak the parameters or snoop around until I find something useful. I just **go in, test, and get out.** While a full course in backtesting is beyond the scope of this book, you don't need a degree in financial engineering to conduct basic backtests of patterns you identify and ideas you come up with.

When testing your hypothesis, be aware of a few things:

1. The law of small numbers. You need a decent sample of observations for your analysis to mean anything. If you see that TSLA stock went down the last four Aprils in a row, that's meaningless. If it went down 33 of the last 41 Fridays, that might mean something. While there is no hard rule for legit sample size, any study using less than 30 observations is risky and likely to be less reliable.
2. The harder you have to look, the more likely whatever you find is bogus or biased. Let's say you want to see how the stock market performs the Monday after a 3% drop on Friday. You find nothing interesting. So then you test how it performs after a 4% drop on Friday. Still nothing. Then, you up the threshold to 5% and find the subsequent Monday averages a 2% further fall. Then you test, "What if stocks fall 2% or more Thursday AND 5% or more Friday" … The more you mess around with your parameters, the more likely you are to find "interesting" results. This is called "p-hacking" in the research business. You keep tweaking the inputs until you get an interesting result. That is not good research. **Don't torture your data in an effort to make it confess.** Keep your analysis simple. For the best ever and super simple explanation of how p-hacking, snooping and data-mining work, see "xkcd green jelly beans" at the end of this chapter.
3. Be aware of the trend in your data. If you do any study of S&P 500 data since 1930, you will generally find that bullish strategies perform well and bearish strategies perform poorly! This makes sense since stocks have gone up a zillion percent in that time period. Similarly, you will find it easy to "discover" bullish NASDAQ or bearish oil company strategies. The secular trend in the data is an important driver of the output of any strategy you analyze.
4. No matter how well something worked in the past, there's no guarantee it will work in the future. In a world of infinite data, many relationships, and a huge number of sophisticated analysts, people are going to find strategies that worked in the past. If you have a strong opinion on why the strategy is likely to work in the future, the value of your analysis is higher.

   For example, Turnaround Tuesday is well known and has existed for many years. It is founded on a reliable and repeatable pattern of human behavior and a persistent fear and greed cycle that repeats around weekends, even if statistically savvy investors know about it. Also, as a short-term strategy, it is fairly expensive to execute (in terms of transaction costs) so large institutions are unlikely to quickly arbitrage it away.
5. Don't build regression models unless you know what you are doing. Regression models can be useful but often require sophisticated knowledge to avoid data mining, overfitting, and other errors.

Most patterns in finance are random. You need to find evidence and use logic before accepting a pattern as meaningful.

The stock split pattern

Stock splits are a strange phenomenon that drives EMH proponents crazy because splitting a stock 2-for-1 should have no impact on the price of the shares. In theory. If I have one dollar bill, or four quarters, I don't expect the four quarters to sell at a premium to the dollar bill—it makes no sense! But things don't always have to make sense in markets. It's not a perfectly efficient world; it's just a bunch of humans buying and selling stuff and humans are not particularly logical at an individual level, or in aggregate.

The best explanation for why a stock split would increase the price of a stock is that the split news attracts attention to the stock. By definition, the stock is usually near the highs and there is a bullish story around it, so more attention = more buying.

Here is the abstract of a paper on the topic:

> *In this research I study whether stock splits attract market's attention by exploring how investors are trading around event announcement dates. By employing high frequency intraday trading data from NYSE Trades and Quotes (TAQ) database I compute net abnormal buying around split announcements. The empirical tests on a matched pair sample of splitting and matching firms show that stock splits serve as attention attracting tool and investors are buying abnormally more around the announcements. Additional analysis confirms this finding – abnormal buying is significantly higher for larger splits.*

I have noticed lately that not only do stocks rally on the split announcement, but they sell off after the split in what looks like a "buy the rumor / sell the fact" pattern. This would make sense as people buy the stock on the split because they think other people will buy the stock on the split (greater fool theory) and once the split happens, they have no reason to hold the stock anymore.

I asked Justin to take a look at the price action of stocks into and after the split date to see if this pattern is real or just my imagination. Here is the result:

Performance of well-known stocks that split in 2022

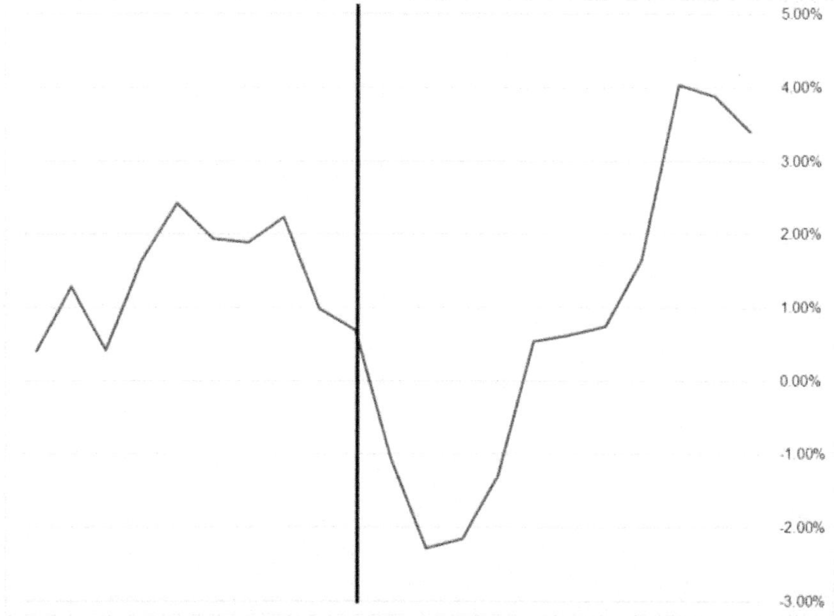

RJF MBIN WRB CM AMZN SHOP SAL GOOG GME

The sample size here is only 9 stocks, so **caution is warranted**. Not a great sample size! I have seen better patterns than this one, but I am using this one as this week's trade because it's relevant and timely and my belief is there is enough logic to the pattern that it's not random. My conviction on the trade is 5.7 out of 10.

TSLA splits tomorrow (24AUG) and trades post-split 25AUG. As such, selling TSLA here (888) with a stop at 914 (above the two recent opening gaps) makes sense based on this pattern. The effect is only good for a few days, and Powell speaks Friday, so the safe trade (and what I will do for tracking purposes) is square up at the close on Thursday, August 25. We don't want random Powell risk on a pattern like this.

In real life, you would want more of a thesis than a simple pattern like this. Perhaps you were already bearish TSLA and were waiting for a rally and now you got the rally and you now you also have this post-split pattern working in your favor. The pattern is another planet in line that helps you fine-tune your tactics and optimize your execution timing.

Conclusion

Backtesting might sound daunting if you're not a quant, but trust me, it's easy. Don't be intimidated by Excel—if you spend a couple of weeks trying stuff and Googling how to make Excel do something… Before you know it you'll be more than capable of quickly testing theories against prices and data. You don't need crazy math skills to do your own backtesting.

Use the scientific method to test patterns. Don't optimize parameters. Don't snoop for results if your initial idea turns up nothing. Be honest with your analysis and remember that humans are built to see patterns, even where none exist.

Further reading: *Fooled by Technical Analysis*[40] is an excellent learning tool if you want to know more about the fun and perils of backtesting, and building systematic strategies.

---

[40] https://www.priceactionlab.com/Blog/the-book/

Week 27: Time of Day

Time of day effects can be large and predictable

Quick update on previous trades

The short SPY trade is back from the dead and now in the money, as we peaked right into mega resistance at the trendline and 200-day MA at 4300/4330 in SPX. As someone who uses technical analysis but is also kind of skeptical of techs at times, I must say combining sentiment and techs with a macro bearish view of tightening liquidity has been an excellent framework all year. Every bounce in EURUSD stops exactly where it should. The S&P 500 rallies stop exactly where they should.

The MSTR short from Week 25 hit the take profit and was an absolute thing of beauty. High leverage, zero pain. The post-split TSLA short broke even after a few jitters on the open.

Here are the results from last week's sentiment vs. confidence survey. Similar to weeks one and two, people were looking for lower stocks and generally tighter financial conditions. The consensus has been generally correct. I will be interested to see if people are still so bearish now that everything has moved so much.

Sentiment vs. confidence (1 is least confident, 5 is most confident)

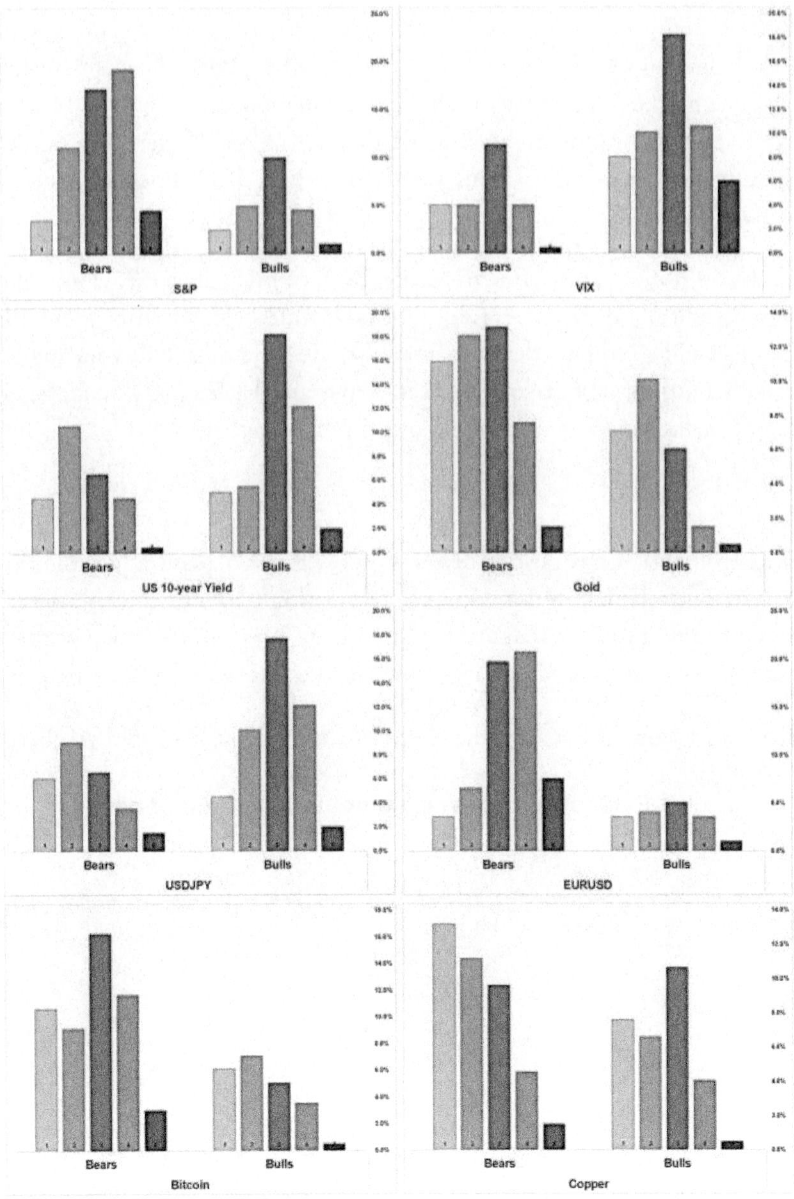

Now, let's talk about time-of-day patterns and considerations.

Time of Day

Microstructure is the study of flows, liquidity, intraday activity patterns, price discovery, transaction costs, volatility, and anything else that is part of the underlying structure of how, when, and why markets move. Chapter 8 of *Alpha Trader* is all about microstructure.

It's an important topic and the place where short-term traders can most easily find an edge.

There is not one easy answer to: How do you find an edge using microstructure? It depends on the market you trade, your time horizon, your trading style, your amount of capital, and your transaction costs. But even those trading longer time frames can use microstructure analysis to optimize entry and exit points, determine stop losses, and avoid common traps and leaks.

In this week's 50in50, I explain one particular facet of microstructure: Time of day. I put together four radically different examples of how time of day matters, and I hope that these examples will stimulate ideas for how to trade time of day in your market. When you're done here, think about your market. What are the features, nuances, anomalies, patterns, and inefficiencies you see at various times of day?

Intro

Just about every market has various textures and features depending on the time of day. There are windows where flow dominates. There are high-volume, highly volatile periods, and there are times of the day that are random, drifty, and stupid. Much of this relates to flows going through the market because flows tend to center around particular times.

Just to give you a sense of how volume varies by time of day, here are two charts.

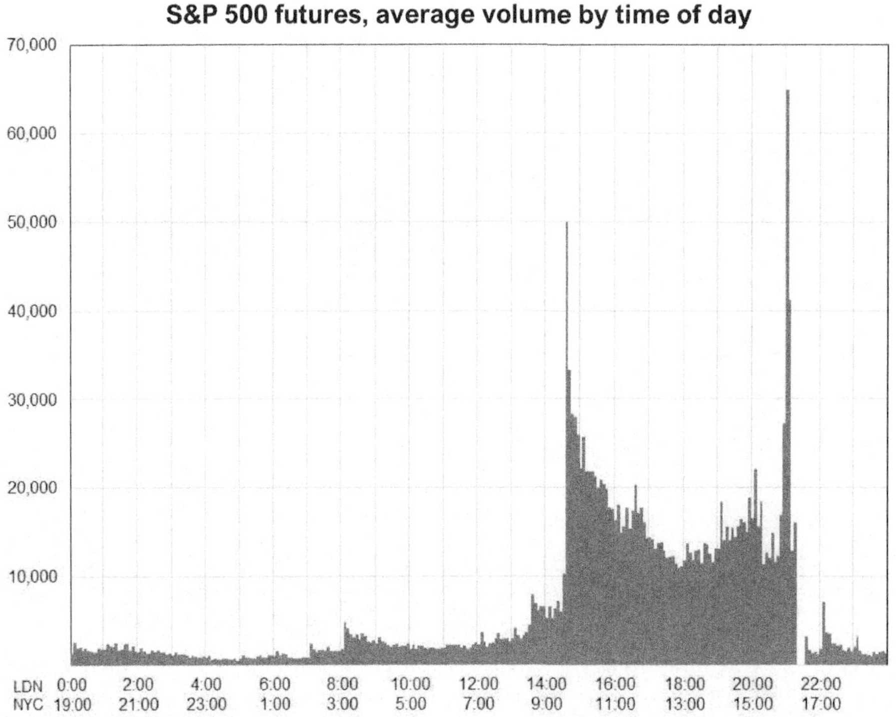

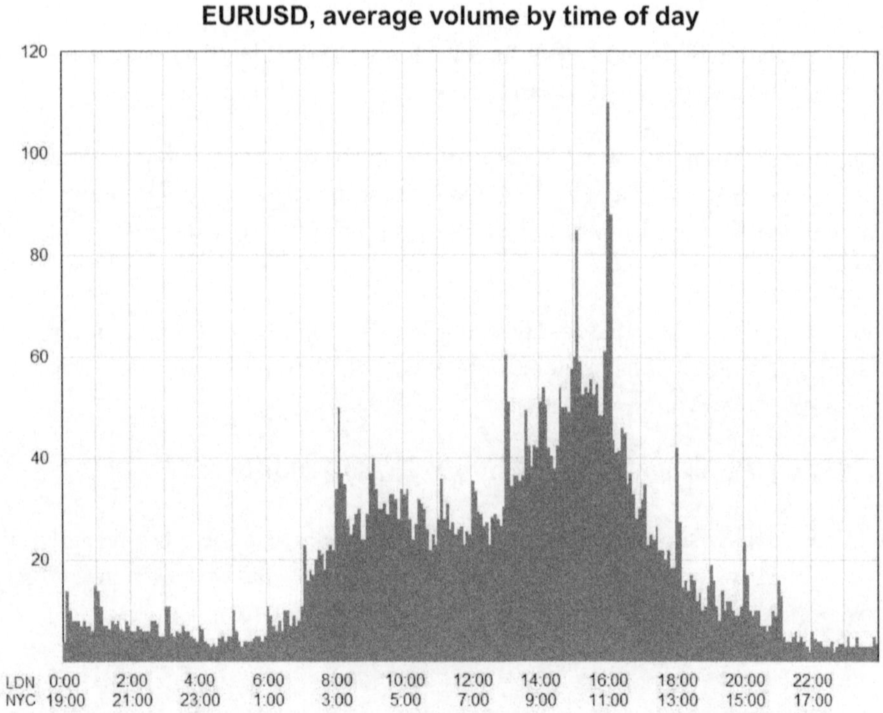

Volume and volatility tend to be correlated, though that is not always the case. Here's the volatility of AAPL and SPY, by time of day:

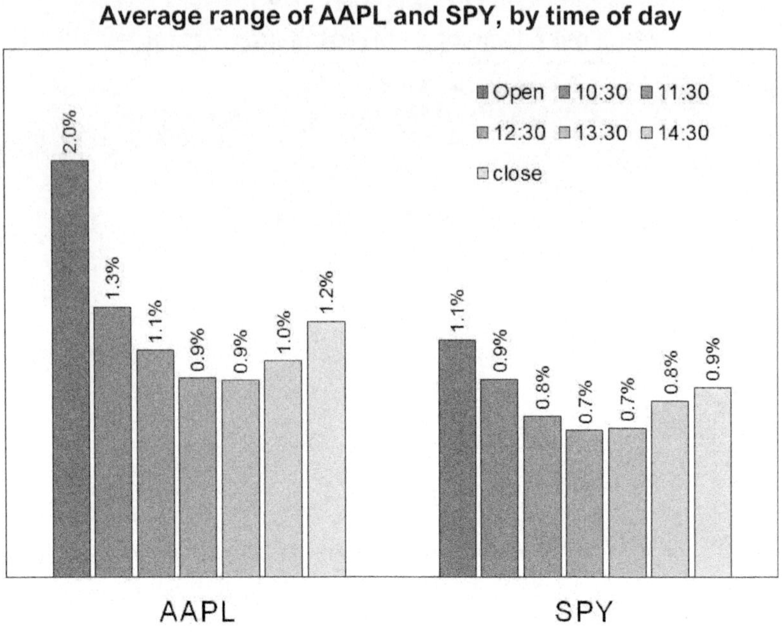

As a general rule, good traders are active when things are moving, and when volumes are high. High volatility is a predictor of high P&L for good traders (expected value but not every single day) and transaction costs are lower when markets are busy.

As such, the first thing you want to do, if you know nothing else, is focus on the busiest times of day for your market. There are traders that make a living only trading the open and close of stocks, for example, and many of those traders consider the rest of the day mostly noise.

Let's look at three specific time-of-day strategies. The point is not for you to start trading these strategies yourself. The point is to show you some examples, and then let you find your own strategy in your own market.

Time of Day Example 1: The Gap and Trap in Stonks

I like to read academic papers about finance but generally find them boring and at times find them hard to understand. This paper is not boring; it's well written and easy to understand: *Night Moves: Is the Overnight Drift the Grandmother of All Market Anomalies?*[41]

The fact that equities outperform overnight and suck wind intraday is well known and has been known for years. Here is a chart from the paper. Variations of this chart have been going around for more than two decades.

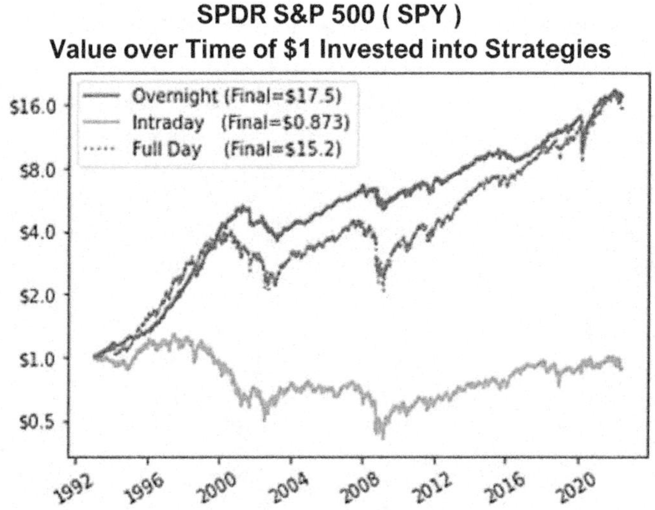

And here is NASDAQ performance by hour of day over the past twelve months. The big down bars at 9 and 10 show the 9 am to 11 am period is no bueno.

[41] https://papers.ssrn.com/sol3/papers.cfm?abstract_id=4139328

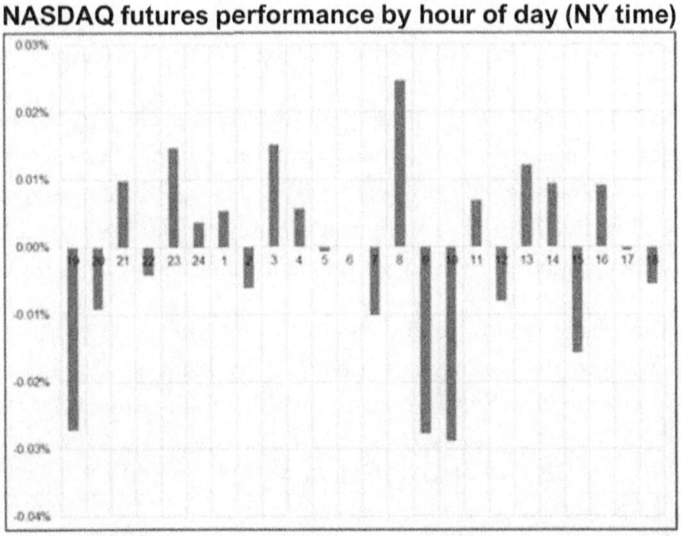

While this effect is well known, a good explanation has been lacking. The authors of the paper do an excellent job of explaining some theories in plain English and the theory that makes the most sense, by far, is that **retail traders tend to net buy stocks, and retail traders tend to leave "buy on open" orders.**

This creates a premarket buy imbalance which means market makers must move the price as high as possible into the open (at which point they are now short the stock) and then step away once the opening bell rings and the imbalance is filled. This is similar to any fixing in the FX or oil markets.

There is a large imbalance centered on a particular moment in time and the market peaks right at that time. So… It's not that stocks do well overnight and poorly during the day, it's that individual stocks attract buy imbalances on the open and those imbalances drive individual stocks up into 9:30 am. In aggregate, this effect can be seen in the futures, but it operates at the single stock level.

The more retail-y the stock, the bigger the impact:

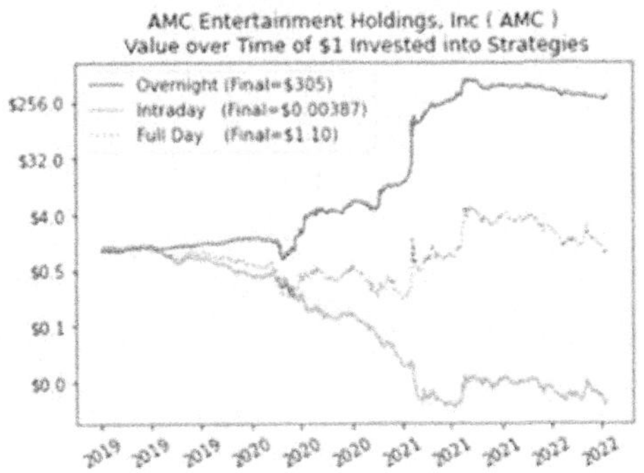

When I used to trade single-name equities at a place called SwiftTrade during the dotcom bubble, one of the main strategies I used was called the "gap and trap."

Put simply, you look around for the biggest pre-market topside gappers, wait until about 10 seconds before the open, go short, and cover about ten minutes later. If there was big news overnight, it attracts retail "buy on open" orders and it also triggers resting stop losses that will all be filled at the opening price. Market makers are going to be short the net balance at 9:30 am and so their incentive is for that open to be as high as possible.

I wrote about this phenomenon in June, in am/FX, my global macro and trading daily[42]. KZR and SNOW were two examples that popped up that day. Here is how they traded. KZR was a buyout story and SNOW was an investment bank upgrade.

KZR and SNOW: Gap and traps on 28JUN

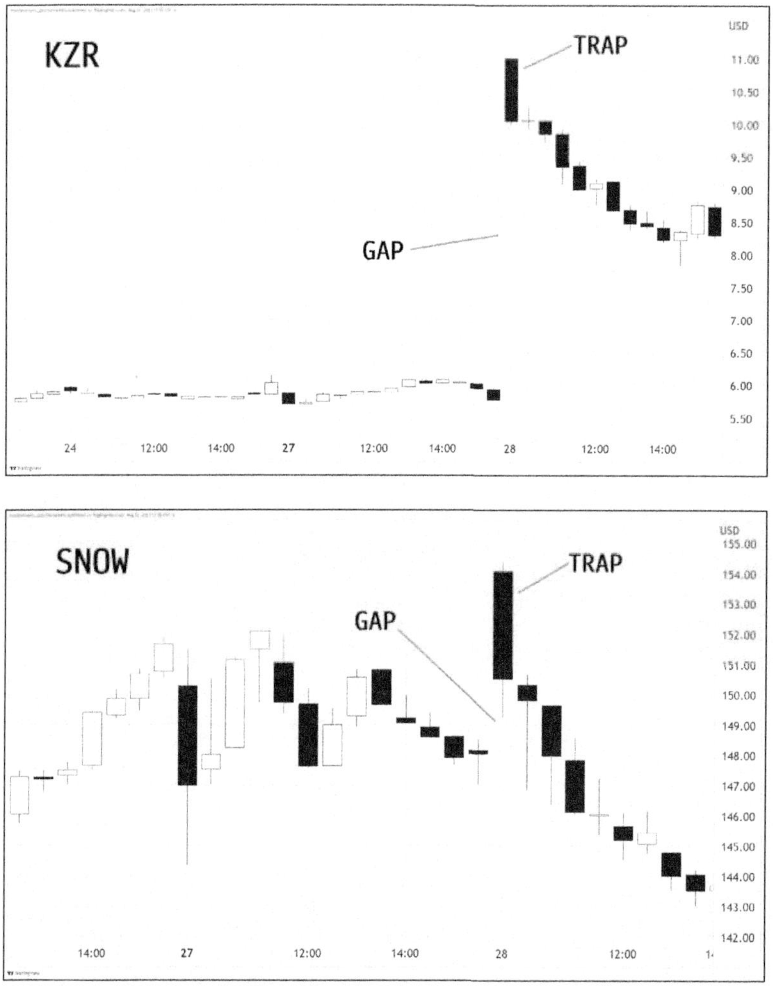

[42] https://www.spectramarkets.com/subscribe/

The gap and trap is hard to risk manage because you are getting involved with extreme volatility and trading right into a frenzy. That's why they are fun and profitable. But they also require strong discipline because they are the kind of trades that can keep ripping and wipe you out if you don't know what you're doing.

Time of Day 2: Closing Time in Oil

There are particular windows of time each day where flows are likely to be transacted. The best-known of these would be the open and close of US stocks (9:30 am and 4:00 pm Wall Street time) but there are many others.

Traders at banks and hedge funds have a distinct edge here as they know much more about flows than a trader sitting behind a screen at home. Still, there are simple ways to identify the time of day effects in your market.

Flow generally has both a signal and a noise component. Flow is often a real market participant (not a speculator) transacting in the market and that can have important directional information. For example, when a Japanese oil importer buys USDJPY, there is both a signal and a noise component.

Signal: Japan's petroleum trade deficit is impacting the currency market in an observable way.

Noise: USDJPY just shot up 50 points and will mean revert whenever the buyer is done.

As a general rule, flow moves the market and when the flow is done, there is partial mean reversion of the move caused by the flow. This is not always true because a flow can create momentum that triggers more flow or stop losses and spec activity in the same direction.

The window for flows varies dramatically by the product you trade, but every market has windows of time where flows are most dominant. Think about strategies to predict the flow and trade ahead of it, trade the mean reversion after the flow, or simply avoid getting your head ripped off by random, unexpected volatility. A particularly nutty time of day effect is the NYMEX close at 2:30 pm NY time.

Here's how average crude oil volumes look on the NYMEX, each day.

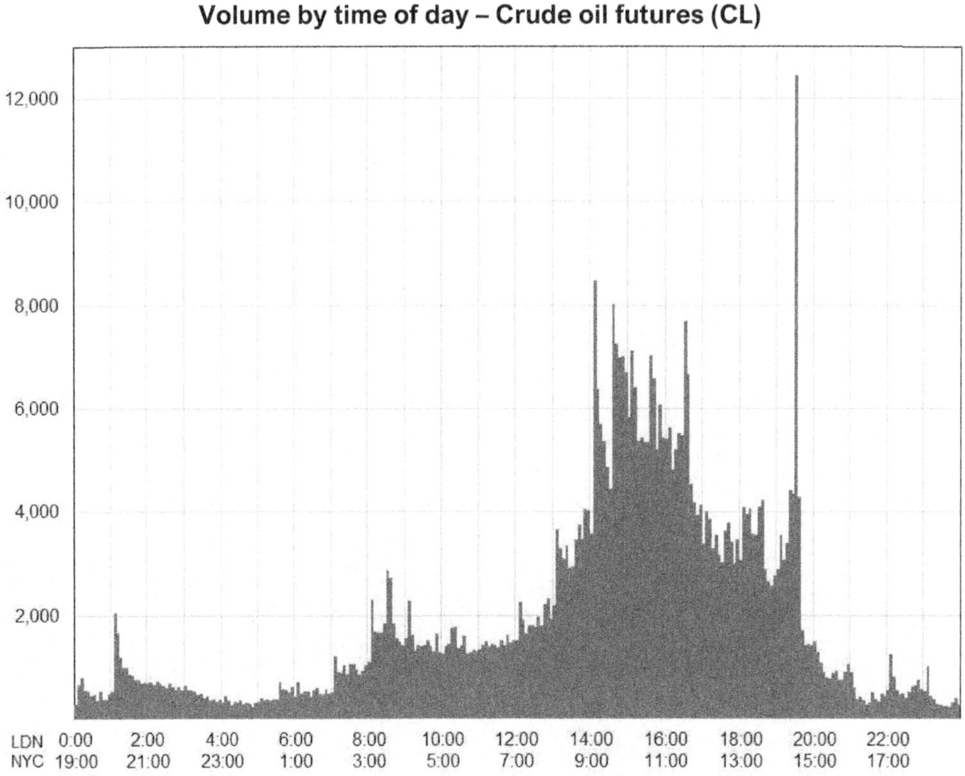

That insane volume spike at 2:30 p.m. is the NYMEX close.

Many participants use Trade at Settlement (TAS) orders to guarantee the closing price on their fill and the hedging of these TAS orders creates a monster volume spike in the minutes leading up to the close. If this volume is not balanced, you will sometimes see a huge move at that time. If someone yells "What's going on in crude!" right at 2:30 p.m., just shake your head and say "NYMEX close, dude. NYMEX close." :]

How would you trade this? If you're long and it rips into 2:30 pm, you cover. If you're flat, and you wanted to be short above market because of X, Y and Z (tech levels, macro, whatever) … And oil rips higher into 2:30 pm… You sell the rip.

Or maybe you develop a model that predicts which way the flow will go and get long or short before and square up into it… etc. You predict it, you fade it, or you use it as an entry opportunity for a trade you wanted to do for other reasons. And you avoid breakout trades that trigger around that time because mean reversion is more likely than continuation.

I am not telling you to do any of these things, I am saying they are examples of ideas that might work.

PS: If someone wants to backtest this and tell me whether systematic mean reversion trading around large moves at the NYMEX close is a profitable strategy… Please do!

Time of Day 3: What's Japan doing in USDJPY?

Another example of a time of day pattern, which I briefly referenced above, is Japanese activity in USDJPY in Tokyo. Here's the total return of USDJPY, by time zone, since 2018:

USDJPY total return by time zone, 2018 to now

Courtesy of Deepak Ramaswami, Spectra FX Solutions

Focus on the line with the huge drop in it (Asia time), as that is the main window in Tokyo where Japanese hedgers are busy. You can see there was a profitable strategy to be long USDJPY every day in Japan time since the start of 2021. This is not a fooled by randomness situation; USDJPY rallies when oil is rallying because Japanese importers must buy USD to purchase oil. Note that line looks somewhat similar to a chart of crude oil:

Crude oil 2018 to now

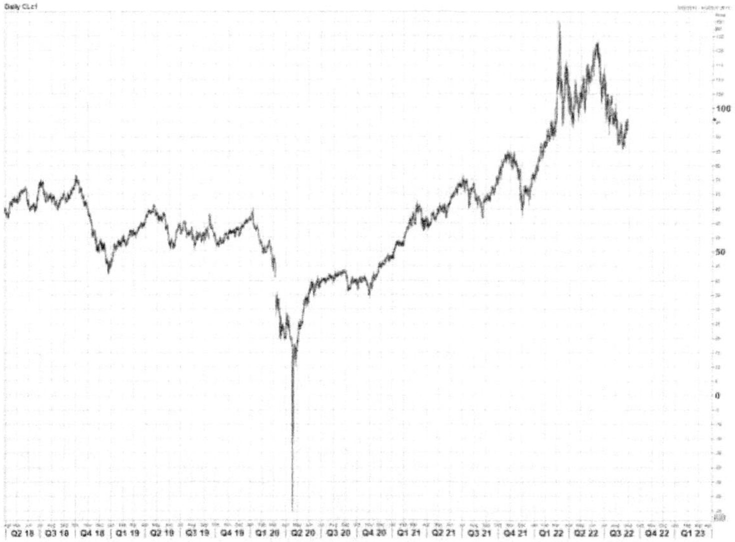

We ran a systematic model that traded USDJPY only in Japan time for years and it produced excellent returns net of transaction costs and a high Sharpe. We also ran a flipper 2010-2016 that went short USDJPY in Japan and long USDJPY in NYC. That "flipper" was pure gold. Here's the time of day data for USDJPY in that period:

USDJPY return by time zone, 2010 to 2019

You can see that going short the Asia line (the one that dips sharply in 2016) and long the NY line (the one that keeps going up) was pretty sexy for many years. And here's oil for the same period:

Crude oil 2010 to 2016

Same story! The flipper was turbocharged by Abenomics but **the underlying driver of Japan USDJPY was still the price of oil** the whole time.

Explainer: What is Abenomics?

Abenomics is one of the great macro trades of all time. It describes the set of policies introduced by Shinzo Abe in 2012/2013 as he was determined to rid Japan of its deflationary malaise. The policy successfully targeted a weaker currency and stronger stock market and drove USDJPY from 75.00 to 125.00 in less than three years while pushing Japanese inflation away from negative readings and up towards the BOJ target of 2.0%.

Bank of Japan governor Haruhiko Kuroda was a key player in this policy, and he is set to step down as BOJ governor in April 2023.

I hope those three strategies give you an idea of how time of day influences markets.

There are countless other examples. In bull markets, crypto goes up most in the first seven days of the month because inflows are driven by retail payday cycles and institutional inflows at the start of the month. Gold trades heavy around the time producers sell each day. FX markets rip or dip for no reason into 11 a.m. sometimes as mutant flows are benchmarked to that time. Option expiry can create predictable patterns in stocks and currency markets. And so on.

Understand your market at a time of day level and find an edge.

P&L by time of day

Here is a completely different way to think about time of day impacts in trading.

An extremely useful analysis for short-term traders is to look at your P&L by time of day. The way I collected this information when I worked at a hedge fund was to manually record my P&L in a spreadsheet every 30 minutes. If you can have this done automatically; that is even better. After collecting intraday data for a while, I noticed that my P&L very consistently rose from 7:00 AM and peaked around 11:00 AM. It then came off gradually until the end of the day. The chart looked something like this:

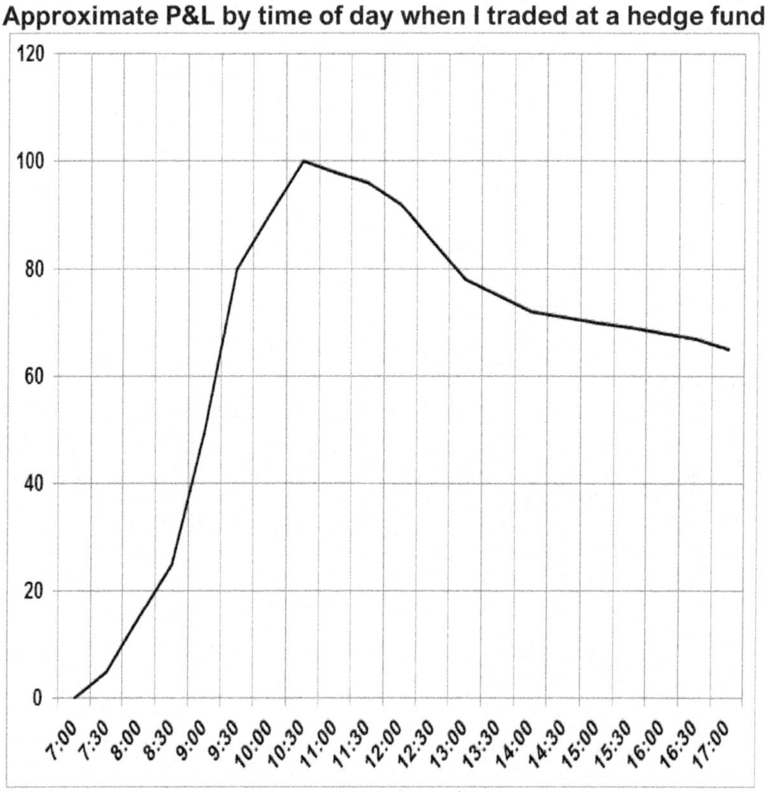

y-axis is percent of total daily P&L, on average

I was unaware of this pattern until I started recording intraday P&L data. There is a strong logic to a pattern like this because the volatile and liquid period for FX markets in the New York time zone is 7:00 a.m. until 11:00 a.m. After that, London goes home and things tend to die down.

Armed with the information from this chart, I started to square up much, much earlier each day. Instead of taking my risk down in the afternoon, I tried my best to reduce risk around 11:00 AM. This helped me lock in more P&L and it reduced my overall stress level because once I knew that all my trading after 12 noon was net negative, I could reduce my risk and use the afternoons for research, exercise, and other more useful endeavors. An added benefit of squaring up earlier is that liquidity is much better at 11 a.m. NY than it is at 4 p.m. NY.

This is a good example of how data collection and P&L analysis can make you a better trader.

OK, so what's the trade here?

Tesla time of day in 2022

Given the research quoted on the meme stocks and my recent focus on trading TSLA from the short side post-split, I decided to have a look to see if TSLA follows the same pattern as other meme stocks (rally overnight, sell off during the day). It does!

Here is time of day P&L for TSLA this year:

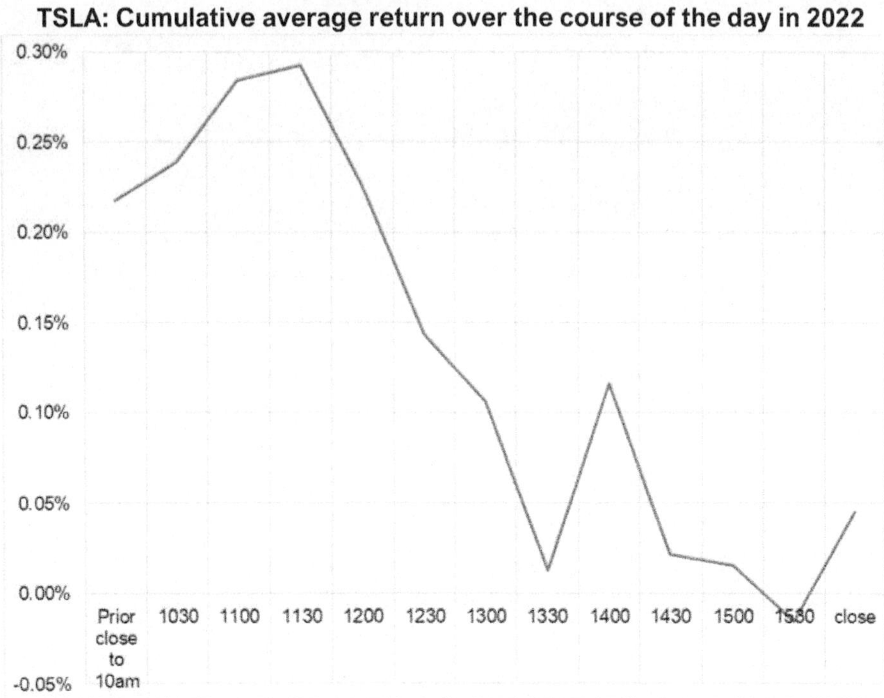

It follows the same pattern as the other meme stocks (gap overnight then selloff most of the day).

Here is the P&L of the strategy of long TSLA from 11 a.m. to the close each day (lighter line) vs. long TSLA from the close to 11 a.m. (darker line):

Long TSLA during the day (lighter gray) and long TSLA close to next day at 11am (darker gray)

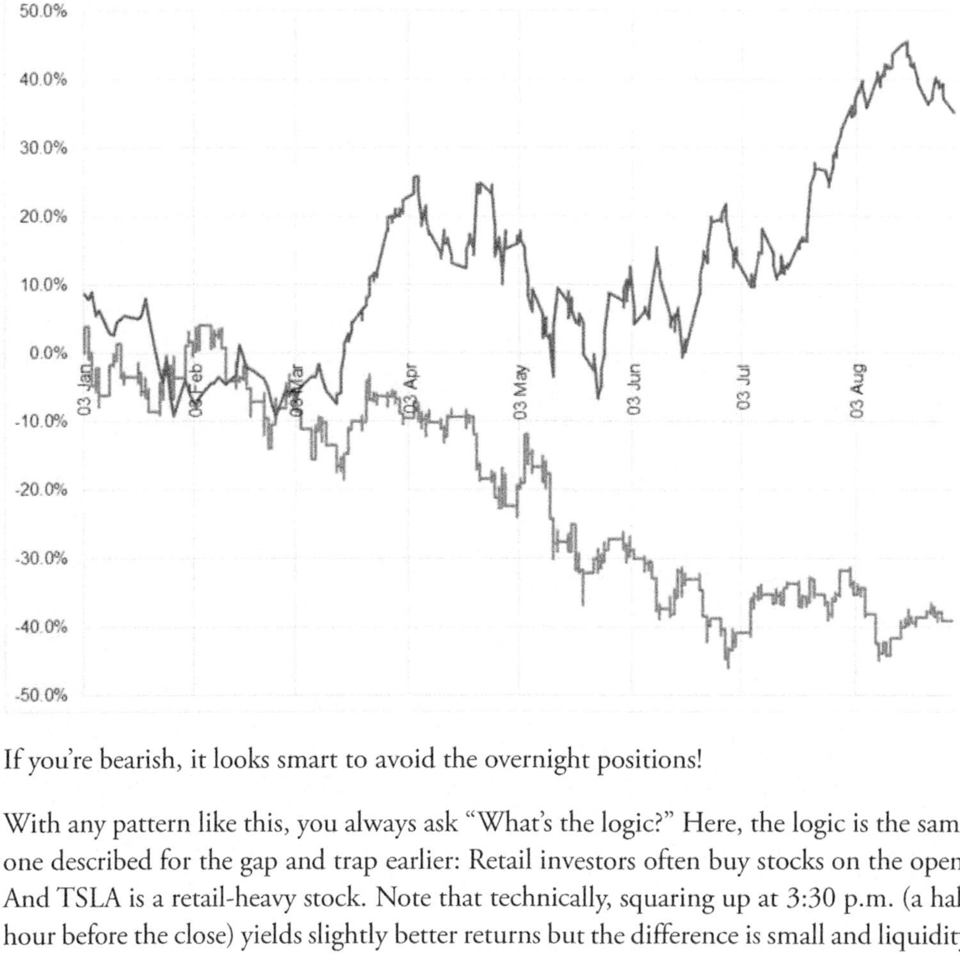

If you're bearish, it looks smart to avoid the overnight positions!

With any pattern like this, you always ask "What's the logic?" Here, the logic is the same one described for the gap and trap earlier: Retail investors often buy stocks on the open. And TSLA is a retail-heavy stock. Note that technically, squaring up at 3:30 p.m. (a half hour before the close) yields slightly better returns but the difference is small and liquidity is best at the close.

So this week's trade is a bit more complicated. I'm bearish TSLA post-split as I think the equity bear market has resumed after the perfect touch of the 200-day in S&P, the macro backdrop remains horrendous (central banks hiking into global recession), and TSLA keeps making lower highs and has an eventual date with the lows.

The trade this week is: Starting tomorrow, go short TSLA every day at 11 a.m. and cover at the close for the next three weeks. There are transaction costs (TC) here, but

TSLA trades 10 or 20 cents wide most of the time and if you trade at mid and take a bit of execution risk, you can get in and out of TSLA for almost zero TC (not always true!!!). Relative to an average daily range of 6%, TSLA's bid/offer of 0.05% (5 basis points) is not life-threatening.

I'm not necessarily saying this is a valid systematic strategy, but if I'm bearish TSLA, this is an (admittedly high-maintenance) way to play it and remove the stupid overnight gap risks on a random headline about the Twitter takeover situation or whatever. Again, **these 50in50 trades are for demonstration purposes.** Trade at your own risk. Ideally, you would want to have this running systematically for much longer than three weeks but this a long enough period to collect some results and move on.

While I am stressing this is an example, there are many systematic trades like this that work very well. Like I said, we used to do tons of them in FX and they delivered good returns and a good Sharpe. Transaction costs can sometimes be a challenge.

Another challenge: This type of trade is hard to size and risk manage. There is a whole field of study on sizing and risk managing systematic trades like this, but I'm going to keep it as simple as possible.

TSLA's average daily range is 6% and you can't really put a tight stop on stuff like this. In fact, adding stop losses to systematic strategies almost always leads to lower returns. So I'm gonna set this one up as follows:

- Max risk per day = $300
- Max risk total = $2,000. So if the strategy loses $2k, it gets turned off.
- Stop loss 10% away from entry point each day so there is some risk management but the odds of getting stopped out are low.
- Taking today's price as an example: $284. A 10% move is $28.40 therefore we will be short 10 shares because 10 X 28.4 is $284.00 (as close as we can get to $300 using a whole share number). Stop loss at entry point plus 10%. Cover at the close.
- The strategy will start tomorrow and the last day it will trade (if it doesn't blow through the full $2,000) will be 20SEP22. That is the day before the FOMC meeting. Running a strat like this through FOMC is ill-advised.

This might be stupid. It's an experiment. Let's see how it goes. I will create a spreadsheet and track this bad boy for the next few weeks and see how we do. I will also compare this strategy to simply straight-up shorting the stock with a stop loss at $315.50 (above the recent highs).

Conclusion

Time of day matters. There are good times of day to trade, and bad times. There are common traps that lead to bad outcomes for traders and investors who don't know what they are doing—traders that leave BUY AT OPEN orders, for example. There are ways to find an edge trading time of day patterns.

Identifying time of day patterns will:

- Help you find edges to trade
- Help you save money by avoiding leaks
- Focus your effort on trading the most lucrative times of day
- Open up new avenues for analysis and investigation
- Give you some basic insights into how systematic trading works

Understand the patterns, regularities, anomalies, signals, and noise at various times of day and you are on your way towards better short-term trading.

Week 28: Buy the rumor / sell the fact

A common behavioral pattern in TradFi and crypto

Quick update on previous trades

The short SPY trade is full-on Lazarus, way back from the dead and now well in the money. SPX peaked right into mega resistance at the trendline and 200-day MA at 4300/4330 in SPX.

The TSLA short view is working, though the time of day effect has been marginal.

Now let's talk about "buy the rumor / sell the fact."

Buy the rumor / sell the fact

Part of today's 50in50 is excerpted from my latest crypto note: MacroTactical Crypto #32: Stiff Competition and Hard Truths[43].

[43] https://mtcbd.substack.com/p/eth-stiff-competition-and-hard-truths

The reason "buy the rumor / sell the fact" works as a general pattern in financial markets, especially in markets populated mostly with inexperienced traders, is that everyone wants to be long when the good stuff is about to happen, but once the anticipated good stuff transpires… There is no reason to be long anymore. After the expected catalyst or event happens, everyone tries to sell at the same time post-event… And whoosh.

Buy the rumor / sell the fact has been a pattern since the dawn of markets and it always involves early buyers selling to later buyers. The later buyers then look to cash out but find… No bids. So the price falls.

This is often known as a buyer's strike. Why would anyone buy AFTER a big event, when they know about it before? They wouldn't. That's why buy the rumor / sell the fact works.

Almost all highly-anticipated events in crypto have been textbook buy the rumor / sell the fact trades.

The futures launch

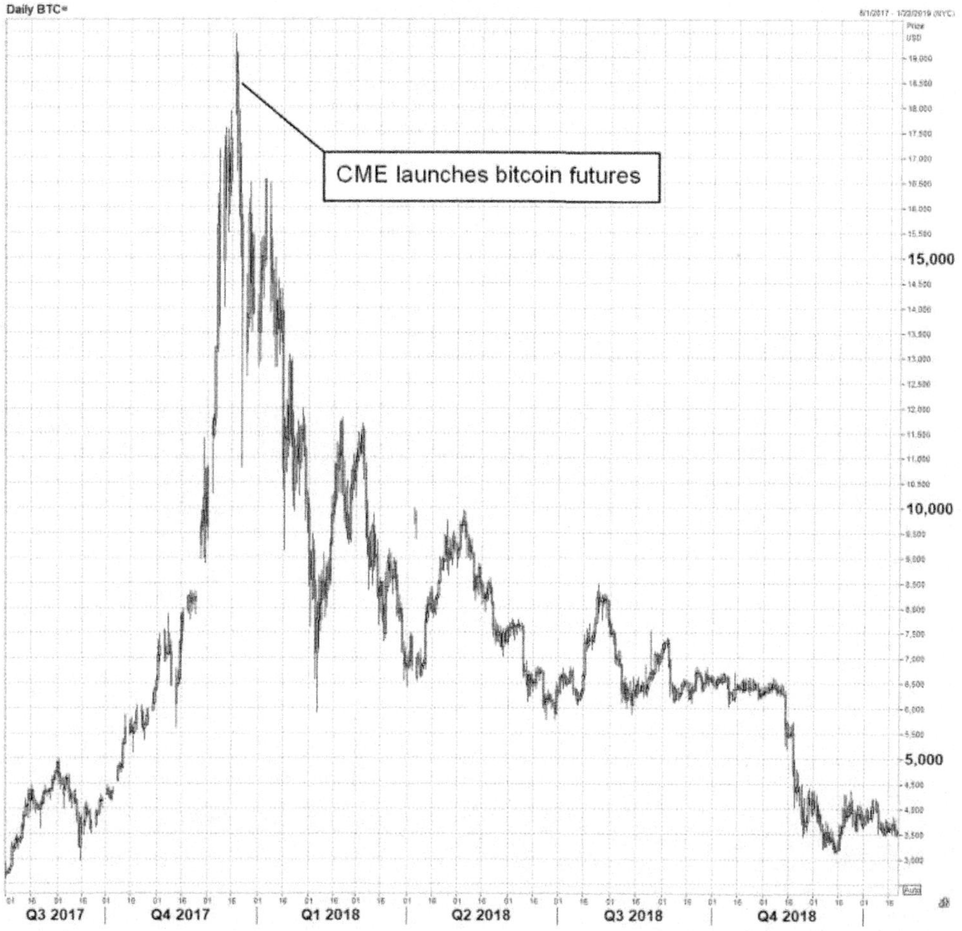

Elon on SNL

A comedy show, indeed sir.

The futures ETF launch

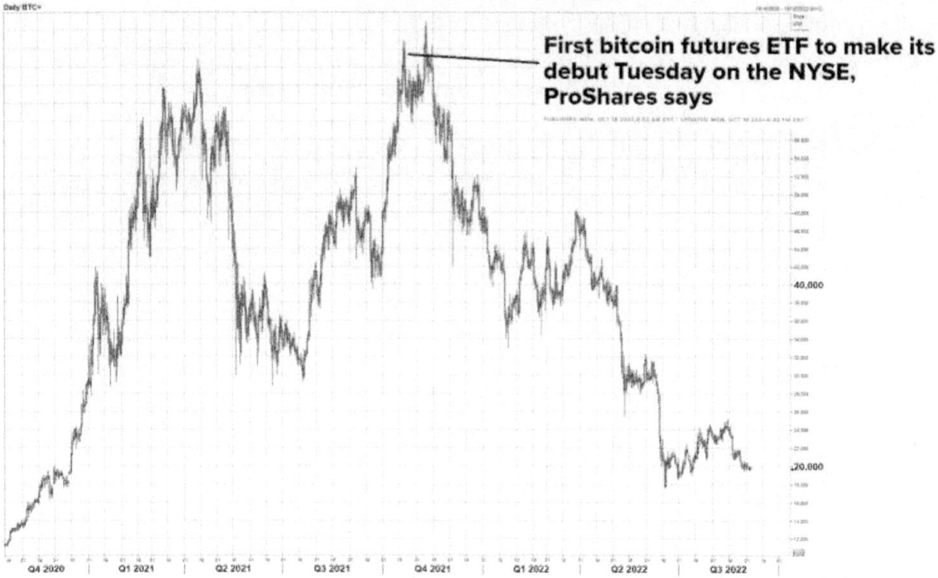

El Salvador adopts bitcoin day (07SEP21) also saw a textbook, though less epic version of the pattern.

El Salvador adopts BTC as legal tender!

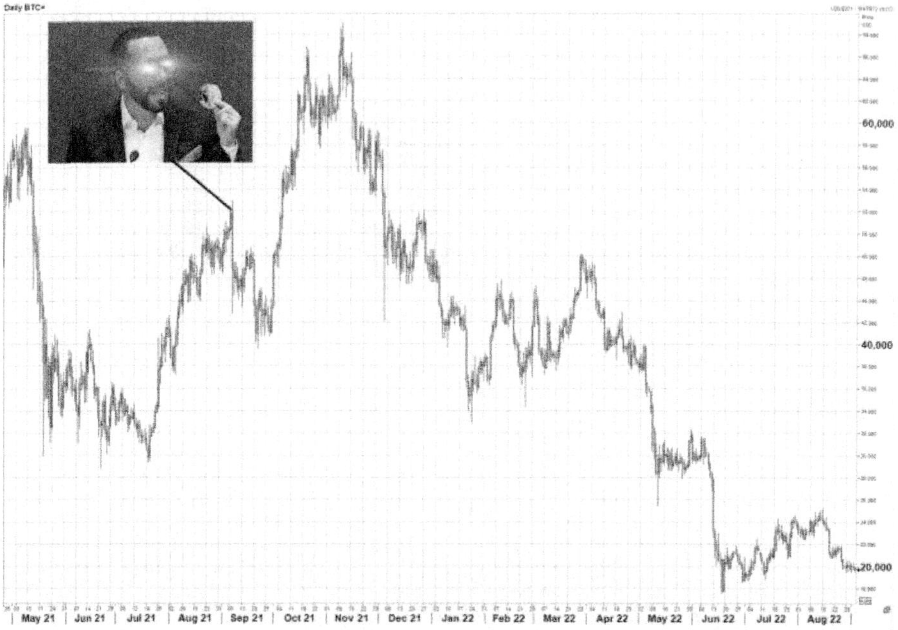

And you see similar silliness after stock splits. Traders buy stocks when they announce a split because they know they will find a greater fool to sell to as the split date nears. Once the split date arrives, the catalyst is passed and priced in and the stock goes down. Here's buy the rumor / sell the fact on the GameStop split:

You can't, you won't, and you don't stop

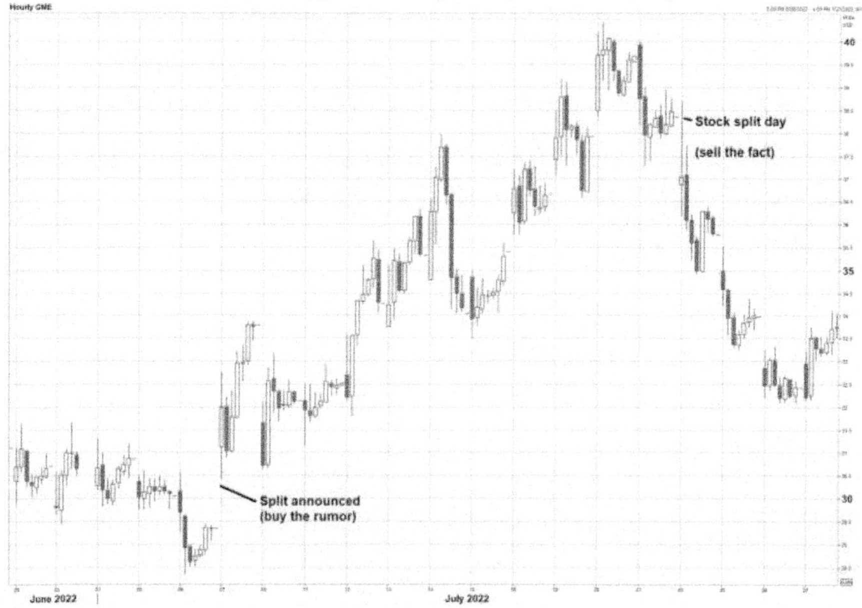

Come and rock the GameStop

This is a list of recent cryptomemetic examples but buy rumor / sell fact is a thing in TradFi too. Markets are forward-looking and price things in before those things happen. Once the thing happens, there's nothing to look forward to anymore so traders liquidate and move on to the next shiny object.

The Merge™

Ethereum is about to transition from proof of work to proof of stake. The date for the event is approximately September 13. Here is a chart of ETH since the announcement of a merge date:

ETH rallies on the Merge announcement

You can see there was significant buying in the days after the announcement as some believe The Merge will unlock all sorts of value and send ETH to the moon. The market piled into the September 30th 4000 ETH calls. There is a huge debate about the importance of The Merge, but this piece isn't really debating that one way or the other. This piece is about the idea of a known catalyst approaching from way out and landing in a week or so.

Who is going to buy ETH immediately after The Merge?

There is a 100% chance of significant selling by short-term specs in the hours and days after the Merge. They are simply (and logically) front running the event. I'm not talking about long-term buyers and inflows… Those will come when they come. Crypto hedge funds are not sitting on the sidelines waiting for the Merge to happen so they can buy

ETH at 1650. They're either long already or they might be leaving bids lower, but they are not waiting for the Merge to get out of the way so they can go to market.

IMPORTANT NOTE: Not every anticipated event leads to a historic selloff from the all-time highs. An important and notable example of this: Bitcoin halvings are known events that have resulted in prolonged bull markets before and after, not buy the rumor / sell the fact.

The big argument for post-Merge ETH longs is the digital bond hypothesis. "It will be an ESG-compliant, commodity-linked digital bond!" is the most extreme bull case. I can't get past the simple TradFi notion that ETH is way (wayyy) too volatile for any institution to care much or at all about the yield. I discuss this in detail in MTC32, but let me give you the gist here.

The reason bond yields are useful is because they are proportionate to the volatility of the underlying instrument. ETH as a 70-vol bond that yields under 7% makes little sense under any normal framework for evaluating fixed-income securities. Plus, if it's a digital bond, it's a security, and will thus attract interest from regulators.

When an institution looks at a carry product (a bond, currency carry basket, etc.) the standard metric they use is the carry/volatility ratio. That's the best snapshot of how much principal risk you are taking to earn a given yield. Here is carry versus vol for some well-known yieldy instruments, along with ETH. I have very generously assumed a 7% annual yield for ETH.

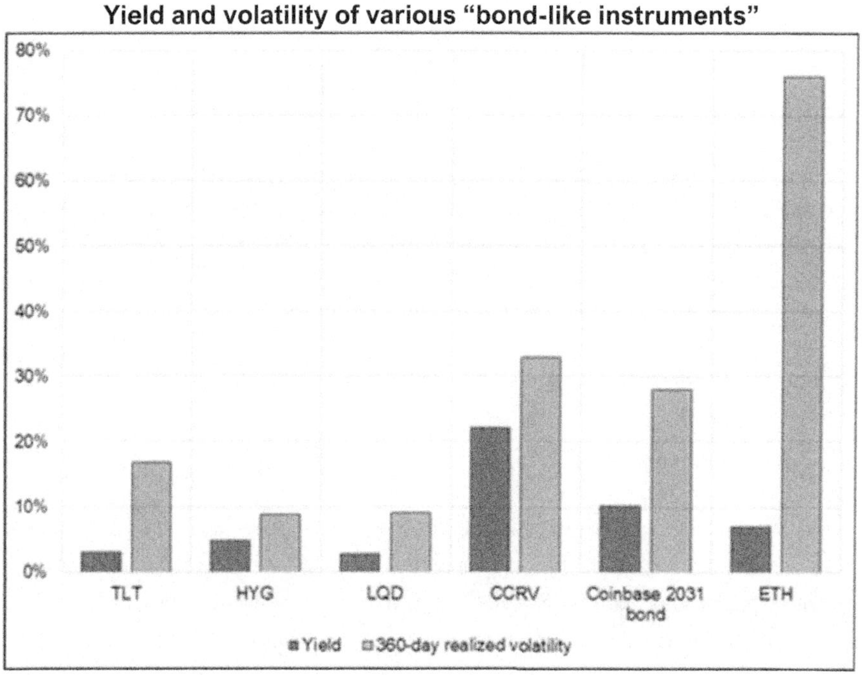

If this all sounds a bit Boomer/TradFi to you… Guess who runs the institutional money? TradFi Boomers.

The packaging and marketing of ETH as a digital bond rings hollow to me because it doesn't stand a chance against other bond-like instruments. The only way ETH works as a digital bond is if volatility collapses or if you package and hedge it and repackage it and/or lend and overcollateralize it into a synthetic derivative. Synthetic on-chain hedged ETH solutions are attractive to some, but introduce a lot of complicated, hard-to-measure basis risk (and execution and risk management inconveniences).

The synthetic ETH bond is probably only going to appeal to the most diehard institutional fans of crypto. One River Digital has been talking about this kind of digital yield product for a while and it surely has appeal. But it's niche and it existed before The Merge so I don't envision some massive stampede into synthetic digital yield post-Merge.

My feeling is that ETH bulls expect a huge wave of institutional adoption when really ETH as a bond-like instrument is a niche product that has become less attractive in recent months as the regulatory Eye of Sauron turns towards ad-hoc enforcement and criminal complaints against various crypto entities and coins.

Given everything I have read and considered… My view is: Sell ETH on the merge announcement. It should be classic buy the rumor / sell the fact.

Strategy vs. tactics

It's fun to look at those DOGE and BTC charts and dream about going short and never covering. The hard part is that you don't know if it's the DOGE scenario (collapse and never revisit that level), the El Salvador scenario (drop 25% in a few weeks then rip to new highs), or the BTC halving scenario (no pattern of trading other than some hard to identify bullishness before and after in the midst of a trend).

My view on buy rumor / sell fact is that it's a fairly short-term phenomenon and the effect is trumped by new information rather quickly. So while there were some epic sell-and-HODL opportunities in the past on these buy rumor/sell fact trades, the high expected value approach is to get in and out somewhat quickly. You capitalize on the juicy, reliable part of the pattern near the event date and who cares what happens once you take profit.

The Merge Trade: Details

The Merge will occur when Ethereum Mainnet hits the Terminal Total Difficulty (TTD) value of 58750000000000000000000[44]. That was thought to be 19SEP but the date keeps moving left. It was 15/16SEP and now looks to be **as early as 13SEP**. For my

[44] https://twitter.com/vitalikbuterin/status/1558072902972473344

purposes, The Merge is priced in and therefore I would rather just sell now, not wait for the announcement. The most likely price action immediately on the headline that The Merge has succeeded is ETH flash up 100 then down 300 or so (my guess, not investment advice!)

Always trade your own view and make sure you understand the risk you are taking (including gap and margin call risk). The first rule of trading is AVOID RISK OF RUIN.

Given the timing of the news is not precisely knowable and my belief it's fully priced in, 50in50 goes short ETH here (1650) with a stop loss 50% at 1906 and 50% at 2056. Take profit on the whole thing at 1155. Not super high leverage here, but you need to have the stop far enough away to avoid the zippy whipsaw jiggle fest vol explosion on September 13.

Week 29: Home Sweet Home

Flat can be a position of strength... Or a sign of trader weakness

Quick update on previous trades

I have decided to square everything up. The 50in50 trades have a decidedly bearish lean, and I have been waffling on the bearish view of late as the USD looks less impulsive to the upside and things improve in the Ukraine. The CPI release gives me a chance to square up at good levels—a get out of jail free card kind of thing. I will provide a full update of all the trade results next week (Week 30). For now, the trade this week is to square everything up and get close to home.

In this piece, I'll explain why getting close to home is a good habit for many traders, but can be a bad habit for others.

Home Sweet Home

Risk appetite in trading is a continuum that looks something like this:

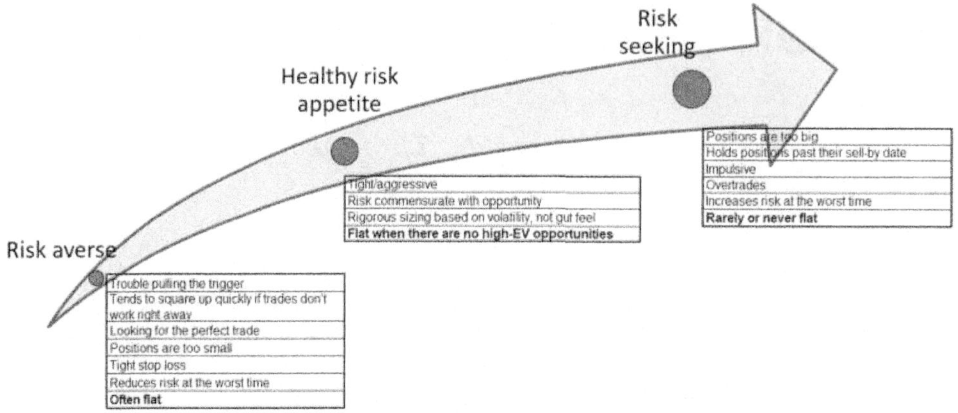

You can see from this graphic that different traders get flat for different reasons. Let's look at the traders across this spectrum, examine how they behave, and see what we can learn from it.

Before we look at risk-averse vs. risk-seeking traders, remember that risk appetite is not constant. Many traders behave differently under different conditions. Here are three effects that influence trader risk appetite:

1. Zero-bound effect. Traders that are down on the year tend to trade more nervously than traders who are up. If you are up $4 million on the year and drop to $2.5 million (a loss of $1.5 million), that will feel different than going from plus $1 million to minus $500,000. You need to have the courage to take smart risk, even when you are down.
2. End-of-period effect. Traders tend to take less risk at the end of the year. If a trader has had a good year, they want to bank it. If they have had a bad year, they don't want to make it worse. This effect is why most hedge funds will not pay out more than once per year. Hedge funds that institute twice-yearly payouts find that trader risk appetite drops in both June and December, instead of just in December.
3. House money effect. Traders that are massively profitable in a given period will tend to take on extra risk. This is known as the house money effect, a bias that shows up in both experimental and real-world settings. The house money effect is especially strong immediately after large gains, and then it dissipates over time.

In my book *Alpha Trader,* there is a trader questionnaire and one of the attributes I ask traders to rate themselves on is risk appetite. The scores run from 1 to 10. Here is a quick discussion of different risk appetite scores, what they mean, and how to address problems related to specific ranges. Before reading this: What would you rate yourself from 1 to 10 on the risk-averse to risk-seeking spectrum?

Risk appetite score: 1-4 – Risk averse trader

More traders than you would expect fall into the 1-4 range. That's OK! You can still succeed in trading if you are risk averse. But don't be in denial. Be self-aware and be honest about your score. A score between 1 and 4 signals you are a risk-averse trader. Even if your risk appetite score is higher than four, please read this section.

The risk-averse trader:

- Is afraid to lose money. It is impossible to trade successfully if you are afraid of losing money. You will always be weak. If your fear comes from within, you need to work on it. If your fear comes from inadequate capitalization, the irony is this: your fear of losing money means you are going to lose all your money. Wait until you are adequately capitalized and find another source of income until then. Traders with too little capital end up gambling. The biggest risk in trading is that you will lose money. You need to understand and accept this risk before you can have any chance of success as a professional.
- Has trouble pulling the trigger.
- Always looks for the perfect trade.
- Needs many things to align before trading.
- Often feels much more comfortable having the same position as manager or peers. Rarely takes the opposite position.
- Looks for an excuse to take off a trade as soon as she puts it on. She will say things like "It should have gone up by now", "It's not trading well", "I don't like the price action" or "This idea isn't working" even when the security has barely moved. She will take a tiny loss or tiny profit using any possible excuse because fundamentally she is risk-averse and her subconscious would prefer not to have the position (or any position)! There is a difference between taking risk and putting on positions. If you are always on edge the second you put on a position, you need to think about how to develop staying power.

A basketball player who always waits for the perfect shot might shoot 100% from the field and score 4 points per game. That is not good! As a coach, you want that player to take 15 shots and miss 5 (and thus score ~20 points). Traders who are risk averse do not take enough shots.

If you are a risk-averse trader, see Chapter 7 of *Alpha Trader* for a series of tips on how to overcome your risk aversion. You can succeed as a risk-averse trader, you just need the right tools and tactics.

Risk appetite score: 5-7 — Moderate risk trader

If you gave yourself a 5, 6 or 7 on the continuum of risk averse to risk seeking, you can probably up your game. Your risk aversion is not a weakness, but you might be able to stretch yourself a bit and avoid an early career plateau.

In the early 2000s, I worked for a bank that was generally risk averse. They ran a business model that is surprisingly common in banks: **"take risk, but don't lose money."** This is the optimal business model for a manager that wants to protect the bank but also allow for a bit of upside if trading conditions are optimal. This same business model is employed by many pod-based hedge funds. If you have 100 traders all working with very tight stops but some of those traders are still able to generate 20% returns in a year, the overall returns and Sharpe ratio of the hedge fund will be outstanding.

Some traders detest this business model because it makes them nervous. Taking risk without losing money sounds like an oxymoron. It really isn't. It just means that you need to behave like a call option. Take as much risk as you want when you are profitable, but play extremely tight when you are not.

The moderate risk taker thrives in that sort of model because they deliver exactly what management wants: decent upside with limited downside. I have generally been fairly flexible in my approach but I definitely have concluded that this is the optimal strategy for most traders. Increase your risk when you have a strong P&L base and decrease your risk when you are near or below zero. This substantially reduces risk of ruin, maintains the right tail of the P&L distribution, and offers you the best chance at long-term success.

The trader with risk appetite in the 5-7 range may struggle to hit the right tail of the distribution because they will more likely be satisfied once they hit their budget or goal. This is the kind of trader I was, when I worked at the generally risk-averse bank I mentioned. If my budget was $5 million and I got there eight months into the year, I was encouraged to "bank it" or "ring the register" or "take it easy into year end."

This makes sense on some level but greatly reduces your ability to see what kind of trader you can be, because despite the risks of the house money effect, most traders are at their best when they have a big base of P&L to work with but can remain patient and on the lookout for great opportunities worthy of a big bet.

Given the incentives and guidance from management, at that bank I acted like a trader with risk appetite of 5-7 even though my true risk appetite is much higher. High enough that it tends to be a weakness when I'm not at my best.

When I went to Lehman Brothers in 2006, I had a great start to the year. My budget was $6 million and I was up more than that by March. I went to my boss at the time and asked him how he felt I should proceed. I gave him the explanation of how things went at my last job and how they would tell me to "take it easy" once I hit my budget.

Steam came out of his ears.

"No way, dude! This is your chance to see what kind of trader you are! You have six million dollars in the bank! Set a stop loss at three million and go turn that six into ten."

I sat there thinking for a bit and he waved me out of his office.

"Go! Go make money!"

That year I made 50 million dollars and I am forever thankful to that manager for teaching me that lesson. The lesson was not: "You have money in the bank so go gamble it." The lesson was: "When you are in a strong capital position with chunky P&L, increase your risk in a methodical way and try to blow through the ceiling. The time to go for it is not January 1; the time to go for it is when you have money in the bank and markets are full of opportunity."

When you take this approach, it is crucial that you remain aware of downside and drawdown. Set a point at which you will go back to a more defensive approach. In the case outlined above, I was up $6 million and set my "go back to defensive" level at +$3m. This gives you ammo to push hard when you're doing well but also defines your downside so you don't just blow through all the money you've made.

This idea of pushing hard when you are in a strong position is 100% contingent on the opportunity set. You don't push just because you're doing well. You push because you're doing well *and* there are great opportunities.

Risk appetite score: 8-9 — Strong risk appetite

A trader with a risk appetite score of 8 or 9 has the most upside but also requires more supervision and has more downside risk than a trader with a lower score. I would say the sweet spot for risk appetite is somewhere in the 7 to 8 area, though traders with very high scores, when harnessed, can deliver blockbuster returns. Then again, they can be scary to watch.

A trader with strong risk appetite needs rules. If you are in this category, develop specific but simple rules to regulate your desire to take risk.

All of the following limits should be clearly defined and deemed to be unbreakable:

1. Maximum daily, monthly, and yearly loss. This can be a formula based on total capital and current P&L. Depending on trading style, the liquidity of products

traded, and time horizon, daily stops are not appropriate for all traders. There is a full discussion of risk management in Chapter 11 of *Alpha Trader*.

2. Permitted products and strategies. Can a hedge fund PM sell volatility with unlimited downside, for example? Can a home day trader short low-priced stocks? Can an FX trader take a position in a pegged or managed Asian currency?

   Depending on where you trade, this question may not be relevant. It is an esoteric question that does not come up all that often, but can be the difference between blowing up and not blowing up.

   Many of the blowups that I have witnessed first-hand have been the result of trades where the trader never should have been trading that product in the first place. Hedge fund managers risking 24 basis points to make 1 on Bank of Canada day. Retail day traders going short a thinly-traded biopharma stock. Option traders selling topside USDCNH volatility. Retail FX punters going long EURCHF at 1.2010. These are all blowups caused by traders dealing in products that they never should have touched.

   If you are day trading from home, what stocks are fair game? The way you answer this question might be the difference between long-term success and instant, nuclear devastation of your trading account. See GameStop shorts, for example.
3. Maximum position size by product.
4. Value at risk (VAR) or stress-test P&L. These are higher-level frameworks used at banks and hedge funds, but both methods have many issues when applied in real life. If you trade from home, don't worry about VAR, it's a tool used by institutions. Some issues with VAR and stress testing: a) VAR often depends on historical volatility which is not always a good predictor of future volatility. b) Stress tests can overweight rare events and ignore the fact that stop losses are effective loss control mechanisms in liquid markets. c) VAR and stress testing often rely on historical correlation which is backward-looking and unstable.
5. Cooling off levels. If a trader draws down X from high water or over-earns by Y, she should enter a two or three-day cooling off period. During cooling off periods, all risk is cut in half. This helps stabilize P&L after weak periods and avoids winner's tilt after strong periods. If a trader has enough experience, P&L history, and self-awareness to know she does not suffer from winner's tilt or overconfidence after very strong periods, the topside cooling off levels can be excluded. Cooling off levels are different from stop losses on the downside as they relate more to bad streaks and drawdown from peak, not absolute levels of P&L.

Risk appetite score: 10 — Too much risk appetite

If you gave yourself a score of 10 on risk appetite, you need to be careful. You are probably in the sensation-seeking, trading-for-excitement, or gambling category. Trading can be a lot like gambling (if you want it to be) and it has similar dopamine payoffs if you have an addictive personality. Along with the rules I listed above, traders with a risk appetite score of 10 need to honestly analyze their motivation for trading and be self-aware enough to know whether they are acting more like finance professionals or gambling addicts.

Traders on the extreme end of the risk-taking spectrum use trading as another method of sensation seeking. This is not good.

Trading can be incredibly fun. That's good. But that is also a problem! Enjoyment should always be a side benefit of trading and not the primary objective. The first objective must always be profit. Very often, traders will get involved in the market out of boredom or out of a need for stimulation. This gets them into trades that have weak (or no) logic and low or negative expected value. Remember: tight / aggressive. Look for juicy, low-hanging fruit and pluck it. Don't climb up into the treetops and risk a big fall. Be patient.

How powerful is trading as a stimulant? *Very*. This is from a 2001 study:

> *The psychological processes underlying the anticipation and experience of monetary prospects and outcomes would appear to play an important role in gambling and in other behaviors that entail decision making under uncertainty. In this regard, it is striking that the activations seen in the NAc, SLEA, VT, and GOb in response to monetary prospects and outcomes overlap those observed in response to cocaine infusions in subjects addicted to cocaine.*

NAc (nucleus accumbens), SLEA, VT, and GOb are four reward-related brain regions.

And the following is from Andrew Lo's testimony to Congress on Hedge Funds, Systemic Risk, and the Crisis of 2007-2008:

> *... the same neural circuitry that responds to cocaine, food, and sex—the mesolimbic dopamine reward system that releases dopamine in the nucleus accumbens—has been shown to be activated by monetary gain as well.*

Both the anticipation and receipt of monetary gains trigger the reward circuitry of the brain. Human nature is to seek activation of this circuitry both consciously and unconsciously. You must come to grips with the fact that trading often involves sitting there doing nothing, just waiting for a great opportunity. Unfortunately, the numbers moving up and down on that screen are like squirrels, and you are a dog.

Various commentators, including Jean-Paul Sartre, have commented that war is "...hours of boredom interspersed with moments of terror." Trading can often be the same. There is a strange temporal rhythm to trading where time speeds up and slows down depending on what is going on.

I remember instances after a major economic announcement or market event where I did 5 or 6 big trades, got into a position and out of a position and made hundreds of thousands of dollars. The time elapsed felt like 15 minutes. Then, later in the day when things were quiet, I would go look at the 1-minute chart and could not see enough detail to capture what had happened. I would have to go to a 1-second chart to see the levels at which I did those 5 or 6 trades and I would realize that the entire sequence, which felt like 15 minutes, actually took more like 90 seconds.

This time dilation is a common feature in sports, military action, trading, and other fast-moving pursuits that require rapid-fire, high-stakes decision making. Of course, the stakes are much higher in the military but the mental effect where time slows down is similar.

Once you get that feeling of excitement, the *in the zone* moments where the P&L piles up so fast you can't believe your eyes—you want that feeling again. Problem is, you can't get that feeling by trading low probability set ups. Instead, those low EV trades give you that "why did I do that" feeling. You can't trade to chase a rush. Your only goal each day should be to maximize P&L.

You need to be honest with yourself. Just like it's OK to be risk averse, it is OK to be sensation-seeking or boredom-averse. You just need to be aware of it and institute a set of rules to control your behavior and manage your weaknesses. You also need to accept that this sensation-seeking or disinhibition is a weakness you will need to deal with throughout your career. Attitudes toward risk are highly innate and very difficult to modify even with the healthiest, most growth-oriented mindset.

Sensation-seeking and gambling often go hand in hand. To get a sense of whether you are trading to feed your desire for excitement (i.e., as a form of gambling) take a look at the following excerpt from the DSM-V. The DSM-V or DSM5 is the Diagnostic and Statistical Manual of Mental Disorders. It contains descriptions, symptoms, and other criteria for identifying mental disorders and it is the authoritative guide to mental illness throughout most of the world.

Here, I have taken the section on identifying gambling disorder (previously known as pathological gambling) and replaced the word "gambling" with "trading". Do any of these line items sound familiar to you?

A diagnosis of ~~gambling~~ trading disorder requires at least four of the following during the past year:

1. Need to trade with increasing amount of money to achieve the desired excitement
2. Restless or irritable when trying to cut down or stop trading
3. Repeated unsuccessful efforts to control, cut back on or stop trading
4. Frequent thoughts about trading (such as reliving past trading experiences, planning the next trade, thinking of ways to get money to trade)
5. Often trading when feeling distressed
6. After losing money trading, often returning to get even (referred to as "chasing" one's losses)
7. Lying to conceal trading activity
8. Jeopardizing or losing a significant relationship, job, or educational/career opportunity because of trading
9. Relying on others to help with money problems caused by trading

Many traders would recognize their own thought patterns in that list. A trader who scores himself as 10 out of 10 for risk appetite might see himself in five or six of those behaviors. Think about these criteria for gambling disorder and be honest with yourself about how trading impacts your life. It should be an enjoyable, intellectually stimulating profession, not a way to achieve a gambler's high.

Jesse Livermore is celebrated as a trading hero but it is worth remembering that he took his own life after going bankrupt for a third time, after his second divorce. He is a trading hero and a cautionary tale wrapped into one.

The process and mechanics of trading and gambling overlap. Both involve risk management, probability, randomness, risk of ruin, emotion, bias, and irrational human beings. Bad trading can often be very much like casino gambling. It is impulsive, emotional and has a negative expected value.

If you want to gamble, go to a casino.

Excellent trading deals with incomplete information and variance of a game like blackjack, but has a positive expected value, like a professional poker player at a table of weaker opponents.

One final note here: The term "gambling" usually describes a form of entertainment where the gambler's odds or expectation are negative. Some forms of gambling, like poker, can have a positive expectation if the player is highly skilled. I would say that when a highly-skilled and highly-disciplined poker player sits down at a table full of tourists or recreational poker players, that is not gambling.

The skilled player has a significant mathematical edge. Poker is much closer to trading than most forms of gambling because it offers a small group of highly-skilled players the ability to generate abnormal returns consistently. In other words, poker is skill, not luck. Research confirms this unequivocally.

A substantial portion of investor underperformance can be explained simply by the fact that investors are active when they should be doing nothing. This is proven again and again by the consistent and sizeable outperformance of index funds vs. active managers and by the poor returns in retail accounts. Most of the time you should be doing nothing!

This is a simple concept but one that is extremely difficult to put into practice in real life. In *Alpha Trader*, I outline specific ways to reduce the problem of overtrading.

Your default mode should always be to do nothing.

Flat is the most powerful position in trading. When you have no position, you are unbiased, ready to pounce, and unconstrained by any prior view or notions. You are not anchored on any price or level. You are most open-minded and nimble when you have no position.

Yet people often feel bad when they are flat, especially if they remain flat for many days. "I'm not putting my capital to work", they might think. Or "My boss is gonna think I'm lazy." Human nature equates doing nothing with laziness, and in most jobs that's a pretty accurate assessment! An employee who sits there and does nothing over multiple days is probably not doing a great job in most roles. In trading, though, the opposite can be true. Quite often, the trader doing nothing is the wolf waiting silently in the long grass. Ready to pounce. An Alpha Trader.

Take pride and comfort in your ability to remain flat. The very nature of the tight/aggressive framework in trading is that you should be flat as often as possible and only engage when the expected value of a trade is high.

Flat is good. A trader with no position has no bias.

When you are in a position, you are not objective. You are under the influence of many forms of bias. You own something (the trade and the view that led to it) and people don't like giving up what they own. Therefore, if you are feeling uncomfortable about a position, the best bet is to take it off. Then, once you're flat, you can analyze with an open, unbiased mind.

Confirmation bias is strongest when we have a position. When you are flat, it is easier to honestly evaluate competing hypotheses. Only when you are totally flat can you process incoming information with zero bias. It is important to truly understand and believe that. No matter how smart you are, no matter how self-aware; everyone is subject to confirmation bias. Do not think you are exempt.

If you are confused… Get flat. As I say in *The Art of Currency Trading*[45]:

Rule #7 of FX Trading: Flat is the strongest position. When in doubt: Get out.

Flat can be good or bad

Note that flat for a risk-averse trader can be the result of excessive fear and a persistent desire to avoid risk. Flat for a risk-seeking trader can be a safe harbor from overtrading and an opportunity to see the market sans bias, through clear eyes. Know yourself and know what flat means for you.

Back to flat

I am prone to overtrading. I sometimes trade for fun, or to avoid boredom. The question you have to ask is: Do you want to have fun? Or do you want to make money? When I get flat, it usually means I am trading well and doing the right thing.

The current portfolio of 50in50 trades has a strong bearish bias and I am uncomfortable with this bias right now because:

- Fed is priced for 80 bps at the next FOMC meeting and it's very hard to see the market pricing more than that.
- 2023 cuts from the Fed are now mostly priced out. It will take a lot to price hikes into 2023 as the Fed is getting close to neutral and hikes into restrictive territory have a higher bar than hikes from accommodative to neutral.
- The energy crisis in the EU looks less bad as energy prices fall and EU and UK governments intervene.
- The newsflow out of Ukraine has improved.
- S&Ps just dropped 100 points in a straight line, providing a nice exit.

The 50in50 book hasn't been flat in ages. It's time to get flat, reevaluate, and achieve complete open-mindedness. Maybe next week I'll be bearish again. Or maybe I'll be bullish. In the meantime, I am nimble and unbiased.

I square up all the trades here, including the RBLX / CVNA relative value trade. We start fresh next week with a results update and brand-new concepts and ideas.

---

45 https://amzn.to/3S07tgK

Week 30: Trading Global Macro

A fiendishly complex, ever-changing puzzle

Update on previous trades

It's time for the once-every-ten-week update on the 50in50 trades. Squaring up the buy the rumor / sell the fact ETH trade last week was a big mistake. Here is the spreadsheet of trades since the last update:

Week 20 to Week 30 results

Week	Entry date	L/S	Asset	Entry	USD at risk	Stop loss	Take profit	Exit or current level	P&L	Exit date	Holding period (days)	Notes
20	7/4/22	Short	TSLA	701.50	2,000	820.00	437.00	829.00	(2,200)	22-Jul	18	
21	7/19/22	Long	XME	44.50	2,000	34.95	63.70	49.90	1,131	20-Sep	63	
22	7/25/22	Short	META	Options	2,000	29JUL $160 and $155 puts		Small profit on the 160s	(1,600)	29-Jul	4	
23	8/1/22	Short	SPY	412.50	2,000	436.60	37.00	403	830	20-Sep	50	Sold put against it
25	8/16/22	Short	MSTR	345.00	2,000	381.00	251.00	251	5,222	26-Aug	10	
26	8/23/22	Short	TSLA	296.00	2,000	304.67		296	-	25-Aug	2	Cover at 25AUG close
27	8/29/22	Short	TSLA	Daily strat	2,000			295	(297)	13-Sep	15	
28	9/5/22	Short	ETH	1,650	2,000	1906 and 2056	1,155.00	1,587	381	13-Sep	8	

Total P&L	3,086
Winners	4
Losers	3
Win%	57%
avgWIN	1,891
avgLOSE	(1,366)
avg holding period	21

The MSTR short was the only trade that really moved the needle as it showed what a well-timed, high-leverage trade can do. Overall, the low leverage of the trades (using just 2% of capital) means the volatility of the P&L is going to be low. Risking 2% of free capital is a very conservative approach and often the best approach for new traders.

For reference, here is the quarterly update for my real-time trades in am/FX. My assumption has always been that the 50in50 trades would have less edge than my real trades because FX and global macro is my expertise and many of the single name equity trades I do in here are for example purposes and not necessarily reflective of a setup where I have an identifiable edge.

am/FX Trade Ideas: Quarterly Results June to September 2022

		Asset	Entry	Stop loss	Position size	Take profit	Actual exit	P&L	Exit date	Holding period (days)	Notes
10-Jun	S	EURJPY	141.25	144.44	4,427,900	137.77	141.1600	2,759	17-Jun	7	
11-Jun	S	USDJPY	134.05	135.55	8,936,667	130.55	135.5700	(100,212)	15-Jun	4	
17-Jun	L	EURUSD	1.0485	1.0374	8,913,635	1.0720	1.0518	29,415	22-Jun	5	
22-Jun	S	USDJPY	136.11	137.15	13,087,500	133.15	135.82	27,673	5-Jul	13	
5-Jul	S	EURJPY	139.55	141.11	8,945,513	136.66	140.01	(29,161)	18-Jul	13	
20-Jul	B	EURUSD digi			1-month 0.9900			(100,000)	18-Aug	29	
1-Aug	S	EURCHF	0.9725	0.9777	18,076,923		0.9777	(102,085)	3-Aug	2	
3-Aug	S	GBPUSD	1.2230	1.2361	7,715,354		1.2194	27,775	10-Aug	7	
10-Aug	S	EURAUD	1.4630	1.4816	7,906,388	1.4351	1.4520	59,140	15-Aug	5	
11-Aug	S	EURUSD	1.0346	1.0466	8,429,989	1.0166	1.0166	151,740	16-Aug	5	
18-Aug	S	ES1	4,272	4,366	21	4,010	4,010	278,723	29-Aug	11	
31-Aug	L	EURCHF	0.9797	0.9714	11,084,337	0.9944	0.9794	3,611	1-Sep	1	
5-Sep	L	GBPUSD	1.1518	1.1379	3,553,712	1.1839	1.1555	13,149	13-Sep	8	1/2 risk unit
5-Sep	L	GBPJPY	161.84	159.29	3,173,333	165.99	165.99	82,675	7-Sep	2	1/2 risk unit
5-Sep	L	GBPCAD	1.5133	1.4884	2,988,755	1.5684	1.5115	(3,614)	13-Sep	8	1/2 risk unit
8-Sep	L	AUDUSD	0.6758	0.6684	13,365,541	0.6994	0.6800	56,135	13-Sep	5	
							Total P&L	397,723		8	average hodling period
							Winners	11			
							Losers	5			
							Win%	69%			
							avgWIN	66,618			
							avgLOSE	(67,015)			

These trades assume free capital of $4 million, 2.5% of capital per trade = $100,000 at risk for each idea

The hit ratio is much better in my real trades, as one might hope or expect.

If you would like to receive am/FX in your inbox every day and get my global macro thoughts, live trade ideas, and some random silliness… You can subscribe at www.spectramarkets.com/subscribe/.

OK, update complete. Let's talk global macro!

Trading Global Macro

Sitting down to write a 2500-word Substack about trading global macro is a bit like sitting down to write a 2500-word essay titled "Everything you need to know about religion." It is such a broad topic that one could write two full books and still not cover everything. I mean… I did that. I wrote two books and still didn't cover everything!

So today, I'm going to run through a sample trade, much like I did in Chapter 12 of *Alpha Trader*. But here I'll use an example of a trade that I wrote about this morning in am/FX. The idea covers multiple facets of global macro, including trade idea generation, technical analysis, positioning and sentiment, correlation, and more.

I hope a specific example will give you a sense of how I look at markets. Then, think about your own style, and how you can develop a process of your own to understand, and profit from macro trading.

By the way, if you want to keep up to date on global macro, I recommend you read:

1. My daily (am/FX) - https://www.spectramarkets.com/subscribe/
2. Macro Alf Substack - https://themacrocompass.substack.com/
3. Mr. Blonde's Substack - https://stuckinthemiddle.substack.com/

These three publications will give you a solid understanding of the big, medium, and tactical/micro picture.

My Trading Philosophy

My philosophy is to look at the big picture, but trade the evolution of that picture, and not the picture itself. In other words, I focus on changes and perceptions as much as, or more than, current reality. This is an essential distinction because market prices are formed at the margin by the changing expectations of a broad range of participants. There is money to be made by anticipating those changing expectations.

It's not about whether interest rates (yields) are high right now, for example... It's about:

- Are yields going higher from here?
- Do people generally expect them to go higher?
- Do market prices in other markets accurately reflect the high level of yields and the rate of change of higher yields? (Changes matter. Speed of change also matters.)
- How much higher would rates have to go to change the minds of the skeptics who think these high yields are transitory? That is, where would the doves capitulate?
- How far would yields have to **fall** to shake the confidence of those who are already positioned for higher yields?
- How big is market positioning in the direction of higher yields?
- What proximate events or catalysts might move yields higher or lower from here? How will people increase or reduce positions as the events near? Is there an asymmetry around these events or catalysts where prices might move more aggressively in one direction?

My process is not really about forecasting where the economy is going... It's about understanding where the economy is now (the reality), where people **think** the economy is now (the narrative), and studying the array of market prices to find discrepancies, dislocations, or places where I see a mispricing or asymmetry. Then, I try to anticipate changes in the reality and the narrative, and predict where prices will move as this interplay between reality and narrative evolves.

The questions I am always asking: Where are we? Where are we going? Where do people think we are going? **What do other people think other people are thinking?** How does my view diverge from everyone else's view? Is there an opportunity to profit if I am right? How much will I lose if I'm wrong?

Sounds complicated, right? It is! There is no simple ABC way of trading global macro. It's a huge crazy puzzle with different pieces every day. It's hard. That's what makes it fun. **Nothing worth doing is easy at first.**

My Trading Framework

This is the basic framework I use for trading:

<table>
<tr><th></th><th colspan="5">The lifecycle of a trade</th></tr>
<tr><td>1
Idea generation</td><td colspan="2">New narrative identified or existing narrative is stale or nearing exhaustion</td><td>Economic event or news changes outlook</td><td>Deviation from fair value</td><td>Pattern recognition and indicator scanning</td></tr>
<tr><td rowspan="3">2
Filtering</td><td>Where are we in the narrative cycle?</td><td>Positioning and sentiment</td><td>Events and catalysts</td><td>Correlated markets</td><td>Technical analysis (charts)</td></tr>
<tr><td colspan="5">Do these factors all support your idea? Or are there too many crosswinds?</td></tr>
<tr><td colspan="5">Last step: Consider alternative hypotheses. Why and how might I be wrong?</td></tr>
<tr><td>3
Tactics</td><td>What is the best product / market to express this view?</td><td colspan="2">Determine entry, stop loss and take profit</td><td colspan="2">List re-assessment triggers (where or when am I wrong?)</td></tr>
<tr><td>4
Position sizing</td><td colspan="2">Determine conviction level (TYPE I, TYPE II or TYPE III)</td><td>Determine risk capital to allocate to the idea ($ at risk)</td><td>Solve for position size using stop loss and $ at risk</td><td>Consider market liquidity and capacity</td></tr>
<tr><td>5
Execution</td><td colspan="2">Execute trade</td><td colspan="2">Automate / outsource stop loss</td><td>Enter trade in journal</td></tr>
<tr><td>6
Tracking</td><td>Did the thesis or facts change?</td><td>Stick to the original plan unless something major changes</td><td>How is risk-reward evolving?</td><td colspan="2">Caution!!! Noise vs. signal</td></tr>
<tr><td>7
Performance analysis</td><td colspan="2">Post-mortem on the trade. Extract any useful lessons, then move on</td><td>Record results in detail</td><td colspan="2">Monthly analytics.

What's working and what isn't?</td></tr>
</table>

Today's post (this chapter) is mostly about 1: Idea generation. How do you come up with global macro ideas? In FX, trades often revolve around economic or monetary policy divergence. Because every FX trade has a numerator and a denominator, you are comparing the state of macro in one country vs. another. In today's trade, I am looking at USDJPY.

The current narrative in USDJPY

USDJPY has been skyrocketing all year on the divergence between US and Japanese monetary policy. All other things being equal, investors would rather own a currency with high rates, not low rates. US 10-year bonds at 3.6% are much more fun to own than Japanese bonds (JGBs) at 0.25%. Here is a chart of USDJPY (black) vs. US 10-year yields (gray) since the Fed dropped "transitory" last November.

USDJPY vs. US 10-year yield

You can see the gray line, US yields, went from below 1.0% to 3.6%. Now here's Japanese 10-year yields during that same period.

Oh, they went up too! From 0.08% to 0.25%. Lol. So while US yields increased 2.6% (260bps*), Japanese yields went up 0.17% (17bps). The reason for the tiny move in Japanese yields is the Bank of Japan has instituted a policy called Yield Curve Control (YCC) where **they cap the 10-year yield at 25 basis points.**

**A basis point is 1/100 of a percentage point. So 25bps = 0.25%.*

You can see in the first chart that the gray line (US yields) tracks USDJPY very well. As investors expect or see a higher yield in the USA, they buy more USDJPY. When that yield premium looks like it's at risk, they sell USDJPY.

There are leads and lags and this sort of observation leads to a type of trading called lead/lag or intramarket or correlation trading. That is a separate topic for another 50in50 but my point here is to show you that the direction of US yields is a critical determinant of the direction of USDJPY.

Knowing this, one might expect that USDJPY would be at the highs right now, but it's not. It's close, but not quite there because of two main factors:

1. The Japanese Ministry of Finance (MOF) has been complaining about the weak yen and threatening intervention.
2. The Fed and BOJ both meet this week and there is a risk that the BOJ removes the 25bp cap on yields. If the BOJ removes YCC (the yield cap), USDJPY will probably go down as that would diminish the US yield advantage over the yen.

The setup

People are worried about the MOF and event risk, and have little to no topside exposure in USDJPY. This creates an interesting setup where the momentum in the critical correlated market (US yields) continues, but the correlated pair (USDJPY) is stalling as people worry about muddling from policymakers.

This creates an opportunity to go into the BOJ and Fed meetings long USDJPY on the view that once the events are out of the way (and BOJ governor Kuroda keeps YCC capping yields at 25bps)... USDJPY can rip. This requires one to believe the following:

1. BOJ will not move the yield cap. My experience is that leaks ahead of BOJ meetings (of which there are plenty!) are usually pretty accurate. Here are two recent sources stories: BOJ is nowhere near shifting monetary policy to support yen[46] (Reuters) and BOJ set to end COVID-relief plan, but no change to loose policy[47] (Japan Times).
2. The Fed will not be dovish. My view is the Fed will hike 75bps and sound somewhat hawkish as inflation becomes stickier and they are still wildly behind the curve. High inflation requires tight policy (that is, a Fed Funds rate above neutral) and the Fed is still running loose policy. It has been more than a year of sky-high inflation and yet the Fed (despite some big hikes) is not even at neutral yet.
3. The market is not all-in long USDJPY already. If the macro setup is bullish but everyone is already in the trade, the opportunity is less interesting. You want a view that isn't already fully subscribed. Long USDJPY is barely subscribed at all because people are afraid of the MOF and are positioning in lotto tickets (USDJPY puts) for an end to YCC. **The market is the wrong way if USDJPY rallies from here.**
4. Yields will not reverse to the downside. Here is sticky core inflation (ex-shelter) vs. US yields. I believe that pressure on yields will remain high until we see real signs of falling inflation. Everyone is hoping for peak inflation because of commodities and supply chain improvements but it looks like inflation is about much more than just commodities or rent at this point.

---

46 https://www.reuters.com/world/asia-pacific/boj-is-nowhere-near-shifting-monetary-policy-support-yen-2022-09-12/

47 https://www.japantimes.co.jp/news/2022/09/12/business/boj-covid-relief/

Atlanta Fed Sticky Core ex-shelter (black) vs. US 10year yield (gray)

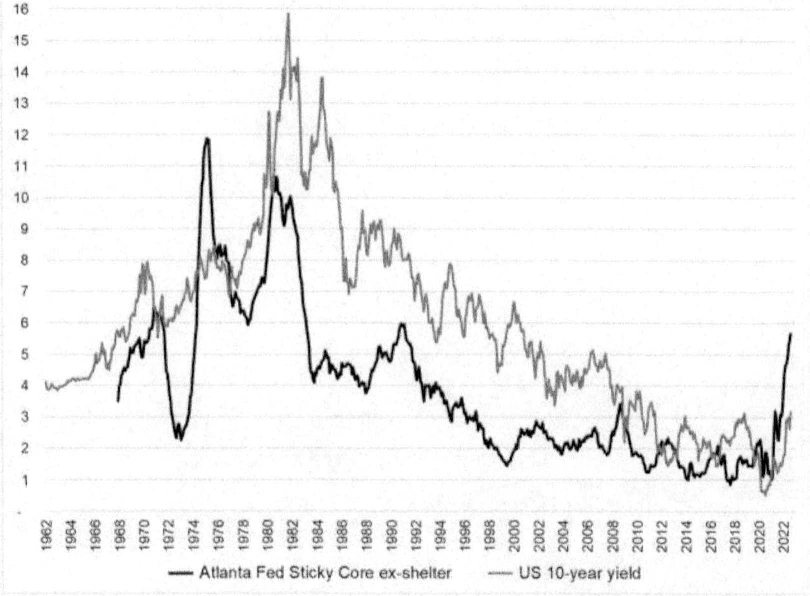

I always prefer trades where I will know almost right away if I am right or wrong and with the BOJ and Fed meetings this week… This trade should resolve one way or the other pretty quick.

Technicals

Once I have a global macro trade idea, I turn to the charts for tactics and risk management. USDJPY is famous for its triangular consolidations, so when I put up the chart and see this…

USDJPY hourly since early August

... I'm like: Sweet! In case you weren't following USDJPY from 2012 to 2015, that was the period in which the BOJ did massive easing and you can see it was triangles, all the way up:

USDJPY daily 2012 to 2015

I am not sure why USDJPY hangs out in so many triangular consolidations during big up trends of every fractal, but it does. Therefore, the triangle on the hourly chart above is encouraging.

The beauty of these triangles is that they make risk management relatively straightforward. You go long here (143.65) with a stop somewhere below the 14SEP low of 142.58 and the bottom of the triangle.

I am using 141.74 as my stop loss to allow for a little excess volatility around this week's central bank fest. If the BOJ were to move YCC, there is gap risk, but I think you would probably get out somewhere on a low 141 handle.

Reassessment triggers

It's important to list your reassessment triggers ex-ante (before the fact) so that you are ready if the alternative hypothesis (you're wrong) happens. Here are my reassessment triggers:

1. If the BOJ raises or removes the YCC policy, get out. This will mean hitting the first bid available or leaving a stop loss in a system and praying for the gods of trading to be merciful.
2. If 141.74 trades, the idea is wrong. That's the stop loss.
3. If the Fed is dovish, I will not reassess, I will try to ride it out while maintaining the 141.74 stop. A dovish Fed is just more behind the curve and I do not think the market will find such dovishness credible for more than a day or two. Therefore, the dip in USDJPY on a dovish Fed could be temporary and so I don't want to cut in that case.

Conclusion

With this week's central bank meetings and the recent consolidation near the highs in USDJPY you have:

- A good macro story (higher yields, higher USD) with minimal participation at the moment due to upcoming event risk.
- US yields making new highs, which provides cross-market confirmation for a higher USDJPY view. Small deviation from fair value with yields at the highs and USDJPY 150 points below the highs.
- Bigger picture positioning light due to fears of MOF intervention. My view is that we don't need to worry about the MOF here at 143.65. When you know people are avoiding a trade because of a specific risk, and you are willing to take on that risk yourself… That's a good situation.
- Chart pattern of ascending series of triangles continues. Risk management parameters are thus fairly clear. Leverage is decent, though not epic, because I need to leave some room for volatility around the central bank meetings and I need to manage the gap risk if I am wrong about the BOJ and YCC.
- Two major events (BOJ and Fed) that will let me know quickly if I am right or wrong. Winning or losing quickly is a benefit as it frees up your capital (mental and financial) for other trades instead of locking you into something that drags on for weeks.

There are many, many ways to trade global macro. I like to identify short-term opportunities where I anticipate different outcomes than the consensus or where I feel I have an edge in understanding why the prevailing narrative is probably wrong. Every trade is probabilistic… There are no sure things, ever. But if you can identify a series of 50/50 bets that pay 2:1 or 60/40 bets that pay 1.5:1 or 70/30 bets that pay 1:1… Over time you will make money.

Week 31: Trading Events

Fun and scary and profitable and dangerous

Update on previous trades

I was in Brazil (São Paulo and Rio) for a bit, but I'm back!

The USDJPY trade I outlined for 50in50, Week 30 was either great or terrible, depending on how you played it. I stupidly forgot to put the take profit in the write-up. So, I'm marking it as a loss because even though USDJPY rallied significantly after I went long, it got smoked by MOF intervention. And I forgot to communicate my take profit: so I take the L.

Sometimes in trading, little screw-ups like forgetting to cancel an order, or leaving an order as DAY instead of GTC by accident can cost you money. Outtrades and screw-ups are a cost of doing business. Minimize them, and cut them as soon as you discover them. And don't be too hard on yourself.

One time I left an automated stop loss on a machine for 70 million euros in the morning, to protect a long position. The day went on and about 5 hours later, I squared up my position for a decent profit.

I went for a run outside, and when I got back, EURUSD was unchanged but my P&L was $500,000 worse than when I left and I was short 70 million euros 70 pips out of the money. Turned out there had been some clickbait bearish headline about a downgrade of Spain (it was during the eurozone crisis) and EURUSD went down 100 and up 100 while I was off desk, stopping me into an unwanted short euro position and pushing me 70 pips underwater.

Horrible.

Anyway, outtrades and errors happen. I have an even worse story than that one! Forgive yourself and modify your process so you don't make the same mistake twice.

Now let's talk about event trading.

Note: I am sending this right at 4 pm NY, the market close, on the day before CPI. That will mean most people will read it after it's too late to do the exact trade I described. That's OK! This is supposed to be a learning exercise, not a trade copying exercise.

Trading Events

Once you have a solid understanding of the fundamentals that drive your market and you have a good handle on the current narratives, you are ready to trade events. With your knowledge of current themes along with positioning and sentiment, you are ready to figure out how new information will move prices. Remember that the current price is the sum total of all the known information in the world (public and private).

When news comes out (e.g., economic data, monetary policy announcements, or unscheduled headlines) the price zigs and zags as it looks for a new equilibrium level. This search for equilibrium is sometimes said to be guided by an "invisible hand" because it is uncanny how price rapidly incorporates new information and adjusts to the new outlook.

When news hits, there is a significant opportunity for profit. Traders that have the best understanding of the fundamental backstory going into an event will have the best chance of coming out the other side in the black. Before you trade the news, you need to have a solid understanding of what is driving the markets you trade and any correlated markets.

The prevailing economic and fundamental landscape has a massive influence on how the market interprets new information. For example, during the 2010-2012 period, the stock market consistently rallied on bad economic news because it was perceived that bad economic news meant the Fed would announce more quantitative easing (QE) and more QE usually means higher stock prices.

Traders who weren't fully cognizant of the macroeconomic landscape in those days were always complaining "This price action makes no sense! Why are we rallying on bad news?!?" Those that were focused and did their homework understood the reaction function perfectly. A nuanced understanding of the market gives you a huge edge when trading the news.

There are many types of news and events that can generate profitable trading opportunities. The main ones are:

1. Economic data
2. Central bank meetings
3. Corporate earnings
4. Central bank speeches and comments
5. Other headlines and news events (corporate announcements, mergers, geopolitical news, etc.)

CRITICAL CONCEPT: Understand What Is Priced In

Before you can trade a data release, central bank meeting, or any other event, you need to understand what is priced in. This is an absolutely critical concept for anyone who trades any financial market. If you trade or you are ever planning on trading any security in any market, you need to fully and completely grok the concept of "Priced In". If you read this section and still don't really get it, ask someone to explain it more fully. Do not trade events until you are completely comfortable with the concept of what is priced into a market.

Financial market prices are generally set by the sum total of all the buying and selling done by every human and computer market participant. Different buyers and sellers will decide to buy or sell depending on the price, and as prices move, different actors with different time frames will enter or exit the market.

Decisions to buy and sell are generally driven by the market's assessment of fair value for the security and this assessment should (in theory) be composed of all the available information that relates to that security. As new information comes in, prices move in real-time and should reflect and anticipate all available information, often before the information itself is released. Let's look at an example:

Currencies are highly sensitive to interest rate movements. Therefore, it makes sense that currencies should move when central banks adjust their primary interest rate. Here is an example of how a currency can move when a central bank unexpectedly changes interest rates.

Hourly USDCAD around a surprise interest rate cut from the Bank of Canada (January 2015)

Note: USDCAD higher means weaker CAD and stronger USD

When something unexpected like this happens, it is not priced in. This move higher is what you would anticipate because an unexpected rate cut makes holding Canadian dollars less attractive given the lower yield. The market sells CAD and buys USD, driving USDCAD higher.

This was NOT PRICED IN. In contrast, let's look at an interest rate move that **was** priced in.

In 2008, The Reserve Bank of New Zealand (RBNZ) cut rates dramatically in response to the global financial crisis and then they cut rates again after the 2011 Christchurch earthquake. By 2013, economic activity had rebounded significantly and it was clear to the RBNZ that rates were too low. Inflation was picking up and the RBNZ felt it would become appropriate to start raising rates at some juncture, but not right away. The story plays out as shown in the chart below. The first hint that the RBNZ wanted to hike rates was delivered on July 25, 2013, and it is marked by point 1 on the chart.

The RBNZ kept warning more and more loudly that rate hikes were coming, so NZD strengthened vs. the AUD (AUDNZD went down).

Daily AUDNZD, June 2013 to July 2014

AUDNZD down means weaker AUD, stronger NZD

The pair falls as the market anticipates a NZ rate hike then rallies when the RBNZ hikes.

1. "Although removal of monetary stimulus will likely be needed in the future, we expect to keep the OCR unchanged through the end of the year." – July 25, 2013
2. "OCR increases will likely be required next year."—September 2013
3. "Although we expect to keep the OCR unchanged in 2013, OCR increases will likely be required next year." – October 2013
4. "The Bank will increase the OCR as needed in order to keep future average inflation near the 2 percent target midpoint." – December 2013
5. **RBNZ hiked on March 13, 2014**

This concept of the market pricing in an event and then reversing (somewhat counterintuitively) after the event is known as "buy the rumor / sell the fact." We covered that concept in Week 28 as a reason to go short ETH at 1650. That idea worked out well.

You can see that the RBNZ slowly prepared the market for the interest rate hike over a period of 8 months and the NZD gradually appreciated over this time period (lower AUD, higher NZD). Finally, the RBNZ hiked in March 2014 but it was completely expected—fully priced in. The market priced in the hike over the course of many months and when the hike finally arrived, NZD sold off in response.

This reaction is counterintuitive to someone who is not following the NZD closely. "They hiked and the currency sold off? What the???" But any professional following the NZD would know that the hike was fully priced in and so the reaction in the currency market is perfectly understandable. There is no need for NZD to rally after a rate hike that is fully priced in.

In fact, quite often the reaction to an event that was priced in is the opposite of what the macroeconomic textbooks might suggest because those that had been buying the NZD in anticipation of the rate hike sell (take profit) on the day of the event.

In every market event, the outcome is determined, to a significant degree, not by the event itself but by the combination of the outcome of the event and the market pricing. If something is 100% priced in, the market will not react when it happens. The interplay between expectations (what's priced in) and reality is part of what makes trading events super complicated and interesting.

Trading Economic Data

In the "good old days" before algorithmic trading, you could make money trading economic data in the seconds right after the release. If a US data release was strong, you could just quickly buy 20, 30 or even 50 million USDJPY and then sell it out just as quickly to slower traders at other banks as it rallied. You could buy TY on a weak CPI and make money if you had quick reflexes honed by years of video gaming (I do).

Those days are long gone. There are now hundreds of algorithms programmed with code that reads something like:

1. If nonfarm payrolls headline number beats by 80,000 jobs or more, buy USDJPY at current market or up to 50 points higher
2. If NFP number beats by 150,000, buy USDJPY up to 100 points higher
3. If NFP number misses by X, sell Y… And so on.

Instead of gyrating back and forth for a while before finding equilibrium, the market now finds equilibrium super fast after the release of economic data. Hedge funds and banks use regression analysis before the data release to estimate how far each asset should move on various outcomes and they execute trades via algorithm at the moment of release. They will buy or sell until all asset classes are approximately in line with where history suggests they should be and this will happen in microseconds. There is nothing left on the table for the human traders because all the liquidity in the market is hoovered by the bots in the first few microseconds.

Imagine you are in a gymnasium with poor lighting, trying to shoot rats with a slingshot. There are a few other people in the room doing the same thing but you are a pretty good shot and your vision is good. You are doing OK. You are hitting your fair share of rats.

Suddenly, a cyborg marches into the gym. He is equipped with infrared night vision and a fully-automatic laser gun with motion-sensitive targeting. He shoots 50 rats in 10 seconds without missing. You and the other human rat hunters stand there, jaws on the floor.

That is what trading economic data is like now that algos are programmed to trade every economic release. With hundreds of electronic players all using similar algos, competition is at the microsecond level and humans are shut out. Pre-2005 or so, you could just about make your year trading economic data alone. Now there is far less money to be made by humans after data releases. This is one of many examples of how you need to adapt to changing market conditions over time. Adapt or die.

So now, instead of four strategies, there are three main strategies around economic data.

1. Go with. Trade the extreme data.

Algos will take out the first pocket of liquidity when economic data are released, but there are still opportunities for profit when important data come in extremely strong or extremely weak. This is because the bots can only buy or sell so much (they have risk limits too!). The first wave of algo trades can be followed by more waves of macro and hedge fund trades in the same direction and you can get in after the algos but before everyone else.

If you know what a big miss looks like, because you have studied all the past releases and printed out a little sheet showing 1, 2, 3, and 4-standard deviation misses for the data… And you know positioning and expectations and what is priced in (beyond the simple median economist forecast)… You can sometimes GO WITH extreme data points.

Last month's CPI is a clear example of this. The market had killed all the shorts, bulls were getting feisty, and the talk was of peak inflation. The SPX had rallied from 3600 to 4300, right into the 200-day moving average. There was no room for error as momentum, positioning, and expectations were all one way. Then this happened:

S&P futures, 5-minute chart through CPI in July 2022

Oops! Any trader going into that CPI number with a good knowledge of pricing and a flat book could have made a ton of money simply selling S&P futures at 4075 or so after the number. It's never an easy trade selling something down 100 handles, and this is only easy in hindsight. But it's a textbook example of how you can go with the data in cases of extreme outliers into wrong-way positioning.

2. Beat the algos! Go the other way after economic data

Another way to profit from economic data is to take the other side (or fade) the initial kneejerk move. The term "fade" means to take the other side of a big move or view in the market. Sell a rally or buy a dip. Quite often on a trading floor you will hear someone say "This move is a fade" or "This move is baloney; I'm fading it."

Fading economic data is a scary strategy because you are going against short-term momentum and against the theoretically logical direction dictated by the economic release. That said, with the proliferation of algos trading the initial headline, quite often the fade strategy is most profitable.

The reason fading the kneejerk move often works is that algos and humans pile in based on the initial reading but there are quite often times when the details are not as strong as the headline or the headline is not really all that strong in the first place. Then you often see a rapid turnaround in the market because the algos are risk-averse and so they hit or pay almost any price to get out of a trade that is not instantly in the money. As usual, it pays to know the setup going in. Which way is the market leaning? What is the asymmetry?

A key skill in trading is to identify asymmetries. Always be on the lookout for moments when the market looks much more likely to go a particular direction after an event due to positioning or some other bias in the market.

As a human trader, there is sometimes a profitable opportunity to take the other side of a move if the headline is not representative of the full story. For example, say the headline jobs number is extremely strong but the details of the report (unemployment rate, average hourly earnings) are weak. You can sell the spike in USDJPY because the bots will be long too many USD and will need to sell. The best way to be ready for this type of reaction is to listen to the immediate reaction and commentary from economists and strategists.

This is easiest if you work at a bank or hedge fund because you can hear your economist's reaction almost immediately, but there is also real-time reaction on CNBC, Twitter, Reuters, Bloomberg, and so on. If the headline is very strong but the details are weak, the dollar will often fail to hold initial gains as the market views the knee-jerk as incorrect or exaggerated and fades it.

Remember that the last trade before the release, what I call the "NewsPivot," is a simple but effective reference point for trading economic data and other news releases. Make a note of where each of the majors is trading before any major release and consider those levels to be the critical pivots for each pair for the rest of the day. This works because the reaction to the news is often just as important as the news itself.

If very good news comes out and the market goes back through the level it was trading before the news—that's bearish price action. This is a concept known as good news/bad price, which we covered in Week 17. The opposite situation (bad news/good price) is bullish.

Why would a market rally on bad news? There are all sorts of reasons for counterintuitive moves after news and economic releases but the two main ones are 1) The underlying details of the release are not consistent with the headline release (strong headline/weak details) and 2) Supply and demand, not news, determine market prices.

3. Take a view. Go into the event with a position.

I am confident from experience that the highest expected value way to play events is to go in flat and trade either strategy 1 or strategy 2 above. On the other hand, the highest returns come from betting before the number. Higher returns, but much higher risk and a lower hit ratio. Before you can take a position into an event, you need to estimate jump risk. That is, if you're wrong... Where can you get out?

If you can't estimate it with confidence, forget about the idea. Rule one of trading is: Eliminate risk of ruin. Don't put on trades if you cannot quantify your risk. Don't be short USDHKD. Don't front run the underwriter's stabilization bid after an IPO. Don't go max short a stock through earnings, etc.

Estimating jump risk

There are two ways to estimate jump risk. The first is to look at historical data for a given event and study the maximum, average, and median moves. The Bloomberg function ECMI is useful for this type of analysis. Looking at how markets moved over the same event in the past is usually a good way to estimate gap risk but it is, by definition, backward-looking. A more accurate way to estimate jump risk is to use the options market.

The difference between volatility pricing for the day before an event and the day of an event can be used to extract an approximate jump risk for the currency. The calculation is beyond the scope of this piece. To be perfectly honest; when I want this information, I don't calculate it myself, I just ask an options trader.

If you work at a bank or have an institutional relationship with a bank you can simply ask: "What is the options market pricing as jump risk for event X?" and they will give you an answer, usually in basis points. If not, you can ask someone smarter than me to get it for you.

Once you have a sense of the jump risk, you can take a cash position. If you are not comfortable with gap or jump risk, you can trade options. The issue there is that options through events tend to be overpriced because market makers charge a premium for the jump risk! You don't want it and neither do they. If you want to buy it, you have to pay up. Still, if you're right, options will often realize much more than the event premium anyway. And you can't blow up.

Factors to consider

Going into an event, there are a few main factors to consider:

1. What is positioning? This will help you determine the weak side, or asymmetry through the number. If everyone is short, your market is more likely to see an impulsive topside move post-event.
2. What's the FOMO trade? People hate to miss the "obvious" trade. For tomorrow's CPI, the FOMO trade is strong CPI so people are positioning for that because they will feel stupid if they miss an epic inflation print.
3. What is the skew of the distribution for the event? Sometimes you can get a lean on the event using various methods. That's beyond the scope of this piece, but a simple example would be to use a good model of the correlation between PPI misses and CPI misses to forecast the probability that CPI will miss one way or the other.
4. What is the most recent move? Generally, the move going into an event will tell you a lot about positioning. If your market rallied hard into nonfarm payrolls, it's more likely traders are long that market, not short. Weak hands that want to square up, lotto ticket buyers, and those with a strong view on the data all wait til nearly the last minute before putting on their bets. As such, you get a read on the positioning and the lean by looking at how things moved beforehand.

The trade: Long FXA calls into CPI

The USD has been ripping all year, and the last CPI was a barnburner. Recency bias suggests that number is front of mind, and given the monster move after CPI last month, and the inflationary macro environment, fear of a strong CPI makes sense.

The issue is that the follow-through after a big runup like this one into CPI hasn't been great this year. Obviously, the number itself matters tomorrow, but the conditions going in are important too.

Here's AUDUSD three days into, day of, and three days after CPI releases this year.

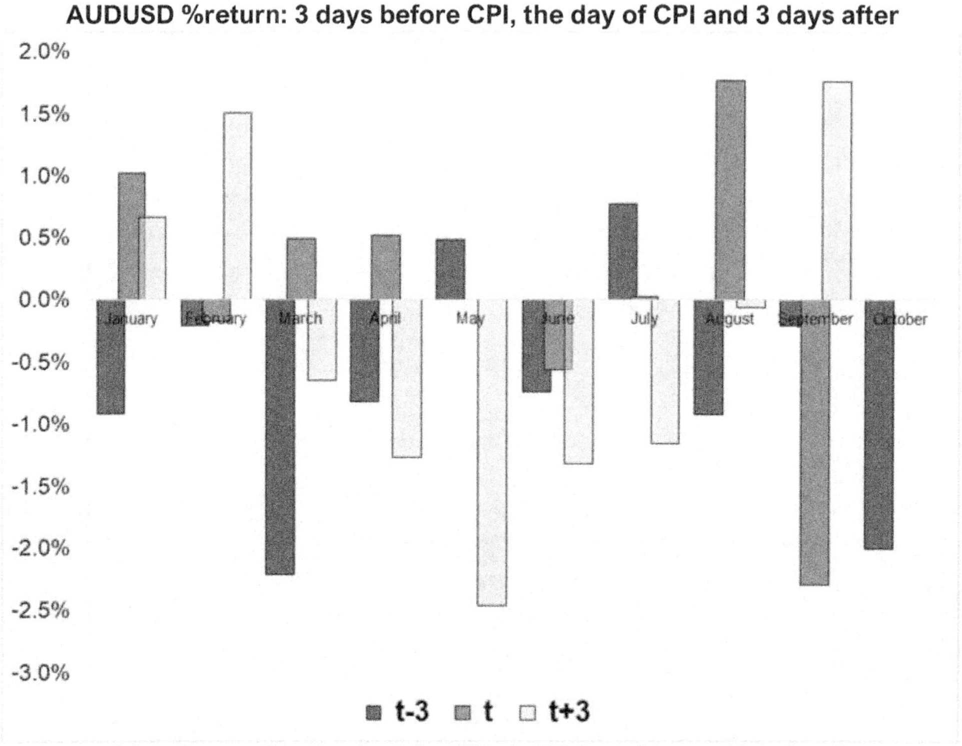

t-3 is total return of the three days before CPI. t is CPI day. t+3 is sum of three days after.

Look at the darkest bars. The USD ran up (lower AUDUSD) into most CPI releases. But then look at the lighter gray bars. The move often reversed on the day of CPI. The takeaway is that in months like January, March, April, and August, the big runup in the dollar was a fade once CPI came out. The only exception was June, where you had a 1% drop in Oz going in, and another 0.7% drop on the day of CPI.

The market has been extremely bullish USD most of the year and the USD has gone up most of the year, but price action around CPI and FOMC days has been much more dollar bearish. Dollar bulls have been adding to risk since nonfarm payrolls last week and I think tomorrow's CPI could see a huge reversal. Also, there has been a firehose of bad news in GBP and GBPUSD can't go down (bad news/good price). That could be a tell that the market is over its skis on long USD trades.

But I am too scared to get involved in spot because the risk of a strong number is still meaningful. When you trade events, there is never a sure thing. You are trying to find 50/50 bets that pay 2:1 or 60/40 bets that pay 1.8:1 and so on. It's always probabilistic. Everything I do in trading is probabilistic.

When you have a probabilistic mindset, you know you are going to be wrong a lot and you get used to it. That makes it easy to cut your losses and easy to flip views and find new ideas. I have zero attachment to my trades. I never fall in love with them. I know some will work and some won't. I just want to put myself in a ton of 60/40 bets that pay 1.5:1 and let the chips fall. Speaking of chips, I found a poker game when I was in Rio!

Check out this hand.

I had KK vs. AA and the flop was K 3 K. Lulz.

For tomorrow's CPI release, I think the USD will sell off much more on a weak number, so while I have no counter-consensus forecast for CPI, the asymmetry makes me favor short USD.

AUDUSD is very often the best trade through US data because AUD is a high beta currency that trades consistently with risk appetite and general USD direction. You can trade AUDUSD via the ETF "FXA" and you can trade options on FXA. They are not super liquid, but they are liquid enough.

For this trade, I'm going to buy $2000 worth of 21OCT FXA 63 calls for 40 cents. I'm crossing a huge bid/offer on the screens (.30/.40) but remember **these trades are for educational purposes only**. In real life, I would bid at mid, and maybe do a call spread (buy 63/sell 64, etc.)

I want to keep things simple enough, and manageable in 50in50. Precise execution strategy isn't the point of this write-up, but precise execution strategy is super important in real life.

Conclusion

When you determine that there is an asymmetry around an economic release, you can often come up with and structure positive EV trades. Always understand the following when trading events:

1. It's about probabilities. You will be wrong a lot. That's OK. This FXA trade is probably 50/50, but I think it will pay 2:1.
2. Don't do anything unless you are sure you can risk manage the trade. Jump risk and gap risk are scary and they should be scary. **Avoid risk of ruin.**
3. Don't overstay your welcome. If you are correct on an event, the right move is usually to cash out within 24 hours. With this trade, if CPI is weak and AUDUSD goes up, I'll exit or hedge on the open Friday (14OCT). That will give the trade all day Thursday to get busy and will eliminate weekend risk. This is a ~24-hour time horizon trade.

This post was longer than usual and yet I have left out considerable detail and information in an attempt to keep it manageable. Trading events is risky. It's fun, scary, profitable, and dangerous. Even if you're a professional—be careful.

Week 32: Correlations flip

Correlations are not stable or static. See: energy in 2022!

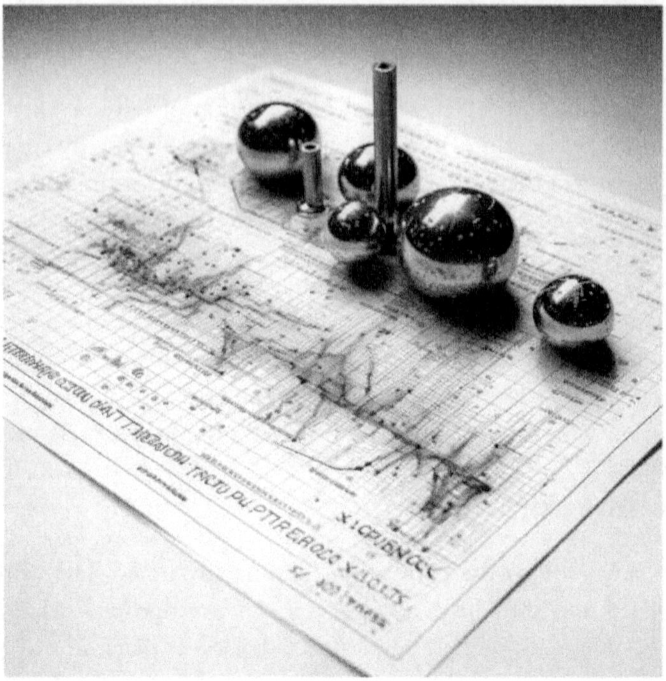

Update on previous trades

I had the right lean on positioning into CPI, but the number was too strong and AUDUSD ended up unchanged after one of the most insane equity sessions I can remember since March 2020. The trade was a loser, despite a pretty good thesis.

I feel confident putting that trade in the "good decision / bad outcome" bucket. While a loser is still a loser, I feel completely different about a trade where my process was solid and I lost money, vs. a trade where I made a fundamental mistake or followed a failed process. In this case, I had a good read on, but the variance around the number itself was high enough to wreck the idea. If CPI had come in anywhere close to expectations (or below), the trade would have been explosive.

It is with some sadness that I see the RBLX / CVNA spread at more than +$20 after I squared that thing up in Week 29, but that's life. Sometimes you're gonna square up good trades before they have time to hatch. Try not to look at or feel emotion towards trades once you get out.

Correlations are not stable or static

The number one question I get from new traders is: "Where do you get your trade ideas?" and it's not a simple question to answer. First of all, I would say that if you work to become an expert in your particular market, you will find more and more that **the trade ideas come to you**.

The more you understand your market, its microstructure, the factors, stories and narratives that drive it, and the correlated markets that offer directional signals... The more often you will see a bunch of information and market activity come together in a clear picture, the way a fuzzy view comes into focus through binoculars, or the way a jigsaw image reveals itself as you put more pieces together.

One of the most complicated, but useful ways to generate trade ideas is to study the prices and inputs that are correlated to your market and find signals that help you predict future direction. As with everything in markets, correlation trading is probabilistic. You don't say "Gold is higher, so gold mining stocks are definitely gonna rally!" You think: "The rally in gold suggests short-term risk/reward in gold mining stocks is positive."

Where to look for correlations

There are so many ways to use correlation to your advantage. The world has evolved significantly since I started trading and there is much less edge in correlation trading than there used to be. Here are some examples of correlations that can help you trade and forecast markets.

Single name vs. index

When I was day trading in the late 1990s, most of my edge came from listening to the squawk from the S&P pit and getting ahead of single name moves thanks to my better real-time understanding of where S&P futures were trading, and where they were headed.

This is one of the simplest examples of a correlation: Equity index vs. single name equity. Naturally, these correlations are arbitraged away by algorithms now, especially when the single stock is a member of the index. Still, you can watch the relationship between single stocks and equity indexes and sometimes extract information and make predictions from the relative performance.

Single-name sympathy plays

When Nike makes a negative earnings announcement, the market will assume that this is bad news for the sports apparel industry. Therefore, when Nike drops, stocks like Lululemon (LULU) and Under Armour (UAA) will probably drop, too. Markets are very, but not 100% efficient in pricing in sympathy plays. For example, you might notice that

LULU reacts almost instantly to bad news from NKE but a stock like Dick's Sporting Goods might react with a short lag.

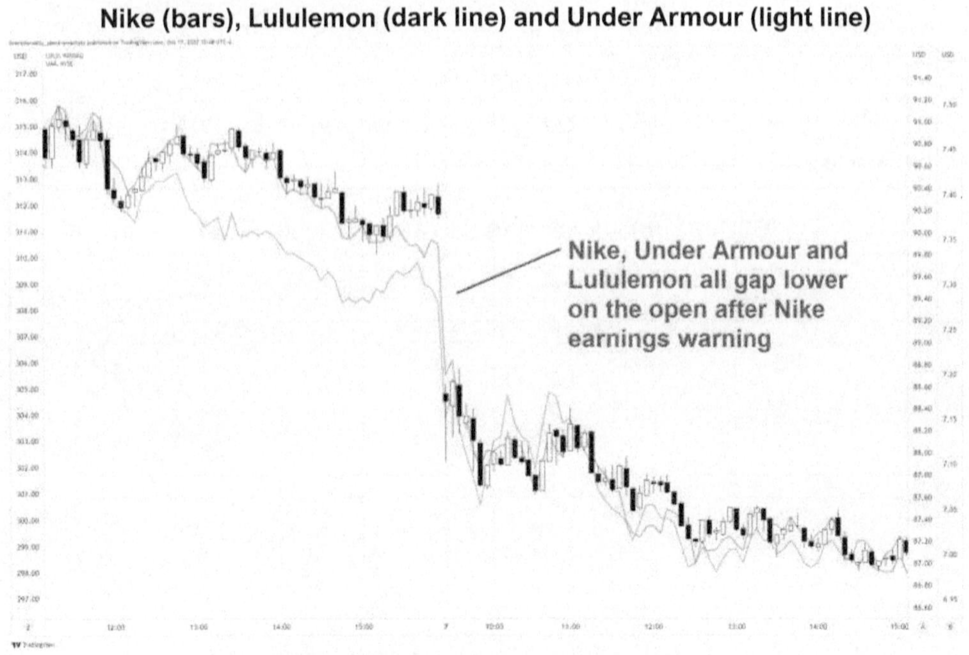

5-minute chart around the Nike earnings warning

If you know your sector and know your stocks, you can jump on sympathy plays if you are quick. When I was day trading in the late 1990s, this was a major source of P&L for me, and I still trade sympathy trades now.

You can also trade sympathy in other markets, for example: If good news comes out on UK gilts (the UK 10-year bond)… US bonds will normally rally in sympathy. If the Bank of Canada hikes rates unexpectedly, AUDUSD will usually rally as the market sees a read-through from Canadian to Aussie monetary policy.

Commodities and yields vs. currencies

I remember sitting on the trading floor at Lehman Brothers in 2005/2006 and more than half the FX traders didn't even have a live feed for gold, copper or oil. My co-workers would ask me "What's oil doing?" or "Where's gold?" which seemed completely ludicrous to me (because it WAS ludicrous!). How could people trade FX without knowing where other markets are trading?

This all changed in 2007/2008. Correlations between FX and other asset classes jumped toward 1.0 and FX traders suddenly understood how important it was to watch other markets. Now there are armies of algorithms that trade FX correlation in real time. There is a phalanx of hedge funds analyzing fair value of currencies using complex quantitative cross-market analysis models. There are fintech startups that will tell you what is driving currencies right now according to their multivariate Granger causality or AI regression or machine learning models. Even with infinitely more competition, though, intermarket correlation is still a great source of understanding and edge for discretionary human FX traders.

Relationships such as US 10-year yield vs. USDJPY worked well in 2006, and still work well now. Here's the overlay over the past few years:

USDJPY (black bars) vs. US 10-year yield (line)

Market variable vs. economic data

Many economic releases are highly correlated to market variables. For example, consumer confidence in the United States is highly correlated to gasoline prices. More recently, one might suspect that German business confidence would be related to European energy prices.

If you have no other information, and you look at this chart, you might reasonably guess that the next German PMI figure (which comes out October 24), is likely to be higher, not lower than last month.

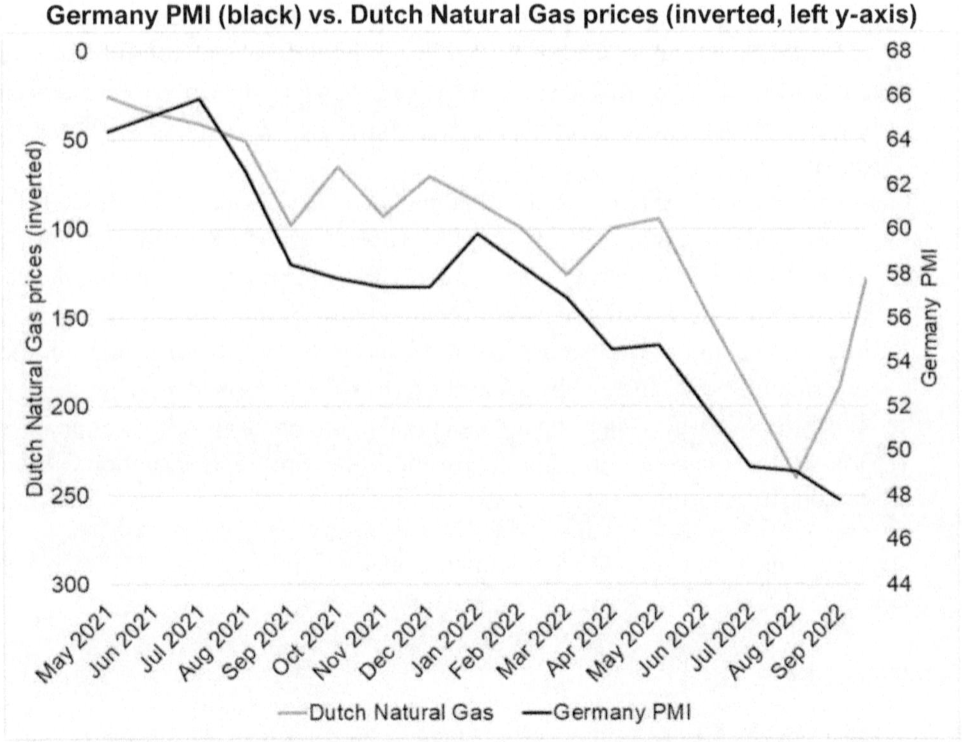

Idea from Steen Jakobsen. Note that gas prices are inverted, i.e., lower gas price = higher confidence.

While economists should in theory be forecasting economic data using these high-frequency, predictive variables… Economists don't update their forecasts very often and not all economists use these variables in their models. This is especially true as energy prices were not nearly as important for German sentiment pre-2022.

Questions to ask when you are considering correlations

As the title of this piece suggests, though, correlations are not stable and they are not static. What worked yesterday is not guaranteed to work tomorrow.

Whenever you see or read about a correlation in financial markets, you need to ask yourself:

1. Does the correlation make any econometric/logical sense? This is the most important question of all. I don't care if the r2 is 99.9%… If the relationship has no underlying logic, either forget about it or search for a reasonable explanation. Otherwise it is likely a spurious correlation. Spurious correlation is when people infer a cause / effect relationship between two variables when there is no logical or actual connection between them.
2. Is the correlation likely to continue into the future? Correlations are inherently unstable. You need to make a logical assessment of whether or not a given

correlation will continue into the future. This comes mostly from experience. Correlations like interest rates vs. currencies have existed pretty much forever and will tend to be reliable most of the time whereas the correlation between, say, natural gas and CAD might work at times and be completely useless most others.

3. Are there periods of both rising and falling prices in the sample? It is more likely a correlation is spurious if it is simply two prices going straight up or straight down. You can easily find a bunch of price charts that have been rallying steadily for a given time period and then overlay them to imply some relationship. If prices go up and down together, it's more likely that you haven't simply found two smooth trends that happened at the same time by coincidence.
4. What third variables might be influencing the movement in your two variables? You will hear over and over that correlation does not imply causation. That is certainly true–but it certainly provides a clue!

To read much more about how correlation impacts markets and what causes cross-market correlation, read Week 2.

Correlations flip!

In number 2 above, I ask: Is the correlation likely to continue into the future? **That's an important question!**

2022 has provided some incredible examples of changing correlations. For example, the relationship between interest rates and the value of the UK pound flipped.

GBPUSD (gray) vs. UK 10-year yield (black)

Normally, when UK rates go up, it reflects good news about the UK economy and stronger growth and inflation. Today, when UK rates go up, it reflects fear of insane fiscal policy in the UK and a possible sudden stop of capital flows. This flip in correlation was an important event in global capital markets.

The relationship between energy prices and many currencies has also completely flipped.

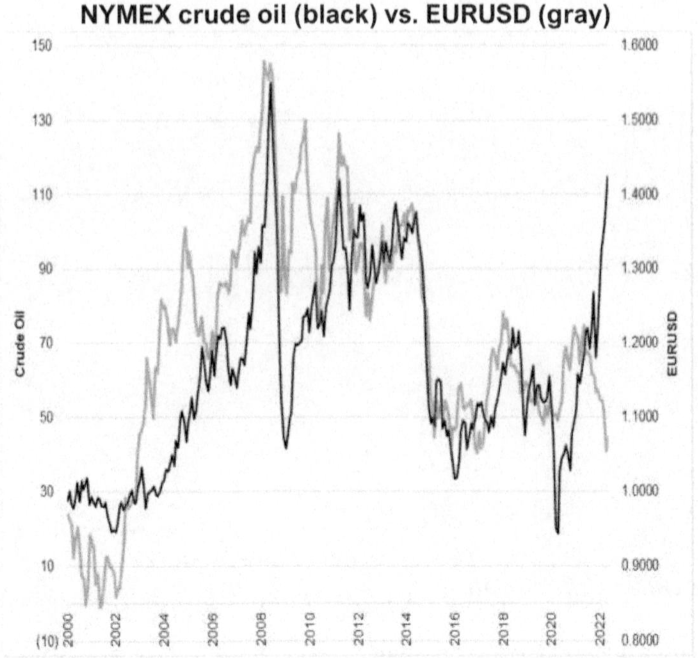

From 2000 to 2020, moves up and down in oil generally reflected ups and downs in global demand. The US dollar tends to rally when global demand is weak, because it's a safe haven in global recession. It used to sell off when oil rallied because of the implications for global growth, and also because the US was a net importer of crude.

As such, higher oil meant US consumers sold USD to buy foreign oil. But here's the US oil situation and how it has evolved over time:

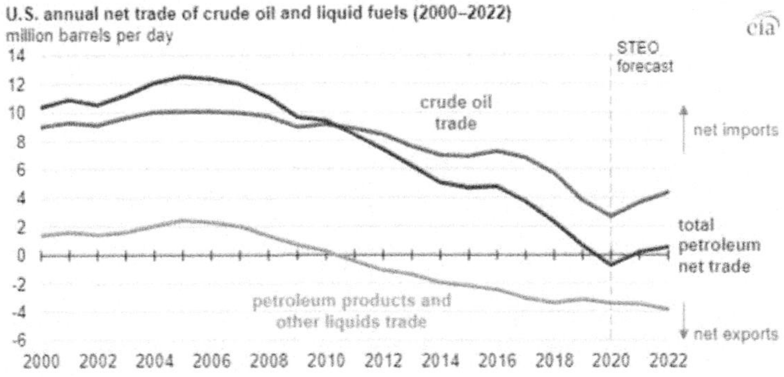

The US used to be a huge net importer of crude; now it's a net exporter. Meanwhile, with the war in the Ukraine, the EU is having trouble finding a reliable source of energy. Instead of buying energy from Russia, using euros, Germany needs USD to buy energy from other nations such as Qatar, or Canada[48]. Here's Germany's Trade Balance:

Germany Trade Balance 1980 to now

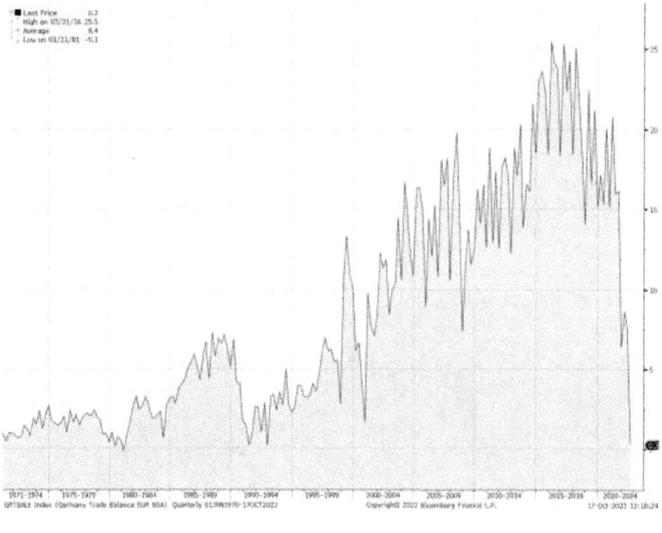

Oops. All gone.

But it's not quite that simple

Based on the discussion above, one might expect that Canada and Norway's currencies would be ripping higher the way the USD is exploding to the moon. But they are not. The correlation story is always hypercomplex and depends on many details. The most important detail is often the specific nature and direction of the cashflows. If Canada is selling crude at higher prices, but all that revenue is going to foreign shareholders and Canadian energy companies are not investing in new projects… The benefit to CAD will be minimal. That is exactly the case right now.

The incredible changes in the flow of energy around the world have led to some major changes in FX and other market correlations. The USD used to be highly-connected to the price of oil. Higher oil meant a weaker USD for most of the period from 2000 to 2020.

But shale production made the US much more energy independent and the war in Ukraine destroyed Europe's manufacturing business model. They relied on cheap Russian gas and as the gas is cut off, their terms of trade has collapsed. As such, the relationship

---

[48] https://ecfr.eu/article/europes-other-transatlantic-friend-germanys-and-canadas-new-energy-partnership/

between the dollar, the euro, and energy prices has flipped. This type of shift in correlation happens regularly, though mostly on much smaller scales than the massive change in energy correlations over the past 12-18 months.

Selling USDNOK as equities rally

The market has been obsessed with energy prices since the war started in Ukraine in late February 2022. An "obvious" trade into the war was to buy Norwegian krone because Norway is a massive exporter of energy with a massive current account surplus and very little geopolitical risk. The next chart shows how that played out.

The chart shows NOK in black and oil in gray. You can see that in 2015, oil and NOK sold off in tandem. Same thing in 2020, then they both rallied back in 2021. But then, in 2022, there was a massive decoupling. Note that NOK is usually quoted as USDNOK, but the green line is NOKUSD so that you can easily see how oil and NOK move together pre-2021.

NOK vs. oil, 2012 to now

Note that NOK is normally quoted as USDNOK but I am showing NOK vs. oil here so that they go up and down together on the chart and it's easier to see what's happening.

The reasons for this decoupling are complicated, but mostly come down to the fact that the Norwegian fund that manages the oil revenues has been a massive holder of foreign equities and hedges those equities quite actively. If equities fall, Norwegian asset managers need to sell NOK to rebalance their hedges. So while the oil correlation fell, the equity market to NOK correlation looked like this in 2022:

S&P futures (black) vs. NOK (gray) since July 2022

If you wanted to express a view on equities, you could use NOK and get a pretty good synthetic S&P 500 trade!

In Friday's and today's am/FX, I outlined why I am bullish risky assets, including stocks, for the next few weeks. But instead of going long S&P or NASDAQ futures, I decided to go short USDNOK (that is, long NOK and short USD).

Here is what I wrote:

> When you look at equity correlation to FX markets, CAD and NOK always pop up as two of the most tradable correlations. I don't love long CAD because I am worried about the mortgage reset problem there and the risk that the Bank of Canada Outlook Survey today could be dour (10:30 am NY time). I don't think we are far from a BoC pause, despite consistently hawkish words from Macklem, et al.
>
> I am pre-empting the breakdown by going short here, simply because I think the triangle offers close enough resistance that you can get short here (10.59) with a stop at 10.92, targeting 9.8800. A move back towards 9.80 would be a full round trip of the move up that started with the September 13 explosion higher on US CPI. The spike high after last week's US CPI figure was 10.8600 and that is why I think a stop at 10.9200 makes sense. That is also above the quintuple top at 10.90 (start of October.)
>
> In contrast, there is nothing coming out in Norway until the 20th of October. USDNOK is forming a nice triangle on the hourly chart and 2022 has been marked by a consistent stream of great setups featuring either triangles or horizontal lines. Here's the chart:

USDNOK hourly

Lower USDNOK is a higher SPX trade (~70% correlation), so if stocks collapse, this idea will not work. Why not just be long S&P futures? The risk/reward looks better to me in USDNOK because you can have a tighter stop and I would argue that NOK got more oversold than S&Ps. The high in the RSI for USDNOK was 80 while the SPX RSI never got much below 30. They are similar trades, but I like short USDNOK better.

Conclusion

Correlations are not static and they are not stable. They come and go, and they can even completely flip sometimes. A good understanding of macro will get you ahead of the curve on correlations and help you predict changes over time. A good understanding of correlation will help you find good trade ideas and think of interesting ways to structure them.

I am bullish stocks over the next few weeks, but think the setup is even better for the highly-correlated Norwegian krone. It got more beaten down than stocks, it's super correlated to stocks, and its tracing out a beautiful triangle on the charts. If we can take out the triangle and strong support in the 10.35/10.40 area, 9.80 quickly becomes a reasonable target.

Correlation and intermarket trading are huge topics. You can read more in Week 2 of 50in50, in many of my daily am/FX notes and in my first book, *The Art of Currency Trading* (Chapter 8 is "Understand Correlation and Intermarket Relationships").

Trading correlation is challenging, but over time, it gives you a much deeper understanding of your markets, and global capital markets as a whole.

There are macroeconomic reasons for relationships between markets and there are micro reasons for these relationships. The global economy is a complex system of nearly infinite connections. When one asset price moves, the trigger for the move could be something relevant to other assets as well. Similar to chaos theory where a butterfly flaps its wings in the Amazon and triggers a monsoon in Thailand, every action in the global economy can be caused by and can also trigger other complicated actions and reactions.

The more you watch, understand, and trade correlation, the better you will understand the wildly complex, interrelated, and ever-changing systems that make up the global economy and capital markets.

Week 33: Write it down

Diligent process is a meaningful edge in trading

Update on previous trades

The USDNOK short from last week is working well so far as my bullish risky asset view has been accurate to this point. Next week's Fed meeting is going to be particularly interesting and while I haven't finalized my view on the FOMC yet, it is prudent to take off the USDNOK short before that meeting. Therefore, I will cover this position at 9am on November 2 (assuming it doesn't get stopped out first).

Write it down

I am a fanatical believer in the importance of writing things down. Good traders are prepared to trade before they start trading. They have a process and a plan before they hit any buy or sell keys.

I have a daily sheet that I complete each morning before things get busy. This sheet helps me gauge where I am at emotionally and also puts numerical brackets around my day as I set a profit target and a stop loss number. This helps enforce discipline so that I know at what point I will stop myself out (how much money can I lose today?) and when I should be taking some profit (what P&L would make this a successful day? A great day?).

Thoughts are abstract and fuzzy. Writing is solid and concrete. If you think, "I'm going to cut my AAPL short at $285", that is completely different from writing **CUT AAPL**

285 on a piece of paper and having those words stare up at you as the stock rallies from $282.50 to $284.75.

The same goes for any plans or ideas you have. There is so much noise in your head, so many competing voices vying for airtime. Don't assume you can formulate a plan in there and then execute it successfully without writing anything down. Again, this doesn't have to mean anything more than scratching a few notes down on a piece of paper or recording some thoughts in a spreadsheet.

Research shows that when you write down a goal, you are more likely to achieve it.

When you write something down, it solidifies. It transforms from abstract into concrete. All the sludge falls away and only the important information is left. When you write something down, you have made a choice to select that particular information, goal, or action as more important than all the others. This highlights it for your brain. When you write something down, you signal to your brain "THIS IS IMPORTANT". Your brain records it as such.

The pathways and connections developed in your brain are different when you write something down because the encoding process is different. The encoding is stronger, more robust, and information is recalled more easily. If you want something to happen, write it down.

Another benefit of writing down stop losses, take profits, ideas and goals is that it is harder to wiggle out of them when they are staring right at you. You can't convince yourself that you *never really were going to stop out at $285 absolutely for sure* if you have a huge note on your desk that says **CUT AAPL @ 285**!!! It is your past self sending a message to your future self. Unambiguously. In black Sharpie.

The importance of a trading journal

A trading journal is the best way to keep track of your progress, especially early in your career. It can be a detailed record of every single trade you do, or it can be a few paragraphs you write at the end of the day. A trading journal can take whatever form you like. Record a few thoughts each day, or record the specifics of each trade you do. Either way, a journal will enhance your ability to analyze performance, and improve your process. You will start to notice repeated mistakes. You will identify bias in your views. "*Hmmm, I'm always short bonds and never long. That's probably not good. I need to be more flexible.*"

Your journal entries should focus on your decision-making and process. What triggered the idea? How strongly did you feel about it? Was it all logic, or partly gut? Describe the specifics of the process and the route you took to develop, execute, and exit the trade.

To enforce the habit of journaling, when I worked at a bank, I sent an email to one of my peers on the desk at the end of each day. I called it 12-12, meaning: 12 hours back and 12 hours forward. The 12 back part was a quick summary of how my day went, whether I stuck to the plan, whether I overtraded and so on. The 12 forward part was my overnight and next-day trading plan including stop losses, dollars at risk, and maximum position size.

Good traders have a plan

They may not always stick to the plan but they always have one.

I encourage every trader to create at least a brief written plan before they start trading. It can be one or two paragraphs, written to yourself or sent to others. But I cannot emphasize this enough: Have a written plan every day. It can be incredibly simple. Write it on a Post-It Note if you want. But do it. This simple daily practice will make you a better trader.

Every trader, regardless of experience level, should keep a trading journal. A journal helps track the evolution of your trading and captures emotions, themes and thoughts throughout the process. Many people think of a trading journal as something just for noob traders. It is not. You should use it as a professional trade strategy planning and assessment tool. There are many ways that a journal can help you.

Above all, a trading journal provides an opportunity for you to be honest with yourself. It's one thing to think and think and think about your trading but things become more concrete when you write them down. By writing down each trade along with a rationale and thought process, you can pick up on recurring errors, themes, and leaks in your trading.

A trading journal also helps you identify bias. Are you always the same way in a specific currency? Do you tend to short commodity currencies? Long the USD? You can also look at your time horizons and study whether you make more money on certain time horizons or on specific types of trades. The more you write down, the more you can go back later and investigate various hypotheses and answer questions about your trading.

A trading journal also helps you stick to your plan. If you write your plan in your journal before you do a trade (or immediately thereafter), you are much (MUCH!) more likely to stick to that plan. Bad discipline often comes from having no plan whatsoever and just hitting the buy and sell keys in response to random market stimuli. A plan written down has 100 times the value of a plan loosely formulated in your head.

In my daily newsletter, am/FX, I outline my trading plan for the day and discuss the themes in focus. When I moved from an interbank trading job to a hedge fund for a few years, I stopped writing. I found that this had a major negative impact on my trading. I would walk in some mornings and just start hitting the buy and sell buttons, reacting to price action and headlines instead of trading logically according to a plan.

If you go into a trading day or into a specific trade without a written plan, it is a recipe for poor trading. If you have a written plan for every day and every trade, you will find your trading is tighter and your risk management is better. The process of writing down your plan also filters out some bad trades in advance as you realize as you write out the plan that the idea is not solid enough to deserve an allocation of risk capital.

Collect data

If you collect trade-by-trade data, once trades are closed you record the information about the trade and after a while, you will have enough numerical and qualitative data to go back and assess your performance. Wait until you have a few months of trades in your journal before you assess anything because otherwise, you will run into sample size issues.

As you progress you can ask yourself subjective questions such as:

- Is there a mistake you make repeatedly? One of the best predictors of failure is the trader that keeps making the same mistakes over and over.
- Do you stick to your plan? Or do you always take profit too early? Do you stop out at worse levels than you planned?
- Do you always lose money in a specific currency? Are some times of day or days of the week or times of the month better or worse for you?
- Are your high-conviction trades more profitable than your low-conviction trades? If yes, why? Are you sizing the different trades appropriately?

And so on. This type of analysis can really improve your game and reduce errors. Be creative when slicing and dicing the information and try to make an honest assessment of your performance. Always think about what is working and what is not. Do more of what works and less of what does not.

You should always work hard to understand and analyze your trading performance. Be thoughtful about your trading and about your strengths, weaknesses, and leaks. This will lead to greater self-understanding and more profits.

A specific example of how collecting data helped my trading

When I worked at a hedge fund, I was curious whether there was any particular pattern to my P&L over the course of the day. A logical thesis would be that you make your money in the morning as an FX trader in the United States because that is the most volatile and most liquid part of the day. But I didn't know whether or not that was true for me.

I manually recorded my P&L in a spreadsheet every 30 minutes. After collecting intraday data for a while, I noticed that my P&L very consistently rose from 7:00 AM and peaked around 11:00 AM. It then came off gradually until the end of the day. The chart looked something like this:

Approximate P&L by time of day when I traded at a hedge fund

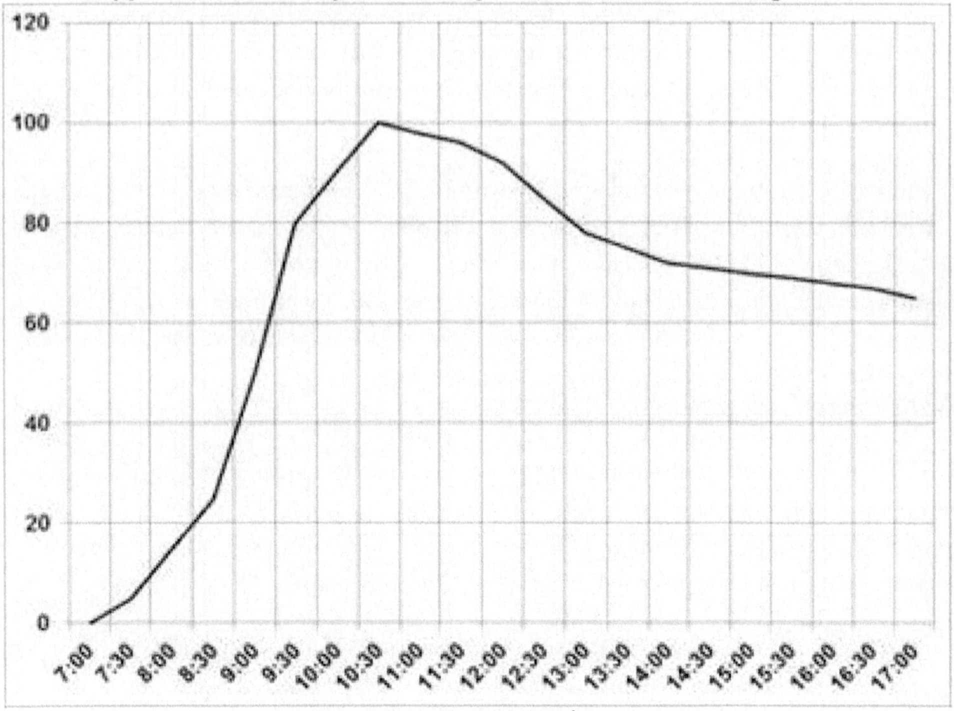

y-axis is percent of total daily P&L, average

It makes sense! But instead of a theory that I may or may not have acted on, the data gave me a concrete snapshot of how much money I was pissing away every afternoon.

Armed with the information from this chart, I started to square up much, much earlier each day. Instead of taking my risk down in the afternoon, I tried my best to reduce risk around 11:00 AM. This helped me lock in more P&L and it reduced my overall stress level because once I knew that all my trading after 12 noon was net negative, I could reduce my risk and use the afternoons for research, exercise, and other more useful endeavors. An added benefit of squaring up earlier is that liquidity is much better at 11 AM NY than it is at 4 PM NY.

This is a good example of how data collection and P&L analysis can make you a better trader. Use data to investigate sensible hypotheses and ideas.

Be thoughtful about what data you collect so that you do not waste time dealing with a firehose of useless information. Do you think you might trade best on Mondays and worst on Fridays? Investigate it. What about the start of the month vs. the end of the month? Whenever you think about your trading and performance, go back and look at your P&L data to better understand your strengths, weaknesses, and leaks.

Two sources of edge, each necessary but neither sufficient

People usually think about trading edge as a toolbox of strategies and tactics that reliably beat the market. That is correct; a methodology that generates alpha is a necessary condition for success in trading. **Necessary, but not sufficient.** The other necessary source of edge in trading is process.

If you have amazing tactics and strategy with an 80% hit rate and an average payout of 2:1 on each trade, but terrible process, bad discipline, low conscientiousness, and sloppy risk management... You will lose. Generating alpha is hard. Setting up and using a rigorous trading process is hard, but less hard. It is 100% within your control. Work on continuously improving your process. Automate, create rules, record data, etc.

Not coincidental timing

I am writing this piece about trading process, planning, and journaling because those topics have been on my mind of late. JR and I just published *The 2023 Spectra Markets Trader Handbook and Almanac*. The book is a product of my strong view on the importance of planning, preparation, and writing things down.

As I mentioned earlier: each trading day, I print out a daily sheet and write down my plan, thoughts, ideas, and results. I realized this would be much more efficient if I had a book preloaded with each day.

That way, I could also have all the important events like seasonality, economic events, option expiry, and holidays, along with coaching and inspiration sprinkled throughout. Then, I thought maybe other people would value such a book as well. So, JR and I made it!

You can check out *The Trader Handbook and Almanac* on Amazon. The 2024 Handbook should be available around October 2023.

The book takes everything I have written about in this piece and puts it all right in front of you every day. The book will make your process better and help you make more money.

How writing leads to trade ideas

I write a lot about markets. Much more than any normal trader would or should. Generally, I'm writing about currencies and global macro, but sometimes when I start with top-down ideas, I end up with something more micro.

Over the past four weeks or so, I have been writing about the coming mortgage reset calamity and residential investment collapse in Canada. I have been suggesting that the Bank of Canada will turn less hawkish as they see the same things I see: Overindebted Canadian consumers reached high in the sky for any house they could buy in 2020/2021 and financed it at super low rates. Variable rate and short-term fixed-rate mortgages such as 3-year fixed are popular in Canada and were more popular than ever in 2021. Canadians are up to their eyeballs in debt as you can see in this chart Macro Alf[49] made.

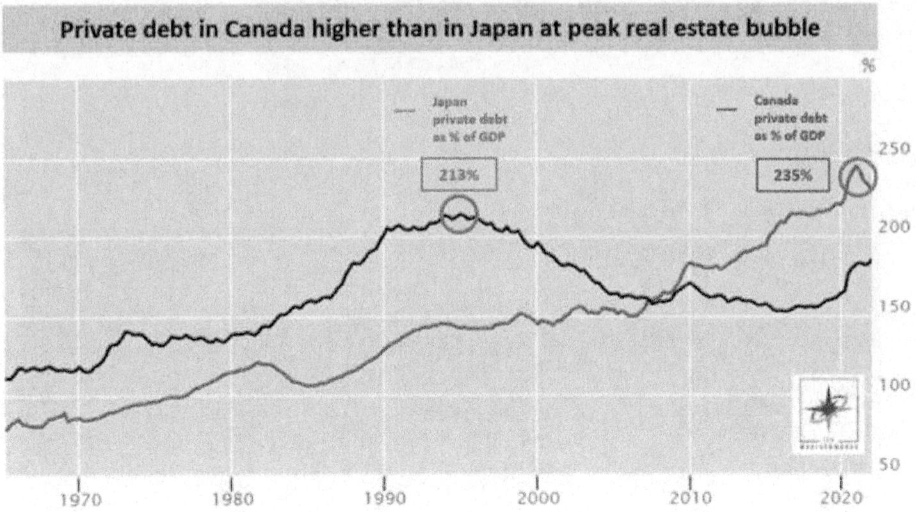

As an FX guy, my first inclination was to think about how this might affect CAD. But if you believe that the Canadian economy is likely to be hard hit by mortgage resets, falling residential real estate investment, and a decline in spending on housing services, the trade will be in rates, not CAD. This is because CAD has been driven by risky assets and US yields, not domestic news. Hawkish BoC didn't matter for USDCAD so it will not matter for CAD if they turn dovish, either.

---

49 https://themacrocompass.substack.com/p/sudden-change-of-heart

I don't really trade rates though. But I keep writing about this theme so it compelled me to find another expression of the trade.

Before I go any further here, I want to acknowledge that shorting the Canadian housing market is an evergreen doom and gloom narrative that people have been trying to make money on for years. This 2013 Maclean's cover is a true classic.

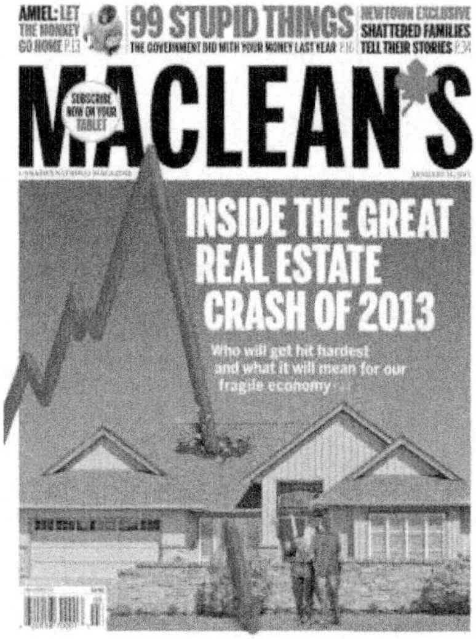

Oops

The online version featured this pic:

Flames!

The thing is… "People have tried this many times and it never worked before" is not a good reason to exclude a thesis. It is a reason to look for triggers and signals before getting involved.

I remember from the day I started at Spectra in September 2021 and right through the start of 2022, it looked obvious that USDCNH should be going higher. Everyone was trying various approaches, but the thing would not budge. Then, months later, without warning, it finally ripped. Yes, CNH is managed, so that could explain that particular lag, but this is emblematic of how sometimes markets just don't do what you think they should do for ages—then they do it with a vengeance.

USDCNH (black bars) vs. US/China 10-year rate differential (gray line)

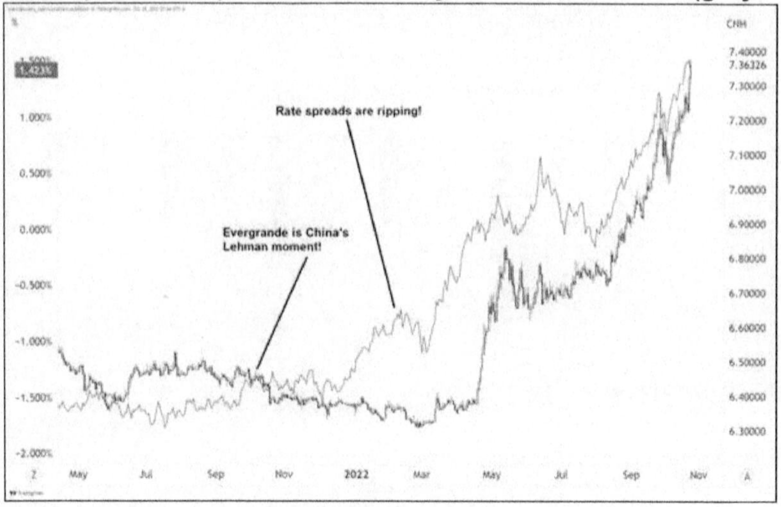

Timing is always hard. **In trading, early is a synonym for wrong.**

Canada Housing Short

This piece is getting on 3000 words and that's where I like to cap these bad boys so let me give you the super short trade thesis here.

Housing is a huge part of the Canadian economy. Here is a chart:

Residential Investment % of GDP in USA, Canada, Ireland and Spain, 1985-

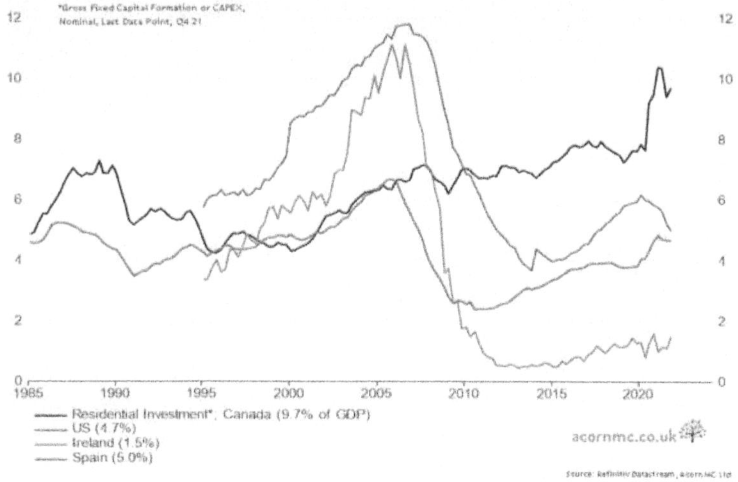

Source: Richard Dias on Twitter

US Housing has turned aggressively lower. NAHB Housing Index is collapsing. Today's US GDP number showed a collapse in Fixed Residential Investment. Canada is highly exposed to such a collapse and the two economies are strongly correlated.

The bank most exposed to mortgage risk in Canada is CIBC. Here's a chart:

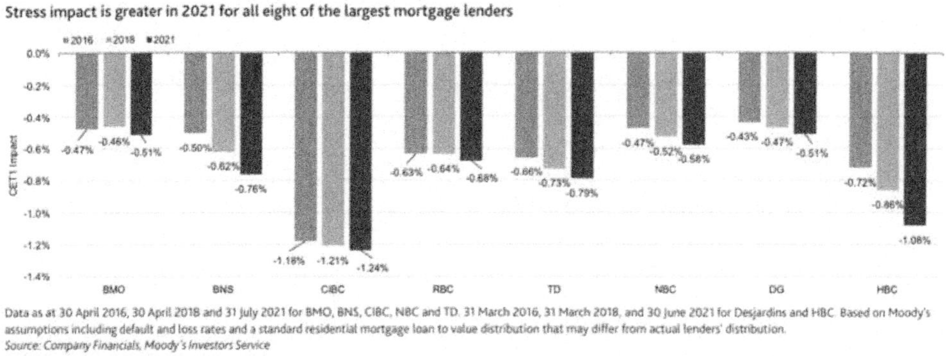

Source: https://betterdwelling.com/canadian-mortgages-are-riskier-for-lenders-probability-of-correction-rising-moodys/

And here's a chart of CIBC stock (trading in the USA).

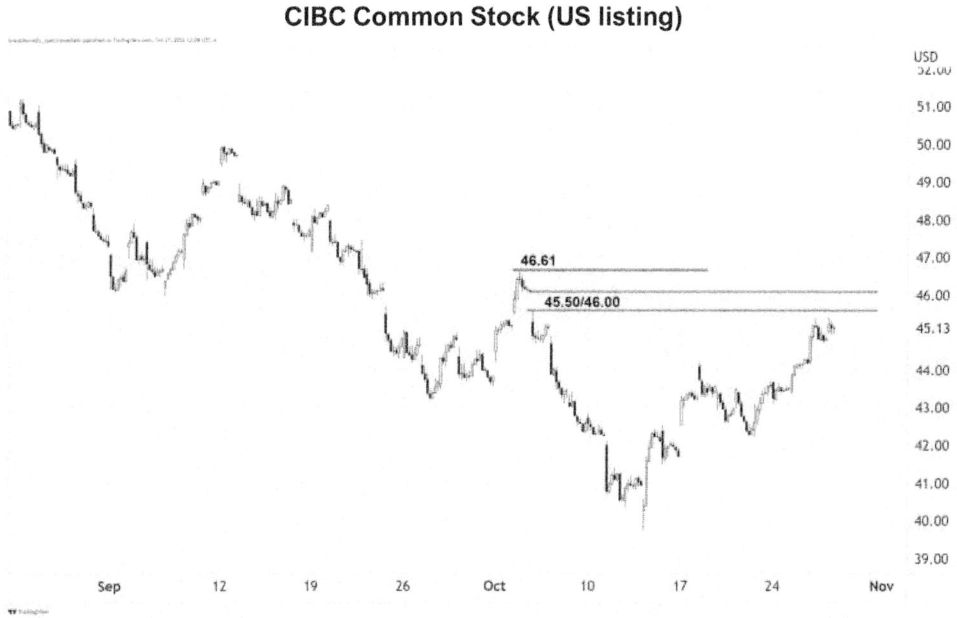

Pretty good timing here as it just rallied right up into a major gap and an old high. This trade is easy to risk manage. Short here, stop above all those lines ($47.11 to give it a bit more room). Take profit at $40.55 (down near the lows). Risking $2.00 to make $4.60. Bear in mind that since this is a Canadian stock, and you are trading the US-listed version, some of your performance is going to come from movements in USDCAD. That's fine by me now that USDCAD is down here, but still something important to know and keep in mind if you trade this.

Also remember: *I may or may not have an edge in trading 6-month views on Canadian bank stock performance! My normal trading time horizon is one day to one month.*

Conclusion

There are two types of edge in trading and you need both to succeed.

1. The ability to generate alpha through ideas, tactics, and strategies.
2. The ability to act rationally using a reliable and consistent set of processes. One critical part of good process in trading is to write things down.

Trading edge (alpha) and process edge are both necessary but neither is sufficient for success on its own. You need to have both engines running smoothly or you won't succeed in trading.

The more you write down your ideas and plans, the more you will develop your process edge. And you will find that as you write out your thoughts, plans, and views other new, different trade ideas will also pop out. For me, the process of writing about the Canadian housing market, and my difficulty in finding a good expression in FX has led me to this:

Short CIBC at 45.10, stop loss 47.11, take profit at 40.55.

A joke before we go:

How do you spell: Canada?

C, eh? N, eh? D, eh?

That is a terrible joke. Sorrey, eh.

Week 34: Nosce te ipsum

Excellent traders are self aware and humble

Update on previous trades

The USDNOK short from Week 32 was decent. Squared it up at a profit at 10.33 ahead of FOMC (as outlined / planned last week). CIBC stock is ripping higher on the strong Canadian data and China reopening optimism but I am skeptical this China bullishness will continue. I think it's a positioning unwind story in China for now, not a new macro event.

Nosce te ipsum

Nosce te ipsum is Latin for "know yourself."

The Ancient Greek aphorism "**know thyself**" is one of the three Delphic maxims. The other two maxims are "nothing to excess" and "certainty brings insanity." It's easy to connect all three of these aphorisms to trading and while today's piece focuses on *know thyself*, here's how the other two connect to trading psychology.

"Nothing to excess" means two things to me in trading and markets:

- Don't obsess about trading. Turn your phone off before you go to bed and turn it on in the morning. Don't install a Bloomberg terminal in the can. Those stories of guys with trading screens in the bathroom are neat but do you really want your life dictated by S&P futures? *Reminiscences of a Stock Operator* is an awesome book, but Jesse Livermore's excess in his trading and personal lives led to his eventual suicide. Trading is what you do, not who you are.
- Trends don't last forever. There is a point where excessive attention and excessive price moves become destructive for a trend. The best cure for high prices is high prices because when a commodity or stock price runs too far, it triggers changes in supply and demand that eventually lead to mean reversion. 2021 is a classic example of excessive liquidity and excessive animal spirits where excess eventually leads to ruin. Oil prices after the war shock, same deal.

"Certainty brings insanity" is a perfect aphorism for markets because you should always be thinking in probabilistic, not deterministic terms. Most people have a confidence vs. outcome curve in trading that looks something like this:

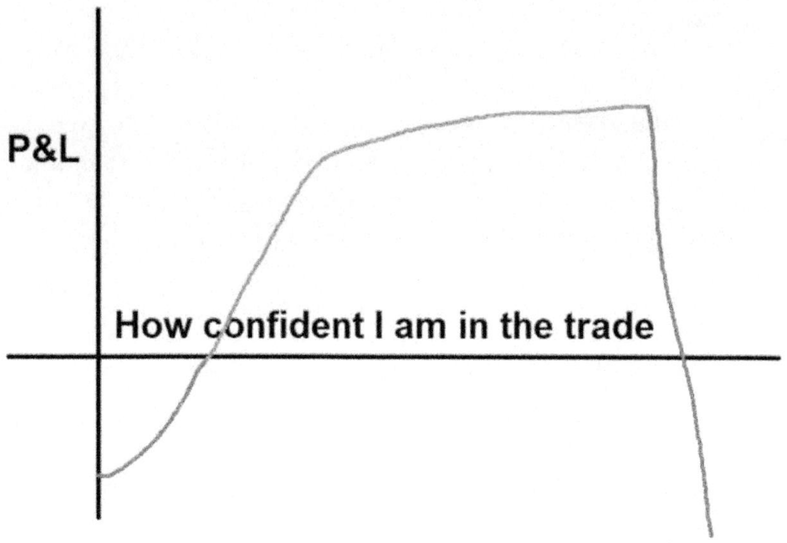

Overconfidence is kryptonite in trading and humility is a superpower. If you are cheering your positions because you "nailed it!" or you are doing the trading equivalent of the football team pictured below, that's not good.

San Francisco celebrates prematurely in the 3rd quarter of the Super Bowl; their overconfidence soon leads to ruin

Don't do this in the middle of a football game!

Confidence is critical but overconfidence is deadly.

If you think all your trades are 5-star home run/*amazeballs* ideas, your ability to determine the expected value of those trades is likely to be hampered by this overly rose-colored view of the trade's prospects. Overconfidence leads to overtrading, poor assessments of probability, and rigid, closed-minded analysis. Overconfident traders are also less likely to explore alternative hypotheses and will embrace confirmatory information much more openly than contradictory information.

Overconfident traders:

- take too much risk
- trade too frequently
- behave recklessly
- make poor assessments of probability
- do not keep an open mind
- overweight evidence that confirms their idea and ignore evidence that does not
- fail to consider alternative hypotheses
- refuse to admit when they are wrong

Most wise aphorisms and self-helpy truisms apply directly to trading. The Three Ancient Greek aphorisms are no exception.

Now, let's get back to Ancient Greek aphorism number one.

Know thyself

The most exciting, crushing, fun, and also soul-destroying aspect of trading is the way it forces you along a journey of self-discovery. This is big juicy stuff, and it's easy to be cynical about phrases like "journey of self-discovery." Cynicism on this topic isn't warranted or useful. Whether you want to admit it or not, the pursuit of trading as a profession is a journey of self-discovery. No trader or human being is fully formed when they start trading. **Trading forces you to learn about yourself—mostly the hard way.**

If you are going to pursue a career in trading, you can't keep making the same mistakes over and over. While you can quickly learn to fix procedural and process errors, the mental errors of poor discipline, irrational behavior, persistent bias, and emotional interference are not easily fixed with a few tweaks of a spreadsheet or systematic automation of a process.

I wrote last week about the two sources of edge in trading and how they are both necessary for success. You need alpha (tactics or strategy that take money out of the market) and you need a rigorous set of mental and functional processes.

Journaling and writing can be a big part of developing good processes and that's why I spent Week 33 on the importance of writing things down. This week, let's talk about a trickier part of process: the ongoing effort to know yourself, build on strengths, and eliminate leaks.

Not all traits can be modified but humans can change significantly over time. Your starting point should be that all traits are malleable and you can improve almost any part of yourself over time with enough effort. On the other hand, there is value to admitting the things you cannot change about yourself because those weaknesses need to be addressed not by "I'm gonna get better" but by introducing systems that acknowledge the weakness and buffer or eliminate its negative impact.

But always start with a growth mindset. Start by assuming that your flaws can be fixed.

The Growth Mindset

If you have kids, you may be familiar with the idea of the growth mindset because it is a perennial trendy topic in education. The idea was popularized by American psychologist Carol Dweck. Here is how she defines it in a 2012 interview:

In a fixed mindset, students believe their basic abilities, their intelligence, their talents, are just fixed traits. They have a certain amount and that's that, and then their goal becomes to look smart all the time and never look dumb. In a growth mindset, students understand that their talents and abilities can be developed through effort, good teaching and persistence. They don't necessarily think everyone's the same or anyone can be Einstein, but they believe everyone can get smarter if they work at it.

When you reflect on particular negative traits you possess and think "that's just who I am" or "that's just me," you cannot grow. Instead, embrace the surprising plasticity of the human brain and keep learning, evolving, and improving.

This concept is similar to the Japanese concept of Kaizen or "good change" which was a key ingredient in the superior quality and productivity of the Japanese automakers as they eclipsed North American car makers in the 1980s. With Kaizen or Growth Mindset (aka, continuous improvement), you always look to make incremental positive changes and continue to grow.

Without a growth mindset, you will wrongly believe that many of the traits, strengths, and weaknesses you possess are fixed or too difficult to change. That's not the right attitude. Pick a weakness, and work on it. You will notice improvement over time.

When someone says, "I'm not a people person" or "I'm not very good at math," that's a fixed mindset. Clearly, people are built a certain way by genetics and personality, and this is augmented by environment. That is your starting hand. A growth mindset says that you can overcome your starting hand by playing well, and thereby outperform your baseline or starting point.

Here's a quick summary of how the two mindsets contrast:

Growth mindset	Fixed mindset
Believes "I can change"	Believes "I am who I am"
Embraces challenges	Avoids challenges
Persists despite setbacks and failures	Retreats from obstacles
Learns from criticism	Rejects negative feedback
Inspired by the success of others	Threatened by the success of others

Even if you were the most disorganized kid in high school, all over the place in university, and live like a pig now, you can still become an organized person. You have to drop the idea that you are a certain way and embrace positive change. You don't need to take radical action; make continuous small changes. Start small and keep improving every day.

Here is conscientiousness by age:

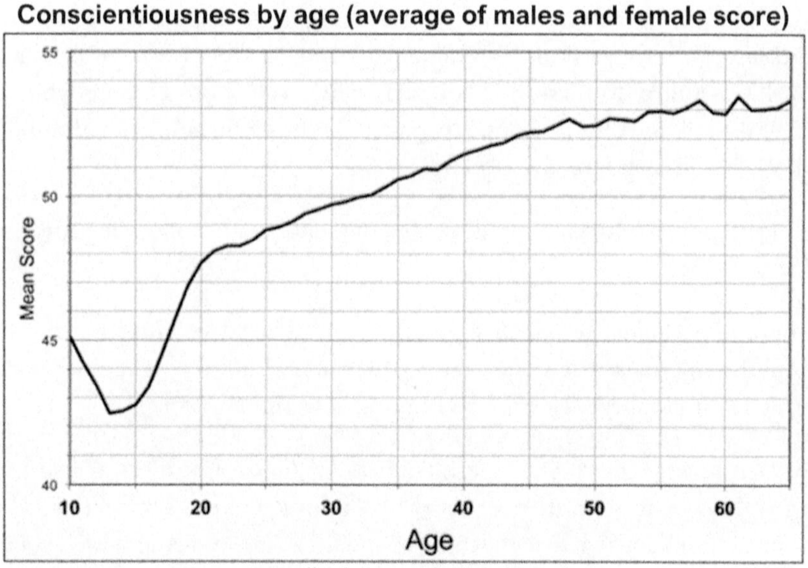

Image: Donnelly, data provided by Christopher Soto

Remember though, this is an average. Averages camouflage the substantial variance within a sample. Conscientiousness evolves differently in specific individuals over time. Some people will massively increase their conscientiousness as they grow. Some will flatline their entire life or even become less conscientious. This is in contrast to other facets of personality like extraversion, which tends to remain steady over a person's adult lifetime (on average).

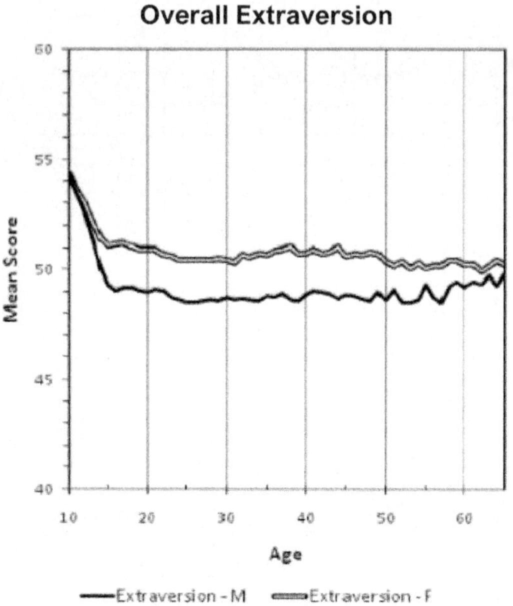

Source: https://www.researchgate.net/figure/Means-for-overall-Conscientiousness-A-and-its-facets-B-by-age-and-gender-Single_fig1_49696299

If you'd like to see where you score on the Big Five personality traits (openness, conscientiousness, extraversion, agreeableness, and neuroticism), check out bigfive-test.com. It's useful to do these types of personality evaluations because while they will mostly reveal what you already know, they will also bring up subtleties and information about you that you may not have realized.

You can learn much more about how the Big Five relate to trading success in my book *Alpha Trader*.

In that book, I include a personality questionnaire that relates directly to trading as it looks at all the key traits that make a successful trader. I humbly request that you please fill out this 5-minute survey7 before continuing with this chapter.

You can learn how to interpret the results in *Alpha Trader*, but most of it is pretty self-explanatory. Note that there are not that many "must have" traits to become a successful trader. The key isn't having specific traits or qualities, it's knowing where you're strong and where you're weak and making the right adjustments.

For example, risk-averse traders can succeed just as well as risk-seeking traders. They just have to think and behave differently. For every successful trader that tends to err on the side of too little risk, there is one like me who tends to err on the side of too much.

After working on trading floors for many years and studying research on trader success and failure, here are my best estimates for the ideal characteristics of the Alpha Trader:

	1	2	3	4	5	6	7	8	9	10	
Risk averse							X				Risk seeking
Not very confident								X			Extremely confident
Contrarian					X						Tend to follow others
Impulsive										X	Rational
Can snap under stress										X	Copes with high stress
Poor self-control										X	Excellent willpower
Average math skill									X		Quantitative superstar
Loves money										X	Loves trading
Acts on gut feel									X		Acts on logic
Lucky	X										Unlucky
Limitless energy	X										Often exhausted
Highly creative			X								Average imagination
I control my life	X										I don't control my life
Decisive			X								Hesitant
Adapts well to change	X										Not great with change
Focused			X								Scattered
Always very curious	X										Not all that curious
Organized	X										Disorganized
Trading experience	X										No trading experience
Highly emotional							X				Robotic

Remember, this is just me throwing subjective darts. This is not science or math. Reasonable people could easily disagree on my choices of where to put the X's. It's just a starting point for you to assess yourself.

Once you have completed the questionnaire, compare it to that grid and see where you are substantially different.

There is not enough room to discuss the importance of each trait in this note, of course. One of the main objectives of *Alpha Trader* is to help you identify your strengths and weaknesses and figure out how to level them up. This piece is about starting the process of understanding yourself and the questionnaire is one step in that direction. Consider this the self-evaluation phase.

The self-improvement phase is in your hands.

Now, pick **one trait** (a strength, or a weakness) from the survey you completed, and ponder how you will level it up.

One goal

I am a big believer in working on just one or two measurable and achievable goals at a time. Let me explain.

When I was a senior manager at a bank, we used a formal corporate goal-setting system, and it usually allowed for somewhere between five and fifteen goals to be entered. I found that was just way too many goals for me to supervise or coach as a leader and way too many goals for an employee to manage as an individual.

I eventually instituted my own "One Goal" system. I told the people that worked for me that all those goals in the corporate system were great, but all I cared about was their one most important goal. I asked them to e-mail me that goal and explain why it was important and how they planned to achieve it. This was effective. I saw much more impact from this One Goal system than I ever saw from more formalized, multi-goal systems.

This is consistent with Jocko Willink's approach in the book *Extreme Ownership*. **Prioritize and execute.** If you pick seven things you want to work on, guess what? None of them will receive the necessary attention. If you say: "I'm going to work on my intellectual flexibility this month because my permabear bias is hampering my short-term trading," you'll benefit. If you say "I'm going to work on these six traits this year to become a better trader," you'll flounder. Pick one thing and work on it.

Here are some examples of how to level up… Just to get you started. These are excerpted from *Alpha Trader* and are just the tip of the iceberg to wet your whistle.

Level up your self-discipline

1. If you have poor self-discipline, admit it. Then create systems to deal with it. Too many people just hope they will be stronger and more disciplined next time instead of creating friction to prevent unwanted actions, and automating desirable habits.
2. Outsource discipline as much as possible. For example, every time you put on a trade, load up an automated stop loss right away. If you have a team that works for you, keep your hands off the buttons and let them get you in and out of trades according to parameters you set in advance. Remember that once you put a trade on, the bias kicks in. You often start to overthink, overreact, and overanalyze. Stick with the parameters you selected when you entered, automate or outsource the stop loss, and take profit so that you do not overtrade.
3. Create a clear set of risk management rules and keep them as simple as possible. If you have a daily stop loss of $100,000, it's easy to know when you are done for the day. On the other hand, if you use a very complex set of rules governing your risk management and have no clear eject button, you are more likely to crash. Always have either a daily, weekly, or monthly stop loss (or all three) to manage risk of ruin.
4. Meditate or do yoga. A mind in a state of agitation has less self-control and less willpower. Learn about mindfulness. Check out dailystoic.com.
5. Read books about willpower and self-control. It is a trait that is innate to some extent but can also be built. *Willpower: Rediscovering the Greatest Human Strength* by Roy Baumeister and John Tierney is excellent, as are *The Science of Self-Discipline* by Peter Hollins and *The Disciplined Trader* by Mark Douglas.
6. When you are done reading these books, create a short list of takeaways: two or three actions you plan to take to improve your process and become more disciplined. Keep things as simple as possible.
7. Get a coach. There are many levels of coaching available for traders. When I worked at a hedge fund, we had a coach that came in once a month and I found the process useful. I found I did most of the talking and the coach prompted me and helped me find my way. There are online trading coaches available too, but do your homework before hiring someone.

Level up your willpower

1. Don't say things like: "I'm just like that" or "I'm really disorganized" or "That's just who I am" when it comes to conscientiousness. Being organized or on time or proactive is a choice. Think of your mind as plastic, not fixed.
2. Again, read the book *Willpower: Rediscovering the Greatest Human Strength* by Roy Baumeister and John Tierney. It is packed with research and anecdotes about how to improve not just your willpower, but your organizational skills and your

metacognition. I learned a ton of immediately applicable information from that book, including how to keep my inbox empty. It also taught me how we have a finite supply of willpower each day and thus willpower often runs low, especially at night. And the book taught me the importance of Zeigarnik Loops.

3. Acknowledge your willpower is not perfect and create systems to protect yourself from this weakness. Create friction in places where you engage in activities you should not. An example of friction is when people turn off their phone while at dinner to avoid checking it. By making it a hassle, you are less likely to perform the habitual or addictive behavior. On the other hand, reduce friction to reinforce desirable habits.

   For example, if you want to get in shape, don't make yourself decide whether to work out or not each day. Work out every day. And go to bed in your workout gear so you have one less step to take in the morning before working out. When the decision is already made, there is less friction. In trading this means you need to build systems and install processes that protect you from unwanted behaviors like overtrading while working to automate desirable behaviors. Delete the trading app from your phone if you overtrade on it. Institute an unbreakable rule that every position must be matched with an automated stop loss in a system.

Level up your quantitative skills

1. Learn about expected value (EV) and decision trees. These are especially useful when trading economic or market events with discrete outcomes.
2. Learn Python. This is rapidly becoming the standard for data analysis in finance. Excel is fine but not as good as Python. Not even close.
3. Take a course in statistics, probability, or data visualization.
4. Read academic research papers about the assets you trade. Freely available academic research is a hugely underutilized resource. Most research can be found and read online. Go to Google Scholar and type in a topic you find interesting (e.g., stock market inefficiencies, trading psychology, currency valuation or high-frequency trading). If you find a good paper, go to the bibliography and read some of the papers cited.
5. Learn about Bayes Theorem and Bayesian updating. There are many, many good websites on the topic (e.g., towardsdatascience.com). The basic idea of Bayesian updating is that good forecasters start with a prior probability and then update it as new information comes in. This is in contrast to people that form an opinion and then ignore new information. Good thinking and good forecasting are not possible without Bayesian updating.
6. Read *Superforecasting* by Phil Tetlock and Dan Gardner. This is one of the best books on statistics and forecasting, and it has tons of applications both in the real world and in trading. The book also does an excellent job of explaining Bayes so you kill two bullet points with one stone if you read it. I would

say *Superforecasting* is one of the books that has most influenced my quantitative thinking style (along with *Fooled by Randomness* by Nassim Taleb, *Risk* by Dan Gardner, and *Thinking in Bets* by Annie Duke).

7. Backtest your ideas. If you notice that stocks tend to fall every Monday and rally every Tuesday, backtest it. If it feels like oil rallies every day from 2 PM to 3 PM, check it out. Is it true or false? Whenever a hypothesis appears in your head, dig in and figure out if it's true. Playing with ideas and data like this can inspire new ideas and a better understanding of the inner workings of the markets you trade. If you don't know how to backtest, just open Excel and start messing around. This is the kind of thing you can teach yourself with a bit of effort.

Level up your creativity and curiosity

1. Study other asset markets or businesses with linkages to your market. The more you understand the iron ore market, the better you can trade the Australian dollar. The more you understand American Airlines, the better you can trade the airline ETF: XAL. Drill into the principal factors that drive your market and learn about them in detail.
2. Read about random and varied topics. It seems so obvious but I never really understood this until recently. If you read voraciously, you load new information into your mind and that information can then cross-pollinate with old information and spark new ideas. Most ideas come from combining two forms of disparate knowledge. If you read about art, or outer space or fractals or whatever… Cool finance-related ideas may pop into your head from time to time thanks to the stimulation.
3. Go for a walk. Sitting at your desk staring at numbers going up and down will drop you into a rut at some point. Get up and go outside for a few minutes. I have had many moments of clarity on the way to the bathroom or on my way to pick up Panera for lunch.
4. Talk to people in your network. New ideas come from contact with new streams of thought. Don't be a taker, though. Offer ideas to your network. Don't be the guy that just emails ten people saying, "What you thinking?" To form a strong network, you need to both offer and receive information and ideas.
5. Be curious and develop interests outside finance. Learn some history. Listen to British rap music. Exercise your brain like it's a muscle.

The trade

As I have learned more about myself over the years, one thing I have come to learn is that if I want to hold a trade for longer than a week, I have to do it in options. I am impatient, I am biased to overtrade, and I get bored easily. I have worked on my discipline and it has improved at the margin, but it's still pretty bad. I am addicted to excitement and change.

I change jobs every three years. I am always knee-deep in some new project. I like shiny intellectual objects. That's who I am. So it's not fair to expect myself to patiently sit on a delta one position for, say, four months.

When I worked at a hedge fund, the guy next to me and I used to exchange thoughts all the time. More than once, it went down something like this:

> *BRENT: Wow, GBPCHF is a great setup. Bullish chart, fundamentals, positioning, etc. etc. I'm buying here.*
>
> *GUY NEXT TO ME: OK, I'll check it out.*
>
> *— TWO DAYS LATER —*
>
> *Brent takes profit, up 1.9% on the trade.*
>
> *— A MONTH LATER —*
>
> *GUY NEXT TO ME: Wow, great idea on the GBPCHF! I'm taking profit here, it looks overdone."*
>
> *Brent checks GBPCHF and sees he would have been up 7.4% if he held it.*

I'm not good at holding cash positions for more than a week, especially because I hate weekend risk. I learned this over time by observation, and by journaling and tracking my trades, including what happened afterward.

Bullish Brazil

Recently, I have been getting more and more bullish on Brazil after I visited in early October. The full thesis from early October is here[50].

Almost a month later, I still think there is an opportunity to own Brazil for a trend trade into 2023. Assets there are cheap, the political situation looks stable, real rates are high, economic policy is somewhat orthodox, and the people I met there are generally proud, friendly, and humble. Not sure that last part matters, but whatever.

EWZ is the Brazil ETF and it tracks the US dollar vs. Brazilian real exchange rate (USDBRL) extremely closely and works as a simple proxy where both perform similarly.

---

[50] https://www.spectramarkets.com/issues/am-fx-brazil-is-excellent/

If I were to buy EWZ here at 34.10 and hold it for a move to 38.00, I would inevitably get bored at some point and sell at 34.85 or something before an epic move higher.

Therefore, if I think Brazil is going to trend for a few months, **I need to know myself**. I need to do an option. The election is out of the way, and the entry point is still pretty good in EWZ. There are still positive catalysts possible (Bolsonaro officially concedes, Meirelles named as Finance Minister) and I think the removal of election uncertainty is the big story and now Brazil can trend higher.

To keep it simple, I'll buy a January 2023 $35 $39 EWZ call spread, spending 2% of capital or $2,000. Entry point is 34.25 in EWZ and around $1.15 in the spread.

Conclusion

Know yourself.

Week 35: Hills and Valleys

Trading is an emotional, tiring, incredibly fun game.

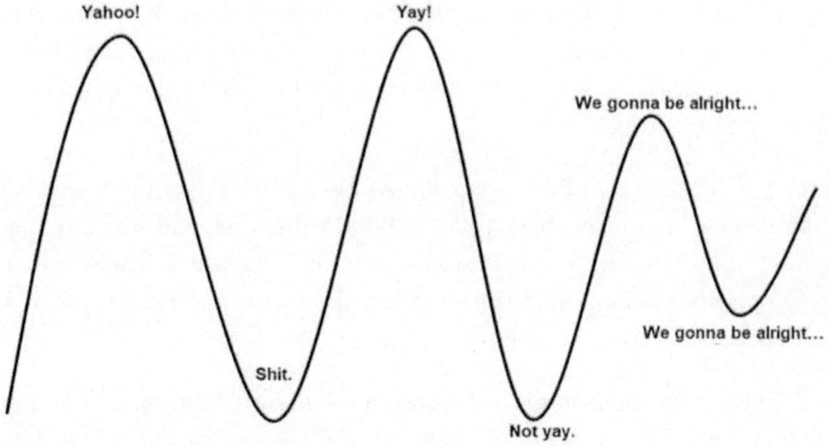

Update on previous trades

CIBC stock is still trading higher on the strong Canadian data and China reopening optimism while EWZ is a bit lower as there is still post-election uncertainty with regard to the finance minister appointment. Neither trade looking especially great at the moment as the 50in50 story continues to be one of hills and valleys.

Hills and Valleys

In 1996, when I was less than one year into trading FX at Citi New York, I was all bummed out about a trade that had gone against me. My boss at the time (and still my friend now) said to me:

"Hills and valleys, beeper. Hills and valleys."

A few weeks later, I was fist pumping an awesome trade after taking profit and he turns to me and says:

"Hills and valleys, beeper. Hills and valleys."

Simple, sage advice. Don't get too high. Don't get too low. There's always another high coming and another low right around the corner.

(He called me beeper because I was the only trader who was nice to the brokers and hence got the nickname: BP (broker's pal) which eventually turned into "beeper." Believe me, befriending the brokers was positive EV optimal metagame, especially if you needed playoff tickets.) :)

Pain

In December 2007, I was beaten down and frustrated. It was my worst trading year ever and it looked like I might finish negative on the year. When you work in a market-making seat at a bank, it is fairly uncommon to have a down year and I was proud of never having finished in the red. After this long and frustrating period, all I wanted to do was finish the year in the black. Even by $1.

Every time I got close to zero P&L, I would lose money again. By mid-November, I had gone from down $2.5 million back to $250,000 in the black and was thinking about making one last push to finish with a number that might be at least respectable. I finally felt mildly optimistic for the first time in ages, after almost an entire year of battling repeated cycles of frustration and despair.

Then, a brutal turn. A salesman slinked over to me with his tail between his legs and told me there was an outtrade in my book. Negative $700,000. That put me back to minus $450,000 with less than two months in the year. *Gross.* I grinded out the next few weeks and was finally up again YTD, just tiny, about $200k, on the very last day of the year.

At 10 a.m., our toughest client called and wished me a happy new year by ripping my face off to the tune of $600,000. Despite what felt like a heroic effort to the very last day, I ended the year in the red.

This is impossible. I am the worst trader in the world.

I e-mailed my wife: "This is impossible. I don't think I can do this anymore."

I walked out of the office miserable that day. New lows.

But the sun came up on January 1. Slowly, the frustration dissipated a bit, and the prospect of a new year gave me some hope. Despite that exhausting and disappointing year, I hung on and kept going.

Twelve months later, I was staring at my best year ever: Over $50 million of P&L. Sometimes the thing is just to keep going. As Joe Mauro said in his classic 2016 e-mail to the Goldman Sachs analyst class: "Keep running."

More pain

One of the hardest things about trading is that humans generally feel 2X the pain from losses as they feel joy from gains. And even when there is joy from gains, traders are afraid to feel it or express it for fear of jinxing themselves. This can mean trading becomes this endless series of grinding days full of self-hatred with blips of happiness interspersed but barely acknowledged.

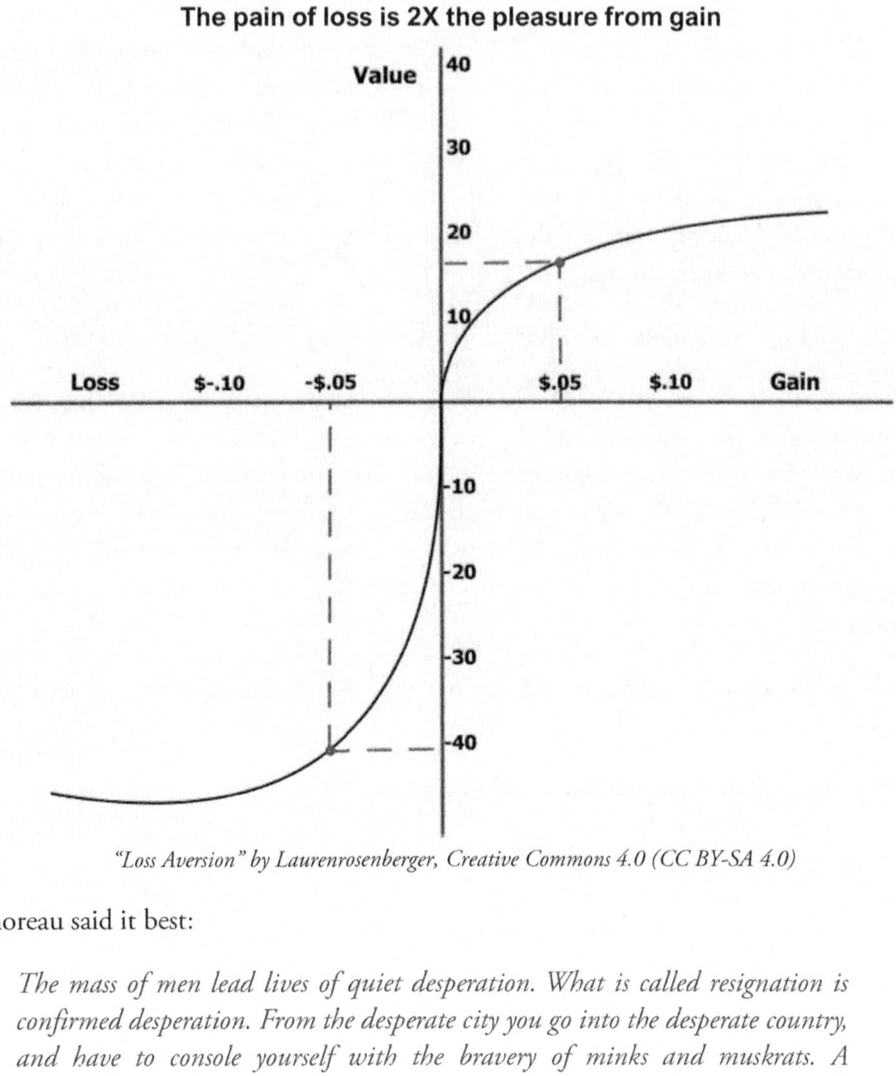

"Loss Aversion" by Laurenrosenberger, Creative Commons 4.0 (CC BY-SA 4.0)

Thoreau said it best:

> *The mass of men lead lives of quiet desperation. What is called resignation is confirmed desperation. From the desperate city you go into the desperate country, and have to console yourself with the bravery of minks and muskrats. A stereotyped but unconscious despair is concealed even under what are called the games and amusements of mankind. There is no play in them, for this comes after work. But it is a characteristic of wisdom not to do desperate things.*

Trading does not have to be that depressing!

You need to allow yourself to be happy. Whenever people ask me "Don't you find trading stressful?" I reply: "Yeah, but it's good stress." Like playing professional baseball is stressful. Or flying a fighter jet is stressful. And sure, the stakes are high but it's not life or death. It's important. But it's not life or death.

Don't beat yourself up because you did not trade perfectly. Perfection is not the goal in trading. The goal is excellence, consistency, and self-control. Process is more important than outcomes. If you rigorously executed your process today and lost money… You can still be happy with your performance.

In trading, and in life, the quest for perfection is commendable but the expectation that the world, any situation, or any trade will be perfect is flawed. You need to know when you have reached "good enough" or you will wait forever for the perfect trade, perfect spouse, or perfect job. This doesn't mean you settle for a crappy relationship or put on sub-par trades, it means you must have the wisdom to understand that life is not meant to be perfect. Perfection is rare and fleeting and anything perfect should come as a positive surprise, not as an expectation.

As the Italian proverb made famous by Voltaire says: *Perfect is the enemy of good.*

This applies to self-evaluation too. Many traders spend way too much time beating themselves up. Unless you finish the day at the ding dong highs, you will always wish you took profit earlier or had a bigger position or did something a little different. Assess your performance rationally. Set high standards but do not expect perfection from yourself, or every day will be a disappointment. When you do a good job: *be proud.* Don't niggle away at small performance glitches when you have generally run well. This is draining and pointless.

Good traders have the right perspective. They take the job seriously but do not allow it to consume them.

There are two sides to the emotional coin in trading. Hills and valleys. Hills and valleys.

Trading slumps

There is nothing more gut-wrenching than a major trading slump. No matter how many losing streaks you have experienced, each slump brings with it the same array of negative emotions. Self-hate, frustration, self-doubt, physical nausea, a lump in the throat, the urge to smash keyboards, sadness, confusion and vertigo are all normal symptoms of a trading slump.

Slumps can come completely out of the blue. One day you seem to know what will happen, before it happens. The next day, you have fat fingers, you hesitate, you miss the great opportunities and double down on the bad ones. Suddenly, you've lost money eight days in a row and you feel like you might never make money again. Trading is hard.

The first thing to understand is that there are probabilities at work. A trader with 55 percent winning days will average two or three 5-day losing streaks per year and probably one 6-day losing streak. A 6-day losing streak is enough to make the best trader feel like a complete moron. But he isn't. It's just probability.

It is easy to say this… And a totally different thing to embrace and accept it. That is why slumps can be very dangerous. They can morph from a simple run of good decision / bad outcome into something much more nefarious. If the run of bad outcomes leads to process breakdown and bad decisions, what was initially just bad luck becomes a negative feedback loop. If you are normally a 55 percent winner and you came in this morning angry, frustrated, and a bit hopeless... What do you think your odds of making money are going to be today? 40%? 35%?

The first key to dealing with slumps is good self-awareness. Recognize physical signs of frustration and acknowledge them. You cannot deal with a trading slump if you are not aware of it or you are in denial.

Once you realize that you are in a slump, the first action is slow down. Breathe. Take a day off or cut your positions down dramatically. If I usually trade 100 million USD positions, I might cut myself down to 20 million. If I lose money again, I'll drop to 10 million.

Why not stop trading completely?

This is a matter of personal preference but I rarely stop trading completely. I might take one day off to mentally reset but if I am at work I keep trading, just in smaller size. Short-term trading has a rhythm and you are apt to lose that rhythm if you stop trading completely. Instead, cut yourself down to something small enough that it will not matter if you are right or wrong. The object at this point is not to make money but to reset your emotions while still maintaining a connection to the market.

If things are going really, really badly, and I feel really dejected or down, I will stop trading altogether for one or two days and jump into a research project. I keep a file of ideas and projects so that when I hit a very rough patch, I can step away from the market and still feel like I am doing something useful. It's hard to do research when you are in the zone trading so I try to see bad slumps as blessings that finally let me get to that backtesting or correlation research project I have not had time for.

Some traders prefer to completely disconnect from the market by pulling out temporarily but as Jared Dillian once said: the markets are like a story. You can't just flip ahead 10 pages and know what is going on.

My view on taking scheduled time off is different. Vacations are a necessary part of a healthy trading process. Your brain cannot process billions of bits of market information efficiently 52 weeks / year. You need to turn off the noise now and then.

Three or four days away from the market should be enough to clear your brain and allow you to come back fresh. The only way to achieve this is to go on vacation and stay flat while on vacation; otherwise, your brain will be running all the scenarios about possible SPX outcomes instead of just digging holes with your kid on the beach or enjoying the music at Ibiza or whatever it is you do to unwind.

Go on vacation flat at least once per year. Any positive P&L you might generate with your holiday positions is more than offset by the mental damage you do to your brain when you refuse to let it disconnect from the matrix.

With experience, you will know when a slump is over. Things will seem easier again. Each losing trade will not trigger an emotional or physical reaction (tight throat, white knuckles). Given my belief that trading is very much about probabilities and process, I don't stay in defensive mode for very long. Once I feel OK, I go back to my normal size. The best cure for a trading slump is a perfectly-executed Five-Star trade.

A different type of slump is one precipitated not by a run of bad luck but by a concrete externality. This type of slump is totally different from a normal slump and is triggered by something outside the market, not just random variance. Your health, financial security, marriage, mental well-being, an addiction or something of that sort. If a slump like this comes along, get flat right away and figure things out before you come back.

Trading is not an escape and there are cheaper ways to forget about your worries. Until the issue is resolved or dealt with in a way that will not interrupt your train of thought at work, stay flat. Trading is stressful enough; if you are shaking with anger as you just hung up the phone after a fight with your sibling about who will take care of your sick mother.... Take the rest of the day off.

Next-level trading is when you know yourself and you consistently put that knowledge to use. Don't let externalities ruin you. You will never know what kind of trader you have the potential to become unless you give yourself the opportunity to succeed. Part of this is knowing when to trade and when not to trade.

How I deal with slumps

Here is my step-by-step strategy for handling slumps:

1: Square up

First, I cut all existing positions so that any residual frustration related to those losing views can dissipate.

2: Trade smaller

Then, I cut my position size for new ideas to about 20% of normal for a few days (or more) until I get a strong feeling and high conviction idea. Some people recommend not trading at all for a bit but I find this disconnects me too much from the market and I lose my feel. I would rather trade small, wait for a Five-Star idea, then fully re-engage. If I am feeling extremely frustrated (angry lump in throat) or recognize my state of mind is poor (bad health, external real-life issues) I'll stop completely, but this is rare.

3: Talk about the slump

I find just talking about a slump makes me feel better about it. Frustration boils inside but releases when you open up. Some firms have trading psychologists around but you can also just talk to your peers or friends or boss. When you discuss your trading out loud, it helps crystallize your thoughts and leads to forward progress and a calmer state of mind.

4: Read and do research

When I'm trading well, my entire focus is on the market and on staying in the zone. When things are not going well, it's a chance to catch up on reading, do some cool research projects I haven't had time for and get back to basics by re-reading stuff like the *Market Wizards* books.

5: Get some perspective

I am one of 8 billion people sitting on a huge, spinning rock hurtling around a spherical ball of hot plasma in an infinitely large universe. Meanwhile, this is the safest time in human history to be alive. My wife and kids are healthy. It's sunny and warm outside. No matter what happens in G10 FX today, the sun will still come up tomorrow. Markets always get better, you just have to ride out the tough times and stay resilient and optimistic.

Believe it or not, there is more to life than trading. Think about the long game and your entire career. While it is fun to trade all night and live a fast and exciting life, you cannot do that forever. Trading does not provide a path to happiness, no matter how much money you make. Financial freedom is one small part of happiness, but most research shows true happiness comes from other areas: Health, relationships, family, friends, and a feeling of purpose.

In fact, the relationship between money and happiness becomes very weak once you break above a certain level. That level depends on the individual but is generally lower than most people think. The money/happiness curve flattens out pretty fast. I wrote a longer piece on money vs. happiness at EpsilonTheory.com[51].

Get some perspective

A life of trading is a life full of hills and valleys. Every time you lose more money than you ever have before, it hurts. Right in the gut. And every time you make a new "best day" or hit your lifetime high water mark, there is a giddy sensation that is hard to regulate. If you are a good trader, you will trade with more and more capital and bigger and bigger positions as the years go by and therefore by definition your biggest up and down days will get bigger and bigger over time.

Some traders (including myself up until about 5 or 6 years ago) are afraid to feel happy or admit their satisfaction after a great day or a great trade because they don't want to jinx themselves. This creates an asymmetry where you feel bad after bad days but you don't give yourself the right to feel good after good days.

Over the years, this can be incredibly draining because you only let yourself feel the bad emotions. If you have a good day, feel good about it. Be happy. Go celebrate. Buy the better bottle of wine. But don't celebrate until you have taken profit! Celebrating while in a winning position is a recipe for upcoming disaster. Take profit, then go be happy.

So again, it is fine to feel good about your trading. It is fine to give yourself credit where credit is due. Don't dissect your great days to find the tiny thing you could have done better. Just be happy for one day.

Make lower highs and higher lows emotionally as time goes on. Avoid euphoria but give yourself permission to be happy and to feel fulfilled when you are trading well. A life of hating yourself when you're down and fearing the next drawdown when you're up is not healthy.

A major requirement for staying positive is you must have a risk management system that you trust. If you know you can trust yourself and your risk management, the sick feeling of having blown through your stop loss can be avoided. Many world-class traders are only right 50% or 55% of the time. There is no reason to feel bad on days you lose money. Imagine if Michael Jordan got down on himself every time he missed a shot. He would be a sad person, full of self-loathing.

The time you should feel bad is when you planned to risk $200,000 on a trade and you

---

51 https://www.epsilontheory.com/money-can-buy-happiness-in-variable-and-diminishing-quantities/

lost a million dollars. These are the cases when you should feel bad because deep down inside these days make you wonder if you can really trust yourself and if you are truly in control of the process. This is the worst possible feeling. It's scary.

You need to have clear risk management rules and then treat every day as a separate unit and compartmentalize your feelings. You run into problems when your risk management is bad and it spills into the next day and the next because it puts you under pressure or forces you to change your process or abandon your plan.

Don't break the rules.

Simple right?

No. It is very, very difficult. Everyone knows that if you eat too much and don't exercise, you will gain weight. But there are still plenty of overweight people around. Knowing the rules is easy. Following them is hard.

Always remember though.... Hills and valleys. Hills and valleys. Don't let yourself get too high or too low. Regardless of your P&L, the sun will still rise tomorrow, your kids will still love you and even in the most extreme situation where you end up losing your job as a trader, life STILL goes on.

A trade

Normally trade ideas in 50in50 relate to the topic of the lesson. Today, I wanted to write about slumps because I have received a lot of requests from readers asking me to cover that topic. And it's an important topic.

Even after 25 years, I still get bummed when things don't go well. I am still a bit on edge about the random performance of the trades in 50in50, even though I expected the results to be medium because I am forcing it at times in assets where I have no edge. That lingering voice saying "dude, you suck" still haunts me sometimes, even after all these years of trading.

Anyway, if we're talking about hills and valleys, nobody has bigger ones than Michael Saylor. His stock has gone from zero to infinity to zero and back to infinity and now is heading back towards zero, I think. The collapse of FTX is a massive event and will significantly damage confidence in crypto for months or years.

The break of 18800 puts 10000 as the next target for bitcoin and MSTR looks wildly expensive, even down here. 10k bitcoin is not good for MSTR.

So I go **short MSTR @ 200 with a stop at 282, looking for sub-100.**

This is not investment advice. This is an educational Substack. MSTR is wickedly volatile and the borrow is EXTREMELY expensive. Please do your own due diligence. There is also gap risk. In the time it has taken me to finish this, MSTR is now 186. I'll mark the trade to market when I finally hit send. It's volatile!

Crypto is broken and we are entering a new leg down. MSTR fair value based on its bitcoin holdings minus its massive debt is closer to $50 than $200. It's one of the last meme stocks still worth selling (along with TSLA).

Conclusion

Trading and life are full of hills and valleys. Try to make lower highs and higher lows emotionally as your trading career progresses. You don't need to be a robot, just maintain perspective. Listen to your emotions, but don't let them control your actions. Act rationally.

Week 36: Trading Gaps

Gaps offer clear insight into past and future equilibrium prices

Update on previous trades

The CIBC stock idea has been stopped out. The move in the USD (CM is denominated in CAD) and the bounce in SPX was its ruin. Many people pointed out in the Substack comments that the large Canadian banks are extremely diversified and the mortgages they hold are mostly insured so this is partly a result of me not knowing what I'm doing in this particular area. Mortgage servicers and brokers are probably a better long-term way to short the Canadian housing problem. HRED (TSX) is a good candidate for the trade if you're still interested. It is an inverse Canadian REIT ETF that trades in Toronto. Thanks to people in the comments and on Twitter.

EWZ is sucking wind as a long, and MSTR is doing OK, lower as the crypto utopia follows the dystopian trajectory of prior utopian dreams. Will crypto tech ever deliver on its ambitious promises to change the world? I'm agnostic, though getting more skeptical. Here's a powerful essay[52] that argues a hard "NO".

---

[52] https://squareman.substack.com/p/crypto-21st-century-philosophy-for

Gaps and Single Prints

The way things generally work in liquid markets is that prices move up and down to adjust for new information along with supply and demand. Investors focus on fundamental information in the hopes that a stock price will eventually converge on their estimate of "fair value" but in the short run, supply and demand determine asset prices, not fundamentals. As Benjamin Graham said:

In the short-run, the market is a voting machine, but in the long-run, the market is a weighing machine.

This is a nuanced but important distinction. Fundamentals influence supply and demand, but **price is a reflection of buyers and sellers in an ongoing auction** and can deviate substantially from what you or I think the fundamentals say. That's why stocks can rally on bad news and currencies can sell off on good news. The flows run the show.

While markets tend to be a continuous series of prices going up and down, sometimes there are discontinuous moves where new information takes price from a discrete location to some other discrete location without any trades in between. These gaps can be useful to identify when trading and they can also be devastating for risk management if you always assume continuous prices and prices jump.

Stocks are most dangerous when it comes to gaps, because they are closed half the time. Currencies are least susceptible to this problem, but can still gap significantly on weekends and (less so) on news.

In 2000 there was a particularly egregious example of gap danger as a press release came out saying Emulex earnings were going to miss by a huge margin. At the time, I worked in a day trading office and many of the guys around me sold the stock on the news. It was around $50 before the news broke, they sold at $30 or so and it was soon trading at $25.

Two guys were fully margined short (i.e., they had $100,000 in their account and were short $200,000 worth of stock) Then, disaster. The stock was halted. Nobody knew why for about 2 hours then the NASDAQ announced that the press release *was fake*. The stock reopened at $62 and both traders got margin called by the office and lost their entire accounts.

One, this is why gaps are dangerous. Two, careful with leverage, especially leveraged shorts.

The wiki page for the hoax is here[53].

---

[53] https://en.wikipedia.org/wiki/Emulex_hoax

Emulex stock, daily August to October 2000

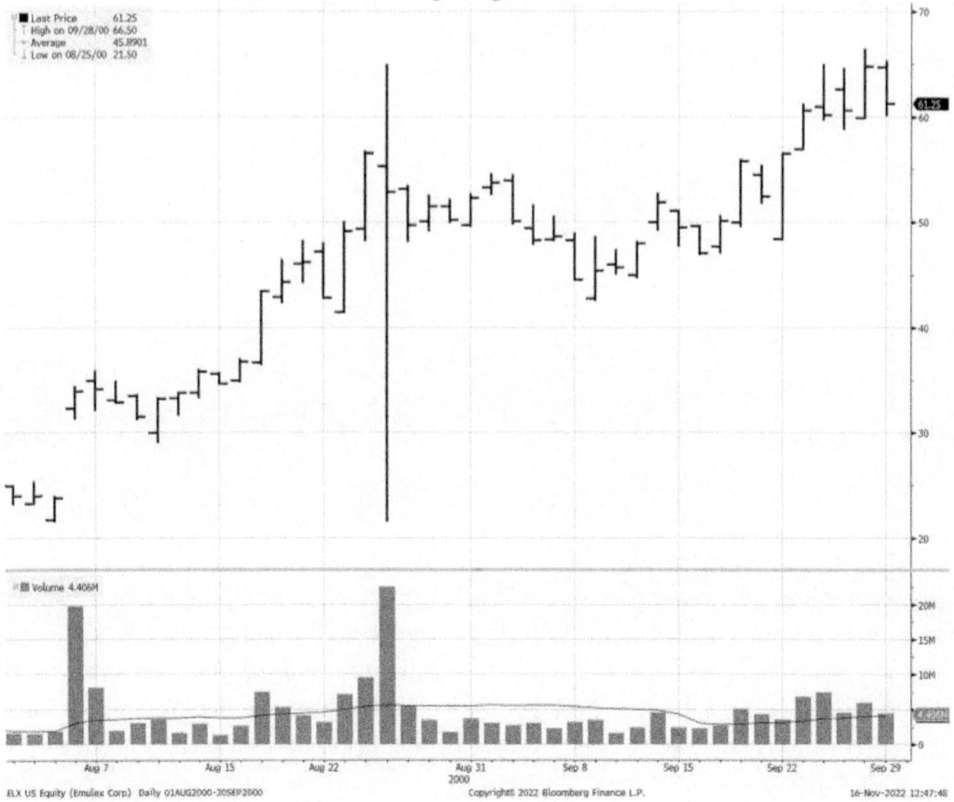

Trading gaps

Gaps are a simple way of seeing that a market was in equilibrium and then moved instantaneously to a new equilibrium. There's a lot of information there. The main thing I use gaps for is as support and resistance. There are clichés like "gaps always get filled" but they are empirically untrue. Sometimes gaps get filled; sometimes they don't. Trading on the expectation that every gap will get filled is a recipe for losing many a finger to falling knives and many a trading account to exploding rocket ships.

I don't think there is a systematic way to trade gaps all the time. Simply **use either side of a gap as support and resistance to enter trades ideas you already like.**

Let's say I'm bearish Carvana, because I always am. I think they are going bankrupt but I have come to this view at some arbitrary moment in the last few months. The first thing I would do is look for retracements in the downtrend that test the bottom of a prior gap.

Here is the chart:

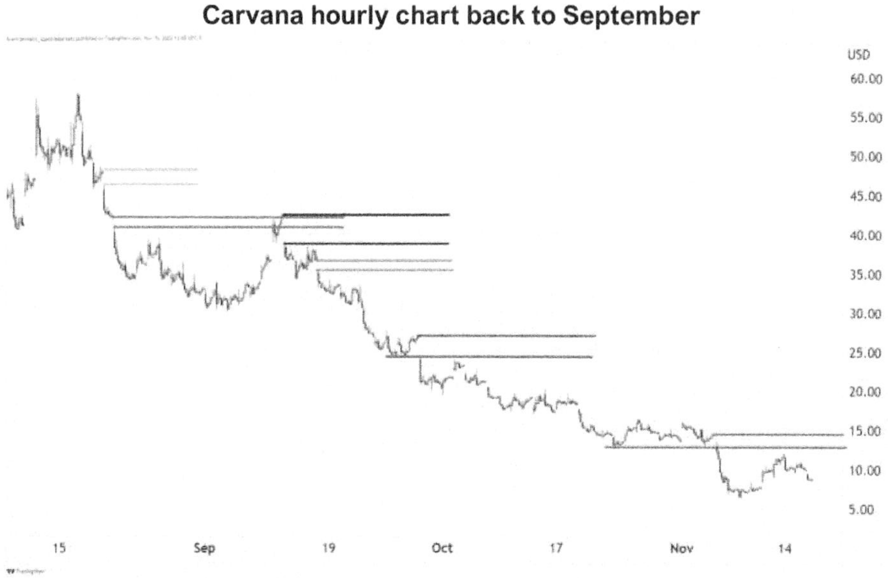

Each pair of lines marks a gap lower in Carvana's price. Note that many of those gaps saw price rally back to, but not through, the gap. The second lines from the left are the best example, where the gap was filled perfectly, but the next pair of lines saw a rally to the bottom of the gap and the second-to-last ones got super close before failing. The simple strategy is identify the gap, the enter trades as price approaches the gap, with a stop on the other side.

Here's a simpler diagram to explain it clearly:

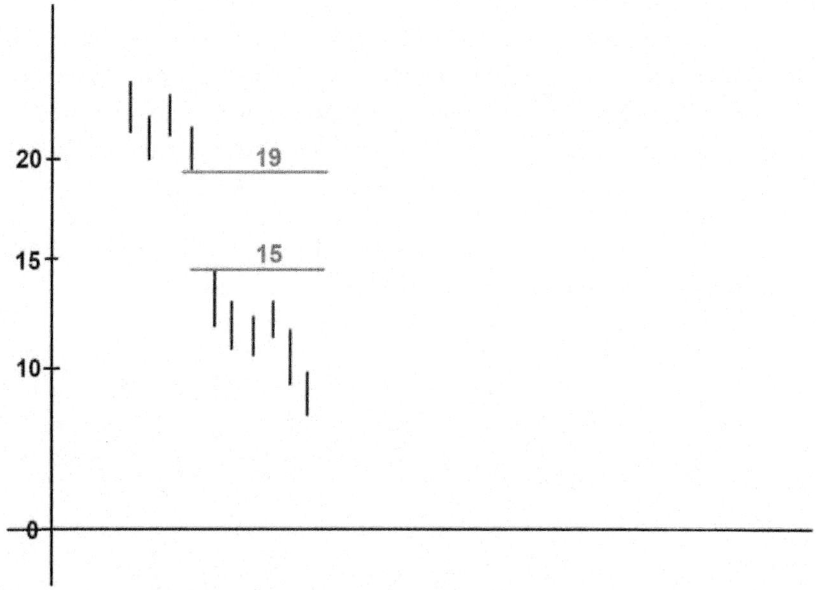

The stock gapped from 19 to 15 and is now trading at 7. I don't like the risk reward of going short here, because if I do: Where the heck am I gonna stop out? $22? Risking 15 to make 7 is not good. So instead, I will wait for the stock to bounce up towards the gap. I will go short at $14 with a stop at $21. **Sell as price approaches the gap, with a stop loss on the other side**. Same story, but reversed in an up trend.

The attractiveness of these trades is that you are participating in the primary trend while playing reactions against that trend to avoid selling the hole or buying the highs.

What exactly happens around gaps?

I have written in the past about how I like technical setups that have an underlying logic based on market structure and participant psychology. You can read more about that concept here[54]. The gist is that super-complicated stuff like Gann fans tend to rely more on mathematics or pattern recognition while simple stuff like horizontal lines simply reflect the underlying supply and demand, and order book dynamics in a market.

If you've ever been a market maker, for example, you know that support and resistance are often simply the byproduct of huge customer orders in the market. If EURUSD keeps bouncing off 1.0250, it might be as simple as "China is bidding for 4 billion euros at 1.0250."

Gaps also reflect a particular psychology in the market because they leave traders trapped. Human nature is to anchor on prior price points, even though that is totally irrational. When a stock or asset gaps, wrong-way bets are trapped and are simply praying for the thing to get back to where it was before the gap. If you're long Nike stock and it closed at $99 yesterday, and then it gaps open to $93 on the open because of whatever… Irrational traders (i.e., the majority) will look to get out of longs as price approaches $99. That is, even though they were bullish before, they are psychologically anchored on their entry point of $99 and hate the pain they feel as the stock goes to $93. Thus they become sellers now at $99 because that's where they feel the relief of breaking even.

Fading or going with the initial gap

Another valid strategy around gaps is to fade them almost right away, or go with them with a tight stop. The implicit idea here is that the invisible hand has not found the right price instantaneously, and it will either mean revert, or rip much farther. This often requires you to have some view of the underlying story or fundamentals, but not always.

---

[54] https://medium.com/@mbrentdonnelly/how-technical-analysis-can-reveal-underlying-market-structure-87710a7f2a32

Sunday gaps in FX (especially ones related to risk aversion or scary weekend stories) are notorious for mean reversion. Here is the P&L of fading every Sunday gap of 0.5% or more in USDJPY:

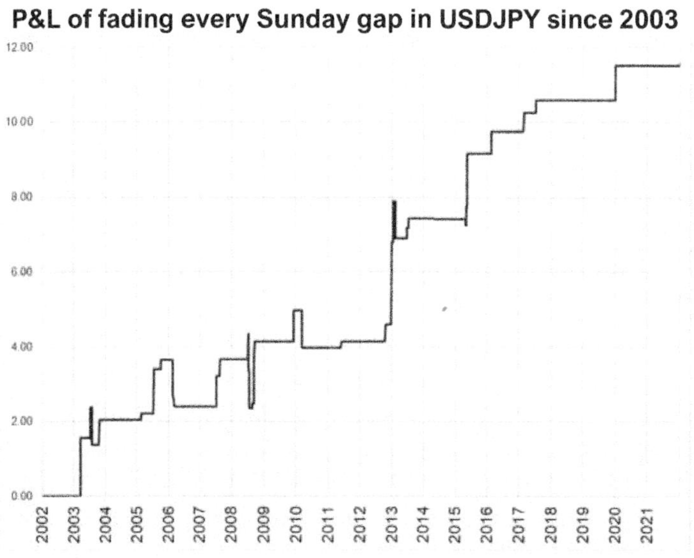

This is typical for most Sunday gaps in FX, but not always typical of gaps in stocks. Sometimes gaps will trade like this one after Nike's earnings warning:

You could have gone long at the open $83.19 with a $1 stop loss and made 9 bucks in a two weeks. On the other hand, when INTC warned in June 2022, the stock did this:

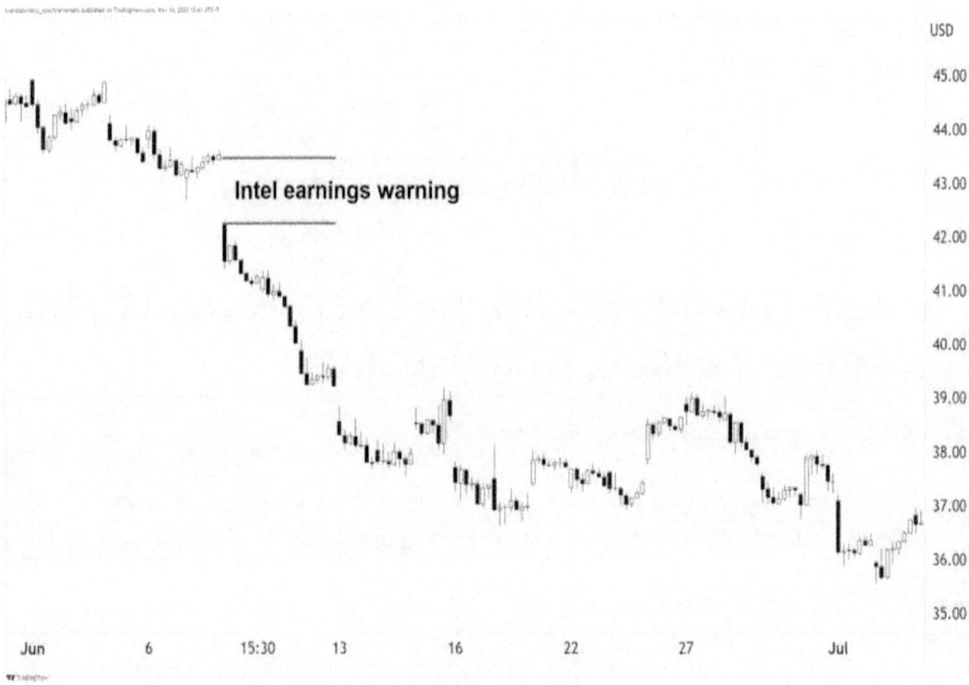

You need to have a view on the importance of the news, and whether or not the market is pricing it correctly, before you trade immediately on a gap.

These can be absolutely mega trades when they work and the beauty is that a tight stop loss is the correct play on these so you can get strong leverage. Be careful fading or going with gaps pre- or post-market because it's very difficult to risk manage. Better to wait until the open, do the trade, and automate your stop loss right away. Otherwise, that trade where you were risking $2 to make $7 becomes a trade where you lose $9.

Double gapper weirdness

Over the course of the last two days, Walmart and Target released earnings. While Walmart is 6.5X larger than Target from a revenue standpoint, and the two companies cater to different clienteles, they are both downmarket, price-oriented mass retailers. If WMT is doing well, one might expect TGT to be doing OK, in general.

Before we get to the trade idea, I must share this analyst preview of the two retail giants' earnings releases courtesy of Barron's:

BARRON'S

RETAIL

Target Has an Advantage Over Walmart This Earnings Season, Analyst Says

By Sabrina Escobar Follow Nov. 7, 2022 9:59 am ET

Both Target and Walmart are in a solid position heading into third-quarter earnings season, Cowen says, but Target may just have the upper hand.

This is funny if you know what happened. I don't post this to slag the analyst at Cowen. I am wrong plenty of times too. I just post it as a reminder that experts are wrong all the time and you should not blindly follow them (including me).

Trading your own ideas and risk managing them so that you have positive EV on your trades is so important. When you trade your own view, you are strong and will do all the right things. When you trade someone else's view, you will risk manage it poorly, take profit too early, and never know when the situation has changed unless you have an open line to the person whose view you are trading. Always. Trade. Your. Own. View.

Anyway, here's what happened. The chart is straight out of a Tufte nightmare, so let me explain it. The gray line is Walmart, selling off into earnings on worries. The light gray line shows the selloff then WHOOSH. Massive gap higher.

The black line is Target, rallying into earnings on bullish excitement. The accompanying lines show the rally then KABOOM. Massive gap lower.

WMT (gray) and TGT (black) rip opposite directions on earnings

(intraday back to 03NOV22)

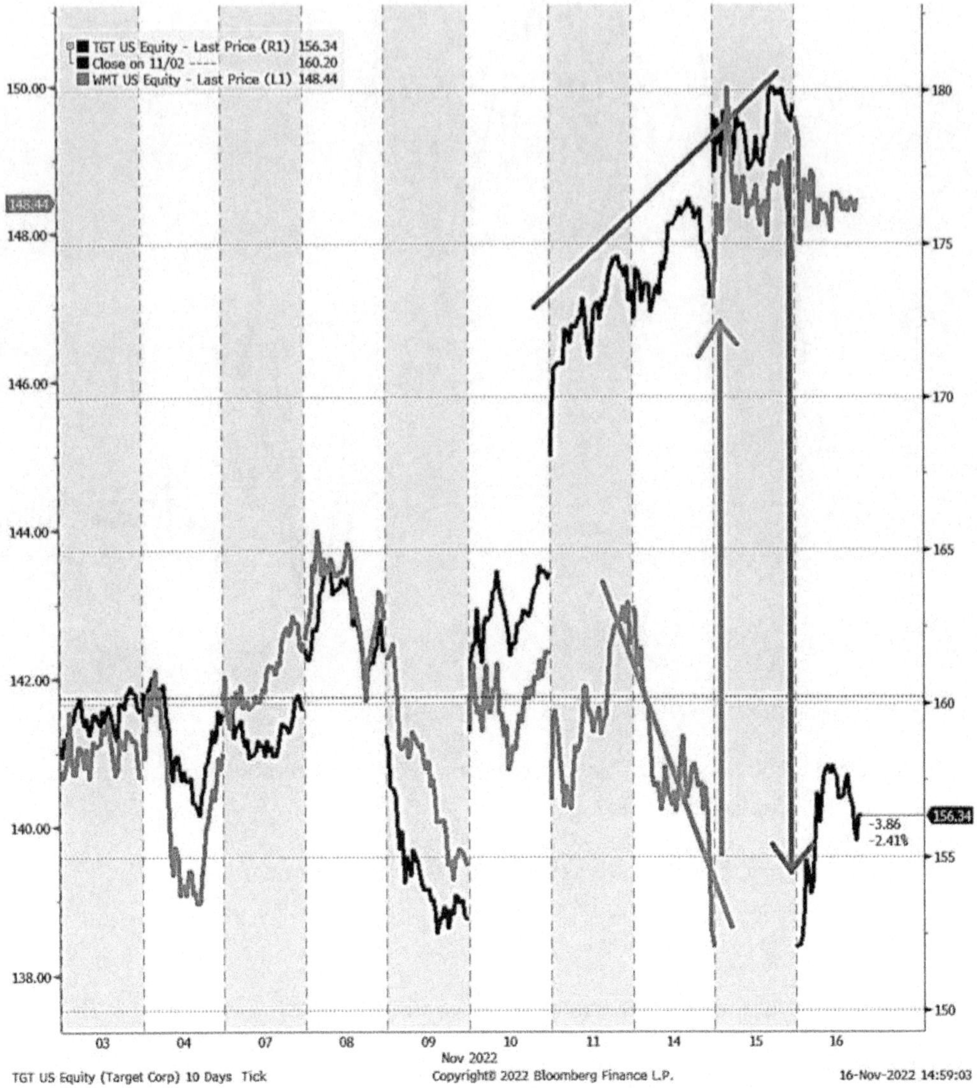

For context, here's how the two stocks move in the bigger picture:

WMT (gray) and TGT (black) rip opposite directions on earnings (daily back to 01MAR21)

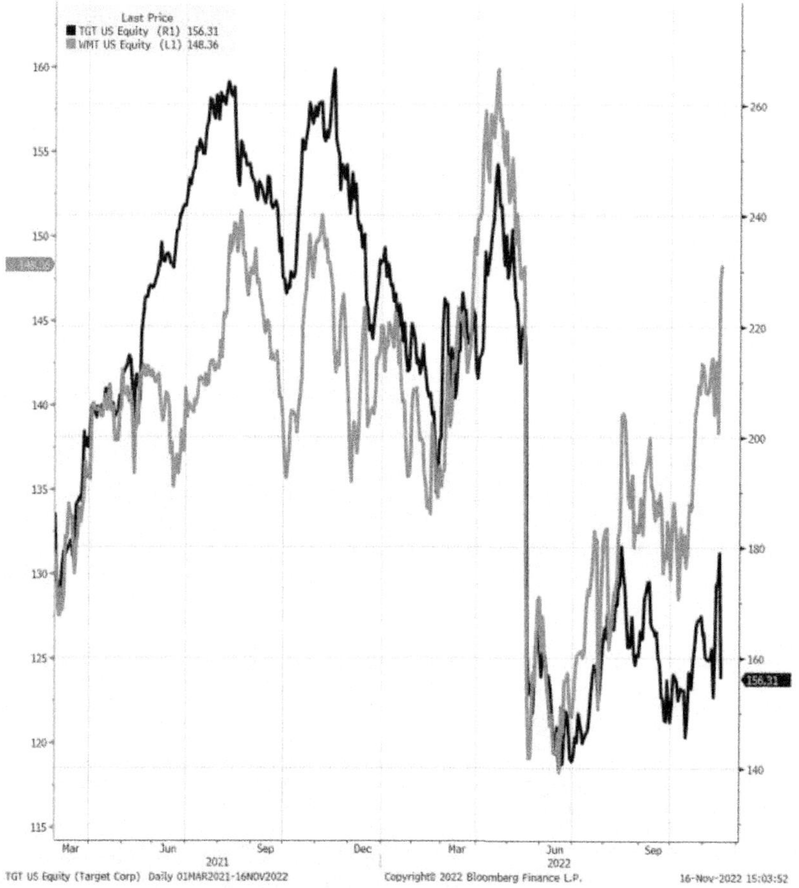

You can see the ebbs and flows are similar, but WMT has exploded relative to TGT. I explained three ways to use gaps:

1. Use gap tops and bottoms as support and resistance zones
2. Go with the gap using a tight stop
3. Fade the gap with a tight stop

So those are simple and effective ways to trade around gaps.

Another more complicated way you can use gaps is as targets and strikes to help structure trades you put on with options. Here, I'm going to do an RV trade going short WMT and long TGT for convergence. If you have no idea how relative value trading works, I suggest you read Week 15: RV Trading is Hard before you read the end of this chapter.

The trade: Short WMT, long TGT via options using gaps to define targets

I'm not an expert in US retail stocks. I'm using this setup as an example of how you can use gaps in your trading. Let's say I don't think it's sustainable to have WMT and TGT gapping in opposite directions on earnings. Their businesses are too correlated and I expect the prices to converge. If I'm right, I would expect one or both of the stocks to close the gaps.

Here are the gaps, before we continue:

WMT gap: 138/146

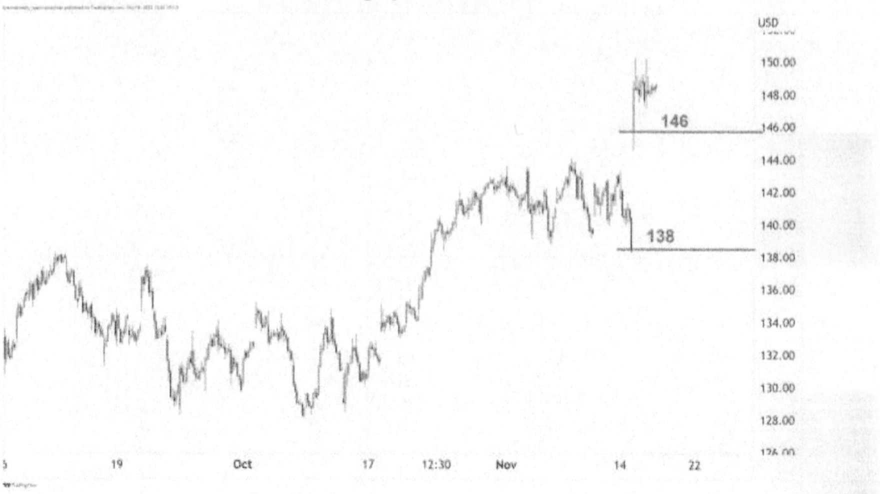

TGT gap: 150/179

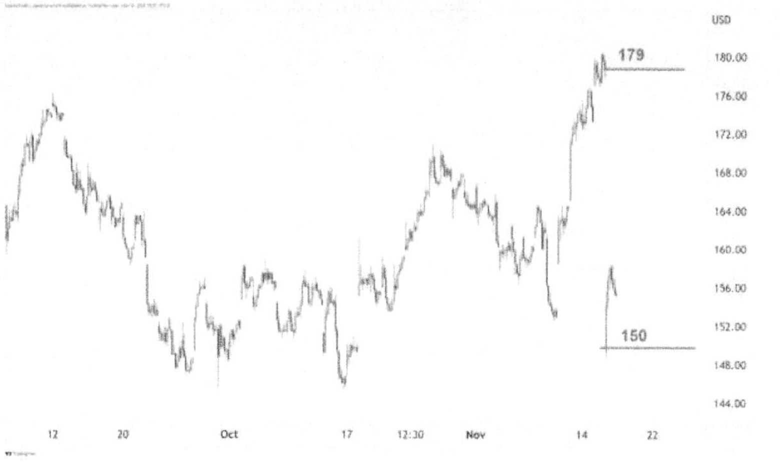

For what it's worth, another great tool for looking at gaps, along with the equilibrium zones that preceded them, is Market Profile. I have written about this at length in various posts and in my books. A complete guide is here[55], or you can grab *Mind Over Markets* by Dalton. That is my favorite market profile book.

The gist of the methodology is that it shows how much time a security spends at each price. The longer the asset spends around the same price, the thicker the stack of letters becomes so you get a market profile chart for TGT that looks like this:

TGT Market Profile, November 3 to now

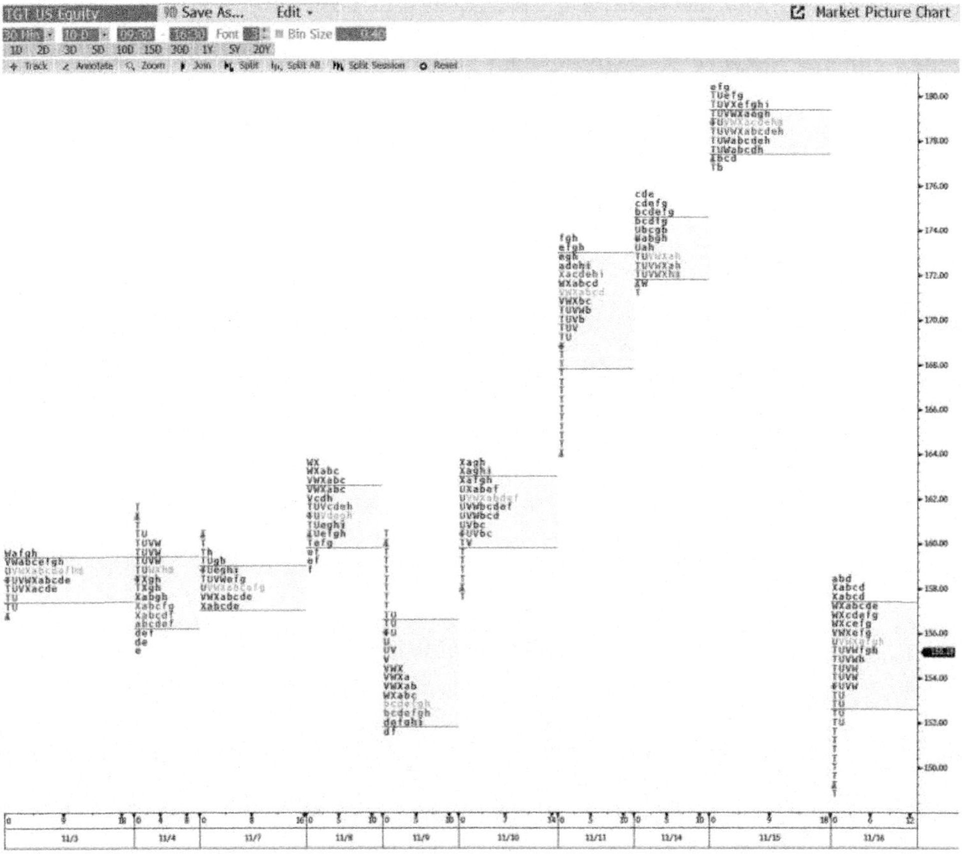

Maybe I'll write a full Market Profile piece for 50in50 before we're done. It's an excellent tool that's easy to use. In this chart, you can see that equilibrium before the run up into earnings started was 156/164. That gives you some extra context if TGT starts to run higher. The first resistance will be the top of the old equilibrium range (164) and the next one will be the top of the gap (179).

So for this trade, I want to buy call spreads in TGT and buy put spreads in WMT. I'm going to use a 1-month time horizon because that's the kind of trade I think this is. So

[55] http://www.r-5.org/files/books/trading/charts/market-profile/CBOT-Market_Profile-EN.pdf

what strikes do I pick? When you're buying a call spread, you want to own a strike that is far enough away to give you leverage but close enough that you will get well through it by expiry. You want to sell a strike that you think will not be breached.

So with TGT, you can buy the old equilibrium high (164) and sell the top of the gap (179). If you want to tighten up the top strike, you can use the low on that last day before earnings, which is 176. If you stare closely at the TGT chart, you can see that last day before earnings was a little island encompassing 176/179.

With WMT, you're doing a put spread. The equilibrium range before earnings was 138/144 (this is easy to see on the WMT chart above). The stock is 148.50 right now so you buy the 144 put (assuming we head back into the old equilibrium range) and sell the 138 put (the bottom of the gap).

The strikes are on the $5 increments, so I see this as the complete trade structure:

Ticker	Expiry	Strike	C/P	Buy or sell	Price	Total cost
TGT	16-Dec-22	165	Call	Buy	3.7	
	16-Dec-22	170	Call	Sell	2.3	1.40
WMT	16-Dec-22	145	Put	Buy	2.4	
	16-Dec-22	140	Put	Sell	1.23	1.17

If this were a simpler trade and, say, I was just buying WMT puts, the thought process would be similar. You target a closure of the gap when selecting your strikes. This trade pays $5 on a total cost of $2.51 if either stock fills the main $5 of the gap. If both stocks keep running, we lose the whole premium on both structures. If TGT is just suffering from bad management and idiosyncratic weakness, that may well happen.

And of course, there are a ton of outcomes in between. The dream scenario is that TGT rips, WMT dumps, and you make $10 minus the premium spend. Doubtful!

A nice thing about a trade like this is that you don't care what the broader market does. You have no beta to SPX here, really. Or tiny beta as TGT vol is higher than WMT, but whatever. Another nice thing is that you are buying options after earnings, so the options are much cheaper than before (5 vols or so). You are also buying close-to-the-money options so again, vol is not pricey.

For the purposes of tracking, we spend $2,510 on this idea, doing 10 contracts of each spread. Hold to expiry.

Conclusion

Gaps are useful as they show you where price went out of equilibrium and then found its new happy place. As price travels back towards the gap (the rejected equilibrium), you will very often see it stall. There are a variety of ways to trade gaps. You can use them as support and resistance, you can go with them, you can fade them, and you can use them as targets and strikes when you structure trades using derivatives.

Use gaps to your advantage as they offer tight risk management parameters and reasonable estimates of where price may stall in the future.

Week 37: Common Traits of Top Traders

Survey results and a yawning jaws correlation breakdown trade

Update on previous trades

Week 36: +TGT vs. -WMT is doing OK.

Week 35: Short MSTR small in the money, not moving much.

Week 34: EWZ call spread sucking major wind.

Full update with the detailed spreadsheet in Week 40.

Common Traits of Top Traders

A few weeks ago, I sent out a survey to see if successful traders have different personality traits than beginners. Surveys are generally boring and annoying, so I try not to send them out too often. Feedback on this particular survey was unusually strong and positive. Most of my surveys get around 250 responses and this one got ~600.

The cool thing to me is that many of the traders I know well and have a deep respect for pinged me after to tell me they completed the survey. The results show that many experienced traders completed the questionnaire, along with many other traders of various skill levels.

Before I show you the traits that differentiate successful traders from inexperienced and not-yet-successful traders, let me provide a couple of excerpts from *Alpha Trader* for context. The survey I constructed was based on analysis from the early chapters of *Alpha Trader* where I attempted to dissect what makes a successful trader. Today's piece is meant to complement my findings in the book, and hopefully add new insights.

In that book, I study success outside trading (in fields like academics, sports, and life outcomes) and I study research on success in trading to come up with this equation for trading success:

Rational + intelligent + skilled + conscientious + calibrated confidence

I then offer the following clarification (excerpted from *Alpha Trader*):

> Note my equation for trading success excludes some traits that are important but not critical to trading success. I did not include risk appetite, for example. People at each end of the risk-taking continuum (extremely risk averse or highly risk seeking) might underperform those in the middle, but risk appetite is not an important character trait in the literature on trading performance.
>
> Furthermore, risk tolerance can be dialed up or down fairly easily with a simple set of rules. I have seen traders at every point on the risk-taking spectrum succeed.
>
> Before the year 2000 or so, IQ was less important in trading because trading was more skill-based and less quantitative. Now, a higher level of quantitative intelligence is required although I would argue that Wall Street currently overvalues IQ and academics, and does not focus enough on grit, street smarts and fire in the belly.
>
> My equation leaves out many positive attributes that most certainly make for better traders. It does not include positive attitude or ability to handle stress, for example. These are useful but not critical attributes when it comes to trading success. There are plenty of grumpy, stressed-out traders that still make money. Sure, that's not ideal (and certainly does not meet my personal definition of success), but only the indispensable traits are in the equation. Many other attributes will help you succeed in trading but the formula I laid out is the mashed potatoes—everything else is gravy.
>
> On at least one of those viewpoints, the survey results show I was wrong. But I'll get to that in a bit. First, here's the basic info on the traders that completed the survey. Total sample was 589. The first three questions were used to bucket traders into groups by success/experience. Here are the results:

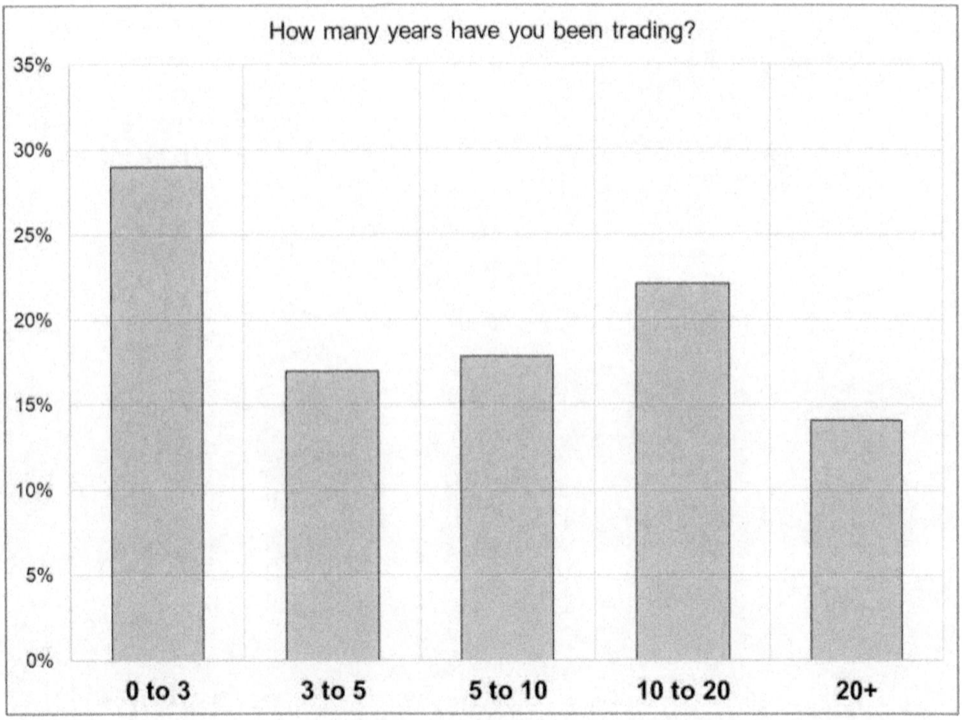

Impressive number of traders with 20+ years of experience on my distro! I thought that was cool.

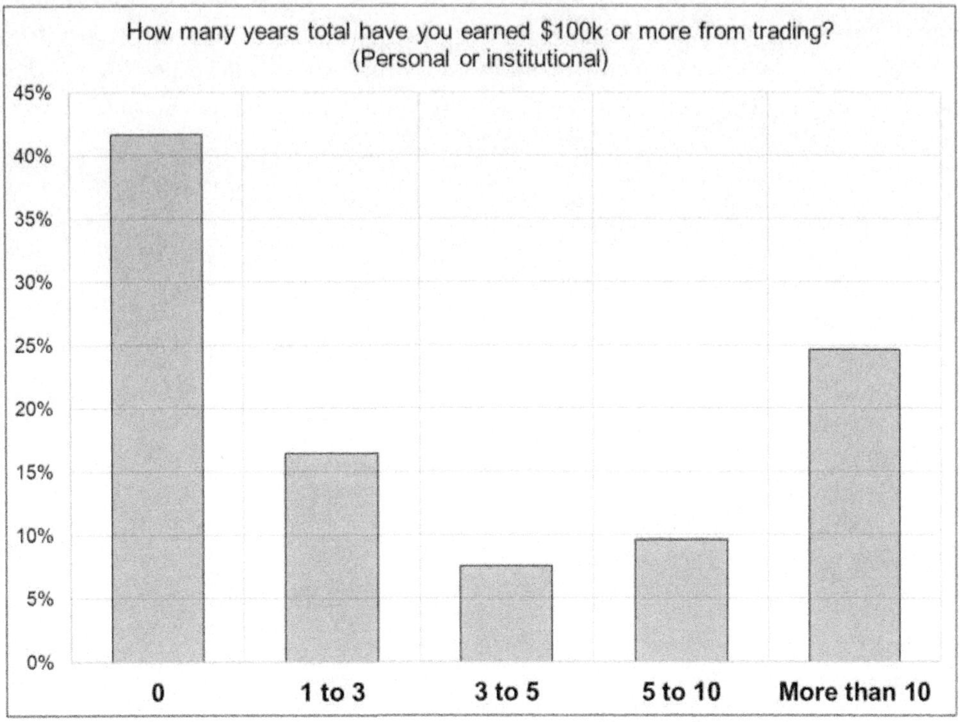

Again, decent representation from professional traders. And a lot of new traders, of course. Next, profitability:

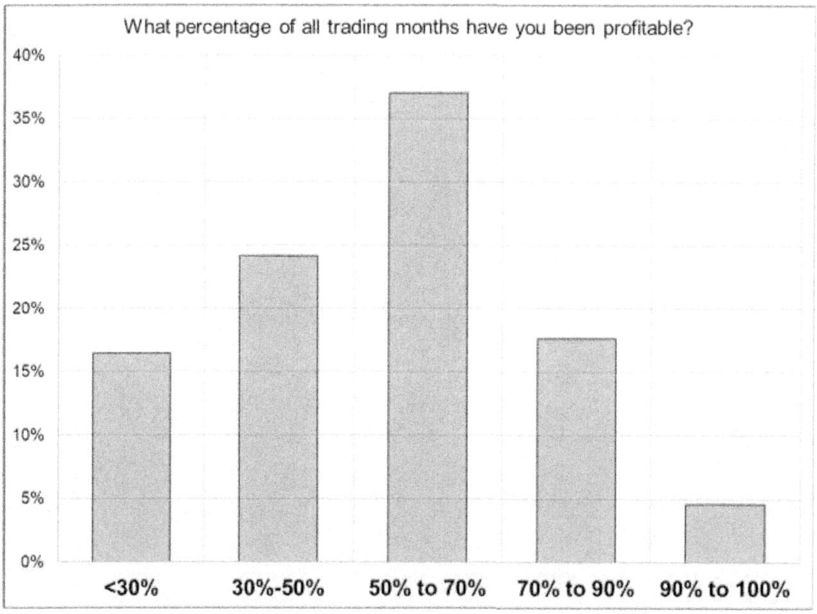

And I always enjoy throwing in this last question as a study in overconfidence bias (see next chart). Almost everyone thinks they are average, or better than average, as usual! Fun. This overconfidence bias also appears in the main data as there are very few low rankings on the scales and many, many more 7's than you would expect in a normal distribution. The data is somewhat normally distributed, but around a mean of 7, not 5.

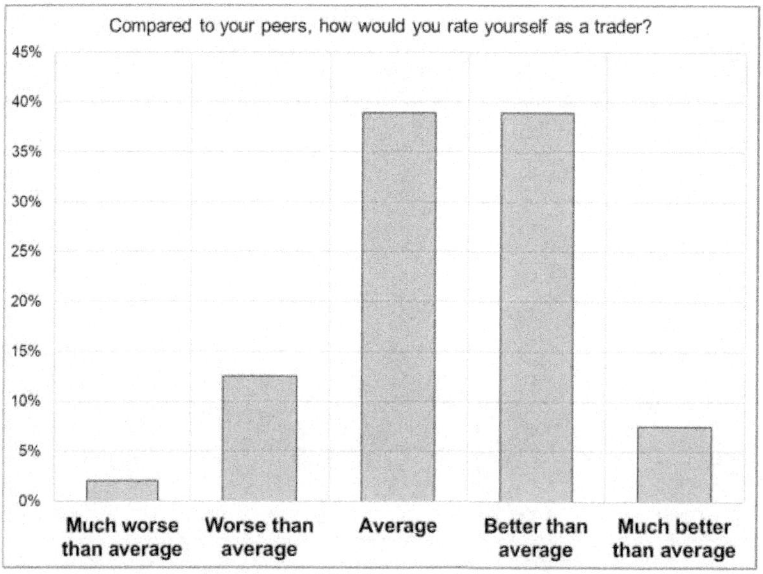

Once all the data was collected, Justin and I worked to split the respondents into four cohorts defined by experience and profitability. We called the groups: Beginner, Trader, Pro, and Veteran (ascending order of combined experience and profitability). The output I was most excited to see was the traits where there are large differences between the cohorts. The absolute responses were going to be mostly meaningless to me; I figured the relative traits comparing noobs to pros would offer the most interesting takeaways.

Some results were as expected, and there were some surprises. I am going to show the results in a graph first, then the data is provided in a table afterward, so you can see it more clearly and specifically.

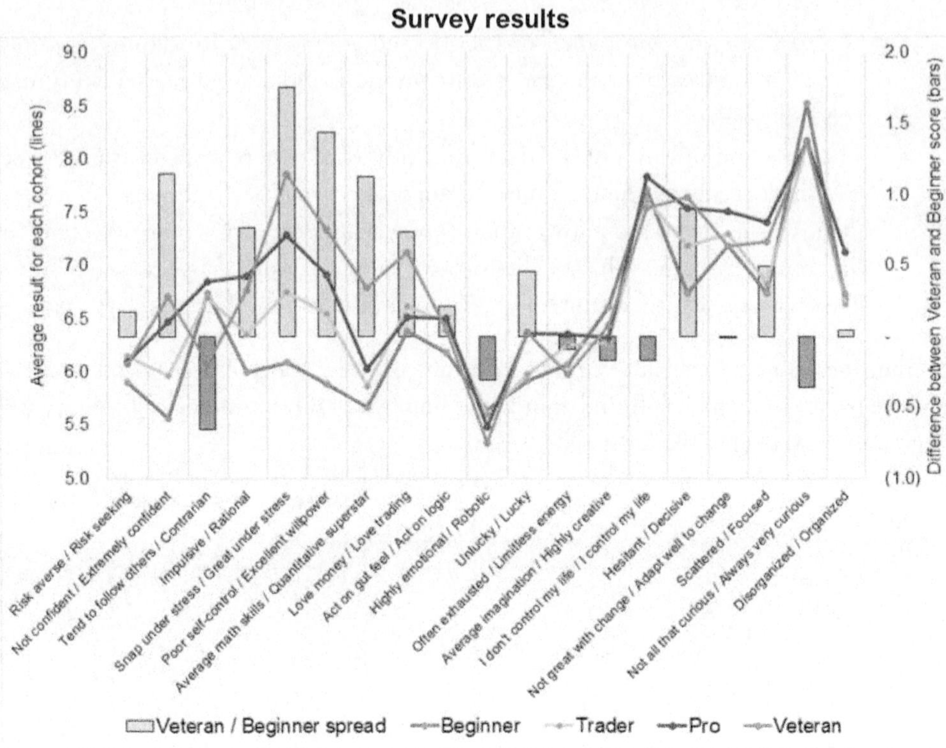

Takeaways

Focus on the light gray bars in the chart, which show the difference between the Veteran and Beginner lines:

- Number one divergent trait is: Ability to handle stress. I find that interesting as it contradicts what I wrote in *Alpha Trader*. I suppose if I think about it, handling stress is one of my greatest strengths. I like stress.
- Willpower, quantitative skills, confidence, rationality, and decisiveness are the five other areas where Veterans greatly exceed Beginners.

- Risk appetite is about the same for traders of all levels. This is consistent with what I wrote in *Alpha Trader*. You can succeed in trading with any level of risk appetite. You just have to manage yourself differently and develop systems and processes to regulate or increase your risk. And know yourself.
- New traders tend to be more contrarian than experienced traders. This is a lesson I learned early on. I always wanted to be contrarian when I started because my ego loved it when I made money while everyone else was losing. I wanted to be right when everyone else was wrong. Now, I just want to make money. Reflexive contrarians are not good traders because they miss every trend. **Traders who focus too much on market sentiment are bearish all the way up and bullish all the way down.** Good traders can fade or go with trends.
- You can be either emotional or robotic and still succeed in trading. It doesn't matter, as long as you are aware of your emotions and make sure they don't make you irrational.
- The direction of travel of the data from cohort to cohort was consistent, which gives me confidence these are meaningful results. That is: "beginners" score lower than "traders" who score lower than "pros" who score lower than "veterans" on the important traits. That is, the lines in the graph don't criss-cross very much. That consistency is a feature of good data and meaningful research results.

Overall, the results of the survey provide insight into the traits and characteristics that separate professional traders from beginners. I hope you found it useful and informative. Here is all the data in table form.

	Veteran / Beginner difference	Veteran	Pro	Trader	Beginner
Risk averse / Risk seeking	0.2	6.1	6.1	6.2	5.9
Not confident / Extremely confident	1.1	6.7	6.5	6.0	5.6
Tend to follow others / Contrarian	(0.7)	6.1	6.9	6.7	6.7
Impulsive / Rational	0.8	6.8	6.9	6.4	6.0
Snap under stress / Great under stress	1.8	7.9	7.3	6.8	6.1
Poor self-control / Excellent willpower	1.4	7.3	6.9	6.5	5.9
Average math skills / Quantitative superstar	1.1	6.8	6.0	5.9	5.7
Love money / Love trading	0.7	7.1	6.5	6.6	6.4
Act on gut feel / Act on logic	0.2	6.4	6.5	6.5	6.2
Highly Emotional / Robotic	(0.3)	5.3	5.5	5.6	5.6
Unlucky / Lucky	0.5	6.4	6.4	6.0	5.9
Often exhausted / Limitless energy	(0.1)	6.0	6.4	6.2	6.1
Average imagination / Highly creative	(0.2)	6.4	6.3	6.3	6.6
I don't control my life / I control my life	(0.2)	7.5	7.8	7.6	7.7
Hesitant / Decisive	0.9	7.6	7.5	7.2	6.7
Not great with change / Adapt well to change	(0.0)	7.2	7.5	7.3	7.2
Scattered / Focused	0.5	7.2	7.4	6.8	6.7
Not all that curious / Always very curious	(0.4)	8.2	8.2	8.1	8.5
Disorganized / Organized	0.0	6.7	7.1	6.6	6.7
No trading experience / Significant trading experience	3.8	9.5	8.6	6.6	5.7

To wrap things up… If you have read *Alpha Trader*, you might remember the questionnaire from Chapter 1. Here is the profile of the least and most successful traders in my survey, structured the same way as it's displayed in the book:

Average traits of least and most successful traders

(least successful in light gray, most successful in dark gray... if both the same, box is dark)

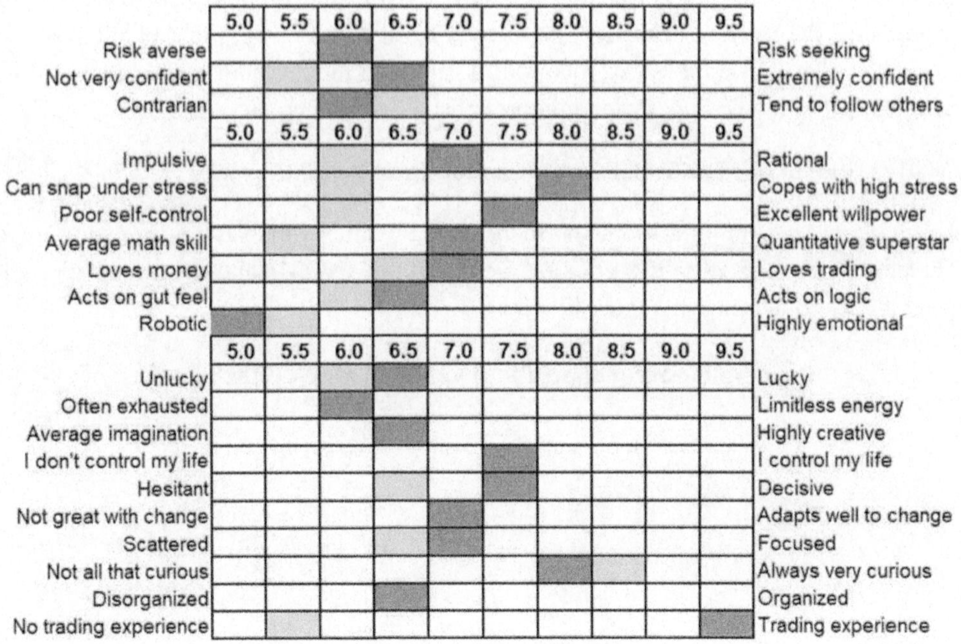

The last question I asked was: "Who is the one person on Twitter you find most useful? (please provide Twitter handle if you can)". am/FX readers skew towards nice, so many put my Twitter handle in there. Other than me, here are the handles that came up at least five times:

Most useful Twitter handles, according to survey respondents

@MacroAlf	29
@AdamMancini4	9
@MrBlonde_Macro	7
@WifeyAlpha	7
@lynaldencontact	6
@zerohedge	6
@NickTimiraos	5

Go Alf![56]

[56] https://themacrocompass.substack.com/

Thanks to all those who completed the survey and thank you for reading the results.

This week's trade

The survey results have taken a good bit of your time, so let me quickly talk about a theme that is capturing the market's attention right now and a way to play it.

There is normally a strong correlation between oil companies and the price of crude. This is probably the easiest correlation in finance to explain. If the price of oil goes up, companies that pump oil out of the ground get more money. And their expenses don't change much. So oil company margins are mostly determined by:

(Market price of oil) minus (Cost of extraction / production)

This is a gross oversimplification, and there are many other variables but those dominate. Therefore, if you overlay the price of Exxon Mobil (XOM) and crude oil, you will generally see something that looks like this:

Crude oil, hourly chart (line) vs. XOM stock (black bars)

November 2021 to July 2022

I am using XOM and you could use XLE (the oil and gas ETF) and get the same answer. There are divergences, but the general direction of travel is usually the same. Oil up, XOM up. Oil down, XOM down.

Here's how it looks since then:

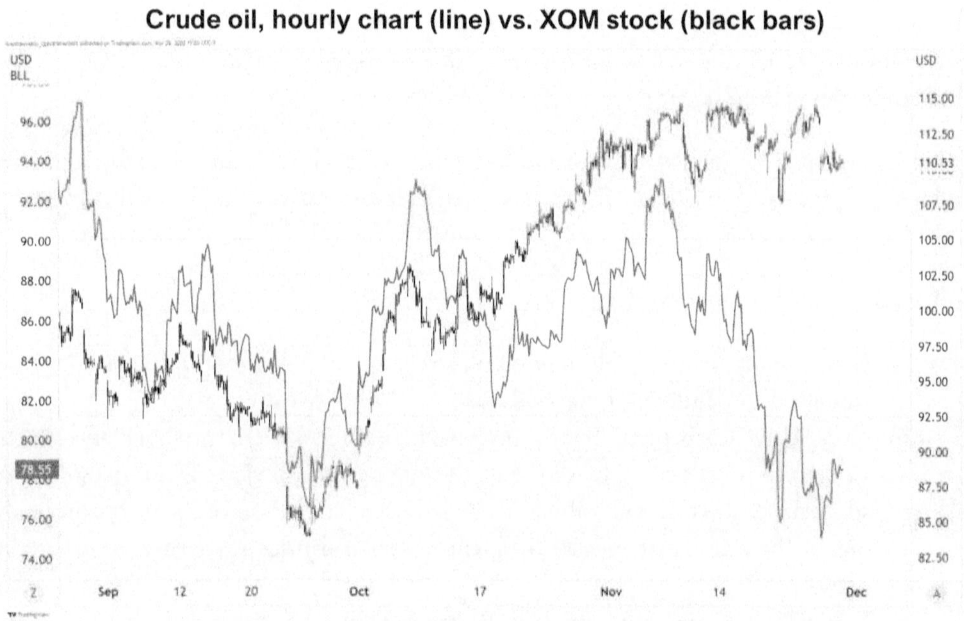

August 2022 to now

And here is the zoomed out version so you can see both charts as one.

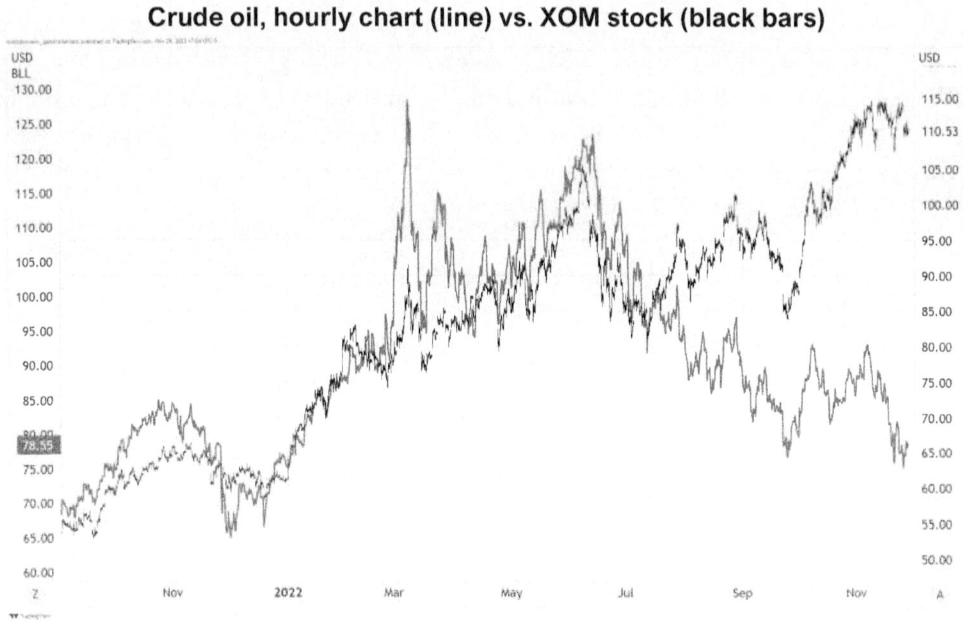

September 2021 to now

That is one Looney Tunes / Mugatu crazy pills divergence.

If you run a correlation of the variables through various filters and lookbacks, you will see that the residual (the difference between *expected* XOM price and *actual* XOM price) has rarely if ever been larger.

There are many ways to play a divergence like this. You can buy oil and sell XOM (relative value trade), you can sell XOM if you have other reasons, or you can buy oil if you have other reasons to do so.

I like selling XOM. Here's why:

1. Many, many people I talk to are bullish energy and energy producers. This was supposed to be the big trade of 2022.
2. Good news / bad price in oil. You have had a massive energy shock and war in Europe, ESG crippling investment, and raging bullish views from investors and speculators all year. And oil is unchanged. Unchanged on the year! It's probably one of the most extreme cases of good news / bad price I have ever seen, in any market.
3. When two correlated variables diverge, I like to focus on the one with momentum. Oil has the downward momentum. XOM is just hanging there like Wile E. Coyote. And I am bearish oil, even down here.
4. There's a good chance people are praying and holding their longs for January 1, 2023, so they can sell with fewer tax consequences. That's how megatech played out at the turn of 2021/2022: People saw the writing on the wall in December 2021 as Powell dropped transitory and Waller floated QT, but they held on 'til the first week of January then unloaded with a vengeance. Megatech went straight down from the opening bell on the first day of January 2022. Here's the evidence.

So oil trades incredibly heavy, the market is confidently long oil producers and oil exploration stocks, and investors are praying they can make it to January without XOM dropping back to reality so they can lower their capital gains pains. My view is that this all resolves with XOM sub-100. It took two months to rally from 85 to 115, so perfect symmetry would put us back to 85 in late January. That's an optimistic target for bears, but not an unrealistic one. Symmetry is a simple and useful way to estimate future moves and determine profit targets.

XOM hourly chart showing symmetry if it starts selling off in early December

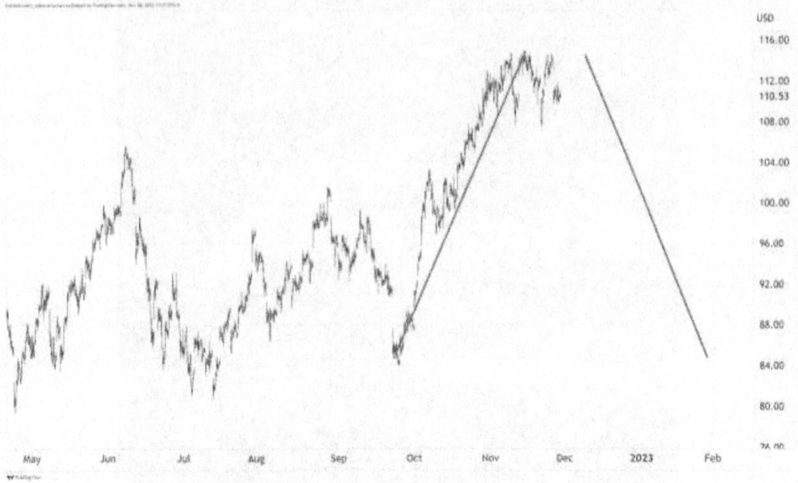

To keep my life simple and avoid any wild price action around this weekend's OPEC meeting and year-end shenanigans and window dressing, I'm going to buy February options.

Buy February 100 XOM puts for $3.00 ||| Sell February 85 XOM puts for $0.80

I am buying a strike that's easily reachable and selling the strike at the stretch target because I doubt XOM can go much lower than $85 by expiry. Spending $2,200 on 10 contracts of the put spread.

All prices as of 10 am 30NOV when I wrote this. For official tracking, I will mark to market when I hit send.

Conclusion

To be a good trader, you need to handle stress. You need willpower, quantitative skills, confidence, and decisiveness. You must be rational. And you need a healthy, supportive trading environment. Know yourself, plug your leaks, and level up your strengths.

See you below $100 XOM.

Week 38: How to sell vol without risk of ruin

Buying options is fun, but that doesn't always make it right

Update on previous trades

Week 37: XOM put spread doing well.

Week 36: TGT getting hammered.

Week 35: Short MSTR small in the money, not moving much. I will leave an order to square it up at $160.55 if we get down there.

Week 34: EWZ call spread sucking major wind.

Full update with the detailed spreadsheet in Week 40.

Selling vol with limited downside

Buying options is fun. It's easy to risk manage. You know your downside. But buying options puts you on the clock. It's like betting the over on a sporting event. You need stuff to happen before time expires or you lose all your money. Time decay is not your friend. It's called "bleeding theta" for a reason.

The other problem with owning volatility (vol) all the time is that it is wrong-way risk for your trading P&L. Let me explain: Directional short-term traders make more money when things are moving and volatility is high. So you are already exposed to volatility by this reality. If vol is high, your trading will be more profitable, on average. Active traders are implicitly long vol. So if you always buy vol via options, you are adding to the risk of a boring market that makes trading harder, and bleeds you out on time decay.

Buying options requires an exciting market. If you buy calls and then the market takes a nap, you're losing money even if you're directionally right.

As a manager of many spot FX trading desks over the years, the best hedge for the business was always to be short vol. If vol exploded, the desk did well, and if vol was low, the desk did less well but the hedge (short vol) offset that somewhat.

Thing is, though, selling vol can be incredibly risky. If you sell an option naked, you are exposed to unlimited downside. **I hate unlimited downside** because it's stressful and it creates a real risk of ruin. *I never put on trades with unlimited downside.* Imagine you sold MDB calls a couple of days ago.

MDB common stock, intraday since November 22

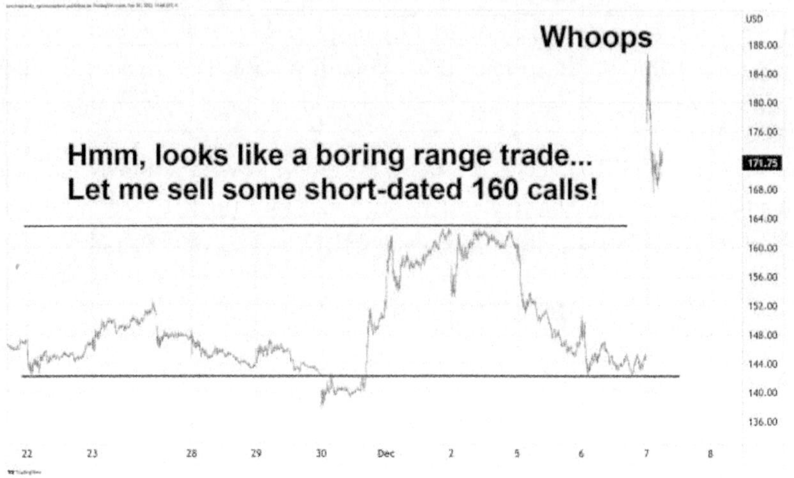

The first rule of trading is always: avoid risk of ruin.

Most people who buy options are making relatively aggressive, relatively low-confidence bets. "I think this stock is going to this price starting right now," basically.

What you're doing in selling options is taking the other side of those trades and saying "I don't think that's going to happen." So from a confidence standpoint, you can generally have more than the option buyer. But from a risk management standpoint, although most retail option buyers lose their money, you're the one who has to be more careful.

But! **You can sell options and still know your max downside.** Let me get right into the trade idea.

Sell MSTR volatility with limited downside

Crypto winter is upon us, and lethargy and apathy have kicked in. Trading volumes have dropped, people are questioning the use cases and the web3 and financial applications and benefits of crypto. Mania has turned into despair. Despair is different from fear in that it's a low-vol regime, not a high-vol regime. Fear pushes prices lower fast but apathy leads to grinding, boring price action. Look at what NASDAQ did from 2001 to 2003, for example. Tedious and soul destroying.

If you think this kind of boring price action is set to continue, selling volatility is a good play, as long as the market hasn't fully priced in the lower vol regime. Implied vol on MSTR puts is still trading around 100%, which is about its average for 2021 and 2022. The vol spiked when the FTX debacle started, and it's back to normal now. No sign of any repricing to extreme wintery levels.

When selling vol, the way to limit your downside is to only ever sell spreads. That is, if you sell a 150 put, you need to buy a 140 put (for example) as protection. The unfortunate aspect of this is that you are buying pricier options because the more out of the money an option is, the pricier it is, volatility wise. But that's life. If you want protection, you have to pay for it.

If we assume that MSTR is likely to remain rangebound with a downward bias, we can sell a call spread close to the money and a put spread a bit further away. This allows some room for when the next shoe drops in crypto. Here's a chart of the stock:

MSTR daily back to late 2020

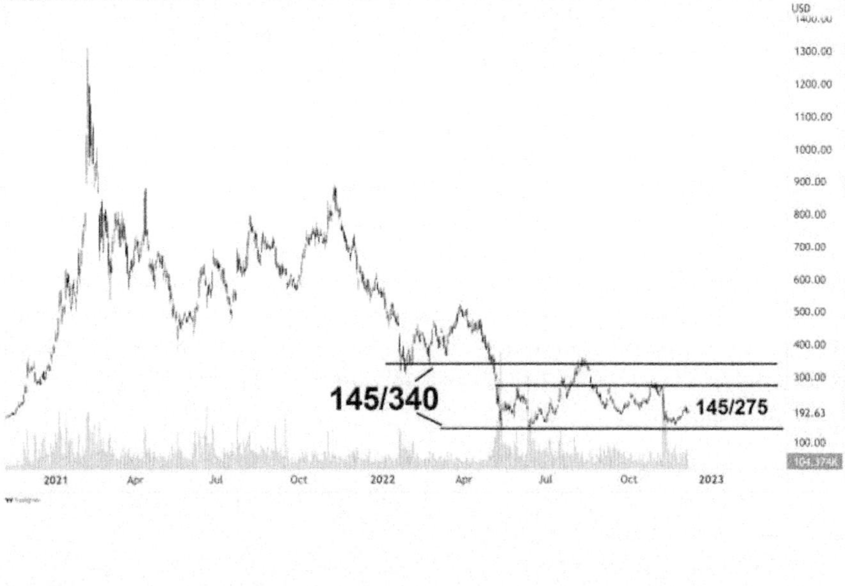

You can see that since April 2022, we have been in a 145/340 range, with most of the action between 145 and 275. This is a starting point for what strikes we might want to pick.

The further out you go time-wise, the more premium you collect, but the more impossible it becomes to predict what might happen. Think of markets as a complex system like the weather. We can forecast a few days out, but it gets harder and harder the farther you go.

50in50 is going to end when Week 50 happens around three months from now. So let's look at selling spreads for March 2023 expiry. Here are the prices of some puts and calls that would make sense to sell if we think MSTR is going to stay rangebound with a downward bias.

BUY 240 call $15.50
SELL 230 call $18
194 Current stock price
SELL 145 put $22.50
BUY 135 put $18.00

If we sell both of these spreads, we collect: $4.50 on the put spread and $2.50 on the call spread. Market prices are wide for these options, but this is where I see them trading right now. So you collect a total of $7 if you can get the spreads on at these prices. Your maximum risk is $10 if the stock blows through either spread. So you collect $7 and risk $10 which means you are risking $3 per contract X 100 shares = $300. Risking $300 to make $700 per contract. 10 contracts would be risking $3,000 to make max $7,000.

Some words of caution

While your downside is capped on this sort of strategy, one quirk is that if the stock ends up in between your strikes, you will get exercised. You probably don't want this to happen as it will require a lot of margin and leave you with a position you don't want. Therefore, when doing this sort of strategy, **you need to monitor it very closely about a week before expiry** and if it looks like you're going to fall in the middle, just cut the trade by unwinding both legs.

Another aspect here is the execution can be hard. You need to leave a limit order in the spread, not try to leg into the two options. If you try to leg in by doing one option, then the other, you can end up with a single trade that you didn't want.

For more on risk of ruin in options and short positions, please see this video[57].

---

57 https://www.zer0es.tv/masterclasses/structuring-your-bearish-bets/

So for this trade, if we are risking $3,000, we would do 10 contracts of each spread. We collect $4,500 on the puts and $2,500 on the calls for a total of $7,000. If MSTR blows through one side, we lose $10,000 on the stock, but that is partially offset by the $7k we earned.

I'm using MSTR here as an example. It is not certain you can put these spreads on at the prices I have indicated. Those are mids as I type this. Use limit orders and make sure you know what you are doing. The puts are more attractive to sell because of the high vol, even though the stock doesn't trade with much asymmetry.

There is downside convexity in the stock because at some point MicroStrategy is worth negative dollars due to their losses on BTC. But there is upside convexity because 40% of the float is shorted and it's really, really expensive to maintain a short position.

My view on MSTR is that it will mostly do nothing for the next few months, with occasional bursts to the downside as new shoes drop on the FTX, MtGox, and other liquidation stories. So the short MSTR position from Week 35 still makes sense but so does selling vol.

Did I mention: Make sure you know what you are doing before you do anything that remotely involves selling vol. If you're not sure what you are doing... Just don't.

:]

Conclusion

It's fun to buy options. It's much less fun to sell options. Humans love fun, they love lotto tickets, and thus, they tend to overpay for options. There are almost always more buyers than sellers in equity options and for that reason, it's often strongly positive EV to sell equity options, especially puts.

But selling puts can lead to catastrophe! So you need to do the less leveraged strategy and sell spreads.

Week 39: Timing is Everything

Early or late = wrong

Update on previous trades

Week 38: Medium-term short vol trade in MSTR is fine, no real update.

Week 37: XOM put spread doing OK.

Week 36: TGT dumped and WMT didn't dump enough. L.

Week 35: Short MSTR in the money, not moving much. Left an order to square it up at $160.55 last week. Almost there!

Week 34: EWZ call spread is bad.

Full update with the detailed spreadsheet next week (Week 40.)

Timing is Everything

There is a cliché in trading: Early is the same as wrong. Most people understand this, but there should also be a saying: Late is the same as wrong. Putting on trades too early or too late has both real and opportunity costs.

This week, I am going to expand on the lessons from Week 38 and show you another way to use options to help with the structuring and tactics of a trade idea.

It's (no longer) raining yen

The big trade of 2023 was supposed to be long JPY. In early December, I did a survey of am/FX readers and here is the currency they most wanted to be long:

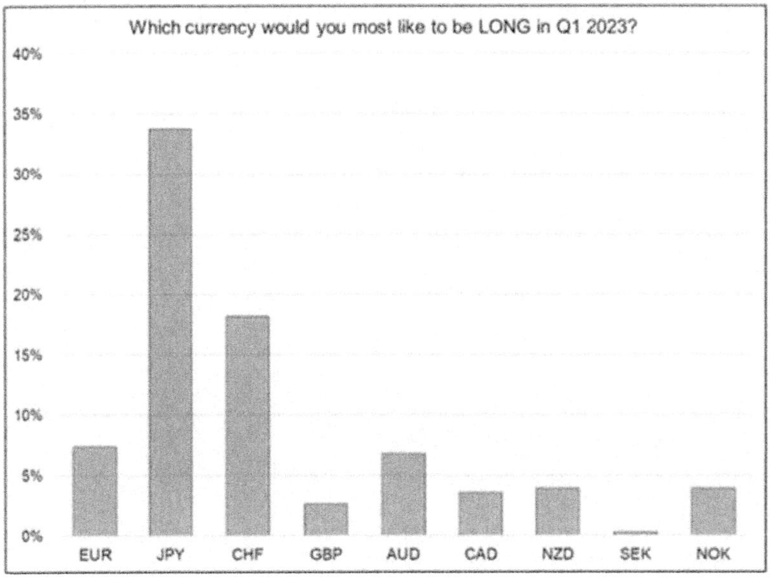

> ### *Explainer*
>
> To be clear for those who don't trade much FX: Long JPY means you want the yen to get stronger. Long USDJPY means you want the yen to get weaker. The JPY also trades against every other currency, for example you can trade CADJPY, EURJPY, GBPJPY and so on. All the JPY crosses as a group, excluding USDJPY, can be called cross/JPY or cross yen. So if I'm thinking the JPY will strengthen in 2023, but I don't have a view on the USD, I might go short cross/JPY. Most professional FX traders always put JPY as the denominator and talk about long or short USDJPY or cross/JPY. You would never hear an institutional FX trader say: "I'm long yen," though futures traders will say it this way, and that's fine. Whenever you are talking about FX, just make sure you are clear on the direction and the pair.
>
> Short USDJPY
> Long USDCAD
> Short EURCAD
> etc.

The main driver of the bullish JPY thesis was an expected pivot from the Bank of Japan (BOJ).

BOJ Governor Kuroda leaves at the end of March 2023 and his Yield Curve Control (YCC) program has been the catalyst for an epic moonshot in USDJPY this year. By pinning Japanese yields super low (around 0.25%) while US yields have exploded higher to around 4.0%, Kuroda engineered a massive rip higher in USDJPY (115 to 150 this year). Investors generally prefer currencies with higher yields, most of the time.

If you are an investor, and you are trying to maximize returns, you are generally happier holding a bond that yields 4% vs. one that yields 0.25% (all other things being equal).

The presumption is that if the BOJ loosens the cap on yields and allows Japanese yields to go higher, Japan's yields can rise to catch up with the rest of the world and that will make the JPY more attractive (or at least… Less unattractive).

Here's USDJPY since I sent out the survey:

USDJPY 15-minute chart since early December

137 to 131 in one day is a large move!

The BOJ changed its YCC program ahead of schedule, raising the top of the yield control band from 0.25% to 0.50%. USDJPY got slammed! Many hedge fund managers and spot traders out there were busy wargaming all the USDJPY puts they planned to buy in January, and now the move they expected in Q1 2023 has already started.

It's like everyone was off to the side tying their shoes and stretching their calves when the starting gun went off.

This led to a lot of FOMO trading as people walked in and saw USDJPY at 131.25 and decided they had better get on board. The problem was, the daily chart looked like this:

USDJPY daily chart back to mid-2021

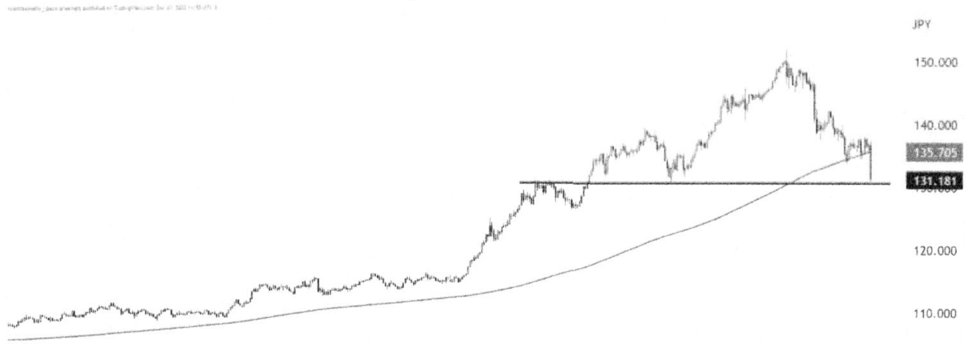

At the time, I tweeted:

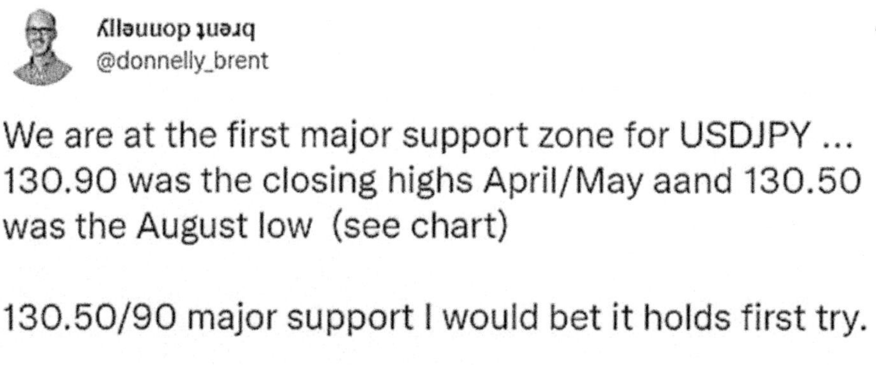

Traders and portfolio managers were selling hard, right into major support. They were **late** for the first move and compounded the problem through reactionary selling. Now they are **early** for the next leg. Here is the updated chart:

USDJPY hourly chart back to late November

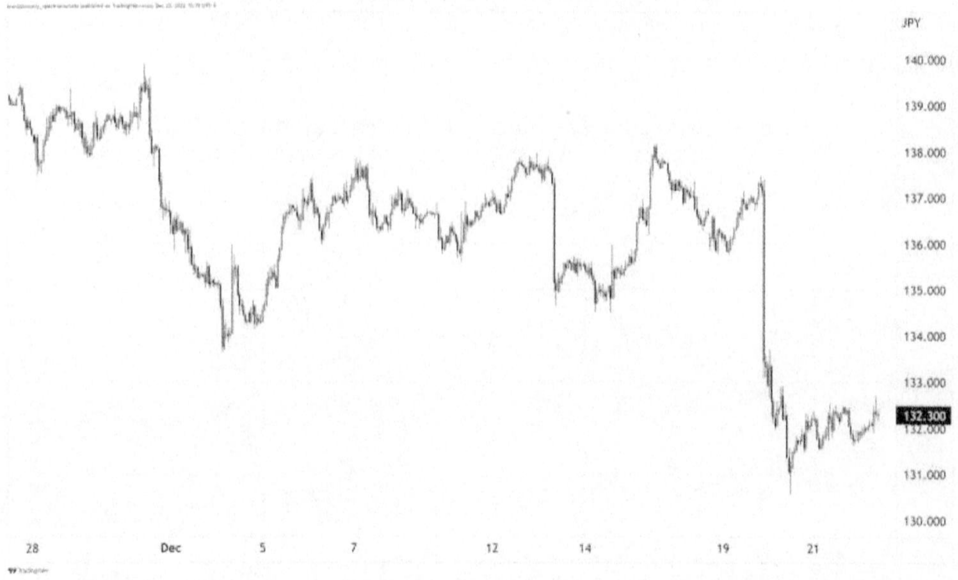

Trading is all about timing. When you're early, you get chopped up by the noise and bleed theta. When you are late, you miss the juicy part of the move and get sucked into good trades at bad levels. Tactics are an absolutely critical part of trading and you have to resist the urge to sell into collapsing markets or buy explosions out of FOMO.

It's not always wrong to go with the momentum, but if you're going to chase momentum you need to do it in a thoughtful, strategic way. Always ask yourself whether your trading strategy is about tactics and rational thinking, or FOMO and price chasing.

Another reason the rush to buy USDJPY puts after the BOJ announcement is risky: USDJPY puts got significantly more expensive because of the surge in demand. The way you look at the price of puts vs. calls in FX is the price of the risk reversal.

The simple interpretation of the risk reversal is that it tells you the price of USDJPY calls relative to the price of USDJPY puts. When demand is high for one side of the market, that side will get more expensive. This is also called skew. The more demand there is for options in a particular direction, the more difficult that direction is to hedge, and the less natural selling there is of those options, the more expensive options in that direction will be.

S&P puts, for example, are almost always more expensive than calls because there are tons of natural buyers of puts (portfolio hedgers, specs, etc.) but few natural sellers. Selling S&P puts is very difficult to risk manage and there are only limited participants who can do so.

Here is the USDJPY risk reversal. You can see how the line moved down dramatically in the last few days. When that line goes down, it means that **USDJPY puts** are getting more expensive.

USDJPY 3-month 25-delta risk reversal since late 2021

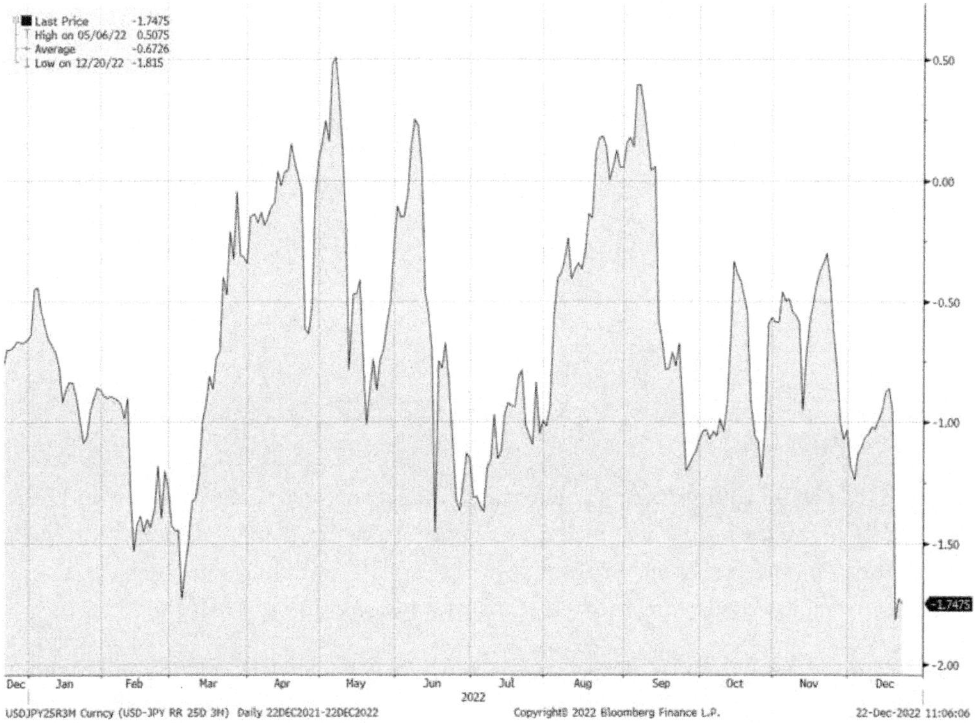

So not only did spot USDJPY drop 500 points, but your puts are going to cost much more today than they did a few days ago.

A timing trade

Now that the Bank of Japan has signaled a willingness to move its 10-year yield target, one might expect the JPY to appreciate in 2023. That is, the consensus narrative for JPY strength in '23 has been somewhat validated by Kuroda's actions. On the other hand, you can also argue that a nearby catalyst (change in YCC) has now passed and the market has already repriced from 137 to 132 in one day.

What is the best way to play it going forward? You missed the first move, so do you want to chase it? Or do something else?

My view is that now that the YCC move has happened, we will consolidate, and USDJPY will range trade for a while. Then, once the market finds out who the new BOJ governor is in February, it will be game on again and USDJPY will skate lower.

When you have a directional view, and a strong sense that the timing of the directional move will happen not now, but later, it's a good setup for **calendar spreads.**

Calendar spreads are a simple options strategy where you sell an option for one date and buy an option for another date. In order to avoid outright short volatility exposure, for me this always means selling a nearer-dated option and buying one farther out. That way, if things move dramatically, you are protected. You are net long options.

For example, you sell a USDJPY put for expiry in February 2023, and buy one that expires in June 2023. This cheapens up the strategy significantly compared to simply buying a June 2023 option and allows you to benefit from the consolidation, instead of paying time decay.

I am going to go through the details here using over-the-counter FX options, but the concepts are identical whether you use options on CME futures or even options on a yen-tracking ETF like YCS. All the concepts apply to retail or institutional trading of any options product.

The strategy

Let's say we think USDJPY will be at 120.00 at the end of June 2023. A 6-month 125 USDJPY put costs about 2.00%. You can sell a 2-month 125 USDJPY put for around 0.65%.

So if you do these two options (buy 6-month and sell 2-month) you pay about 1.35% instead of 2.00% (that is: 2% minus 0.65%). The dream scenario is that USDJPY is exactly 125.00 in two months so the option you're short expires worthless and the one you are long is at the money.

Calendar spreads are a good strategy to keep in mind for any market you trade. As I said last week:

> Owning outright volatility (vol) all the time is wrong-way risk for your trading P&L. Directional short-term traders make more money when things are moving and volatility is high. So you are already exposed to volatility by this reality. If vol is high, your trading will be more profitable, on average. Active traders are implicitly long vol. So if you always buy vol via options, you are adding to the risk of a boring market that makes trading harder, and bleeds you out on time decay.
>
> *Buying options requires an exciting market. If you buy calls and then the market takes a nap, you're losing money even if you're directionally right.*

Calendar spreads are still "owning volatility" but you are doing it in a more nuanced way.

If you are bearish TSLA but think it's oversold right now and set to consolidate... Either wait for better levels or do a calendar spread. If you think MSFT is going to do nothing into earnings, then beat and explode higher; do a calendar spread. The risk with calendar spreads is that you can be right and lose money but there's always a variety of risks around every execution style and trading outright long vol comes with its own huge bag of risks, too.

You have to accept that sometimes you will be correct and still lose money. That's just part of trading.

The current head of the BOJ, Kuroda, was nominated on February 27, 2013. His term expires at the end of March 2023 and therefore the Japanese government will need to nominate a new governor at some point in February. If Nakaso is nominated, that would be hawkish (higher yields) and therefore good for the yen (bearish USDJPY). Other candidates could have varying impacts on the direction of BOJ policy and USDJPY. Here is a quick story that will give you the background on possible choices:

https://www.japantimes.co.jp/news/2022/12/12/business/boj-leadership-candidates/

One note about risk and execution. If USDJPY goes below 125 before the 2-month option expires, I will be exercised and end up with a potentially large USDJPY position. Usually if I am near my short strike as expiry gets close, I will roll or unwind the option to avoid exercise. Whenever you trade option spreads, make sure you understand the exercise risk and what happens to your margin if you get exercised.

And one final technical note and another reason selling 2-month to buy 6-month is nice: Due to the carry in USDJPY, the strike on the 2-month ATM USDJPY put is about 200 points higher than the strike of the ATM in the 6-month.

Conclusion

Timing is everything in trading. While in bubbles and massively trending markets, timing can be temporarily less important, it is generally critical to trading success. Many young traders made their first foray into trading in the 2020 bull market. And in parts of 2020 and 2021, timing was almost irrelevant. Everything was going up all of the time. You could buy calls on just about any stock, wait a couple of weeks, and hit the take profit button.

2022 was a mirror of 2021, somewhat, but timing became more important. Despite strong trends like USDJPY higher, stocks lower, EURUSD lower, etc., timing was key. If you were selling the hole in stocks or EURUSD in 2022, you were bearish and you got smoked despite a trending bear market. As global macro (including stocks and everything else) enters a more uncertain regime in 2023, **timing and direction** will both be paramount to success.

Strategies like calendar spreads increase the complexity of tactics and pose new risks not posed by other strategies, but they can also be the best way to express a view. If you think USDJPY is going to hang around 128/132 for a while and then trend lower starting in February, it makes sense to sell a 2-month 125 USDJPY put and buy a 6-month 125 USDJPY put.

The most important takeaway, though, is to make sure you are trading rationally, and not out of FOMO or frustration. If you can step outside yourself and see yourself trading on FOMO, you will be able to course correct—you can stop the behavior or correct it before it costs you too much capital.

Week 40: Over-oversold

The TSLA elastic band has never been more stretched

Update on previous trades

It's time for the decaweekly update! The P&L performance remains somewhat random, which is mildly disappointing, but not unexpected. The trades I'm choosing are often in products like single name equities, where I have no edge. I continue to publish the results for transparency and for discussion purposes… And to be honest, even in my am/FX trades, where years of evidence shows I am probably displaying some edge in global macro … I just had my first negative quarter since 2019. So I am hot as a cucumber.

Here is the big spreadsheet[58].

[58] https://50in50.substack.com/p/week-40-over-oversold

Conviction	Week	Entry date	L/S	Asset	Entry	USD at risk	Stop loss	Take profit	Exit or current level	P&L	Exit date	Holding period (days)	Notes
8.0	1	2/9/22	Short	XAUEUR	1,602	2,000	1,702	1,421	1,704	(2,000)	28-Feb	19	
4.0	2	2/16/22	Short	CLK2	90.50	1,000	95.45	79.05	95.55	(2,000)	1-Mar	13	
8.0	3	2/21/22	Short	DOCS	56.00	2,000	60.51	50.21	60.58	(2,000)	28-Feb	7	Wrong stop loss.
7.0	4	2/25/22	Long	BTC	39,200	2,000	31,400	49,800	39,200	-	14-Mar	17	
7.0	5	3/1/22	Long	BTC	43,400	2,000	38,900	49,800	38,870	(2,000)	14-Mar	13	
5.0	6	3/8/22	Long	EWC	37.85	2,000	35.19	44.80	39.65	1,353	11-Apr	34	
9.0	7	3/14/22	Long	XPO May $60 puts	2.60	2,000	-	53.50	6.10	2,692	18-Apr	35	
8.0	8	3/28/22	Short	NQ	14,970	2,000	15,660	13,344	13,908	3,078	18-Apr	21	
9.0	9	4/4/22	Long	TWTR	50.85	2,000	45.84	57.77	45.80	(2,000)	13-Apr	9	
7.0	10	4/11/22	Long	ASHR	32.18	2,000	29.84	36.44	29.80	(2,000)	25-Apr	14	Wrong stop loss.
6.0	11	4/18/22	Long	ESM2	4,381	2,000	4,279	4,579	4,276	(2,000)	5-May	17	
3.0	12	4/25/22	Long	ARKK	45.67	2,000	29.00		51.39	687	11-Aug	108	
2.0	14	5/15/22	Long	BTC	28,500	2,000	24,900	39,300	24,900	(2,000)	13-Jun	29	
9.0	15	5/18/22	Long	JAN23 CVNA 20 put	4.70	1,500	-	-	3.00	(543)	13-Sep	118	
9.0	15	5/18/22	Long	JAN23 RBLX 40 call	7.00	1,500	-	-	10.40	729	13-Sep	118	
10.0	16	5/27/22	Short	ETHBTC	0.061	2,000	0.077	0.033	0.069	(1,000)	25-Jul	59	
4.0	17	6/6/22	Short	LLY	297.99	2,000	306.25	283.10	306.25	(2,000)	22-Jun	16	Low was 1 cent from the take profit!!!!!!
8.0	18	6/14/22	Long	TY	114.56	2,000	112.84	118.00	118.00	4,000	30-Jun	16	
10.0	19	6/24/22	Long	GBTC	12.77	2,000	10.90	16.60	14.80	2,181	31-Jul	37	
5.0	20	7/4/22	Short	TSLA	701.50	2,000	820.00	437.00	829.00	(2,200)	22-Jul	18	
7.0	21	7/19/22	Long	XME	44.50	2,000	34.95	63.70	49.90	1,131	13-Sep	56	
9.0	22	7/25/22	Short	META	Options	2,000	29JUL $160 and $155 puts		Small profit on the 160s	(1,600)	29-Jul	4	
8.0	23	8/1/22	Short	SPY	412.50	2,000	436.60	37.00	402.50	830	13-Sep	43	Sold put against it
8.0	25	8/16/22	Short	MSTR	345.00	2,000	381.00	251.00	251.00	5,222	26-Aug	10	
5.7	26	8/23/22	Short	TSLA	296.00	2,000	304.67		288.09	2,191	25-Aug	2	Cover at 25AUG close
7.0	27	8/29/22	Short	TSLA	Daily strat	2,000			295.00	(297)	13-Sep	15	
8.0	28	9/5/22	Short	ETH	1,650	2,000	1906 and 2056	1,155.00	1,587	381	13-Sep	8	
8.0	30	9/20/22	Long	USDJPY	143.65	2,000	141.74		141.71	(2,030)	23-Sep	3	This trade made money in real life but I forgot to put my TP in 50in50 write up oops
7.0	31	10/12/22	Buy	FXA call spread	0.40	2,000			-	(2,000)	21-Oct	9	
8.5	32	10/17/22	Short	USDNOK	10.53	2,000	10.92	9.88	10.33	1,026	2-Nov	16	
6.5	33	10/27/22	Short	CM	45.10	2,000	47.11	40.55	47.14	(2,010)	10-Nov	14	Stop too tight - ended up hitting TP not oo long after
8.0	34	11/4/22	Buy	EWZ call spread	35/39	2,000			-	(2,000)	27-Dec	53	
7.0	35	11/9/22	Short	MSTR	192.10	2,000	282.00	160.55	160.65	700	27-Dec	48	
6.0	36	11/17/22	Buy	TGT / WMT spread					142.60 in WMT	(170)	16-Dec	29	
8.0	37	11/30/22	Long	XOM put spread	2.05	2,050	FEB '23 100/85 put spread	85.00	1.46	(590)	27-Dec	27	
9.0	38	12/7/22	Sell	Call spread and put spread in MSTR	See Substack	3,000				-			
8.0	39	12/22/22	Sell 23FEB23 and buy 23JUN23 125.00 USDJPY puts			2,000				-			
8.0	40	12/28/22	Long	TSLA	108.00	2,000	94.25						

Total P&L	**(6,239)**
Winners	**14**
Losers	**20**
Win%	**41%**
avgWIN	**1,891**
avgLOSE	**(1,366)**
avg holding period	**30**

Takeaways:

1. It's worth noting that risking $2,000 per week on a single trade does not create much P&L volatility in a $100,000 account. I would not recommend this risk management style to anyone; I just wanted to keep things simple for 50in50 and I wanted to err on the small side in case anyone was confused into thinking I was suggesting a specific risk management methodology. Risking 2% of your capital each day, as a day trader, is plenty volatile, but risking 2% of your capital on one trade, once per week is nonsensical. The idea was simplicity for explanation

purposes. For a full discussion of position sizing and proper risk management, please read Chapter 11 of *Alpha Trader*[59].

2. A couple of tactical errors crushed the P&L over the last period. One, I forgot to leave a take profit on the USDJPY long (Week 30). The trade was good but subsequently crashed and shows up as a loss. This kind of thing happens in real life, too. You leave a TP and a stop loss overnight. Your TP gets hit before bedtime. You go to be happy then and come in the next day. You open up your P&L and see a big red number instead of a green one. Then you realize you forgot to input your order. Trading is such a game of inches that tiny screw-ups can be the difference between a W and an L.
3. The CM trade had the right idea but the wrong stop loss. We were short at 45 with a stop just above 47 and a take profit at 40.55. The stock went to 49 then 40. Again, good strategy isn't enough. You need good tactics, too. The comments and feedback from this trade also revealed to me that CM was a bad expression of a Canadian housing short. There were better ways to do the trade. Then again, one of the alternative suggestions was to short Home Capital Group (HCG, the Canadian mortgage company). Somewhat hard to believe, but that company was trading at $27 when I went short CM and got bought out at $44 shortly thereafter. So could have been worse, I suppose. A good example of terrifying gap risk and bad luck for people that were levered short HCG.
4. The MSTR short was OK but utilized very little leverage. It's hard to make a lot of money shorting extremely volatile stocks because you can't take a big position.

Over-oversold

RSI is a simple indicator that gives you a snapshot of oversold or overbought conditions in a particular security, index, or market. The standard way to use RSI is that when it breaks below 30, you wait for it to come back above, and buy. And the opposite for breaks above 70. As someone who hates being late to a party, I have a different approach. I like to look for moments when the RSI breaks under 20 or above 80 and jump in right away.

I would not do this solely based on the RSI; I would need some sort of thesis to go along with the technical signal. Here's a recent example of one that worked in FX.

---

[59] https://amzn.to/3rngGo3

AUDNZD with 14-day RSI

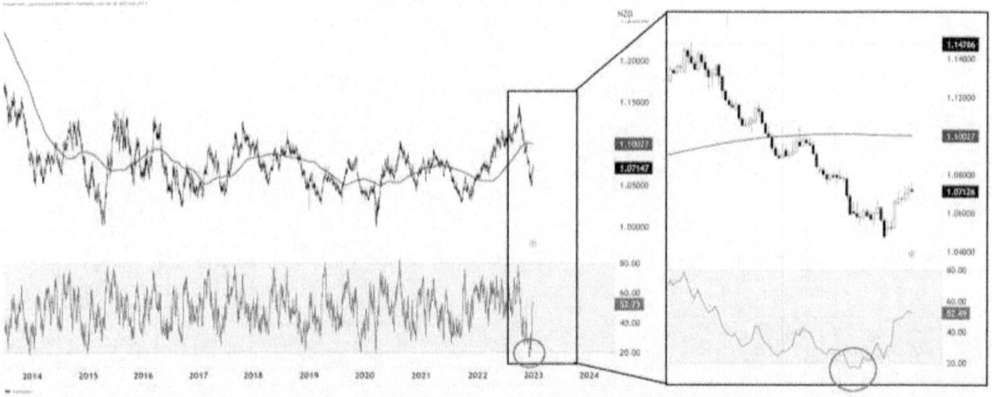

I set the parameters for the band on the bottom to 20 and 80 so that you can see the breaches. **There are very few.** Most of them coincide with overshoot and reversal, though the execution of the fade can take a few years off your life and there is nothing guaranteeing that this works every time. I have not backtested it, though that is a project I will start today. I'll report back to you with my findings.

I'm not giving investment advice here, but the reason I have RSI on my mind today is that TSLA just hit its all-time low on the 14-day RSI.

TSLA with 14-day RSI

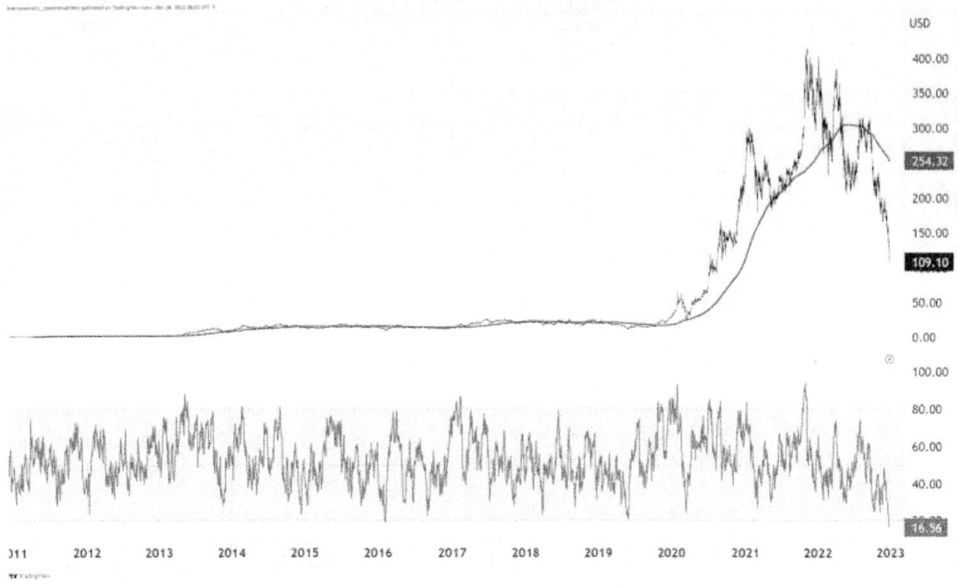

The stock still trades at 4.6X sales, which is *-ahem-* a tad higher than, say, Mercedes-Benz at 0.5X sales. But the ratio is now more in line with TSLA history before it was embraced by the "any valuation is OK when the story is fun enough" crowd as part of the meme stock bubble.

TSLA price-to-sales, 2011 to now

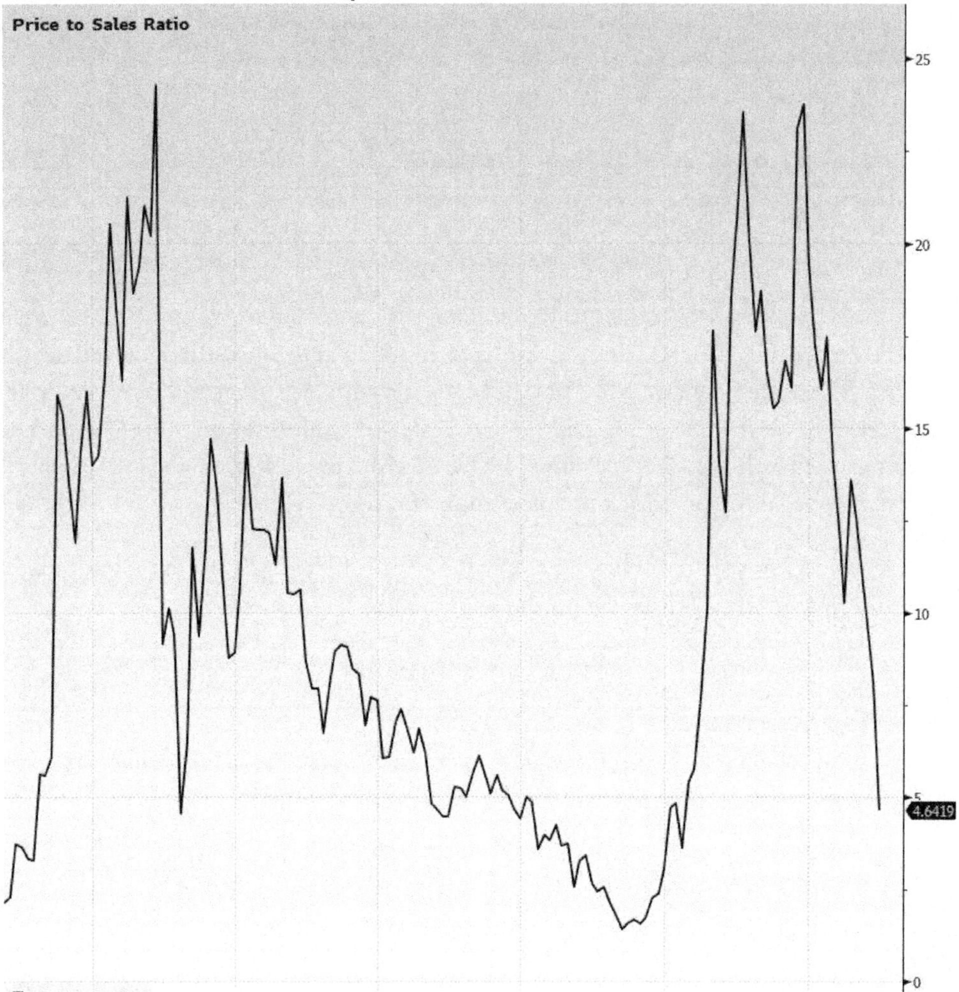

Note that a price/sales ratio of 25X is defensible when you are a $4B company like TSLA was in 2011. It is completely indefensible when you are one of the largest companies in the world, by market cap. Trees do not grow to the sky.

Anyway, I'm not a CFA, but I have traded through two huge tech bubbles now. Price-to-sales is a simple and logical way to cut through the community-adjusted GAAP noise and see one easy-to-understand valuation metric. Like I said, price/sales is less meaningful for tiny companies but matters for big ones. Here's a modern way of looking at it.

Both images from: https://twitter.com/Bardamu_31

And just for fun, here's CSCO price/sales.

CSCO price-to-sales, 1990 to now

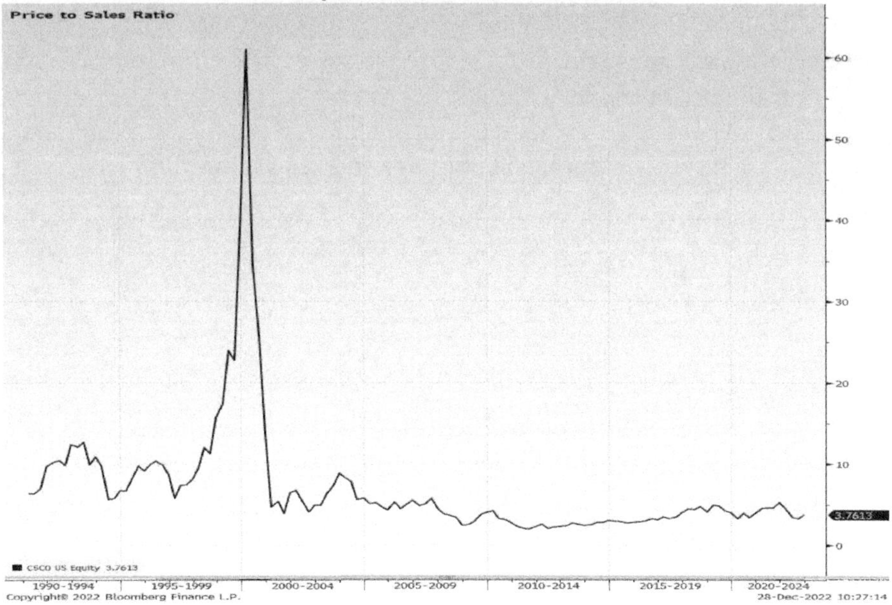

Anyway, if you are interested in owning an automaker that trades at 4.6X sales, this might be your moment.

Tax loss selling and window dressing are probably playing a big part in the selloff in TSLA as its owner has temporarily left the building to pursue a $44B hobby that has aggressive political overtones. Fund managers who don't believe in the Musk message, or whose investors or managers don't believe in the message, are probably cutting TSLA holdings before year-end holdings are published.

The stock is down almost 50% this month, the RSI is at an all-time low, and the deadline for tax loss selling is Friday. As far as countertrend punts go, you could do worse. A bounce back to 150/165 would be in the realm of possibility for TSLA in JAN/FEB.

Did I mention this is not investment advice?

What is RSI, anyway?

RSI looks back at the last 14 days of price action and examines where the price finished, relative to its normal up and down moves. A figure below 20 or above 80 is difficult to achieve given the math. You need a crazy streak of large down days to get below 20.

If you would like to build the calculation into a spreadsheet, this website shows you how, step by step. It works; I used it.

https://smallbusiness.chron.com/make-rsi-excel-51528.html

It's worth noting when using indicators like RSI, MACD, etc., that the math behind the indicators tends to be highly similar. Momentum is momentum, no matter how you measure it. Don't overcomplicate your process or clutter up your charts by adding five momentum indicators and oscillators. One or two max will do just fine. For example, here's TSLA with the RSI and MACD.

TSLA stock (top), RSI (middle) and MACD (bottom)

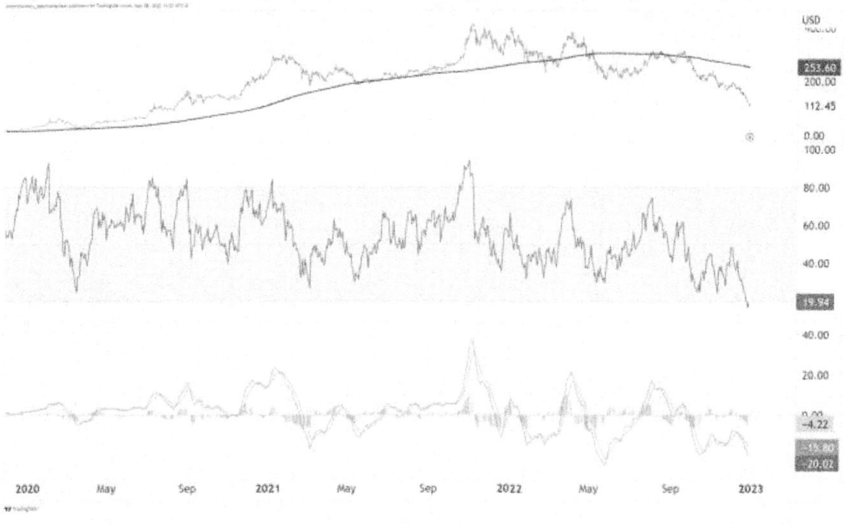

Do you think the MACD is adding incremental value on top of the information already provided by the RSI? Probably not. Pick one or the other. In trading, your goal is to develop robust, but simple ways of looking at the market so you can filter the noise and extract the signal. More indicators = more noise (generally).

Another way to use RSI

When the price of a security or market you are trading diverges from indicators or other markets that should be confirming, that's a red flag. For example, if price is trending up, and RSI is making lower highs, that's called bearish divergence. Here is an example from the first major bitcoin top in 2021.

Bitcoin with RSI and divergence marked with lines

Good trends are confirmed by indicators and other markets. Tired trends are not.

You can also compare two securities this way to look for divergence. For example, in FX, it's popular to look for agreement or disagreement between the DXY (dollar index, which is mostly EUR-driven) and EURUSD. If the dollar is making new highs against the EUR (i.e., EURUSD is at the lows) but the DXY is not confirming, that can be a sign that the dollar is tired. Here is an example of that. I remember this one specifically because many traders caught the divergence in real time and saw it as a sign that USD strength was over after the Global Financial Crisis.

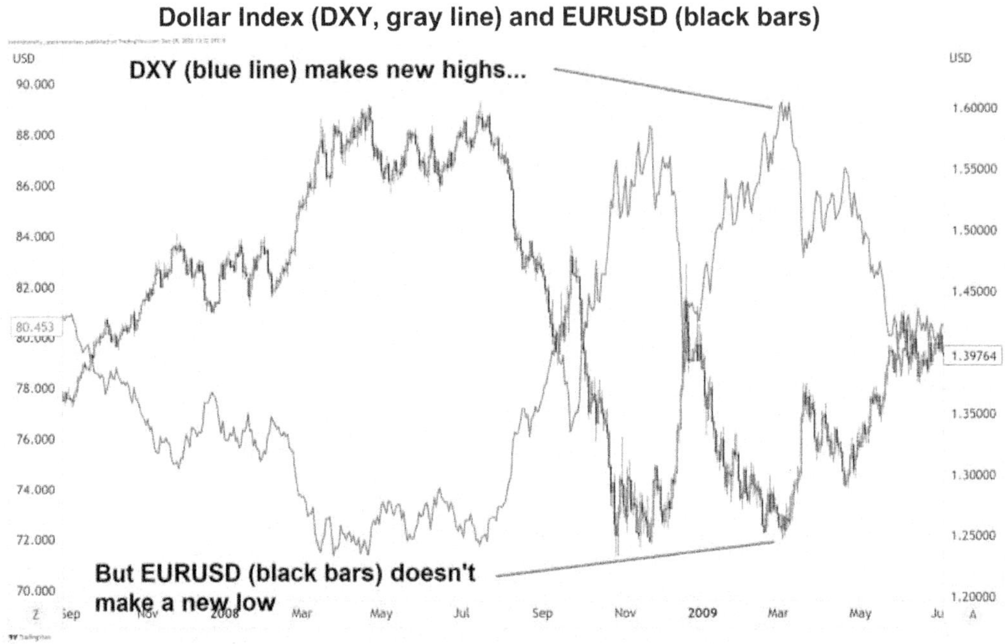

Bearish divergence for the USD in Q2 2009

You can use this methodology for any two markets you watch. AUDUSD making new highs but copper isn't? Be careful with your AUDUSD longs. MSTR making new lows, but bitcoin isn't? Maybe it's time to get long MSTR. And so on.

This week's trade

As you might have guessed, this week's trade is long TSLA. Stop loss at 88.50 and take profit at 159.00. People love to love Elon Musk or they love to hate him. I don't care. I just want to find trades that will make money. While most of 2022 was a great time to be short TSLA as it became a wildly-overvalued meme stock… Now is probably a reasonable time to stick a toe in the water long.

Please do your own research. Many of the trades in 50in50 are examples that I am using to explain a specific concept and have no embedded edge. I do truly like this idea, but it's risky and TSLA is a falling knife. The turn of the year and the end of window dressing and tax loss selling make a good case for timing the trade here and the lowest-ever RSI is waving at me like a bullfighter's flapping red muleta.

So I'm charging. Let's see. *Be extremely cautious around TSLA earnings on January 25.*

Conclusion

There are different ways to use RSI. I like to use it at the super mega extremes as an idea trigger and if there are other reasons to get on board, I will do so. You can also use RSI as a confirmation or divergence indicator when analyzing trends. This is a useful way to measure the strength of trend using some basic mathematics.

RSI rarely gets below 20 or above 80. When it does, pay attention.

Week 41: Sweat the small stuff

Execution and trade management can be an edge or a leak

Update on previous trades

Week 37: XOM put spread is quiet.

Week 38: Sell vol in MSTR has been good so far.

Week 39: Sell 2-month USDJPY and buy 6-month USDJPY. This has been a good idea so far. USDJPY is unchanged.

Week 40: Long TSLA has been a wild ride. There was bad news on deliveries and Tesla gapped down to a low of 101.81. Then, a positive Barron's article and a broad market rebound took it to 123.60. The good news it that the move on January 6th is the first time TSLA has recovered from a large opening gap down since it was up around $200. This is bullish. The bad news short-term is that 123.50 is starting to look like a bit of a ceiling. I'm waiting for Musk to announce a new CEO for Twitter. That is a meaningful bullish catalyst that is possible one of these days. No guarantees this will ever happen, though. Musk is known for promising whatever and delivering whenever.

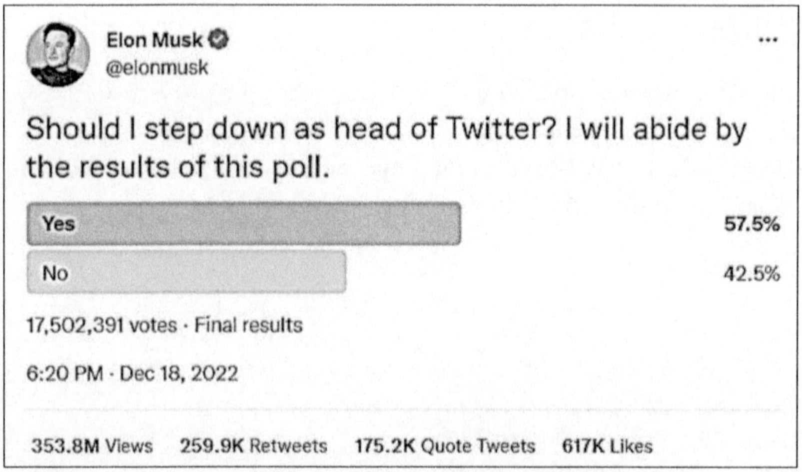

I am hoping this promise is more reliable than his past promises on self-driving, robotaxis, the Cybertruck, hyperloop, taking Tesla private, Neuralink human trials… :|

For your viewing pleasure, here's the chart with the important features marked.

TSLA hourly chart back to mid-November

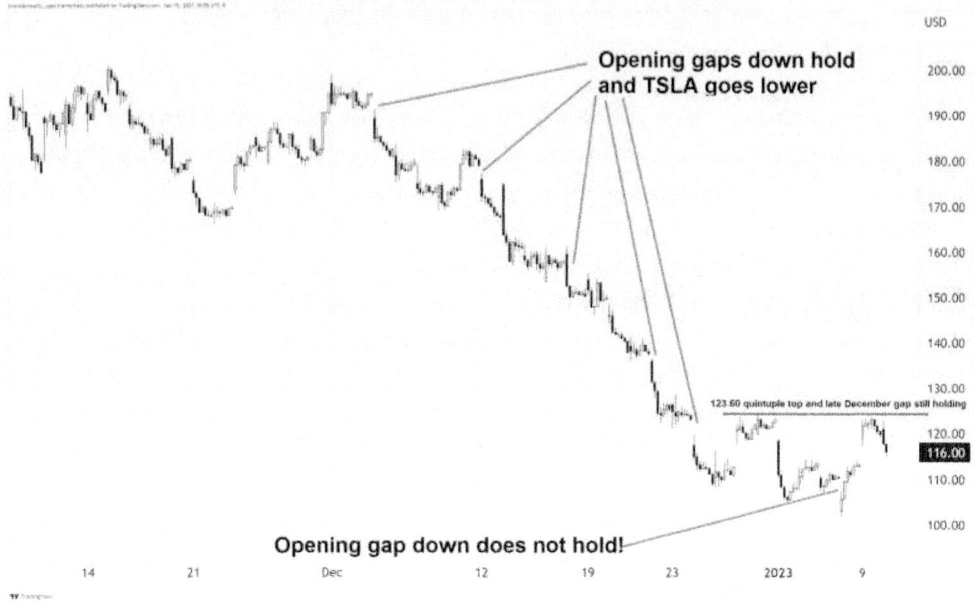

I am still bullish and I will get *Will Ferrell seeing Santa* levels of excited if we close above $125.

Sweat the small stuff

One of the most useful books you will ever read is called *Don't Sweat the Small Stuff... And it's all small stuff*[60]. It sounds cheesy, and it kind of is, but it is one of the OG self-help books before self-help became a saturated category. Published in 1997, it tells you most of what you need to know if you want to stay sane.

Here are a couple of quotes:

> *"True happiness comes not when we get rid of all of our problems, but when we change our relationship to them, when we see our problems as a potential source of awakening, opportunities to practice, and to learn."*
>
> *"One of the mistakes many of us make is that we feel sorry for ourselves, or for others, thinking that life should be fair, or that someday it will be. It's not and it won't. When we make this mistake we tend to spend a lot of time wallowing and/or complaining about what's wrong with life. 'It's not fair,' we complain, not realizing that, perhaps, it was never intended to be."*
>
> *"We deny the parts of ourselves that we deem unacceptable rather than accepting the fact that we're all less than perfect."*

Much of the advice in the book feels kind of cliché now but that's mostly because the book was ahead of its time and is frequently cited or copied. Anyway, the book popped into my head because today I'm going to talk about the importance of sweating the small stuff in trading. In contrast to life, you SHOULD sweat the small stuff in trading.

Getting in and getting out

There are many ways to get in and out of a trade. You can scale in, you can go all in at one level, you can use limit orders or market orders, you can stop into the highs or try to bottom tick the lows. Much of it comes down to the particular set up, but let me go over some need-to-know information about getting in and out of trades.

To scale or not to scale

Scaling in or out of trades is a stylistic determination you have to make either broadly or on a trade-by-trade basis. I rarely scale into trades over a wide range because part of my strategy is finding optimal entry points that offer the most possible leverage.

That said, the problem with picking a single entry point is that there is too much false precision. Say I leave a limit order at 0.6861 in AUDUSD. Do I really think exactly

---

60 https://amzn.to/3itB7z6

0.6861 is the correct entry point for an AUDUSD long? Or is it more like I see the support zone as 0.6850/70 and I arbitrarily picked 0.6861 because that is the midpoint of the range and I wanted to get ahead of the round number (0.6860)?

Nobody can pick the turns down to the pip. Therefore, I prefer to scale my orders in a tight range. If I am going long 60 million AUDUSD in this example, I bid 0.6863 0.6861 and 0.6857 for 20 million each. This way, if 62 is the low, I'm not smashing my fist on the keyboard. At least I got a bit of a position on.

On the other hand, I won't leave a series of orders like 0.6861 0.6841 and 0.6821 generally because I would rather just find a tighter band than that or, if I think there is a decent chance it's going to 0.6821, just bid down there. This is also related to my time horizon, which is on the short side. It's all a series of fractals. If I was trading a 3-month AUDUSD view, then bidding 0.6861 0.6841, and 0.6821 might make sense. But my trading is mostly clustered around the 1-day to 1-week time horizon.

I am more likely to scale out using wider parameters as a trade goes deeper in the money but I try not to do this too much or the original risk/reward of the trade becomes compromised. I prefer to move my stop loss once a major level breaks and that way if it keeps going, my original take profit remains in place and the risk/reward I was playing for is the risk/reward I actually get.

The main idea here is that you should be thoughtful about execution. You want to maximize leverage by optimizing your entry point, but you don't want to be a dick for a pip all the time. You want to minimize transaction costs but not put your strategy in jeopardy with your tactics.

I like to zoom in as much as possible, then spread my orders a bit inside a narrow zone.

Never leave your orders on round numbers. Your probability of getting a fill is lower than if you leave them just in front of the round number. You can read more about round number bias here[61] or in *Alpha Trader*[62] (pages 214 to 216).

Next, I'm going to provide a detailed explanation of the different order types. If you are a market professional, or you have read *The Art of Currency Trading* you probably want to skim this week. This is a nuts and bolts need-to-know lesson that will mostly benefit newish traders.

---

[61] https://www.spectramarkets.com/wp-content/uploads/2021/11/MacroTactical-Crypto-Number-3-11NOV21.pdf

[62] https://amzn.to/3rngGo3

Order Types

There are many different order types. New order types are always in development so be on the lookout for exciting new ways to execute. For now, understand the following order types. I'm going to use examples from currency trading because some of this is excerpted from my book on FX trading, but the concepts apply to all markets.

Market orders are an easy, clean, and expensive way to trade. Every time you cross the spread, money is leaking out of your P&L. You might think it's tiny, a few basis points here and there. But believe me, it adds up.

Here are two P&L simulations using realistic assumptions as follows:

- Average bid/offer spread is 10 cents. Zero commission. 252 days per year.
- Average up day is +$3,000, average down day is -$2,000 and WIN% is 50%.

Two P&L simulations for a day trader who turns over 3,500 shares per day

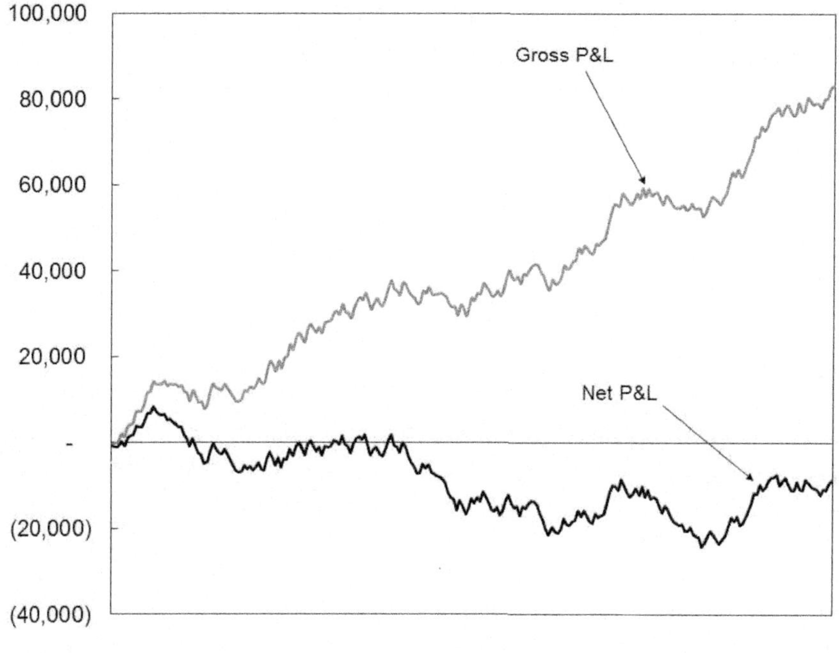

You can see that first chart shows a trader that probably has a decent edge extracted 90,000 dollars of alpha from the market but gave it all to market makers. This is common. Trading is a negative-sum game. You need to outearn your transaction costs by a wide margin or you will never make real money trading. Here's another run of the simulation.

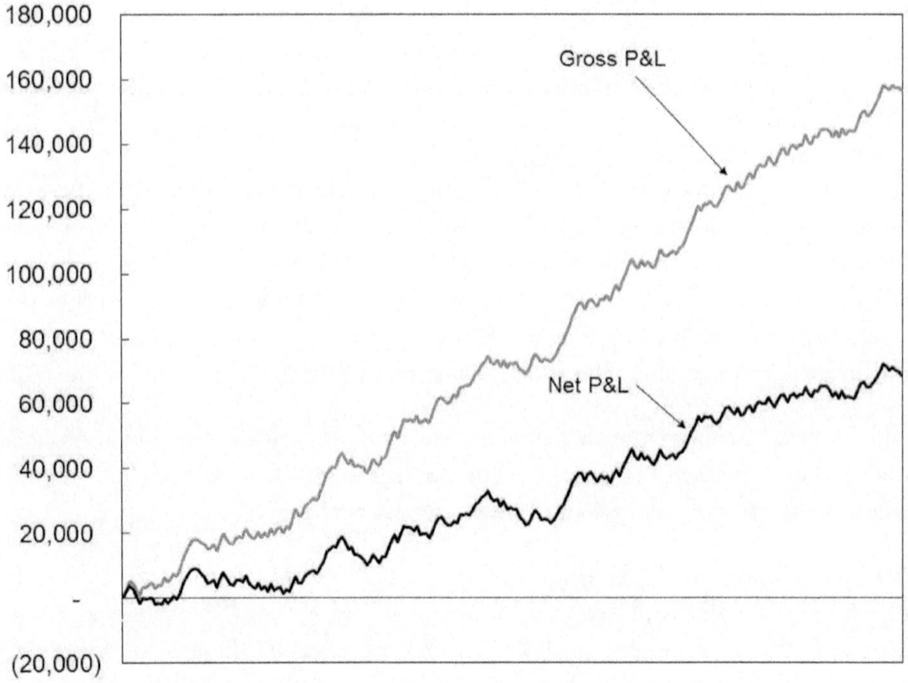

Tiny leaks in a tire are barely noticeable but eventually, the tire ends up flat.

If you are worried about the trade ripping in a straight line before you can get it on with a limit order, use a market order. This rarely applies but in the case of headlines, news, or a breakout trade, it might.

If you think nothing is going on or the market might even move against you a bit before your idea works, use a limit order or algorithm to trade.

Streaming Risk Price (also known as crossing the spread or risk transfer): This is the most common way to transact FX and is used by customers in retail and wholesale. It is also common in crypto. This type of trade is similar to a market order and immediately gives you the position you want at a known price. If a machine is showing you 1.3817/19 in EURUSD and you pay the offer, you have bought at 19 and you're now long euros.

This type of trade is clean and easy and gets you the position you want right away with no aggravation or delay. In the long run, transacting on risk prices all the time generates profits for the market maker banks and retail platforms but it is a simple and efficient way to trade, especially for beginners.

The trader taking the other side of a risk price trade is called a market maker. Her ideal scenario is that the market doesn't move and she is hit on the bid and paid on the offer over and over again and thus she captures the spread by buying and selling at slightly different rates. In reality, there is meaningful risk to being a market maker because prices are not static and traders tend to move in herds, creating large imbalances. Trading on a risk price is similar to sending a market order but it differs in that with a risk price you know what your fill will be before you trade—with a market order, you don't get your fill until afterwards.

Market makers earn a spread when you hit their bid or pay their offer but this is compensation for the fact they must bear two types of risk. First, market makers take on liquidity risk when you trade with them. This is the notion that only a fixed amount of a security can be dealt on a given price. So if you hit a bank's bid for 50 million EURUSD, the liquidity risk is defined by how far the market moves directly as a result of the bank selling as they try to get out. This is also sometimes called the "footprint" of the trade.

Market makers also bear market risk. This means if you sell to someone at 45 and the market collapses instantly to 25, the market maker takes the loss, not you. The market maker bears the risk of any price movements after a trade.

Limit orders (also called "take profit orders") are common in both retail and wholesale markets. A limit order is placed at a specific level and will only be triggered when the market moves to or through your level. For example, EURUSD is 1.3820/22 and you want to buy if it dips to 1.3815. You leave a limit order to buy at 1.3815. This is usually called "leaving a bid." If you are selling, you "leave an offer." The advantage to limit orders is that you do not cross the spread, but the disadvantage is that you are not guaranteed to get filled. In the example described, if EURUSD goes straight up from 1.3820 to 1.3890, you miss the whole move as your 1.3815 limit order would never get filled.

Limit orders are best when you are in no hurry and you don't think the market is going to move much, or if you have a specific entry point in mind. Say EURUSD is 14/16 and you think it's going nowhere for a while. You want to get long but you're in no huge hurry. You can leave a 14 bid and because there is a tremendous amount of random micro movement in FX markets (this is called bid/offer bounce), your probability of getting filled is high. The less liquid the security, the more important is the decision whether to leave a limit order or simply cross the spread.

You gain more by bidding and offering in illiquid markets (because the spread is wider) but you are less likely to get filled because there is less bid/offer bounce. There is no right answer when choosing between order types. It is situation-specific and you have to make an assessment of what is the best order type based on your directional market view, your sense of urgency, and current and expected liquidity and volatility. Limit orders are sometimes called take profit orders, even when they are used to initiate a new position.

Some traders will *only use limit orders* for entries because they fear often-opaque spreads and feel like market orders are for noobs that want to give away free money to the algorithmic market makers. While I generally prefer limit orders, there is definitely a time and place for a market order. There is no one size fits all tactic that is always best and pre-committing or excluding order types just limits your toolkit for no reason.

Two special types of limit orders are **if done orders** and **loop orders**. An "if done" order is simply a limit order that, once executed, creates another order. For example, say I want to sell 20 million AUDUSD at 0.7299 and if that gets done I want to stop loss at 0.7336. I would enter an "if done" order.

A loop order is similar to an "if done" but a loop order creates only new limit orders and it creates them over and over, not just once. Say I want to buy 10 million USDCAD at 1.3125 and if that gets done, I want to sell them out at 1.3165 and repeat this process again if it drops down to 1.3125. I simply enter a loop order as follows: Buy 10,000,000 USDCAD at 1.3125. Loop sell 10,000,000 USDCAD at 1.3165. I will keep buying at 1.3125 and selling at 1.3165 as long as the market cooperates. Loop orders are usually used by traders who own options.

Stop loss order: Stop loss orders are key to proper risk management. A stop loss order is an order to buy higher or sell lower if price moves to a certain level.

For example, I am long euros (positioned for EURUSD to go up) and my entry point is 1.3825. Based on my analysis, EURUSD should not go below 1.3780; if it does, my idea is probably wrong. So I leave an order: Stop loss sell 10 million EURUSD @ 1.3779.

If 1.3779 trades, a market maker will sell my 10 euros for me (or an electronic system will execute on my behalf). The rate is not guaranteed because the stop loss simply becomes a market order when the level is triggered.

Note that stop losses can also be used to enter new positions. For example, a trader thinks that a break below 1.1300 in EURUSD will cause the pair to accelerate lower. He could leave a stop loss (sometimes called a "stop enter") order to initiate a new position, selling to get short when 1.1299 trades.

Quite often, a trader will send her order as an **OCO order** (one cancels the other). This means that the trader sends a take profit and a stop loss for the same position and if one side gets executed, the other side is cancelled. Whenever I have an open position and I am off the desk, I pass an OCO order so that my take profit level and stop loss are watched. Once one side trades, the other cancels.

A **two-way price** is a way clients execute large transactions by voice in institutional markets. In this case, a customer asks a bank to show them both a bid and an offer on a set amount. The bank making the price does not know if the customer is going to buy or sell and so the bank shows both sides and the customer decides whether or not to deal and if so, which side. At any moment in time, there are somewhat standard spreads for two-way quotes in a currency, but spreads change frequently and vary by time of day, market maker skill, and market conditions. A spread in a fast market will generally be wider than a spread in a quiet market.

Let's look at an example in FX. The market is jumping around and a corporation needs to sell 130 million NZDUSD. The CFO is worried that liquidity is not good and does not want to show his exact interest to a bank. The size of the trade is a bit too big to do on a machine and since the market is volatile, he feels a TWAP has too much market risk.

He decides to call a bank and ask for a two-way price. The market is currently around 0.6644. In this instance, the market maker at the bank determines that the appropriate spread in 130 million NZDUSD is 10 points wide so he shows the corporation 0.6640/0.6650 without knowing which way the corporation needs to trade.

The CFO thinks 10 points wide is a very fair spread in 130 NZDUSD so he says: "Yours at 0.6640." 'Yours' is the FX term for "I SELL." And 'Mine' means "I BUY." So now the corporation has transferred the risk and the bank is long the 130 million NZDUSD at 0.6640. The bank trader then needs to figure out the best way to get out of the risk in a way that makes as much (or loses as little) money as possible.

Personally, I always enjoy making two-way prices as it is the old school way to deal and is very clean and easy. It puts all the onus on the market maker and instantly puts the customer at ease because the risk is fully passed to the market maker right away.

TWAP and VWAP: TWAP stands for time-weighted average price. VWAP stands for volume-weighted average price. TWAPs and VWAPs are algorithmic orders used primarily for larger transactions. These orders are managed electronically by slicing a large order up into smaller pieces and executing the trade over a given time frame. Say a corporation wants to buy 100 million USDCAD but doesn't want to leave a big footprint in the market. USDCAD is trading 1.1010/13 (in other words, USDCAD is ten/thirteen). A trader or customer could enter the following variables into a TWAP or VWAP algo and hit GO:

Buy 100 USDCAD over 10 minutes with a limit price of 1.1017.

The system will then start to buy in small slices, 1 million here, 1 million there, buying 10 million USDCAD per minute for 10 minutes until it has bought the 100 million USDCAD. The TWAP will try to cross the spread as little as possible, although in reality TWAPs and VWAPs tend to pay quite a bit of spread. The TWAP will continue only if USDCAD remains below 1.1017. If the pair rallies, then the TWAP will shut off and wait for USDCAD to come back down. If USDCAD never comes back down, the trade will not happen. The generic format for a TWAP or VWAP order is:

BUY (or SELL) X amount of CURRENCY PAIR over Y minutes with a limit price of Z.

Z can also be set to "no limit." The advantage of this type of order is that it leaves less of a market footprint, but the major disadvantage is that it takes a long time and so the market can move significantly against the execution as time passes. In other words, there is significant market risk and if the market does not cooperate, the order might never get done.

The ideal time for a TWAP order is when the market is not moving or when you expect it to move gradually in favor of the trade. If you need to buy, but you think the market is going to grind lower, a TWAP is a good idea. If you need to buy and expect the market to go higher soon, a TWAP is a bad idea. Get a risk transfer price or do the trade at market.

VWAP is very similar to TWAP but differs in that the amounts executed are sliced into pieces that match the amount of volume being transacted in the market. This allows the algorithm to trade more actively when volumes (and liquidity) are high and less actively when volumes are low. Generally, TWAP and VWAP strategies yield similar results. Many retail brokers now offer TWAP or similar orders.

Dark pools are another type of order available only in the wholesale market. Traders show an interest to buy or sell an amount but do not assign a price to the order. The order goes into the dark pool and waits for someone to match in the opposite direction. When a match occurs, both sides of the trade are filled at midmarket (as derived from a separate primary market price feed). Dark pools have become increasingly popular in recent years as they allow traders to transact without showing their interest to the market.

Adding to TSLA

Let's say I like the price action in TSLA and I approve of its ability to recover from the bad deliveries number reported last weekend. Let me go through four ways I could add to my long position.

1. **Limit order**

   I could leave a limit order at a major support. Here is the chart of the past three days of TSLA price action.

TSLA 5-minute chart, January 5 to now

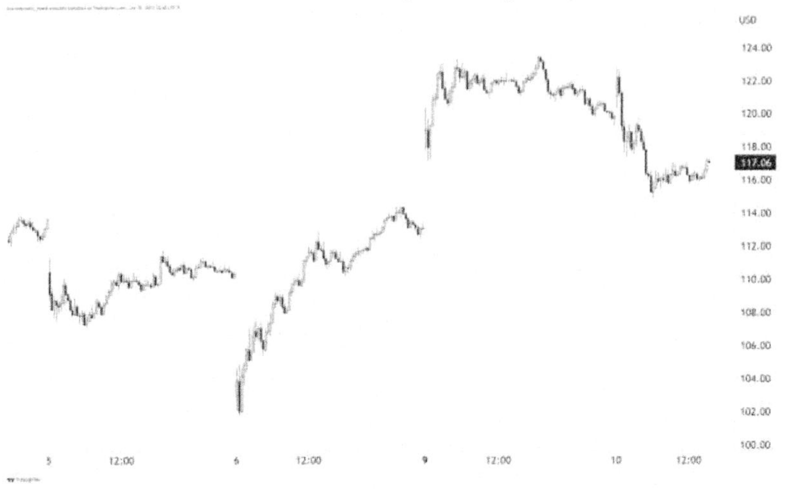

Doing some basic technical analysis, two main levels pop out for me. 1) The bottom of the gap open on January 9 (113.50) and 2) the low (101.85). I don't think we are going to get back to the lows, and we already made a decent low today at 114.95. Based on this information, I could leave a bid at 115.03 (just ahead of today's low, the bottom of the gap, and a round number) and stop out below 101.85. I like this option.

The biggest risk with this idea is that if TSLA goes straight to 150 from here, I never got the extra shares on. Then again, I'm already long so it's not the end of the world.

2. **Market order.** I could buy TSLA here at 117.06. That feels totally arbitrary to me and it's doubtful that this random price point that I just happened to screenshot is the optimal entry. Furthermore, my default is to avoid market orders because they are usually a waste of money. I reject this idea.
3. **Stop entry order.** I could buy TSLA on the break of the multiple highs up around 123.50. This is not a bad idea, though I will incur slippage on a stop entry order as it will simply become a market order once my level is touched. The biggest downside to this style is that by buying high, I'm increasing my average entry price. Last week I got long TSLA at 113.10 so if we add at, say, 124.10, our average is now 118.60 and we have double the size. If I get stopped in intraday on a "New CEO for Twitter" headline, I'm going to be happy. If I get stopped in on a random gap open higher one day, I could be sad.

Adding on breaks like this can be a feasible strategy but with so much chop in TSLA and absurd volatility on the open at times; I don't love this.

4. **Wait for a daily TSLA close above 124.00, then buy**. Many of the issues with number 3 apply here, the only advantage is that you get a cleaner break on the charts because you wait for the close. Then again, you might be adding at $131.50 or something and that disimproves the average even more. My target on the trade is 159 and the stop is 88.50 so adding above 125 really messes with the risk/reward.

No option is ever perfect. In this case, I like option 1 the best. Buy a dip to 115.03. Instead of the 88.50 stop loss, I will put the stop on this new chunk at 98.49. Keep in mind that in real life, I would bid 115.07, 115.05, and 115.03 for my order (for example) to avoid the false precision problem but when I'm writing up trades that is generally just confusing. To avoid the number salad, when I write, I just give one level. And the stop loss in real life should always be on the correct side of the round number (88.49, not 88.50) as I said in Week 40.

Conclusion

Market orders are expensive but sometimes appropriate. Limit orders are cheap in theory but can be painfully expensive when they don't get filled and the market rips your way. Don't be dogmatic about order types. Experiment. Figure out ways to increase your fill rate and lower your transaction costs.

There is not one correct execution method for all markets and all regimes.

It depends on the market and situation. In a product with a wide bid/offer spread, you are more likely to miss the trade if you don't aggress, but you are also saving more by using a passive strategy. It comes down to your view of what is going to happen in the very short-term.

Be thoughtful about your execution. Try to measure the leakages where you can. Fill your toolbox with as many tools as possible, and use a hammer when you want to hit a nail and a screwdriver when you want to turn a screw.

In trading, you gotta sweat the small stuff.

In life, don't sweat the small stuff (and it's all small stuff).

Week 42: Obvious trades are not always bad

Just don't be late.

Tesla fighting a Ford, Japanese animation style.

Update on previous trades

Week 37: XOM put spread is quiet but losing as China reflation helps oil.

Week 38: Sell vol in MSTR has been good so far.

Week 39: Sell 2-month USDJPY and buy 6-month USDJPY. This has been a good idea so far. USDJPY is unchanged.

Week 40 and 41: Long TSLA has been a good trade despite a wild ride. The newsflow has been poor as deliveries drop and price cuts continue, but the overall macro environment has been excellent as favorite short plays get squeezed. Last week, the play was to add at 115.06 and the low was 115.63 on the price cut news. Damn.

As discussed last week, this is the issue with limit orders; you might not get filled on the idea. We could have sent a market order with TSLA at $117.06 and got filled, but we didn't. We could have bought the break of 125.00, but we didn't. There is no perfect execution strategy and in this case the patience to wait for the dip to strong support was a decent idea, but did not work out.

I am going to square this idea up here now at $141.50 because TSLA earnings come out this week and I have no strong view on how the stock will respond to the release. The numbers could show a dire outlook or Musk could announce he found a CEO for Twitter and the stock explodes higher. Hard to say. The long TSLA trade was founded on the historic fall in RSI, but now, almost a month later, with TSLA up here, I don't like the coin toss aspect of holding through earnings.

TSLA stock, 5-minute chart (12DEC to the close on January 20)

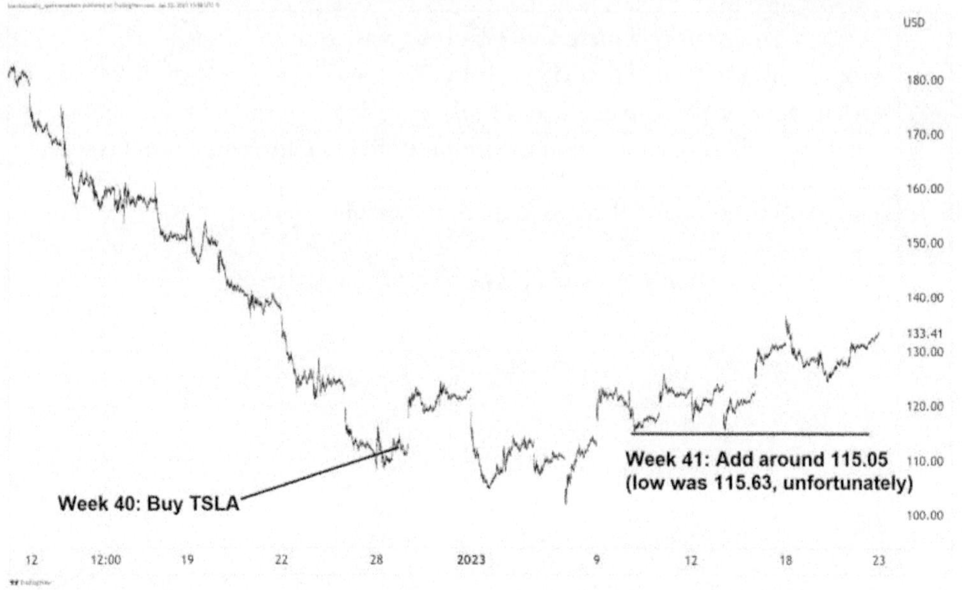

Obvious trades are not always bad

Markets are extremely efficient, most of the time, and there is no edge in putting on an obvious trade that is fully understood and priced in by the market. On the other hand, the market is not an instantaneous discounting mechanism. There are a few reasons why markets don't immediately discount all new information.

1. Confirmation bias. Old narratives die hard. Traders and investors that have made money on a prior narrative tend to be slow to abandon that narrative as new information arrives.
2. Financial market prices are mostly continuous. When news comes out, price doesn't just jump to a new, correct level and sit there. It flies all over the place as market players with different views and incentives disagree on the importance of the new information. What's obvious to you might not be obvious to everyone else. This period as price moves from one equilibrium to the next can be lucrative

for early movers with strong conviction. Being the first through the door comes with its own risks, but it's often the best way to capture the biggest returns or avoid the biggest pain.

3. Many market participants are slow moving. A pension fund with a secular bull view on automakers might need to convene an investment committee meeting before it changes that view. This process could involve an analyst processing news, writing a report, and then presenting it to the investment committee. Then, the investment committee makes its decision to reduce the allocation to automakers and communicates this to the execution team. Then, the execution team needs to sell the stocks. If the position is large, this selling could last days or even weeks.
4. Price makes news. No matter how bad the news is, if the price hasn't moved yet, some will just assume that the security "trades well" or the news doesn't matter. Many market participants believe that price is the ultimate information signal and they will not cut a winning position until price forces them to do so.

Here are two "obvious" trades that worked out incredibly well.

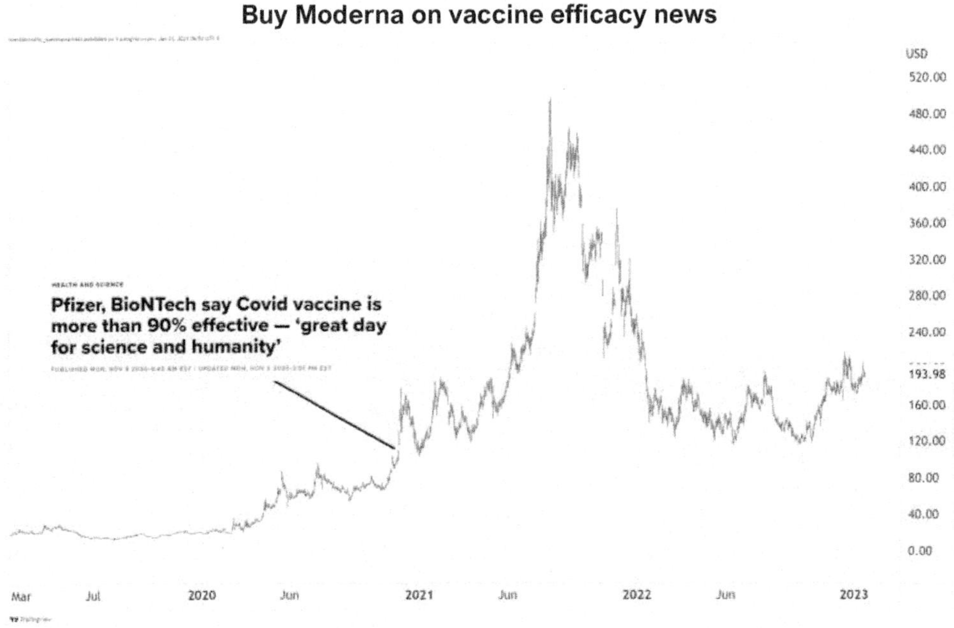

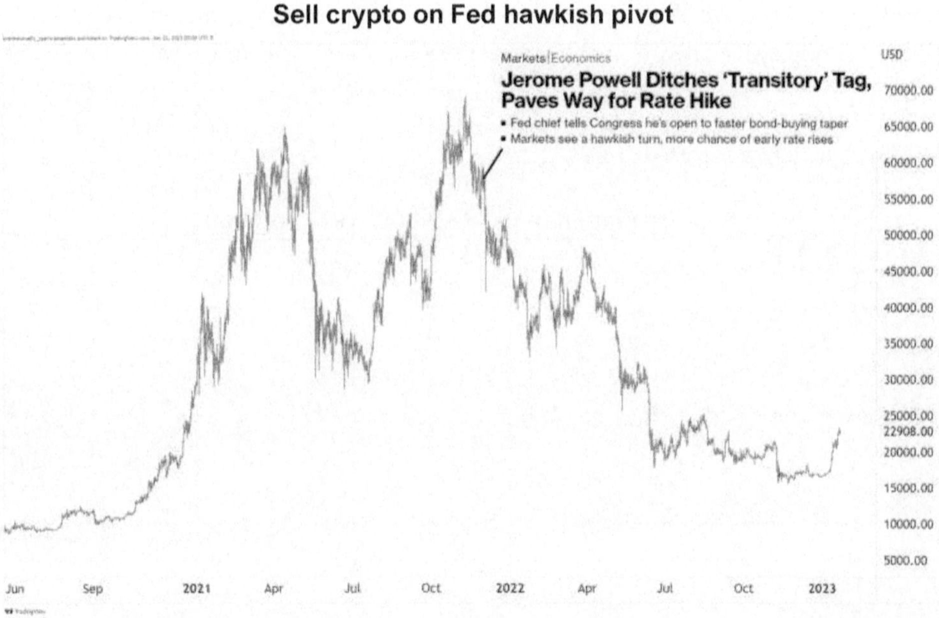

I put "obvious" in quotes because the word is subjective. But let's just say my brother, who is a musician and never trades stocks, bought vaccine stocks in November 2020. And I was writing about the obvious bearish implications of a tighter Fed for crypto in November 2021[63]. So this isn't just hindsight. The Abenomics trade in 2012/2013 was probably one of the greatest macro trades of all time. And it was obvious.

Many trades around Fed and monetary policy cycles can be obvious, though there is usually a ton of volatility when the Fed turns and it's not usually as binary and clean as it was in November 2021.

If every person who wanted to be a trader had the courage to act immediately on his own ideas, a lot more people would be good traders. Very few people have the courage to act on what's obvious to them, until it's too late. And then they end up buying NIO at $56.

Peter Lynch, the Captain Obvious of fundamentals

One of the greatest investors of all time is Peter Lynch. From 1977 until 1990, he ran Fidelity's Magellan Fund, and it averaged a 29.2% annual return. As of 2003, **Peter Lynch's Magellan Fund had the best 20-year return of any mutual fund, ever**.

---

[63] https://www.spectramarkets.com/wp-content/uploads/2022/01/MacroTactical-Crypto-Number-8-06JAN22.pdf

Barry Ritholz, who probably knows more about investment management than 99.9999% of humans on earth, called him the greatest stock picker of all time[64], ahead of Warren Buffett.

Here's a chart Barry featured:

Fidelity Magellan vs. S&P 500. 1977 to 1990

Sidenote: Here is a fascinating Spencer Jakab[65] tidbit that shows that despite Lynch's amazing returns, his investors did much worse because retail investors underperform due to horrendous timing.

> *During his tenure Lynch trounced the market overall and beat it in most years, racking up a 29 percent annualized return. But Lynch himself pointed out a fly in the ointment. He calculated that the average investor in his fund made only around 7 percent during the same period. When he would have a setback, for example, the money would flow out of the fund through redemptions. Then when he got back on track it would flow back in, having missed the recovery.*

Lynch wrote three books and his main principle is "invest in what you know." Since most people are expert in particular fields, applying this basic "invest in what you know" principle helps individual investors find good undervalued stocks.

Lynch views the observation of successful companies in everyday life as a starting point for investment opportunities. He invested in Dunkin' Donuts after being impressed by their coffee as a customer, noticing their busy Boston locations, and studying the company's financial status.

---

64 https://ritholtz.com/2021/03/peter-lynch-goat/

65 https://awealthofcommonsense.com/2016/07/peter-lynchs-track-record-revisited/

Lynch believes individual investors can make similar smart choices by paying attention to business trends in their careers and hobbies. He outlines how to read and interpret company paperwork in his books. **Lynch states that his undergraduate studies in philosophy and logic were more important to his career than his MBA in math and finance**, as he disagrees with the academic theories of random walk hypothesis and efficient market hypothesis. He relies more on practitioners than theoreticians.

This sort of fundamental analysis has appeal, but it's important to note that this does not mean you just say "Yummy coffee!" and go buy the stock. The coffee being delicious is simply a logical starting point for a thesis and you build on that thesis by analyzing other inputs. For a full summary of Lynch's investment process, you can read this[66]. But believe me; he's not just checking out a new sandwich at Wendy's, then buying Wendy's stock.

The biggest mistake traders and investors make with the common sense approach is the failure to understand this critical point:

Great companies can be terrible investments.

Trading and investing are about the interaction of 1) opportunity / value and 2) price. Amazon was a great company and a terrible investment in 2001. Seemingly bad companies like GameStop can be terrible shorts. Markets are always about the interaction of price and value. It's story + price, not just story. Always. This is the most costly error investors make: Chasing great stories at any price.

In early 2021, I was somewhat shocked to see that famous value investor Howard Marks was getting bulled up on tech and disruptors[67]. I managed to arrange a phone call with him and we spoke for about an hour. This piece is a summary of our conversation[68].

I recommend you give that piece a read because there are many timeless bits of knowledge in there. I am particularly proud of that piece because even while Howard Marks, an investor I admire, was saying "this time might be different," I stuck to my view that the rally in disruptor tech stocks was BS and likely to crash to earth under the weight of reality.

Here is the takeaway from that interview that is relevant to today's piece:

"It's not what you buy, it's what you paid."

Or for trading: It's not how obvious the story is, it's where you get in.

---

66 https://home.csulb.edu/~pammerma/fin382/screener/lynch.htm

67 https://www.oaktreecapital.com/docs/default-source/memos/something-of-value.pdf

68 https://www.epsilontheory.com/a-conversation-with-howard-marks/

Marks said to me on the phone: "I'm going to sell you my car, do you want to buy it?" I mumbled for a second and he clarified: "The question makes no sense." Every asset you buy is a combination of the intrinsic worth of the asset and the price you pay. Looking at one or the other in isolation is dumb. People define "value" as cheap, but they are often talking about price, not worth.

Again, buying and selling on obvious fundamental stories can lead you to bankruptcy because you might always be chasing the new shiny thing and selling when things are at their worst. What Lynch managed to do was find bullish stories and good products before the market sniffed them out. Then, he could get in, do more analysis, narrow down his picks, and ride the waves up.

And Peter Lynch is not the only investor or trader who starts with common sense observations as the backbone for a trade idea. Jeffrey Neumann (featured in Jack Schwager's excellent book *Unknown Market Wizards*[69]) uses the same approach.

Macro tourists often jump on big, obvious macro trades like Abenomics, ECB QE, and the 2009 China stimulus. Don't assume that just because a thesis is obvious, it won't work. What you want is a thesis that is common-sensical or obvious, but not yet fully priced in.

This is totally different from saying: "Peloton is a cool product and WFH FTW!—let me get some of that stock at $150!" That's what analysts do, as evidenced here:

Tell me you don't understand extrapolation without telling me...

PTON stock: analyst ratings

Date	Brokerage	Action	Rating	Price Target
2/5/2021	Rosenblatt Securities	Boost Price Target	Buy	$186.00 → $190.00
2/5/2021	Gordon Haskett	Reiterated Rating	Buy	$190.00
2/5/2021	JPMorgan Chase & Co.	Boost Price Target	Overweight	$145.00 → $200.00
2/5/2021	Truist	Boost Price Target	-	$145.00 → $160.00
2/5/2021	MKM Partners	Boost Price Target	Neutral	$110.00 → $130.00
2/5/2021	BMO Capital Markets	Boost Price Target	Underperform	$33.00 → $45.00
2/5/2021	Roth Capital	Boost Price Target	Buy	$140.00 → $165.00
2/5/2021	Needham & Company LLC	Boost Price Target	Buy	$140.00 → $180.00
2/5/2021	The Goldman Sachs Group	Boost Price Target	Neutral	$162.00 → $180.00
2/5/2021	Barclays	Boost Price Target	Overweight	$148.00 → $163.00
2/5/2021	Raymond James	Downgrade	Outperform → Market Perform	-
2/1/2021	Cowen	Boost Price Target	Outperform	$130.00 → $175.00
1/19/2021	UBS Group	Downgrade	Neutral → Sell	$115.00 → $124.00
1/13/2021	Bank of America	Boost Price Target	Buy	$150.00 → $175.00

The stock was $150 when this table was printed on capital.com. Nice UBS and BMO!

69 https://amzn.to/3kBpRkZ

But this isn't 50 investments in 50 weeks

But this book isn't about investing; it's about trading. The reason I have given you this background information on Peter Lynch is that good **trades**, like good investments, can also start with a common sense observation.

Obvious, common sense trades can and sometimes do make sense. But there has to be more to the process than a single common sense observation. This is consistent with my overall philosophy that excellent trades have many inputs. Let's look at what seems to me to be an obvious trade.

Tesla price cuts are straight out of a business school case study

In business school, we used the case study method, which means you study real company stories and debate what went right and what went wrong thereafter. The recent, somewhat gigantic price cuts from TSLA provide the kind of case study you would do in biz school.

Demand is falling, so a major player decides to cut prices dramatically. What does this mean for that company, and for its competitors?

The obvious takeaway to me is that lower-margin competitors will be hurt the most by the price cuts and the company cutting prices may gain or lose, depending on shifts in demand. This story from the Verge[70] covers it pretty well. Here's a key quote from Dan Ives:

> *"We believe all together these price cuts could spur demand/deliveries by 12 percent to 15 percent globally in 2023 and shows Tesla and Musk are going on the 'offensive' to spur demand in a softening backdrop," Ives said. "This is a clear shot across the bow at European automakers and U.S. stalwarts (GM and Ford) that Tesla is not going to play nice in the sandbox with an EV price war now underway."*

I am not an automotive analyst, but my first thought when I heard about these price cuts was: this is obviously really bad for Ford. Here's why:

- Ford has been winning the EV narrative game. Markets and consumers have been excited about Ford's push into EVs. In late 2021, Ford made a massive commitment to EVs[71] while many companies like BMW have been slower to go electric.

---

70 https://www.theverge.com/2023/1/14/23554886/tesla-price-cut-ev-market-deman-elon-musk

71 https://media.ford.com/content/fordmedia/fna/us/en/news/2021/09/27/ford-to-lead-americas-shift-to-electric-vehicles.html

- With finite EV credits available, and TSLA cars now eligible for more EV credits, Ford buyers will lose out.
- Tesla has much higher profit margins than Ford so it can afford a price war.

Global carmakers on gross margin in %

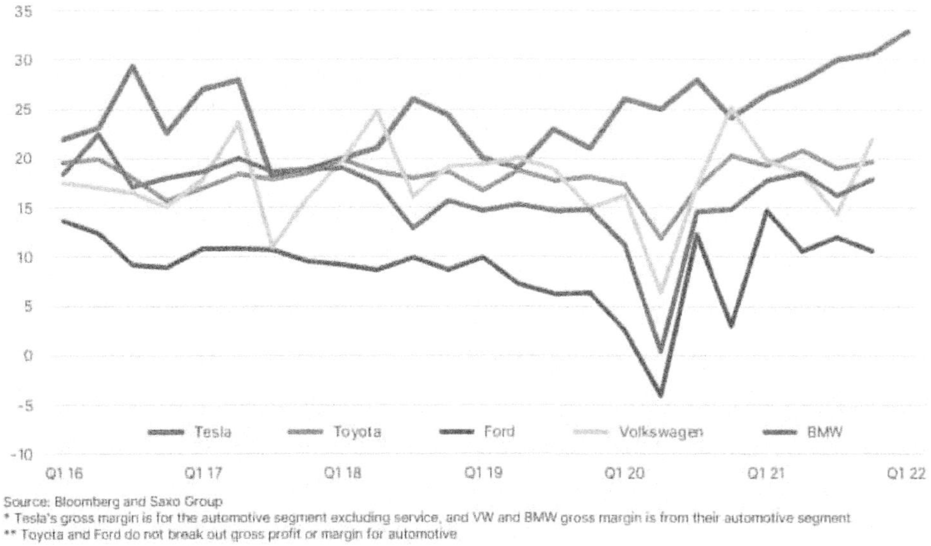

Meanwhile, searches for Ford stock are in a nice downtrend after peaking during COVID. Since most investors and traders buy stocks and trade exclusively from the long side, search interest tends to be bullish.

Google search interest for Ford and Tesla stock

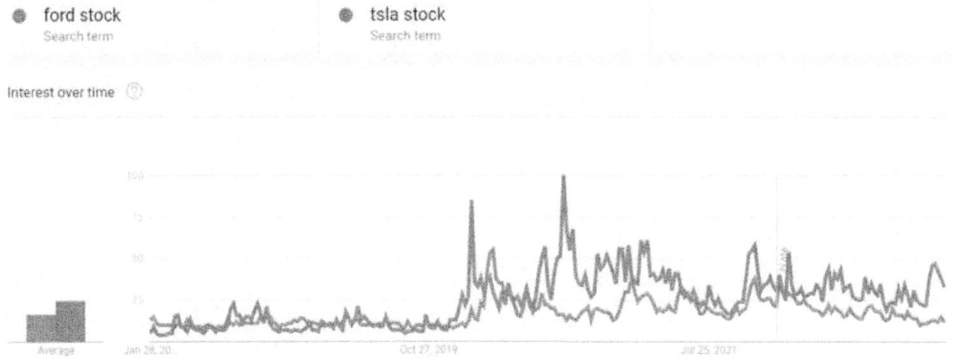

From a trading point of view, here's what I see on the daily chart.

Ford daily chart back to the start of 2020

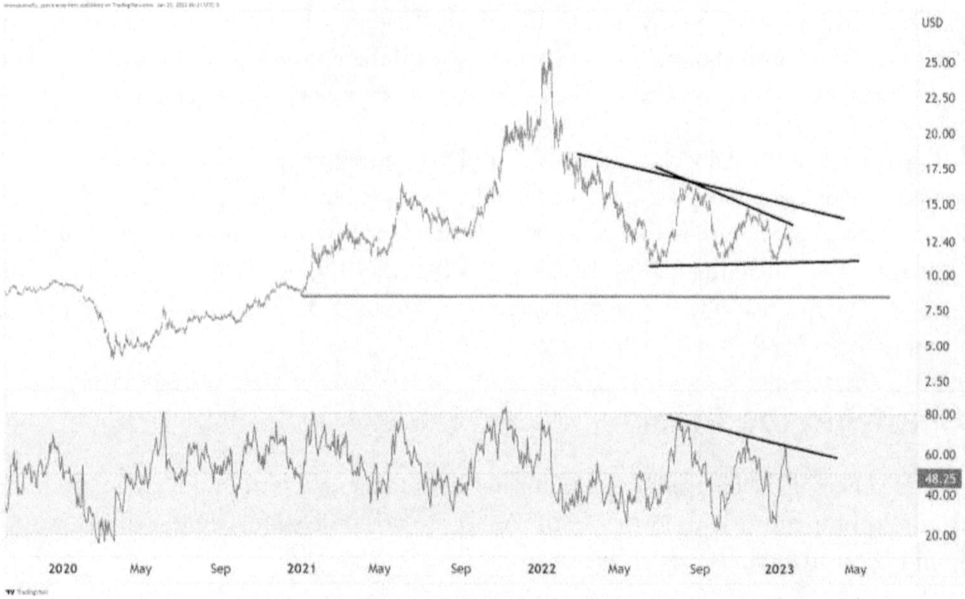

The daily chart is tracing out a series of triangles with each subsquent high weaker than the last. You can see this pattern of weakening rallies in two ways. 1) The bounces are not getting back up to the old declining trendline and 2) the RSI is making a series of lower highs. This gives us a clear exit because if F goes back above the November high (14.70), the idea is wrong.

If we zoom in, the chart looks like this:

Ford hourly chart back to the start of November 2022

The gap on the TSLA news gives us a nice nearby resistance at 13.40, followed by the down trend line at 13.50. In conjunction with the daily chart, we can put our stop at 15.26 and that's well above all the resistance on both the hourly and daily charts. A much tighter stop at 14.06 is probably reasonable, too, if you want more leverage.

Looking back at the daily chart, the full round trip of the move that started in early 2021 would take us back to 8.00 and this is a good take profit area. For this trade, we'll put the TP at 9.03 to get ahead of that noisy $8/$9 launch area where Ford made a major base in January 2021. Risking 2.77 to make 3.43 (off $12.60). Like I said, you could also put your stop at 14.06 and then you are risking 1.57 to make 3.43 but I will err on the side of more room here.

Clarifying the thesis

The idea here is that a major competitor has initiated a price war and the obvious trade is to sell competitors with low margins. As we are not professional auto analysts, we are jumping on an obvious catalyst because:

- The stock hasn't moved that much since news came out and the narrative that Ford is in trouble is not in the market. If Ford was at $10.50 and there were tons of articles about Ford margins collapsing, then we are in the *bad kind of obvious trade* where everyone is already involved. What you want are trades that are seemingly obvious, but not yet fully subscribed. This looks to me to be one of those.
- There is a clear stop loss. We are not saying Ford is doomed and we will keep selling the stock no matter where it goes. We are saying, this looks like obvious bad news for Ford that is not fully priced in. If we are correct, Ford should not go above 15.00. If it does, the thesis is wrong and we get out. The huge triangle and gap lower on the news makes the trade easy to risk manage. If we break above the triangle and the prior highs, the idea is wrong.
- The chart supports the idea. The hourly RSI was mega overbought (above 80) when the TSLA news came out and we are down just a buck. Each rally is weaker than the last as measured by the trendline and the RSI.

I said in the intro that I'm squaring up the TSLA long idea from Week 40. Why not keep the TSLA long trade and do the RV trade of long TSLA/short Ford? There are two main reasons:

1. TSLA earnings on Wednesday, January 25 is a coin toss. I don't have a strong view on which way those results will lean. It will likely be an extremely volatile and (to me) totally random move. You don't want to hold stuff through huge, random gaps.

2. It's not obvious that price wars are bullish TSLA. The market has taken Tesla higher since the news, but much of it has been an all-out squeezefest of anything the market was short. Stocks like BBBY, CVNA, MSTR and TSLA were all much hated and have been the leaders on this rally. Falling deliveries leading to massive price cuts and a price war is not clearly bullish TSLA.

Conclusion

There is nothing wrong with obvious trades. You can use a common sense observation as a starting point for a trade idea and then dig deeper into other factors such as sentiment, chart patterns, and price momentum to figure out whether or not the obvious thing you've observed is priced in.

When the obvious thing is: "WFH is going to change the world!" and WFH stocks have already quadrupled, be careful. When the obvious thing is "Price wars are bad for Ford because it was perceived as a leader in the EV market" and Ford is down a buck since the news, it's reasonable to think about getting short. The biggest risk to this trade is simply a broad stock market rally, of course. But at SPX 4000 I think market risks are pretty balanced.

Week 43: Flipper

Flexible and open-minded is best mindset for short-term traders

Update on previous trades

Week 37: XOM put spread is quiet but losing as China reflation helps oil.

Week 38: Sell vol in MSTR has been good so far.

Week 39: Sell 2-month USDJPY and buy 6-month USDJPY. This has been a good idea so far. USDJPY is unchanged.

Week 40 and 41: Took profit on long TSLA. Missed a huge move after earnings, but that's going to happen sometimes when you reduce risk ahead of a major event. The original take profit of $159 traded the day after I squared up.

Week 42: Ford a bit higher since we went short, but they cut prices this morning, which is positive reinforcement for the thesis and will hopefully cap the stock.

Flipper

Before we get started, here's a nice introductory quote from Alex Barrow of MacroOps[72] as he dissects what makes Stan Druckenmiller so successful:

> When you study Druckenmiller you get the sense that he was built in a laboratory, deep in a jungle somewhere, where he was put together piece by piece to create the perfect trader. Every character trait that makes up a good speculator, Druck possesses in spades... things like:
>
> Mental flexibility
>
> Independent thinking
>
> Extreme competitiveness
>
> Tireless inquisitiveness
>
> Deep self-awareness

Today, I'm going to talk about that first bullet point. Mental flexibility.

When I worked at various banks, we often went to visit the largest hedge funds in the world, because they were our clients. Generally, I would meet with senior portfolio managers (PMs), the guys who were one step below the founder. A question I liked to ask these PMs when I was in my 30s was:

"Why do you think —blank— is such a successful trader?"

This would be in reference to the big name on the fund, one of the most famous traders in the world in almost every case. The answer was always strikingly similar. Something like:

"He's flexible. He's not married to one view. We have our morning meeting and he gets on there and tells everyone all the reasons he's short corn futures or whatever and then at the end of the day I look at the position report and see he's flipped! He's long corn and confident it's going higher. I ask him why and he'll say something like 'I changed my mind.' And then he'll go through all the reasons he flipped. And he'll make money on the short, and the long."

This is the epitome of excellent short-term trading. And it's also why you should never trade someone else's view.

---

[72] https://macro-ops.com/lessons-from-a-trading-great-stanley-druckenmiller/

Trade your own view. If you trade someone else's idea, you will inevitably do everything wrong. You will stop out at the wrong levels because your conviction will not be high when the trade goes against you. Also, if you are trading someone else's view, you might not know when their view changes. Frequently you will hear someone moaning about someone else's idea they followed and then have insult added to injury as they find out the original trader exited long ago or even flipped her position.

Successful traders do their own work and come to their own conclusions.

Intellectual flexibility is important because it's the ultimate antidote to many forms of bias. Confirmation and extrapolation bias tend to be more problematic for those with rigid views, for example.

Rigid intellectual approaches are just as bad as rigid views. You don't want to be a reflexive contrarian nor do you want to follow every trend. You want to have an open-minded approach that invites new information and debate and ultimately seeks the correct answer, not a conclusion that fits to a particular trading strategy.

Intellectual flexibility keeps you from sticking to the same technique or tactics all the time. In some markets, breakout trading works, and in some, it doesn't. If you're just a breakout trader, you're going to bleed and leak during all low-vol periods. Better to be a trader that seeks to do what will make money, not a trader that has a rigid preference for a single approach.

Intellectual flexibility and adaptation to the current regime are the essence of excellent trading.

> *"A foolish consistency is the hobgoblin of little minds, adored by little statesmen and philosophers and divines. With consistency a great soul has simply nothing to do. He may as well concern himself with his shadow on the wall. Speak what you think now in hard words, and to-morrow speak what to-morrow thinks in hard words again, though it contradict every thing you said to-day. — 'Ah, so you shall be sure to be misunderstood.' — Is it so bad, then, to be misunderstood? Pythagoras was misunderstood, and Socrates, and Jesus, and Luther, and Copernicus, and Galileo, and Newton, and every pure and wise spirit that ever took flesh. To be great is to be misunderstood."*
>
> *- Ralph Waldo Emerson*

Strong opinions, weakly held

"Strong opinions, weakly held", is a framework for thinking developed by technology forecaster and Stanford Scholar Paul Saffo. Here is his description[73] of how to think:

> *Allow your intuition to guide you to a conclusion, no matter how imperfect — this is the "strong opinion" part. Then – and this is the "weakly held" part – prove yourself wrong. Engage in creative doubt. Look for information that doesn't fit, or indicators that point in an entirely different direction. Eventually your intuition will kick in and a new hypothesis will emerge out of the rubble, ready to be ruthlessly torn apart once again. You will be surprised by how quickly the sequence of faulty forecasts will deliver you to a useful result.*

There is a risk to this framework: You become an erratic, overtrading lunatic as you change your mind every 14 seconds. Your changes of mind must be triggered not by the direction of the prevailing winds outside or by the vagaries of your mood on any given day. Your changes of mind must be driven by facts. As new information comes in, you revise your view and when the new bullish information has overwhelmed the old bearish information, you flip.

Like I said, it's a fine line. You can be too rigid. Or you can be an overtrading flip-flopper. You need to find the middle ground.

As with many aspects of trading, if you collect detailed data about your trades, you will quickly find out whether you are appropriately flexible. First, look at all the positions you took in the past year in every market. Are there markets where your ratio of long to short is heavily skewed? If you went long TSLA 14 times last year and short 3 times, you are probably biased. You are either biased to like the company, or you are biased to mean reversion and buying dips and kept trying to pick a bottom all the way down.

If you trade intraday, do you ever take the opposite position in the same market in the same day? If you do, does the flipper make money? These are the kinds of questions you should be asking as you collect more and more data about your trading. Very often your trading data will tell you many things you already knew. But it will also tell you a few snippets that can be revelatory and game-changing for your P&L.

Short TSLA

I spent Week 40 and Week 41 talking about long TSLA, and why it made sense to add to the position. It was a perfect confluence of a historically oversold setup right at the

---

[73] https://www.saffo.com/02008/07/26/strong-opinions-weakly-held/

turn of the year when tax loss selling was destined to abate. The stock has since rallied from $113 to $179 despite weaker-than-expected deliveries and massive price cuts.

Now, the stock is overbought, and approaching major overhead resistance just as the broad market has exploded higher, wiping out bearish sentiment at the turn of the year and installing a consensus soft landing, everything-gonna-be-alright narrative.

Meanwhile, TSLAs margins are contracting, competition in the EV market has exploded, the Musk factor has become a negative for the brand as its left-leaning consumer base becomes more aggravated by Musk's alt-right dog whistles on Twitter, Musk refuses to hire a new CEO for Twitter (so far, anyway), etc. This is to say, not all is rainbows and lollipops for Tesla. Many of the reasons the stock collapsed in 2022 are still valid and the competitive landscape is getting worse, not better.

Furthermore, my view on macro in 2023 is that we will see more mean reversion and questioning of narratives as the market is in an extremely confused and probabilistic mode as players weigh the five main outcomes for the US economy.

1. No landing
2. Soft landing
3. Recession lite
4. Hard landing
5. Crash landing

I am not a believer in using valuation to trade stocks (I think it's mostly useless) but here's a link to a recent TSLA valuation[74] from the DCF GOAT for your reading pleasure. And here's the chart:

TSLA hourly chart with RSI and distance from 100-hour moving average

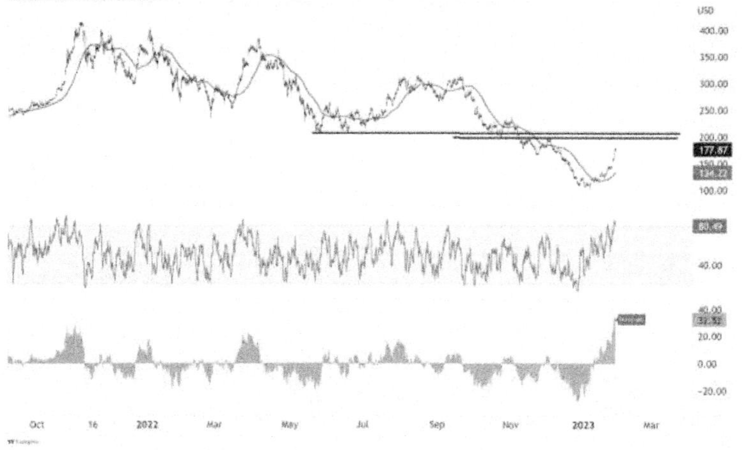

---

[74] https://aswathdamodaran.blogspot.com/2023/01/tesla-in-2023-return-to-reality-start.html

Quite a lot to chew on here.

1. TSLA is approaching massive horizontal line resistance at 200/206. You can read more about horizontal lines in Week 25. In this case, the $206 major support from May/June 2022 becomes major resistance and the $200 level (which was support in October 2022, then resistance (twice) in November and December 2022) is also major resistance. Two major resistance points within six bucks of one another is meaningful.
2. Hourly RSI is above 80. This is not ALL THAT uncommon as you can see this is about the 10th time it's happened in the past year. Still, the risk of a pullback is higher here than it would be normally.
3. TSLA is trading 32.5% above its 100-hour MA (see bottom panel of chart). In the epic selloff, we got to 27% below the 100-hour and you can see anything more than 20% is epic.

So to summarize:

- Massive short squeeze off record oversold levels in late December.
- Tax loss selling ends and the macro story flips from a consensus recession view in December to a consensus soft landing view in January.
- Every most-hated asset has ripped (crypto, TSLA, MSTR, CVNA, etc.)
- TSLA is now extremely overbought.
- Massive overhead resistance at $200/$206 gives us an easy risk management trigger and stop loss level.

So, 50in50 goes short TSLA here (178) with a stop loss at 221 (enough to give a bit of room for a false break of 200/206). The target is major support in the 110/120 area so the take profit is 117.77. Risking 43 to make 68. Note these are levels when I'm writing this thing.

NOTE: As I finish writing this; TSLA just dumped on the open and it's trading at170.50. I will always mark the entry point to market when I hit send and that is the price I will use for P&L tracking. Obviously selling at 170.50 is not as good as selling at 178. If I were doing this trade in real life I would probably wait and sell into 175/178 on a rally but for the purpose of tracking this exercise, 50in50 goes short when I hit send to keep things simple.

I thought about trying to thread the needle by selling closer to $200, but with all the central bank meetings and nonfarm payrolls this week, I think the risk is that risky assets reprice lower and so I would rather just put the trade on here.

The biggest risks to this trade are:

- Musk hires a new CEO for Twitter.
- The Fed is dovish.

- NFP and AHE come in on the weak, but not too weak side and Goldilocks takes the market higher.

Conclusion

The best traders in the world are flexible. They are not always long certain currencies or short other markets or religiously married to specific assets. They do whatever they think is going to make money and they are able to override confirmation bias, extrapolation bias, FOMO, and other trader kryptonite as they rationally assess future probabilities.

I loved TSLA at 113 in December and I hate it at 178 in January. This is perfectly rational. If you love Elon Musk, or hate Elon Musk, don't trade TSLA stock. Always be open to trading any security from the long or short side. If you can't, take that security off your list of permitted products.

Week 44: Back on the horse

Is it OK to get back into a trade after you were stopped out?

Update on previous trades

Week 37: XOM put spread is doing nada.

Week 38: Sell vol in MSTR has been good so far.

Week 39: Sell 2-month USDJPY and buy 6-month USDJPY. This has been a good idea so far. USDJPY is tiny higher vs. entry point, which is fine.

Week 42: Ford is about unchanged but you had to stomach a huge rally to 14.60.

Week 43: Short TSLA is perilously close to the stop loss.

Back on the horse

One of the great contradictions of trading is that in order to succeed you must have incredible grit and staying power. You must subscribe to the Japanese proverb: "*Nana korobi, ya oki*" which means "Fall down seven times, stand up eight." You must never give up!

But then again, good traders give up all the time. Super fast. On losing trades. You need to be able to ruthlessly cut your losers without much thought or remorse. This is kind of the opposite of grit or determination or any of those great human characteristics. How can a single person embody grit and tenacity at the same time they are willing to cut losing trades without a second thought?

This is one of the many contradictions that make it very hard to nail down the archetypal trader characteristics. You need to love risk, but be super disciplined. You need to have high confidence in yourself, but show humility to the markets. You need to hold onto risky trades when you are feeling incredibly uncomfortable, but simultaneously cut your losers early. Paradox City.

This piece is in response to three questions I am very often asked by younger traders: "Is it OK to get back into a position after you have been stopped out? Is it OK to add to a losing position? Is it OK to move your stop loss on a losing position?" My answer to all three is mostly "NO!" But there are times when these three normally-destructive behaviors can be appropriate.

If you do any of these things frequently, you will not succeed as a trader.

If you do them once in a while because the situation rationally calls for it, you'll be fine.

Self-awareness is the key to everything

The best antidote to almost every psychological problem in trading is self-awareness. I know I have bad discipline. I know when I'm trading for fun and not for profit. I know when I am bullish and short at the same time (and yes, this happens once in a while!). You can't stop every dumb monkey brain action before it happens, but you can at a minimum step outside yourself and catch yourself doing dumb stuff and course-correct afterward.

This is relevant to today's questions because if you are going to re-enter a trade after being stopped out, or move your stop, or add to a loser, you need to be self-aware. Here are my three rules for these situations.

1: Check your mood meter

Has enough time elapsed that you are no longer emotionally impacted by the stop-out? Is there any emotional valence to the trade at all?

If you walk in at 7 am and see that you got stopped out of your long TY futures at the exact low while you were asleep and now TY is trading 24 ticks higher and you are screaming at your broker and just smashed a handset over the desk and your assistant is picking up black pieces of broken plastic all around your feet… Don't get back into the trade.

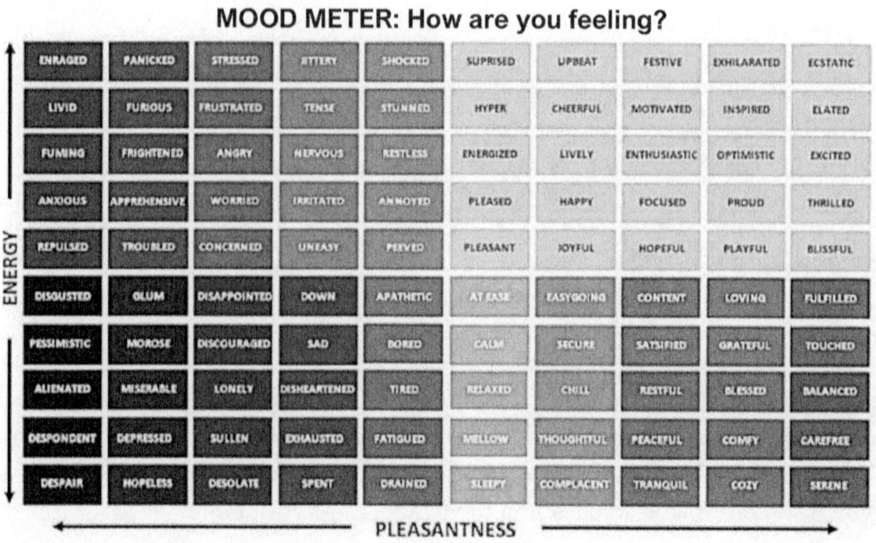

Emotions have a half-life. This is an extremely important idea in trading, and outside trading. I wish someone had taught me this when I was in my 20s. However angry you are about something right now, you will be less angry in two hours. You will be much less angry in 24 hours. This is empirically true.

This is why common sense says never to send an angry email right away. Wait until tomorrow and see if you are still angry. Then send it.

Studies show this consistently and if you think about your own life, you will probably realize that very few emotions stay around very long.

Here's the result of one study, to give you the gist. Don't worry about the exact numbers. The point is that we are in a permanent state of emotional flux. Emotions come in; emotions go out

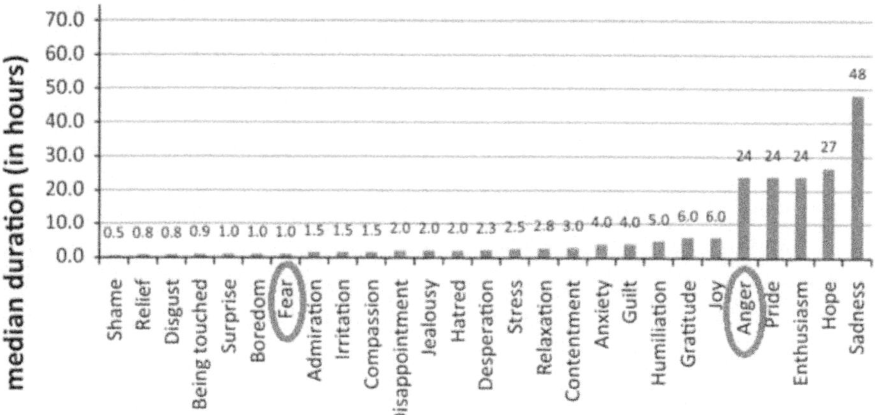

This article takes it to an extreme with this explanation[75]:

> "Feelings are like ocean waves," says psychologist Alyson Stone, "they rise, crest and recede, all day long." We can all relate. But according to brain scientist Dr. Jill Bolte Taylor, these waves last just 90 seconds. After that, we're simply re-stimulating our internal circuitry.
>
> Explains Taylor: "When a person has a reaction to something in their environment, there's a 90-second chemical process that happens in the body; after that, any remaining emotional response is just the person choosing to stay in that emotional loop."

Again, whether an emotion affects you for 90 seconds or 4 hours isn't the point here. The point is that emotions come in and go out like waves. You don't want to make trading decisions when you have just been hit by a wave and you are spinning around underwater and you just scraped your forehead on the hard ocean-bottom sand.

So the first rule of putting back on a position after getting stopped out, moving your stop loss, or adding to a losing position is: Wait until you are unemotional about it.

For me, that cooling-off period is usually one day. When I was in my 20s, I might get stopped out at the lows in EURUSD, then it would bounce 20 pips and I'm like: "Dammit! That was the low! Get me back in!" See all those exclamation points? Those are bad. Those mean I was all emotional about the situation. Guess what happened every time? Stopped out again, rebuy, stopped out again, etc.

Or I would see USDJPY ripping and move my stop and move it again and then move it again to the point where the risk/reward on half my trades was worse than 1:1.

Re-entering a position right after stopping out, then setting a new, lower sell stop is the equivalent of moving your stop down. Actually, it's worse, because you probably incurred some extra slippage in all that frustrated buying and selling.

Moving your stop repeatedly or stopping out and re-entering intraday are kryptonite. Same thing with adding to losers. You will never succeed in trading if you do any of this with any regularity.

So to simply state the rule.

RULE 1: If stopped out of trade today, do not touch again until tomorrow. Do not enter a trade and then move the stop or add when it's losing money on the same day you got in.

---

[75] http://thedanielislandnews.com/opinions/how-90-second-rule-can-change-your-life

I am always checking my mood meter. Am I pissed and bursting with FOMO? Or just calmly reassessing the probabilities? Remember, of course, these are rules for me. Your rules should relate to your trading style, time horizon, personality, strengths, and weaknesses.

2: Don't get married to a view

You can't keep going back to the same idea over and over again, no matter how much you believe in it. Even if you're calm about it. This will eventually lead to a terrible psychological state where you are paralyzed by the fear of missing the trade when it finally happens.

When I was trading in 2007, my boss (who is one of the best people I have ever known on or off Wall Street) was convinced that AUDJPY was going to collapse. This was a logical thesis! The carry trade was a mania by that point and huge hedge funds were long billions of AUDJPY and USDJPY and selling JPY puts at the same time to extract even more carry from the trade.

Here is a chart of AUDJPY.

AUDJPY weekly, mid-2005 to late 2007

Every time it dipped, my boss thought the big one was coming and added to his shorts at the lows. By mid-2007, as you might guess, his P&L was not very good. Trading FX on a bank desk, you are expected to be flexible and able to make money in various regimes. You can't sit there positioned the same way all the time, waiting for the big one.

Sadly, he lost his job at the end of 2007. He is one of the nicest people in the market and he's an excellent trader, he just got dialed into a particular view and couldn't shake it.

Wanna guess what that chart looks like if we jump forward one year?

AUDJPY weekly, 2006 to end of 2008

Look at the y-axis! AUDJPY dropped more than 40% in less than a year. Mind-boggling moves, but my boss was not there to participate because the move took too long to happen. The problem with short-term traders who get addicted to a single view is that it very often doesn't matter whether the view is right or wrong. After enough tries and failures, those traders become terrified of missing the big one and so they trade the view in a highly suboptimal way.

The best way to trade is always to have the flexibility to trade a market from the long or the short side. Even if you are super bearish bigger picture, you should be able to recognize times when you are wrong on the relevant (shorter) time frame and go long because you know the asset is going to go up, not down for a while. You can't just keep going short the same asset over and over and hope the timing works out. It rarely does.

If you are so locked into a view that you cannot shake it… Stop trading that asset and find something else to trade where you can maintain an open mind. Rigid views are rife with confirmation bias and FOMO and don't allow a rational interpretation of new inbound information.

RULE 2: Don't try the same trade more than three times.

Again, this rule is for me. If you have a different style or time horizon, it might not be right for you. Feel free to stick with the same view over and over if it's making you money. But the whole point of a stop loss and risk management system is to acknowledge the fact that no matter how confident you are, you will still be wrong.

Treat your market views like short-term relationships, not marriage. You do your best while you are in the view but you stay open to the idea that it might not work out. Stopping out of a marriage is way too hard. You have too much emotional investment. You do not want to be emotionally invested in any trade. You want to see it through rational eyes. You want to monetize it or cut it, and move on.

If you get stopped out two or three times, put that market in the penalty box for a few months and find something else to trade.

3: Consider options

For trades where you believe strongly in the idea but fear you might keep getting jiggled or stopped out, or you're not sure where to put your stop... Use options. I have written a fair bit in 50in50 about the choice between cash and options. It is a critical choice in some cases because options give you staying power and noise-resistance. But you pay a price for that. You still need good timing, and if the thing doesn't move at all, you lose money in options when you would have broken even in cash.

RULE 3: If you are worried about noise and repeated stop outs, use options.

Cash vs. options is a huge and important topic but I am not going to get into it here. But if I love a trade and get stopped out and still love it, my first thought will usually be to consider putting on the trade in options to avoid the chop. You can read more about cash vs. options in 50in50 Week 6: Options or Cash? If you are new here, I recommend that chapter—it was one of the most educational.

TSLA is a Tubthumper

Tesla gets knocked down, but it gets up again.

In Week 43, 50in50 went short TSLA at 171 with a stop at 221. While the trade has not been stopped out yet, it has moved 43/50ths of the way from entry to the stop loss. I actually like the idea more than I did when I first put it on, and the rally has been dramatic.

In this case, I am not re-entering a position after being stopped out. I am re-evaluating my parameters because I like the trade more than ever and my stop is within a random blip of getting done. So I plan to increase my position and move the stop at the same time.

I want to reiterate here: This is an extremely dangerous habit! Do it rarely or never. And only do it if you believe in your own self-awareness and ability to think rationally in the face of escalating losses. Part of me thinks I shouldn't have even written this piece because I'm giving a green light to do something that often ends up catastrophic when repeated.

But I think it's important to explain that constant reassessment of the probabilities through the prism of a rational mind can bring clarity that can sometimes extricate you from a badly timed, but good idea. You don't want to do this often, but you want to have it in your playbook for the rare times it's appropriate.

In this case, I am going to calmly and rationally move my stop loss and double my risk because I think the trade has high expected value despite my initial entry being mistimed.

There are four main reasons:

First, NASDAQ seasonality turns bearish today. Seasonals are never the be-all end-all but they are a useful tool in a holistic trader's toolkit. There are myriad reasons for persistent seasonality in equities and we are about to enter a period where bullish bonus inflows and new year 401k allocations run out but before bullish mid-March tax refunds start rolling in. The chart looks like this:

TSLA seasonality looks similar but I have not included it because the sample size is much smaller (TSLA stock has only been around for 12 years).

Second, 2023 has been characterized by aggressive buying focused on the most injured stocks from 2022. This is a combination of a seller's strike (end of 2022 was all about tech fund redemptions and tax loss selling and that selling stopped 31DEC22) and rebound in everything most hated from 2022.

This chart from Macro Alf[76] captures it perfectly:

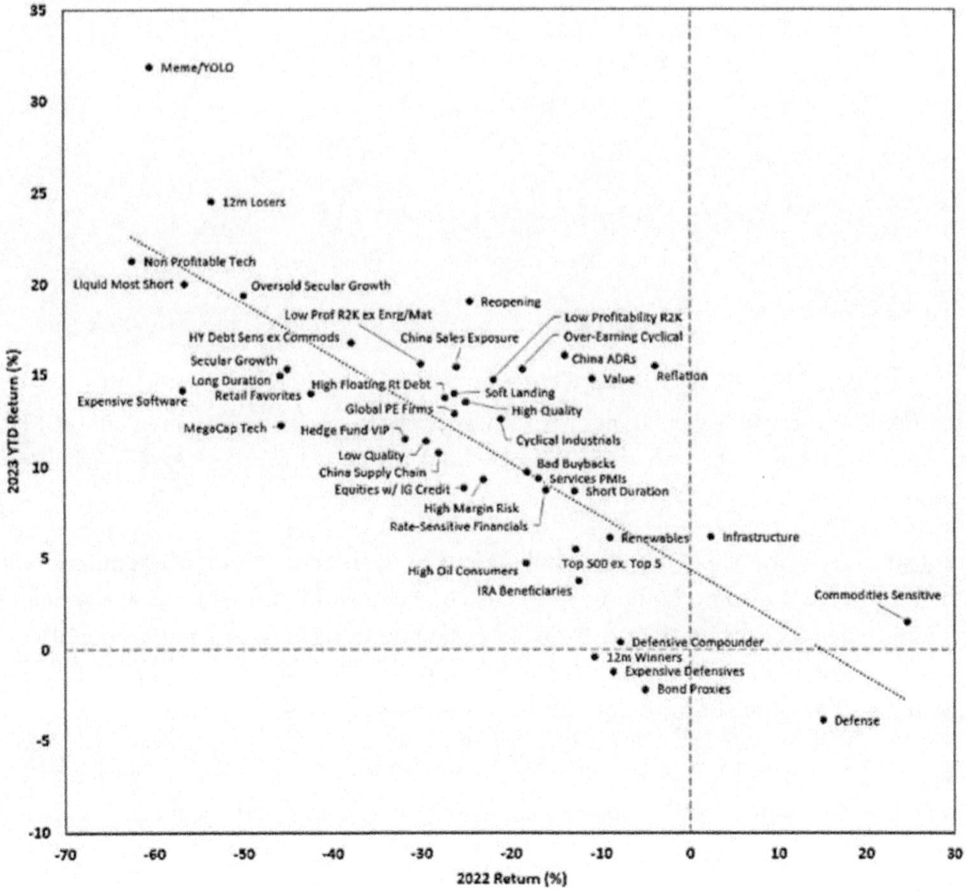

2023 has mostly been about unwinding the extreme panic selling from late 2022.

Third, US yields have risen dramatically of late, and once again long duration assets like TSLA are slow to react. Here is a chart of the US 10-year yield (inverted) against Tesla.

76 https://twitter.com/MacroAlf/status/1624898894361681920?s=20

US 10-year yield (inverted, line) vs. TSLA (bars)

Notice how every time yields go up, TSLA hangs around for a while, or even rallies? Then, eventually, there is the "oh sh*t" moment and TSLA craps out. I eagerly await that moment!

Fourth and finally, one of the TSLA bull narratives has been that Elon Musk might return home to TSLA at some point as he gets bored of spending time in the weeds helping Twitter engineers debug the platform. Now he says he's going to hang around Twitter until the end of 2023[77]. Sure, much of what Musk says is unserious or outright false, but these headlines don't inspire a lot of hope for immediate succession plans.

Big resistance is at $237 so I think a stop above $250 offers plenty of room for a bit of noise. If this position gets stopped out, I will not go short Tesla again for at least six months.

Conclusion

A lot has changed, even as TSLA rallied over the past two weeks. Seasonality turns bearish today, the shorts are impaled, US yields are higher, and the CEO change promised by Musk in 2022 might not happen until 2024. So while the backdrop for TSLA has gotten worse, the price has gone up as shorts continue panic covering. That panic covering should be done or close to done.

[77] https://www.usatoday.com/story/tech/2023/02/15/elon-musk-twitter-ceo-replacement/11265479002/

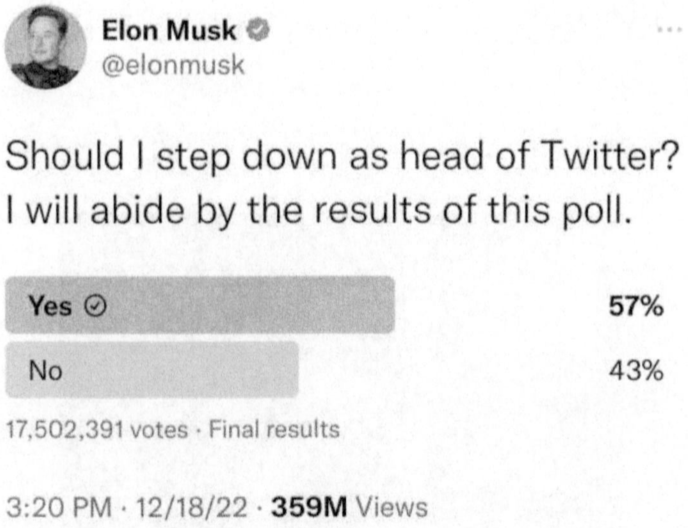

Technically, he probably wasn't lying because he will abide by the results of the poll at some point maybe late 2023 or 2024.

While adding to losers and moving stop losses is generally what bad traders do all the time, good traders also do it on occasion if they are rational and new information compels them to do so. I have no strong emotions here. I was long TSLA at 114 and I went short at 171. I'm flexible. I am neutral on Elon Musk one way or the other. He's smart, he's entertaining and he does a lot of really dumb stuff. So I have no emotional attachment to him, the stock, or this trade.

I looked at options but found them too expensive. So, I am adding a new trade of short TSLA on the open 16FEB23 and I will put the stop loss on the whole double position at $251.11. This means the original position has really bad risk/reward now in hindsight—but that's life.

Sometimes you have to react to new information.

The original trade was risking $2,000 on a move from 171 to 221 so moving the stop to 251 adds another $1,200 of risk there and we risk $2,000 on this new clip so the total risk on this idea ends up being

$2,000 (original idea) + $1,200 (moved stop) + $2,000 (adding here) = $5,200.

Week 45: Regime Flux

Adapt to (and predict) market regime change

Update on previous trades

Week 37: XOM put spread is doing nada.

Week 38: Sell vol in MSTR has been good so far.

Week 39: Sell 2-month USDJPY and buy 6-month USDJPY. This has been a good idea so far. USDJPY is higher vs. entry point, which is fine.

Week 42: Ford is about unchanged. It's flying around.

Week 43 and 44: Short TSLA doing better but not great.

Regime Flux

In Week 18, I wrote about Macroeconomic regimes. Specifically how to identify and trade them. This week, let's talk some more about macroeconomic regimes but also get into volatility and trend vs. rangebound.

Knowing what volatility and trend regime you're in is an absolutely critical concept and I don't know why I waited until Week 45 to write about it. Excellent traders are highly adaptable, understand the current trading regime, and have one eye on the horizon for regime change.

One of the reasons the markets are not yet completely dominated by computers and the big reason that humans still exist on market-making desks at banks is that algos are not great at detecting and switching regimes, especially when a regime arrives that is not highly similar to something in the algorithm's history or playbook.

The day EURCHF dropped from 1.2000 to 0.8500 as the Swiss National Bank executed the craziest rug pull in FX history, I can guarantee you that there was not a single algorithm in the world that was programmed for that. The algos holstered their lasers and hid under the desk, leaving the humans alone to fight it out with cudgels, maces, and hand axes.

The primary trading regimes

You can usually put an X in this diagram to identify the primary regime.

		Trend		
		Rangebound	Trending	Megatrend
Volatility	Low			
	Normal			
	High			
	Crisis			

There are other features that define a trading regime, particularly liquidity, correlation, and positioning, but those tend to be outputs of the primary regime as determined by the grid.

For example, correlation is usually high and liquidity is low in times of raging volatility or crisis. Correlation is lower in quiet markets. Positioning gets increasingly extreme during trends and megatrends and is less prone to extreme readings when things are rangebound. And so on. This is not always true, but it's mostly true enough.

Let's talk about trend first, then volatility. About a third of this week's lesson is excerpted from *Alpha Trader*.

Rangebound vs. Trending

The main distinction to make here is rangebound vs. trending, but it's useful to have a third category called "megatrend." I will discuss megatrends a bit later.

Rangebound markets favor mean reversion strategies (buy low/sell high) while trending markets favor breakout or "go with" strategies (buy high/sell higher). You should always have a good sense of whether each market you trade is trending, rangebound, or neither. You can still trade mean reversion in trending markets but you should be cognizant of what you're doing.

It is usually straightforward to figure out whether a market has been trending or rangebound. Start by looking at the chart and making a subjective, common-sense assessment. Sometimes a rangebound or trending market is easy to identify at a glance. The harder part is identifying when the market is transitioning from one to the other.

Another simple way to identify the range or trend status of a market (and a possible change) is with technical analysis tools. I prefer simple technical analysis to more esoteric methods, so here are a few simple approaches to gauge whether a market is rangebound or trending (note that this methodology is suited to short-term trading with a 1-hour to 5-day time horizon).

1. Has the price made a new 20-day high or low in the last ten days? If yes, it is trending that way; if no, rangebound.
2. Put a 100-HOUR and 200-HOUR moving average on an hourly chart and look at this matrix:

	100-HOUR above 200-HOUR	**100-HOUR below 200-HOUR**
Price of asset above both 100-HOUR and 200-HOUR	**UP TREND**	Range
Price of asset between the 100-HOUR and 200-HOUR	Range	Range
Price of asset below both 100-HOUR and 200-HOUR	Range	**DOWN TREND**

You can substitute different moving averages depending on what you find generally fits the trend of the product and the time frame you trade. If you are trading a longer time horizon you can also put three moving averages on your daily chart. Say, 20, 50, and 100-day moving averages. When they are in order it is a trend (**20 > 50 > 100** = uptrend or **20 < 50 < 100** = downtrend). When they are not in order, there is no trend or the trend is weak.

3. Eyeball it. This sounds kind of stupid but generally, no advanced mathematics degree is required to determine if a market is trending or rangebound. Often a cursory glance at a chart (or your experience sitting there trading the market for the past month or two) reveals the type of regime.

It's not difficult to figure out if you are in a range or trend regime, but the challenge is to trade appropriately and to figure out when the regime is changing. Assume trends and ranges are somewhat persistent and wait for evidence of a regime shift before altering your approach. It is better to wait for a signal to tell you the regime has changed than to try to anticipate or front-run that regime change.

Volatility, liquidity, and trend are the three features you should always be able to describe with confidence for each market you trade. You should always know where volatility is relative to recent history, whether liquidity is good, bad, or ugly, and whether your market is in a trend or a range. If you update your view of these three variables daily, you will adapt in real time better than most of your competitors.

Megatrends

In megatrends, markets will behave differently from regular trends. For example, in megatrends positioning can often be less important or even irrelevant in the early innings because the driver of the megatrend (usually a major central bank action) is bigger than all spec activity combined.

Examples of megatrends are: The Global Financial Crisis, Abenomics, and FiscalFest 2021. It didn't matter that everyone was short stocks in 2008 because the guano was hitting the fan with so much speed that forced asset liquidations dwarfed any speculative activity.

During megatrends, you need to run a different playbook and be much less willing to fade and trade mean reversion. Think of megatrends as an exceptional regime that comes around once every few years at the most in your market. Change your tactics and become less flexible in the early days of a huge trend driven by fresh news.

Realize no trading method works always and forever. No matter how well your methodology works right now, there is a chance it won't work tomorrow. Be vigilant to changes in the market and monitor the success of different trading strategies.

For example, if you notice that breakout trading has not been working for you over the past two years, spend some time thinking about why. Has your methodology changed? Did you stop following your own rules? Or… Are there new algorithms doing the same thing you used to do, but faster? Are the basic breakout trading strategies such common knowledge that they no longer provide any edge? **If everybody is doing the same thing, the odds are low that it will make money.**

I believe that adaptation is one of the keys to survival and professional longevity in almost every industry. A good athlete adapts as her sport changes, just like a good trader adapts as markets change. Be thoughtful about the current environment, how it is changing, and how it might change in the future. Think about how you can adapt your trading to stay ahead.

As Billy Beane says to the aging baseball scout in Moneyball, "Adapt or die."

Volatility

Market professionals call volatility "vol." Vol is a critical part of a market's microstructure. It is the dispersion of returns over time, usually measured as the standard deviation of logarithmic returns. In simple English: How much does the thing move?

Volatility is not constant or static. A currency pair like USDJPY might realize 6% volatility one year and 18% the next. Vol is a key concept to understand and you should always know your product's vol profile, how it has evolved over time, and how it might change in the future.

A few things you need to know about vol:

1. Markets tend to be more volatile around events because equilibrium is a function of all known information, and events introduce new information and upset the equilibrium. For example, overnight vol for AUDUSD might be 8% on a normal day and 20% on the day the Reserve Bank of Australia (RBA) meets. Facebook trades with higher vol on earnings day relative to other days.
2. Volatility within and across markets is correlated. If equity volatility is exploding higher, it is likely that FX, bond market, and commodities volatility will go up too. There is often a single factor driving volatility in capital markets. This can be economic uncertainty, geopolitical drama, or something else. Volatility and uncertainty are usually associated.
3. It is hard to make money trading low-vol markets. Most traders make more money when things are moving. One of the keys to success in trading is identifying the vol regime and adjusting your trading accordingly. You probably won't make money trading breakouts when the VIX is at 11. You probably can't trade mean reversion when the VIX is at 80. My P&L is highly correlated to volatility. If you notice a meaningful drop in volatility in something you trade, consider trading something else or monitor the situation closely and see if your P&L is drifting lower along with vol.

To be 100% clear, when people talk about volatility, they usually mean *historical* volatility, but it is important to understand the two different types:

Historical volatility. This is the dispersion of returns in the past. You can measure it different ways but unless you are an options trader, I wouldn't worry about where the number comes from. Just know that when people say "volatility" they are mostly referring to daily historical or realized volatility. The amount the security has moved around in the past, based on daily data.

Implied volatility. This is the market price for volatility going forward. This measure is used in option pricing, and is a better proxy for future volatility than historical volatility. The distinction is not important here and for the purposes of an exercise like vol-adjusted position sizing, it rarely matters which data you use.

Adapt in real-time to changes in your market's vol

Fast markets are temporary, but changes in volatility can be more permanent. Do you know how to size your risk correctly to reflect current levels of volatility? Does your methodology respond systematically to changes in volatility? It should. For example, higher volatility means you should be trading smaller positions. Lower volatility means larger positions.

Bad traders always put on the same position size.

Many traders are not very good at adjusting their position size and risk management strategies in response to volatility. If S&P futures are moving 1% per day, should you have the same position size or stop loss parameters as if they are moving 3% per day? Clearly, the answer is no. Actively adjust your trading as volatility changes.

The easiest way to volatility-adjust (or vol-adjust, as most professionals say) is to use a spreadsheet that determines position size and stop loss parameters based on a volatility input. This does not have to be complicated.

The figure you use for volatility adjustment will never be perfect because we don't know future volatility until it happens. That said, there are many ways to estimate future volatility, and those estimates will generally be accurate enough for our purposes. For example, this chart shows the VIX on a given day plotted against the percent range in the S&P futures the day after:

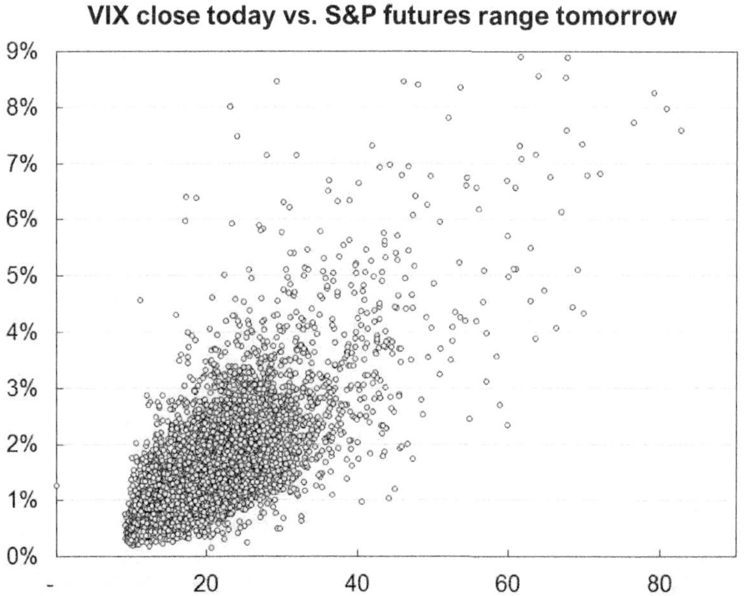

You can see from that plot that tomorrow's range has a strong relationship with today's VIX. The relationship between VIX and S&P ranges is not linear or normal as you see by the many outliers. The point is not to be perfect here.

Here is a simplified but realistic example of how a trader can apply this information and use good thinking to determine position size.

Frank trades only S&P futures and has $1,000,000 in his account. He buys or sells on the open each day and risks 2% of his account ($20,000) on each trade. He does not believe much in technical analysis so he simply sets his stop loss and take profit this way:

> STOP LOSS = (entry level) + (half of one average daily range)
> TAKE PROFIT = 2 * stop loss

In other words, he risks half a day's range to make one day's range. These parameters are not unreasonable and a simple methodology like this will work in real life. The point of the example is to show that changes in volatility should change your sizing and risk management parameters.

Frank looks at yesterday's close in VIX and plugs it into a formula in Excel. Here is Frank's risk in six different volatility regimes:

VIX today	Average Range SPX tomorrow	# of contracts where half day range is $20,000
Under 12	0.5%	23
12 to 15	0.7%	16
16 to 20	1.1%	10
21 to 30	1.6%	7
31 to 40	2.3%	5
above 40	3.9%	3

Assume index at 3500 so 1% = 35 points

35 points X $50 = $1,750

Therefore each 1% move costs $1,750 per contract

You can see here that as volatility rises, Frank takes smaller positions. If he normally trades 50 e-mini contracts and market volatility falls substantially, he will find the volatility of his P&L falls if he doesn't adjust the number of contracts he trades. In contrast, if he sticks with the same number of contracts and the same P&L parameters as volatility rises, he will get stopped out of good trades all the time before they have a chance to work. All other things being equal, the probability that your trade hits its stop loss level is a direct function of volatility.

I cannot emphasize this enough. Your position size should change as volatility changes. This is the easiest and most automatic adaptation you can make as markets change. VIX is the most popular measure of equity market volatility. 10 is very low. 80 is extremely high.

Macroeconomic regimes

You've got your volatility and trend/rangebound regime and then you have your macroeconomic regime. A significant error that specialists and micro traders often make is to know everything about their product (say, BTC or copper, for example) and not enough about macro. Whether or not you nail the supply/demand story for copper or the institutional adoption story for bitcoin doesn't much matter if there are larger macro forces at play.

You always need to know the macro regime and factor that into your analysis so that you know what matters on the structural and cyclical side. The macroeconomic regime also has a strong impact on the trend and volatility regime.

Throughout most of 2020-2022 we were in a unidirectional macro regime where either the tide was coming in due to fiscal and monetary largesse, or it was going out due to Fed tightening. The day Powell dropped "transitory" was a flashing red beacon from the top of macro mountain announcing to everyone below that the game had changed. Here are the main regimes over the last few years.

Regimes since January 2020

		Vol	Trend
JAN2020 to APR2020	COVID panic	Crisis	Yes
APR2020 to NOV2020	Fiscal tsunami and Fed easing	High and falling	Yes
NOV2020 to DEC2021	Vaccine success, spec bubble mania	Average and falling	Yes
JAN2022 to mid-2022	Inflation panic, risk parity demolition, hawkish Fed	Average but rising	Yes
mid-2022 to DEC2022	Peak Fed, peak inflation	Low and falling	No
Late DEC2022 / Early JAN2023	Recession risk is high!	Low	**No**
JAN2023	Soft landing!	Low	
FEB2023	No landing!	Rising but low	
MAR2023	?	Low	

These are my best approximations and there is room for debate around some of the details. The point is, that even without the benefit of hindsight, it was pretty easy to say we were in a good regime for trend following in 2020, 2021, and much of 2022 and if you followed a simple macro framework you were probably in the right mode most of the time.

Now, we're changing macro regimes every four weeks as everyone toggles within a probabilistic framework and nobody has a clue where the economy or the Fed are going.

What macroeconomic regime are we in now?

Identifying regimes can be a combination of subjective and objective measures and you are not just observing the current regime, you are forecasting the coming regime so that you are ready for it. Your first clue that nobody has a clue right now and we may be in for some rapid regime-switching on the macro side is the number of probabilistic frameworks you see out there right now.

Forecasters and analysts are usually in the chest-pounding deterministic business of making bold predictions but the band of uncertainty around the US economy is so wide that few are making hard predictions. Instead, you see a lot of probabilistic frameworks and such.

The second clue that we may be in an unstable macro regime is that we switch narratives every few weeks. December 2022 the recessionistas were in control then January was soft landing island and February is no landing at all. In such a probabilistic regime, the market jumps on a patch of data and falls victim to extrapolation and recency bias as it assumes a new regime has arrived.

In reality, good macro traders will know it when they see it and right now, nobody is seeing it. That says to me that the recent surge in yields, the USD, and US economic confidence is ripe for mean reversion. The January inflation and jobs data in the US was strong to very strong and that triggered a significant repricing of yields and the USD.

Now, the bar is high for the February data (that comes out in March). Any sign of a return to disinflation or a move toward outright labor market weakness will be a shocker while more inflationary data will probably push yields and the USD a bit higher, but not much.

How to trade it

When looking for mean reversion, you can start with the charts. I have been writing in am/FX[78] over the past few days about mean reversion in the USD as we approached epic levels in USDCNH, AUDUSD, and USDJPY. Here is the chart of USDJPY I published a few days ago, for example:

USDJPY right into the 100-day and 200-day moving average

USDJPY touched the 137 level and then reversed hard down to 135.25. Ideally, you want trades that are easy to risk manage and offer high leverage and when a market goes right into a major tech convergence zone, you can get in with clear knowledge of where you're wrong. Short USDJPY into 137 was an example of that.

[78] https://www.spectramarkets.com/subscribe/

Another dynamic I always look for is whether other markets confirm the move in the market I'm watching. Recently, stocks have sold off and risky currencies like NZD have gone down significantly but volatility has remained low. That's a huge flashing light again. Risky assets falling usually triggers an uptick in volatility and when it doesn't, that's a non-confirmation.

Going forward, I think yields will struggle to make further gains and there is an asymmetry around US data where weak data will matter more than strong data because the market is leaning hard into the "no landing scenario" when the reality is probably closer to a soft landing or something weaker, eventually.

Looking at the charts, and keeping it simple, 5-year and 10-year yields are climbing towards the October 2022 highs but have not yet breached them. I like 5-year yields best for a reversal but generally yields all move together so when you're making directional bets in bonds on an economic data view, the outcome is often not sensitive to the duration you choose. It can matter, but it's rarely the difference between winning and losing.

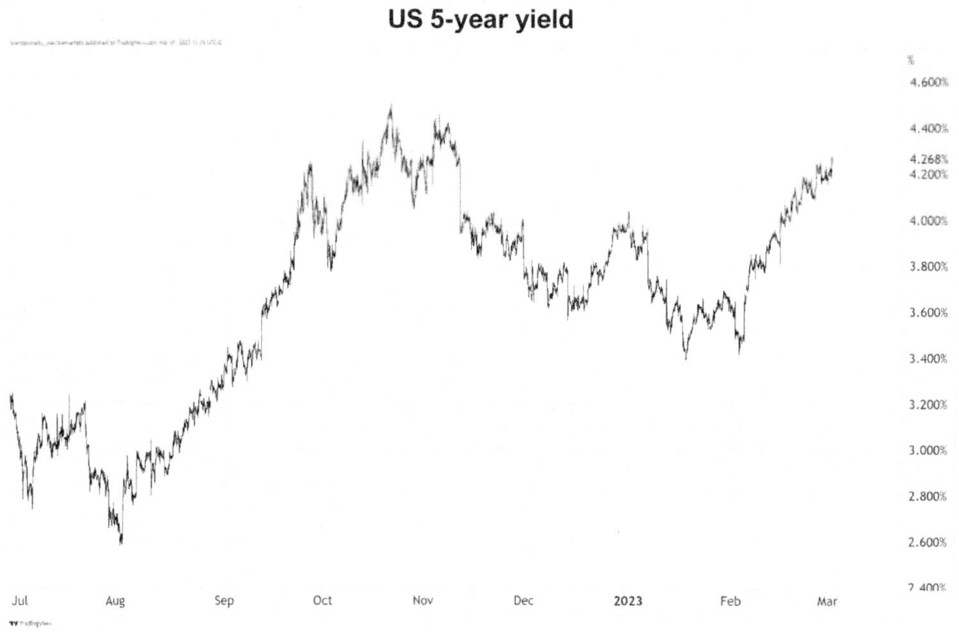

In ETF land, you can pick SHY or IEF or TLT and accomplish similar results. There is important nuance to picking the right duration but for this piece, today, I am ignoring all that and I will go long IEF here (94.80) with a stop loss at 92.44 (which will trigger if the 5-year yield makes a new high). Again, I'm oversimplifying here. You could find smarter ways to play mean reversion in the US economic data but that's not the point of this lesson.

Here, I'm using the simplistic approach. US economic data has overshot and will mean revert and this will trigger a reversion in bond market expectations and push IEF higher. That's the view.

Risking a normal unit of $2,000 on the trade. Take profit at 99.49, risking 2.36 to make 4.69.

Conclusion

You need to know the regime you're in and adapt to new regimes as they arrive. Regime can mean volatility, trend, correlation, macroeconomics, and liquidity. It can also mean other details of how and why markets move.

Bad traders have a single approach to markets and eventually that approach stops working because the market will not cooperate forever. Good traders adapt and do what the market is rewarding.

Week 46: The Evolution of Edge

Keep learning, keep scouring for new ways to win

Charles Darwin trading S&P futures

Update on previous trades

Week 38: The MSTR sell vol idea broke on the final day. MSTR went from 235 to 275 on expiry day and wiped out all the profit on the trade. In real life, we would probably not leave a multi-month trade to the whims of the final day's action. But this is an educational project.

Week 39: Sell 2-month USDJPY and buy 6-month USDJPY. This has been a good idea so far. The 2-month USDJPY put expired worthless (good news) and now we have a June 125.00 USDJPY put. We paid much less than we would have paid otherwise.

Week 42: The Ford short is in the money now.

Week 43 and 44: Short TSLA doing better but not great.

Week 45: The IEF trade worked pretty much instantly and hit the take profit already.

The Evolution of Edge

Edge is fickle and ever-changing. You think you have a trading edge today and then it disappears, almost overnight. AI systems and human intelligence are scouring the data for any edge and whatever you have discovered will not stay in the dark for long.

The best defense against efficient markets is to keep learning, stay curious, and remain humble. Assume your current edge is not permanent and continue to look for other methodologies that will deliver alpha over time.

What is trading edge and where can I find me some?

Markets are incredibly efficient and therefore you need to assume that finding an edge that will deliver alpha in excess of trading costs is close to, but not impossible. When you backtest a system and the returns graph shows a perfect 45-degree angle from the lower left to the upper right… Be skeptical.

On the other hand, thousands of traders make money every year. It is possible, just difficult. The clearer your edge, the more likely that edge is real and sustainable. Here are three examples of edge on the smaller fractals.

- This guy[79] figured out exactly how FTX was rebalancing their perps and was able to trade the predicted rebalancing for a large profit for a long time. This sort of microstructure edge is hard to scale and can be enormously profitable for small traders. Small traders have a huge advantage over large traders because they don't need huge P&L to move the needle. No way a large portfolio manager could do these trades because the P&L would not be big enough and the capacity of the market (liquidity) is not substantial enough.
- Another example of microstructure edge like this is when you are highly-skilled at reading order flow (e.g., NASDAQ Level 2). CanteringClark[80] is known for his microstructure skills in crypto and Michigandolf[81] stands out on the equity side and I recommend them as great follows if you are interested in this sort of edge. They do other stuff worth learning about, too.
- Predicting FX movements around month end is a source of edge. While the month-end patterns in FX have long been studied (I started trading the basic month-end model in 2005), the patterns change and the strategies fail just enough that month-end is never quite free money. This is another fairly micro source of edge. It is also a good example of how the more people know about an edge, the less it works.

---

79 https://twitter.com/adlay_eth/status/1601800521798799361?s=20

80 https://twitter.com/CanteringClark

81 https://twitter.com/TraderadeTweets

Whether you trade at the biggest asset management firm in Midtown Manhattan or out of a spare room in your parent's house in Wichita, Kansas… Trading is an impossibly complex game of imperfect information played by many thousands of technologically-sophisticated and highly-motivated opponents. What is your edge?

Successful traders can clearly and confidently explain their edge.

Do you have enough edge to outperform the market and exceed transaction costs? This is the most important question in trading, especially if you do not work at a bank. Banks have some built-in edge (better information, market-making revenue, best access to liquidity) but if you work at home or at a hedge fund or at an asset management firm… What is your edge? Don't lie to yourself. Think about it and be honest.

Sources of edge

To give you some sense of where the edge has come from over the years, let me go through a quick historical list. The list is meant to get you thinking about your own edge. The point is not to go through the list and pick one. It's a starting point for thinking about and understanding trading edge.

There is a cliché that if you are at a poker table and you don't know who the sucker is… You are the sucker. Similarly, if you are a trader and you do not know what your edge is, you probably don't have an edge. I will focus on sources of edge for human traders and the date ranges I provide are my best estimate of when that source of edge was most prevalent.

Most of these sources of edge still exist, but are greatly diminished from peak. This chronological section on edge is excerpted from *Alpha Trader*.

Trend Following

1984 to 2003

Trend-following systems were the go-to source for human (and computer) alpha in the 1980s and 1990s. Many large trend-following commodity trading advisors (CTAs) extracted meaningful abnormal returns for more than two decades. Returns from trend-following systems have steadily declined over the past 40 years. Many studies cover the slow decline of trend-following performance. This table from a Winton study shows the decline in trend following Sharpe ratios over time.

Performance of trend following strategies across 20 asset classes

	1984-1993	1994-2003	2004-2013
Fast	1.85	0.85	0.00
Medium	1.54	1.18	0.70
Slow	0.95	0.94	0.38

10-year gross Sharpe ratio. Fast: Weekly, Medium: 6-week, Slow: 13-week

This does not show there are now zero profitable trend following strategies, but clearly the edge has dropped over time. This is not a surprise given the proliferation of academic literature on the topic in the 1990s and 2000s. As a strategy becomes well known, its Sharpe ratio grinds towards zero.

Asymmetrical information and lack of transparency

1980 to 1996

Before the internet, markets were opaque and it was hard for those outside financial institutions to get an accurate view of prices. Traders at banks and large investment firms had a meaningful advantage given their knowledge of accurate price levels and because of wide bid/offer spreads.

Meanwhile, relatively few macro traders had big research budgets and access to policymakers. Those who did had a massive edge over less informed and less sophisticated corporations and speculators.

Instantaneous communication speeds, near-unlimited availability of information, and rigorous compliance and monitoring of non-public information have dramatically flattened the landscape for both macro and bank traders.

Technical Analysis

1980 to 2006

The most common trading strategy on most trading desks I worked on before 2006 was technical analysis. Most techniques were fairly basic, while some of the smarter-sounding people might throw in some Elliott Wave or more esoteric systems built in Lotus 1-2-3. Most of these strategies produced what amounted to trend-following or breakout signals. Continuation patterns, breakouts, head and shoulders etc. were the favored setups and these piggy-backed on the underlying high Sharpe of trend-following strategies in that era.

As algorithmic strategies became more common in the mid-2000s and trend following Sharpes fizzled, traders using simple technical analysis lost their edge because technical strategies are easy to replicate with a computer and computers are better than humans when it comes to risk management and unbiased trade selection. Now, I believe technical analysis has been reduced to a risk management tool and does not work effectively for trade selection or forecasting.

Correlation and intermarket analysis

2004 to 2014

This was my bread and butter back in the Lehman Brothers days but after the 2008 Global Financial Crisis, everyone became acutely aware of the importance of correlation and intermarket analysis for short-term trading.

Just about every global macro trader (and blogger) in the world is highly proficient in this style of analysis now. And there are many, many computerized systems using dynamic correlation to trade every asset class. Again: Too much money chasing too little alpha.

I still use correlation as an important input for my trade ideas but I think its usefulness has declined significantly over the past 20 years.

Data and Event Trading

1990 to 2005

It's 1997. I expect a strong nonfarm payrolls (NFP) number and USDJPY is 118.80/85. As 8:30:00 a.m. approaches, I key up a bid for 100 million USDJPY at 119.01. I stare intensely at the US economic release page on Bloomberg.

5, 4, 3, 2, 1…

If the number is significantly better than expectations, I hit send. If not, I do nothing. Often, pre-2005 or so, you could scoop all the lazy offers left by risk-averse traders and make an instant $100k or $200k profit in the seconds after any major economic release. Now, there are hundreds of algos set up with a series of commands like: (If NFP beats by 1 standard deviation + Unemployment rate drops, buy 100 USDJPY, limit X). All available liquidity is sucked up in microseconds as an army of algos wipes the battlefield clean.

There are some second derivative ways to make money trading the economic data now, but 95% of the alpha is now owned by algorithms. This creates a form of singularity where price finds its new equilibrium point almost instantly after economic data hits the market. Instead of flailing all over the place as it tries to find the right price, USDJPY just ratchets to the new "correct" price in a few minutes as similarly-tuned programs react at faster than human speed.

Pattern Recognition

1980 to ???

There is a famous story of Paul Tudor Jones and Peter Borish using price and volume patterns to uncover an analogy between the price and volume pattern in the stock market in 1987 and price and volume in the stock market in 1929. Using this analogy, macro analysis, and his concerns about derivatives, portfolio insurance, and equity futures without price limits, Tudor predicted the Crash of '87 and returned 62% in October 1987!

In 2023, this type of analogy would be tweeted twenty-two times by day traders and online bloggers and would be revealed in the output of every machine learning, AI and pattern recognition machine at every hedge fund and bank in the world. Computers are significantly better than humans when it comes to unbiased pattern recognition.

I do believe, though, there is still an edge in pattern recognition. Experienced human traders can still combine complex pieces of information to form conclusions that would elude the best computers.

Leverage, carry, and selling risk premium

Forever

Borrow at 2% and buy an asset that yields 7%. Carry and roll down. Sell insurance to hedgers. Sell SPX puts. These are the tried, tested, and true ways to generate consistent returns. These strategies produce non-normal returns and lead to occasional blowups and meltdowns and are often more beta than alpha. Tactics like timing on entries and exits and superior risk management, though, can make simple levered carry and option selling strategies more like alpha than beta.

Quant / discretionary combo

2012 -

While quantitative analysis was once mostly the domain of systematic and algorithmic trading programs, human traders now use more sophisticated quantitative methods. Combining the best quantitative analysts, the best datasets, and the best discretionary traders into one business pod looks to me like the ideal model for discretionary alpha capture in the current era.

Quantitative analysis is greatly enhanced by experienced humans who can ask the right questions. Models are great for many types of trading, but are not as good at other tasks such as predicting or reacting to regime change or handling one-off events.

All these styles of trading still work, off and on. The challenge is to find a trading style that gives you an edge in the current market, and then stay clear-eyed, open-minded, and adaptable so you can transition or pivot as the market changes. Your edge this month might not be your edge next month, or next year.

Thinking about my own evolution

When you first start in trading, you want to buy something at a certain price and sell it at a higher price. Most everything you do is directional and fairly simple. This is fine! Most of what I do is still directional and simple. But over the years I have added more layers.

The natural evolution after you learn directional trading is to get into options. Trading options is fun, but you realize after a few years that buying options all the time is not always the way to go. The biggest reason for this is that owning options tends to be wrong-way risk for directional traders. Higher vol usually means higher P&L (active markets are easier to trade than dead markets) so if you buy vol all the time, you are really screwed if things quiet down. Your trading is less profitable right at the moment you are bleeding theta out your ears.

I address this issue more fully in Week 38: How to sell vol without risk of ruin. Many vol-selling trades are still directional, though. You are selling a spread in the opposite direction of where you think the market will go, etc.

So eventually, I moved from only directional bets, to buying options, to selling options, and then one day I realized… If you are selling options, it can open up a completely new framework. Instead of betting on what will happen, you can start to bet on what you think will NOT happen. While this is not useful on its own, it can be a useful tactical edge when coupled with an existing forecasting edge. That is, sometimes if you know your market very well, you might have a strong sense of what will not happen, even if you don't know exactly what WILL happen.

Before we get into how to profit from something you think will NOT happen, I want to excerpt a short bit of the latest piece published by Traderade[82]. Traderade is a service I follow. It's run by Michigandolf and others. I have no financial relationship with the site or the people there; I just like the writeups.

This excerpt provides an excellent example of two things. One, adapting to new regimes and new market structure. 80% of FinTwit is complaining about 0DTE options or proclaiming how they will bring down entire nations while the remaining 20% is busy trying to figure out how to profit from them. Be the 20%, not the 80%. Adaptation is

---

[82] https://www.traderade.com/

about constantly having one eye on the horizon so you see new techniques, inputs, and market regimes as they appear. It's not about whining when market structure changes.

The other reason I like the excerpt is that it's a good example of a trader with a solid reason for thinking something will NOT happen. While they played it via a directional strategy, they could have also sold options on the other side of the Put Wall described in the piece.

One quick word on selling options. I have often written about selling options and done a video[83] on the topic and my hard and fast rule is this: I never NEVER sell anything with unlimited downside. There are ways to do so, but it's a completely different business model. It's a business model I am not interested in because I value career longevity (avoiding risk of ruin) over everything else.

Here's the excerpt from the Traderade piece (with permission).

Options Activity

With the recent rise in short-dated Options activity, the largest Put Option strike or largest Call Option strike have often been acting as *walls* for price, or a natural area of support based on market mechanics like dealer hedging. This phenomenon can also apply to longer dated Options interest but the example I'll show here is relevant for day trading.

I took a long trade today at ES 3981 and one of our Discord members messaged me asking why I chose to *catch a falling knife* at that level. In their defense, here's the chart at the time of the trade:

[83] https://www.zer0es.tv/masterclasses/structuring-your-bearish-bets/

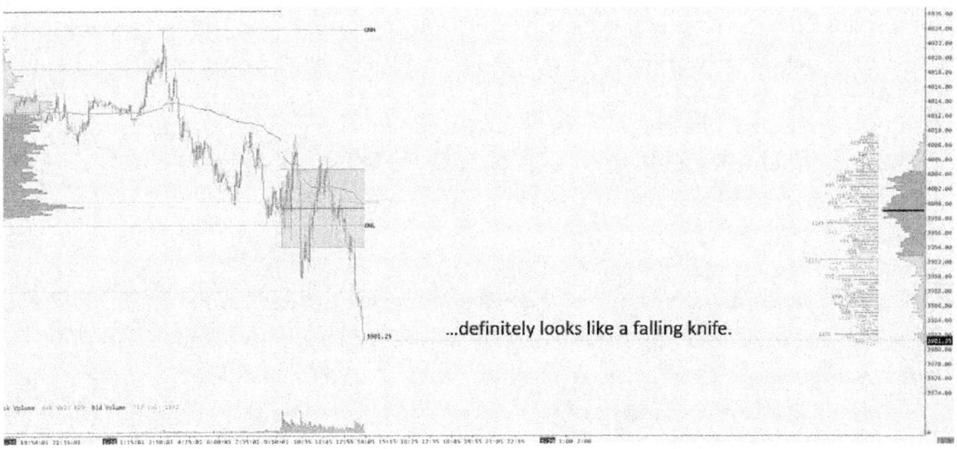

On the 5min ES (S&P500 Futures) Chart above we can clearly see a rather aggressive selloff in the S&P500 and I'd agree that on the surface a long position here looks like a knife catch.

But…

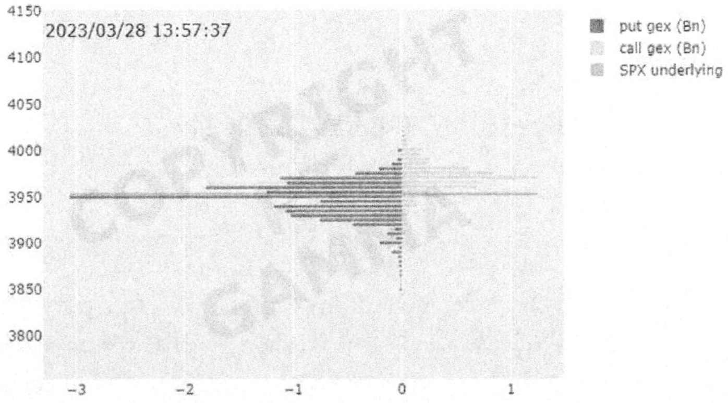

The 0DTE SPX GEX Chart above from twitter.com/rt_gamma shows in a large Put *wall* at 3950, which is roughly 3980 currently on the front month ES contract I was trading. Since I can count on 2 fingers how many times price has meaningfully pushed through the large Put Wall so far this year, I chose to use this information as a buying opportunity, anticipating many of these aggressive options traders would be closing their now profitable 0DTE Puts, forcing dealers to buy back the shares they sold to hedge. (Note: Similar examples can be found shorting against the large Call Wall for the day)

In this case the thesis worked, allowing me to "Buy a Dip" rather than "Catch a Knife":

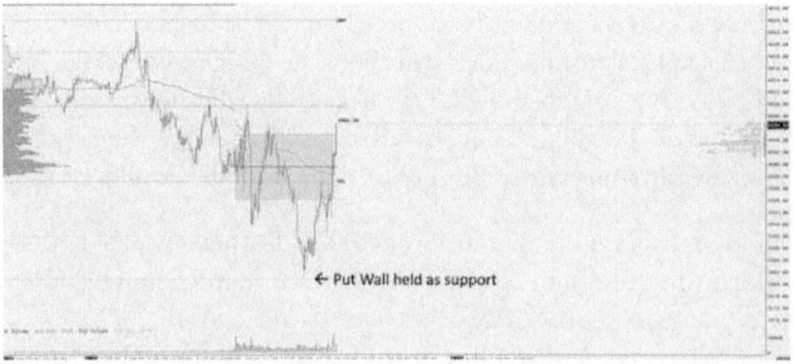

Will this edge always work? Probably not, but nothing "always" works in trading and it's been an important new factor in my day trading that has been working with a high degree of success this year so I thought I'd include it to illustrate this article's main point: **If you're going to buy a declining financial instrument (stock, bonds, ETFs, futures, etc.) always do it with strong support RIGHT below you for the best Risk/Reward and results.**

So here, Horse identified the Put Wall and bought against it. Another approach would have been to sell put spreads against that level, or identify a stock you like and sell put spreads there. Obviously, in this case the futures exploded higher and Horse's strategy was best. But it's an excellent example of a case where you might say: "I dunno if we'll bounce much, but we are going to have a tough time getting through that Put Wall, so I'm not going to bet on S&P futures going up, I'm going to bet that ES futures will NOT go down."

Betting on what won't happen

For the sake of this week's exercise, let's assume I think stocks are going nowhere. I think we are trapped in a loop where stock rallies lead to a more hawkish Fed but massive shorts and underweights are always on the bid any time stocks sell off. This has been the environment for the past 9 months, basically.

SPX: Blame it on the range

I lean bearish stocks, but I think there has been so much bad news that it's hard to imagine what it will take to break the back of the market. The thing is, if stocks rally, I doubt they will go far because the calm that might help stocks rally will allow the Fed to keep hiking gradually and as the Fed hikes, more naked swimmers[84] will emerge. So: I don't think stocks are necessarily going down. But I don't think they will go above 4100, either.

I am going to use options on SPY, the S&P 500 ETF. There is some basis between SPX (the index), ES (the index futures) and SPY (the ETF) but for simplicity, let's say I don't think SPY is going over 410.00. We can sell the 410/412 April 21/2023 call spread and receive around $0.65 per contract. If we're risking $2000 on the trade, that's 10 contracts.

Now the sad part about trades like this is that you do not get leverage. If the trade works, you win $650. But there is a reason for that! It's more likely to work, than not to work. SPY is 400 right now and you are betting it won't be above 410 on April 21, 2023. Very often, this is the nature of selling options with limited downside. Just like buying options often gives you unlimited profit potential (leverage!) ... Selling options usually does not.

It's all about expected value. Don't get fooled by the optics... This could be a fine trade, depending on the odds you assign to the win and lose outcomes.

Note: 410/412 is a very skinny spread. There are reasons to do wide spreads and reasons to do skinny spreads but they are beyond the scope of this note. The point of today's note is to get you thinking about different ways you can find an edge beyond pure directional trading. A discussion of the right way to sell spreads is a whole 'nother post.

This trade on its own will not move the needle. But as part of a larger framework, I hope it gets you thinking about different ways to look at the market and different ways to structure your bets.

Conclusion

Your edge can come from many different angles. Studying your market and finding inefficiencies is one. Observing the entire macro universe and finding dislocations is another. As shown in today's note, finding different ways to express and structure your views can also be a source of edge.

If you are a directional punter and you think "This thing ain't going up, but it might just be stuck here for ages trading a range," there is nothing to do. If you have other non-linear tools in your toolbox... There just might be something profitable to do!

---

[84] https://money.com/swimming-naked-when-the-tide-goes-out/

Week 47: Where to put my stop?

Some basics on determining the appropriate level for a stop loss

Update on previous trades

Nothing significant to report other than the SPY put spread is smalls underwater and the TSLA short is bobbing around aimlessly with a bit of a bearish bias.

Where Should I Put My Stop?

One of the most frequent questions I get from new traders is "Where do I put my stops?" It's an important question and can often be the difference between a W and an L on a trade. It's critically important to understand that forecasting the direction of a market is just the very, very start of making money in trading. Tactics and trade structure can influence your P&L as much as or more than trade selection and idea generation.

As we are through 46 Weeks of 50in50 so far, I want to use these last few weeks to cover any important topics that I have not yet hit.

Today, I'm specifically discussing where to put stop losses, but all the same concepts apply to where you put your take profits. Use the same two-step method for TPs.

A simple method for determining your stop loss

Once I have come up with a strong trade idea, usually through some combination of narrative analysis, catalysts, positioning, and cross-market analysis, the next thing I think about is where to put the stop loss. You want your stop loss to clearly tell you "My idea was wrong" and not be more like "There was some noise and chop, so my stop got hit."

Every time you choose a stop loss level, you are navigating the tension between maximum position size and leverage vs. the probability of getting tapped out by noise. Tight stop = max leverage. Tight stop = riskier.

If you are getting stopped out all the time, that's a clear indication that your stop losses are too close. That may sound obvious to some, but it's something important to keep in mind. If you hear yourself saying: "Man, I'm right a lot lately, but I'm losing money," that could well mean your stops are just too close.

When in doubt, use a wider stop.

Better to be too small and alive than big and dead.

There are two basic steps when determining your stop loss and you need to do both to optimize your tactics.

Step one: Do the math

The first method is to understand the volatility of the product you are trading and how that relates to your trading time horizon. When volatility is higher, you need smaller positions and wider stops, percentage-wise.

I tend to trade with a time horizon of one hour to one week, with many trades in the 3-to-5-days-long category. As such, I'm using hourly charts looking back about three months and looking to catch a decent 3-day move. While I hate when people religiously use 1:2 or 1:3 as their risk/reward ratio, somewhere in there is a good starting point.

So if I'm looking to catch a good 3-day move, and I want, on average, trades that pay 2:1 or 3:1, my stop loss should be approximately 1.0X to 1.5X an average daily range.

You should always know the average daily range of anything you trade.

This is trading 101. If you don't know the average daily range of an asset you are trading, that is not good. If you are trading a micro fractal (day trading, for example), you should also know the average hourly and 4-hourly range for your product because everything I am writing about today works on every fractal. Day traders can use tighter stops because their targets are closer. Swing traders should use wider stops because their targets are further.

It's also helpful to know the distribution of daily ranges because the average camouflages a ton of important information. For example, there is a skew to the average daily ranges in risky assets like SPX and USDJPY. They go down faster than they go up. You can build a histogram of daily ranges in Excel using daily data extracted from wherever.

I trade a lot of USDJPY; here's my histogram of USDJPY ranges. I used two years of data but keep in mind that regimes change and they can change fast. Changes in volatility are more important when considering position sizing than when thinking about stops, but they always matter.

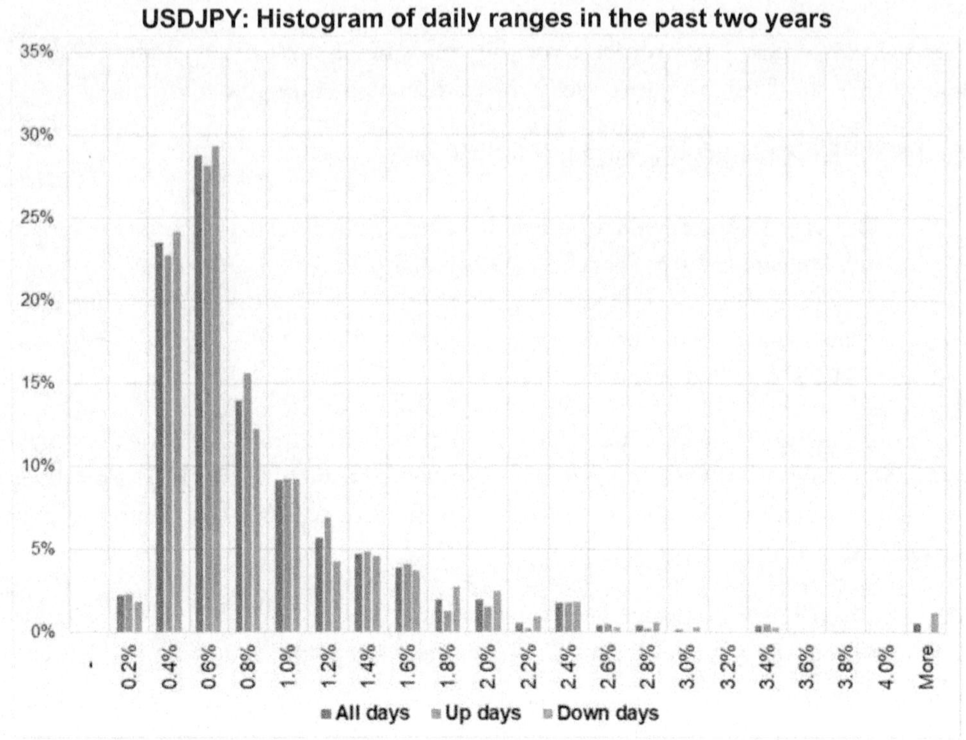

A few things stand out here.

1. While the average daily range is 0.78%, most days are closer to 0.4%-0.6%. If you are expecting a typical day, you could use 0.5% or 0.6% as your expectation when determining the stop loss because the outliers skew the average significantly.
2. Down days are slightly bigger than up days. The difference is not big enough to worry about when setting your stop, but it's good to be aware of this feature of the market.
3. Ranges are not normally distributed. Most ranges are average and then abnormal days can be epic.

So if I'm buying USDJPY with a target of 1.5% (three normal day's ranges), a rough starting point for my stop is going to be my entry minus one day's range (0.5% to 0.6%). This is assuming volatility is normal right now and I have no reason to expect a huge surge of vol.

If I was holding this position through a major event, the determination gets way more complicated because then you have to estimate how much USDJPY normally moves on an event like the one that's about to happen. To do this, you can look at historical data, but that's getting a bit beyond the scope of today's note. There are many exceptions to the general approach I am outlining today, but it works in most situations.

What we are trying to do with these volatility measures is answer the question: "What is a reasonable stop loss given my target, time horizon, and entry point?"

So if USDJPY is 131.05, my starting point here is:

> Target = 3X a normal day's range. If I have decided 0.5% is a normal day, then my target is 133.02. That's 131.05 X 1.015.
>
> Stop loss = 1.5X normal day's range. That is 131.05 X (1 - (0.50% X 1.5)) = 131.05 X 0.9925 = 130.07.

Again, I really want to emphasize: This is kind of a rough starting point for what makes sense. Your estimate of volatility going forward, over the life of the trade, is critical here. When there's nothing special going on, using the mode or average or median range makes sense.

But now, keep in mind those levels are totally arbitrary. They don't take into consideration anything about the reality of the market. They are just a mathematical approximation of what makes sense.

Step two: Do the techs

OK, so my rough estimate says stop at 130.07 and take profit at 133.02. Now, I will look at a chart. Today's lesson is not about technical analysis, but the main things I'm looking for are:

1. Horizontal lines (support and resistance)
2. Equilibrium zones
3. Moving averages

Here's the USDJPY chart right now.

USDJPY hourly with 120-hour and 240-hour moving averages

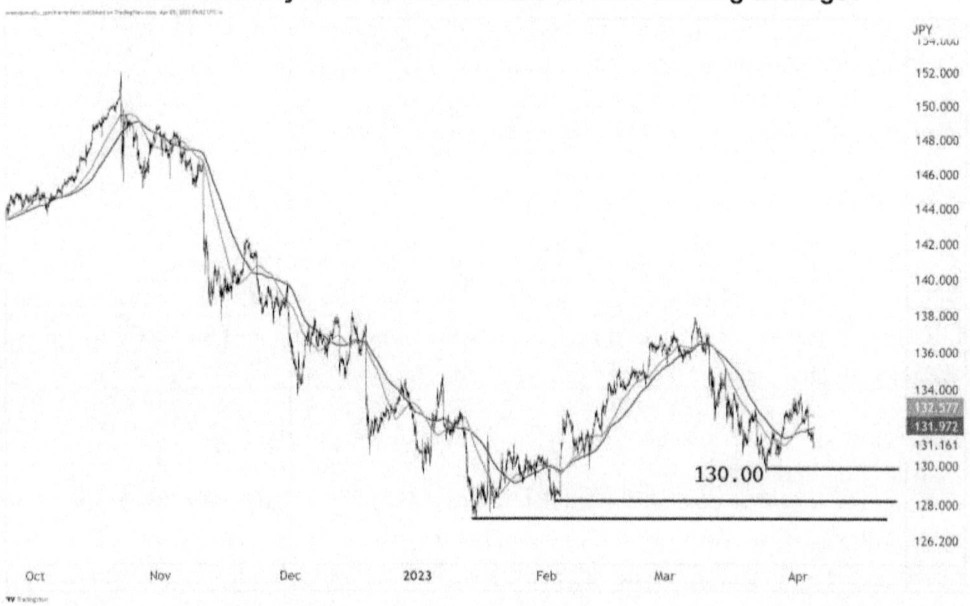

So for the stop loss, it's pretty easy. We have a major low right at 130.00. My first instinct looking at this chart is that I might want to wait to get long closer to 130.00 to get better leverage, but let's just say I have some reason to think it's going to go up soon. Maybe US 10-year yields are ripping or whatever.

Please note in real life I am bearish USDJPY right now and yields are going down. This is just an example.

I have mentioned this before, but it's useful to know that round numbers are more likely to hold than other points on the chart. So we always want our sell stops below the round numbers. My calculation suggested 130.07, but of course given round number bias and the support at 130.00, we want to go below there.

Read more about round number bias on spectramarkets.com[85].

Now the issue is that everyone looking at this chart is going to want to leave stops on long positions below 130.00. So **if you put your stop at 129.97, you are going to get stopped out with everyone else**. If you know your market, you want to put your stop a few spreads below the obvious place so that at least if those stops get wiped and it rebounds, you're OK. So in this case, I would use 129.74, which gives it enough room.

So that's it, really. You calculate a range of reasonableness and then you adjust based on technical analysis. You don't always need to use 2:1 or 3:1 as your ratio. Really you should

[85] https://www.spectramarkets.com/wp-content/uploads/2021/11/MacroTactical-Crypto-Number-3-11NOV21.pdf

be thinking in expected value terms so the estimated probability of winning needs to be factored in, as well. If you think you can risk one to make one on a trade and you see an 80% chance of it working... That's a good trade!

Read more about expected value on towardsdatascience.com.[86]

Short KRE

KRE is the US regional banking ETF. Without getting too far into the weeds on US regional banking... Things don't look great. The regional bank stocks are not bouncing, FRC is still near the lows, and more cockroaches are emerging and are likely to emerge. Western Alliance issued a worrying update today, for example.

So let's just say we want to get short KRE. Where do we put the stop?

First, it's important to consider that KRE has entered a new, higher volatility regime since the fall of Silvergate. You can't look at data before this new crisis, because it will give you totally useless information. The big gap down in KRE was March 9, so let's look at the distribution of daily ranges since then.

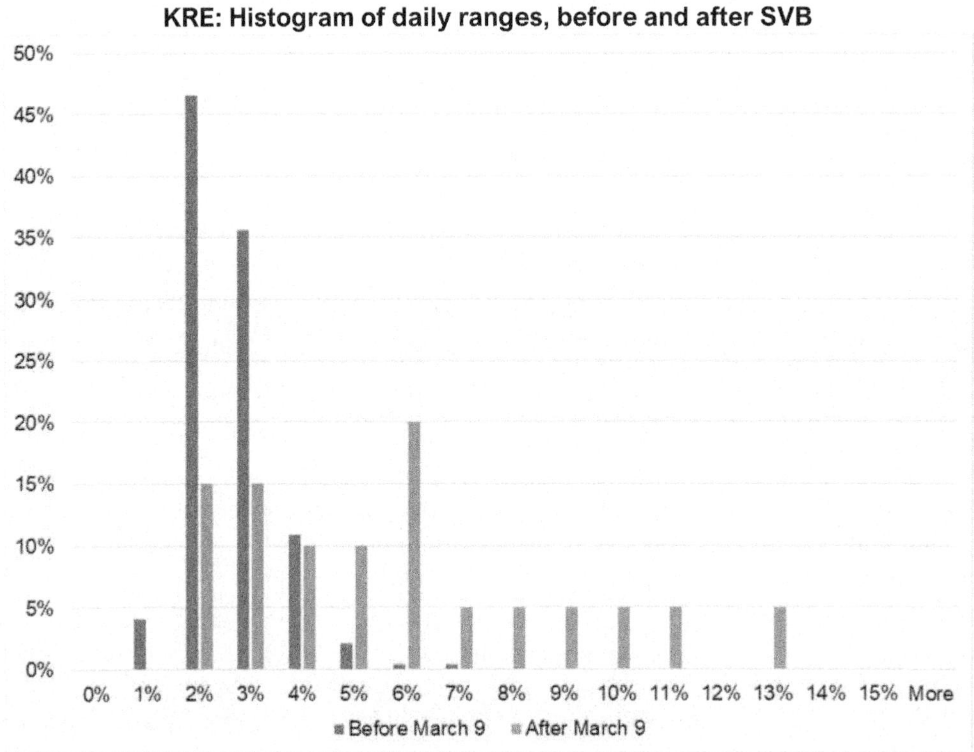

[86] https://towardsdatascience.com/what-is-expected-value-4815bdbd84de

Obviously, the sample size post-March 9 is small, but you get the idea. Daily ranges were 2%-3% and now they are 6%-11%. So let's say we want our stop 1.5 X 7%, to be somewhat safe-ish. That's 10.5% above the current price of 42.00 and thus: $46.41. Let's have a peek at the chart.

KRE hourly chart

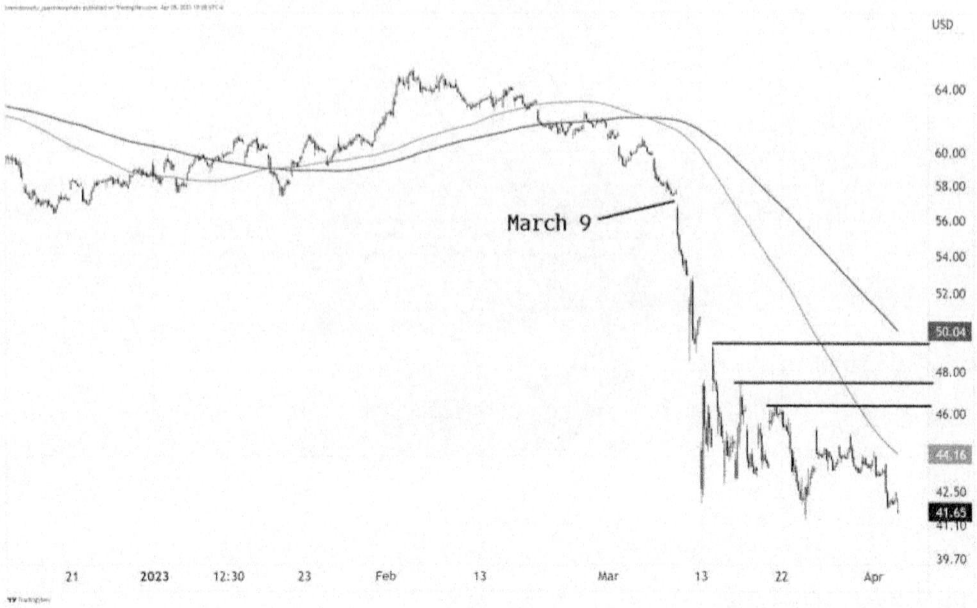

Those two highs are 46.44 and 47.51 and the third one is 49.44. The third one is way too far away given my estimate of what's reasonable, so in this case I would put my stop at 48.06. That's farther than the math suggests but the volatility of volatility is very high in KRE and so wider is better than closer. You might be tempted to put the stop above the 240-hour MA and megatop there around 50.00 but that is just too far away because my target is 33.10, so I can't be risking 9+ to make <8.

You could also consider a tighter stop at 46.10 (above the moving average and more recent double top). That would give you better leverage but in a crisis market, I would rather survive and make less money than get dinged on a random headline.

Conclusion

50in50 goes short KRE at 41.60 with a stop at 48.06. Take profit 33.10. Risking 6.46 to make 8.50. I think this probably has a 65% chance of working, so I'm happy with the thin upside vs. downside ratio.

Final note, this is a textbook bear flag in KRE. So that helps too.

Week 48: Market Profile

Filter noise and sharpen your tactics

Update on previous trades

Nothing major to report other than the SPY put spread is a tiny bit underwater and the TSLA short is gradually looking better by the day. Price wars in the auto industry are unlikely to be bullish TSLA, especially with recession lurking around every corner.

KRE has rallied a bit and is slightly out of the money.

What is Market Profile?

Market Profile (sometimes called Market Picture) is a streamlined system for charting price, volume, and time data. Compared to normal bar or candle charts, it changes the way time and price are represented. I like it because:

1. Market Profile provides a concise, visually appealing summary of what's going on in the market.
2. It cuts out a lot of noise.
3. There are simple ways to apply Market Profile to your process if your goal is to use technical analysis as a risk management tool. In other words, Market Profile is great for identifying pivots. And pivots are what you need when you're determining reassessment triggers like stop losses and take profits.

There are many ways to process the torrent of financial data that rushes through the global pipes every day. Bar and candlestick charts are the most popular presentation format for financial time and price movements but there are other equally valid ways of slicing and dicing the data.

Most of the charts on my trading cockpit are in candlestick format. Market Profile is my second favorite way of looking at time and price data. There is a huge body of writing on Market Profile, so if you like the concepts here, check out the suggestions for further reading further down.

The main benefit of Market Profile is that it gives you a quick and highly visual way of looking at many days' worth of intraday price action. Here is the Market Profile for Apple common stock (AAPL) back to February 27.

AAPL Market Profile, February 27 to now

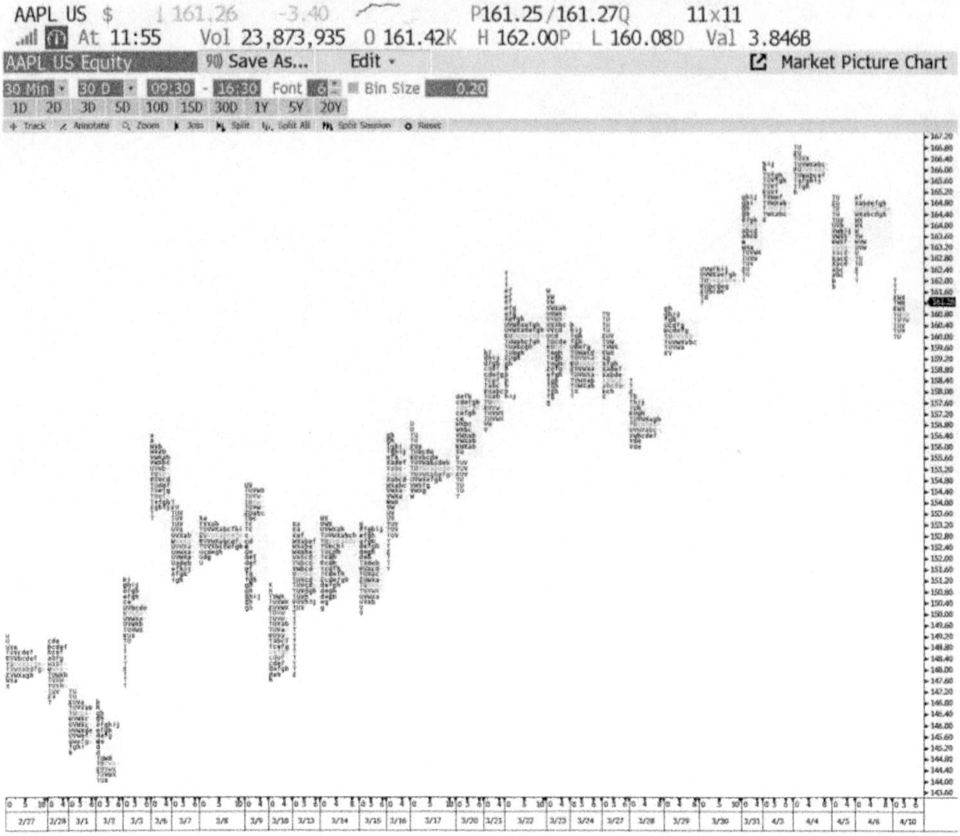

You can access Market Profile in Bloomberg by typing (for example):

EUR {CURNCY} MKTP {GO}

on your terminal. I believe it's available on TradingView and other platforms, too. Sometimes it might go by a slightly different name.

Market Profile is best for analyzing shorter time frames, and most intraday charting systems won't show you more than 30 days. There are ways of using Market Profile on daily and weekly data, but these are way too big picture for me and I don't use those.

My trading time horizon is usually 1 day to 1 week (on average), so I start with that 30-day view and also often zoom in to something like a 5-day chart with 5-minute increments, like this:

AAPL Market Profile, April 3 to now

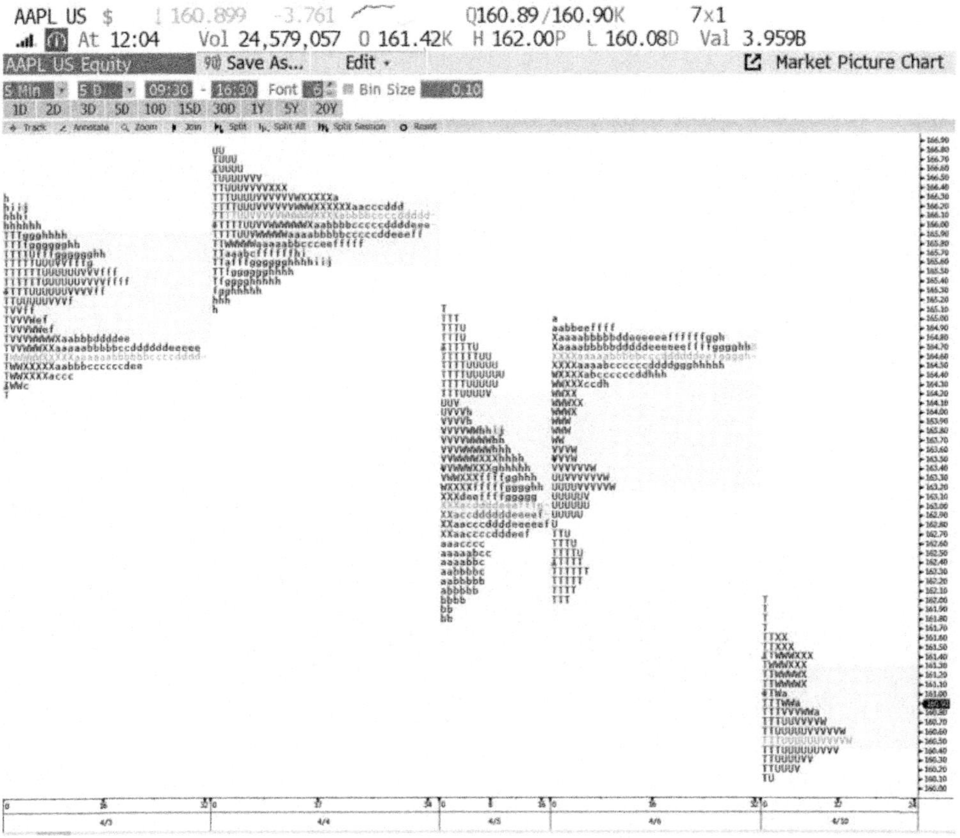

Some people like to create the Market Profile manually as the day progresses using graph paper and a pencil. That's a great idea! Manual intraday charting gives you a more intimate feel for how the day is developing and gives you a more visceral connection to the price action.

It also gives you a better understanding of how the Market Profile is built from the ground up. When I have the time, I build Market Profile charts manually throughout the day. I find doing so helps keep me in the zone.

Each letter on the chart represents a block of time throughout the day (30-minute blocks are used in the first chart example above, and 5-minute blocks in the second).

If there are many letters in a row beside a price, it tells you that the price traded there many times throughout the day. **Each column of letters represents a day** and the date is indicated on the x-axis below each column.

Look at the column of letters for April 10th on the second chart, for example. You can see that 160.50 traded for much of the day (there are many letters stacked up in a row) whereas 160.10 was touched briefly, and quickly rejected. Same deal with 161.60 to 162.00. There is just one letter next to those prices and this tells you that AAPL was there briefly, but didn't like it there and went down right away.

To build the chart manually, simply create a blank grid on graph paper with logical intervals on the y-axis. Then put an A beside every price that trades in the first hour of trading, put a B next to every price that trades in the second hour of trading and so on. I suggest you try this for a few days and see how it feels. If your time horizon is shorter, you can use 30-minute or even 10-minute blocks, too. This can help with focus and concentration. It is a fantastic exercise that will make you a better trader.

Market Profile gives you the ability to quickly identify equilibrium zones. These are the areas where many letters form large clusters and long rows. The longer a row of letters, the more times a given price traded there that day.

At levels where there are very few letters, on the other hand, the market traded there only briefly before more aggressive sellers or buyers came in and quickly pushed the price away. This is all you really need to know to start using Market Picture. The key is to focus on the equilibrium and non-equilibrium zones.

Single Prints are Money

The simplest trading strategy I use with Market Profile is to look for what are called SINGLE PRINTS. **A single print is a point on the market profile where there is only one letter** because price traded there but then moved away before the start of the next time period. When you see a single print, you can clearly see that the market rejected this price point aggressively and therefore this is a price point that you should consider as a key pivot.

If you learn nothing else in this chapter, just remember this: **Single prints make excellent pivots.**

Looking at the first chart again, you can see that in the last two days, there were a bunch of single prints. The letter "U" around 163 yesterday, and in the 161.60/162.00 area, where you see three letter "T"s. Don't worry about what time of day it was; all you need to know is that AAPL could not hold equilibrium yesterday on the 162 handle and it couldn't find it there today, either. So right away, when I look at this chart, I have 161.60/163.00 as an important pivot zone.

Yesterday we flew up through it, and today we have gapped back down below it. This means that rallies back toward that zone will likely be sold as players that missed selling on the way down will try to sell when price gets back up there. Here's the same chart with some new annotations.

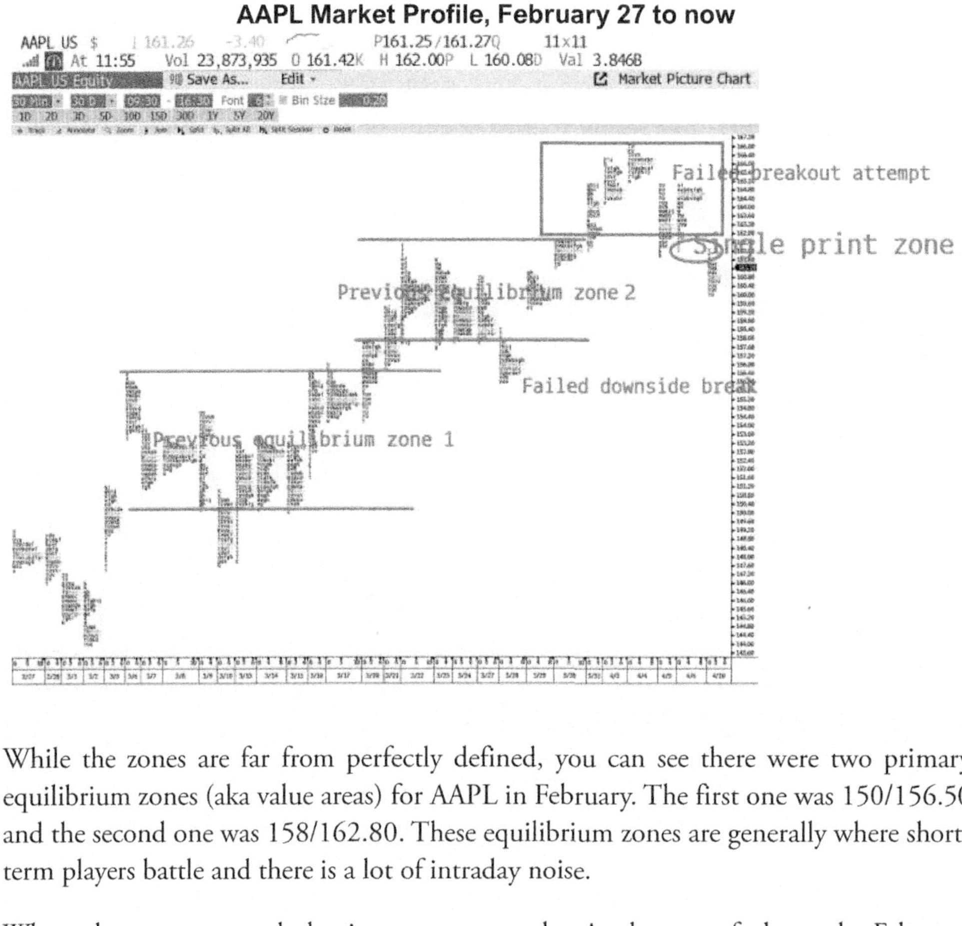

While the zones are far from perfectly defined, you can see there were two primary equilibrium zones (aka value areas) for AAPL in February. The first one was 150/156.50 and the second one was 158/162.80. These equilibrium zones are generally where short-term players battle and there is a lot of intraday noise.

When there was enough buying power to take Apple out of the early February equilibrium zone 1 and into equilibrium zone 2, that implies medium-term buying interest came in and take out the supply near 156.50.

When that happens, short-term traders recalibrate. Short positions stop out and buyers that missed the boat in zone 1 move their bids up to the bottom of the new zone. Then, the stock bounces around for a while as retail and smaller players play Pong until stronger hands emerge from the shadows. In this case, the strong hands were buyers and they took price up and out of zone 2.

This time, though (see the box), medium and long-term demand got filled and there was nobody left to hold up the bottom of the range. Apple dropped out of the box and back into the old equilibrium zone. Now, the single prints yesterday should define the top of the new equilibrium zone, while we look to 158 once again as a possible area where demand might reappear.

The box looks like a failed attempt to define a new supply/demand equilibrium and now we wonder if there will be demand when AAPL gets back to the bottom of zone 2 at 158. Based on this market profile chart, I would expect the new value area to be (once again) 158/162.80 and I will watch closely if we get near 158 to see if demand emerges or if we just gap right through.

This is just a taste

Here I have introduced:

1. Understanding equilibrium zones
2. Single prints
3. The interaction of short-term noise traders inside the value areas
4. Medium and long-term supply and demand at the edges of those areas, and
5. How different time frame buyers and sellers can take you out of one zone into another.

That is enough to get you started!

If you like this topic, I encourage you to read this huge PDF from the CBOT[87], and/or "Mind Over Markets[88]" by Dalton, Jones, and Dalton. Those publications will give you a much more in-depth view of Market Profile and the many ways it can be used. I've simply provided a basic overview of the most simplistic ways I use it.

Peak Apple

Whenever companies become a gigantic proportion of an index, beware.

MSFT and AAPL currently make up a larger percentage of the S&P 500 than any other two companies in history. The last duo that was this dominant in the S&P 500 was IBM and AT&T in 1978. Here's how IBM worked out.

---

[87] http://cdn.preterhuman.net/texts/finance_and_marketing/stock_market/Cbot%20-%20A%20Six-Part%20Study%20Guide%20To%20Market%20Profile.pdf

[88] https://amzn.to/3KNVaDN

IBM stock, 1978 to 1982

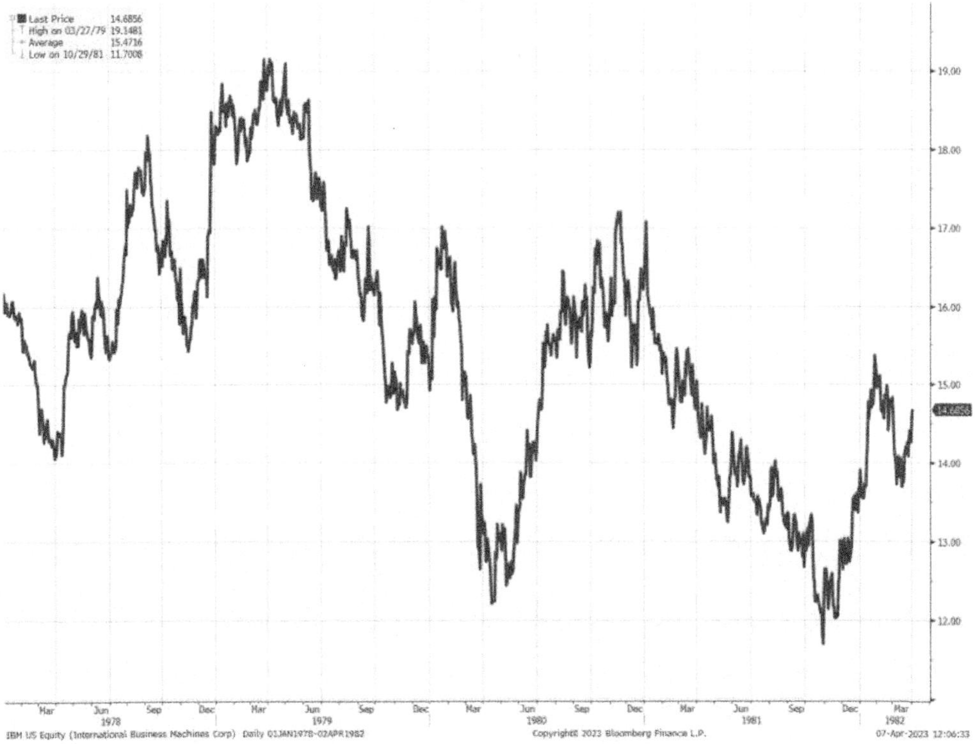

Meanwhile, if you see your favorite stock or asset class on the cover of a mainstream magazine… Be afraid. That is very often a sign of a top.

Here's an explanation of why mainstream magazines are an excellent reverse indicator[89]. *This is not investment advice and nothing works every time. Good economic forecasting and excellent trading both rely on probabilistic, not deterministic thinking.*

Here's a doozy from the end of 2021.

Tesla stock and Musk Man of the Year Award timing

Tim Cook is also selling a lot of stock. Sales of one of Apple's flagship products are down 40% YoY. And the daily chart keeps making lower lows, as you can see here.

Apple daily chart, mid-2021 to now

---

[89] https://medium.com/@mbrentdonnelly/a-somewhat-empirical-look-at-the-magazine-cover-indicator-2d0ca835f7d1

There's plenty to dislike about Apple right now as the GQ magazine cover could signal peak idolization of Tim Cook the way the Time Magazine cover signaled peak idolization of Elon Musk before his reputation and TSLA stock crashed back to earth.

When you're selling a raging behemoth stock like AAPL, you always need to understand that there is a good chance you'll be wrong. You want to try to find a good setup, get short, and risk manage it judiciously. You don't keep selling if you get taken out. You give up and you move on. One of the best ways to go broke trading is to pick a fight with a popular stock.

On the other hand, if you have a bunch of timing indicators in your favor and the stock is already showing weakness, you can get short with a reasonable stop loss and create a trade with excellent risk/reward.

In this piece, I'm looking at two distinct time frames. The market profile charts are zoomed in, while I'm also talking about some bigger-picture ideas like the magazine cover and Tim Cook's insider selling. That's OK. The bigger picture stuff is the thesis, then we can zoom in using Market Profile and achieve more leverage and better tactics.

Looking back at the very first chart from the start of this piece, there are single prints in the 161.60/162.00 area, and again at 163.00 and 163.60. This gives us a solid bunch of pivots to consider. For a trade like this, I would use those points to set a tight stop loss at, say, $164.11 (above all the single prints). This stop loss gives us good leverage because the stock is trading at 161.70 right now. Then again, that's a pretty tight stop for a trade that could go all the way to 130.00 or something if it works.

So in this case, I would put half my stop at 164.11 and give the other half some more breathing room above the April highs at 167.26. Splitting up your stop avoids the risk of getting dinged on the top tick and reduces a bit of your false precision risk. I am a fan of doing this with stops and take profits as long as it makes sense and you can find logical levels to do so.

In this case, I think it's perfectly logical to seek more leverage on half the position and give a wider berth to the other half.

If we are risking $2,000 on this trade, that means we are risking $1,000 on each half of it and we calculate the number of shares to go short as:

SLICE 1

161.50 minus 164.11 stop loss = $2.61 per share.
$1000 at risk / $2.61 = 383 shares

SLICE 2

161.50 minus 167.26 stop loss = $5.76 per share
$1000 at risk / $5.76 = 173 shares

You see the tighter stop gives us twice as much leverage, but it also greatly increases our chance of getting stopped out. By slicing the trade into two pieces, we get more leverage, but still have hope if the first clip gets popped.

When doing a trade like this in real life, one also has to consider overnight gap risk because there are no promises a $164.11 stop loss is going to get filled anywhere near that level through news or earnings. The next Apple earnings release is May 4, so we need to be hypervigilant as that day nears. Most likely the trade will either be in the money or stopped out by then, but you never know.

Note that AAPL is trading a bit higher as I prepare to hit send on this week's note. I always mark the trades to market based on where things are trading at the time I hit send.

Conclusion

Market Profile is a great way to analyze short-term price patterns and come up with useful pivots that will help you risk manage trades and maximize leverage while reducing noise.

Always be sure that the time horizon you are using for risk management matches the time horizon of your thesis. Don't trade a 2-year view with a 35 basis point stop loss unless you have some strong reason to do so. That said, if you can use tactical methods to find tight stop losses on bigger picture trades and your timing is good… You can find yourself with trades like this AAPL short where we are risking $2.61 to make $20 if all our dreams come true.

Week 49: Numbers and Narratives

Wanted: Storyteller with mad quant skills - Lavish remuneration possible

Update on previous trades

The SPY put spread is a tiny bit underwater and the Ford and TSLA shorts are in the money despite a big rally in the indexes.

The KRE trade from Week 47 is doing well while the AAPL trade from Week 48 is stopped out. Overall, the 50in50 portfolio is doing well these days considering it's short a bunch of stocks and the SPX is near the top of the range.

Numbers and Narratives

This week, I want to discuss something on the border between practical and philosophical advice.

There are many ways to succeed as a trader, but I think the path with the highest probability of success is one where you are strong on both the quantitative and qualitative sides. You can succeed as a pure quant, and you can succeed as a pure behavioral trader who simply uses anecdotes and gut feel. But most do not succeed this way.

The most likely path to success is to choose one market and master everything you possibly can about that market, using a combination of data/quantitative analysis and subjective analysis of narratives, positioning, anecdotes, pattern recognition, and experience. Don't pick a methodology, because different methodologies work in different regimes. Pick a market and master it. This approach is inherently adaptable over time while mastery of a technique or strategy is much less flexible and regime-dependent.

Let me give you a few quotes about this sort of holistic thinking. This first quote block is an excerpt from Barry Ritholz's excellent interview[90] with Aswath Damodaran, one of the best voices you could possibly listen to as an aspiring trader or market practitioner. He's smart, humble, and open-minded.

> DAMODARAN: I am interested in numbers. I'm naturally a numbers person. But I've also been interested in storytelling. To me, storytelling is much more — I mean, if you think about the history of humanity, for thousands of years, the way we pass down information was with stories, not numbers. It's only in the last century that numbers have come to the forefront.
>
> RITHOLTZ: Is that correct, it's just the last century? That's fascinating.
>
> DAMODARAN: In fact, I think the first numbers were collected by the insurance people in the 1700s, but it was very proprietary only. Now we have access to Excel and so on. It has allowed for this acceleration of number crunching. So, to me, you know what attracts me to valuation, it's a bridge between stories and numbers. You tell stories about companies that you convert into numbers, and those numbers eventually become valuations, and I find that attractive. I'm not a natural accountant or an actuary. I'm not a natural strategist who can tell the stories. I like to connect stories and numbers, and valuation is the place to go to do that.
>
> RITHOLTZ: So is it safe to say narratives drive value?
>
> DAMODARAN: Narratives drive value. Absolutely.
>
> RITHOLTZ: Now, sometimes narratives drive value to towns and cities they really shouldn't go.
>
> DAMODARAN: Sometimes narratives can become very dense, and that's why you need numbers to keep your discipline. In fact, when I start my valuation class, I have 350 MBAs who take my class and it's in an amphitheater. I start with the question, how many of you are more naturally number crunchers? And about 200 put up their hands; ex-bankers, recovering accountants, auditors, actuary, scientists, mathematicians. And

[90] https://ritholtz.com/2023/04/transcript-aswath-damodaran/

the other 150 are natural storytellers, liberal arts majors because MBA programs have become incredibly diverse.

And I tell them what my endgame for the class is, I said, by the end of this class, and I turned to my number crunchers, I said, look, I hope you have enough belief in your own imagination that you're willing to let go because they've spent a lifetime being told that being subjective is a weakness, making judgments about something is a weakness. And then I turn to my storytellers, I said, by the end of this class, I hope you have enough confidence with numbers so you'd become a disciplined storyteller.

To me, what makes for good valuation is you're either a disciplined storyteller or an imaginative number cruncher. And I think that combination is getting increasingly hard to find because we're categorized very early in life. I see this with my wife who teaches fifth grade, and already people are being slotted as natural number crunchers. They're going to take number crunching classes. We can go for a number crunching degree, have a number crunching job. There are no Renaissance people left on Wall Street, and investing people who can talk about drama and talk about numbers at the same time. And I think that's a loss.

RITHOLTZ: There are a handful, but they certainly are few and far between.

I agree with Barry's conclusion and this was my biggest beef when recruiting students into trading jobs when I worked for big banks. The pipeline of people that come through the top analyst programs is glaringly homogeneous, with an emphasis on quantitative book smarts and less emphasis on creativity or street smarts. This is a broad generalization! There were certainly excellent, well-rounded graduates coming through every year.

Even if the programs attempted to achieve some sort of diversity, the diversity tended to be related more to demographic features, not manners of thinking. When you recruit from a group of 10 or 12 universities all located in the Northeastern United States, you are going to get a lot of really smart people that grew up with rich parents and incredible test-taking skills.

Again, I'm not dissing every single recruit! There were many, many good ones. And I understand that a recruiting process that is more bespoke would be less scalable and less efficient. The takeaway, though, is that if you are a polymath/Renaissance person, you have an advantage. And you don't have to be born a polymath, either. You can be intentionally curious and build the weaker muscles in both your left and right brain.

This quote, from a somewhat obscure book called *The Tao Jones Averages*, is also good. The quote is via a write-up from Sapient Capital[91].

---

[91] https://sapientcapital.com/insights/investings-big-blindspot/

> "The left-brained analytic system on Wall Street has become overdeveloped. Like a tree that has grown too large for its place in the forest, it has crowded out intuition, vision, creativity, and gestalt sensing, which are the properties of the right hemisphere. As professionals of the Street continue to try to overpower darkness, opportunities will exist for those who can sense new directions."

Many of the best traders, analysts, salespeople, and strategists on Wall Street are polymaths who are part math professor, and part humanities PhD. You can succeed as a mainstream thinker on Wall Street, but the outliers are people that can think differently.

Here's one more quote, this time from Stan Druckenmiller:

> I think the great thing about my original mentor Spiros Drelles in Pittsburgh was he made me focus on what moves the stock price. Like you can't just say, "Okay this is a great company and the earnings are great…" So tell me how people are going to think differently in 18 or 24 months about the situation than they're thinking now.
>
> That would be my number one advice to young people. Do not invest in the present. The present is not what moves stock prices, change moves them, and I want you to try and envision a different world in a year and a half from now, and where these security prices would trade versus now given the world you envisioned.
>
> That would be my number one advice to a young person getting in the business.

In other words, conventional thinkers extrapolate. Original thinkers do not.

A word of caution here because I think a lot of people would assume this means you have to be contrarian all the time to succeed on Wall Street. That is not true. In fact, being contrarian all the time leads to a reflexive countertrend stance that will mean you miss all the big trends and you are fighting every major move. You can't just put a negative sign in front of whatever the consensus says and assume that's the right answer.

You need to be contrarian at times, and when you are contrarian you have to be right. Being contrarian all the time is a good way to feel smarter than everyone else while you lose money. Being selectively contrarian at times because your view of the future diverges from the crowd's view is a way to find huge opportunities and inefficiencies in the market.

In *Alpha Trader*, I lay out the formula for trading success as:

Alpha Trader = rational + intelligent + skilled + conscientious + calibrated confidence

I stand by that formula, but looking from another angle, I would say that success in trading also comes from a strong fusion of quantitative and creative skills. If you want a great read on how this fusion of numbers and stories works in the equity valuation game, check out this wonderfully-detailed presentation from Professor Damodoran[92].

An attempt to be contrarian and correct

I have written many times about how trading stocks successfully always comes from an understanding of the interplay between price and value. Value is what you get. Price is what you pay. People tend to overpay for stories.

The ARKK ETF is a good example of this. They were so blinded by the religion of disruption that the story became the only thing and valuation and price became irrelevant. They used ridiculous inputs to create a veneer of quantitative rigor around what was really just a preconceived view that disruption stories are so powerful there is no price too high. They focused on a story (TSLA is great!) and then reverse-engineered the data to sell it.

If you have not seen it, my interview with Howard Marks in March 2021 is here[93]. It covers the difference between good stories and good stocks. They are sometimes the same thing, but very often they are not. Cheap stocks are usually cheap for a reason and no matter how good a company is, it's a bad bet at the wrong price.

Buffet says it best:

> *"It's far better to buy a wonderful company at a fair price than a fair company at a wonderful price."*

While the focus tends to be on buying good assets for low prices, the converse is often just as valid. Selling good assets short at inflated prices can be profitable, too. While it's hard to make money shorting a bubble, there are plenty of times when it makes sense to short a good story when you believe that story is fully subscribed and more likely to mean revert than continue. You don't need to expect a complete reversal in the story, you just need to have a contrary view on price… And good timing.

Some examples of this: shorting crypto in 2021 on the back of Fed tightening and the Bubblicious narrative, shorting Tesla when Elon was on the front cover of Time Magazine, shorting wheat when it was on the front cover of The Economist, or many lesser-known stories that captured the market's imagination, then mean reverted like crazy… 3-D printing, the recent uranium frenzy, work-from-home stocks, etc.

---

[92] https://pages.stern.nyu.edu/~adamodar/pdfiles/country/narrative&numbers.pdf

[93] https://www.epsilontheory.com/a-conversation-with-howard-marks/

Right now, we are in the midst of an AI frenzy. This can be ascertained via basic observation (it's the only thing anyone is talking about)... But you can also see it through anecdotes:

There's a cliché on Wall Street: "If it's in the news, it's in the price." The real money is made by those who have unique views that are not obvious to everyone else in the world. Doing the obvious thing *can* work, but doing the obvious thing at nosebleed levels can be enormously costly. We now have AI on four magazines in less than three weeks.

Further reading on why magazine covers are often reverse indicators: *A somewhat empirical look at The Magazine Cover Indicator.*[94]

Meanwhile, here's Google search activity for AI:

---

[94] https://medium.com/@mbrentdonnelly/a-somewhat-empirical-look-at-the-magazine-cover-indicator-2d0ca835f7d1

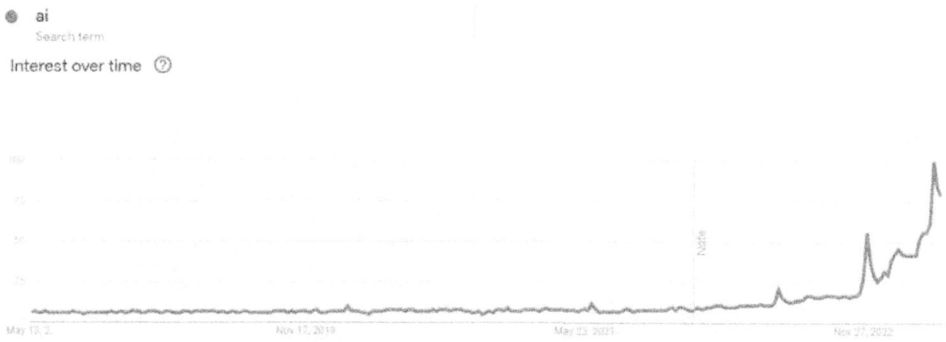

It has ramped up to all-time highs and is now starting to come off. Why would this matter? Search interest, demand for an asset, and the price of an asset often move in lockstep. More interest = more buyers. Here's an example of how interest in crypto and the price of ETH move together:

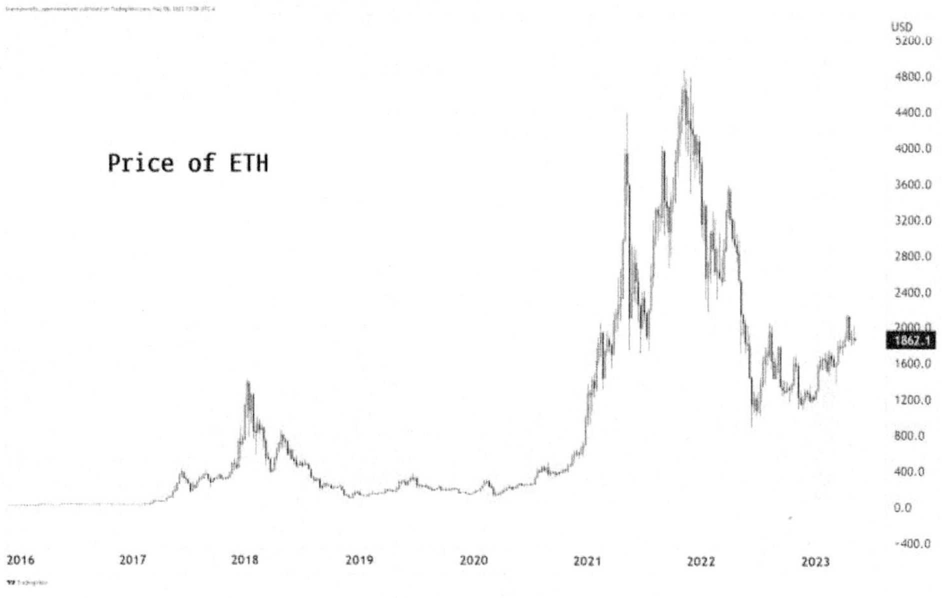

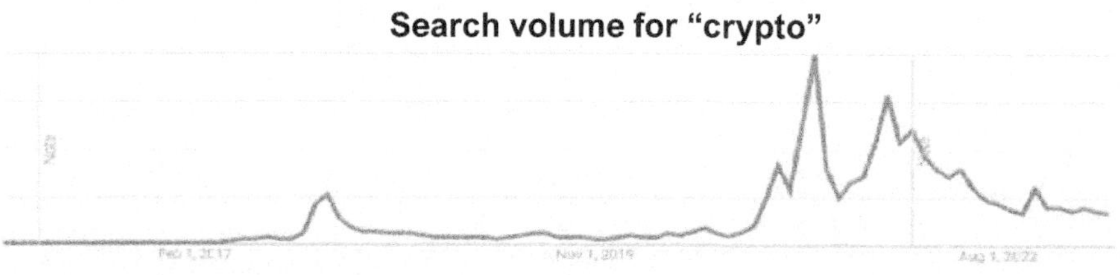

"But dude! AI is going to change the world!"

Of course it is! That's why everyone is so excited. World-changing technology is the stuff that price overshoots are made of. By the way, when you frequently hear the words "world-changing" with regard to a company's technology, that is often a strong clue that the stock might be overvalued.

Zoom kinda changed the world, but it was still a terrible investment

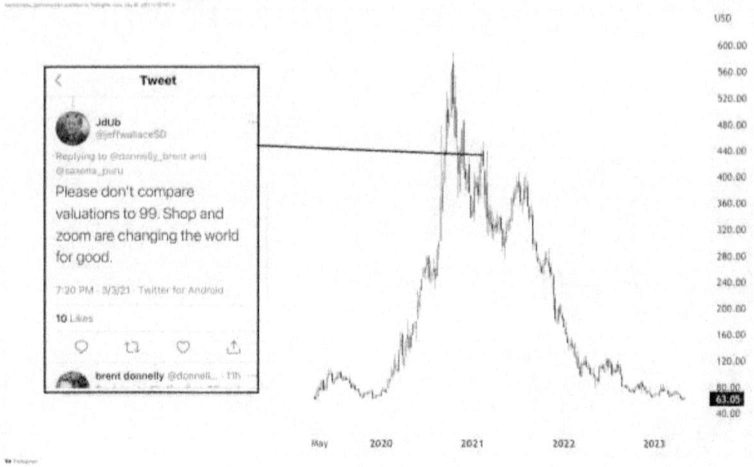

When we think of the leaders in the AI race, we might think of NVDA or MSFT. Those stocks have gone to the moon of late, but so have many other megacap techs. When looking to short a narrative, you want pure play stocks that are faddish, not perennial behemoths like MSFT and NVDA. While I think MSFT and NVDA are wickedly overvalued and I would be underweight or flat both of them… They are tough shorts.

The data also points to another huge issue with shorting MSFT particularly. Their shares outstanding are in inexorable decline as they buy back more and more stock. If price is a function of supply and demand, you are running uphill trying to short a stock with less and less supply outstanding.

MSFT shares outstanding 2000 to now

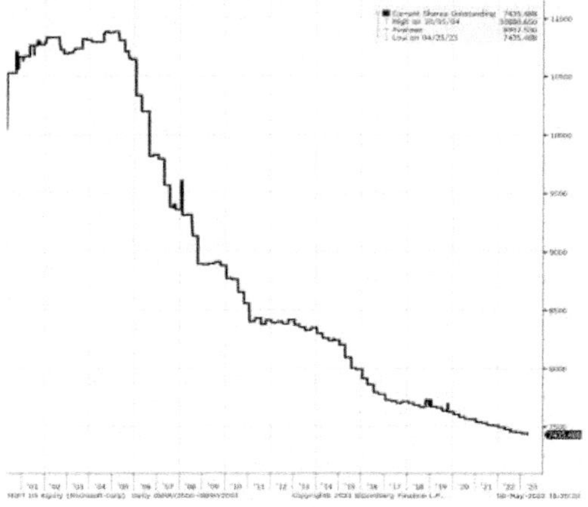

A more attractive way to short AI is to find the weakest links. For example, look at Big Bear AI, C3.AI, or BOTZ (The Robotics and AI ETF). All three are nowhere near their highs despite the (justified) hysteria over AI. I would always rather sell something like this that is already weak than try to short MSFT or NVDA as they rage like flying sky mutants up toward the mesosphere.

AI, BBAI and BOTZ (daily chart back to 2021)

So... To recap... The search data shows us AI interest has gone wild. Four magazine covers tell us it's at the forefront of the zeitgeist. Shares outstanding data tells us MSFT is always going to be a tough short. And when we look at price charts, we can see the underperformance of the gimmicky pure plays.

Without any further information, I would consider a basket where we go short all three stocks. Digging a bit deeper, BBAI is trading at 2.68. I don't like shorting cheap stocks because they tend to have much greater short squeeze risk. Remember you can lose infinity on a short, but you can only make 100%. Shorting low-priced stocks is a recipe for disaster, so BBAI is out.

Meanwhile, if you check short interest, 34% of AI's outstanding shares are sold short. So there's major squeeze risk there, too. But it's the best expression of the trade because when we drill into the components of BOTZ[95], it's really more of a robotics ETF than an AI ETF. We want to be short the maximum of the AI narrative, and that's not going to be achieved via a robotics ETF.

C3.AI (ticker: AI) is a dangerous short, but shorting is generally always dangerous. To do it safely, you could use options, but for simplicity here I'm going to talk about shorting the stock. **Don't do this unless you know what you are doing.** For a full video on how to structure bearish bets without getting your face ripped off, see my video "Structuring Your Bearish Bets"[96].

AI common stock, hourly back to March 2022

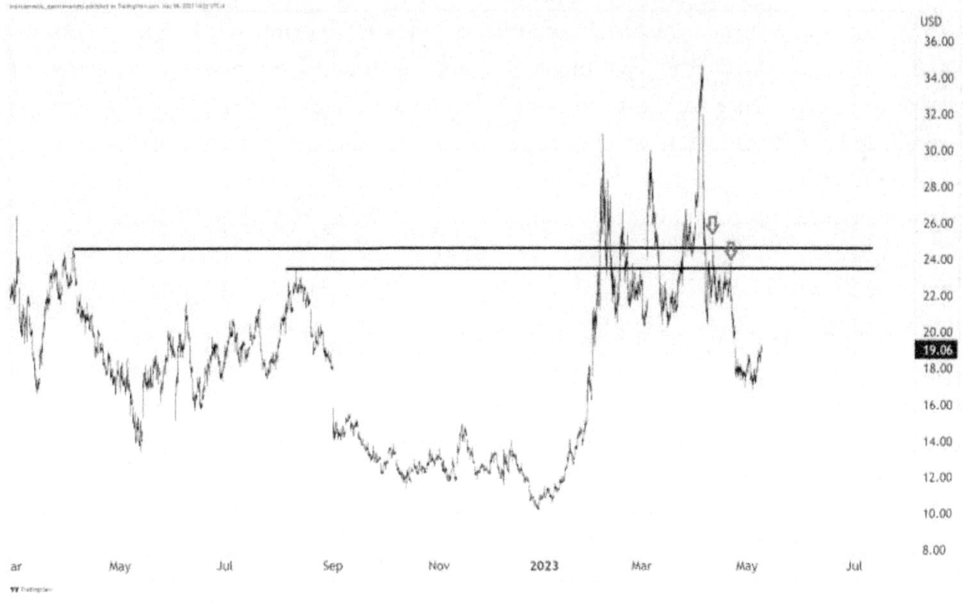

In that chart, I note that the old highs in 2022 were $23.50 and $24.50 (horizontal lines), then we had the hyperactive AI bubble action that took us into the low 30s. After that last spike, and after we crashed back to earth, the little arrows show highs of $25.10 and

95 https://www.globalxetfs.com/funds/botz/

96 https://www.zer0es.tv/masterclasses/structuring-your-bearish-bets/

$23.80. If we are back to a less bubbly regime as AI excitement peaks in the short term, we should not go back through that band of pre- and post-bubble highs ($23.50/$25.10).

Therefore, I think $26.25 is an appropriate stop loss and I will take profit back down towards the low of $11.11. This thing costs about 10% / year to borrow (estimated) so it's expensive to short, but not prohibitively expensive.

50in50 goes short AI at 19.25 with a stop loss at 26.26 and take profit at 11.11.

This is Week 49 out of 50, so I'll call this a multi-month trade and I will check back in with a randomly-timed post sometime after Week 50.

Conclusion

Common sense observation of the narrative tells you that AI is in a super heavy hype cycle right now. Using anecdotal observations (magazine covers) and data (search frequency) we can conclude that now may be a good time to put on the contrarian hat and go the other way. We are not betting that AI will never matter—it will! We are betting that the narrative is fully subscribed and about to leak a bunch of air.

Using short interest data, technical analysis, data on ETF composition, and a common sense understanding of the asymmetry of shorting low-priced stocks, we narrow our choice to C3.AI. Note we are playing this from a pure max-narrative angle and we are not doing a DCF or anything of that sort. A comprehensive analysis of the company would add another layer of sophistication to this trade idea but that's beyond the scope of this week's lesson.

Bonus read… Related. "Storytelling" by Scott Galloway[97].

Next week, I'll offer some final thoughts on trading, a final trade idea, and comprehensive results for all the trades.

We are nearly at the end of the ride! I hope you have enjoyed the ups and downs so far.

---

97 https://www.profgalloway.com/storytelling/

Week 50: Three Existential Questions

On money, self-sabotage and meaning

Final update

It's hard to believe, but this is the fiftieth and final week of this project. 15,000 subscribers and 150,000 words later, I hope you have found 50in50 to be informative and educational. I had fun writing it and the process of thinking through all these concepts one by one has even helped me unlock some new ideas and approaches myself. I hope you too were able to extract some useful framework upgrades.

The lessons presented by 50in50 are self-contained and mostly speak for themselves. Each week, I tried to pick a particular concept and focus there. But while each lesson on its own contains much specific learning, there were also some broader lessons.

I tried to keep each week of 50in50 to around 3000 words or less, and my post-mortem and takeaways are almost that long on their own. And I want to conclude the series with some bigger-picture thoughts on the existential aspects of a career in trading.

Therefore, I will put the post-mortem and takeaways as the conclusion to the Fifty Trades in Fifty Weeks book (this one). That also puts some original material in there to motivate people to want to buy the book.

Turning 50in50 into book format is not meant to be a cash grab. I wasn't planning to make a book out of this, but I have had many people suggest and request that we do so. So why not! We'll price the softcover fairly and make a more expensive hardcover version for enthusiasts and collectors. And the Substack will stay up and remain free.

Also, FYI, we are going to be launching a slightly more formal markets education series soon. It will be called **Spectra School**.

Analyzing the Results of Fifty Trades in Fifty Weeks

One big takeaway from the series is completely unsurprising: **I don't have an edge doing fifty random trades in asset classes where I have no specific expertise.** This was not surprising to me and I wrote about this a few times at the start of 50in50. The sample trades in 50in50 are designed to highlight a particular topic, and most of them had no intrinsic edge.

On the other hand, my FX trading P&L is consistently profitable over many years because I have an edge and tons of experience in FX and macro. When I traded NASDAQ stocks full-time during the dotcom bubble, I also had a defined edge (bid/offer capture in the direction of futures momentum + front running Level 2).

But in 50in50, when I put on a sample trade in oil, ARKK, BTC, or some other asset class in order to demonstrate a particular concept… I am unlikely to have a huge edge. The P&L on the entire exercise was extremely close to zero, including estimated transaction fees.

I am still bearish TSLA and Ford, but for a clean finish here, I am going to mark everything to market and shut it down. No new trade this week, just some big-picture closing thoughts about trading for a living.

Here is the detailed P&L spreadsheet:

Conviction	Week	Entry date	L/S	Asset	Entry	USD at risk	Stop loss	Take profit	Exit or current level	P&L	Exit date	Holding period (days)	Notes
8.0	1	2/9/22	Short	XAUEUR	1,602	2,000	1,702	1,421	1,704	(2,000)	28-Feb	19	
4.0	2	2/16/22	Short	CLK2	90.50	1,000	95.45	79.05	95.55	(2,000)	1-Mar	13	
8.0	3	2/21/22	Short	DOCS	56.00	2,000	60.51	50.21	60.58	(2,000)	28-Feb	7	Wrong stop loss.
7.0	4	2/25/22	Long	BTC	39,200	2,000	31,400	49,800	39,200	-	14-Mar	17	
7.0	5	3/1/22	Long	BTC	43,400	2,000	38,900	49,800	38,870	(2,000)	14-Mar	13	
5.0	6	3/8/22	Long	EWC	37.85	2,000	35.19	44.80	39.65	1,353	11-Apr	34	
9.0	7	3/14/22	Long	XPO May $60 puts	2.60	2,000	-	53.50	6.10	2,692	18-Apr	35	
8.0	8	3/28/22	Short	NQ	14,970	2,000	15,660	13,344	13,908	3,078	18-Apr	21	
9.0	9	4/4/22	Long	TWTR	50.85	2,000	45.84	57.77	45.80	(2,000)	13-Apr	9	
7.0	10	4/11/22	Long	ASHR	32.18	2,000	29.84	36.44	29.80	(2,000)	25-Apr	14	Wrong stop loss.
6.0	11	4/18/22	Long	ESM2	4,381	2,000	4,279	4,579	4,276	(2,000)	5-May	17	
3.0	12	4/25/22	Long	ARKK	45.67	2,000	29.00		51.39	687	*11-Aug*	108	
2.0	14	5/15/22	Long	BTC	28,500	2,000	24,900	39,300	24,900	(2,000)	13-Jun	29	
9.0	15	5/18/22	Long	JAN23 CVNA 20 put	4.70	1,500	-	-	3.00	(543)	13-Sep	118	
9.0	15	5/18/22	Long	JAN23 RBLX 40 call	7.00	1,500	-	-	10.40	729	13-Sep	118	
10.0	16	5/27/22	Short	ETHBTC	0.061	2,000	0.077	0.033	0.069	(1,000)	25-Jul	59	
4.0	17	6/6/22	Short	LLY	297.99	2,000	306.25	283.10	306.25	(2,000)	22-Jun	16	Low was 1 cent from the take profit!!!!!!!
8.0	18	6/14/22	Long	TY	114.56	2,000	112.84	118.00	118.00	4,000	30-Jun	16	
10.0	19	6/24/22	Long	GBTC	12.77	2,000	10.90	16.60	14.80	2,181	31-Jul	37	
5.0	20	7/4/22	Short	TSLA	701.50	2,000	820.00	437.00	829.00	(2,200)	22-Jul	18	
7.0	21	7/19/22	Long	XME	44.50	2,000	34.95	63.70	49.90	1,131	13-Sep	56	
9.0	22	7/25/22	Short	META	Options	2,000	29JUL $160 and $155 puts		Small profit on the 160s	(1,600)	29-Jul	4	
8.0	23	8/1/22	Short	SPY	412.50	2,000	436.60	37.00	402.50	830	13-Sep	43	Sold put against it
8.0	25	8/16/22	Short	MSTR	345.00	2,000	381.00	251.00	251.00	5,222	26-Aug	10	
5.7	26	8/23/22	Short	TSLA	296.00	2,000	304.67		288.09	2,191	25-Aug	2	Cover at 25AUG close
7.0	27	8/29/22	Short	TSLA	Daily strat	2,000			295.00	(297)	13-Sep	15	
8.0	28	9/5/22	Short	ETH	1,650	2,000	1906 and 2056	1,155.00	1,587	381	13-Sep	8	
8.0	30	9/20/22	Long	USDJPY	143.65	2,000	141.74		141.71	(2,030)	23-Sep	3	This trade made money in real life but I forgot to put my TP in 50in50 write up oops
7.0	31	10/12/22	Buy	FXA call spread	0.40	2,000			-	(2,000)	21-Oct	9	
8.5	32	10/17/22	Short	USDNOK	10.53	2,000	10.92	9.88	10.33	1,026	2-Nov	16	
6.5	33	10/27/22	Short	CM	45.10	2,000	47.11	40.55	47.14	(2,010)	10-Nov	14	Stop too tight - ended up hitting TP not oo long after
8.0	34	11/4/22	Buy	EWZ call spread	35/39	2,000			-	(2,000)	27-Dec	53	
7.0	35	11/9/22	Short	MSTR	192.10	2,000	282.00	160.55	160.65	700	27-Dec	48	
6.0	36	11/17/22	Buy	TGT / WMT spread					142.60 in WMT	(170)	16-Dec	29	
8.0	37	11/30/22	Long	XOM put spread	2.05	2,050	FEB '23 100/85 put spread	85.00	1.46	(590)	27-Dec	27	
9.0	38	12/7/22	Sell	Call spread and put spread in MSTR	See Substack	3,000				-			
8.0	39	12/22/22	Sell 23FEB23 and buy 23JUN23 125.00 USDJPY puts			2,000				(2,000)	23-Jun	183	
8.0	40	12/28/22	Long	TSLA	113.10	2,000	88.49	159.00	141.50	2,308	23-Jan	26	
7.0	41	1/10/23	Limit Buy	TSLA	115.03	2,000	98.49	159.00					*Never got filled*
7.0	42	1/23/23	Short	F	12.60	2,000	15.26	9.03	11.58	767	22-May		
7.0	43	1/30/23	Short	TSLA	171.10	3,200	251.11	117.77	182.00	(272)	22-May		*Moved stop nice play*
8.0	44	2/15/23	Short	TSLA	210.78	2,000	251.11	117.77	182.00	1,427	22-May		
8.0	45	3/1/23	Long	IEF	94.80	2,000	92.44	99.49	99.49	3,975	23-Mar		
6.0	46	3/29/23	Sell SPX call spread	410/412	0.65	2,000			Expired below 410	650	23-Apr	25	
8.0	47	4/5/23	Short	KRE	41.60	2,000	48.06	33.10	40.40	372	22-May		
7.0	48	4/11/23	Short	AAPL	161.50	2,000	164.11		165.69	(2,000)	17-Apr	6	
8.0	49	5/8/23	Short	AI	19.30	2,000	26.26	11.11	26.31	(2,014)	17-May		
	50												*No trade*

Total P&L	**(3,028)**
Winners	**20**
Losers	**24**
Win%	**45%**
avgWIN	**1,785**
avgLOSE	**(1,614)**
avg holding period (days)	33

Zooming in on the summary statistics:

Total P&L	(3,028)
Winners	20
Losers	24
Win%	45%
avgWIN	1,785
avgLOSE	(1,614)
avg holding period (days)	33

Perhaps more telling is the breakdown by asset class:

	Single name	Equity Index	FX and bonds	Commodities and crypto
Total P&L	(1,556)	2,558	4,970	(9,000)
Winners	14	3	3	-
Losers	16	1	2	5
Win%	47%	75%	60%	0%
avgWIN	1,581	1,519	3,000	
avgLOSE	(1,481)	(2,000)	(2,015)	(1,750)

I focused a lot on single stocks in 50in50 because it's easiest to tell a simple story in stocks, while in FX and other asset classes, you very often need to provide much more background information. I also didn't want to do much global macro because that is what I write about every day in am/FX (my real job) and it felt like there would be too much duplication.

Logically, the macro trades (equity indexes, FX, and bonds) did the best while the single stocks, commodities, and crypto did the worst. That makes sense!

Like I said in *Alpha Trader*, the most likely path to success in trading is to choose one market and master everything you possibly can about that market. **Pick a market and master it.** For me, that market is FX.

This comes through in the P&L of my real-time trades published in my daily newsletter, am/FX. Here are the results of my am/FX trades going back to the day I started at Spectra Markets (September 2021). These trades are all published and marked to market in real-time. The risk is $100,000 on each trade.

Total P&L	2,628,369
Winners	52
Losers	40
Win%	57%
avgWIN	113,128
avgLOSE	(81,357)
average holding period (days)	11

I publish am/FX trade results, in detail, each quarter, but the detailed xls with all 92 trades won't fit in here so I am only showing the summary stats. These stats are consistent with my performance over many years in FX. I started keeping track in 2006 and most years I put up something close to a 50% win rate. Historically my daily avgWIN$ / avgLOSS$ = 1.8. For more on P&L tracking and analysis, please see Chapter 11 of *Alpha Trader*.

As mentioned earlier, there will be a more substantial analysis of the hits, misses, ups, downs, and takeaways at the conclusion of this book.

Three Existential Questions

When it comes to trading for a living, three existential questions pop up most.

1. When things are not going well, how do you know when to quit?
2. How do you deal with bad managers and bad trading environments?
3. How do you deal with making a ton of money from a pursuit that adds no value to the world?

The third one is obviously one of those high-class problems that will sound stupid to some people, but it's relevant and important. There is a weird existential angst that can invade your psyche when you receive huge financial rewards for pressing buttons and watching numbers go up and down on a screen. This issue can feel especially acute if you come from a lower or lower-middle-class household, as I did, or if your parents did societally-beneficial jobs that involved some combination of *make, protect, or teach*[98].

Let's take these questions one by one.

1. When things are not going well, how do you know when to quit?

The word "quitter" has a strong negative valence. Society hates a quitter. They make posters like this to remind you:

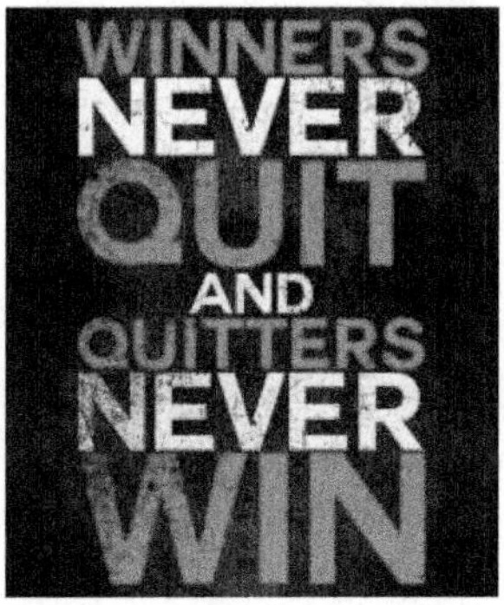

[98] https://www.epsilontheory.com/the-long-now-pt-2-make-protect-teach/

But this is bullshit. In fact, good traders quit on trades every day. That's what stop losses are for.

You must cut your losses in trading and there is a time and a place to cut your losses in every facet of life. Whether it's a single trade, a particular trading job, or trading as a career, there is definitely a right time to quit. Quitters win by quitting the game where they have no edge and picking a game they can win.

The ability to stop out of a bad position is a learned skill that makes you better at trading and better at life. Sticking around in a bad trade, job, friendship, marriage, or investment for too long can be disastrous.

Thing is, though, switching costs are high. You can't stop out of a marriage or a job the first time something bad happens. You incur risks and costs every time you change your mind, whether that's transaction costs, reputational risk, or alimony. But eventually there is always a line below which you should stop out.

One of the most frequent request-for-advice emails I get goes something like:

> *Hey Brent:*
>
> *I have been trading for 2 years. I am gross positive but net negative. I feel like I can do this, but my wife is getting antsy, I have a 2-year-old about to start daycare and I just got offered a tech job that pays $77,000/year. Should I quit trading? Or keep pushing to get over the hump and become the trader I know I can be?*

This is hard to answer!

One trader that worked for me who did not have the x-factor told me, a few years after he pivoted to a job that fits him much better, that he wished someone had told him earlier that he wasn't suited to be a trader. He could have moved on to a new career that fit his personality and skills more quickly instead of wasting five years in a trading job that he and I probably both knew was not the best fit.

This is a useful insight. Not everyone was born to be a trader… Even if they successfully complete a sales and trading analyst program at a major bank.

I almost gave up. A few times.

In December 2007, I was beaten down and frustrated. It was my worst trading year ever and it looked like I might finish negative on the year. When you work in a market-making seat at a bank, it is uncommon to have a down year and I was proud of never having finished in the red. After this long and frustrating period, all I wanted to do was finish the year in the black. Even by $1.

Every time I got close to zero P&L, I would lose money again. By mid-November, I had gone from down $2.5 million back to $250,000 in the black and was thinking about making one last push to finish with a number that might be at least respectable. I finally felt mildly optimistic for the first time in ages, after almost an entire year of battling repeated cycles of frustration and despair.

Then, a brutal turn. A salesman slinked over to me with his tail between his legs and told me there was an outtrade in my book. Negative $700,000. That put me back to minus $450,000 with less than two months in the year. *Gross.* I grinded out the next few weeks and was finally up tiny YTD, about $200k, on the very last day of the year.

At 10 a.m., our toughest client called and wished me a happy new year by ripping my face off to the tune of $600,000. Despite what felt like a heroic effort to the very last day, I ended the year in the red.

This is impossible. I am the worst trader in the world.

I e-mailed my wife: "This is impossible. I don't think I can do it anymore."

I walked out of the office miserable that day. But the sun came up on January 1. Slowly, the frustration dissipated a bit, and the prospect of a new year gave me some hope. Despite that exhausting and disappointing year, I hung on and kept going.

Twelve months later, I was staring at my best year ever: Over $50 million of P&L. Sometimes the thing is just to keep going. As Joe Mauro said in his classic 2016 e-mail to the Goldman Sachs analyst class: "Keep running."

But the thing is, that's a survival story. There are so many traders that do not succeed, that it's important to be realistic.

Unfortunately, there is no correct answer here. Think about the musician or artist who toils in obscurity for 10 years and then finally makes it big. The baseball player who toils in the minor leagues for years, never quits, and gets called up to be the hero in September at age 31. Trading can be like that. It's nonlinear. Most people never make it, but the few that do are rewarded big time. And you need hella grit to get over the hump.

Since not everyone is cut out for trading, part of the decision-making process for many traders is figuring out when to quit. When you have invested significant time and money into your trading career, how do you know when enough is enough? This is a hard question to answer because success in trading only comes with extreme perseverance and experience. Therefore, by its very nature, **trading rewards those who refuse to quit**.

You have to recognize that for most people there will never be a clear sign from the heavens that tells you exactly when enough is enough. If you have been trading for more than two years and you are not making significant progress, that is a bad sign. I would say that anyone who has been trading for more than three years and does not feel confident that they are on the right path, is probably on the wrong path.

Not everyone can succeed at trading. If things are not working out after two or three years of effort, think about what comes next. Can you parlay your trading experience into another job or pursuit? Investing, financial planning, research, etc.?

I realize my answer to Question 1 could feel unsatisfying, but it's a personal question only you can answer. If one day you find yourself thinking: "Ermmm... Maybe I suck at trading... Maybe I should do something else"... Set a deadline or establish clear objective metrics for when you will quit. That way, you have a clear exit strategy and you don't just keep trading until you blow up.

Say "If I'm not X profitable by date Y, I'm done." This will help keep you rational and avoid the constant repetitive loop where you ask yourself the same question over and over.

Deciding when to quit a career is hard. There is no way around this fact.

2. How do you deal with bad managers and bad trading environments?

I answered this question in Week 13: The Most Important Trading Decision. Here is a short summary:

Trading is hard. Your odds of success are heavily influenced by the seat you choose. I have worked as a retail trader, as a market maker at a bank, and as a hedge fund PM. My decision to switch jobs was usually driven by a failure on one of the metrics I describe below.

Here are common features of the best places to work as a trader.

1. Healthy trading environment (this is the big one; I go into detail in that chapter).
2. Your manager believes in you and gives you enough runway to screw up now and then. You will screw up at some point and what goes down between you and the firm at that point is critical.
3. No micromanaging. A great trading manager who trusts his people checks the P&L once a week, not four times a day.
4. The company or division you work for targets revenue growth more than cost cuts. It's much more enjoyable to work for a company that is trying to grow, not one that is trying to cut. And you'll get paid better.
5. Passionate peers and a mentor who all love trading as much as you do.
6. Filled with people that are hungry, smart, and humble.

It is almost impossible to succeed in trading without a healthy trading environment.

3. How do you deal with making a ton of money from a pursuit that adds no value to the world?

First of all, let me address the fact that there is an implicit assumption in that question. The implicit assumption is that trading doesn't add value to the world.

Some will disagree with that and make arguments about liquidity and price discovery and all that. Sure, financial markets do that as a whole, maybe… But financialization has morphed so cartoonishly over the past 25 years that I am pretty confident in saying that financial services are a rent-seeking operation more than a societal value add at this point. It's fine if you disagree. This is just my subjective opinion.

Here is what Paul Volcker had to say on the subject:

> I hear about these wonderful innovations in the financial markets and they sure as hell need a lot of innovation. I can tell you of two — Credit Default Swaps and CDOs — which took us right to the brink of disaster: were they wonderful innovations that we want to create more of? You want boards of directors to be informed about all of these innovative new products and to understand them but I do not know what boards of directors you are talking about. I have been on boards of directors and the chances that they are going to understand these products that you are dishing out or that you are going to want to explain it to them, quite frankly, is nil.
>
> A few years ago I happened to be at a conference of business people, not financial people, and I was making a presentation. The conference was being addressed by a very vigorous young investment banker from London who was explaining to all these older executives how their companies would be dust if they did not realize the joys of financial innovation and financial engineering, and that they had better get with it.
>
> I was listening to this and I found myself sitting next to one of the inventors of financial engineering who I did not know, but I knew who he was and that he had won a Nobel Prize, and I nudged him and asked what all the financial engineering does for the economy and what it does for productivity. Much to my surprise he leaned over and whispered in my ear that it does nothing. I asked him what it did do and he said that it moves around the rents in the financial system and besides that it was a lot of intellectual fun.
>
> Now, I have no doubts that it moves around the rents in the financial system, but not only this as it seems to have vastly increased them. How do I respond to a Congressman who asks if the financial sector in the United States is so important that it generates 40% of all the profits in the country, 40% after all of the bonuses and pay? Is it really a true reflection on the financial sector that it rose from two-and-a-half percent of value added according to GDP numbers to six-and-a-half percent in the last decade? Is that

> a reflection of all your financial innovation or is it just a reflection of how much you pay?
>
> What about the effect on our economies [taking] all our best young talent? In Britain, I was just talking to a high-tech company about the immense attraction to go into finance when both Britain and the United States are suffering from a basic inability to produce things competitively.
>
> **The most important financial innovation that I have seen the past 20 years is the automatic teller machine**, that really helps people and prevents visits to the bank and it is a real convenience. How many other innovations can you tell me of that have been as important to the individual as the automatic teller machine, which is more of a mechanical innovation than a financial one?
>
> I have found very little evidence that vast amounts of innovation in financial markets in recent years has had a visible effect on the productivity of the economy, maybe you can show me that I am wrong. All I know is that the economy was rising very nicely in the 1950s and 1960s without all of these innovations. Indeed, it was quite good in the 1980s without Credit Default Swaps or CDOs. I do not know if something happened that suddenly made these innovations essential for growth. In fact, we had greater speed of growth in the 1960s and more importantly it did not put the whole economy at risk of collapse.

Anyway, it's debatable, but my view is that trading is great for the successful individuals, but at best net zero for the world at large.

Losing money on purpose?

If you are uncomfortable with trading as a career because it conflicts with your beliefs and values, you may find that you self-sabotage as a reaction to the dissonance.

> "Win or lose, everybody gets what they want out of the market. Some people seem to like to lose, so they win by losing money."
>
> - Ed Seykota

I remember first reading about the subconscious desire to lose money trading in Mark Douglas's book *Trading in the Zone*[99]. I was 27 or something, and I thought "That's stupid. Nobody does that."

Now, I understand how wrong I was.

---

[99] https://amzn.to/45wSXVI

When you trade, a huge percentage of the mental processing that happens goes on in your subconscious. If your dad taught elementary math and made $44,000/year and you make $48,000 in fifteen minutes arbing the S&P rebalance… Your value system and beliefs can feel a tremendous dissonant burden. On the one hand, you are consciously ecstatic, but on the other hand, your subconscious may be screaming:

"THESE BE ILL GOTTEN GAINS! Rewards like this require hard work. You just pressed a few buttons. This is nonsense. Begone ill-gotten gains!"

And then you find yourself going into some random trade, and losing 33k for no reason, and you leave the office still up 15k, but furious with yourself.

When I hired new grads to come work for me on FX trading desks, I always gave them small limits to trade for real right away because I don't believe that paper trading works. Taking real risk requires different skills than watching markets and putting on theoretical paper trades. Most of the hard part of trading is psychological and there can be some crazy stuff going on in your head when you take real risk.

So the first thing you need to do once you start making money is come to terms with it. It's OK. Capitalism divides up the money in really weird ways. Place kickers in the NFL make millions of dollars every year. Kim Kardashian is rich for being a celebrity by being a celebrity. Mr. Beast is 1000X richer than the best teacher in the world. Life isn't fair. Get over it.

Then, once you accept the initial weirdness of the disconnect between hard work or tangible output and income… You start to find out other things about success and financial gain.

I am "successful"! What does it all mean?

> I just found a million dollars that someone forgot
> It's days like this that push me o'er the brink
>
> Guns 'n Roses, Pretty Tied Up, 1991

Once you start to achieve persistent success in trading, remember three things.

a) The money is great at first, but it will become less meaningful over time. Money/happiness is a non-linear curve that flattens out fast.
b) No matter how good you are at it, trading will not give your life meaning.
c) You only need to get rich once.

a) Money vs. happiness

Don't be surprised if your overall happiness doesn't change much as you get richer. Half your baseline happiness comes straight out of the box, and the impact of money on the remaining part of your happiness is small and nonlinear.

Happiness has many inputs. Money is a small one.

The money vs. happiness equation is critically important to understand. Know your money vs. happiness curve. This is such an important topic. I wrote about it in "Money Can Buy Happiness"[100] and will excerpt a bit below.

Your personal money vs. happiness curve will depend on your values, your beliefs, where you live, your family size, and other things. Think about it in specific detail. Where will your money/happiness curve start to flatline?

In aggregate, the curve looks something like this:

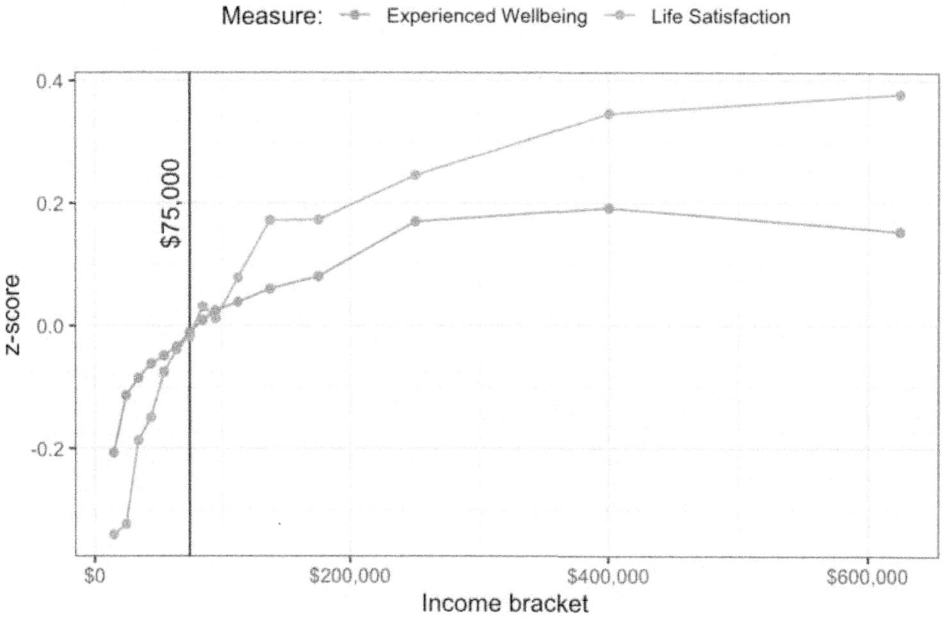

Source*: https://kieranhealy.org/blog/archives/2021/01/26/income-and-happiness/*

[100] https://medium.com/@mbrentdonnelly/money-can-buy-happiness-1d3d548babf6

The race for more money is a race you can never win because if your goal is just "more"... You are this guy:

It's a weird feeling the first time you make life-changing money. You are beyond ecstatic for a few days and then you gradually revert back to however you felt before. Emotions, including the positive feelings you get from making money, are almost completely transitory.

Joy, like pain, is mean reverting.

Think about your history (childhood and young adult years especially) and how it might influence your trading performance. For example: if your dad was an electrician and your mom was an entrepreneur... Your subconscious might have trouble with the idea that in trading you magically pull money out of thin air without any traditional hard work and without producing or creating anything. You might find your subconscious repeatedly sabotages you in an effort to divest what it perceives as ill-gotten gains.

Many traders from blue-collar families struggle with this when they first find success. It is a strange and sometimes surreal feeling to generate huge income without producing anything tangible. Trading is not the only job where this is the case, but the sometimes sudden and gigantic income from trading makes it different from most other professions.

Believe it or not, there is more to life than trading. Think about the long game and your entire career. While it is fun to trade all night and live a fast and exciting life, you cannot do that forever. Trading on its own does not offer a path to meaning, no matter how much money you rake in. Financial freedom is one facet of happiness. Most research shows true happiness comes from: Health, relationships, family, friends, and a feeling of purpose.

While it might feel like your P&L ups and downs are a matter of life and death — they are not. Traders spend way too much time thinking about P&L and money and all the things it might mean to them. Focus on trading when you are at work and focus on relationships and activities you love when you are not.

If you have a good day, feel good about it. Be happy. Go celebrate. Order the Château d'Yquem. But don't celebrate until you have taken profit! Celebrating while in a winning position is a recipe for disaster. Take profit, then go be happy.

Always remember.... Hills and valleys. Hills and valleys. Don't let yourself get too high or too low. Regardless of your P&L, the sun will still rise tomorrow, your kids will still love you and even in the most extreme situation where you end up losing your job as a trader, life STILL goes on.

At the end of the day... It's only money.

b) I'm a successful trader! What does this mean?

As you become successful in trading, look for other sources of meaning. If trading is the main thing that gives you excitement and fun, you are going to overtrade and possibly gamble at work. **Trading must always be about the relentless and rational pursuit of profits**, not relief from existential boredom.

For me, accepting that trading is a kind of meaningless but satisfying way to exist in the world, make money, and get paid as a writer was an important step toward finding peace.

Life does not automatically come with meaning. The meaning of your life is whatever you decide it to be. But don't decide on money. If you think the meaning of life is to make as much money as possible, you will never be happy.

The meaning of my life is to love my wife and grow and learn and teach and spend time with my kids and spend time with my friends and write books. That's my meaning. You need to find your own.

Making money allows me to pursue these other things I care about, and I am able to make the money in a job that is perhaps meaningless, but definitely fun, interesting, and intellectually satisfying. And through my writing, my job also gives me the creative outlet I need.

Think about your meaning of life and figure out how to use trading to move towards it. Trading doesn't have to be the source of meaning. It can be the grease that allows the wheels of meaning in your life to turn freely. It can be the thing that gives you financial freedom and mental peace so you don't have to worry about paying the rent. It can move you to the middle of Maslow's hierarchy of needs, but it can't take you higher.

c) You only need to get rich once

The final thing to consider is this: Once you have a good idea of your money/happiness curve and where it flattens out… Aim for that and reduce your downside risk when you get there. If you make $4 million dollars punting crypto, there is no excuse for giving it all back.

Buy some hard assets with $2m and keep trading the other $2m. Orient your life away from MOAR MOAR MOAR and towards things you care about like music, or art, or friends, or writing, or whatever. Optimize for life satisfaction, not money, once you get to the middle of Maslow's pyramid. This graphic is another way of looking at the money vs. happiness curve.

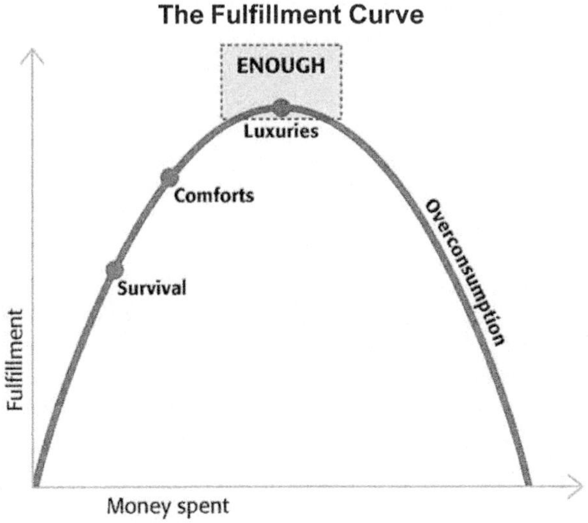

Conclusion

Trading is fun, and it can be incredibly profitable. But it is very unlikely you will find the meaning of life in a high Sharpe ratio or a successful USDJPY pyramid after nonfarm payrolls, or even inside a bank account stuffed with millions of dollars of P&L. Money can be part of your life equation, but for a huge majority of people, it's not the most important input.

Even if you believe that trading has no societal value, you can use trading as a means to a greater end. Trading can give you the intellectual stimulation you need and it can give you enough money to provide the freedom of choice to do those things that will give your life meaning. It's not the money or the trading that have meaning, it's what you do with the freedom and opportunity they provide.

Decide the meaning of your own life. Then move in that direction by taking massive, courageous action every day.

That's it for this week! That's it, period! 50in50 is over.

I hope you had fun and learned some new frameworks, tactics, strategies, and ways of thinking about markets and about life.

Post-mortem and Takeaways

The lessons presented by 50in50 are self-contained and mostly speak for themselves. Each week, I tried to pick a particular concept and focus there. But while each lesson on its own contains many specific lessons, there were also some broader points you can extract from this book.

1. **I don't have an edge doing fifty random trades in asset classes where I have no specific expertise.** This was not surprising to me. My FX trading P&L is consistently profitable over many years because I have an edge and tons of experience in FX and macro. When I was trading NASDAQ stocks full-time, I also had a defined edge. But in 50in50, when I put on a sample trade in oil, or BTC, or some other asset class in order to demonstrate a particular concept… I am unlikely to have a huge edge. The P&L on the entire exercise was extremely close to zero, including estimated transaction fees.

Here is the detailed P&L spreadsheet:

Conviction	Week	Entry date	L/S	Asset	Entry	USD at risk	Stop loss	Take profit	Exit or current level	P&L	Exit date	Holding period (days)	Notes
8.0	1	2/9/22	Short	XAUEUR	1,602	2,000	1,702	1,421	1,704	(2,000)	28-Feb	19	
4.0	2	2/16/22	Short	CLK2	90.50	1,000	95.45	79.05	95.55	(2,000)	1-Mar	13	
8.0	3	2/21/22	Short	DOCS	56.00	2,000	60.51	50.21	60.58	(2,000)	28-Feb	7	Wrong stop loss.
7.0	4	2/25/22	Long	BTC	39,200	2,000	31,400	49,800	39,200	-	14-Mar	17	
7.0	5	3/1/22	Long	BTC	43,400	2,000	38,900	49,800	38,870	(2,000)	14-Mar	13	
5.0	6	3/8/22	Long	EWC	37.85	2,000	35.19	44.80	39.65	1,353	11-Apr	34	
9.0	7	3/14/22	Long	XPO May $60 puts	2.60	2,000	-	53.50	6.10	2,692	18-Apr	35	
8.0	8	3/28/22	Short	NQ	14,970	2,000	15,660	13,344	13,908	3,078	18-Apr	21	
9.0	9	4/4/22	Long	TWTR	50.85	2,000	45.84	57.77	45.80	(2,000)	13-Apr	9	
7.0	10	4/11/22	Long	ASHR	32.18	2,000	29.84	36.44	29.80	(2,000)	25-Apr	14	Wrong stop loss.
6.0	11	4/18/22	Long	ESM2	4,381	2,000	4,279	4,579	4,276	(2,000)	5-May	17	
3.0	12	4/25/22	Long	ARKK	45.67	2,000	29.00		51.39	687	*11-Aug*	108	
2.0	14	5/15/22	Long	BTC	28,500	2,000	24,900	39,300	24,900	(2,000)	13-Jun	29	
9.0	15	5/18/22	Long	JAN23 CVNA 20 put	4.70	1,500	-	-	3.00	(543)	13-Sep	118	
9.0	15	5/18/22	Long	JAN23 RBLX 40 call	7.00	1,500	-	-	10.40	729	13-Sep	118	
10.0	16	5/27/22	Short	ETHBTC	0.061	2,000	0.077	0.033	0.069	(1,000)	25-Jul	59	
4.0	17	6/6/22	Short	LLY	297.99	2,000	306.25	283.10	306.25	(2,000)	22-Jun	16	Low was 1 cent from the take profit!!!!!!!
8.0	18	6/14/22	Long	TY	114.56	2,000	112.84	118.00	118.00	4,000	30-Jun	16	
10.0	19	6/24/22	Long	GBTC	12.77	2,000	10.90	16.60	14.80	2,181	31-Jul	37	
5.0	20	7/4/22	Short	TSLA	701.50	2,000	820.00	437.00	829.00	(2,200)	22-Jul	18	
7.0	21	7/19/22	Long	XME	44.50	2,000	34.95	63.70	49.90	1,131	13-Sep	56	
9.0	22	7/25/22	Short	META	Options	2,000	29JUL $160 and $155 puts		Small profit on the 160s	(1,600)	29-Jul	4	
8.0	23	8/1/22	Short	SPY	412.50	2,000	436.60	37.00	402.50	830	13-Sep	43	Sold put against it
8.0	25	8/16/22	Short	MSTR	345.00	2,000	381.00	251.00	251.00	5,222	26-Aug	10	
5.7	26	8/23/22	Short	TSLA	296.00	2,000	304.67		288.09	2,191	25-Aug	2	Cover at 25AUG close
7.0	27	8/29/22	Short	TSLA	Daily strat	2,000			295.00	(297)	13-Sep	15	
8.0	28	9/5/22	Short	ETH	1,650	2,000	1906 and 2056	1,155.00	1,587	381	13-Sep	8	
8.0	30	9/20/22	Long	USDJPY	143.65	2,000	141.74		141.71	(2,030)	23-Sep	3	This trade made money in real life but I forgot to put my TP in 50in50 write up oops
7.0	31	10/12/22	Buy	FXA call spread	0.40	2,000			-	(2,000)	21-Oct	9	
8.5	32	10/17/22	Short	USDNOK	10.53	2,000	10.92	9.88	10.33	1,026	2-Nov	16	
6.5	33	10/27/22	Short	CM	45.10	2,000	47.11	40.55	47.14	(2,010)	10-Nov	14	Stop too tight - ended up hitting TP not oo long after
8.0	34	11/4/22	Buy	EWZ call spread	35/39	2,000			-	(2,000)	27-Dec	53	
7.0	35	11/9/22	Short	MSTR	192.10	2,000	282.00	160.55	160.65	700	27-Dec	48	
6.0	36	11/17/22	Buy	TGT / WMT spread					142.60 in WMT	(170)	16-Dec	29	
8.0	37	11/30/22	Long	XOM put spread	2.05	2,050	FEB '23 100/85 put spread	85.00	1.46	(590)	27-Dec	27	
9.0	38	12/7/22	Sell	Call spread and put spread in MSTR	See Substack	3,000				-			
8.0	39	12/22/22	Sell 23FEB23 and buy 23JUN23 125.00 USDJPY puts			2,000				(2,000)	23-Jun	183	
8.0	40	12/28/22	Long	TSLA	113.10	2,000	88.49	159.00	141.50	2,308	23-Jan	26	
7.0	41	1/10/23	Limit Buy	TSLA	115.03	2,000	98.49	159.00					*Never got filled*
7.0	42	1/23/23	Short	F	12.60	2,000	15.26	9.03	11.58	767	22-May		
7.0	43	1/30/23	Short	TSLA	171.10	3,200	251.11	117.77	182.00	(272)	22-May		*Moved stop nice play*
8.0	44	2/15/23	Short	TSLA	210.78	2,000	251.11	117.77	182.00	1,427	22-May		
8.0	45	3/1/23	Long	IEF	94.80	2,000	92.44	99.49	99.49	3,975	23-Mar		
6.0	46	3/29/23	Sell SPX call spread	410/412	0.65	2,000			Expired below 410	650	23-Apr	25	
8.0	47	4/5/23	Short	KRE	41.60	2,000	48.06	33.10	40.40	372	22-May		
7.0	48	4/11/23	Short	AAPL	161.50	2,000	164.11		165.69	(2,000)	17-Apr	6	
8.0	49	5/8/23	Short	AI	19.30	2,000	26.26	11.11	26.31	(2,014)	17-May		
	50												*No trade*

Total P&L	**(3,028)**
Winners	**20**
Losers	**24**
Win%	**45%**
avgWIN	**1,785**
avgLOSE	**(1,614)**
avg holding period (days)	33

Zooming in on the summary statistics:

Total P&L	**(3,028)**
Winners	**20**
Losers	**24**
Win%	**45%**
avgWIN	**1,785**
avgLOSE	**(1,614)**
avg holding period (days)	33

More interesting is the breakdown by asset class:

	Single name	Equity Index	FX and bonds	Commodities and crypto
Total P&L	(1,556)	2,558	4,970	(9,000)
Winners	14	3	3	-
Losers	16	1	2	5
Win%	47%	75%	60%	0%
avgWIN	1,581	1,519	3,000	
avgLOSE	(1,481)	(2,000)	(2,015)	(1,750)

I focused a lot on single names in 50in50 because it's easiest to tell a simple story in stocks, while in FX and other asset classes, you very often need to provide much more background information. I also didn't want to do much global macro because that is what I write about every day in am/FX (my real job) and it felt like there would be too much duplication. Logically, the macro trades (equity indexes, FX and bonds) did the best while the single names, commodities, and crypto did the worst. That makes sense! I have an edge in macro but not in trading US companies.

Like I said before: The most likely path to success in trading is to choose one market and master everything you possibly can about that market. Pick a market and master it. For me, the market is FX. And that comes through in the P&L of my real-time trades published in my daily newsletter, am/FX. Here are the results of my am/FX trades going back to the day I started at Spectra Markets (September 2021). These trades are all published and marked to market in real time. Risk is $100,000 on each trade.

Total P&L	**2,628,369**
Winners	**52**
Losers	**40**
Win%	**57%**
avgWIN	**113,128**
avgLOSE	**(81,357)**
average holding period (days)	11

I publish the am/FX trade results, in detail, each quarter, but the detailed xls with all 92 trades won't fit in here so I am only showing the summary stats. These stats are consistent with my performance over the years in FX. I started keeping track in 2006 and most years I put up something close to a 50% win rate. Historically my daily avgWIN$ / avgLOSS$ = 1.8. For more on P&L tracking and analysis, please see Chapter 11 of *Alpha Trader*.

2. **The biggest failure in my 50in50 trading was not the win percentage, but the ratio of win size to loss size.** The average win was about the same size as the average loss, and you cannot make money doing that.

I think the reason for this is that I was using wider stop losses than usual and a longer time horizon because the trade frequency for this exercise was so low. That is, if I'm only trading once per week, it seems stupid to have a trade that gets stopped out after three days. But in real life, tactical precision can be a tremendous edge if you are expert in your market. In 50in50, there was very little tactical precision, and I am not expert in most of the markets I was trading in.

Also, because of the wide stops and longer time horizon, I got bored of a bunch of the trades and cut them early. For example, I got long TSLA at the ding dong lows in late 2022 before it rallied from 100 to above 200, but I took profit at $141.50 because I was kind of bored of it. I think another subconscious driver was that I wanted to maintain an OK hit rate to avoid embarrassment and that led me to take profit prematurely on some of the best trades. This is a good example of how when your motivation in trading is anything other than "maximize profits," you trade suboptimally.

Knowing that I get bored of trades in real life, I try to avoid slow-burner trades that are likely to sit there for ages. I focus on trades with proximate catalysts where I expect movement sooner rather than later.

3. **The most popular posts.** The posts people liked the best fit two themes. They were either about global macro, or they attempted to answer an age-old trading question. Here are the top five posts.

    - **Week 30: Trading Global Macro** was the most popular (other than Week 1, but the first issue of any series always gets excess upvotes). There isn't really a good book out there on how to trade global macro, so this post was popular. Two other global macro write-ups also made the top five.
    - **Week 45: Regime Flux**, and **Week 18: Fun with Quadrants** (both about global macro) resonated with many readers. I should write a book called "Global Macro 101" at some point, I guess. I think the popularity of these posts also shows the readership is sophisticated enough to detect that I am expert in global macro and not expert in single name stock picking, so the global macro posts probably rang a bit truer than some of the others.

- **Week 24: Do Good Traders Vary Bet Size?** This is an age-old question and a super fun subject to debate. And thus it was naturally a popular writeup.
- Similarly, **Week 44: Back on the Horse… Is it OK to get back into a trade after you were stopped out?** addresses another age-old trading question and also received outsized engagement. Trader psychology and risk management (like global macro) are subjects directly in my wheelhouse and the trader psychology and risk management posts got the most upvotes. Makes sense!

4. **The best trade.** I think the best trade in the series was the long TSLA in December 2022 and the attempt to double the TSLA long on January 10, 2023. Ironically, while these two trades were the best logic and highest EV of the 50 trades in the series, they didn't produce that much P&L. The first long was cut ahead of TSLA earnings at $141.50, right before the stock exploded above $200. And the second long was a *dick-for-a-tick* situation because I was writing about different types of orders you can use and decided to use a limit order at 115.03 to buy a dip. The stock dipped to 116 then rallied above 200 LOLLLLL.

This is an example of where 50in50 underperformed what would happen in real life because I would never put my entire trade at the mercy of a single limit order. I mentioned this in the TSLA writeup, but just to reiterate here…

I almost always scale in using a tight band near my optimal entry point. This avoids false precision and the all-or-nothing problem of putting your entire entry at one level. If I'm using a market order, I just get in all at once. But if I'm using a limit order on the way in or on the way out, I'll scale it across a narrow window so that at least I get a partial if my choice of levels is slightly off.

So while this trade didn't produce the most P&L (that honor goes to the MSTR short in August 2022)… I am always about process not outcome. My process here was excellent, and it took a lot of courage to go long TSLA at the end of 2022 when it was in free fall. My logic was sound, and the stock doubled in less than two months after I put out the idea. I know a bunch of people made money on the idea in real life because they wrote me to tell me so. Another reason this is a good trade is that I don't really like Elon Musk's public persona, generally, so to go long stock in his company required me to overcome a bias. Unbiased, rational trading is the path to success.

5. **The worst trade.** The worst trade of the 50in50 was the one-two combo of **Week 1: Short XAUEUR** and **Week 2: Short oil**. Short gold and oil in the weeks leading up to the Russian invasion of Ukraine definitely qualifies as no bueno! When I look back at whether a trade was good or bad, it's not about the outcome; it's about the thought process and risk management that went into the trade. It's not about what you know after the fact, it's about what you knew when you put on the trade, and what you did about it.

You can lose money on good ideas and you can make money despite bad risk management and therefore assessing performance of individual trades by analyzing outcomes is the wrong approach. Obviously, outcomes matter at certain levels of zoom but always remember that you control the process, not the outcome.

Outcomes are subject to tremendous variance and so when you do a post-mortem on a trade, or a month of trading, or even a year of trading... Focus as much as possible on evaluating the process, not the results. You need to be careful to avoid beating yourself up with a bunch of after-the-fact things that seem obvious in hindsight. In this case, though, no hindsight was required to see the trades were at risk of a Russian incursion.

The reason I really hate these trades now is that they show a) a lack of intellectual flexibility on my part and b) a total failure (in Week 1) to acknowledge one of the biggest, most obvious risks to the short gold trade: A Russian invasion of Ukraine.

When I published Week 1, it was already clear that a Russian attack on Ukraine was possible. But my experience over many years was that most geopolitical tension is a waste of time and markets tend to overprice geopolitical risks. Even the Russian moves in Crimea and Ukraine in 2014 were barely relevant to markets beyond a few days.

This was lazy thinking. Not just in hindsight. I didn't do the work or even read much about Russia / Ukraine because I just lazily dismissed it as irrelevant. Needless to say, pre-attack jitters took gold up, up, and away and my Week 2 trade was short oil (!) which got blown to smithereens by hypersonic Russian Kinzhal rockets.

•

There are many more takeaways from the 50in50 series, but much of the specific value proposition depends on your starting point and your experience level going in. I hope noobs added some basic hammer-and-screwdriver trading tools like position sizing and trade idea generation, while pros added some new stuff... The trading equivalent of say, a precision laser level or a Japanese pull saw.

Conclusion

I spent a solid year on this project. I hope you extracted many useful ideas, concepts, and tactics from the 50in50 series. The idea when looking at case studies is not to obsess over the particulars or the specific outcomes. The idea with 50in50 is to see how I look at trade selection, filtering, risk management, and analysis, and upgrade your thinking and your framework by extracting the parts that you find useful, and discarding those you do not.

This book was an exercise in real-time trade idea generation and narrative thinking. Books are wonderful, and you should keep reading them. However, there is immense value in engaging with other people's ideas in real time. That's why financial research/commentary is such a massive (and useful) industry.

That is part of why I write my daily, am/FX, and that is also why my email inbox is always full of the commentary and analysis of other macro thinkers. And that is, I think, why 50in50 became such a popular project. Because when you're trying to deeply learn something, there's nothing better than spending time around other people who are doing it live, with real risks and real consequences.

If you want more of my real-time thoughts, **subscribe to am/FX at www.spectramarkets.com**. It's an excellent way to keep up with what's going on in global macro and finance, and plug into other networks and sources of information. Watching experienced traders generate real ideas in real time is incredibly useful and will help you become a better trader and investor.

Learning to trade is never about copying a methodology or learning a specific tactic that's going to work now and forever. It's about creating an adaptable framework that will allow you to understand all aspects of your market and react faster, smarter, and with more courage than the competition. It's about understanding the current equilibrium, seeing when things are about to change, and then taking courageous, forceful action.

Thanks for reading. I truly appreciate the time and money you have invested in this book.

Trade at your own risk. Be smart. Have fun. Call your mom.

About the Author

Brent Donnelly is President of Spectra Markets. He has been trading currencies since 1995 and writing about macro since 2004.

Brent is the author of *Alpha Trader* (2021) and *The Art of Currency Trading* (Wiley, 2019). He writes a widely-read and highly-respected global macro and FX daily called am/FX. Over the course of his career, he has been a market maker, trader, and senior manager at some of the top banks in foreign exchange.

Brent has extensive experience trading currencies, FX options, stock index futures, NASDAQ stocks, and commodities. He is a respected macro thinker with the unique perspective of a senior risk taker. He has been quoted by or featured in the Economist, Real Vision, Epsilon Theory, the Wall Street Journal, Financial Times, Bloomberg Radio and TV, and CNBC.

Before joining Spectra, Brent was a senior FX trader at HSBC, head of G10 Spot Trading at Citi New York and a Managing Director at Nomura New York. He was also a portfolio manager at a major hedge fund in Connecticut for three years. He created and wrote a cartoon called "Daft Planet" which aired on TV in Canada, and he dreams of one day winning the Man Booker Prize.

Photo: Suv Bose

Index

Printed in Great Britain
by Amazon

46083006R00311